Hyacinthe

LATIN READER SERIES

Beginning *Latin* Poetry Reader

D0700716

Gavin Betts and Daniel Franklin

Mc Graw Hill

New York Chicago San Francisco Lisbon London Madrid Mexico City
Milan New Delhi San Juan Seoul Singapore Sydney Toronto

Library of Congress Cataloging-in-Publication Data

Beginning Latin poetry reader / [compiled] by Gavin Betts, Daniel Franklin.
      p.   cm. (Latin Reader Series)
      Includes bibliographical references.
      ISBN 0-07-145885-9
      English and Latin.
      1. Latin language—Readers—Poetry.

   PA2095 .B375   2006
   871'.01—dc22   2006048209

Copyright © 2007 by The McGraw-Hill Companies, Inc. All rights reserved.
Printed in the United States of America. Except as permitted under the United
States Copyright Act of 1976, no part of this publication may be reproduced
or distributed in any form or by any means, or stored in a database or retrieval
system, without the prior written permission of the publisher.

Photographs of fragments of the Severan Marble Plan on page xxv are
reproduced with the permission of Professors Marc Levoy and Jennifer Trimble
of Stanford University and Professor Eugenio La Rocca of the Sovraintendenza
ai Beni Culturali di Roma.

The Fell types in the boxed material on page 119 were digitally reproduced
by Igino Marini (*www.iginomarini.com*).

3 4 5 6 7 8 9 10 11 12 13 14 15 16 17 18 19   FGR/FGR   0 9 8

ISBN 978-0-07-145885-6
MHID   0-07-145885-9

Interior design by Village Typographers, Inc.

McGraw-Hill books are available at special quantity discounts to use as
premiums and sales promotions or for use in corporate training programs.
To contact a representative, please visit the Contact Us pages at www.
mhprofessional.com.

This book is printed on acid-free paper.

CONTENTS

POETRY SELECTIONS

KEY TO DIFFICULTY

Easy✦ *Somewhat difficult*✦✦ *Rather difficult*✦✦✦

ESSAYS

MARGINALIA

PREFACE

Classical scholars have been described as people who take nothing on trust, who will only believe that life is short if they are provided with at least six references certifying that this is so. In editions of Latin texts intended for students, this attitude has often led to commentaries overladen with superfluous material that illustrates—rather than explains—a text, while basic (and often not so basic) points of grammar are ignored.

Beginning Latin Poetry Reader uses a different approach. It has been compiled for the person who has begun the study of Latin, who knows how to conjugate verbs and decline nouns and adjectives, and who has a basic vocabulary of perhaps 750 Latin words. When reading a Latin poem, this person wants all the necessary grammatical and other information available at a glance, and this is provided in footnotes on the same page as the text or on the page opposite.

The selections range from Ennius at the beginning of Roman literary activity down to Claudian, who stands at the end of Rome's Western empire. We have chosen them partly because of their low level of difficulty, and partly to give a broad sample of the different periods and genres of Latin literature. We have included essays on topics related to the study of Latin poetry (for example, religion at Rome and the form of the Roman book), as well as marginalia that showcase famous lines from Roman poets and miscellaneous information of interest to the reader.

For each selection, the meter is identified, with a numbered reference to the Metrics section, and at least the first two lines are metrically scanned. Details are given of the edition that is the source of the authoritative text; a few textual changes have been made for consistency and clarity, including the substitution of **v** for consonantal **u**.

In the footnotes and Glossary, long vowels in Latin words have been marked with a macron (ˉ, as in **abscēdō**), except for hidden quantities (long vowels that cannot be decided by meter), which have been ignored. Hidden quantities are of interest to the history of the Latin language, but add an unnecessary complication for those at the beginning of their Latin studies.

We suggest that the reader take a moment to become familiar with the components and features that make *Beginning Latin Poetry Reader* an all-inclusive resource for the study and enjoyment of Latin poetry.

(The **Contents** assigns a level of difficulty to each selection, allowing the
reader to choose selections suitable to his or her ability.

(The **Introduction** (pages xiii–xviii) and **Time Line of Latin Literature**
(pages xix–xxi) orient the reader to the literary highlights and themes
represented by the selections. The Introduction also includes a list of
books suggested for further study.

(The **maps** of Italy, Greece, and the Troad and of Rome in Late Antiquity (pages xxii–xxiv) have been specifically tailored to the places mentioned in the selections.

(The **Abbreviations** (page xxvi) interprets all the grammatical and other
abbreviations used in this book.

(The **Grammar** section (pages 221–255) explains, with examples, nearly
100 points of Latin syntax, especially as it is encountered in poetry.
Throughout the selection footnotes, there are copious numbered references to these grammar points.

(The **Metrics** section (pages 256–266) provides details and examples of
the 14 different meters used by the 70 selections in this book.

(The **Translations** (pages 267–302) offer accurate, natural translations of
the selections.

(The **Glossary** (pages 303–342) provides the basic meanings of all Latin
words in this book, as well as uncommon meanings specific to the selections. (Basic vocabulary is marked in the Glossary; the meanings of all
other words are given both in the footnotes and in the Glossary.)

It is our pleasure to present this book to the reader who seeks the unique
edification and enjoyment that reading Latin poetry offers.

                                                    Gavin Betts, M.A.
                                                    Daniel Franklin

INTRODUCTION

Rome began as a settlement on the Tiber River in west central Italy. The Romans themselves placed its founding at 753 B.C., but the actual date was probably earlier. After a slow beginning, the city extended its power beyond its original boundaries and came into contact with the Greek communities in southern Italy and Sicily. These were a part of the complex of Greek city-states that by the end of the fourth century B.C. had developed in many lands bordering on the Mediterranean and had long since reached a degree of sophistication in literary, artistic, and intellectual pursuits unequalled in the ancient world. It was inevitable that this more advanced civilization should influence the uncouth northern intruders whose military exploits far exceeded their achievements in refined living.

After struggles against Gauls from the north and Carthaginians from the south, Rome's power in Italy was firmly established, and she began to extend her dominion overseas. By the end of the first century B.C., the entire Greek world had been overrun and absorbed into her empire, but the Romans did not destroy the brilliant culture it represented. On the contrary, as the poet Horace expressed it,

Graecia capta ferum victōrem cēpit et artīs
intulit agrestī Latiō. *Epistulae* 2.1.156f.
Captive Greece took its rough conqueror captive
and brought the arts to rustic Latium (i.e., Rome).

As Romans gradually became more sophisticated, they adopted and adapted more and more of Greek intellectual, literary, and artistic achievements to suit the development of their own culture. In every field of artistic endeavor—literature, sculpture, painting, and architecture—Greek masterpieces of past centuries were taken as models, but these were not slavishly imitated. The Romans saw themselves as continuing Greek traditions and endowing them with a flavor of their own. An example is the portrait bust, which depicts a person whose features the sculptor wishes to record for posterity or for contemporary propaganda. Greek busts of this kind tended to be idealistic or to emphasize a dominant characteristic, but Roman examples were painstakingly accurate and showed unflattering blemishes, such as wrinkles and moles.

LATIN LITERATURE BEGAN with Livius Andronicus (*fl.* 240–207 B.C.), of whose work we unfortunately possess only scanty fragments. Through him, Rome was introduced to epic and drama, and his initiatives were soon taken up and surpassed by Ennius, Plautus, and Terence. After Terence's death in 159 B.C., other literary genres were developed in Latin, and with Cicero (106–43 B.C.) the period known in modern literary histories as the Golden Age of Latin Literature began. Although Cicero's achievements in prose were immense, he was an indifferent poet. Still, among his contemporaries were two outstanding poets whose works survive: Lucretius and Catullus. The former broke new ground at Rome with his long didactic poem *De rerum natura* (*On the nature of the universe*); the latter, in addition to following recent Greek trends in poetry of a learned kind, wrote much in a personal and informal manner, telling of life in Rome, of his friends, and, above all, of his fatal passion for one of the great beauties of the day.

Cicero's life coincided with the most disturbed period of Roman history. After his death, peaceful conditions were gradually restored by Octavian, the future emperor Augustus, and we have the greatest of Roman poets, Vergil, who wrote pastorals (the *Eclogues*), didactic poetry (the *Georgics*), and epic (the *Aeneid*), all based on Greek models. His contemporary Horace aspired to emulate the Greek lyric poets; he also continued the Roman tradition of satire, which for him was an informal type of verse ranging over a variety of subjects, usually of a personal nature, and which was the only literary genre of purely Roman origin. Elegiac poetry, a Greek genre defined by the meter in which it was composed (see page 262), was embraced by Tibullus, Propertius, and Ovid, and used by them for amatory and other themes. In addition, Ovid wrote the *Metamorphoses*, a vast collection of stories, mostly Greek, that (as the Greek title indicates) tell of physical transformations. Of other Golden Age poetry little has survived; an example in the present collection is from a minor elegiac writer, Lygdamus.

The death of Ovid in A.D. 17 is usually taken as the beginning of the Silver Age of Latin Literature. There was no sharp break between it and the Golden Age, but the distinction is useful because many later authors were not of the same caliber as their predecessors. Writers of both prose and verse displayed an excessive fondness for the trappings of contemporary rhetorical theory, which favored a terse, concise style. Brevity of expression was highly prized, with an emphasis on short pithy sentences (called **sententiae**), which were meant to have an immediate impact on the listener or reader. An epitaph for the poet Lucan tells us that *the style that hits [the reader] shows real excellence,* and this view is amply illustrated in Lucan's epic, the *Bellum civile*, and in the tragedies of his uncle, the younger Seneca.

From the first century A.D. we also have the fables of Phaedrus, Manilius' didactic poem on astrology, and the epics of Valerius Flaccus, Statius, and Silius Italicus; Statius also wrote a collection of occasional poetry, the *Silvae*. The most attractive poet of the period, however, is Martial, whose many short poems (misleadingly called epigrams in English) give frank and lively vignettes of the Rome of his day. A still sharper and broader picture is provided by Martial's younger contemporary, Juvenal, who lived on into the next century and established the modern concept of satire. Subsequently, up to the fifth century A.D., when Rome succumbed to barbarians from the north, few writers stand out, although a new note, akin to that of early nineteenth-century romanticism, was struck in the *Pervigilium Veneris* (*The Vigil of Venus*), a poem plausibly attributed to an obscure poet, Tiberianus, of about A.D. 300. The period closes with Claudian (*fl.* A.D. 400), who revived earlier literary forms.

After Roman civilization collapsed, the survival of the literature it had produced was at risk not only in Italy, but also in western Europe. Books had always been laboriously written out by hand (see "The Roman Book," page 18); when a particular work was not considered sufficiently interesting or useful to warrant further copies being made, it was in danger of disappearing as the number of existing copies decreased. This had always been a possibility in earlier centuries and had already occurred with a host of minor writers, but now even important works were at risk. Certain authors who were still read in schools, such as Vergil and Horace, were always safe. Some books, such as prose treatises on medicine and agriculture, fulfilled a practical need and so were also preserved. The survival of many other authors, however, was largely a matter of chance. In some cases—Lucretius and Catullus are examples—only a single copy remained, lying hidden, perhaps for centuries, in some monastery, but often all copies of an author disappeared. The random way in which writers in this category were preserved or lost has meant that some inferior works have come down to us, while major ones have perished. We have Silius Italicus' long and mediocre epic, but Ennius' *Annales*, which was one of the most significant works of early Latin literature, has been lost, and our knowledge of it comes from a few quotations in prose authors. Greek literature suffered a similar fate.

In the fourteenth century, when western Europe began to recover from the torpor of the Middle Ages, the literatures of ancient Greece and Rome were taken as models for authors to emulate. Of these, Roman literature was the more immediate, because a knowledge of Latin was widespread, whereas Greek was known only to an initiated few. Latin, in a somewhat changed form, had continued to be used after the collapse of the western portion of the Roman Empire, and what remained of Latin literature was still read, although in an uncritical and desultory way. With the Renaissance, scholars appeared who revived the study of the language used by the great authors of antiquity, like Cicero and Vergil. They also began to produce texts that were as close as possible to those from the hands of the original authors (see "Editing a Latin Text," page 160).

It was fortunate that these activities were underway when the invention of printing (c. 1450) brought about a revolution in book production. The old manuscript, laboriously produced by hand, was replaced by the printed book, which represented an enormous advance both in accuracy and in ease of manufacture. By the end of the fifteenth century, most of the surviving Latin authors were in print and available to a wider audience than ever before. Literary genres such as epic, tragedy, and comedy appeared for the first time in the vernacular languages of western Europe, and their new forms owed much to Latin models. As an example, we may take Shakespeare's *The Comedy of Errors*, which took its structure from Roman comedy and its plot from a particular play of Plautus, the *Menaechmi*.

Other aspects of Western cultural life were influenced by the renewed interest in things Roman. Painters and sculptors often turned to the ancient world for inspiration; the early Renaissance artist Botticelli (1445–1510) broke from the medieval tradition and used subjects from classical mythology, such as the birth of Venus. Even science was affected. When scholars in such diverse fields as astronomy and medicine expounded their new ideas, it was in classical Latin that they wrote, not in its medieval form or in their own native tongue. Copernicus (1473–1543) published his theory of the solar system in his *De revolutionibus orbium coelestium* (*On the revolutions of the heavenly bodies*), and William Harvey (1578–1657) explained the circulation of blood in his *Exercitatio anatomica de motu cordis et sanguinis in animalibus* (*An anatomical disquisition on the movement of the heart and blood in living beings*).

In the sixteenth century, the language and literature of the Romans were at the center of Western education and culture. However, the spoken languages of western Europe, which had, in some cases, been used as vehicles for literature from the Middle Ages, grew in importance, and the use of Latin slowly declined in later centuries. During the first four decades of the twentieth century, it was still taught widely in schools, but the emphasis placed on science after World War II led to a sharp fall in its popularity. Only in recent years has it been realized that a knowledge of Latin not only provides the key to the most important society of the ancient world, but also enables us to gain a full understanding of the beginnings of modern Western culture.

Suggestions for Further Study
Texts

The Loeb Classical Library (Harvard University Press) contains editions of every important Latin author. In each volume, the Latin text faces its English translation, accompanied by brief notes and a comprehensive introduction. This series is invaluable for students at all levels, since it provides reliable texts at a reasonable price. Other series (see page 163) are more expensive and sometimes difficult to obtain.

Notable among recently produced editions of individual authors are Daniel H. Garrison's *The Student's Catullus* and *Horace: Epodes and Odes* (Oklahoma University Press). These books include notes suitable for students and a glossary as well.

Many older school editions that have proved their worth are available as reprints. These include editions of the individual books of Vergil's *Aeneid* edited by H. Gould and J. Whiteley (Duckworth Publishers). Each book has its own glossary.

Two publishing companies that have issued both new editions and reprints of older ones are Bolchazy-Carducci Publishers, Inc. (Wauconda, Ill., *www.bolchazy.com*) and Bristol Classical Press (a division of Duckworth Publishers, *www.duckw.com*).

References

We recommend the following books. Those marked with an asterisk are expensive and should not be purchased before the reader has reached an advanced level.

Dictionaries

Collins Gem Latin Dictionary: Latin-English, English-Latin. D. A. Kidd (Harper-Collins, 1990). An inexpensive, pocket-sized dictionary.

An Elementary Latin Dictionary. C. T. Lewis (Oxford University Press, 1969).

*The Oxford Latin Dictionary. Edited by P. G. W. Glare (Oxford University Press, 1982). The largest Latin-English dictionary available.

Grammars

Allen & Greenough's New Latin Grammar. J. H. Allen and J. B. Greenough (Ginn, 1903; Dover reprint, 2006). An excellent grammar with clear explanations and copious examples from Latin literature.

A New Latin Syntax. E. C. Woodcock. (Harvard University Press, 1959; Bristol Classical Press reprint, 1991). An advanced treatment of Latin syntax.

The Shorter Latin Primer. B. H. Kennedy (Longman, 1973), based on Kennedy's *The Revised Latin Primer* (Longmans, Green and Co., 1931). An elementary grammar.

General

Roman Society. D. R. Dudley (Pelican, 1975).

The Oxford Classical Dictionary. Edited by S. Hornblower and A. Spawforth (Oxford University Press, 2003). An alphabetically arranged work of reference for the Greek and Roman world, containing articles on the major historical, literary, and other figures, as well on topics relating to the history and society of Greece and Rome.

The Concise Oxford Companion to Classical Literature. Edited by M. C. Howatson and I. Chilvers (Oxford University Press, 1993).

A Handbook of Greek Mythology: Including Its Extension to Rome. H. J. Rose (Methuen, 1958; Penguin reprint, 1991). An account of the mythological background used by all Latin poets.

The Penguin Dictionary of Classical Mythology. P. Grimal, edited by Stephen Kershaw, translated by A. R. Maxwell-Hyslop (Penguin Books, 1991). An alphabetical arrangement of the basic information contained in the previous title; an inexpensive, useful reference work for readers of Latin poetry.

The Cambridge History of Classical Literature. Vol. II, *Latin Literature.* Edited by E. J. Kenney and W. V. Clausen (Cambridge University Press, 1983).

Latin Literature: A History. Gian Biagio Conte, translated by J. B. Solodow, revised by D. Fowler and G. W. Most (Johns Hopkins University Press, 1994). An encyclopedic history intended primarily for advanced students and scholars.

A TIME LINE OF LATIN LITERATURE

The names of authors included in the selections are in boldface. The exact date of birth and death of many authors is uncertain; in some cases, an approximate year is given, but for others, only the time of writing can be given (indicated by *fl.*, i.e., **floruit** (*flourished*)).

	AUTHOR	POLITICAL BACKGROUND
	THE BEGINNINGS OF ROMAN LITERATURE	
THIRD CENTURY B.C.	Livius Andronicus (*fl.* 240–207 B.C.) *epic, drama* Naevius (*fl.* 235–204 B.C.) *epic, drama*	First Carthaginian War (264–241 B.C.) Second Carthaginian War (218–201 B.C.) Rome is established as a Mediterranean power by the end of the century
SECOND CENTURY B.C.	**Ennius** (239–169 B.C.) *epic, drama, didactic, satire* **Plautus** (*fl.* 220–184 B.C.) *comedy* **Terence** (c. 195–159 B.C.) *comedy* Cato (234–149 B.C.) *speeches, history*	Third Carthaginian War (149–146 B.C.) Roman power is extended to Greece and elsewhere
	Lutatius Catulus (c. 150–87 B.C.) *elegiac*	Sulla's dictatorship (82–79 B.C.)
	THE GOLDEN AGE OF LATIN LITERATURE	
FIRST CENTURY B.C.	Caesar (100–44 B.C.) *De bello Gallico, De bello civili* Cicero (106–43 B.C.) *speeches, letters, philosophical and rhetorical treatises, poetry* **Lucretius** (c. 94–c. 55 B.C.) *De rerum natura* **Catullus** (c. 84–c. 54 B.C.) *elegiac, lyric and occasional poetry, mini-epic* Sallust (c. 86–c. 35 B.C.) *history* **Publilius Syrus** (first century B.C.) *mimes*	Caesar conquers Gaul (58–51 B.C.) Caesar crosses the Rubicon (49 B.C.) and begins a civil war against Pompey and supporters of the Senate Caesar emerges victorious but is assassinated in 44 B.C.

AUTHOR	POLITICAL BACKGROUND
Vergil (70–19 B.C.) *pastoral, didactic, epic* **Horace** (65–8 B.C.) *lyric, didactic, satire* **Propertius** (*fl.* 25 B.C.) *elegiac* **Tibullus** (c. 50–19 B.C.) *elegiac* **Lygdamus** (late first century B.C.) *elegiac* **Ovid** (43 B.C.–A.D. 17) *elegiac, narrative poetry* Livy (59 B.C.–A.D. 17) *history*	Caesar's heir, Octavian, forms a triumvirate with Marcus Antonius and Lepidus (43 B.C.) to prosecute the civil war against Caesar's assassins Brutus and Cassius are defeated at Philippi (42 B.C.) Further fighting comes to an end with Octavian's victory at Actium (31 B.C.) over his former partner, Marcus Antonius, who had allied himself with the Egyptian queen Cleopatra All Mediterranean countries are now under Roman control Octavian's position as sole ruler is symbolized by his adoption of the name Augustus (27 B.C.) Death of Augustus (A.D. 14)

Left margin: FIRST CENTURY B.C.

THE SILVER AGE OF LATIN LITERATURE

Manilius (early first century A.D.) *Astronomica* **Phaedrus** (c. 15 B.C.–c. A.D. 50) *fables* **Persius** (A.D. 34–62) *satire* **Seneca** (c. 2 B.C.–A.D. 65) *tragedy, letters, philosophical treatises* Petronius (d. A.D. 66) *Satiricon* **Lucan** (A.D. 39–65) *epic* **Valerius Flaccus** (late first century A.D.) *Argonautica* Quintilian (c. A.D. 35–c. 95) *Institutio oratoria* **Statius** (c. A.D. 50–c. 96) *epic, occasional poetry* **Silius Italicus** (c. A.D. 26–c. 102) *epic* **Martial** (c. A.D. 40–c. 102) *epigrams*	The Julio-Claudian line, which Augustus had begun, continues with the emperors Tiberius, Caligula, Claudius, and Nero, but ends with Nero's suicide in A.D. 68 Claudius conquers Britain (A.D. 44) Political unrest leads to the establishment of the Flavian line by Vespasian in A.D. 69 This continues with Titus and Domitian, but ends with the latter's assassination in A.D. 96

Left margin: FIRST CENTURY A.D.

	AUTHOR	POLITICAL BACKGROUND
SECOND CENTURY A.D.	**Juvenal** (b. c. A.D. 60) *satire* Pliny the Younger (c. A.D. 62–c. 112) *letters, speeches* Tacitus (c. A.D. 56–c. 120) *history* Suetonius (c. A.D. 60–c. 130) *biography*	A more liberal regime begins with Nerva in A.D. 96 and continues for most of the second century The Roman Empire is at its greatest extent under Trajan (emperor from A.D. 98 to 117)
THIRD TO FIFTH CENTURIES A.D.	Tiberianus (*fl.* A.D. 300) probable author of the *Pervigilium Veneris* **Claudian** (c. A.D. 370–c. 404) *epic, elegiac*	The imperial system continues, but Constantine (d. A.D. 337) founds Constantinople as the New Rome (A.D. 330) The western half of the empire comes under increasing pressure from the north, which culminates in the sack of Rome in A.D. 410 by the Visigoths

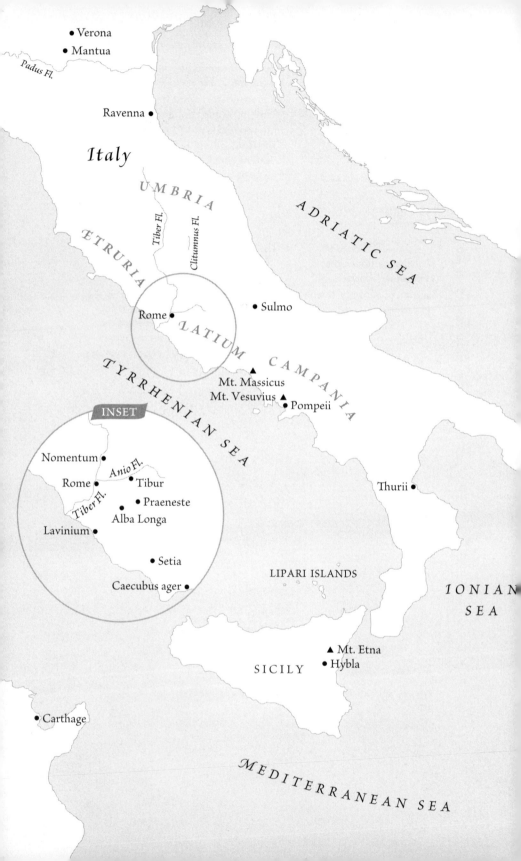

• Verona
• Mantua

Padus Fl.

Ravenna •

Italy

U M B R I A

E T R U R I A

Tiber Fl.

Clitumnus Fl.

Rome •   • Sulmo

L A T I U M   C A M P A N I A

Mt. Massicus ▲
Mt. Vesuvius ▲
              • Pompeii

T Y R R H E N I A N   S E A

A D R I A T I C   S E A

INSET

Nomentum •
              Anio Fl.
Rome •   • Tibur
              • Praeneste
Tiber Fl.
              Alba Longa
Lavinium •

              • Setia

Caecubus ager •

• Thurii

LIPARI ISLANDS

I O N I A N
S E A

▲ Mt. Etna
S I C I L Y   • Hybla

• Carthage

M E D I T E R R A N E A N   S E A

ITALY, GREECE, AND THE TROAD

Adapted from Mountain High Maps® Copyright © 1995 Digital Wisdom, Inc.

0   50   100   150   200   250 miles

Boreas
NORTH

THRACE

Hellespont

Mt. Olympus ▲

THESSALY

Greece

Apidanus Fl.

Troy • ▲ Mt. Ida

TENEDOS   TROAD

AEGEAN
SEA

LESBOS

Mt. Oeta ▲

SCYROS

Mt. Parnassus ▲
• Delphi

Mt. Helicon ▲

Mt. Erymanthus ▲

Athens
•
Corinth • • Piraeus

Mt. Maenalus
▲

ARCADIA

DELOS
PAROS •
NAXOS
Mt. Marpessa ▲

PELOPONNESE

IONIAN
SEA

Taenarus •

Cnossos
•
CRETE

ROME IN LATE ANTIQUITY

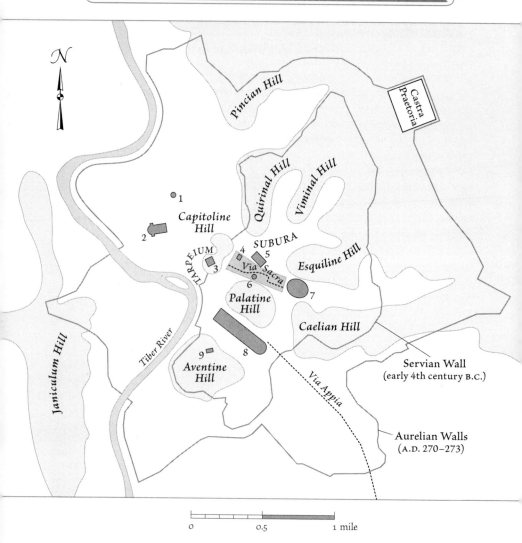

N

Pincian Hill

Castra Praetoria

Quirinal Hill

Viminal Hill

1

Capitoline Hill

2

SUBURA

TARPEIUM

4

5

3

Via Sacra

Esquiline Hill

6

7

Palatine Hill

Caelian Hill

9

8

Aventine Hill

Janiculum Hill

Tiber River

Via Appia

Servian Wall
(early 4th century B.C.)

Aurelian Walls
(A.D. 270–273)

0   0.5   1 mile

The shaded area encompassing the Via Sacra at the center of the map is the Roman Forum.

1 Pantheon
2 Theater of Pompey
3 Temple of Jupiter Optimus Maximus
4 Senate-house (Curia)
5 Temple of Peace
6 Temple of Vesta
7 Colosseum
8 Circus Maximus
9 Temple of Diana

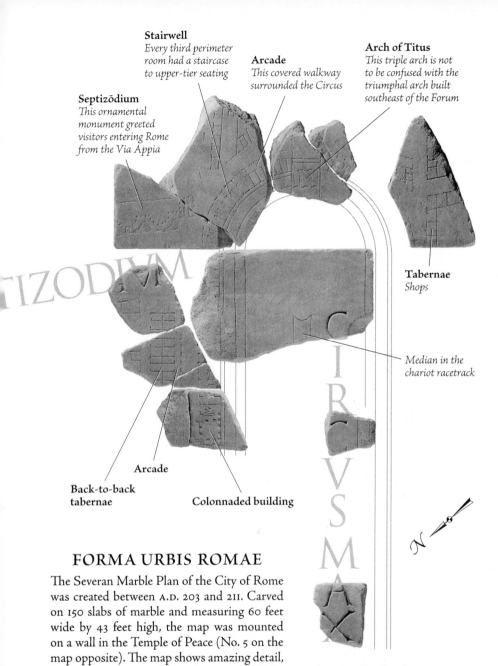

Stairwell
Every third perimeter room had a staircase to upper-tier seating

Arcade
This covered walkway surrounded the Circus

Arch of Titus
This triple arch is not to be confused with the triumphal arch built southeast of the Forum

Septizōdium
This ornamental monument greeted visitors entering Rome from the Via Appia

Tabernae
Shops

Median in the chariot racetrack

Arcade

Back-to-back tabernae

Colonnaded building

N

FORMA URBIS ROMAE

The Severan Marble Plan of the City of Rome was created between A.D. 203 and 211. Carved on 150 slabs of marble and measuring 60 feet wide by 43 feet high, the map was mounted on a wall in the Temple of Peace (No. 5 on the map opposite). The map shows amazing detail, from monuments and aqueducts to small shops and stairwells. Southeast was placed at the top of Roman urban maps.

About 10 percent of the map survives, in 1,186 pieces. Shown here are the pieces that remain of the area of the Circus Maximus (No. 8 on the map opposite).

The identity and location of a quarter of the surviving pieces are unknown, but Stanford University's Classics Department and Computer Graphics Laboratory, in collaboration with the Sovraintendenza ai Beni Culturali del Comune di Roma, are using three-dimensional modeling to "solve" the map. See their Web site at *http://formaurbis.stanford.edu.*

ABBREVIATIONS

In the notes to the selections, parentheses are used to enclose glosses and grammatical and other explanations. Square brackets are used to enclose Latin words omitted by an author for the sake of brevity, as well as English words that have no specific equivalent in the Latin original but that must be supplied in the translation. Square brackets also enclose references to numbered grammar and metrics points.

A.D.	**annō Dominī**, in the Christian era	indef.	indefinite
		indir.	indirect
abl.	ablative	inf.	infinitive
acc.	accusative	interr.	interrogative
acc.+inf.	accusative and infinitive	intr.	intransitive
act.	active	irreg.	irregular
adj.	adjective, adjectival	l.	line
adv.	adverb(ial)	lit.	literal(ly)
b.	born	ll.	lines
B.C.	before Christ, before the Christian era	loc.	locative
		m./M.	masculine
c.	**circā**, about	m.pl./M.PL.	masculine plural
cf.	**confer**, compare	n./N.	neuter
compar.	comparative	n.pl./N.PL.	neuter plural
cond.	conditional	n.o.p.	no other (principal) parts
conj. (after a number)	conjugation (e.g., 3 conj.)	neg.	negative
		nom.	nominative
conj.	conjunction	obj.	object
d.	died	pass.	passive
dat.	dative	perf.	perfect
decl.	declension	pers.	person
demon.	demonstrative	pl.	plural
dep.	deponent	pluperf.	pluperfect
e.g.	**exemplī gratiā**, for example	poss.	possessive
etc.	**et cetera**	pple.	participle
f. (after a number)	and the following line	prep.	preposition(al)
		pres.	present
f./F.	feminine	pron.	pronoun, pronominal
f.pl./F.PL.	feminine plural	refl.	reflexive
ff. (after a number)	and the following lines	rel.	relative
		sg.	singular
fl.	**floruit**, flourished	sub.	subordinate
Fl.	**Flūmen**, River (maps)	subj.	subjunctive
fut.	future	sup.	supine
gen.	genitive	superl.	superlative
i.e.	**id est**, that is	tr.	transitive
imp.	imperative	trans.	translate
imperf.	imperfect	viz	**videlicet**, that is to say
impers.	impersonal	voc.	vocative
ind.	indicative		
indecl.	indeclinable		

POETRY SELECTIONS

The Dream of Ilia

There were Roman poets before **Quintus Ennius** (239–169 B.C.), but he was the one responsible for setting Roman poetry firmly in the Greek tradition. Of his many works, the most significant was the **Annālēs**, an account in epic style of Roman history from its mythical beginnings up to his own day.

The following fragment, one of the few longer passages that survive from the **Annālēs**, comes from early in the poem where Ennius tells the story of Rome's foundation. After Aeneas escaped from Troy to Italy, he had two daughters by Eurydica (this version of the legend differs from that of Vergil). One of these, Ilia, is described as waking from a terrifying dream that she recounts to her unnamed sister. The dream hints at Ilia's union with the god Mars (**homo pulcher** in l. 5), by whom she will bear the twins Romulus and Remus. The obscure clause "[your] fortune will rise again from a river" may refer to the story that the twins were set adrift on the Tiber but driven ashore by a flood.

Et cita cum tremulis anus attulit artubus lumen.
talia tum memorat lacrimans, exterrita somno:
"Eurydica prognata, pater quam noster amavit,
vires vitaque corpus meum nunc deserit omne.

TEXT   *The Annals of Q. Ennius*, ed. O. Skutsch (Oxford University Press, 1985)
METER   hexameter [§M I]
      ēt cĭtă | cūm trĕmŭ|līs ‖ ănŭs | āttŭlĭt | ārtŭbŭ(s) | lūmĕn
      tālĭă | tūm mĕmŏ|rāt ‖ lăcrĭ|māns ēx|tērrĭtă | sōmnō
      (Early Latin poetry allowed the elision of final **s** before a word
      beginning with a consonant, as in **artubu(s)** above.)

1   **cita** *quick*, adj. agreeing with the subject **anus** (**-ūs** F. *old woman*, perhaps here a nurse), but trans. *quickly* [§G 55]; take **cum tremulīs** (*shaking*) with **artubus** (**artus -ūs** M. *limb*—a few 4th-decl. nouns have a dat./abl. pl. in **-ubus**, not **-ibus**); the object of **attulit** (**afferō -ferre** *bring*) is **lūmen** (lit., *light*, but trans. *torch*).

2   **tālia** is the object of **memorat** (historic pres. [§G 60]; **memorō -āre**, lit., *she speaks such [things as follows]*, i.e., *she spoke thus* (the understood subject is **Īlia**); **lacrimans** (**lacrimō -āre** *cry*) and **exterrita** (**exterreō -ēre** *frighten*) agree with the subject of **memorat**; take **somnō** (abl. of separation [§G 40]) with **exterrita**, *frightened out of sleep*.

3   **Eūrўdĭcā prōgnātă** voc. phrase, lit., *born of Eurydica* (abl. of origin [§G 41])— Ilia's unnamed sister, who is not the old woman of l. 1, is present; **pater quam noster amāvit** adj. clause referring back to **prognāta**—the relative **quam** is postponed [§G 4]; prose order would be **quam pater....**

4   **vīrēs** (nom. pl. of **vīs**) *strength*; **corpus meum ... omne** *my whole body*; **dēserit** (**dēserō -ere** *abandon*) is singular because it agrees with **vīta**, the nearer of the two subjects [§G 58] **vīrēs vītaque**, but trans. *strength and life abandon....*

nam me visus homo pulcher per amoena salicta   5
et ripas raptare locosque novos. ita sola
postilla, germana soror, errare videbar
tardaque vestigare et quaerere te neque posse
corde capessere: semita nulla pedem stabilibat.
exim compellare pater me voce videtur   10
his verbis: 'o gnata, tibi sunt ante gerendae
aerumnae, post ex fluvio fortuna resistet.'

5f. **homō pulcher** (*a handsome man*) is the subject of **vīsus** (supply **est**, i.e.,
seemed—the passive of **videō** can have the sense of *seem*), which is followed by an
inf. phrase **mē ... raptāre** (*to carry me off*); take **per amoena** (*pleasant*) **salicta**
(**salictum -ī** N. *willow grove*) **et rīpās** (**rīpa -ae** F. *[river] bank*) **... locōsque novōs**
(here *unfamiliar, strange*) together: *through pleasant willow groves and ...*—at this
point in the narrative, Ilia is presumably raped by Mars (the **homō pulcher**) and
becomes pregnant by him, but she conceals this from her sister; **sōla** (f.sg. nom.)
agrees with the subject of **vidēbar** (**ego** understood) in l. 7.

7 **postillā** *afterwards*; **germāna soror** lit., *full sister*, but trans. simply *sister*; **vidēbar**
I seemed (cf. **vīsus** [**est**] in l. 5).

8f. **tarda** *slow*, adj. agreeing with the subject of **vidēbar**, but trans. *slowly* [§G 55];
vestīgāre (**vestīgō** *search for*), **quaerere** (**quaerō** *look for*), and **capessere** (**capessō**
grasp) govern **tē**; **neque** here *but not*; **corde** abl. of place where [§G 38] *in [my]
heart*—*to grasp you in [my] heart* expresses the vagueness of a dream; **sēmita -ae**
F. *path*; **pēs pedis** M. *foot*; **stabilībat** old form of the imperf. **stabiliēbat** (**stabiliō**
-īre *make steady*)—lit., *no path made [my] foot steady*, i.e., *there was no path I could
follow*.

10 **exim** (= **exinde**) *then*; **compellō -āre** *address, speak to*; **pater** *[our] father*, i.e.,
Aeneas; **vōce** instrumental abl. [§G 47] *with [his] voice*, i.e., *aloud*; **vidētur** historic
pres. [§G 60].

11f. **hīs verbīs** another instrumental abl., but trans. *in these words*; **gnāta** (= **nāta**)
voc. *daughter*; **sunt ... gerundae** gerundive construction [§G 80] with **aerumnae**
(*troubles*; **aerumna -ae** F.) as subject and **tibī** as dat. of agent [§G 29], lit., *troubles
are to be borne by you*; **ante** and **post** are used adverbially; **fluvius -(i)ī** M. *river*;
resistō -ere here *rise again, be restored*—its normal meaning is *stop* (intr.), *resist*.

13 **ecfātus** perf. pple. of **ecfor -ārī** *say*; **germāna** voc. *sister*; **repente** *suddenly*;
recēdō -ere *withdraw, go away*.

14 **nec sēsē** (= **sē**) **... conspectum** lit., *nor did he give himself to [my] sight* (**con-
spectus -ūs** M.)—Ilia had only heard her father, not seen him; **corde cupītus**
[though] desired by [my] heart (instrumental abl. [§G 47]).

15f. **quamquam** (*although*) introduces two adverbial clauses of concession (with
the indicative), which are joined by **et** (l. 16); **multa** adverbial acc. [§G 16] *many
[times]*; scansion indicates **manūs** (not **manŭs**), and context shows that this is acc.
pl. after **tendēbam** (**tendō -ere** *stretch*); **caerula** *blue*; **templa** here *regions*; take
blandā (*coaxing*) with **vōce** (instrumental abl. [§G 47]).

17 **vix** *just now*; **aegrō cum corde meō** *with my heart sick*.

haec ecfatus pater, germana, repente recessit
nec sese dedit in conspectum corde cupitus,
quamquam multa manus ad caeli caerula templa   15
tendebam lacrimans et blanda voce vocabam.
vix aegro cum corde meo me somnus reliquit."

~: ENNIUS *Annālēs* I fr. xxix

LITTERA SCRIPTA MANET ·I·

In past centuries, a knowledge of Latin was expected of anyone who claimed to be educated, and many Latin phrases and sentences were in common use. Some came from Roman sources, some came from medieval and later writers, while others were part of the western European tradition and have no known origin. Those of the third type sometimes existed in different forms and were interpreted in different ways. An example is **et ego in Arcadia**, which was commonly inscribed on tombstones, where it was interpreted as *I too [was] in Arcadia*, that is, *I* (the dead person) *led a happy life*. Arcadia, the central region of southern Greece, was believed to be inhabited by happy rustics who led simple, uncomplicated lives. The saying was also used by people looking back on a happy and carefree youth before they assumed the responsibilities of adulthood.

However, there was another, possibly more authentic, form: **et in Arcadia ego**. This too was commonly seen on tombstones, but with the meaning *I [am] even in Arcadia*. Here the speaker is Death, who comes even to those who have enjoyed lives of happiness, similar to those of Arcadia's inhabitants.

In later pages, we will examine several Latin sayings and quotations that have been, and in some cases still are, current in society.

A Quarrel Between Slaves

Titus Maccius *Plautus* *(fl.* 220–184 B.C.) *took Greek comedies of the fourth and third centuries* B.C. *and, while preserving the original Greek settings, adapted them for a Roman audience. His rollicking humor manifests itself in the following scene, where a country slave, Grumio, comes to upbraid his city counterpart, Tranio. In the absence of their elderly master, Tranio has encouraged the master's son to indulge himself and squander his father's money. Grumio is depicted as old-fashioned and loyal, Tranio as deceitful and self-serving.*

GRUMIO – TRANIO.

GR. Exi e culina sis foras, mastigia,
　　　qui mi inter patinas exhibes argutias.
　　　egredere, erilis permities, ex aedibus.
　　　ego pol te ruri, si vivam, ulciscar probe.
　　　exi, inquam, nidoricupi, e culina. quid lates?　　5

TEXT　　Plautus *Comoediae*, ed. W. M. Lindsay (Oxford Classical Texts, 1904)
METER　iambic senarius [§M 8]
　　　　ēx(i) ē | cŭlī|nā ‖ sīs | fŏrās | māstī|gĭā
　　　　quī m(i) īn|tēr pătĭ|nās ‖ ēx|hĭbēs | ārgū|tĭās

The scene is set in a street outside the house belonging to the absent master, where his son and Tranio are leading a life of dissipation. Grumio, a slave from the master's country estate, is banging on the door to attract Tranio's attention.

1　**Exī** (2 sg. imp. **exeō exīre**) *come out;* **culīna -ae** F. *kitchen;* **sīs** (= **sī vīs**) *if you please* (spoken ironically); **forās** lit., *outside,* trans. *into the open;* **mastīgia -ae** M. *rascal* (here voc.).

2　**mī** shorter form of **mihi;** **patina -ae** F. *dish;* **exhibeō -ēre** *display;* **argūtiae -ārum** F.PL. (no SG.) *verbal wit*—we are to imagine that Grumio's knocking has already elicited a response from Tranio, who is working in the kitchen.

3　**ēgredere** (2 sg. imp. **ēgredior -ī**) *come out;* **erīlis** (adj. *of a master*) **permitiēs** (-ēī F. *ruin*) voc., trans. *[you] ruin of [our] master.*

4　**pol** *by Pollux!,* a common interjection to add emphasis (both **pol** and **hercle** (l. 18) are written without a capital letter); **rūrī** loc. [§G 51] *in the country;* **ulciscor -ī** *take vengeance on;* **probē** *thoroughly*—one punishment for an offending slave was to be sent to his master's country estate, where he would be given the heaviest work; Grumio thinks that this will happen to Tranio when the old master returns and that Tranio will be put in his (Grumio's) charge.

5　**nīdōricupī** voc. of **nīdōricupius** (a humorous formation unique to Plautus—cf. also ll. 19 and 24) *a person who loves the smell of cooking,* trans. *smell-lover;* **quid** *why.*

TR. Quid tibi, malum, hic ante aedis clamitatio est?
     an ruri censes te esse? abscede ab aedibus.
     abi rus, abi dierecte, abscede ab ianua.
     em, hocine volebas?
GR.   Perii. cur me verberas?   10
TR. Quia vivis.
GR.   Patiar. sine modo adveniat senex.
     sine modo venire salvom, quem absentem comes.
TR. Nec veri simile loquere nec verum, frutex,
     comesse quemquam ut quisquam absentem possiet.
GR. Tu urbanus vero scurra, deliciae popli,   15

6 **Quid tibi** (dat. of possessor [§G30]) ... **clāmitātiō est** lit., *why is there shouting for you?*, a humorous way of saying *why are you shouting?*; **malum** interjection indicating indignation, trans. *damn it!*; **hīc ante aedīs** *here in front of the house.*

7 **an** here introduces a direct question and implies surprise (here ironic), trans. *do you think you are [still] in the country?*; **abscēdō -ere** *go away.*

8 **abī** (2 sg. imp. abeō abīre) *go away*; **rūs** acc. of motion toward [§G13]; **dīērectē** *immediately*; **iānua -ae** F. *door.*

9 **em** interjection to draw attention (here to the blow that Tranio gives Grumio) *there [you are]!*; **hocine** (= hoc + -ne (interr. particle)) **volēbās** *is this what you wanted?*

10 **periī** (lit., *I'm ruined*) is Grumio's reaction to being hit—an English equivalent might be *yikes!*; **verberō -āre** *hit.*

11f. **sine** (2 sg. imp. sinō -ere *allow*) ... **senex** just (**modo**) *let the old man come*—the conj. **ut** is omitted from the subordinate clause **adveniat** (adveniō -īre) **senex**; the second **sine** is used in the same sense but with a different construction, [**senem**] **venīre salvom** (= **salvum**; trans. by an adverb [§G55], *safely*); **absens** (absentis) *absent*; **comēs** 2 sg. pres. ind. act. comedō -esse *eat*—in l. 12 the verb is used metaphorically in the sense *ruin* (i.e., by squandering his property), but in l. 14 it is used literally.

13f. **vērī simile** *likely* (lit., *similar to truth*); **loquere** = **loqueris** (2 sg. pres. ind. loquor loquī *speak*); **vērum** here an adj., *true*; trans. *what you say is neither likely nor true* (lit., *you say [something] neither likely nor true*); **frutex fruticis** F. *shrub*, here metaphorically *blockhead*; the postponed **ut** [§G4] introduces a noun clause [§G92] qualified by **vērī simile** and **vērum**, lit., *that anyone can* (**possiet** = **possit**) *eat anyone absent*, i.e., *that a person can eat someone who is absent*—Tranio is perversely misinterpreting Grumio's use of **comedō**.

15 **urbānus ... scurra** a city (lit., *urban*) *smart aleck* (**scurra -ae** M.); **vērō** *really*—Grumio is sarcastically referring to Tranio's witty last remark; **dēliciae** (-ārum F.PL.) **poplī** (= **populī**) *a general favorite, a darling of the people*, i.e., the sort of person whose talk and behavior make him popular; both phrases are in apposition [§G52] to **tū**; trans. *you, a real city smart aleck, a darling of the people.*

rus mihi tu obiectas? sane hoc, credo, Tranio,
quod te in pistrinum scis actutum tradier.
cis hercle paucas tempestates, Tranio,
augebis ruri numerum, genus ferratile.
nunc, dum tibi lubet licetque, pota, perde rem,   20
corrumpe erilem adulescentem optumum;
dies noctesque bibite, pergraecamini,
amicas emite, liberate, pascite
parasitos, obsonate pollucibiliter.
haecine mandavit tibi, quom peregre hinc it, senex?   25
hocine modo hic rem curatam offendet suam?
hocine boni esse officium servi existumas,

16f. **rūs mihi** acc. and dat. after **obiectās** (**obiectō -āre** *throw [something]* (acc.) *in [someone's]* (dat.) *face*); **sānē** *certainly*; **hōc** (abl. of cause [§G 48]) ... **quod** lit., *for this [reason, namely] that*, trans. *because*; **crēdō** (*I think*) is parenthetical; **pistrīnum -ī** N. *mill* (for grinding flour)—the very hard labor of turning the millstone was a punishment dreaded by slaves; **actūtum** *in the near future*; **trādier** (= **trādī; trādō -ere** *hand over*) is used in a future sense, trans. *that you will be consigned*.

18f. **cis** + acc. *within*; **hercle** *by Hercules!*; **tempestās tempestātis** F. *season*; **rūrī** see l. 4—Grumio sarcastically declares what will happen to Tranio: *you will increase the population* (lit., *number*) *in the country* (i.e., by being sent there for punishment), and then specifies the segment of the population that will be increased, **genus ferrātile** (another coinage unique to Plautus), *the iron mob*, a euphemism for *chain gang* (slaves were often chained to prevent them from running away).

20 **dum ... licetque** lit., *while it is pleasing* (**lubet**) *and permitted* (**licet**) *to you*, i.e., *while you want to and can*; **pōtō -āre** *drink*; **perde rem** *waste property*.

21 **corrumpō -ere** *corrupt, destroy*; **erīlem adulescentem** *young master* (both words were originally adjectives); **optumus** *excellent* (superl. of **bonus**, here used to express a very high degree [§G 54]).

22 **diēs noctēsque** acc. of time how long [§G 11]; **pergraecāminī** 2 pl. imp. **pergraecor -ārī** *play the Greek*, i.e., *make merry*—Greeks were supposed to know how to "live it up" in much the same way as the French are reputed to today.

23f. The imperatives **emite** and **līberāte** (**līberō -āre** *set free*) govern **amīcās** (*sweethearts, mistresses*—the reference is to slave girls); **pascite parasītōs** *feed* (**pascō -ere**) *parasites* (**parasītus -ī** M.)—parasites lived off others' hospitality (in the word's original meaning); **obsōnō -āre** *stock up* (i.e., with food for banquets); **pollūcibiliter** (still another coinage unique to Plautus) *sumptuously*—in these lines, Grumio uses the plural imperative as though he is addressing the absent young master as well as Tranio.

25 **haecine** = haec + **-ne** (interr. particle); **mandō -āre** *enjoin, bid*, trans. *give you these instructions*; **quom** (= **cum** [§G 95]) conj.; **peregrē** *to foreign parts, abroad*; **īt** = iit (3 sg. perf. ind. act. **eō īre**).

26 **hōcine** = **hōc** + **-ne** (interr. particle); take **hōc** with **modō**, *in this way*; **rem cūrātam ... suam** *his property looked after*; **offendō -ere** *find*.

ut eri sui corrumpat et rem et filium?

nam ego illum corruptum duco, quom his factis studet;

quo nemo adaeque iuventute ex omni Attica   30

antehac est habitus parcus nec magis continens,

is nunc in aliam partem palmam possidet.

virtute id factum tua et magisterio tuo.

TR. Quid tibi, malum, med aut quid ego agam curatio est?

an ruri, quaeso, non sunt, quos cures, boves?   35

lubet potare, amare, scorta ducere.

mei tergi facio haec, non tui fiducia.

GR. Quam confidenter loquitur.

TR.   At te Iuppiter

dique omnes perdant! fu! oboluisti alium.

❧ PLAUTUS *Mostellāria* 1–39

27f. **hocine** = **hoc** + **-ne** (interr. particle); take **hoc** with **officium** (-**(i)ī** N. *duty*)—from context we determine that we have **hŏcine** here, but **hōcine** in l. 26; **existumō** (or **-imō**) **-āre** *think*; **ut** introduces a noun clause [§G 92] qualifying **officium** (cf. l. 14); **erus -ī** M. *master*.

29 **dūcō -ere** here *consider*; **quom** (= **cum** [§G 95]) conj.; **factum -ī** N. *action*; **studeō -ēre** + dat. (here **factīs**) *devote oneself to*.

30ff. **quō** abl. of comparison [§G 42] *than whom*—its antecedent is **is** (l. 32); take **adaequē** (*equally*) with **parcus** (*sober*); **iuventūte ... Atticā** *from all the Athenian youth* (**iuventūs iuventūtis** F.); **antehāc** *previously*; **est habitus** *was considered* (**habeō -ēre**); **continens** *self-restrained*; **in aliam partem** *on* (lit., *into*) *the other side*, trans. *for the very opposite*; **palma -ae** F. *palm, first place*.

33 **virtūte ... tuā** instrumental abl. [§G 47], lit., *through your merit*, i.e., *thanks to you, through you*; **id factum [est]** *this has been done*; **magisteriō tuō** instrumental abl. [§G 47] *through your instruction* (**magisterium -(i)ī** N.).

34 **Quid tibi ... cūrātiō est** + abl., lit., *why is there concern for you with ...*, i.e., *why do you care about ...*; **malum** as in l. 6; **mēd** = **mē** (abl.).

35 **an** as in l. 7; **quaesō -ere** *ask*—a sarcastic addition of Tranio's, *I ask [you], tell me*; **cūrēs** potential subj. [§G 68] *you should be tending*.

36 Cf. l. 20: with **lubet** supply **nōbīs**, since both slave and young master are leading a wild life; **amāre** here *fornicate*; **scortum -ī** N. *prostitute*; **dūcere** here *bring home*.

37 **fidūciā** (abl. of manner [§G 45] *on the responsibility*; **fidūcia -ae** F.) governs two genitives, **meī tergī** and **tuī [tergī]**—Tranio means that if his misdeeds are discovered, he, not Grumio, will be flogged.

38 **Quam** *how* introduces an exclamation; **confīdenter** *audaciously*.

39 **perdant** subj. to express a wish [§G 67]; **fu** interjection indicating disgust, *yuck!*; **oboluistī ālium** *you have a stink* (**oboleō -ēre**) *of garlic* (**ālium -(i)ī** N.) [*about you*]—the perf. tense indicates that Grumio has been smelling of garlic throughout the conversation.

An Insolent Slave

Like Plautus, **Publius Terentius Āfer** *(c. 195–159 B.C.), known in English as* **Terence,** *wrote comedies based on Greek originals but in a way that more faithfully reflected their spirit. His quieter humor is seen in the following selection, where a father* (**Simō**), *who has chosen a wife for his son, warns an insolent and cheeky slave* (**Dāvos**) *not to interfere in the arrangements he has made.*

SIMO – DAVOS.

SI.   Meum gnatum rumor est amare.

DA.   Id populus curat scilicet.   185

SI.   Hoccin agis an non?

DA.   Ego vero istuc.

SI.   Sed nunc ea me exquirere

iniqui patris est; nam quod antehac fecit nil ad me attinet.

dum tempus ad eam rem tulit, sivi animum ut expleret suom;

TEXT   Terence *Comoediae,* ed. R. Kauer and W. M. Lindsay
        (Oxford Classical Texts, 1926, reprinted with supplement 1958)
METER   iambic octonarius [§M9] (except for ll. 196–198)
        mēūm gnā|tūm rū|mŏr ēst | ămār(e) | īd ‖ pŏpŭ|lŭ(s) cū|rāt scī|lĭcĕt
        hŏccĭn ă|gĭs ān | nŏn ĕgŏ | vēr(o) īs|tūc ‖ sēd | nūnc ĕă| m(e) ēxquī|rĕrĕ
        (In the first line, **meum** is pronounced as one syllable (synizesis).)
        iambic senarius [§M8] (ll. 196–198)
        sī sēn|sĕr(o) hŏdĭ|ē ‖ quīc|qu(am) ĭn hīs | tē nūp|tĭīs
        fāllā|cĭāē | cōnā|rī ‖ quō | fĭānt | mĭnŭs

185   *There is a rumor* (**rūmor rūmōris** M.) *that my son* (**gnātus** = **nātus**) *is in love*—Simo has heard that his son, like most young men in Greek comedies of this type, has fallen in love with an unsuitable woman; Davos' sarcastic reply, *Of course* (**scīlicet**), *people are interested in that,* implies that such a commonplace event would hardly excite gossip.

186f.   **Hoccin** = **hoc** + **-ne** (interr. particle); **agō -ere** here *pay attention to;* **an nōn** *or not;* with **Ego vērō istuc** (= **istud**) supply **agō; nunc**—it is not appropriate now for Simo to investigate his son's love affairs when he is arranging the latter's marriage; **ea mē exquīrere** *for me to inquire into* (**exquīrō -ere**) *these [things];* **inīquī** (*harsh*) **patris** gen. of characteristic [§G19]; **antehāc** *previously;* **nīl** here an emphatic negative; **attinet** (**attineō -ēre**) **ad** + acc. *concern.*

188   **tempus** here *circumstances,* i.e., the bachelor status of his son; **ferō ad** + acc. *be suited to;* **eam rem** i.e., having love affairs; **sīvī** 1 sg. perf. ind. act. **sinō -ere** *allow;*

nunc hic dies aliam vitam defert, alios mores postulat:
dehinc postulo sive aequomst te oro, Dave, ut redeat iam
                                        in viam.   190
hoc quid sit? omnes qui amant graviter sibi dari uxorem ferunt.

DA.   Ita aiunt.

SI.   Tum si quis magistrum cepit ad eam rem improbum,
ipsum animum aegrotum ad deteriorem partem plerumque
                                        adplicat.

DA.   Non hercle intellego.

SI.   Non? hem.

DA.   Non: Davos sum,
                                      non Oedipus.

SI.   Nempe ergo aperte vis quae restant me loqui?

DA.   Sane quidem.   195

---

ut (postponed [§G4]) introduces a noun clause [§G92]; **animum ... suom**
(= **suum** [§G95]) *his inclination*; **expleō -ēre** lit., *fill up*, trans. *follow.*

189   **hic diēs** *this day*, which is the day fixed by Simo for his son's marriage; **aliam
... aliōs** trans. both *different*; **dēferō -ferre** *bring*; **mōrēs** *conduct, behavior*; **postulō
-āre** *require* (but in l. 190 *ask*).

190   **dehinc** *consequently*; **sīve** *or if*; **aequomst** (= **aequum est**) *it is right*—it was
hardly normal or dignified for a master to beg (**ōrō**) a favor of a slave; **redeō -īre**
(*return*), here used metaphorically with **in viam** (*to the [proper] path*).

191   **hoc quid sit?** *[you ask] what this is?*—the subjunctive **sit** implies that Simo is
repeating a question of Davos (**hoc quid est?**) in indirect form, which Simo does
to make his point absolutely clear; take **graviter** with **ferunt**, *take it badly*, followed by the acc.+inf. [§G10] **dārī uxōrem.**

192   **Ita aiunt** *so they say*—Davos ironically pretends that he does not know this
himself; **quis** indef. pron. *anyone*; **magistrum ... improbum** *a rascally guide*; **capiō
-ere** here *get.*

193   **ipsum animum aegrotum** *[his] heart, itself [love]sick*—the victim is already
suffering before he gets a rascally guide, who is the subject of **adplicat** (**adplicō
-āre** *lead*); **ad dēteriōrem partem** *in a worse direction*; **plērumque** *often.*

194   **hercle** interjection *by Hercules*; **intellegō -ere** *understand*—Davos is pretend-
ing to be stupid, but he does not fool Simo; **hem** *really?*, an interjection expressing
surprise, here feigned; Oedipus was proverbial for his feat of solving the riddle of
the Sphynx.

195   The question has no introductory word; so (**ergō**) *of course* (**nempe**), spoken
sarcastically; **apertē ... loquī** *to state frankly*; **vīs** 2 sg. pres. ind. **volō velle** *wish*;
quae restant lit., *what [things] remain* (**restō -āre**) *[for me to say]*; **Sānē quidem**
lit., *certainly, indeed*, trans. *yes, indeed.*

SI.   Si sensero hodie quicquam in his te nuptiis
      fallaciae conari quo fiant minus,
      aut velle in ea re ostendi quam sis callidus,
      verberibus caesum te in pistrinum, Dave, dedam usque
                                       ad necem,
      ea lege atque omine ut, si te inde exemerim, ego pro te molam.   200
      quid, hoc intellextin? an nondum etiam ne hoc quidem?
DA.   Immo callide:
      ita aperte ipsam rem modo locutu's, nil circum itione usus es.

~: TERENCE *Andria* 185–202

196f.   **senserō** 1 sg. fut. perf. act. **sentiō -īre** *perceive,* but trans. by the present [§G66]; **quicquam ... fallāciae** (partitive gen. [§G24]) lit., *anything of deceit* (**fallācia -ae** F.), i.e., *any deceit*; **nuptiae -ārum** F.PL. *marriage*; **tē ... cōnārī** acc.+inf. [§G10]; **quō ... minus** (joined in classical Latin as **quōminus**, lit., *by which ... not,* i.e., *so that ... not*) introduces a noun clause after an expression implying prevention [§G90]; **fīant** 3 pl. pres. subj. act. **fīō fierī** *happen*—the understood subject of **fīant** is **nuptiae**; trans. *so that it* (the marriage) *does not happen,* i.e., *to prevent it from happening.*

198   The subject of **velle** is **tē** (l. 196); the indirect question [§G91] **quam sīs callidus** is the subject of **ostendī**, lit., *how clever you are to be shown,* trans. *to show how clever you are.*

199   **verberibus caesum** lit., *beaten* (**caedō -ere**) *with lashes* (**verber verberis** N.), trans. *flogged*; **tē in pistrīnum ... dēdam** *I will deliver* (**dēdō -ere**) *you to the mill* (**pistrīnum -ī** N.; see note to Plautus *Mostellāria* 17, page 8); **usque ad necem** lit., *right up to* (**usque** reinforces **ad**) *death* (**nex necis** F.), trans. *until you die.*

200   **eā lēge atque ōmine** *on this condition* (**lex lēgis** F.) *and expectation* (**ōmen ōminis** N.)—the phrase anticipates the noun clause introduced by **ut** [§G92]; **inde** *from there,* i.e., *from the mill*; **exēmerim** 1 sg. perf. subj. act. **eximō -ere** *take away*; **prō** + abl. *in place of*; **molam** 1 sg. pres. subj. act. **molō -ere** *grind* (in a mill).

201   **quid** here *well*; **intellextīn?** (= **intellexistī** + **-ne** (interr. particle); **intellegō -ere** *have you understood?*; **an** (*or*) introduces the second half of a double question and **intellexistī** is to be supplied; in **nōndum etiam** (*not even yet*) followed by **nē hoc quidem** (*not even this*), the two negatives provide emphasis—trans. *or even now do you not [understand] this?*; **Immō** contradicts Simo's second question, and **callidē** reinforces Davos' assertion (trans. *but [I do], thoroughly*)—by using **callidē**, Davos is mocking Simo's use of **callidus** in l. 198.

202   **ita** here *for,* giving the reason for the previous statement; **apertē** *clearly*; **modo** *now*; **locūtu's** = **locūtus es**; **itiōne** (**itiō itiōnis** F. [*the act of*] *going*) is qualified by **circum** (adv. *around*), lit., *a going around,* i.e., *circumlocution*—the ablative is governed by **ūsus es** (**ūtor ūtī** + abl. *use*).

Verse Epitaphs

Many thousands of Roman epitaphs have survived, some of which take the form of a short poem. The three given here illustrate three common types, both in prose and verse. The first is a plain statement about the dead person; in the second, the tombstone itself is conceived as speaking and inviting the passerby to stop and read what is written on it (Roman tombs were very often placed alongside a road); in the third, it is the dead person who addresses the traveler. On Roman funerary practices, see page 79.

The texts of these epitaphs have been taken from E. H. Warmington, Remains of Old Latin, volume IV (Loeb Classical Library, 1940); the spelling and some forms have been changed to the classical norm.

A Epitaph of **Lucius Cornelius Scipio**, *a member of a famous noble family (c. 160 B.C.)*

L[ucius] Cornelius Gn[aei] f[ilius] Gn[aei] n[epos] Scipio.
Magnam sapientam multasque virtutes
aetate cum parva possidet hoc saxum.
cui vita defecit, non honos, honore,
is hic situs qui numquam victus est virtute.   5
annos natus XX is locis mandatus.
ne quaeratis honore qui minus sit mandatus.

A 1 The first line, which is in prose, gives the full name of the dead person and something of his ancestry; abbreviations (here expanded) were regularly used when giving this information; **nepōs nepōtis** M. *grandson.*

2f. The poem, which begins here, is in the Saturnian meter, the oldest verse form in Latin. Only a few examples survive, and its metrical structure has never been satisfactorily explained. The subject of the clause is **hoc saxum** (*this [tomb]stone*), which is said to *hold* (**possideō -ēre**) *great wisdom* (**sapientia -ae** F.) *and many virtues with a short life.*

4f. The antecedent of **cui** is **is** in l. 5, *for whom* (**cui** is a dative of disadvantage [§G 31]); **dēficiō -ere** *run short, fail*; **honōs** old form of the nom. sg. of **honor**, which is used here in two different senses: (1) *honor, probity* and (2) *public office*; **honōre** abl. of respect [§G 46]; lit., *for whom life, not [his own] probity, ran short with respect to public office*, i.e., *he was worthy of assuming public office but did not live long enough to do so*; **hīc** *here*; with **situs** (*buried*) supply **est**; **victus est** *was surpassed*; **virtūte** abl. of respect [§G 46].

6 **annōs ... XX** acc. of time how long [§G 11]; **nātus** perf. pple. of **nascor nascī** *be born*; **locīs** dat. *to the places*, a euphemism for *to the Underworld*; with **mandātus** (**mandō -āre** *entrust*) supply **est**.

7 **nē quaerātis** negative command [§G 72]; take **honōre** (here *public office*) with **sit mandātus** (**mandō -āre** *entrust [someone]* (acc.) *with [something]* (abl.)); **quī** (here *why*) introduces an indirect question [§G 91]; **minus** = **nōn**; trans. *do not ask why he was not entrusted with public office.*

B *Epitaph of **Claudia**, a married woman about whom nothing*
   further is known (c. 135–120 B.C.)

Hospes, quod dico paullum est; adsta ac perlege.
hic est sepulchrum haud pulchrum pulchrae feminae.
nomen parentes nominarunt Claudiam.
suum maritum corde dilexit suo.
Natos duos creavit; horunc alterum   5
in terra linquit, alium sub terra locat.
sermone lepido, tum autem incessu commodo.
domum servavit, lanam fecit. dixi. abi.

METER   iambic senarius [§M8]
      hōspēs | quŏd dī|cō ‖ pāul|l(um) ēst ād|st(a) āc pēr|lĕgĕ
      hīc ēst | sĕpūl|chr(um) hāud ‖ pūl|chrūm pūl|chrāe fĕ|mĭnāe

B 1   **Hospes** here *stranger*, i.e., a passerby unknown to the dead person; the subject
of **dīcō**, *I*, is the tombstone itself; **paullus** *short*; **adstā** (**adstō -āre**) and **perlege**
(**perlegō -ere**) are both 2 sg. imp. act., *stand by and read [it] through.*
2   **hīc** *here*; **sepulchrum -ī** N. *grave*; **haud** = **nōn**; this line (*here is the not beautiful
tomb of a beautiful woman*) plays on the popular (but completely false) etymology
of **sepulchrum** from **pulcher** and the negative prefix **sē-**.
3   **nōmen** cognate acc. [§G17] with **nōminārunt** (= **nōmināvērunt**; **nōminō -āre**
name) with **Claudiam** in apposition [§G52] to it, lit., *named [her] the name Claudia*, i.e., *gave her the name of Claudia*; **parens parentis** M./F. *parent*.
4   **corde ... suō** abl. of manner [§G45] *with [all] her heart*; **dīlexit** (**dīligō -ere**)
loved.
5f. **Nātōs duōs** *two sons*; **creō -āre** *give birth to*; **hōrunc** archaic form of **hōrum**;
alterum ... alium ... *the one ... the other ...* (the variation is because of the meter); **linquit** (**linquō -ere** *leave*) and **locat** (**locō -āre** *put*) either are historic presents [§G60] or represent the state of affairs at Claudia's death.
7   Supply **erat**—both phrases are ablatives of description [§G44]; **sermō sermōnis**
M. *conversation*; **lepidus** *charming*; **incessus -ūs** M. *bearing*; **commodus** *proper*; the
two ablative phrases are joined by **tum autem** (lit., *but then*), trans. *her conversation was charming, yet her bearing was proper*—charming conversation may not
have always accompanied the bearing considered proper for a Roman matron.
8   **domum servāvit** *she kept* (**servō -āre**) *house*; **lāna -ae** F. *wool*—spinning wool
for clothing was a traditional occupation for a Roman housewife; **dixī** i.e., *that is
what I have to tell you*; **abī** (2 sg. imp. **abeō abīre**), lit., *go away*, trans. *go on your
way*—the wish not to unduly delay the reader is a frequently occurring theme in
epitaphs.

C *Epitaph of Helvia Prima, another otherwise unknown Roman matron (c. 45 B.C.)*

Tu qui secura spatiaris mente, viator,
  et nostri vultus dirigis inferiis,
si quaeris quae sim, cinis en et tosta favilla;
  ante obitus tristis Helvia Prima fui.
coniuge sum Cadmo fructa Scrateio,   5
  concordesque pari viximus ingenio.
nunc data sum Diti longum mansura per aevum
  deducta et fatali igne et aqua Stygia.

METER elegiac couplet [§M2]
  tū quī | sēcū|rā ‖ spătĭ|ārīs | mēntĕ vĭ|ātŏr
  ēt nōs|trī vūl|tūs ‖ dīrĭgĭs | īnfĕrĭ|īs

C 1 **sēcūra … mente** abl. of manner [§G45] *with carefree mind;* **spatiāris** 2 sg. pres. ind. spatior -ārī *walk leisurely, stroll;* **viātor** viātōris M. here voc. *traveler.*

2 Take **nostrī** (gen. of **nōs** (pl. for sg. [§G53])) with **inferiīs**—the possessive adjective **nostrīs** would be more normal; **vultūs** acc. pl., here *gaze, glance* (pl. for sg. [§G53]); **dīrigō -ere** *direct;* **inferiīs** (inferiae -ārum F.PL.) dat. of motion toward [§G35] *to my* (**nostrī**) *funeral offerings*—the deceased Helvia supposes that the traveler is looking at the customary offering placed on her tomb.

3 **quaeris** introduces an indirect question [§G91], **quae sim**, and what follows is the answer; **cinis cineris** M. *ashes;* **ēn** *behold!, look!;* **tosta** perf. pple. of **torreō -ēre** *burn;* **favilla -ae** F. *ashes, remains;* trans. *look! [I am now simply] ashes and burned remains.*

4 **obitūs tristīs** (pl. for sg. [§G53]) *sad death* (**obitus -ūs** M.).

5 This hexameter, which has only five feet, is defective; **coniuge** (coniunx coniugis M./F. *spouse*) abl. (with **Cadmō … Scrateiō**) after **sum … fructa** (fruor fruī + abl.), trans. *I enjoyed Cadmus Scrateius [as my] spouse.*

6 Trans. **concordēs** (concors (concordis) *harmonious*) by an adverb [§G55]; **parī** (pār (paris) *matching*) … **ingeniō** abl. of manner [§G45] *with matching temperaments;* **viximus** 1 pl. perf. ind. act. **vīvō -ere** *live.*

7f. **data sum** 1 sg. perf. ind. pass. **dō dare; Dīs Dītis** M. another name for **Plūtō**, the king of the Underworld; **longum … per aevum** *for a long age* (**aevum -ī** N.); **mansūra** f.sg. nom. of the fut. pple. of **maneō** (-ēre), agreeing with the understood subject *I,* lit., *going to stay;* **dēducta** perf. pple. of **dēdūcō -ere** *take down;* **et … et …** *both … and …;* **fātālī** (*destructive*) **igne … aquā Stygiā** (**Stygius** adj. *of the river Styx*) both instrumental ablatives [§G47]—the fire is that of the pyre on which Helvia's body was cremated; **aquā Stygiā** is a rather odd way of referring to Helvia's passage over the river Styx in Charon's boat (see page 79).

  This epitaph illogically combines the two conflicting beliefs about an afterlife. The old Roman belief was that the dead woman lived on in her tomb, and so required funeral offerings (**inferiae**), and that she could still communicate with the living. However, according to imported Greek notions, her shade went down to the Underworld, where it was to stay forever.

The New Eroticism

From **Quintus Lutātius Catulus** (*pronounced* Cátulus) (*c. 150–87* B.C.),
*an aristocrat who was both a politician and a general, we have two poems
that represent a new trend in Latin literature. Roman poets of this time
looked for models to contemporary fashions in Greek poetry, which had begun a century and a half earlier with Callimachus and his contemporaries.
One popular genre was the erotic epigram, as exemplified here.*

A   Aufugit mi animus; credo, ut solet, ad Theotimum
    devenit. sic est, perfugium illud habet.
  quid, si non interdixem, ne illunc fugitivum
    mitteret ad se intro, sed magis eiceret?
  ibimus quaesitum. verum, ne ipsi teneamur   5
    formido. quid ago? da, Venus, consilium.

TEXT   *The Fragmentary Latin Poets,* E. Courtney
         (Oxford University Press, 2003)
METER elegiac couplet [§M2]
        aūfŭ|gīt m(i) ănĭ|mūs ‖ crēd(o) | ūt sŏlĕt | ād Thĕŏ|tīmŭm
        dēvē|nīt sīc | ēst ‖ pērfŭgĭ(um) | īllŭd hă|bĕt

A 1f. The author speaks of his **animus** (trans. *soul or heart*) as a runaway slave;
aufūgit 3 sg. perf. ind. act. **aufūgiō -ere** *run away*; **mī** (shorter form of **mihi**) dat.
of possessor [§G30]; **ut solet** *as it is accustomed [to do]*; **dēvēnit** + **ad** lit., *has gone
[to stay with]*, trans. *gone off to*; **Theotīmus -ī** M. Greek name—both epigrams
have a homosexual theme, which was common in Greek poetry of the time; **sīc
est** *so it is*, i.e., this must be what has happened; **perfugium -(i)ī** N. *refuge*; **habet**
lit., *has*, trans. *avails itself of.*

3f. **quid, sī nōn interdixem** (= **interdixissem; interdīcō -ere**) ...? lit., *what, [as] if
I hadn't forbidden* ...? (**nōn interdixem** is contrary to what happened and hence
the subj. is used), i.e., *didn't I forbid* ...?; what was forbidden is expressed by the
indirect command [§G91] **nē illunc** (= **illum**) ... **intrō** (*that he* (i.e., Theotimus)
should not admit (**intrō mittō -ere**) *that runaway* (**fugitīvus -ī** M.) *into his house*
(**ad sē** lit., *to himself*—**sē** is used because it refers to the subject of **mitteret**)); **sed
magis ēiceret** *but instead* (**magis**) *[hadn't I given orders that] he should throw [it]
out* (after **magis** we must understand **nōn iussissem ut** ...), trans. *didn't I tell Theotimus not to admit that runaway into his house, but, on the contrary, to throw it out?*

5f. **ībimus** and **teneāmur** both pl. for sg. [§G53]; **quaesītum** sup. to express purpose [§G82]; **vērum** *but*; **nē ipsī teneāmur** noun clause [§G89] after **formīdō,**
I am afraid (**formīdō -āre**) *lest I myself may be caught* (lit., *held*); **quid agō?** idiomatic for *what am I to do?*, which would normally be **quid agam?** (deliberative
subj. [§G70]); **Venus Veneris** F. *goddess of love.*

B   Constiteram exorientem Auroram forte salutans,

     cum subito a laeva Roscius exoritur.

   pace mihi liceat, caelestes, dicere vestra:

     mortalis visus pulchrior esse deo.

B 1f.   **Constiteram … forte … cum** *by chance I had stood* (**consistō -ere**) … *when*—the chance was that both events happened at the same time; **exorior -īrī** *rise*; **Aurōra -ae** F. *goddess of the dawn*—the practice of addressing the dawn or morning sun is attested elsewhere; **subitō** *suddenly*; **ā laevā [manū]** *on the left*—for a Roman augur, omens such as lightning that appeared on the left were regarded as favorable; Roscius was a contemporary of Catulus and is known from other sources; **exoritur** historic pres. [§G 60], lit., *rises*, trans. *came into view*—for Catulus, the appearance of Roscius was comparable to that of the dawn.

3   **pāce … vestrā** abl. of attendant circumstances [§G 45] *by your leave*, i.e., without offending you; **liceat** subj. to express a wish [§G 67] *may it be allowed*; **caelestēs** voc. pl. *O heavenly beings* (**caelestis = deus**)—the Romans were always careful to avoid offending the gods in word or deed.

4   **mortālis** (**mortālis** M.) *the mortal*, i.e., Roscius; **vīsus [est]** *seemed*; **deō** abl. of comparison [§G 42] *than a god*.

PROVERBIA DE PROSCAENIO ·I·

Proverbs abound in the plays of Plautus and Terence.

Dictum sapienti sat est.   PLAUTUS *Persa* 729

                                    TERENCE *Phormiō* 541

A word to the wise is sufficient.

Nihil homini amico est opportuno amicius.

                                      PLAUTUS *Epidicus* 425

A friend in need is a friend indeed.
(lit., *Nothing is friendlier to a person than a friend*
[*who is*] *available when wanted.*)

Flamma fumo est proxima.   PLAUTUS *Curculiō* 53
Where there's smoke, there's fire.
(lit., *Flame follows very closely on* (i.e., *is next to*) *smoke.*)

Quod tuom est meum est; omne meum est autem tuom.

                                    PLAUTUS *Trinummus* 329

What's yours is mine, and what's mine is yours.
(lit., *What's yours is mine, and indeed all of what's mine is yours.*)

For more proverbs from the plays of Plautus and Terence, see pages 26 and 36.

The Roman Book

For Roman authors from Ennius up to those of the Silver Age, such as Tacitus and Juvenal, the ordinary form of books and their manner of production were completely different from what we have today. Books throughout the Mediterranean region were the same as they had been four centuries earlier in the heyday of Greek civilization. The Greeks themselves had taken over techniques from Egypt, where both writing and papyrus, the ancient equivalent of paper, had been invented.

No technique even vaguely similar to printing was known. Every copy of a book had to be individually written out by hand. This did not increase the cost of books, since the scribes who produced them were usually slaves. However, apart from the time and labor required to transcribe each and every copy of a book, the method had a serious flaw: Unlike the results of printing, no two copies could ever be guaranteed to be exactly alike. Inevitably, each copy of a book had its own peculiar variations, and as the process was repeated over centuries, more variations crept into the text. With the passage of time, it became progressively more difficult to know exactly what the author had originally written.

The traditional form of a Roman book would be equally surprising to a modern reader. From the time of its invention by the Egyptians about 3000 B.C., a book consisted of a roll of papyrus, a material resembling paper, with a length of 20 to 26 feet and a width of ten inches, though sizes varied considerably. The text was written on this in narrow columns at right angles to the roll's length. A roll consisted of up to 20 papyrus sheets, which were slightly overlapped to allow for gluing. To make up the sheets themselves, the stalks of the papyrus, a large reedlike plant that grew in profusion along the Nile River, were shredded into thin strips. A number of these were placed side by side to make up the dimensions of the sheet required, and these were completely covered with another layer of strips placed at right angles to the first. Since this was done with the strips still moist, the sap acted as a glue when the sheet was placed in a press. After removal, the sheet was smoothed with pumice, or some similar abrasive, and trimmed. Many examples of papyrus rolls have survived and show that as a material for writing, it is comparable to paper, although it differs in being less flexible.

After a roll had been made up, a turned wooden rod resembling a small rolling pin was attached to each end, and the rods' projecting handles allowed the long papyrus strip to be rolled up from either direction. A text could then be transcribed onto one side of the roll—the back was left blank—and the roll was then ready for use. The lower handle of the rod on the outer end was held in the left hand, and the corresponding handle of the other rod in the right. As the beginning of the roll was unwound, the first columns were read. The reader's right and left hands kept unrolling and rolling up respectively until the end was reached, at which point the roll, like a modern videocassette, had to be rewound for the next user. The whole procedure was best performed if the roll was on the knees of the reader when seated (much the same as when we read a book by the fire), and it is in this position that ancient sculptures depict a person reading. Papyrus rolls were not suited to desks as we know them.

The reader's problems were not confined to manipulating the roll, however, as conventions of presenting a text were different from those today. Scribes wrote in capitals, because an equivalent of our lowercase had yet to develop. This in itself would not have created difficulty, but a line of capitals normally gave no indication of where one word ended and the next began; words were not always separated by word spaces.* In addition, punctuation was rarely used. The unfortunate reader was faced with a string of letters and was obliged to split these up, first into words, then into clauses, and then into sentences. As an example, we may take the beginning of the *Aeneid*, which could have appeared on a papyrus roll in the rustic scribal hand of the day as follows,

ARMAVIRVMQVECANOTROIAEQVIPRIMVSABORIS
ITALIAMFATOPROFVGVSLAVINIAQVEVENIT
LITORAMVLTVMILLEETTERRISIACTATVSETALTO

that is,

ARMA VIRVMQVE CANO TROIAE QVI PRIMVS AB ORIS
ITALIAM FATO PROFVGVS LAVINIAQVE VENIT
LITORA MVLTVM ILLE ET TERRIS IACTATVS ET ALTO

It is little wonder that ancient readers always read aloud. The act of articulation would have helped them recognize the divisions (words, clauses, and sentences) that had to be made before a text could be understood.

The upper limit of what could be put on one roll was about 18,000 words (40 or so pages like this one); a longer roll would have been too cumbersome to use. Most works of Roman literature were, of course, much longer and so had to be accommodated on two or more rolls. This led to longer poems and prose works being composed in (that is, split up

---

*Sometimes, as in the Gallus fragment mentioned below, word division was indicated by a centerline dot. This practice also occurs in inscriptions.

into) sections, each of which was contained within one roll. The Latin term that we translate by *book* (**liber**) refers to a single papyrus roll. A longer literary work contained as many books as the rolls necessary to record it; Vergil's *Aeneid* was in 12 books and so required 12 rolls. Shorter works could have been combined on a single roll (for example, Horace's *Ars poētica*, which ran to 476 lines), but no one roll comprised what we today would consider a book of normal length (say, 200 to 300 pages).

There is not a single classical Latin work for which we have the original author's copy, but fragments of papyrus rolls have survived from Herculaneum and elsewhere. One of the most interesting contains lines from a poem by Cornelius Gallus, a contemporary of Vergil, and may have been written during the poet's lifetime (see also page 190).

The papyrus roll was not a user-friendly production. It was awkward to read and cumbersome to consult. Whereas today we simply flip through a book's pages for a reference or to check the accuracy of a quotation, an ancient scholar was obliged to work through a roll until the necessary passage appeared; there was no equivalent to pagination. The limited amount of material that a roll could contain was also a serious disadvantage.

In the first century of the Christian era, a new type of book was beginning to appear, the **cōdex**. An earlier form had already existed for several centuries and consisted of a small number of thin wooden boards (**tabellae***) smeared on each side with wax and held together by a leather thong that was threaded through holes along one edge of each board, similar to modern spiral binding. This allowed the user to turn the boards over and inscribe a message into the wax on either side with a sharp-pointed stylus. Tabellae were not intended for anything approaching the amount of text that even a papyrus roll could hold. They were for letters, messages, note taking, and the like, and could be reused simply by applying a new coating of wax to the boards.†

When papyrus was substituted for wood in making tabellae, recycling became more difficult, but the modern form of the book was born. Sheets of papyrus were folded in two and a number of such foldings were held together by stitching along the spine, just as in better-quality books today. The front, back, and spine were protected by what we now call the binding. With this new form of book, readers had something that was consid-

---

*The singular **tabella** is the term for one board; the plural **tabellae** is the term for a joined set of boards and can be used for one notebook of this sort or many.
†In 1973, archaeological excavations at Vindolanda, a Roman fort near Hadrian's Wall in northern England, produced a number of original **tabellae** from around A.D. 100. These contain letters and military documents, many of which display features not previously known.

Araldo de Luca/CORBIS

Roman statue of the grammarian Marcus Mettius Epaphroditus holding a papyrus roll in his left hand.

erably easier to use, more convenient to consult when a particular reference or passage was required, and capable of holding the contents of many
rolls. By the end of the first century A.D., the codex had begun to be used
for literary works, but the transition from roll to codex lasted several hundred years. It was assisted by the substitution of parchment for papyrus.
Parchment (also called vellum) was made from animal skins and was not
only thin and white but also extremely strong and durable. It was ideal for
the codex—and for preserving works of literature.

Martial was the first classical writer to speak of the transition from
rolls to books with pages. He was obviously impressed with the compact-
ness of the new book form:

> Quam brevis inmensum cepit membrana Maronem!
> *How small a parchment has packaged the vast Maro (i.e., Vergil)!*
>
> *Epigrammata* 14.186.1

He also described a paginated copy of Ovid's *Metamorphōsēs*:

> Haec tibi multiplici quae structa est massa tabella,
>   carmina Nasonis quinque decemque gerit.
> *This large object, which has been put together for you*
>   *from many pages, contains the 15 books of Naso.*   *Epigrammata* 14.192

∾⦂∾

The Inevitability of Death

Titus *Lucrētius* Cārus (*c. 94–c. 55* B.C.) *lived in troubled times, during which the Roman state was disrupted by internal strife and civil war. In his poem* Dē rērum nātūrā (On the nature of the universe), *he expounds the doctrines of the Greek philosopher* Epicūrus *on the physical nature of the universe and the consequences of these doctrines for suffering humanity.*

A fundamental tenet of Epicurean philosophy was that, because there is no afterlife, we have no reason to fear death. In the following selection, Lucretius strengthens the minds of waverers by pointing out that even the greatest and most powerful men have not escaped death.

Hoc etiam tibi tute interdum dicere possis
"lumina sis oculis etiam bonus Ancus reliquit,   1025
qui melior multis quam tu fuit, improbe, rebus.
inde alii multi reges rerumque potentes
occiderunt, magnis qui gentibus imperitarunt.

TEXT   Titi Lucreti Cari *De Rerum Natura*, ed. C. Bailey
        (Oxford University Press, 1947)
METER   hexameter [§M I]
        hōc ĕtĭ|ām tĭbĭ | tūt(e) ‖ īn|tērdūm | dīcĕrĕ | pōssīs
        lūmĭnă | sīs ŏcŭ|līs ‖ ĕtĭ|ām bŏnŭs | Āncŭ(s) rĕ|līquĭt
        (Early Latin poetry had allowed the elision of final **s** before a word beginning with a consonant, and Lucretius follows this practice, as in **Ancu(s)**.)

1024   **Hoc** *this*, i.e., what follows; **tūte** emphatic form of **tū**; **interdum** adv. *at times*; **possīs** potential subj. [§G 68] *you could*—Lucretius is suggesting that the reader could tell himself what follows in order to overcome any fear he might have of death.

1025   **lūmen lūminis** N. *light* (pl. for sg. [§G 53])—the light is the light of day; **sīs** (an old form of **suīs**) **oculīs** instrumental abl. [§G 47] *with his eyes*; **etiam** here *even*; **Ancus -ī** M. the fourth king of Rome; *abandoned* (**relinquō -ere**) *the light with his eyes* is a roundabout way of saying that he died.

1026   **melior** compar. of **bonus**; **multīs … rēbus** abl. of respect [§G 46] *in many ways* (lit., *things*); **quam** here *than*; **improbe** voc. [*you*] *shameless [person]*—the reader is conceived as rebuking himself for imagining that he should fare better than Ancus.

1027   **inde** *since then*; **rērum potentēs** *masters* (**potens (potentis)** adj. used as a noun, lit., *powerful*) *of things*, i.e., *lords of the world*.

1028   **occidō -ere** *die*; **quī**, which is placed second in its clause ([§G 4]; the same word order is used in l. 1029), has as its antecedents the two nouns in l. 1027; **imperitārunt** (= **imperitāvērunt** [§G 95]) 3 pl. perf. ind. act. **imperitō -āre** *rule over*, which takes the dative (**magnīs … gentibus**).

ille quoque ipse, viam qui quondam per mare magnum
stravit iterque dedit legionibus ire per altum   1030
ac pedibus salsas docuit super ire lacunas
et contempsit equis insultans murmura ponti,
lumine adempto animam moribundo corpore fudit.
Scipiadas, belli fulmen, Carthaginis horror,
ossa dedit terrae proinde ac famul infimus esset.   1035
adde repertores doctrinarum atque leporum,

1029   **ille quoque ipse** *even that [man] himself*—Xerxes I, king of Persia, who in 480 B.C. constructed a bridge of boats over the Hellespont to invade Greece; this feat, which Lucretius describes in ll. 1029–1032, was universally regarded as an extraordinary display of power; **quondam** *once*; **per** + acc. *over*.

1030   **strāvit** (3 sg. perf. ind. act. **sternō -ere**) here in the technical sense of *pave*, trans. *who once paved a road over the mighty sea*; **dedit legiōnibus** *allowed [his] legions* (**legiō legiōnis** F.); **iter** (cognate acc. [§G17]) … **īre** *to go on a way*; **altum -ī** N. poetic word for *sea*, trans. *the deep*.

1031   **pedibus** (**pēs pedis** M.) instrumental abl. [§G47] *with [their] feet*; **salsās** … **lacūnās** (**lacūna -ae** F.) is governed by **super**, trans. *over the salt pools*, i.e., *over the sea*; the understood object of **docuit** (**doceō -ēre**) is the legions in l. 1030, trans. *taught them*.

1032   **contempsit** (**contemnō -ere**) *showed his contempt for*; **equīs** (instrumental abl. [§G47]) **insultans** (**insultō -āre** lit., *jump on*) *[by] prancing on [it]* (i.e., the sea) *with horses*; **murmura** (**murmur murmuris** N.) **pontī** (**pontus -ī** M.) *the sea's mutterings*—**murmura** (acc. after **contempsit**) suggests that the sea was making low noises of protest.

1033   **lūmine ademptō** (**adimō -ere**) abl. absolute [§G49] *the light [of day] having been taken away*, trans. *when deprived of the light [of day]*; **animam** … **fūdit** (**fundō -ere**) *breathed* (lit., *poured*) *out [his] soul*—according to ancient belief, the soul left the body through the mouth at the point of death; **moribundō corpore** abl. of separation [§G40] *from [his] dying body*.

1034   **Scīpiadās** (**-ae** M.), an eccentric form of the cognomen **Scīpiō**, is used here because of the meter; the person referred to is **Publius Cornēlius Scīpiō Āfricānus** the elder, the most famous and successful Roman general in the Second Carthaginian War, who finally defeated Hannibal in 202 B.C.; **bellī fulmen** (**fulminis** N.) *the thunderbolt of war*; **Carthāgō Carthāginis** F. the city of Carthage in what is now Libya; **horror horrōris** M. *terror*.

1035   **os ossis** N. *bone*; **terrae** dat.; **proinde ac [sī]** … **esset** (3 sg. imperf. subj. **sum**) *in the same way as [if] he were*—the subjunctive is used because this is a supposition; **famul** old nom. sg. of **famulus -ī** M. *house slave*; **infimus** *lowliest*.

1036   **adde** (2 sg. imp. act. **addō -ere**) *add*—Lucretius is introducing other classes of eminent people; **repertor repertōris** M. *inventor, creator*; **doctrīna -ae** F. here *system of thought*, i.e., the different varieties of philosophy; **lepōs lepōris** M. lit., *charm*, but here denoting the arts that give pleasure (music, painting, and the like).

adde Heliconiadum comites; quorum unus Homerus
sceptra potitus eadem aliis sopitus quiete est.
denique Democritum postquam matura vetustas
admonuit memores motus languescere mentis,   1040
sponte sua leto caput obvius obtulit ipse.
ipse Epicurus obit decurso lumine vitae,
qui genus humanum ingenio superavit et omnis
restinxit, stellas exortus ut aetherius sol."

~: LUCRETIUS *Dē rērum nātūrā* 3.1024–1044

1037f.   The **Helicōniades** (**Helicōniadum** F.PL.) were the Muses, divinities associated with Helicon, a mountain in Boeotia sacred to Apollo, who was the patron
god of musicians and poets, trans. *dwellers on Helicon*; their **comitēs** (**comes comitis** M./F. *follower*) were different types of artists, in particular, poets—the phrase
Helicōniadum comitēs is more restrictive than **repertōrēs lepōrum**; the antecedent of **quōrum** is **comitēs**; **ūnus Homērus** (-ī M.) **sceptra** (pl. for sg. [§G53];
sceptrum -ī N. *scepter*) **potītus** (**potior** -īrī *gain possession of, win*) *Homer alone*
(**ūnus**) *having won the scepter [of poetry]*—Homer was regarded by both Greeks
and Romans as the supreme poet; **eādem** (**īdem** + dat. *the same as*) ... **quiēte**
(**quiēs quiētis** F. *sleep*) instrumental abl. [§G47]; **aliīs** (dat. after **eādem**) *the others,*
i.e., other poets; **sōpītus ... est** (**sōpiō** -īre *put to sleep*); trans. *has fallen asleep in*
(lit., *with*) *the same slumber as the others.*

1039ff.   **dēnique** *finally*—for Lucretius, the final two examples are the most important; **Dēmocritus** (-ī M.) the Greek philosopher who formulated an atomic
theory that was taken over by **Epicūrus** (-ī M.), who for Lucretius was the genius
who had solved all of humanity's problems; **postquam** (*after*; here postponed
[§G4]) takes the perfect tense where in English a pluperfect is used; **mātūra vetustās** (**vetustātis** F.) *ripe old age*; **admonuit** (**admoneō** -ēre *warn*) has **Dēmocritum**
as its object and is also followed by an acc.+inf. [§G10], **memorēs mōtūs languescere** (**languescō** -ere *become feeble*); **memorēs mōtūs ... mentis** lit., *the remembering activities* (**mōtus** -ūs M.) *of the mind*, i.e., the mental processes that make up
memory; **sponte suā** a set phrase, *by his own will, voluntarily*; **lētō** (**lētum** -ī N.
death) dat. with **caput** (**capitis** N. *head*) ... **obtulit** (**offerō** -ferre *deliver*) and also
with **obvius** (here *presenting [himself]*), lit., *he himself, of his own will, presenting
[himself] to death, delivered [his] head [to it]* (i.e., death)—*he committed suicide.*

1042   **obīt** contraction of **obiit** (3 sg. perf. ind. **obeō obīre** *die*); **dēcursō** (**dēcurrō**
-ere *run through, run one's course*) **lūmine vītae** abl. absolute [§G49], trans. *after he
had run through the light of life*—Lucretius seems to be referring to a relay race in
which successive runners received and passed on lighted torches.

1043f.   **genus hūmānum** *the human race*; **ingeniō** (**ingenium** -(i)ī N. *intellect*) abl.
of respect [§G46]; **superō** -āre *surpass*; **omnīs** is the object of **restinxit** (**restinguō**
-ere) *he extinguished all*, which repeats the meaning of the previous clause but
leads on to the metaphor introduced by the postponed **ut** [§G4] (*just as*); **stellās**
(**stella** -ae F.) **exortus** (**exorior** -īrī *rise*) ... **aetherius** (*heavenly, in the heavens*)
sōl, trans. *just as the rising* (**exortus**, though perfect, has a present sense [§G74])
sun in the heavens [extinguishes] the stars.

True Piety

O genus infelix humanum, talia divis
cum tribuit facta atque iras adiunxit acerbas!   1195
quantos tum gemitus ipsi sibi, quantaque nobis
vulnera, quas lacrimas peperere minoribus nostris!
nec pietas ulla est velatum saepe videri
vertier ad lapidem atque omnis accedere ad aras
nec procumbere humi prostratum et pandere palmas   1200

TEXT   Titi Lucreti Cari *De Rerum Natura*, ed. C. Bailey
        (Oxford University Press, 1947)

METER hexameter [§M1]
      ō gĕnŭs | īnfē|līx ‖ hū|mānūm | tālĭă | dīvīs
      cūm trĭbŭ|īt ‖ fāc|t(a) ‖ ātqu(e) ī|rās ‖ ād|iūnxĭt ă|cērbās

1194f. **Ō genus infēlix hūmānum** acc. of exclamation [§G14], trans. *O unhappy human race*; the subordinate clauses are introduced by **cum** (*when*), which is postponed [§G4]; **tālia … facta** *such actions*—in the preceding lines, Lucretius has described features of traditional religion and its all-powerful gods; **dīvīs** (**dīvus -ī** M.) *to the gods*, dat. after **tribuit** (*attributed*; **tribuō -ere**); **īrās … acerbās** pl. for sg. [§G53] *bitter anger*; **adiunxit** *added* (i.e., to the conception of the gods; **adiungō -ere**)—as well as creating the universe, the gods were supposed to be capable of conceiving anger against the human race.

1196f.   Lucretius speaks of the effect of religious beliefs on those who originally conceived them (and whom he has previously mentioned) and on his own and later generations; **quantōs … gemitūs** (**gemitus -ūs** M. *groan*) **… quanta … vulnera … quās lacrimās** are governed by **peperēre** (= **peperērunt** [§G95], *produced*; **pariō -ere**), and each introduces an exclamation containing a dative: **sibi** *for themselves*, **nōbīs** *for us* (i.e., Lucretius' generation—the **vulnera** are emotional wounds), **minōribus nostrīs** *for our descendants* (**minōrēs minōrum** M.PL.); **ipsī** [*they*] *themselves*, i.e., those who first conceived the attributes of the Roman gods.

1198f.   **nec pietās ulla est** (*nor is it any piety* (**pietās pietātis** F.)) is followed by six infinitive phrases that describe various practices of traditional Roman religion; **vēlātum … vidērī vertier ad lapidem** *to be seen veiled* (**vēlō -āre**) *turning* (lit., *to be turning*; **vertier** is an archaic form of **vertī**, pres. inf. pass. of **vertō -ere**—the passive is used here in a reflexive sense [§G59]) *to a stone* (**lapis lapidis** M.)—the stone is either a statue or a sacred stone of the sort that marked boundaries or was supposed to have magical powers; in praying, a Roman, his head veiled, approached with the cult object on his right and spoke his prayer without facing it; he then turned toward it (**vertier**) and prostrated himself on the ground with hands spread open (l. 1200); **omnīs … ārās** trans. *every altar* (**āra -ae** F.)—altars were placed in the open in front of temples, not inside them; **accēdō -ere** (with **ad**) *approach*.

1200   **prōcumbō -ere** *be in a prone position, lie*; **humī** loc. [§G51] *on the ground* (**humus -ī** F.); **prostrātus** *stretched out, flat*; **pandō -ere** *spread open*; **palma -ae** F. *palm (of the hand)*.

ante deum delubra nec aras sanguine multo
spargere quadrupedum nec votis nectere vota,
sed mage pacata posse omnia mente tueri.

~: LUCRETIUS *Dē rērum nātūrā* 5.1194–1203

1201f.   **deum** = **deōrum** [§G 95]; **dēlubrum -ī** N. *shrine, temple*—the person praying is in front of the temple (only an elect few were allowed inside); **sanguine
multō … quadrupedum** instrumental abl. [§G 47], lit., *with much blood of animals*
(**quadrupēs quadrupedis** M/F. lit., *four-footed animal*); **spargō -ere** *sprinkle*—
when an animal was sacrificed, its neck was cut in such a way that the blood
flowed onto the altar; **vōtīs nectere vōta** *to join* (**nectō -ere**) *vows with vows*, i.e., *to
make a large number of vows*—a vow was a promise to do something for a divinity
in return for a future favor.

1203   **sed mage** (= **magis**) *but rather*—Epicureans believed that there were gods
but that they played no part in human affairs; consequently, true piety toward
them consisted in a rational understanding of the universe; **pācātā posse omnia
mente tuērī** [it is piety] *to be able to observe* (**tueor tuērī**) *everything with a tranquil
mind.*

PROVERBIA DE PROSCAENIO ·II·

Proxumus sum egomet mihi.   TERENCE *Andria* 636
Charity begins at home./I'm taking care of Number One.
(lit., *I'm [the one] nearest to myself.*)

Necesse est facere sumptum qui quaerit lucrum.
                                                PLAUTUS *Asināria* 217
You have to spend money to make money.
(lit., *He who seeks profit must make an expenditure.*)

Nemo solus satis sapit.   PLAUTUS *Mīles glōriōsus* 885
Two heads are better than one.
(lit., *No man is wise enough by himself.*)

Quot homines tot sententiae.   TERENCE *Phormiō* 454
There are as many opinions as there are people.

In scirpo nodum quaeris.   PLAUTUS *Menaechmī* 247
Nodum in scirpo quaeris.   TERENCE *Andria* 941
You're looking for trouble where there isn't any.
(lit., *You're looking for a knot in a bulrush.*)

For more proverbs from the plays of Plautus and Terence, see pages 17 and 36.

Love and Rejection

Gaius Valerius *Catullus (c. 84–c. 54 B.C.) was born at Verona in northern Italy and, as a young man, came to Rome. His private means were apparently sufficient to allow him to enjoy the pleasures of city life and to follow his literary interests. As a poet, he belonged to the group of writers (sometimes called the* **poētae novī**) *who, following the lead of Quintus Lutātius Catulus and others, were introducing contemporary Greek literary traditions and practices of the time to Roman audiences.*

Catullus wrote some formal poetry, including a short epic (an epyllion), but the greater part of his work consists of short, informal poems of a personal nature that are concerned with the poet himself and his contemporaries. Several of the latter poems relate to an affair he had with a woman whom he calls **Lesbia**. *(We are told by a later author, Apuleius, that her real name was* **Clōdia**. *In order to conceal the real name of his lover, Catullus, like other Roman poets, used a name that was metrically equivalent:* **Lēsbĭă = Clōdĭă**.) *His passionate devotion was at first reciprocated, but when she finally tired of him, he was overwhelmed with bitterness and despair.*

A   Vivamus, mea Lesbia, atque amemus,
    rumoresque senum severiorum
    omnes unius aestimemus assis.
    soles occidere et redire possunt:
    nobis, cum semel occidit brevis lux,   5
    nox est perpetua una dormienda.

TEXT   C. Valerii Catulli *Carmina*, ed. R. A. B. Mynors
        (Oxford Classical Texts, 1958)
METER   hendecasyllable [§M3]
        vīvā|mūs mĕă | Lēsbĭ(a) | ātqu(e) ă|mēmŭs
        rūmō|rēsquĕ sĕ|nūm sĕ|vērĭ|ōrŭm

A 1ff.   **Vīvāmus ... amēmus ... aestimēmus (aestimō -āre** *value*) jussive subj. [§G69] *let us live*, etc.—Catullus uses **vīvō** here in the sense *enjoy life*, not simply *be alive*; trans. **rūmōrēs (rūmor rūmōris** M.) as sg., *gossip*; **senum** gen. pl. of **senex** *old man*; **sevērior** compar. of **sevērus** *strict, narrow-minded*—the comparative here expresses a high degree [§G54], trans. *too/very narrow-minded*; **ūnius ... assis** gen. of value [§G21] *at a single as* (**as assis** M. a coin of small value).

4   **sōlēs** pl. used for poetic effect; **occidō -ere** *set*.

5f.   Take **nōbis** (dat. of agent [§G29]) with **est ... dormienda** (gerundive [§G80] of **dormiō -īre**), *must be slept by us*, i.e., *we must sleep*; **occidit** 3 sg. perf. ind. act. *has set*; **perpetuus** *continuous*.

da mi basia mille, deinde centum,
dein mille altera, dein secunda centum,
deinde usque altera mille, deinde centum.
dein, cum milia multa fecerimus,   10
conturbabimus, illa ne sciamus,
aut ne quis malus invidere possit,
cum tantum sciat esse basiorum.

~: Catullus *Carmina* 5

7ff.   **mī** shorter form of **mihi**; **bāsium** -(i)ī N. *kiss*; **mille** indecl. adj. in sg. *thousand*; **centum** indecl. adj. *hundred*; **dein** = **deinde**; **altera** (*another*) agrees with **mille** [**bāsia**]; **secunda** (*a second*) agrees with **centum** [**bāsia**]; **usque** here *continuously, without stopping.*

10   **mīlia** *thousands* (noun, pl. of **mille**); **fēcerīmus** fut. perf., but trans. *have made up* [§G66].

11   **conturbō -āre** *go bankrupt*—as if their kisses were money, Catullus and Lesbia will dishonestly declare themselves bankrupt and so be able to start again (**conturbō** is the verb used for fraudulent bankruptcy); **illa nē sciāmus** *so that we do not know their number* (lit., *them*)—if they did, they might feel hesitation in going on.

12   **quis malus** *some malicious [person]*; **invideō -ēre** here *cast the evil eye*—according to a widespread superstition, certain people could cause misfortune simply by looking at someone they disliked or envied.

13   **tantum ... bāsiōrum** lit., *so much of kisses* (partitive gen. [§G24]), trans. *so many kisses.*

Horatiana ·I·

The power of alcohol to stimulate poetic imagination, a claim still made today, was already recognized in ancient times.

Nulla placere diu nec vivere carmina possunt,
quae scribuntur aquae potoribus.   *Epistulae* 1.19.2f.
No poems that are written by water drinkers
can give pleasure or endure for long.

For more Horatiana, see pages 86, 89, 97, 100, and 176.

B   Quaeris, quot mihi basiationes
    tuae, Lesbia, sint satis superque.
    quam magnus numerus Libyssae harenae
    lasarpiciferis iacet Cyrenis,
    oraclum Iovis inter aestuosi   5
    et Batti veteris sacrum sepulcrum;
    aut quam sidera multa, cum tacet nox,
    furtivos hominum vident amores:
    tam te basia multa basiare
    vesano satis et super Catullo est,   10
    quae nec pernumerare curiosi
    possint nec mala fascinare lingua.

~: Catullus *Carmina 7*

TEXT   C. Valerii Catulli *Carmina*, ed. R. A. B. Mynors
        (Oxford Classical Texts, 1958)
METER   hendecasyllable [§M3]
        quaērīs | quŏt mĭhĭ | bāsĭ|ātĭ|ōnēs
        tŭāē | Lĕsbĭă | sīnt să|tīs sŭ|pērquĕ

B 1f.   **quot** (indecl. adj. *how many*) introduces an indirect question [§G91], hence
        sint is subjunctive; **mihi** dat. of reference [§G32] *for me*; **bāsiātiō bāsiātiōnis** F.
        kiss; **satis superque** an idiomatic phrase, *enough and more [than enough]*.
3   Catullus compares the number of kisses required to the sands of the Libyan
        desert and the stars of the night sky; these comparisons are contained in subordi-
        nate clauses introduced by **quam magnus numerus Libyssae harēnae** (lit., *how
        great the number of Libyan sands* (sg. for pl. [§G53])) and **quam sīdera multa** (l. 7)
        (*how many stars* (**sīdus sīderis** N.)), and the main clause begins **tam tē bāsia multa
        bāsiāre** (l. 9) (*to kiss you so many kisses*). A change in order and conjunctions is
        necessary for idiomatic English, *to give you as many kisses as [there are] Libyan
        sands [that] ... or* (**aut**) *stars [that]....*
4   **lāsarpīciferīs ... Cȳrēnīs** abl. of place where [§G38] *in silphium-bearing Cyrene*
        (**Cȳrēnae -ārum** F.PL.)—Cyrene was a Greek city in what is now Libya; its main
        export was silphium, a plant used for medicinal purposes; here the name Cyrene
        is used for the city itself and all the territory it controlled.
5f.   **ōrāc(u)lum** (-ī N. *oracle*) **... et ... sepulcrum** (-ī N. *tomb*) are governed by **in-
        ter**; the oracle of **Iuppiter** (**Iovis** M.) **aestuōsus** (*parched Jupiter*, identified with
        the Egyptian god Ammon) was on an oasis in the Libyan desert (see also page
        177); **Battus** (-ī M.) was the legendary founder of Cyrene, where his tomb stood.
8f.   **furtīvōs ... amōrēs** *the stolen loves* (i.e., *love affairs*); **bāsiō -āre** *kiss*.
10ff.   **vēsānō ... Catullō** dat. of reference [§G32] *for demented Catullus*—Catullus
        is demented by his love for Lesbia; the antecedent of **quae** is **bāsia** (l. 9); **per-
        numerō -āre** *count in full*; **cūriōsī** *curious [people]*, here *busybodies*; **possint** poten-
        tial subj. [§G68] *would be able*; **mala lingua** *an evil tongue*, i.e., someone who could
        utter a curse or spell; with **fascināre** (**fascinō -āre** *bewitch*) supply **possit**.

c   Miser Catulle, desinas ineptire,
    et quod vides perisse perditum ducas.
    fulsere quondam candidi tibi soles,
    cum ventitabas quo puella ducebat,
    amata nobis quantum amabitur nulla.   5
    ibi illa multa cum iocosa fiebant,
    quae tu volebas nec puella nolebat,
    fulsere vere candidi tibi soles.
    nunc iam illa non vult: tu quoque, impotens, noli,
    nec quae fugit sectare, nec miser vive,   10
    sed obstinata mente perfer, obdura.
    vale, puella, iam Catullus obdurat,
    nec te requiret nec rogabit invitam.

TEXT   C. Valerii Catulli *Carmina*, ed. R. A. B. Mynors
        (Oxford Classical Texts, 1958)
METER   limping iambic [§M10]
        mĭsēr | Cătūl|lĕ ‖ dē|sĭnās | ĭnēp|tīrĕ
        ēt quōd | vĭdēs | pĕrīs|sĕ ‖ pēr|dĭtūm | dūcās

c 1f.   Catullus sometimes addresses himself (as here), sometimes Lesbia; **dēsinās
        … dūcās** jussive subj. [§G69] *stop!* … *consider!*; **ineptiō -īre** *be foolish*; l. 2 contains
        two acc.+inf. constructions [§G10], one embedded in the other: **quod vidēs pe-
        risse perditum [esse] dūcās** *consider that what you see to have vanished has been lost.*
3   **fulsēre** (= **fulsērunt** [§G95]; 3 pl. perf. ind. act. **fulgeō -ēre**) *shone*; **candidī …
        sōlēs** *bright suns* used metaphorically for happy times; **tibi** dat. of advantage
        [§G31] *for you.*
4   **ventitābās** (**ventitō -āre** *go frequently*) trans. *you always went*; **quō** lit., *to where*;
        puella here in the sense of *girlfriend*, trans. *your girl*; **dūcēbat** used *to lead [you].*
5   **amāta** agrees with **puella** (l. 4); **nōbīs** dat. of agent [§G29], pl. for sg. [§G53]
        by me; **quantum** lit., *how much*, i.e., *as much as*; **nulla** *no [woman].*
6   **ibi … cum** *then when*; **illa multa … iocōsa** *those many playful [things]*; **fiēbant**
        lit., *used to be done*, trans. *happened.*
7   The antecedent of **quae** is **iocōsa** (l. 6).
8   **vērē** *really.*
9   **nunc** and **iam** are combined for emphasis, trans. *but now*; **impotens** (*lacking in
        self-control, irresolute*) is vocative (Catullus is upbraiding himself), trans. *[although]
        irresolute*; **nōlī** (2 sg. imp. **nōlō nolle**) *be unwilling.*
10   The antecedent of **quae** is the understood object of **sectāre** (2 sg. imp. **sec-
        tor -ārī** *pursue*), **[eam]** *her*, i.e., Lesbia; trans. **miser** by an adverbial phrase, *in
        unhappiness.*
11   **obstinātā mente** instrumental abl. [§G47] *with resolute mind*; **perfer** (2 sg. imp.
        perferō -ferre) *bear up!*; **obdūrō -āre** *be firm.*
13   **requīrō -ere** *seek out*; **rogabit invītam** *ask for your favors [if you are] unwill-
        ing*—**rogō -āre** here *ask for sexual favors.*

at tu dolebis, cum rogaberis nulla.
scelesta, vae te! quae tibi manet vita?   15
quis nunc te adibit? cui videberis bella?
quem nunc amabis? cuius esse diceris?
quem basiabis? cui labella mordebis?
at tu, Catulle, destinatus obdura!

~: CATULLUS *Carmina* 8

14   **rogāberis** (2 sg. fut. pass.; **rogō** is used here in the same sense as in l. 13) **nulla**
you will not be asked for your favors—the adjective **nulla**, which agrees with the
understood subject **tū**, is used as the equivalent of the adverb **nōn**.

15   **scelesta** *wretched [woman]*; **vae tē** *woe to you!*, i.e., *damn you!*; **quae tibi manet
vīta?** *what life is left (lit., remains) for you?*

16   **adībit** (3 sg. fut. act. **adeō adīre**) *will approach*; **cui** dat. of reference [§G 32] *to
whom, in whose eyes*; **vidēberis** (2 sg. fut. pass.) *will you seem*; **bella** *beautiful*—a
colloquial word of the sort Catullus uses in his personal poetry.

17   **cuius esse dīceris?** *whose (i.e., whose love) will you be said to be?*

18   **bāsiō -āre** *kiss*; **cui** (dat. of possessor [§G 30]) **labella** (**labellum -ī** N.) *whose
lips*; **mordeō -ēre** *bite*—Romans were less restrained in showing affection than
the average Anglo-Saxon.

19   **destinātus obdūrā** lit., *[being] steadfast, be firm*, trans. *be steadfast and firm*.

D   Odi et amo. quare id faciam, fortasse requiris.
      nescio, sed fieri sentio et excrucior.

~: CATULLUS *Carmina* 85

TEXT   C. Valerii Catulli *Carmina*, ed. R. A. B. Mynors
          (Oxford Classical Texts, 1958)
METER   elegiac couplet [§M2]
          ōd(i) ĕt ă|mō quā|r(e) id || făcĭ|ām fŏr|tāssĕ rĕ|quīrĭs
          nēscĭŏ | sēd fĭĕ|rī || sēntĭ(o) ĕt | ēxcrŭcĭ|ŏr

D 1   **faciam** subj. in indir. question [§G 91]; **requīrō -ere** *ask*.
2   **excrucior** lit., *I am being tormented* (**excruciō -āre**).

The Effect of Love

A poem that appears to have been written by Catullus in the first stages of his affair with Lesbia is a translation from the early Greek poetess Sappho (fl. 600 B.C.). It was from Sappho's home (the Greek island of Lesbos) that Catullus gave his lover the name **Lesbia** *(lit., the lady of Lesbos), which evoked the romantic past of Greek lyric poetry.*

Ille mi par esse deo videtur,
ille, si fas est, superare divos,
qui sedens adversus identidem te
    spectat et audit
dulce ridentem, misero quod omnis   5
eripit sensus mihi: nam simul te,
Lesbia, aspexi, nihil est super mi
    <vocis in ore;>

TEXT   C. Valerii Catulli *Carmina*, ed. R. A. B. Mynors
        (Oxford Classical Texts, 1958)
METER   Sapphic stanza [§M5]
        īllĕ | mī pār | ēssĕ dĕ|ō vĭ|dētŭr
        īllĕ | sī fās | ēst sŭpĕ|rārĕ | dīvōs
        quī sĕ|dēns ād|vērsŭs ĭ|dēntĭ|dēm tē
        spēctăt ĕt | āudĭt

1   **mī** (also in l. 7) shorter form of **mihi**; **pār** (**paris**) + dat. (here **deō**) *equal to*; **vidētur** *seems* (the more common meaning of the passive of **videō** -**ēre**).
2   **sī fās est** *if it is right [to say so]*—Romans were always careful not to offend divine powers in any way (cf. Catulus B3, page 17); supply **vidētur** with **superāre** (**superō** -**āre** *surpass*); **dīvus** -**ī** M. = **deus**.
3f.   The antecedent of **quī** is **ille** in ll. 1 and 2); the acc. **tē** is governed by **adversus** (prep. + acc. *opposite, facing*) as well as by **spectat** and **audit** but need only be translated with the verbs; **identidem** adv. *continually*.
5   **dulce rīdentem** (modifying **tē** in l. 3) lit., *laughing a sweet thing*, i.e., *laughing sweetly* (adverbial acc. [§G16]); take **miserō** with **mihi** (l. 6); **quod** (postponed [§G4]) *[something] that*; take **omnīs** with **sensūs** (l. 6).
6   **ēripiō** -**ere** *snatch*; the meaning of the other words shows that **sensūs** is acc. pl. (**sensus** -**ūs** M. one of the five senses); **mihi** dat. of disadvantage [§G31], lit., *to the disadvantage of me*, i.e., *from me*; **simul** (= **simulac**) conj. *as soon as*.
7f.   **aspiciō** -**ere** *see, look at*; **nihil … vōcis** lit., *nothing of voice*, i.e., *no voice* (partitive gen. [§G24]); **est super** (= **superest**) *remains* (**supersum**); the angle brackets of l. 8 indicate that this line is missing in the manuscripts of Catullus—the sense, however, can be restored from Sappho's original, which has survived.

lingua sed torpet, tenuis sub artus
flamma demanat, sonitu suopte   10
tintinant aures, gemina teguntur
    lumina nocte.

∾: Catullus *Carmina* 51.1–12

9f.   **sed** is postponed [§G 4]; **torpeō -ēre** *be paralyzed*; **tenuis … flamma** *subtle flame*; **sub** here *(down) into*; **artus -ūs** M. *limb*; **dēmānō -āre** *run down*; **sonitū suōpte** (= **suō**) instrumental abl. [§G 47] *with their own sound* (**sonitus -ūs** M.).
11f.   **tintinō -āre** *ring* (intr.); **gemina … nocte** instrumental abl. [§G 47] *with double* (lit., *twin*) *night*; **lūmen lūminis** N. here *eye*.

Hadrian's Last Verse

After the assassination of Domitian in A.D. 96, Rome enjoyed a succession of rulers who both maintained the Empire and allowed much greater freedom for the individual than had been known in the previous one hundred years. The third of these emperors was Hadrian, who ruled from A.D. 117 to 138.

A scholar and poet as well as a competent general and administrator, he spent much of his time as emperor on expeditions to expand and consolidate Roman rule, as is attested by the wall that he constructed in northern England that bears his name. Of the few surviving scraps of his poetry, the most moving are the lines he is said to have composed on his deathbed:

Animula vagula blandula,
hospes comesque corporis,
quae nunc abibis in loca,
pallidula rigida nudula,
nec ut soles dabis iocos?
                The Fragmentary Latin Poets (ed. E. Courtney), page 382
*Poor wandering sweet soul, guest and companion of the body,
to what places will you now depart, pale, stiff, naked, and not
jest* (lit., *give jokes*) *as you are accustomed [to do]?*

The diminutives in the first and fourth lines are used for pathetic effect, not to indicate size (cf. Catullus 3.16ff., page 36); there are no English equivalents for these words.

For another example of Hadrian's poetry, see page 112.

Lesbia's Sparrow

Catullus conferred immortality on Lesbia's pet sparrow with two poems, one an address to the bird in life and the other a lament for its death. References to the poems occur in later Latin authors, as well as in modern literature.

*The bird was probably not a common sparrow, which is both unattractive and hard to train, but a blue rock thrush (**Monticola solitarius**), which has been a popular pet in Italy.*

A   Passer, deliciae meae puellae,
    quicum ludere, quem in sinu tenere,
    cui primum digitum dare appetenti
    et acris solet incitare morsus
    cum desiderio meo nitenti   5
    carum nescioquid lubet iocari,
    credo, ut tum gravis acquiescat ardor: 8
    tecum ludere, sicut ipsa, possem
    et tristes animi levare curas!   10

~: CATULLUS *Carmina* 2 (with omission of l. 7)

TEXT   C. Valerii Catulli *Carmina*, ed. R. A. B. Mynors
         (Oxford Classical Texts, 1958)
METER   hendecasyllable [§M3]
       pāssēr | dēlĭcĭ|āē mĕ|āē pŭ|ēllāē
       quīcūm | lūdĕrĕ | qu(em) īn sĭ|nū tĕ|nĕrĕ

A 1   **Passer** voc. of **passer passeris** M. *sparrow* or a similar small bird; **dēliciae -ārum** F.PL. *darling* (pl. used with a sg. meaning [§G53]); **meae puellae** gen. sg.

2ff.   **quīcum** = **quōcum**, i.e., **cum quō**; **solet** (l. 4) must be understood with **lūdere, tenēre**, and **dare**—each clause is introduced by a different case of the rel. pron. (**quīcum, quem, cui**); **sinus -ūs** M. *bosom*; **prīmum digitum** *the first [part of her] finger* (**digitus -ī** M.), i.e., *the tip of her finger*; take **appetentī** with **cui**, *to whom, [when] pecking at [it]* (**appetō -ere** lit., *seek, try to reach*); take **ācrīs** (**ācer ācris ācre** *sharp*) with **morsūs** (**morsus -ūs** M. *bite*); **incitō -āre** *provoke*.

5f.   **cum** here *when*; **dēsīderiō meō nitentī** dat. after **lubet**, lit., *it is pleasing to my radiant* (**niteō -ēre** *shine*) *sweetheart* (**dēsīderium -(i)ī** N.); **cārum nescioquid ... iocārī** lit., *to jest* (**iocor -ārī**) *something* (**nescioquis -quis -quid**) *sweet*, trans. *play some sweet game.*

7   This line is not given because no satisfactory emendation or interpretation has been put forward.

8   **crēdō** is parenthetical; **ut** introduces a purpose clause [§G83]; **gravis ... ardor** *[her] burning* (lit., *heavy*) *passion* (**ardor ardōris** M.)—Lesbia's passion for Catullus in his absence is meant; **acquiescō -ere** *subside.*

9f.   **tēcum** = **cum tē** (i.e., the sparrow); **possem** subj. to express a wish [§G67] *I wish I could*; **levō -āre** *lighten.*

B Lugete, o Veneres Cupidinesque,
   et quantum est hominum venustiorum.
   passer mortuus est meae puellae,
   passer, deliciae meae puellae,
   quem plus illa oculis suis amabat.   5
   nam mellitus erat suamque norat
   ipsam tam bene quam puella matrem,
   nec sese a gremio illius movebat,
   sed circumsiliens modo huc modo illuc
   ad solam dominam usque pipiabat;   10
   qui nunc it per iter tenebricosum
   illuc, unde negant redire quemquam.
   at vobis male sit, malae tenebrae

B 1 **lūgēte** 2 pl. imp. **lūgeō -ēre** *lament;* **Venerēs Cupīdinēsque** voc. *Loves* (**Venus Veneris** F.) *and Cupids* (**Cupīdō Cupīdinis** M.)—an odd expression (there was only one Venus) that Catullus probably thought matched the mock-serious tone of the poem (cf. Catullus 13.12, page 43).

2 Take **quantum** (rel. pron. of quantity) with **hominum venustiōrum** (partitive gen. [§G 24]), lit., *how much of more refined* (compar. of **venustus**) *people there are,* trans. *all those of finer feelings.*

3f. **mortuus est** 3 sg. perf. ind. **morior morī**; l. 4 is repeated from the previous poem.

5 **oculīs suīs** abl. of comparison [§G 42] *than her own eyes.*

6f. **mellītus** *honey-sweet;* **suam ... ipsam** *its* (i.e., the sparrow's) *mistress*—in the language of slaves, a master and his wife were euphemistically called **ipse** [*he*] *himself* and **ipsa** [*she*] *herself;* **nōrat** = **nōverat** [§G 95] *knew*—the perfect and pluperfect of **noscō** can be used in a present and imperfect sense, respectively; **tam bene quam** *as well as.*

8 **sēsē** = **sē**; **gremium -iī** N. *lap.*

9 **circumsiliō -īre** *hop around;* **modo ... modo ...** *at one time ... at another time ...,* trans. *now ... now....*

10 **usque** adv. *always;* **pīpiō -āre** *chirp.*

11 The rel. pron. **quī** (antecedent **passer**) connects the following sentence with the previous one, trans. *it;* **it** 3 sg. pres. ind. act. **eō īre**; **per iter tenebricōsum** *along the gloomy way,* i.e., the road to the Underworld—the fact that the sparrow was still on its way to the nether regions seems to indicate that it had only recently died.

12 **illūc, unde** trans. *to the place from where;* **negant ... quemquam** *they say that no one;* **redeō -īre** *return.*

13 **vōbīs male sit** lit., *may it be* (subj. to express a wish [§G 67]) *badly for you,* trans. *a curse on you;* **tenebrae -ārum** F.PL. *darkness, shades.*

Orci, quae omnia bella devoratis:
tam bellum mihi passerem abstulistis.   15
o factum male, o miselle passer!
tua nunc opera meae puellae
flendo turgiduli rubent ocelli.

~: CATULLUS *Carmina* 3

14 **Orcus -ī** M. another name for the Underworld; **bellus** *beautiful* (also in l. 15); **dēvorō -āre** *swallow up*.
15 **mihi** dat. of disadvantage [§G 31], lit., *to my disadvantage*, trans. *from me*; **abstulistis** 2 pl. perf. ind. act. **auferō -ferre** *take away*.
16 **factum male** lit., *wickedly done*, i.e., *wicked deed*; **misellus** diminutive of **miser**, trans. *poor little*—diminutives were commonly used in colloquial Latin for emotional effect, as here and in l. 18.
17 **tuā ... operā** instrumental abl. [§G 47], lit., *through your work*, i.e., *because of you*; take **meae puellae** with **ocellī** (l. 18).
18 **flendō** (gerund [§G 78] of **fleō flēre**) abl. of cause [§G 48] *from weeping*; the force of the diminutives **turgidulus** (**turgidus** *swollen*) and **ocellus** (**oculus**) cannot be expressed in English; **rubeō -ēre** *be red*.

PROVERBIA DE PROSCAENIO ·III·

Utinam quae dicis dictis facta suppetant.

PLAUTUS *Pseudolus* 108

I wish [your] deeds would match your words. (lit., Would that [your] deeds would back up the words you are saying!)

Modus omnibus rebus.   PLAUTUS *Poenulus* 238
Moderation in all things.

Fortis fortuna adiuvat.   TERENCE *Phormiō* 203
Fortune favors the brave.

Tetigisti acu.   PLAUTUS *Rudens* 1306
You've hit the nail on the head.
(lit., You've touched [the matter] with a needle.)

Nullum est iam dictum quod non dictum sit prius.

TERENCE *Eunūchus* 41

Nothing has now been said that wasn't said before.

For more proverbs from the plays of Plautus and Terence, see pages 17 and 26.

Dental Hygiene in the Provinces

The Rome of Catullus' day attracted people from other lands bordering on the Mediterranean. If these newcomers were to be accepted in Roman society, they would have been obliged to abandon at least some of their provincial habits. Here Catullus gives advice to a man from Celtiberia in central Spain whose constantly smiling face could be interpreted as betraying an odd practice of his native land.

Egnatius, quod candidos habet dentes,
renidet usque quaque. si ad rei ventum est
subsellium, cum orator excitat fletum,
renidet ille; si ad pii rogum fili
lugetur, orba cum flet unicum mater,   5
renidet ille. quidquid est, ubicumque est,
quodcumque agit, renidet: hunc habet morbum,
neque elegantem, ut arbitror, neque urbanum.
quare monendum est te mihi, bone Egnati,

TEXT   C. Valerii Catulli *Carmina*, ed. R. A. B. Mynors
        (Oxford Classical Texts, 1958)
METER   limping iambic [§M 10]
        Ēgnā|tĭūs | quŏd ‖ cān|dĭdōs | hăbēt | dēntēs
        rĕnī|dĕt ūs|quĕ ‖ quā|quĕ s(i) ād | rĕī | vēntūm (e)st

1   **Egnātius** (-(i)ī M.) is known only from this and another poem of Catullus; **quod** *because;* **candidus** *white;* **dens dentis** M. *tooth.*

2f.   **renīdeō -ēre** lit., *smile back (at),* trans. *smile;* **usque quāque** *everywhere;* take **reī** with **subsellium** *a defendant's* (**reus -ī** M.) *bench* (**subsellium** -(i)ī N.); **ventum est** impers. construction, lit., *it has been come* (i.e., by Egnatius), trans. *he has come;* **ōrātor ōrātōris** M. *speaker;* **flētus -ūs** M. *weeping;* the scene is a court of law—advocates of the day tried to play upon the emotions of the court, hence **flētum.**

4   **ad piī rogum fīlī** *at the funeral pyre* (**rogus -ī** M.) *of a dutiful son*—cremations were conducted publicly and in the open.

5   **lūgētur** lit., *it is mourned* (**lūgeō -ēre**), another impers. construction, but since the mourning would have been general, trans. *there is mourning;* **orbus** *bereaved;* **ūnicus -ī** M. *[her] only son,* but to avoid repetition, trans. *[her] only boy.*

6   **quidquid** *whatever;* **ubīcumque** *wherever.*

7   **quodcumque** *whatever;* **morbus -ī** M. *disease.*

8   **ēlegans** (**ēlegantis**) *refined;* **ut** + ind. *as;* **arbitror -ārī** *think;* **urbānus** *polite.*

9   **quārē** *wherefore,* trans. *so;* **monendum est tē mihī** impers. use of the gerundive [§G 80], which would normally be expressed as **tū mihi monendus es,** lit., *you are needing to be warned by me,* i.e., *I must warn you;* **bone Egnātī** voc. *[my] good Egnatius*—a condescending expression.

si urbanus esses aut Sabinus aut Tiburs   10
aut pinguis Umber aut obesus Etruscus
aut Lanuvinus ater atque dentatus
aut Transpadanus, ut meos quoque attingam,
aut quilubet, qui puriter lavit dentes,
tamen renidere usque quaque te nollem: 15
nam risu inepto res ineptior nulla est.
nunc Celtiber es: Celtiberia in terra,

10   Lines 10–15 are a category 1 conditional sentence relating to the present [§G94],
     hence the imperfect subjunctives **essēs** and **nollem** (l. 15), trans. *if* (**sī**) *you were ...
     I would not want ...*; **urbānus** here *a city [man]*, i.e., a person born and raised in
     Rome, which was often referred to simply as **urbs** (*the city*) (cf. Ovid *Tristia* 1.3.2,
     page 132, and elsewhere); **Sabīnus -ī** M. *a Sabine*—the Sabines lived in an area
     northeast of Rome; **Tīburs Tīburtis** M. *a Tiburtine*—Tibur was a town northeast
     of Rome but south of the Sabines.
11   **pinguis Umber** *stout Umbrian* (**Umber Umbrī** M.)—Umbria was north of
     Rome on the Adriatic coast; **obēsus Etruscus** *fat* (**obēsus**, a stronger word than
     pinguis) *Etruscan* (**Etruscus -ī** M.)—Etruria was northwest of Rome.
12   Lit., *a dark* (**āter**) *and well-toothed* (**dentātus**) *Lanuvian* (**Lānuvīnus -ī** M.),
     trans. *a dark Lanuvian with good teeth*—Lanuvium was a town south of Rome.
13   **Transpadānus -ī** M. *a Transpadane*, i.e., someone from north of the **Padus**
     (modern *Po*), the largest river in northern Italy; **meōs** *my [own people]*—Catullus
     came from Verona, north of the Po; **attingō -ere** *touch on.*
14   **quīlubet** *anyone*; **pūriter** *cleanly*—the point of the adverb becomes clear when
     Egnatius' own practice is revealed; **lavō -āre** (**-ere**) *wash.*
16   **rīsū ineptō** abl. of comparison [§G42] *than foolish laughter* (**rīsus -ūs** M.)—
     Egnatius' beaming smile is so pronounced that it can be called a laugh; **ineptior**
     compar. of **ineptus.**
17   **nunc** *as it is*; **Celtibēr Celtibērī** M. *a Celtiberian*; **Celtibēriā in terrā** *in the
     Celtiberian land.*
18f. The antecedent of **quod** is **hōc** (*what ... with this* (instrumental abl. [§G47]));
     quisque *each person*; **meiō -ere** (perf. **minxī**) *urinate*; **sibī** dat. of reference [§G32]
     with **dēfricāre** (**dēfricō -āre**), lit., *rub for himself*, but trans. *rub his ...*; **māne** adv.
     in the morning; **dentem** trans. *teeth* (sg. for pl. [§G53]); **russam ... gingīvam** *red
     gums* (sg. for pl. [§G53]; **gingīva -ae** F.).
20f. **ut** introduces an adverbial clause of result [§G84]; **quō ... expolītior ... hōc
     ... amplius ...** a proportional comparison, lit., *by what [degree] the more polished*
     (**expolītior** compar. of **expolītus**) ... *by this [degree] the greater amount* (**amplius
     ampliōris** N.), trans. *the more polished ... the greater amount ...*; **iste** pron. adj. *that*;
     vester = **tuus** [§G53], trans. *of yours*; **dens** trans. by plural as above; **tē ... bibisse**
     acc.+inf. after **praedicet** (**praedicō -āre** *declare*), whose subject is **dens**, trans. *they*
     (i.e., *the teeth*) *declare that you have drunk*; **lōtium -(i)ī** N. *urine*—to make Egnatius'
     practice more disgusting, Catullus says that he drinks his urine rather than simply
     using it as a rinse.

quod quisque minxit, hoc sibi solet mane
dentem atque russam defricare gingivam,
ut, quo iste vester expolitior dens est,   20
hoc te amplius bibisse praedicet loti.

~: CATULLUS *Carmina* 39

LITTERA SCRIPTA MANET ·II·

Habent sua fata libelli.

The meaning usually given to these words is *Little books have their own destinies,* and this is how they would be interpreted without any context. Taken in this way, the words could be used as a motto for the school of modern literary criticism that claims complete autonomy for any piece of writing without reference to an author's intentions or the period in which it was written.

However, the author had a different meaning in mind. The sentence comes from an obscure Roman grammarian of the second century A.D., who, rather eccentrically, wrote in verse. In discussing the reception his book might have, he wrote this:

> **Forsitan hunc aliquis verbosum dicere librum**
> **non dubitet; forsan multo praestantior alter**
> **pauca reperta putet, cum plura invenerit ipse;**
> **deses et impatiens nimis haec obscura putabit:**
> **pro captu lectoris habent sua fata libelli.**
>   TERENTIANUS MAURUS 1282ff.

Perhaps someone would not hesitate to pronounce this book wordy; perhaps another person, much superior [to the first], would consider little [in it] original, since he himself has been more creative (lit., has devised more [things]); a lazy and impatient person will think these [parts of the book] too obscure. Books succeed or fail (lit., have their own destinies) according to the ability of the reader. (The diminutive **libellus** is used for metrical considerations; the lines are hexameters.)

The first three words of the final line are crucial to what the author intended.

Terentianus Maurus wrote nothing else of a memorable nature.

A Social Climber

Two differences between the spoken Latin of the lower classes in Rome and that of the educated were the former's disregard of an initial h *(e.g.,* **ortus** *for* **hortus**) *and the pronunciation of aspirated consonants as simple ones (e.g.,* **triumpus** *for* **triumphus**). *Uneducated people who rose socially would naturally try to change their speech habits, but they were apt to overcorrect and apply an initial* h *where it had no place or wrongly aspirate a consonant. Such a person was Catullus' Arrius, who has been plausibly identified with an ambitious advocate and politician mentioned by Cicero.*

"Chommoda" dicebat, si quando "commoda" vellet
  dicere, et "insidias" Arrius "hinsidias,"
et tum mirifice sperabat se esse locutum,
  cum quantum poterat dixerat "hinsidias."
credo, sic mater, sic semper avunculus eius,   5
  sic maternus avus dixerat atque avia.
hoc misso in Syriam requierant omnibus aures:
  audibant eadem haec leniter et leviter,

TEXT   C. Valerii Catulli *Carmina*, ed. R. A. B. Mynors
         (Oxford Classical Text, 1958)
METER   elegiac couplet [§M2]
         chŏmmŏdă | dīcē|bāt ‖ sī | quāndō | cōmmŏdă | vēllĕt
         dīcĕr(e) ĕt | īnsĭdĭ|ās ‖ Ārrĭŭs | hīnsĭdĭ|ās

1f. Catullus gives two examples of Arrius' faulty pronunciation, **chommoda** (= **commoda**; **commodum -ī** N. *advantage*) and **hinsidiās** (= **insidiās**; **insidiae -ārum** F.PL. *ambush*); **sī quandō** (*whenever* (lit., *if ever*)) is followed by the subjunctive, **vellet**, to express repeated action; **Arrius -ī** M.; **hinsidiās** is in apposition [§G52] to **insidiās**.

3   **tum** anticipates **cum** in l. 4 (lit., *then ... when ...*) and need not be translated; take **mīrificē** (*wonderfully*) with **esse locūtum**, which is part of the acc.+inf. [§G10] after **spērābat**.

4   **quantum poterat** *as much* (i.e., with as much emphasis) *as he could*.

5f. **sīc** *in this way* is repeated for emphasis; **avunculus -ī** M. *maternal uncle*; **eius** is to be taken with each noun, *his mother*, etc.; **māternus** *maternal*; **avus -ī** M. *grandfather*; **avia -ae** F. *grandmother*.

7   **hōc missō in Syriam** abl. absolute [§G49], trans. *when he was sent to Syria* (**Syria -ae** F.); **requiĕrant** (= **requiĕverant** [§G95]; **requiescō -ere**) *had taken repose*, trans. *got a rest*; **omnibus** dat. of reference [§G32].

8   **audībant** = **audiēbant**; **eadem haec** *these same [sounds]*; **lēniter** *smoothly*; **leviter** *lightly*.

nec sibi postilla metuebant talia verba,
  cum subito affertur nuntius horribilis,   10
Ionios fluctus, postquam illuc Arrius isset,
  iam non Ionios esse, sed Hionios.

~: CATULLUS *Carmina* 84

9   **sibi** (dat. of reference [§G 32] *for themselves*) can be left untranslated; **postillā**
afterwards.
10   **subitō** *suddenly;* **affertur** historic pres. [§G 60] of **afferō -ferre** *bring;* **horribilis**
terrible, spine-chilling.
11f.   Within the acc.+inf. [§G 10] after **affertur nuntius**, the **postquam** clause has
its verb, **isset** (= **iisset**), in the subjunctive [§G 85]; **Īoniōs fluctūs** *Ionian waves*
(**fluctus -ūs** M.)—the reference is to the **Īonium mare** (modern *Adriatic*), which
Arrius would have crossed in going to Greece on his way to Syria; **iam nōn** *no
longer.*

Catullus and Caesar

Catullus was a contemporary of Gaius Iulius Caesar. His father and
Caesar were on friendly terms, but that didn't restrain the poet from
writing two short poems attacking Caesar in the coarsest terms and
accusing him and his associate Mamurra of sexual and other abnor-
malities. A third poem, in the form of a single elegiac couplet, expresses Catullus' complete indifference to the man who was one of the
two most powerful figures in Rome at the time.

> **Nil nimium studeo, Caesar, tibi velle placere,**
>   **nec scire utrum sis albus an ater homo.**   *Carmina* 93
> *I am not particularly keen to want to please you, Caesar,*
>   *nor to know whether you are white or black.*

The expression "not to know whether you are white or black" was
proverbial and indicated utter disinterest in the person concerned.
  In his biography of Caesar, Suetonius (c. A.D. 60–c. 130) tells us
that despite these insults, Catullus was forgiven after he apologized.

> *Although Caesar had not concealed the fact that he had suffered a
> lasting slur from Catullus' verses about Mamurra, he invited the poet
> to dinner on the same day as the latter apologized, and he continued
> his previous friendly relations with Catullus' father.*
>   SUETONIUS *Iūlius* 73

The dinner party must have been quite a lively affair.

An Invitation to Dinner

Cenabis bene, mi Fabulle, apud me
paucis, si tibi di favent, diebus,
si tecum attuleris bonam atque magnam
cenam, non sine candida puella
et vino et sale et omnibus cachinnis.   5
haec si, inquam, attuleris, venuste noster,
cenabis bene; nam tui Catulli
plenus sacculus est aranearum.

TEXT   C. Valerii Catulli *Carmina*, ed. R. A. B. Mynors
(Oxford Classical Texts, 1958)
METER hendecasyllable [§M3]
cēnā|bīs bĕnĕ | mī Fă|būll(e) ă|pŭd mē
pāūcīs | sī tĭbĭ | dī fă|vēnt dĭ|ēbŭs

1   **cēnō -āre** *dine*; **mī** voc. of **meus**.

2   **paucīs ... diēbus** abl. of time within which [§G37]; **tibi** dat. with **favent**; **dī** = **deī**.

3   **tēcum** = **cum tē**; **attuleris** (2 sg. fut. perf. ind. act. **adferō -ferre**) trans. by the present [§G66], *if you bring*.

4   **cēna -ae** F. *dinner*; Catullus says **nōn sine** (stronger than **cum**) to emphasize his inability to provide the usual components of a dinner party; the **candida puella** (*pretty girl*) would have been a woman hired for the evening to entertain the guests—this responsibility normally fell to the host.

5   The three ablatives are governed by **nōn sine** (l. 4); **sāl salis** M. here *wit*; **omnibus cachinnīs** all *manner of laughter* (**cachinnus -ī** M.).

6   **venuste noster** voc. *my* (pl. for sg. [§G53]) *charming* (**venustus**) [*friend*].

8   **sacculus -ī** M. *little purse* (diminutive of **saccus -ī** M. *bag*); **arānea -ae** F. *cobweb*.

9   **contrā** adv. *in return*; **mērōs amōrēs** *pure affection* (pl. for sg. [§G53]).

10   **seu** = **vel sī** *or if*; **quid** indef. pron. *anything*; **suāvius, ēlegantius** n.sg. compar. of **suāvis** *pleasant*, **ēlegans** (**ēlegantis**) *graceful*—Catullus is using hyperbole to tempt his friend.

11f. **unguentum -ī** N. *unguent*—the need to counteract the effects of body odor was particularly urgent at dinner parties, where each couch was used by three reclining participants; **meae puellae** (i.e., Lesbia) dat. with **dōnārunt** (= **dōnāvērunt** [§G95]); **Venerēs Cupīdinēsque** *the Loves and Cupids* (**Venus Veneris** F., **Cupīdō Cupīdinis** M. normally *the goddess of love, the god of love*), a vague expression indicating all powers capable of inciting love and desire (cf. Catullus 3.1, page 35).

13f. **quod** (antecedent **unguentum** (l. 11)) is governed by **olfaciēs** (**olfaciō -ere** *smell* (trans.)); **cum** is postponed [§G4]; **rogābis** is followed by an accusative (**deōs**) and by an indirect petition [§G91] introduced by **ut** (postponed [§G4]); **tōtum ... nāsum** *all nose* (**nāsus -ī** M.).

sed contra accipies meros amores
seu quid suavius elegantiusve est;   10
nam unguentum dabo, quod meae puellae
donarunt Veneres Cupidinesque,
quod tu cum olfacies, deos rogabis,
totum ut te faciant, Fabulle, nasum.

~: CATULLUS *Carmina* 13

The Wild Life

In Roman society, as in our own, wild living and debauchery were frowned upon but were engaged in anyway. Some writers censured the enthusiasm for orgies that existed among members of the idle rich. Lucretius tells of how such pleasures lead to disillusionment:

Eximia veste et victu convivia, ludi,
pocula crebra, unguenta, coronae, serta parantur,
nequiquam, quoniam medio de fonte leporum
surgit amari aliquid, quod in ipsis floribus angat.

Dē rērum nātūrā 4.1131ff.

Banquets with magnificent clothes and food, games, plenty of cups,
unguents, wreaths [and] garlands are made ready, [but] in vain,
since from the the middle of pleasure's fount (lit., the fountain
of charms) a bitterness (lit., something bitter) comes up that
chokes amid the flowers themselves.

More damning still is the complaint Juvenal puts in the mouth of an aged debauchee:

Nunc mihi quid suades post damnum temporis et spes
deceptas? festinat enim decurrere velox
flosculus angustae miseraeque brevissima vitae
portio; dum bibimus, dum serta, unguenta, puellas
poscimus, obrepit non intellecta senectus.   *Satires* 9.125ff.

Now what are you telling me to do after the waste of [my]
time and cheated hopes? For the transient flower and [our]
meager share of a limited and wretched life hasten to a close.
While we drink, while we call for garlands, unguents [and]
girls, old age creeps up [on us] unawares.

A Brother's Tears

During a journey to Bithynia in what is now northwest Turkey, Catullus visited the grave of a brother who was buried in the nearby Troad. There he made the traditional gift to the dead (inferiae), which consisted of wine, milk, honey, and flowers.

Multas per gentes et multa per aequora vectus
    advenio has miseras, frater, ad inferias,
ut te postremo donarem munere mortis
    et mutam nequiquam alloquerer cinerem.
quandoquidem fortuna mihi tete abstulit ipsum,   5
    heu miser indigne frater adempte mihi,
nunc tamen interea haec, prisco quae more parentum
    tradita sunt tristi munere ad inferias,

TEXT   C. Valerii Catulli *Carmina*, ed. R. A. B. Mynors
          (Oxford Classical Texts, 1958)
METER   elegiac couplet [§M 2]
        mūltās | pēr gēn|tēs ‖ ēt | mūltă pĕr | āēquŏră | vēctŭs
        ādvĕnĭ|(o) hās mĭsĕ|rās ‖ frātĕr ăd | īnfĕrĭ|ās

1f.   **aequor aequoris** N. *sea;* **vectus** (perf. pple. of **vehō -ere**), lit., *having been carried,* trans. *after traveling;* **adveniō -īre** *come;* **ad** *for [the purpose of]* (also in l. 8); the **inferiae** (-**ārum** F.PL.) were the offering made at a grave.

3   **ut** introduces an adverbial clause of purpose [§G 83]; **tē** acc. after **dōnō** (-**āre** *present*), which here has the accusative of the receiver and ablative of the gift, viz **postrēmō … mūnere mortis** *last gift of death,* i.e., *last gift [owed to] the dead;* **dōnārem** and **alloquerer** (l. 4) are imperfect subjunctive in historic sequence [§G 93] after the perfect participle **vectus**.

4   **mūtus** *dumb,* trans. *silent;* **nēquīquam** *vainly;* **alloquor -ī** *address;* **cinis cineris** here F. *ashes*—the Romans practiced cremation (see page 79).

5   **quandoquidem** *since;* **mihi** dat. of disadvantage [§G 31], lit., *to my disadvantage,* i.e., *from me* (also in l. 6); **tētē** = **tē**; **abstulit** 3 sg. perf. ind. act. **auferō -ferre** *take away;* **heu** interjection *alas!;* the words **miser … frater adempte** (**adimō -ere** *snatch away*) are vocative; **indignē** adv. *undeservedly.*

7f. **intereā** (lit., *as it is*) strengthens **nunc** and need not be translated; **haec** is the object of **accipe** (l. 9); **priscō … mōre** abl. of cause [§G 48] *by ancient custom;* **quae** is postponed [§G 4]; **parens parentis** M./F. here *ancestor;* **trādō -ere** *hand down;* **tristī mūnere** abl. of manner [§G 45] *by way of sorrowful gift.*

9   **frāternō … flētū** instrumental abl. [§G 47], lit., *with fraternal weeping* (**flētus -ūs** M.), trans. *with a brother's tears;* **multum mānantia** lit., *much dripping* (**mānō -āre;** **multum** is an adverb), but trans. *drenched.*

10 **in perpetuum** adv. expression *forever;* **avē** *hail*—the verb exists only in the imperative active and present infinitive; **valē** *farewell* (**valeō - ēre** *be well*).

accipe fraterno multum manantia fletu,
  atque in perpetuum, frater, ave atque vale.   10

~: CATULLUS *Carmina* 101

Sortes Virgilianae

Attempts to predict the future have taken many forms. One method involved taking a copy of a book considered to be in some way authoritative and opening it at random. The first words on the left-hand page were supposed to give some clue about what the future held for the inquirer. Whether the rules of bibliomancy, as this form of absurdity is called, permitted further reading, or even a glance at the right-hand page, is not recorded.

Books favored by bibliomancers include the *Bible* and *Koran*, as well as works of Homer and Vergil. The *Sortes Virgilianae* (*Divination through Vergil*; the form **Vir-** is a common but incorrect spelling) was practiced up to comparatively recent times. The most famous example of its use concerns the English king Charles I (1625–1649). When fleeing from parliamentary forces seeking to depose him, he consulted the Roman poet and was confronted with the lines in which the deserted Dido curses Aeneas:

At bello audacis populi vexatus et armis,
finibus extorris, complexu avulsus Iuli
auxilium imploret videatque indigna suorum
funera; nec, cum se sub leges pacis iniquae
tradiderit, regno aut optata luce fruatur,
sed cadat ante diem mediaque inhumatus harena.
                                                    Aeneid 4.615ff.

But constantly attacked in war and by the weapons of a
bold people, exiled from his territories, torn from the embrace
of [his son] Iulus, may he beg for help and witness the cruel
deaths of his people; and when he surrenders himself to the
terms of an unequal peace, may he not enjoy [his] kingdom
or the light he desires (i.e., a happy life), *but may he fall before*
his time (lit., *day*) *and [lie] unburied in the middle of a beach.*

If the king believed in Vergil, he could hardly have been encouraged. He was, in fact, later apprehended, tried as an enemy of the nation, and beheaded.

Ariadne on Naxos

In addition to shorter poems of an informal and personal nature, Catullus wrote several longer pieces that showed him to be a **doctus poēta,** *a learned poet. This title indicated that a poet had absorbed contemporary and past Greek poetic tradition and could write according to its norms.*

One established verse form was the mini-epic, the epyllion, which treated a story of the heroic age within the relatively short space of a few hundred lines. One such poem is Catullus' Wedding of Peleus and Thetis *(a modern title—none is given in the manuscripts); into his description of the wedding he inserted the unrelated story of Ariadne.*

Theseus, the great Athenian hero, had gone to Crete to save the young men and women who were regularly sent from Athens as tribute to Minos, the Cretan king. In performing the various tasks involved, he was aided by the king's daughter Ariadne, who had fallen in love with him. She eloped with him, but on the return voyage to Athens was abandoned on the Aegean island of Naxos. Her fate has been the subject of many works of art and literature since the Renaissance, one of the best known being the opera Ariadne auf Naxos *of Richard Strauss.*

Namque fluentisono prospectans litore Diae,
Thesea cedentem celeri cum classe tuetur
indomitos in corde gerens Ariadna furores,
necdum etiam sese quae visit visere credit,   55

TEXT   C. Valerii Catulli *Carmina,* ed. R. A. B. Mynors
         (Oxford Classical Texts, 1958)
METER   hexameter [§M1]
        nāmquĕ flŭ|ēntĭsŏ|nō ‖ prōs|pēctāns | lītŏrĕ | Dīaē
        Thēsĕă | cēdēn|tēm ‖ cĕlĕ|rī cūm | clāssĕ tŭ|ētŭr

52   **Namque** (= **nam**) *for*—the sentence (through l. 54) explains what has immediately preceded; **fluentisonō prospectans lītore Dīae** *looking out* (**prospectō -āre**) *from the resounding shore* (abl. of place from which [§G39]) *of Dia* (= Naxos; **Dīa -ae** F.).

53f.   **Thēsea** Greek acc. of **Thēseus** (**Thēsei** M.); **cēdō -ere** here *go*; **celerī cum classe** *with [his] swift fleet*; the subject of **tuētur** (*watches;* **tueor tuērī**) is **Ariadna** (**-ae** F., Latin form of the Greek *Ariadne*)—this is not a historic present, since Catullus is describing a scene on a tapestry; **indomitōs … furōrēs** acc. after **gerens,** *bearing unbridled passions* (**furor furōris** M.).

55   **necdum etiam** *and not even yet;* **sēsē** (= **sē**) **… vīsere** acc.+inf. [§G10] after **crēdit; vīsō -ere** *see.*

utpote fallaci quae tum primum excita somno
desertam in sola miseram se cernat harena.
immemor at iuvenis fugiens pellit vada remis,
irrita ventosae linquens promissa procellae.
quem procul ex alga maestis Minois ocellis,　　　　　60
saxea ut effigies bacchantis, prospicit, eheu,
prospicit et magnis curarum fluctuat undis,
non flavo retinens subtilem vertice mitram,
non contecta levi velatum pectus amictu,
non tereti strophio lactentes vincta papillas,　　　　65

56f.　**utpote ... quae ... sē cernat** adj. clause with subj., giving the cause [§G88] for Ariadne's disbelief (**quae** is postponed [§G4])—**utpote** reinforces the clause, which is to be translated *no wonder* (**utpote**), *since she sees herself* (**cernō -ere**) ...; **fallācī ... somnō** abl. of separation [§G40] *from treacherous sleep*—her sleep was treacherous (**fallax** (**fallācis**)) because it allowed Theseus to leave without her knowledge; **tum prīmum** *then first*; **excitus** (**exciō -īre**) *awakened*; **dēserō -ere** *abandon*; **in sōlā ... harēnā** *on the lonely sand* (**harēna -ae** F.).

58　**immemor** *forgetful*; **at** (*but*) is postponed [§G4]; **pellō -ere** *strike*; **vada** (**vadum -ī** N.) here *waters*; **rēmīs** instrumental abl. [§G47] *with oars* (**rēmus -ī** M.).

59　**irrita ... prōmissa** acc. after **linquens**, *leaving* (**linquō -ere**) *[his] empty promises* (**prōmissum -ī** N.); **ventōsae ... procellae** dat. *to the windy storm* (**procella -ae** F.).

60f.　**iuvenis** (l. 58), i.e., Theseus, is the antecedent of **quem**, which is governed by **prospicit** (**prospiciō -ere** *watch*); **alga -ae** F. *seaweed*, which would have been on the lower part of the beach; **maestīs ... ocellīs** instrumental abl. [§G47] *with sad eyes* (**ocellus -ī** M.); **Mīnōis** (**Mīnōidis** F.) *the daughter of Minos*, i.e., Ariadne; **saxea ut effigiēs** *like* (**ut** is postponed [§G4]) *a stone image* (**effigiēs -ēī** F.); **bacchans bacchantis** F. *female devotee of Bacchus, bacchante*; **ēheu** interjection *alas!*

62　**prospicit** is repeated for pathetic effect; **magnīs ... undīs** abl. of place where [§G38]; **fluctuō -āre** *be tossed*.

63ff.　The participles **retinens** (**retineō -ēre** *hold*), **contecta** (**contegō -ere** *conceal*), and **vincta** (**vinciō -īre** *bind*) agree with **Mīnōis** (Ariadne) in l. 60; **flāvō ... vertice** abl. of place where [§G38] *on [her] blonde head* (**vertex verticis** M.); **subtīlem ... mitram** *finely woven bonnet* (**mitra -ae** F.); **pectus** acc. of respect [§G15] after **contecta**, lit., *concealed with respect to [her] chest*; take **levī vēlātum ... amictū** (lit., *having been [previously] covered* (**vēlō -āre**) *with a light garment* (**amictus -ūs** M.)) with **pectus**—a condensed expression that refers to the previous state of Ariadne's clothing; take **teretī strophiō** (instrumental abl. [§G47] *with a smooth* (**teres** (**teretis**)) *band* (**strophium -iī** N.)) with **vincta**—the **strophium**, which served as a primitive brassiere, was tied on the outside of a garment just below the breasts; **lactentēs ... papillās** acc. of respect [§G15] after **vincta**, lit., *bound with respect to [her] milk-white breasts* (**papilla -ae** F.).

omnia quae toto delapsa e corpore passim
ipsius ante pedes fluctus salis alludebant.
sed neque tum mitrae neque tum fluitantis amictus
illa vicem curans toto ex te pectore, Theseu,
toto animo, tota pendebat perdita mente.   70
a misera, assiduis quam luctibus externavit
spinosas Erycina serens in pectore curas
illa tempestate, ferox quo ex tempore Theseus
egressus curvis a litoribus Piraei
attigit iniusti regis Gortynia tecta.   75

~: CATULLUS *Carmina* 64.52–75

66f. **omnia quae** *all of which,* i.e., the articles of clothing just mentioned; **quae ...
dēlapsa** is the object of **allūdēbant** (**allūdō -ere** *lap at*); **tōtō dēlapsō ē corpore**
fallen (**dēlābor -ī**) *from [her] whole body;* **passim** *at random;* **ipsius ante pedēs** lit.,
before the feet of her herself, trans. *in front of her feet;* **fluctūs salis** *the waves* (**fluctus
-ūs** M.) *of the sea* (**sāl salis** M. lit., *salt*)—the clothes were at the edge of the surf.
68ff. The genitives **mitrae** and **fluitantis** (**fluitō -āre** *float*) **amictūs** depend on
vicem, which functions here as a preposition, *on account of, for;* **cūrans** *caring, being concerned;* **tōtō ... pectore** (here *heart*), **tōtō animō** (here *soul*), and **tōtā ...
mente** ablatives of manner [§G 45], trans. *with [her] whole heart,* etc.; **ex tē ...
pendēbat** lit., *was hanging* (**pendeō -ēre** (intr.)) *from you,* i.e., *on you;* **Thēseu** voc.;
take **perdita** (*ruined*) with **illa.**
71f. **ā** interjection *alas!;* **misera ... quam** (postponed [§G 4]) *unhappy [woman],
whom;* **assiduīs ... luctibus** instrumental abl. [§G 47] *with constant sorrows* (**luctus
-ūs** M.); the subject of **externāvit** (**externō -āre** *drive mad*) is **Erycīna** (**-ae** F., another name for Venus); **spīnōsus** *thorny;* **serō -ere** *sow,* used here metaphorically.
73 **illā tempestāte** abl. of time when [§G 37] *at that time* (**tempestās tempestātis**
F.); take **ferox** (here *cruel*) with **Thēseus; quō ex tempore** (**ex** is postponed [§G 4])
lit., *from what time,* but trans. *when.*
74 **ēgressus** (**ēgredior -ī**) *having left;* **curvus** *curved, winding;* **Pīraeus -ī** M. the
port of Athens.
75 **attingō -ere** *arrive at;* the **iniustus rex** (*unjust king*) was **Mīnōs; Gortȳnius**
here *Cretan;* **tecta** pl. for sg. [§G 53] (**tectum -ī** N. *building*), trans. *palace.*

Worldly Wisdom

Publilius Syrus (first century B.C.*) was a highly successful writer of mimes, which were short dramatic productions performed on the stage and always in demand in Rome. His reputation was such that in the first century* A.D.*, a collection of single-line aphorisms culled from his works was used as a school text. The collection's popularity during the Middle Ages ensured its survival, but all Publilius' original mimes were lost.*

  22   Amare et sapere vix deo conceditur.

  26   Avaro quid mali optes nisi: "vivat diu"?

  41   Amicum an nomen habeas, aperit calamitas.

  92   Brevis ipsa vita est, sed malis fit longior.

186   Etiam capillus unus habet umbram suam.

222   Fortuna plus homini quam consilium valet.

258   Heredis fletus sub persona risus est.

TEXT   *Minor Latin Poets,* J. W. Duff and A. M. Duff
           (Loeb Classical Library, 1934)
           (The line references are to the Loeb edition.)
METER iambic senarius [§M 8]
           ămār(e) | ēt săpĕ|rĕ || vīx | dĕō | cōncē|dĭtŭr
           ăvā|rō quīd | măl(i) || ōp|tēs nĭsĭ | vīvāt | dĭū

22   **sapiō -ere** *be wise;* **deō** dat. after **concēditur** (**concēdō -ere** *grant, allow*).

26   **Avārō** (**avārus -ī** M. *a greedy person*) dat. after **optēs** (potential subj. [§G 68] *would you wish*); **quid** (here postponed [§G 4]) **malī** (partitive gen. [§G 24]) lit., *what of trouble,* i.e., *what trouble;* **nisi** here *except;* **vīvat** subj. to express a wish [§G 67] *may he live*—by living longer, the greedy person will suffer more from his vice.

41   The first four words are a double indirect question (hence **habeās** [§G 91]), which in its fuller form would be introduced by **utrum ... an ...** *whether ... or ...* (*whether* must be supplied in English); **nōmen** i.e., a friend in name only; **aperiō -īre** *reveal;* **calamitās calamitātis** F. *misfortune.*

92   **malīs** instrumental abl. [§G 47] *by troubles* (**malum -ī** N.); **fit** is used here as the passive of **faciō -ere; longior** compar. of **longus.**

186 **capillus -ī** M. *a hair*—the metaphor is meant to indicate that even an insignificant person has worth.

222 Fortune, or Luck, was often imagined to be a divine being; **plūs ... quam** *more than;* take **hominī** (dat. of reference [§G 32]) with **valet,** *is of value to a person;* **consilium** here *intelligence.*

258 **hērēs hērēdis** M./F. *heir;* **flētus -ūs** M. *weeping;* **persōna -ae** F. *mask;* **rīsus -ūs** M. *laughter.*

275 Inopiae desunt multa, avaritiae omnia.

296 Iudex damnatur ubi nocens absolvitur.

298 In rebus dubiis plurimi est audacia.

307 In amore forma plus valet quam auctoritas.

331 Improbe Neptunum accusat, qui iterum naufragium facit.

339 Legem nocens veretur, fortunam innocens.

358 Malus bonum ubi se simulat tunc est pessimus.

397 Multorum calamitate vir moritur bonus.

478 Nec mortem effugere quisquam nec amorem potest.

670 Stultum est vicinum velle ulcisci incendio.

711 Virtuti melius quam fortunae creditur.

---

275 **Inopiae** (inopia -ae F. *poverty*) dat. after **dēsunt** (dēsum + dat. *be lacking*),
trans. *poverty lacks many things* (**multa**); supply **dēsunt** with avāritiae (avāritia
-ae F. *greed*)—a greedy person is supremely needy because he always wants more.

296 **Iūdex iūdicis** M. *judge*; **damnō -āre** *condemn*; **nocens** pres. pple. of noceō
-ēre, here used as a noun, *a guilty person*; **absolvō -ere** *acquit*.

298 **rēs dubiae** lit., *difficult things*, trans. *a difficult position* (e.g., when surrounded
by angry Gauls); **plūrimī** gen. of value [§G 21], trans. *of the greatest [value]*; audācia
-ae F. *boldness*.

307 **forma -ae** F. here *beauty*; **plūs ... quam** *more than*; auctōritās auctōritātis F.
authority (e.g., of parents).

331 **Improbē** *unreasonably*; **Neptūnus -ī** M. *Neptune, god of the sea*; **accūsō -āre**
blame; **quī** *[he] who*; **iterum** here *for a second time*; trans. **naufragium** (-(i)ī N. *shipwreck*) **facit** by *is shipwrecked*—the twice-shipwrecked victim should have taken
Neptune's hint on the first occasion.

339 **nocens** as in No. 296; **innocens** (**innocentis**) *innocent*—the guiltless person
has no reason to fear the law.

358 **Malus** is used as a noun, trans. *a bad person*; **ubi** is postponed [§G 4]; with
bonum ... sē simulat supply **esse**, lit., *pretends* (**simulō -āre**) *himself to be good*;
pessimus superl. of **malus**.

397 **Multōrum calamitāte** abl. of attendant circumstances [§G 45], lit., *with the
misfortune* (**calamitās calamitātis** F.) *of many*, i.e., *to the misfortune of many*.

478 **Nec ... nec ...** *Neither ... nor ...*; **effugiō -ere** *escape*; **quisquam** *anyone*, but
trans. *no one can escape*....

670 **Stultum est** *it is foolish*; **vīcīnum** (**vīcīnus -ī** M. *neighbor*) is the object of **ul-
ciscī** (**ulciscor -ī** *take revenge on*); **incendiō** instrumental abl. [§G 47] (incendium
-(i)ī N. *fire*)—since houses in an ancient city were normally separated only by a
common structural wall, it was inadvisable to practice arson on a neighbor.

711 **Virtūtī** and **fortūnae** are both dative after **crēditur**, which is used impersonally, lit., *it is trusted*; **melius quam** *better than*.

Unrequited Love

Publius Vergilius Marō (*70–19* B.C.), *known in English as* Vergil *or* Virgil, *stands at the head of Latin poetry with his three poems, the* Eclogues, *the* Georgics, *and the* Aeneid.

The Eclogues *belong to the genre of pastoral poetry, short poems set against a rural background, where peasants lead simple lives caring for their flocks. In the selection that follows, a despairing goatherd, Damon, complains of his former partner, Nysa, who has abandoned him in favor of another man.*

Nascere praeque diem veniens age, Lucifer, almum,
coniugis indigno Nysae deceptus amore
dum queror et divos, quamquam nil testibus illis
profeci, extrema moriens tamen adloquor hora.   20
   incipe Maenalios mecum, mea tibia, versus.

TEXT   P. Vergili Maronis *Opera*, ed. R. A. B. Mynors
        (Oxford Classical Texts, 1969)
METER   hexameter [§M1]
        nāscĕrĕ | prāēquĕ dĭ|ēm ‖ vĕnĭ|ēns ăgĕ | Lūcĭfĕr | ālmŭm
        cōniŭgĭs | īndĭg|nō ‖ Nȳ|sāē dē|cēptŭs ă|mōrĕ

17 **Nascere** (2 sg. imp. **nascor nascī**) *be born*—Damon is bidding the Morning Star to rise; take the next words as **praeveniensque diem**—the two elements of **praeveniens** (**praeveniō -īre** *precede*) are split by tmesis, a somewhat rare stylistic feature; **diem ... almum** is governed by both **praeveniens** and **age**, trans. *precede and bring on the life-giving day*; **Lūcifer Lūciferī** M. lit., *the Light-bringer*, i.e., *the Morning Star.*

18ff. The next clauses **dum queror ... adloquor** are introduced by a postponed conjunction (**dum**) [§G4]; **coniunx coniugis** M./F. normally *husband/wife*, but trans. here *partner*, since the woman (Nysa) is now formally marrying someone else; **indignō ... amōre** instrumental abl. [§G47] *by the unworthy love*; **dēcipiō -ere** *deceive*; **queror querī** *complain*; **dīvus -ī** M. *god*; the **quamquam** clause is inserted into the second **dum** clause; **nīl** = **nihil**; **testibus illīs** instrumental abl. [§G47] *with them as witnesses* (**testis testis** M./F.)—presumably both Damon and Nysa had called on the gods to witness their undying love, but the gods had not made Nysa keep her word; **prōficiō -ere** *achieve*; **extrēmā ... hōrā** abl. of time when [§G37] *in [my] final hour*; **moriens** (pres. pple. of **morior morī** *die*) trans. *as I die*—the lover ends his complaint by declaring that he is about to jump off a cliff; **adloquor -ī** *address.*

21 A refrain, as exemplified here, is a feature of pastoral poetry; **Maenaliōs ... versūs** *Maenalian verses* (**versus -ūs** M.), i.e., poetry such as that sung on Mt. Maenalus (**Maenalus -ī** M.; cf. l. 22) in Arcadia, a remote area in Greece that was supposed to preserve a simple and old-fashioned lifestyle; **tībia -ae** F. *flute*, here voc.

Maenalus argutumque nemus pinusque loquentis
semper habet, semper pastorum ille audit amores
Panaque, qui primus calamos non passus inertis.
   incipe Maenalios mecum, mea tibia, versus.   25
Mopso Nysa datur: quid non speremus amantes?
iungentur iam grypes equis, aevoque sequenti
cum canibus timidi venient ad pocula dammae.
   incipe Maenalios mecum, mea tibia, versus.   28a
Mopse, novas incide faces: tibi ducitur uxor.
sparge, marite, nuces: tibi deserit Hesperus Oetam.   30
   incipe Maenalios mecum, mea tibia, versus.

22   **argūtumque nemus pīnūsque loquentīs** *both rustling forest* (**nemus nemoris** N.) *and whispering* (lit., *talking*) *pines* (**pīnus -ūs** F.).

23   **pastor pastōris** M. *herdsman;* **ille** *it,* i.e., Mt. Maenalus, which hears the loves of herdsmen in the sense that they are always singing love poetry on or around it.

24   **Pāna** Greek acc. of **Pān** (**Pānos** M.), a god of herdsmen and flocks, particularly associated with Arcadia; **prīmus** *first;* **calamōs nōn passus [est] inertīs [esse]** *did not allow reeds* (**calamus -ī** M.) *to be idle*—Pan was credited with the invention of the panpipe, or flute, which he made from a reed.

26   **Mopsō** dat. of **Mopsus** (**-ī** M.) *to Mopsus,* the rival to whom Nysa is being given in marriage; **spērēmus** deliberative subj. [§G 70] *are we to expect;* **amantēs** [*we*] *lovers.*

27   Nysa's marriage is so ridiculous that other similar absurdities can now be expected; **iungentur** *will be mated;* **grȳpes** (**gryps grȳpis** M.) *griffins,* creatures of fable who were a combination of eagle and lion parts; **equīs** dat. *with* (lit., *to*) *horses;* **aevō sequentī** abl. of time when [§G 37] *in the following age* (**aevum -ī** N.).

28   **timidī ... dammae** *timid deer* (**damma -ae** here M.); **pōculum** (**-ī** N. *cup*) is used in the plural to mean *drinking*—trans. **ad pōcula** by *to drink.*

29   **incīde** 2 sg. imp. act. **incīdō -ere** *cut;* **fax facis** F. *torch*—the torches are for the evening wedding procession, in which the bride is led from her father's house to that of the bridegroom; this is alluded to in the next clause, lit., *for you a wife is being led,* i.e., *a wife is being brought to you.*

30   **sparge ... nucēs** *scatter* (**spargō -ere**) *nuts* (**nux nucis** F.)—it was traditional to throw nuts among the crowd at a wedding; **tibi** dat. of advantage [§G 31]; **dēserō -ere** *leave;* **Hesperus -ī** M. *the Evening Star;* **Oeta** (**-ae** F.) a mountain in Thessaly traditionally associated with the Evening Star (cf. Statius *Silvae* 5.4.8, page 184)—the rising of the Evening Star above Mt. Oeta is mentioned to indicate that when night comes, Mopsus and Nysa will be united as husband and wife.

32   The goatherd addresses his lost love in a sarcastic vein; **dignō ... virō** dat. *to a worthy husband;* **coniungō -ere** *join;* the **dum** clauses that follow give the reasons for the goatherd's sarcasm; **despicis omnīs** *you look down on* (**despiciō -ere**) *everyone.*

o digno coniuncta viro, dum despicis omnis,
dumque tibi est odio mea fistula dumque capellae
hirsutumque supercilium promissaque barba,
nec curare deum credis mortalia quemquam.   35
   incipe Maenalios mecum, mea tibia, versus.
saepibus in nostris parvam te roscida mala
(dux ego vester eram) vidi cum matre legentem.
alter ab undecimo tum me iam acceperat annus,
iam fragilis poteram a terra contingere ramos: 40
ut vidi, ut perii, ut me malus abstulit error!
   incipe Maenalios mecum, mea tibia, versus.

~: VERGIL *Eclogues* 8.17–42

33f. **tibi** (dat. of reference [§G 32]) **est odiō** (predicative dat. [§G 34]) lit., *is for a dislike for you*, i.e., *you dislike*; **fistula -ae** F. *pipe* (the flute of l. 21); Nysa's dislike extends to her former lover's *nanny goats* (**capella -ae** F.), his *shaggy eyebrow* (**supercilium -(i)ī** N.), and his *long* (**prōmissus** perf. pple. of **prōmittō -ere**) *beard* (**barba -ae** F.)—**prōmissus** is commonly used to describe hair or a beard allowed to grow long (lit., *sent forth, let loose*).

35 Take **deum** (= **deōrum** [§G 95]) with **quemquam** (**quisquam** *any(one)*); **mortālia** *human [affairs]*—the goatherd is claiming that Nysa imagines that the gods will not remember the vows she has made to him.

37 **saepibus in nostrīs** lit., *in our fences* (**saepēs saepis** F.)—*our* here refers to the goatherd and his family, trans. *in our enclosure*; **parvam tē** *you, [when] small*; **roscida māla** *dewy apples* (**mālum -ī** N.).

38 **dux** here *guide*; **vester**, not **tuus**, because Nysa was with her mother (**cum mātre**); **legentem** (**legō -ere**) here *picking*.

39 **alter ab undecimō … annus** lit., *the next year after [my] eleventh [year]*, i.e., he was in his twelfth year.

40 **fragilīs … rāmōs** *fragile branches* (**rāmus -ī** M.); **ā terrā** *from the ground*; **contingō -ere** here *reach*.

41 The construction is in imitation of a Greek idiom to express simultaneous actions; the first **ut** means *just as*, the second and third *so*, and the meaning is that the young goatherd fell in love with Nysa the instant he saw her, lit., *just as I saw [you], so I was lost* (**pereō -īre**), *so foul madness* (**error errōris** M.) *swept me away* (**auferō -ferre**); trans. *as soon as I saw [you], I was lost and foul madness swept me away*.

Italy

Agriculture is the subject of Vergil's Georgics, the second of whose four books is concerned with trees and shrubs. In his discussion of varieties from different parts of the then-known world, Vergil mentions the citron tree of Media, noted for its medicinal properties. This prompts him to digress on the superiority of Italy over Media and all other lands: its climate and fertility, coupled with the absence of dangerous animals, suggest to the reader that the land still possessed something of the abundance and carefree life enjoyed in the Golden Age (cf. Tibullus Elegies *1.3, page 117).*

Sed neque Medorum silvae, ditissima terra,
nec pulcher Ganges atque auro turbidus Hermus
laudibus Italiae certent, non Bactra neque Indi
totaque turiferis Panchaia pinguis harenis.
haec loca non tauri spirantes naribus ignem   140

TEXT   P. Vergili Maronis *Opera*, ed. R. A. B. Mynors
         (Oxford Classical Texts, 1969)
METER   hexameter [§M1]
         sēd nĕquĕ | Mēdō|rūm ‖ sīl|vāē dĭ|tīssĭmă | tērră
         nēc pūl|chĕr Gān|gēs ‖ āt|qu(e) āūrō | tūrbĭdŭs | Hērmŭs

136   **Mēdī -ōrum** M.PL. the inhabitants of **Mēdia** (**-ae** F.), a region south of the Caspian Sea (the northern part of modern Iran); **silvae** (*groves*) refers to the plantations of citron trees mentioned in the preceding lines; **dītissima** (superl. of **dīs** (**dītis**)) **terra** is in apposition [§G52] to **silvae**.

137   **Gangēs Gangis** M. the modern Ganges River; take **aurō** (abl. of cause [§G48]) with **turbidus**, *thick with gold*; **Hermus -ī** M. a river in Asia Minor noted for its alluvial gold.

138f.   **laudibus** (**laus laudis** F. *praise*) abl. with **certent** (potential subj. [§G68]; **certō -āre** + abl. *contend with*); **Ītalia -ae** F. *Italy*; **Bactra**, **Indī**, and **Panchāia** (l. 139) are also subjects of **certent**; **Bactra -ōrum** N.PL. the capital of Bactria, a region that included modern Afghanistan and certain adjacent lands; **Indus -ī** M. *an Indian*; take **tūriferīs … harēnīs** (abl. of cause [§G48]) with **pinguis**, *rich with [its] incense-bearing sands* (**harēna -ae** F.); **Panchāia -ae** F. a legendary island supposed to lie off the coast of Arabia.

140f.   Although Italy had not been the scene of bizarre incidents such as those in Greek legend, it could boast of more worthwhile glories (ll. 143ff.); **haec loca** (i.e., Italy) is the object of **invertēre** (= **invertērunt**; **invertō -ere** *turn over* (in plowing)); **taurī spīrantēs nāribus ignem** *bulls* (**taurus -ī** M.) *breathing* (**spīrō -āre**) *fire from [their] nostrils* (abl. of place from which [§G39]; **nāris nāris** F.)—Jason, after arriving at Colchis in his quest for the Golden Fleece, was obliged to plow a field with two fire-breathing bulls and then sow the teeth of a dragon (**hȳdrus -ī** M.), which produced an immediate crop of armed warriors, whom he had to dispose of; **satīs … dentibus** a somewhat unusual dat. of purpose [§G33] *for sowing* (**serō**

invertere satis immanis dentibus hydri,
nec galeis densisque virum seges horruit hastis;
sed gravidae fruges et Bacchi Massicus umor
implevere; tenent oleae armentaque laeta.
hinc bellator equus campo sese arduus infert,   145
hinc albi, Clitumne, greges et maxima taurus
victima, saepe tuo perfusi flumine sacro,
Romanos ad templa deum duxere triumphos.
hic ver adsiduum atque alienis mensibus aestas:
bis gravidae pecudes, bis pomis utilis arbos.   150

-ere) *the teeth* (**dens dentis** M.)—we would have expected the gerundive construction [§G81] **serendīs dentibus**; **immānis** (gen. with **hȳdrī**) *savage.*

142   **galeīs densīsque … hastīs** instrumental abl. [§G47] *with helmets* (**galea -ae** F.) *and closely packed spears* (**hasta -ae** F.); **virum** (= **virōrum** [§G95]) **seges** (**segetis** F.) *crop of men;* **horreō -ēre** *bristle.*

143   **gravidae frūgēs** *abundant harvests* (**frūgēs frūgum** F.PL.); **Bacchī Massicus ūmor** *the Massic juice* (**ūmor ūmōris** M.) *of Bacchus,* i.e., wine from **mons Massicus** in Campania, which was famous for its vineyards—**Bacchus** (also called **Dionȳsus**) was the god of wine; Vergil is using a specific type of wine to refer to Italian wine in general.

144   **implēvēre** (= **implēvērunt**; **impleō -ēre**) *have filled [them],* i.e., **haec loca** (l. 140; Italy as a whole is meant), which is also to be supplied after **tenent** (here *cover*); **olea -ae** F. *olive tree;* **armenta laeta** *fat herds* (**armentum -ī** N.).

145   **hinc** *from here,* i.e., from these places; **bellātor equus** *warhorse;* **campō** abl. of place where [§G38]; **sēsē** (= **sē**) … **infert** *bears* (**inferō -ferre**) *itself, advances;* trans. **arduus** by an adverb [§G55], *proudly.*

146f.   **albī … gregēs** *white herds* (**grex gregis** M.), i.e., of cattle—white beasts were always used for sacrifices to the upper gods; **Clītumne** voc. sg. of **Clītumnus -ī** M. a river in a region of Umbria famous for its white cattle; **maxima … victima** (**-ae** F.) (*the largest sacrifice*) is in apposition to **taurus;** take **saepe** with **duxēre** (= **duxērunt**, l. 148); **tuō … flūmine sacrō** abl. of place where [§G38] *in your* (i.e., that of Clitumnus) *sacred river;* **perfūsī** *dipped* (**perfundō -ere**)—legend had it that the waters of the Clitumnus turned animals white.

148   The animals mentioned in l. 146 *have often led Roman triumphal processions* (**triumphus -ī** M.) *to the temples of the gods* (**deum** = **deōrum** [§G95])—the procession of a victorious general passed through the Forum up to the Capitol (see the map of Rome on page xxiv), where a sacrifice was made.

149   **hīc** *here,* i.e., in Italy; supply **est** with each noun, **vēr** (**vēris** N. *spring*) and **aestās** (**aestātis** F. *summer*); **adsiduus** *constant;* **aliēnīs mensibus** abl. of time when [§G37] *in months* (**mensis mensis** M.) *not its own* (**aliēnus** lit., *belonging to another*).

150   **bis** *twice [a year];* **gravidus** here *pregnant;* **pecudēs** *[farm] animals;* **pōmīs** abl. of cause [§G48] *with [its] fruits* (**pōmum -ī** N.); **ūtilis** *useful,* i.e., to its owner; **arbōs** = **arbor.**

at rabidae tigres absunt et saeva leonum
semina, nec miseros fallunt aconita legentis
nec rapit immensos orbis per humum neque tanto
squameus in spiram tractu se colligit anguis.
adde tot egregias urbes operumque laborem,   155
tot congesta manu praeruptis oppida saxis
fluminaque antiquos subter labentia muros.

~: VERGIL *Georgics* 2.136–157

151f.   **rabidae tigrēs** *raging tigers* (**tigris tigris** F.); **absunt** (**absum**) lit., *are absent,*
trans. *are not here*, i.e., in Italy; **saeva leōnum sēmina** *the fierce offspring* (**sēmen**
sēminis N. lit., *seed) of lions;* **aconīta** trans. by sg., *aconite* (**aconītum -ī** N.), a poisonous plant that could be mistakenly gathered by *reapers* (**legentīs**; **legō -ere**
here *pick*) with a normal crop.

153f.   The subject of both clauses is **squāmeus … anguis** (**anguis** M.) *scaly snake,*
which governs **rapit** (here *hurries*) and **colligit** (**colligō -ere** *gather*); **immensōs**
orbīs *[its] huge coils* (**orbis orbis** M.); **humus -ī** F. *ground;* **tantō … tractū** abl. of
manner [§G 45], lit., *with so great a pulling* (**tractus -ūs** M.), trans. *with a mighty*
upward movement; **spīra -ae** F. *spiral.*

155   **adde** 2 sg. imp. act. **addō -ere** *add*—Vergil is addressing the reader; in addition to its idyllic environment, Italy has benefited from human effort; **ēgregius**
splendid; **operum labōrem** *the toil of [human] undertakings.*

156   *so many towns raised up* (**congerō -ere** lit., *pile up) by hand on precipitous rocks*
(abl. of place where [§G 38])—Vergil is referring to the many Italian towns, then
as now, perched on mountain ridges.

157   **subter** (prep. + acc. *below, at the base of*) governs **antīquōs … mūrōs; lābentia**
pres. pple. of **lābor lābī** (here *flow*).

VERGILIANA ·I·

In the final episode of the story of Troy, the Greeks trick the Trojans
into believing that they have given up their siege and left for home.
When the Trojans find a large wooden horse in what had been the
Greek camp, opinion is divided as to what should be done with it.
Laocoon, a priest of Neptune, insists that the horse is a Greek ruse
and sums up his opinion with these words:

Timeo Danaos et dona ferentes.   *Aeneid* 2.49
I fear the Greeks even [when] bearing gifts.

For more Vergiliana, see pages 109, 182, 185, and 199.

Religion at Rome

The religion of the Romans was polytheistic. Its gods and goddesses ranged from the great powers of the official religion, who guarded the well-being and interests of the Roman state, to humble spirits, whose function was to care for individuals and their dwellings. Many divinities had temples or shrines where individuals could worship and request divine assistance or favor. Regular festivals were held in honor of a particular god or goddess, which in some cases ended in the sacrifice of an animal, but except for the Vestal Virgins (see below), there were no professional religious associations or priesthoods, such as in most modern faiths. Communal religious practices were under the direction of four colleges of officials, who were chosen from among the leading citizens; the most important was that of the **pontificēs** (cf. Horace *Odes* 2.14.28, page 100), who oversaw the religious calendar and its festivals.

The traditional Roman attitude to divinities was one of caution. Roman gods and goddesses had no general affection or love for the human race and could be easily offended. Even arrogant speech could provoke their anger: When Catullus (*Carmina* 51.1ff., page 32) says that a man who can continually look at his lover, Lesbia, is superior to the gods, he is careful to add the qualification **sī fās est** (*if it is right [to say so]*). Such divine beings would not automatically dispense blessings because of an altruistic nature. They had to be bribed, and this was done by making a vow (**vōtum**) to do something in return for a favor, if granted. The principle of **dō ut dēs** (*I give [to you] so that you give [to me]*) could operate on a state or individual level; this notion is exemplified in Lygdamus' poem to his mistress, Neaera (page 122).

One of the most striking differences between Roman religion and Christianity lies in their differing explanations for the origin of evil and misfortune. Traditional Christianity uses a supernatural force, the devil, to explain human troubles and misdeeds; opposed to him is an omnipotent being who is wholly concerned with what is morally right. The Roman system had no comparable dichotomy. Roman gods and goddesses were not paragons of virtue and had no compunction about the collateral damage of human suffering and misery caused by advancing their schemes and pursuing their whims. A glaring example is the part played by Juno in the *Aeneid*, where she wreaks havoc and destruction to prevent the establishment of a Trojan settlement in Italy, although it is the will of Jupiter that the Trojans be successful. (For Vergil's remonstrance, see *Aeneid* 1.8–11, page 67.)

Rome had come into contact with Greek civilization before the earliest surviving written records, and the Romans probably began to equate their divinities to those of the Greeks at that early stage. The attitude of supposing that the gods of another people were the same as your own (but with different names) was common in antiquity; when Julius Caesar described the religion of the Gauls (*dē bellō Gallicō* 6.17), he used Roman, not Celtic, names (**Mercurius, Iuppiter,** and **Mars,** for instance).

The assimilation of the Roman pantheon to that of the Greeks was completed at an early date: The Roman Jupiter and Juno were the Greek Zeus and Hera, Mercury was the Greek Hermes, and so on. Whether this involved any significant changes in religious practices at Rome is doubtful. It did mean that, for Roman poets, the wealth of stories about Greek gods and goddesses could be transferred to their Roman counterparts, in addition to the tales of such figures as Ulysses, Jason, and other human actors in Greek mythology. (On the use of these Greek elements, see "Mythology," page 124.)

In the following list, the principal Roman divinities are described as they were in the Roman poets; how they were conceived in traditional cults and festivals was sometimes different.

Jupiter (**Iuppiter Iovis** M.): The king of the gods and men (**hominum deumque rex**). The temple of **Iuppiter Optimus Maximus** (*Jupiter best and greatest*) on the Capitol was the most sacred place in Rome.

Juno (**Iūnō Iūnōnis** F.): The wife and sister of Jupiter, whose unfaithfulness was a cause of constant friction between the two. She was the goddess of marriage and childbirth.

Neptune (**Neptūnus -ī** M.): A brother of Jupiter and god of the sea.

Pluto (**Plūtō Plūtōnis** M., also called **Dīs Dītis**): A brother of Jupiter and god of the Underworld, which he ruled without mercy or compassion. His wife, Proserpine (**Prōserpina -ae** F., also called by her Greek name, Persephone), was queen of the dead.

Saturn (**Sāturnus -ī** M.): The ruler of heaven and earth before being dethroned by his son, Jupiter. During Saturn's reign, mortals enjoyed simple lives in a rural setting and were content with plain food, such as acorns; their happiness was complemented by their respect for honesty and justice.

Venus (**Venus Veneris** F.): The goddess of procreation and sexual love. Although married to Vulcan, she advertised her office by promiscuity with both gods and men. One affair, with the Trojan noble Anchises, resulted in the birth of Aeneas.

Minerva (**Minerva -ae** F.): A daughter of Jupiter and patroness of handicrafts. Her favorite sport was warfare. Minerva, Diana, and Vesta were virgin goddesses.

Apollo (**Apollō Apollinis** M., also called **Phoebus -ī**): The son of Jupiter and a mortal woman, Leto. As patron of poetry and music, Apollo was often celebrated by poets.

Diana (**Dĭāna -ae** F., also called **Phoebē Phoebēs**): A sister of Apollo. Among her several functions was that of moon goddess; because of the association of the moon with witches, she was sometimes equated with **Hecatē**, the goddess of the black arts. Diana was also goddess of wild beasts and the hunt.

Mars (**Mars Martis** M.): A son of Jupiter and god of warfare. He was always depicted as quarrelsome and brutal.

Mercury (**Mercurius -(i)ī** M.): A son of Jupiter and messenger of the gods. One of his functions was to take the Shades of the dead to the Underworld (see Horace *Odes* 1.24.18, page 86).

Vulcan (**Vulcānus -ī** M.): The divine blacksmith. He had his forge under Mt. Etna in Sicily or under the volcanic islands to the north.

Bacchus (**Bacchus -ī** M., also called **Dionȳsus -ī** and **Līber Līberī**): The son of Jupiter and a mortal woman, Semele, and god of wine, which he had discovered.

Vesta (**Vesta -ae** F.): The goddess of the hearth. Her temple in the Forum housed a constantly burning fire (the **ignis inextinctus**), which was tended by the six Vestal Virgins (**sacerdōtēs Vestālēs**) and symbolized the continuity of the Roman state. The Vestal Virgins were upperclass women who, during their minimum service of 30 years, were obliged to maintain their virginal state under pain of being buried alive.

Among the minor divinities were the **Larēs** (**Lar Laris** M.) and **Penātēs** (**Penātium** M.PL.), who were spirits without individual names and who presided over the welfare of a Roman household. Their statuettes were placed in a shrine (**larārium**) in the **ātrium** of the home, where they were worshipped daily. The **Larēs** were the guardians of the hearth (**focus**) and home (**domus**); the **Penātēs** saw to the food supply. ༄

Roman statue
of Apollo
holding a lyre.

© Mimmo Jodice/CORBIS

Orpheus and Eurydice

Orpheus, the legendary singer and musician, and his beloved Eurydice had not been together long before she was bitten by a snake and died. In his despair, Orpheus went down to the Underworld in order to gain her release from the land of the dead. His venture, however, ended in failure.

Vergil tells the story in the Georgics, but as it was well known, he does not give the full narrative. Instead, he describes the main scenes: the grieving Orpheus, his descent into the Underworld, the effect of his singing, and the final tragic parting with Eurydice.

Ipse cava solans aegrum testudine amorem
te, dulcis coniunx, te solo in litore secum,   465
te veniente die, te decedente canebat.
Taenarias etiam fauces, alta ostia Ditis,

TEXT   P. Vergili Maronis *Opera*, ed. R. A. B. Mynors
        (Oxford Classical Texts, 1969)
METER   hexameter [§M1]
        īpsĕ că|vā sō|lāns ‖ āeg|rūm tēs|tūdĭn(e) ă|mōrĕm
        tē, dūl|cīs cōn|iūnx ‖ tē | sōl(o) īn | lītŏrĕ | sēcŭm

The legend was Greek and presents traditional Greek beliefs about life after death (see "Roman Beliefs About an Afterlife," page 78).

464   **Ipse** *he himself*, i.e., **Orpheus** (-ī M.), who has been mentioned in the preceding narrative; take **cavā** (*hollow*) with **testūdine** (**testūdō testūdinis** F. *tortoise shell*), instrumental abl. [§G47]—according to legend, the original lyre was made from a tortoise shell from which the animal had been removed, hence **cavā**, *with a hollow tortoise shell*; **sōlans** (**sōlor -ārī** *comfort*) governs **aegrum ... amōrem**—his love was ailing because he had lost **Eurydicē** (**Eurydicēs** F.—the name, like the legend, is Greek).

465f. **tē ... tē** (the repetition is for effect) is the object of **canēbat**, whose subject is **ipse** in l. 464; **dulcis coniunx** voc.; take **sōlō** with **lītore**; **sēcum** = **cum sē**; **veniente diē ...** [**diē**] **dēcēdente** (**dēcēdō -ere** here *set*) abl. of time when [§G37], trans. *when day was rising* (lit., *coming*), *when it was setting*; **canēbat** imperf. to express habitual action in the past [§G62] *used to sing of*.

467   For the Greeks, the Underworld was a vast cavern inside the earth, where mortals went after dying, and Orpheus now enters it to rescue Eurydice; **Taenariās** (with **faucēs**) adj. of **Taenarus**, a promontory in southern Greece where there was a cave supposed to lead down to the Underworld; **faucēs** (**faucium** F.PL.) *jaws, mouth*, i.e., the cave's narrow entrance; **etiam** here *even*; **alta ostia Dītis** is in apposition [§G52] to **Taenariās faucēs**; **ostia** pl. for sg. [§G53] (**ostium -(i)ī** N. *entrance*); **Dītis** gen. of **Dīs**, another name for **Plūtō**, the king of the Underworld.

468   Take **cālīgantem** (**cālīgō -āre** *be dark/gloomy*) with **lūcum** (**lūcus -ī** M. *grove*); **nigrā formīdine** (**formīdō formīdinis** F. *fear*) abl. of cause [§G48]; trans. *the grove*

et caligantem nigra formidine lucum
ingressus, Manisque adiit regemque tremendum
nesciaque humanis precibus mansuescere corda.   470
at cantu commotae Erebi de sedibus imis
umbrae ibant tenues simulacraque luce carentum,
quam multa in foliis avium se milia condunt,
vesper ubi aut hibernus agit de montibus imber,
matres atque viri defunctaque corpora vita   475
magnanimum heroum, pueri innuptaeque puellae,
impositique rogis iuvenes ante ora parentum,

gloomy with (lit., *by reason of*) *black fear*—we are to think of the grove as between the Taenarian cave and the actual gates of the Underworld.

469f.   **ingressus** (*having entered*; **ingredior -ī**) governs the preceding accusatives; **Manīs** acc. pl. of **Manēs Manium** M.PL. *the Shades [of the dead]*; **adiit** (**adeō adīre** *approach*) governs **Manīs**, **rēgem**, and **corda**; ... **-que** ... **-que** *both* ... *and* ...; **tremendum** (gerundive [§G 79] of **tremō -ere**) *fearsome*; take **nescia** with **corda** *hearts not knowing [how]*; **hūmānīs precibus** (instrumental abl. [§G 47]) **mansuescere** (**mansuescō -ere**) *to become gentle through human prayers*—the hearts are those of the rulers of the Underworld, not of the **Manēs**.

471f.   **at** *but*; take **cantū** (instrumental abl. [§G 47]; **cantus -ūs** M. *song*) with **commōtae** (**commoveō -ēre** *agitate, stir*), which agrees with **umbrae** (nom. pl., l. 472; *Shades [of the dead]*, here = **Manēs**); **Erebī dē sēdibus īmīs** *from the deepest* (**īmus**) *abodes* (**sēdēs sēdis** F.) *of Erebus* (**Erebus -ī** M. another name for the Underworld); **ībant** (**eō īre** *began to go* (inceptive imperf. [§G 62]—its subject is **umbrae ...** **simulācraque**); with **umbrae** take **tenuēs** (**tenuis** *insubstantial*)—the Shades are so described because they are merely shadowy outlines of what they had been in life; **simulācra** (**simulācrum -ī** N. *ghost*) ... **carentum** (= **carentium**; gen. pl. of the pres. pple. of **careō -ēre** *lack*, which takes the abl., hence **lūce**), trans. *the ghosts of those lacking the light [of day]* (another way of describing the Shades).

473   Lit., *as* (**quam**) *many [as] the thousands of birds hide* ..., i.e., *as numerous as the thousands of birds that hide* ...; **folium -(i)ī** N. *leaf*; **avium** gen. pl. of **avis avis** F. *bird*; **mīlia** nom. pl. of **mille** *thousand*; **condunt** (**condō -ere** *hide*) governs **sē**.

474   **vesper** ((no gen.) M. *evening*) **ubi** (postponed [§G 4]; here *when*) = **ubi vesper [est]**; **hībernus ... imber** (**imbris** M.) *winter rain*; **agit** *drives* (i.e., the birds).

475f.   The nouns in the nominative are in apposition to **umbrae ... simulācraque** (l. 472) and describe some of the inhabitants of the Underworld; in the phrase **dēfuncta corpora vītā magnanimum** (= **magnanimōrum** [§G 95]) **hērōum** (gen. pl. of **hērōs hērōos** M. a Greek noun, *hero*), the sense tells us that **vītā** is abl. and is governed by **dēfuncta** (**dēfungor -ī** + abl. *be finished with*)—as the Shades of the dead are shadows, not bodies, **corpora** here must refer to their shapes, trans. *the figures of brave heroes [who had] finished with life*; **innuptae** *unmarried*.

477   **impositī** (**impōnō -ere**) **rogīs** (dat. pl. of **rogus -ī** M.) *placed on funeral pyres*; **ante** + acc. *in front of*; **ōra** (acc. pl. of **ōs ōris** N.) here *faces*; **parentum** gen. pl. of **parens parentis** M./F. *parent*.

quos circum limus niger et deformis harundo
Cocyti tardaque palus inamabilis unda
alligat et novies Styx interfusa coercet.   480
quin ipsae stupuere domus atque intima Leti
Tartara caeruleosque implexae crinibus anguis
Eumenides, tenuitque inhians tria Cerberus ora,

478   quōs, the object of **alligat** and **coercet** (l. 480), has as its antecedents the inhabitants of the Underworld just described; **circum** here an adv., lit., *round about*;
līmus -ī M. *mud*; **niger** *black*; **dēformis** *ugly*; **harundō harundinis** F. *reed*.

479f.   **Cōcȳtus (-ī** M.) and **Styx (Stygis** F.) were two of the five Underworld rivers;
Cōcȳtī possessive gen. [§G18] with **līmus** and **harundō**; **tardā ... undā** instrumental abl. [§G47] *with sluggish water*; **palūs (palūdis** F.) *swamp*; **inamābilis** *loathsome*; **alligat (alligō -āre** *restrict, confine*) has three subjects but agrees only with
the nearest [§G58], **palūs**; take **noviēs** (adv. *nine times*) with **interfūsa** (lit., *poured
in between*); **coerceō -ēre** *confine*—in order to prevent the dead from escaping, the
Underworld is, for Vergil, surrounded by the **Cōcȳtus** with its mud and reeds
(since they had nowhere to flow, the Underworld rivers were always imagined as
being sluggish); this circular course is referred to by **circum** (l. 478), which is here
best translated by *in a circle*; as an additional disincentive against attempts to escape, at the entrance to the Underworld the **Styx** was **noviēs interfūsa**, lit., *poured
nine times in between* (the Underworld and the world of the living); trans. *the Styx
with its nine intervening streams* (i.e., its eight loops)—compare Dante's epic *Divine Comedy*, where Vergil is Dante's guide through the nine circles of hell; Vergil
does not mention the other three Underworld rivers here.

481ff.   **quīn** *indeed, in fact*; **ipsae** agrees with **domūs** (nom. pl.); **stupuēre** (= stupu-
ērunt) 3 pl. perf. ind. act. **stupeō -ēre** *be stunned* (the subjects of **stupuēre** are
domūs, Tartara, and **Eumenides**); **intima Lētī Tartara** *Death's* (**Lētum -ī** N.) *innermost region*, **Tartara** (neuter nom. pl.; usually *Tartarus* in English) was the lowest part of the Underworld—the power of Orpheus' singing (cf. l. 471) was such
that it stirred even inanimate things, and hence not only the inhabitants of the
Underworld but even their dwellings and Tartarus itself were affected; Tartarus
was the section of the Underworld reserved for egregious wrongdoers, who were
punished under the supervision of the three Furies (the **Eumenides; Eumenis
Eumenidos** F. a Greek noun); the latter, to present a suitably horrific appearance,
had blue snakes in their hair, hence **caeruleōs** (*blue*) **implexae** (**implectō -ere**
intertwine) **crīnibus** (abl. pl. of **crīnis crīnis** M. *hair*) **anguīs** (acc. pl. of **anguis
anguis** M./F. *snake*), lit., *intertwined with respect to blue snakes in [their] hair*, i.e.,
with blue snakes intertwined in [their] hair (**caeruleōs ... anguīs** acc. of respect
[§G15]); **tenuit inhians (inhiō -āre** *gape*) **tria** (neuter acc. pl. of **trēs**) **Cerberus**
(**-ī** M.) **ōra (ōs ōris** N. here *mouth*), lit., *gaping Cerberus held his three mouths*, i.e.,
Cerberus held his three mouths agape—Cerberus was the three-headed dog sta-
tioned at the gates of the Underworld.

atque Ixionii vento rota constitit orbis.

iamque pedem referens casus evaserat omnis,   485

redditaque Eurydice superas veniebat ad auras

pone sequens (namque hanc dederat Proserpina legem),

cum subita incautum dementia cepit amantem,

ignoscenda quidem, scirent si ignoscere Manes:

restitit, Eurydicenque suam iam luce sub ipsa   490

immemor, heu! victusque animi respexit. ibi omnis

484   Ixīoniī (adj. of Ixīōn Ixīonis m.) ... rota (-ae f. *wheel*) ... orbis (gen. sg. of orbis orbis m. here *rotation*) lit., *the wheel of Ixionian rotation*, i.e., *the revolving wheel of Ixion*—Ixion was a mortal who attempted to seduce Juno and was punished in Tartarus by being spread-eagled on a constantly turning wheel; ventō (instrumental abl. [§G47]) constitit (consistō -ere) *stopped with the wind*—the wind stopped and so did Ixion's wheel, which the wind caused to turn.

485   iamque *and now*—Vergil jumps to the final scene of the story; pedem (pēs pedis m.) referens (referō -ferre) lit., *bringing back [his] foot*, i.e., *returning*; cāsūs (acc. pl. of cāsus -ūs m. here *danger*) ... omnīs is the object of ēvāserat (ēvādō -ere), trans. *he* (i.e., Orpheus) *had escaped all dangers.*

486   reddita (*given back*; reddō -ere) agrees with Eurydicē (nom. sg.); superās ... ad aurās lit., *to the upper breezes*, i.e., *to the upper world.*

487   pōne adv. *behind*; namque emphatic form of nam *for*—the parenthetical clause gives the reason why Eurydice was behind Orpheus; Prōserpina *Proserpine*, wife of Pluto and queen of the Underworld; lēgem here *condition*—this was that Orpheus should not look at Eurydice until they were both back in the upper world.

488   cum (*when*) is followed by the indicative; subita (*sudden*) ... dēmentia (-ae f. *madness*) is the subject of cēpit (capiō -ere here *seize*); incautum ... amantem *the unwary lover* (amans amantis m./f.).

489   Take ignoscenda (gerundive [§G79] of ignoscō -ere, *pardonable*) with dēmentia; quidem *indeed*; scīrent imperf. subjunctive of sciō scīre, here *know how*; sī is postponed [§G4]; Mānēs here refers to the rulers of the Underworld; this line is a condensed form of *[which would have been] pardonable if the Shades knew how to pardon*, with both verbs in the subjunctive [§G94].

490f.   restitit (resistō -ere here *stop* (intr.))—the understood subject is Orpheus; Eurydicēn (Greek acc. of Eurydicē) is qualified by suam (*his own*) and is the object of respexit (respiciō -ere *look back at*); iam here *already*; lūce (lux lūcis f.) sub ipsā = sub lūce ipsā *under the light itself*—Orpheus has stepped out of the tunnel to the Underworld, but Eurydice, because she is walking behind, is still in it; immemor *forgetful*; heu! interjection *alas!*; victus (vincō -ere) animī (locative [§G51]) lit., *conquered in mind*, i.e., *with mind overcome*; ibi *then*; take omnis with labor (l. 492).

effusus labor atque immitis rupta tyranni
foedera, terque fragor stagnis auditus Avernis.
illa "quis et me" inquit "miseram et te perdidit, Orpheu,
quis tantus furor? en iterum crudelia retro   495
fata vocant, conditque natantia lumina somnus.
iamque vale: feror ingenti circumdata nocte
invalidasque tibi tendens, heu non tua, palmas."
dixit et ex oculis subito, ceu fumus in auras
commixtus tenuis, fugit diversa, neque illum   500

492f. Supply **est** with **effūsus** (**effundō -ere** here *waste*) and with **audītus, sunt**
with **rupta**; **labor** here *effort*; take **immitis** (gen. sg., *cruel*) ... **tyrannī** (**tyrannus**
-ī M. *tyrant*) with **foedera** (pl. for sg. [§G 53]; **foedus foederis** N. *treaty, agreement*);
ter adv. *three times*; **fragor fragōris** M. *crash*; **stagnīs** (**stagnum -ī** N.) ... **Avernīs**
abl. of place where [§G 38] *in the Underworld swamps*—**Avernus**, another name for
the Underworld, is used here as an adjective.

494ff. **illa**, i.e., **Eurydicē**; **quis ... quis tantus furor** *what so great madness* (**quis** is
repeated for emphasis), trans. *what terrible madness*; **et mē ... miseram et tē** *both
unhappy me and you*; **inquit** (3 sg. perf. ind. act. **inquam**) *said*; **perdidit** (3 sg. perf.
ind. act. **perdō -ere**) *destroyed*; **Orpheu** voc.; **furor furōris** M. *madness*; **ēn** interjection *behold!, see!*; **iterum** *again*; take **crūdēlia** with **fāta**, *cruel fates*; **retrō** adv.
back; supply **mē** with **vocant**—the fates are said to call Eurydice back because
what the gods (here, those of the Underworld) willed always coincided with what
was fated; **condō -ere** here *close*; **natantia** pres. pple. of **natō -āre** *swim*; **lūmina**
(**lūmen lūminis** N.) here *eyes*.

497 **valē** *farewell*; **feror** 1 sg. pres. ind. pass. **ferō ferre** here *carry off*; take **ingentī**
(**ingens** (**ingentis**) here *thick*) ... **nocte** (instrumental abl. [§G 47]) with **circumdata** (**circumdō -āre** *surround*).

498 Take **invalidās** (*weak*) with **palmās** (**palma -ae** F. here *hand*); **tibī** *to you*—in
poetry, the dative can be used to express motion toward [§G 35]; **tendō -ere** *stretch*;
heu! nōn tua *alas! not yours*, i.e., *no longer yours*—the understood subject is **ego**
(**Eurydicē**).

499f. **ex oculīs** *from [his] eyes*; **subitō** *suddenly*; **ceu** *in the same way as, like*; take
fūmus (**-ī** M. *smoke*) and **commixtus** (**commisceō -ēre** *mix*) together; **in aurās ...
tenuīs** *with* (lit., *into*) *the thin breezes*—Eurydice becomes an insubstantial Shade
once again; **fūgit** perf. of **fugiō -ere** *flee*; **dīversa** lit., *turned in the opposite direction*,
but trans. *in the opposite direction* (i.e., back to the Underworld).

501f. Orpheus (**illum** in l. 500, which is the object of **vīdit** in l. 502) is described
as **prensantem** (**prensō -āre** *clutch at*) **nēquīquam umbrās** (here, the shadows in
the tunnel) (*vainly clutching at shadows*) and **multa volentem** (**volō velle** *wish*)
dīcere (*wishing to say many [things]*); take **praetereā** (*thereafter*) with **vīdit**, whose
understood subject is still **Eurydicē**—they would never see each other again,
since they would not be reunited when Orpheus died (such reunion is a Christian
notion); the age-old belief, which is reflected in the story, was that the Shades of

prensantem nequiquam umbras et multa volentem
dicere praeterea vidit: nec portitor Orci
amplius obiectam passus transire paludem.

~: VERGIL *Georgics* 4.464–503

the dead were devoid of both thought and emotion and so could not resume any
relationship of the upper world; the **portitor** (**portitōris** M. *ferryman*) **Orcī** (**Orcus -ī** M. another name for the Underworld) was **Charōn**, who transported the
dead in his boat across the swamp formed by one of the infernal rivers.

503   **amplius** *further, again;* take **obiectam** (**obiciō -ere** *put in front*) with **palūdem**,
lit., *the swamp put in front* (i.e., of anyone who wanted to pass), but trans. *the
swamp that stood in [his] way;* with **passus** (perf. pple. of **patior patī** here *allow*)
supply **est**.

The Queen and the Schoolboy

In Elizabethan England, children were taught Latin from a very early
age. At the end of their schooling, they had acquired a knowledge
of the language beyond that of most of today's undergraduates. The
queen herself, Elizabeth I, had received such an education at the
hands of private tutors and was able to read Latin fluently by the age
of sixteen.

At the time, corporal punishment was considered an essential part
of the learning process. This is borne out by a story of the queen's
visit to a boys school, where she asked a pupil if he had ever been
beaten. The clever boy replied immediately by quoting Vergil:

Infandum, regina, iubes renovare dolorem.   *Aeneid* 2.3
O queen, you bid [me] recall unspeakable grief.

This is the first line of Aeneas' response to Dido's request to hear the
story of Troy's fall and his own sufferings, but the schoolboy meant it
to refer to his own beatings. Her Majesty was no doubt pleased with
the school's teaching methods and impressed with the boy's profi-
ciency in Latin.

Of Arms and the Man

*Vergil's epic, the Aeneid, tells how the Trojan hero **Aenēās** leaves Troy after its capture by the Greeks and, after many trials, arrives in Italy to begin a settlement that is destined to develop into the Roman nation. Vergil's primary objectives in writing the Aeneid were to establish a foundation myth for Rome and to extol Augustus and the contemporary state, whose fortunes, after decades of civil war, Augustus had restored. However, the complex interplay between the poem's ostensible aims and Vergil's views on humanity and the human condition gives the Aeneid a depth of meaning and a relevance that transcend the period in which it was written.*

Arma virumque cano, Troiae qui primus ab oris
Italiam fato profugus Laviniaque venit
litora, multum ille et terris iactatus et alto
vi superum, saevae memorem Iunonis ob iram,

TEXT P. Vergili Maronis *Opera*, ed. R. A. B. Mynors
(Oxford Classical Texts, 1969)
METER hexameter [§M 1]
ārmă vĭ|rūmquĕ că|nō ‖ Trō|iaē quī | prīmŭs ăb | ōrīs
Ītălĭ|ām fā|tō ‖ prŏfŭ|gūs Lā|vīniăquĕ | vēnĭt
(**Lavinia** is pronounced *lă-vīn-yă*.)

1 **Arma** (*arms*) is used by metonymy [§G 97] for *wars*; **canō** (tr.) *I sing of*—the notion that a poet sang his composition comes from early Greek epic poetry, when this was the normal practice; **Trōiae ... ab ōrīs** *from the shores of Troy* (**Trōia -ae** F.); **quī** is postponed [§G 4]; **prīmus** *first*.

2f. **Ītaliam ... Lāvīniaque ... lītora** acc. of motion toward [§G 13] *to Italy* (**Ītalia -ae** F.) *and the coasts of Lavinium* (lit., *Lavinian coasts*)—Lavinium was the name of Aeneas' first settlement in Italy; **fātō** (abl. of cause [§G 48]) **profugus** (-ī M.) *an exile by fate* (the phrase is in apposition [§G 52] to the subject)—Aeneas was fated to leave Troy and sail to Italy; **vēnit** perf. *came*; two phrases structured around the participles **iactātus** and **passus** (l. 5) are in apposition to the subject of the adjectival clause (**quī**, i.e., Aeneas), but for emphasis **ille** (*that man*) is added—this can be dropped in translation; take **multum** (here adv.) with **iactātus** (perf. pple. of **iactō -āre**) *having been much tossed about*; **et terrīs ... et altō** abl. of place where [§G 38] *both on land* (pl. for sg. [§G 53]) *and on the deep* (**altum -ī** N.).

4 **vī** (abl. of **vīs**) **superum** (= **superōrum** [§G 95]) *through the violence of the gods* (lit., *upper gods*)—for a Roman, there were two types of divinities, the **superī**, *the upper gods*, who controlled the world of the living, and the **inferī**, *the lower gods*, who ruled the dead; take **saevae** with **Iūnōnis** and **memorem** with **īram**, *because of the unforgetting* (i.e., *obsessive*) *anger of fierce Juno* (**Iūnō Iūnōnis** F.)—Juno had supported the Greeks in the Trojan War and was therefore prejudiced against Aeneas; she was also concerned that her current project, the development of Carthage, might be affected by what was destined for Aeneas and his descendants.

multa quoque et bello passus, dum conderet urbem   5
inferretque deos Latio; genus unde Latinum
Albanique patres atque altae moenia Romae.
Musa, mihi causas memora, quo numine laeso
quidve dolens regina deum tot volvere casus
insignem pietate virum, tot adire labores   10
impulerit. tantaene animis caelestibus irae?

~: VERGIL *Aeneid* 1.1–11

---

5   *having suffered* (**passus** perf. pple. of **patior patī**) *many things also* (**quoque**) *in war* (lit., *by war*, abl. of cause [§G 48]) *as well* (**et**); **dum** + subj. *until;* **condō -ere** *establish* (the subjunctive indicates what was to happen in the future); **urbem** i.e., Lavinium.

6   **inferō -ferre** *bring;* **deōs** *[his] gods,* i.e., the household gods (**Penātēs**) of Troy; **Latiō** dat. of motion toward [§G 35] *to Latium* (**Latium -(i)ī** N.); **unde** (which is postponed [§G 4]) is here the relative adverb *from which source,* i.e., from Aeneas and those who established Lavinium with him; trans. with a new sentence *From this source [arose] the Latin race....*

7   The initial settlement at Lavinium, near the west coast of central Italy, was moved farther inland by Aeneas' son Ascanius to Alba Longa (**Albānī patrēs** (*the Alban fathers*) refers to the ruling families of the time); much later came the establishment of Rome (**Rōma -ae** F.) itself.

8   Vergil follows Homer in supposing all his information comes from the Muse (**Mūsa -ae** F.), whom he here addresses—the nine muses were the divinities in charge of cultural matters; a poet often thought it unnecessary to call the muse he was addressing by her individual name; **memorā** 2 sg. imp. act. **memorō -āre** *recount;* **causās** (*the reasons*) is followed by an indirect question stating what has to be explained; **quō nūmine laesō** lit., *through what divine power [of hers, i.e., of Juno] having been offended* (**laesō** perf. pple. of **laedō -ere**)—Juno had **nūmen** (*divine power*) in several areas, e.g., as a war goddess and as goddess of childbirth; trans. *through offense to what aspect of her divinity.*

9ff.   **quidve dolens** *or grieving over what;* **rēgīna deum** (= **deōrum** [§G 95]) is the subject of **impulerit** (l. 11; 3 sg. perf. subj. act. **impellō -ere** *drive*), which is followed grammatically by **virum volvere** (**volvō -ere** here *suffer, go through*) **tot cāsūs** (**cāsus -ūs** M. *misfortune*), **adīre** (**adeō adīre** here *take on*) **tot labōrēs; insignem pietāte** (abl. of cause [§G 48]; **pietās pietātis** F.) *distinguished by his piety*—Vergil places heavy emphasis on this aspect of Aeneas' character; take **tantaene** (**tantae** + **-ne** (interr. particle)) with **īrae** (pl. for sg. [§G 53]) and supply **sunt**; **animīs caelestibus** abl. of place where [§G 38] *in divine hearts* (lit., *minds*).

The Capture of a Royal Palace

When Aeneas, in his wanderings after leaving Troy, arrives at Carthage in north Africa, a banquet is held in his honor by Dido, the beautiful queen of the newly founded city. At her request, Aeneas tells of the capture of Troy by the Greeks and of his subsequent adventures. The following is his description of how Pyrrhus, the son of Achilles, breaks into the palace of Priam, the Trojan king.

Vestibulum ante ipsum primoque in limine Pyrrhus
exsultat telis et luce coruscus aëna: 470
qualis ubi in lucem coluber mala gramina pastus,
frigida sub terra tumidum quem bruma tegebat,
nunc, positis novus exuviis nitidusque iuventa,
lubrica convolvit sublato pectore terga

TEXT   P. Vergili Maronis *Opera*, ed. R. A. B. Mynors
        (Oxford Classical Texts, 1969)
METER   hexameter [§M1]
        vēstĭbŭ|l(um) ānt(e) īp|sūm ‖ prī|mōqu(e) īn | līmĭnĕ | Pӯrrhŭs
        ēxsūl|tāt tē|līs ‖ ēt | lūcĕ cŏ|rūscŭs ă|ēnā

469   **Vestibulum -ī** N. *entrance hall;* the first phrase is more closely defined by **prīmō in līmine,** lit., *on the first [part of the] threshold* (**līmen līminis** N.), trans. *on the edge of the threshold*—**Pyrrhus** (**-ī** M.) is about to break down the door.
470   **exsultat** historic pres. [§G60] of **exsultō -āre** *swagger*—later uses of this idiom are not noted; **tēlīs** and **lūce aēnā** abl. of respect [§G46] with **coruscus,** lit., *shining with respect to [his] weapons and [their] bronze light*—**tēlīs et lūce** form a hendiadys [§G96], trans. *shining with the bronze gleam of his weapons.*
471   **quālis** lit., *of what sort,* rel. adj. of quality agreeing with **coluber** (**colubrī** M. *snake*)—the construction of the simile is somewhat obscured by the word order; lit., *of what sort [is] a snake when ...,* but trans. *just as when a snake ...;* **in lūcem** (*toward the light [of day]*) is placed here for emphasis but is to be taken with **convolvit ... terga** (l. 474) and refers to the snake's movement from its hole after hibernation; **mala grāmina** *harmful plants* (**grāmen grāminis** N.); **pastus** (**pascō -ere**) here has the active sense *having eaten.*
472   **quem** (antecedent **coluber**) is postponed [§G4]; **frīgida ... brūma** *the cold winter* (**brūma -ae** F.); **tumidus** *swollen*—before hibernating, the snake had gorged itself to survive the winter.
473   **positīs ... exuviīs** abl. absolute [§G49], trans. *after shedding [its] skin* (**exuviae -ārum** F.PL.); **novus** here *fresh;* **nitidus iuventā** *shining with youth* (instrumental abl. [§G47]; **iuventa -ae** F.)—it is as if the snake is reborn.
474f. **lūbrica ... terga** *[its] slippery back* (pl. for sg. [§G53]; **tergum -ī** N.); **convolvō -ere** *roll;* **sublātō pectore** abl. absolute [§G49], lit., *breast* (**pectus pectoris** N.) *having been raised* (**sufferō -ferre**)—the snake, lifting its head and the part of its body immediately below (here called **pectus**), advances with a writhing movement;

arduus ad solem, et linguis micat ore trisulcis. 475
una ingens Periphas et equorum agitator Achillis,
armiger Automedon, una omnis Scyria pubes
succedunt tecto et flammas ad culmina iactant.
ipse inter primos correpta dura bipenni
limina perrumpit postisque a cardine vellit 480
aeratos; iamque excisa trabe firma cavavit
robora et ingentem lato dedit ore fenestram.
apparet domus intus et atria longa patescunt;
apparent Priami et veterum penetralia regum,
armatosque vident stantis in limine primo. 485

it has emerged from its hole and is now **arduus ad sōlem** (*rearing up to the sun*); **linguīs ... trisulcīs** *with a three-forked tongue* (pl. for sg. [§G 53]; instrumental abl. [§G 47]); **micō -āre** *flash*; **ōre** abl. of place from which [§G 39] *from [its] mouth*.

476f.   **ūnā** functions as an adverb, trans. *together* (i.e., with Pyrrhus); **Periphās Periphantis** M. a Greek warrior; **agitātor** (**agitātōris** M. *driver*) is in apposition [§G 52] to **Automedōn** (**Automedontis** M.); **Achillis** gen. sg. of **Achillēs** (**Achillis** M.), the greatest of the Greek warriors, who had been killed some time before the capture of Troy; **armiger armigerī** M. *armor-bearer* (i.e., to Pyrrhus); **ūnā** (l. 477) as in the previous line; **Scȳrius** adj. of **Scȳrus -ī** F. *Scyros* (a small island in the northern Aegean Sea, birthplace of Pyrrhus); **pūbēs pūbis** F. *force* (i.e., of men).

478   Take **succēdunt** (**succēdō -ere** + dat. *move up to*) with **tectō** (dat. sg. of **tectum -ī** N. *building*); **culmen culminis** N. *roof*; **iactō -āre** *toss*.

479ff.   **ipse** i.e., Pyrrhus; **correptā ... bipennī** abl. absolute [§G 49], lit., *ax* (**bipennis bipennis** F.) *having been snatched* (**corripiō -ere**); take **dūra** (*stout*) with **līmina**, which, by metonymy [§G 97], here means *door*, i.e., the double door at the entrance to the palace; **perrumpō -ere** *break through*; **postīs ... aerātōs** *the bronze-clad rails* (**postis postis** M.), i.e., the upper and lower horizontal rails of the door, onto each of which a hinge pin (**cardō cardinis** M.) was fitted (cf. Propertius *Elegies* 4.8.49, page 114)—in addition to splitting the door, Pyrrhus' ax wrenches (**vellō -ere**) the rails from their pins (**cardine** sg. for pl. [§G 53]), but the door continues to stand; **excīsā trabe** abl. absolute [§G 49], lit., *a panel* (i.e., of the door; **trabs trabis** F.) *having been cut through* (**excīdō -ere**); **firma ... rōbora** *the solid oak* (pl. for sg. [§G 53]; **rōbur rōboris** N.); **cavō -āre** *make a hole in*—Pyrrhus cuts through a panel and so makes a hole in the door, trans. *he made a hole in the solid oak by cutting through a panel*; **lātō ... ōre** abl. of description [§G 44] *with a wide opening*; **dedit** (**dō dare**) *he made*; **fenestra -ae** F. *window*.

483   **appāreō -ēre** *be visible*; **intus** adv. *inside*; **ātria longa** *long hall* (pl. for sg. [§G 53]; **ātrium -iī** N.); **patescō -ere** *be disclosed*.

484   **Priamus -ī** M. *Priam*, the king of Troy; **penetrāle penetrālis** N. here *chamber*.

485   **armātōs ... stantīs** *armed men standing* (i.e., the Greeks) **in līmine prīmō** (cf. l. 469); the understood subject of **vident** is Priam and the other Trojans inside the palace.

at domus interior gemitu miseroque tumultu
miscetur, penitusque cavae plangoribus aedes
femineis ululant; ferit aurea sidera clamor.
tum pavidae tectis matres ingentibus errant
amplexaeque tenent postis atque oscula figunt.   490
instat vi patria Pyrrhus; nec claustra nec ipsi
custodes sufferre valent; labat ariete crebro
ianua, et emoti procumbunt cardine postes.
fit via vi; rumpunt aditus primosque trucidant
immissi Danai et late loca milite complent.   495

~: VERGIL *Aeneid* 2.469–495

486   **interior** *inner;* **gemitū** (**gemitus -ūs** M. *wailing*) **... tumultū** (**tumultus -ūs** M.
  uproar) instrumental abl. [§G 47].
487f.   **miscētur** *is in confusion;* **penitus** adv. *from within;* **cavae ... aedēs** *hollow*
  rooms (**aedēs aedis** F.)—cavae suggests high ceilings, which would have produced
  a loud echo; **plangōribus ... fēmineīs** instrumental abl. [§G 47], lit., *with female*
  laments (**plangor plangōris** M.), trans. *with the lamentations of women;* **ululō -āre**
  howl; **feriō -īre** *strike;* **aureus** *golden;* **sīdus sīderis** N. *star;* **clāmor clāmōris** M.
  clamor—the lamentations reach the heavens.
489   **pavidus** *frightened;* **tectīs ... ingentibus** abl. of place where [§G 38] *in the huge*
  building (pl. for sg. [§G 53]).
490   **postīs** (here, by metonymy [§G 97], *doors*) is accusative after both **amplexae**
  (perf. pple. of **amplector -ārī**) and **tenent**, trans. *and they embraced and clung to*
  the doors; **osculum -ī** N. *kiss;* **fīgō -ere** here *plant*—the women are bidding farewell to the home they will soon be leaving.
491   **instō -āre** *press on;* **vī patriā** abl. of manner [§G 45], lit., *with paternal force,*
  i.e., with the same force that characterized his father, Achilles; **claustrum -ī** N.
  bar—horizontal bars were fastened on the inside of doors to secure them.
492   **sufferō -ferre** *withstand;* **valeō -ēre** *be [sufficiently] strong;* **labō -āre** *give way;*
  ariete (three syllables) **crēbrō** instrumental abl. [§G 47], lit., *with frequent battering*
  ram (**ariēs arietis** M.), trans. *with frequent blows from a battering ram.*
493   **iānua** (**-ae** F.) is the front double door already mentioned and the **postēs** are
  its rails, which have already been wrenched from their pins—this is mentioned
  again in the phrase **ēmōtī ... cardine** (*dislodged* (**ēmoveō -ēre**) *from [their] pins*
  (sg. for pl. [§G 53], abl. of separation [§G 40])); now the **claustra** (l. 491), which
  have still been holding the rails up, give way and the rails *collapse* (**prōcumbō**
  -ere).
494f.   **fit via vī** *a way is made by violence* (instrumental abl. [§G 47]); **rumpō -ere**
  here *force;* **aditūs** pl. for sg. [§G 53] (**aditus -ūs** M. *entrance*); **prīmōs** are the front
  line of the Trojan guards; **trucīdō -āre** *slaughter;* **immissī** lit., *having been admitted*
  (**immittō -ere**), but trans. *after gaining entry;* **Danaī -ōrum** M.PL. another name
  for Greeks; **lātē** adv. *over a wide area;* **mīlite** instrumental abl. [§G 47], sg. for pl.
  [§G 53]; **compleō -ēre** *fill.*

The Shade of Dido

Before Aeneas reaches his final destination in Italy, he visits the Underworld to see the shade of his father, Anchises, who had died on the voyage from Troy to Italy. Soon after entering the realm of the dead, Aeneas comes to the Fields of Lamentation (lūgentēs campī), the region assigned to those who died for love. There he chances to see Dido, the beautiful Carthaginian queen, who killed herself after he had loved and then abandoned her. •

Inter quas Phoenissa recens a vulnere Dido   450
errabat silva in magna; quam Troius heros
ut primum iuxta stetit agnovitque per umbras
obscuram, qualem primo qui surgere mense
aut videt aut vidisse putat per nubila lunam,
demisit lacrimas dulcique adfatus amore est: 455

TEXT   P. Vergili Maronis *Opera*, ed. R. A. B. Mynors
       (Oxford Classical Texts, 1969)
METER hexameter [§M1]
       īntēr | quās ‖ Phōē|nīssă rĕ|cēns ‖ ā | vūlnĕrĕ | Dīdō
       ērrā|bāt ‖ sīlv(a) | īn māg|nā ‖ quām | Trōĭŭs | hērōs

450 **Inter quās** *among whom*, i.e., the shades of other women mentioned in the preceding lines; **Phoenissa** *Phoenician*—Dido came from the Phoenician city of Tyre; **recens** (**recentis**) **ā vulnere** lit., *fresh from her wound*, i.e., *her wound still fresh*—the wound is the self-inflicted blow that killed her.

451f. **silvā in magnā**—the final vowel of **silvā**, though long (we can deduce its length from the context), is elided; **Trōius hērōs** *the Trojan hero* (**hērōs hērōos** M.); the postponed **ut** [§G4] is followed by two indicative verbs and so means *when*, but the clauses are joined to what precedes by **quam** (*whom*), which is governed by **iuxtā** (prep. + acc., *near*) and **agnōvit** (**agnoscō -ere** *recognize*)—we cannot reproduce this common Latin idiom in English and must say *when the Trojan hero first stood near her and recognized her*; **per umbrās** *through the shadows*—these **umbrae** are genuine shadows and not the spirits of the dead.

453f. **obscūram** *dim*, adj. agreeing with **quam** (l. 451), but trans. *a dim figure*; **quālem**, which agrees with **lūnam** (l. 454), is the relative adjective of quality and here introduces a simile; **prīmō ... mense** abl. of time when [§G37] *at the beginning of the month* (**mensis mensis** M.); **quī** indef. pron. *a man*; take **surgere ... per nūbila lūnam** after **videt** and **vīdisse**, lit., *of what sort a man, at the beginning of the month, sees or thinks he has seen* (supply **sē** with **vīdisse**) *the moon to rise through clouds* (**nūbilum -ī** N.)—the comparison is between Aeneas' sighting of Dido and a man seeing the moon when obscured by clouds (the acc.+inf. [§G10] [**sē**] **vīdisse** is followed by another acc.+inf., **lūnam surgere**), i.e., *just as at the beginning of the month a man sees or thinks he has seen the moon rising through the clouds.*

455 **dēmittō -ere** *let fall, shed*; **dulcī ... amōre** abl. of manner [§G45] *with tender love*; **adfātus ... est** *spoke* (**adfor -ārī**).

"infelix Dido, verus mihi nuntius ergo
venerat exstinctam ferroque extrema secutam?
funeris heu tibi causa fui? per sidera iuro,
per superos et si qua fides tellure sub ima est,
invitus, regina, tuo de litore cessi.   460
sed me iussa deum, quae nunc has ire per umbras,
per loca senta situ cogunt noctemque profundam,
imperiis egere suis; nec credere quivi
hunc tantum tibi me discessu ferre dolorem.
siste gradum teque aspectu ne subtrahe nostro.   465
quem fugis? extremum fato quod te adloquor hoc est."

456f. **infēlix** (**infēlīcis**) **Dīdō** voc. *unhappy Dido*; take **ergō** (*so*) at the beginning
       of the sentence; **mihi** dat. of motion toward [§G 35]; [**tē**] **exstinctam** [**esse**] *that
       you had died*—the passive of **exstinguō -ere** has the meaning *die*; **ferrō** instru-
       mental abl. [§G 47] *with a sword*; [**tē**] **extrēma secūtam** [**esse**] lit., *you to have pur-
       sued final things*, i.e., *that you had sought* [*your own*] *end*; these two acc.+inf. con-
       structions [§G 10] with [**tē**] are in apposition to **nuntius** (l. 456, *message*).
458   **fūneris** (**fūnus fūneris** N. *funeral*) is used by metonymy [§G 97] for *death*; **heu**
       interjection *alas!*; **tibi** dat. of disadvantage [§G 31] *for you*; **sīdus sīderis** N. *star*.
459   **superī -ōrum** M.PL. *gods* (see note to *Aeneid* I.4, page 66); **qua** indef. adj.
       with **fidēs**, *any faith*; **tellūre sub īmā** *under the deepest earth*, i.e., here in the
       Underworld.
460   **invītus** trans. by an adverb [§G 55], *unwillingly*; **rēgīna** (**-ae** F.) voc. *O queen*;
       cessī (**cēdō -ere**) *I went*.
461   **iussum -ī** N. *command*; **deum** = **deōrum** [§G 95]; the antecedent of **quae** is
       iussa; **īre** infin. after **cogunt** [**mē**] (l. 462).
462   **loca senta situ** *places squalid* (**sentus**) *with neglect* (**situ** abl. of cause [§G 48];
       situs -ūs M.); supply **mē** with **cōgunt** *force me*; **profundus** *bottomless*.
463   **imperiīs ... suīs** instrumental abl. [§G 47] *with their orders*—this phrase
       would normally presuppose that the subject is *the gods*, not *the commands of the
       gods*, but Aeneas expresses himself in this way to emphasize that he was com-
       pletely under divine control; **ēgēre** (= **ēgērunt**) 3 pl. perf. ind. act. **agō agere**; **quīvī**
       1 sg. perf. ind. act. **queō quīre** *be able*.
464   The subject of the acc.+inf. [§G 10] is **mē**, the object **hunc tantum ... dolō-
       rem**; **tibi** dat. of disadvantage [§G 31] *for you*; **discessū** (**discessus -ūs** M.) instru-
       mental abl. [§G 47] *by* [*my*] *leaving*.
465   **siste** 2 sg. pres. imp. act. **sistō -ere** *halt* (tr.); **gradus -ūs** M. *step*; **tē ... nē sub-
       trahe** (2 sg. pres. imp. act. **subtrahō -ere**) *do not withdraw yourself*; **aspectū ...
       nostrō** abl. of separation [§G 40] *from my sight* (**aspectus -ūs** M.; **nostrō** = **meō**
       [§G 53]).
466   The relative clause **quod tē adloquor** (**adloquor -ī** takes two accusatives) has
       hoc as its antecedent; lit., *this which I say to you is by fate* (**fātō** abl. of cause [§G 48])
       the last, i.e., *the words I am saying to you are the last allowed by fate*.

talibus Aeneas ardentem et torva tuentem
lenibat dictis animum lacrimasque ciebat.
illa solo fixos oculos aversa tenebat
nec magis incepto vultum sermone movetur   470
quam si dura silex aut stet Marpesia cautes.
tandem corripuit sese atque inimica refugit
in nemus umbriferum, coniunx ubi pristinus illi
respondet curis aequatque Sychaeus amorem.

~: VERGIL *Aeneid* 6.450–474

467f.   **tālibus … dictīs** instrumental abl. [§G 47] *with such words*; take **ardentem et torva tuentem** with **animum** (l. 468), which here means *anger*, lit., *[her] anger, burning* (**ardeō -ēre**) *and looking grim [things]* (**torva** adverbial acc. [§G 16] of **torvus**; **tueor tuērī** *look at*)—Vergil boldly says that Dido's anger was *looking grimly*, but for clarity trans. *her burning anger and grim looks*; **lēnībat** (= **lēniēbat**; **lēniō -īre**) conative imperfect [§G 62] *tried to soothe* (lit., *was soothing*)—we know from what follows that Aeneas did not succeed; the tears that Aeneas was stirring up were his own.

469   **solō** abl. of place where [§G 38] *on the ground* (**solum -ī** N.); **fixōs** perf. pple. of **fīgō -ere** *plant, keep fixed*; **āversa** *turned away*.

470f.   **magis … quam sī** *more … than if*; **inceptō … sermōne** instrumental abl. [§G 47] *by his talk* (**sermō sermōnis** M.) *having been begun*, but trans. *from the beginning of his words*; **vultum** acc. of respect [§G 15]; **movētur** historic pres. [§G 60], lit., *nor is she moved with respect to [her] face*, i.e., *nor did her expression change*; **silex silicis** usually M., but here F. *flint*; **cautēs cautis** F. *rock*; **Marpēsius** adj. of Marpessa, a mountain on Paros famous for its marble quarries (*Marpessian rock = marble*); **stet** agrees with the nearer subject [§G 58] and is subjunctive because of an abridged unreal condition [§G 94]—the full comparison would be *than hard flint or Marpessian rock would be moved if it were standing there*.

472   **corripuit sēsē** (= **sē**) *she snatched herself away* (**corripiō -ere**); **inimīca** *[still] hostile*; **refugiō -ere** *flee back*.

473f.   **nemus nemoris** N. *grove*; **umbrifer** *shady*; **ubi** (*where*) is postponed [§G 4]; **pristinus** *former*; **illī** dat. with **respondet** (historic pres. [§G 60]; **respondeō -ēre** *respond*); **cūrīs** abl. of respect [§G 46]; lit., *responds to her with respect to [her] cares*, trans. *responded to [her] sorrows*; **aequat … amōrem** *reciprocated* (historic pres. [§G 60]; **aequō -āre**) *[her] love*; **Sychaeus -ī** M. Dido's **coniunx pristinus**—his murder by her brother had been the cause of her leaving her native city, Tyre, to found Carthage.

The Emperor Augustus

When Aeneas finally meets his father, Anchises, in the Underworld, the latter explains how the souls of the dead are purified and how some are subsequently reborn into the world. He then shows his son the souls of those who are destined to make Rome great. Prominent among these is the future Augustus, who will restore the prosperity of the Golden Age and extend the empire. (The idea of the transmigration of souls came from Greek sources and was not part of normal Roman belief (see page 78).)

Hic vir, hic est, tibi quem promitti saepius audis,
Augustus Caesar, divi genus, aurea condet
saecula qui rursus Latio regnata per arva
Saturno quondam, super et Garamantas et Indos
proferet imperium; iacet extra sidera tellus,   795
extra anni solisque vias, ubi caelifer Atlas
axem umero torquet stellis ardentibus aptum.

TEXT   P. Vergili Maronis *Opera*, ed. R. A. B. Mynors
        (Oxford Classical Texts, 1969)
METER   hexameter [§M1]
        hīc vǐr hǐc | ēst tǐbǐ | quēm ‖ prō|mīttī | saēpǐǔs | aūdīs
        Aūgūs|tūs Caē|sār ‖ dī|vī gěnǔs | aūrěǎ | cōndět

791   **quem** is postponed [§G4]; **prōmittī** pres. pass. inf. of **prōmittō -ere** *promise;*
      saepius (compar. of **saepe** used to express a high degree [§G54]) *very often.*
792ff.   **dīvī genus** in apposition [§G52] to **Augustus** (-ī M.) **Caesar** (**Caesaris** M.)
      offspring of a god—Augustus was the adopted son of Julius Caesar, who had been
      deified (the Eastern practice of deifying rulers was borrowed by Rome); **aurea ...**
      quondam an adj. clause with a postponed rel. pron., **quī** (l. 793) [§G4]; **aurea ...**
      saecula *golden generations* (**saeculum** -ī N.), i.e., *a new* (**rursus**) *Golden Age;*
      condō -ere *establish;* **Latiō** abl. of place where [§G38] *in Latium* (**Latium** -(i)ī N.),
      the area in central Italy of which Rome was the principal city; **regnāta per arva**
      Sāturnō quondam *through fields* (**arvum** -ī N.) *once ruled over* (**regnō** -**āre**) *by*
      Saturn (dat. of agent [§G29]; **Sāturnus** -ī M.)—Saturn, the father and predecessor
      of Jupiter, was supposed to have reigned in Latium during the Golden Age (cf.
      Tibullus *Elegies* 1.3.35, page 117); **super** (+ acc., here *beyond*) governs **Garamantas**
      (Greek acc. pl. of **Garamantēs Garamantium** M.PL. *a people of north Africa*) and
      Indōs (**Indus** -ī M. *an Indian*); **et** (after **super**, postponed [§G3]) joins this clause
      to the previous one.
795   **prōferō -ferre** *extend;* **iacet ... tellūs** describes the land to which Augustus
      will extend the empire; **extrā sīdera** *beyond the constellations* (**sīdus sīderis** N.)—
      the constellations are those of the zodiac, the belt of star groups that encircles the
      earth.

huius in adventum iam nunc et Caspia regna
responsis horrent divum et Maeotia tellus,
et septemgemini turbant trepida ostia Nili.   800
nec vero Alcides tantum telluris obivit,
fixerit aeripedem cervam licet, aut Erymanthi
pacarit nemora et Lernam tremefecerit arcu;

796 **annī sōlisque viās** lit., *the paths of the year and sun*, i.e., the path of the sun during the year (hendiadys [§G96])—the sun's annual path, as conceived in Ptolemaic astronomy and called the ecliptic, is in the same plane as the zodiac; Vergil is referring to the regions of the earth lying beneath the sky on either side of (i.e., to the north and south of) the zodiac/ecliptic; **caelifer Atlās** *sky-bearing Atlas* (**Atlās Atlantis** M.), a divine being (a Titan) condemned to support the sky.

797 **axem** (**axis axis** M.) here *sky*, which is **stellīs ardentibus aptum** *furnished with blazing* (**ardeō -ēre**) *stars* (instrumental abl. [§G47]; **stella -ae** F.); **umerō** abl. of place where [§G38] *on his shoulder* (**umerus -ī** M.); **torqueō -ēre** *turn*—in Ptolemaic astronomy, the sky with its stars and planets revolved around a fixed earth; standing on earth, Atlas held up the moving sky and so could be said to turn it.

798f. **huius** i.e., Augustus; **in** here *in anticipation of*; **adventus -ūs** M. *coming*; **et ... et ...** *both ... and ...*; **Caspia regna** *Caspian kingdoms*, i.e., countries in the vicinity of the Caspian Sea; both **regna** and **tellūs** are the subject of **horrent** (**horreō -ēre** *tremble*); **responsīs ... dīvum** *because of the replies* (abl. of cause [§G48]; **responsum -ī** N.) *of the gods* (**dīvum** old gen. pl. of **dīvus -ī** M. *god*)—Anchises claims that in oracles the gods had already given warning of Augustus' coming; **Maeōtius** adj. of **Maeōtis** (**Maeōtidis** F.) *of Lake Maeotis*, the Sea of Azov north of the Black Sea.

800 **septemgeminī ... ostia Nīlī** the mouths (**ostium -(i)ī** N.) *of the sevenfold Nile* (**Nīlus -ī** M.), i.e., the Nile delta, which is used by synecdoche [§G98] for Egypt; **turbō -āre** *be alarmed*; take **trepida** (**trepidus** *anxious*) with **ostia**.

801 **vērō** adv. *indeed*; **Alcīdēs** (**-ae** M.) another name for Hercules; take **tellūris** (partitive gen. [§G24]) with **tantum**, trans. *so much of the earth*; **obeō obīre** *visit*—in the course of performing his twelve labors, Hercules traveled to numerous places and eliminated monsters of various kinds.

802f. Three clauses are introduced by **licet** (+ subj., *although*), which is postponed [§G4]; **fixerit** 3 sg. perf. subj. act. **fīgō -ere** here *shoot* (with an arrow); **aeripedem cervam** *bronze-footed stag* (**cerva -ae** F.—the noun, although grammatically feminine, can refer to either sex), in English called "the Hind of Ceryneia," a deer of enormous proportions that ravaged crops at Oenoe in the Peloponnese; **Erymanthī ... nemora** *the groves* (**nemus nemoris** N.) *of Erymanthus* (**Erymanthus -ī** M.), a mountain in Arcadia plagued by a large boar, which Hercules killed; **pācārit** (= **pācāverit** [§G95]) 3 sg. perf. subj. act. **pācō -āre** *pacify*; **Lerna -ae** F. a district in Argolis in southeastern Greece, where Hercules killed the Hydra, a multiheaded water snake; **tremefēcerit** 3 sg. perf. subj. act. **tremefaciō -ere** *make tremble*; **arcus -ūs** M. *bow*.

nec qui pampineis victor iuga flectit habenis
Liber, agens celso Nysae de vertice tigris.   805
et dubitamus adhuc virtutem extendere factis,
aut metus Ausonia prohibet consistere terra?

~: VERGIL *Aeneid* 6.791–807

804f.   **Līber** (**Līberī** M., = **Bacchus** = **Dionȳsus**), the god of wine, is the second
mythological benefactor of mankind to whom Augustus is favorably compared;
nec quī … victor … Līber … in prose order, **nec victor Līber quī …**—with **nec
… Līber** supply **tantum tellūris obīvit** from l. 801, trans. *nor [did] triumphant
Liber [visit so much of the earth], who …*; **pampineīs … habēnīs** instrumental abl.
[§G 47] *with reins* (**habēna -ae** F.) *of vine shoots* (**pampineus** adj. of **pampinus -ī** M.
vine shoot); **iuga** pl. for sg. [§G 53], trans. *yoke* (**iugum -ī** N.), i.e., the yoke placed on
the necks of his two tigers (cf. Tibullus *Elegies* 1.3.41, page 118); **flectit** historic
pres. [§G 60] of **flectō -ere** here *control*; **agens** here *driving*; **celsō … dē vertice**
from the lofty peak (**vertex verticis** M.); **Nȳsa -ae** F. the legendary mountain in
India where Bacchus was born; **tigrīs** acc. pl. of **tigris tigris** F. *tiger*—Bacchus'
journey from India to the West in a chariot drawn by a pair of tigers and his introduction of wine throughout the known world were regarded as symbols of the
triumph of civilization over brute nature.
806   The vision of Augustus' future achievements should dispel any doubts Aeneas had about his destiny to establish a settlement in Italy from which Rome
would eventually rise; Anchises tactfully uses the 1 pl. **dubitāmus …?** *do we hesitate …?* instead of the 2 sg.—Aeneas had shown a certain hesitation during his
laborious journey to Italy; **adhūc** *still*; **extendō -ere** *enlarge*; **factīs** instrumental
abl. [§G 47] *by deeds.*
807   **Ausoniā … terrā** abl. of place where [§G 38] *on Ausonian land* (a poetic expression for Italy); with **prohibet** supply **nōs** (*us*); **consistō -ere** *settle*.

Propertius on the *Aeneid*

With these enthusiastic words, Propertius greeted the appearance of
Vergil's *Aeneid*:

Cedite, Romani scriptores, cedite, Grai!
nescio quid maius nascitur Iliade.   *Elegies* 2.34.65f.
Make way, Roman writers, make way, Greeks!
Something greater than the Iliad is born.

The Roman Mission

Near the end of Anchises' review of the great figures of Roman history (see the previous selection), he contrasts some of the achievements of Greek civilization with what he sees should be the guiding concerns of Rome. To emphasize this, he ignores what the Romans were to accomplish in literature and art.

Excudent alii spirantia mollius aera
(credo equidem), vivos ducent de marmore vultus,
orabunt causas melius, caelique meatus
describent radio et surgentia sidera dicent: 850
tu regere imperio populos, Romane, memento
(hae tibi erunt artes), pacique imponere morem,
parcere subiectis et debellare superbos.

~: VERGIL *Aeneid* 6.847–853

TEXT   P. Vergili Maronis *Opera*, ed. R. A. B. Mynors
        (Oxford Classical Texts, 1969)
METER hexameter [§M1]
      ēxcū|dēnt ălĭ|ī ‖ spī|rāntĭă | mōllĭŭs | āĕră
      crēd(o) ĕquĭ|dēm vī|vōs ‖ dū|cēnt dē | mārmŏrĕ | vūltūs

847   Anchises refers to the Greeks by **aliī** (*others*); **excūdō -ere** *hammer out, fashion*; **spīrantia ... aera** lit., *breathing* (**spīrō -āre**) *bronzes* (**aes aeris** N.); **mollius** (compar. adv. of **mollis** *soft*) trans. *more delicately*—Greek statuary, both bronze and marble, of the classical period and later was famous for its lifelike qualities.

848   **crēdō equidem** *indeed I believe [so]*—Anchises is conceding this to the Greeks; **dūcent** *will shape*; **marmor marmoris** N. *marble*.

849f.   **ōrābunt causās** *they will plead cases*—the Greeks developed the art of rhetoric, both forensic and political; **melius** (compar. adv. of **bene**) *better*; **caelī meātūs** lit., *the movements* (**meātus -ūs** M.) *of the sky*, trans. *the movements [of the celestial bodies] in the sky*—the Greeks developed the prevailing system of astronomy; **describō -ere** *trace*; **radiō** instrumental abl. [§G47] *with a rod* (**radius -(i)ī** M.)—astronomers used a rod and sandbox to illustrate astral phenomena; **surgentia sīdera** *the rising stars* (**sīdus sīderis** N.), i.e., when the stars rise; **dicent** *will predict*.

851f.   **regere imperiō populōs** *to rule peoples with [your] government* (instrumental abl. [§G47]); **Rōmāne** voc. sg. of **Rōmānus -ī** M.—Anchises uses the singular to address the Roman race in general; **mementō** 2 sg. imp. **meminī -isse** here *be sure to*; **tibi** dat. of possessor [§G30]; **artēs** *arts, skills*; **pācī impōnere mōrem** lit., *to impose* (**impōnō -ere** *impose [something]* (acc.) *on [something]* (dat.)) *civilized practice on peace*, i.e., to establish civilized practices in lands to which Rome had brought peace—**mōs** here has the broad meaning of *customs appropriate to a civilized society*; naturally, Romans would understand these from their own point of view, which was not necessarily that of the conquered people.

853   **parcō -ere** + dat. *spare*; the adjectives **subiectus** (*submissive*) and **superbus** (*proud*) are both used as nouns; **dēbellō -āre** *subdue*.

Roman Beliefs About an Afterlife

A strong distinction must be drawn between the traditional Greek notions of an afterlife often presented in Roman poetry (as in the story of Orpheus and Eurydice—see page 60) and those that were actually current in Rome and were reflected in rituals and regular ceremonies. The former were taken over by Roman authors, together with much of the paraphernalia of Greek poetry. The latter represent genuine Roman tradition and also appear in verse, although they did not lend themselves to the same treatment as their Greek counterparts.

Common to both traditions was the idea that humans are the union of a body and an insubstantial but life-giving being that in English we call *soul*, although modern ideas of *soul* are inevitably influenced by Christianity. The Latin terms are **corpus** (*body*) and **animus** (*soul*). **Animus**, which has a feminine by-form, **anima**,* is etymologically connected with words meaning *breathe* or *blow* in languages cognate with Latin. It also has a close parallel in the Greek ἄνεμος (anemos) *wind*.†

The two words **animus** and **anima** overlap in meaning, but the former has a much wider range, as can be seen by comparing the entries in the *Oxford Latin Dictionary*. Both denote the vital element of a living person, but **anima**, not **animus**, is the term used for the soul in the afterlife. This was conceived as a shadowy outline of the body and for this reason is normally called a *Shade* in English (an alternative Latin word for **anima** is **umbra**). It was thought that at the point of death, the **anima** escaped through the mouth and in so doing rendered the body lifeless. The **anima** continued to exist but retained any defects or injuries of the body it previously inhabited; for example, the **anima** of a blind person was also blind. The two traditions, the one derived from Greece and the other indigenous to Rome, differ in the way that the fate and domicile of the **anima** were perceived. Both are represented in Roman poetry.

According to imported Greek ideas, which go back to Homer and had long been part of Greek poetic tradition, the Shades of the dead went down to the Underworld, a vast underground cavern that constituted the kingdom of the god Pluto and his queen, Proserpina.‡ This was approached by a long cave and surrounded by five rivers (the Styx, Cocytus, Phlegethon, Lethe, and Acheron), which served the dual purpose of preventing the

---

*The masculine **animus** and feminine **anima** do *not* represent a distinction between the soul of a man and that of a woman; the terms apply equally to both sexes. A man had both **animus** and **anima**, and so did a woman.

†The Greek word for *soul* (ψυχή) has a different etymology.

‡Here and elsewhere, names are given in their Latin forms.

dead from escaping and of discouraging the living from rescue attempts. A newly arrived Shade had to be taken over the Styx (or sometimes the Acheron) by a suitably morose ferryman, Charon. (There was no canonical version of Underworld geography, and we are not informed how the dead crossed the other rivers, if in fact it was necessary for them to do so.) The Shade then passed though the entrance to the Underworld, which was guarded by a savage three-headed dog, Cerberus. From there it passed to the general assembly of the dead, who shared a colorless existence because they were devoid of intelligence and feeling.

Two categories of Shades received special treatment. Those who had committed an offense against a divinity were severely punished. Most noteworthy were Ixion, who was fastened to a burning wheel that never stopped turning; Tantalus, who could not drink from the river in which he stood or reach the fruit hanging above his head; Tityus, who was pinned to the ground while two vultures fed on his liver; and Sisyphus, who kept pushing a huge stone up a slope from which it always rolled down. The counterparts to these unfortunates were the inhabitants of Elysium, a paradise reserved for the Shades of a few humans favored by the gods. The idea that Shades could be rewarded or punished is, of course, inconsistent with the notion that the dead were mindless and without feeling, but similar inconsistencies appear in descriptions of other features of the Underworld.

There were variations in these beliefs in Greek writers, and these also were taken over by their Roman successors. Often the Underworld was presented as observing some form of justice, since, on arrival, all the dead were tried by three Underworld judges, Minos, Aeacus, and Rhadamanthus. Where appropriate, the judges imposed punishments, which were administered by the three Furies. According to another variant, the dead drank of the river Lethe and so forgot their past lives.

The Roman poets were constantly drawing on such Greek stories about life after death, but they themselves would not have believed them. They would rather have inclined toward the old Roman beliefs for which we have evidence both in literature and in the many thousands of grave inscriptions that have survived.

AT ROME, cremation was the normal practice. The ashes of the dead were put in a vase, which was deposited in either a grave or columbarium. The original meaning of **columbārium** was *dovecote* (a nesting box for doves; cf. **columba** *dove*), but it was also used to designate a communal tomb where niches, similar to those of a dovecote, were cut into a wall; it was in these niches that the vases were stored. Both graves and columbaria

Tombstones along the Via Appia outside Rome.

were placed outside the city. It was thought that the great community of the dead lived on in the places where their remains had been placed; if their graves were inside the city limits, this would have entailed the un-desirable consequence of allowing the dead to join in the everyday lives of the living. However, since it was thought unreasonable to cut the dead off entirely from society with the living, graves were placed where some form of communication was possible. A favorite location was near a busy road, as modern visitors to the Appian Way outside Rome can testify. Epi-taphs often begin with the formula **siste viātor** (*stop, traveler*) and then tell something about the dead person.

At the festival of the **Parentālia** in February and at other times, offer-ings were placed on graves. Since the dead still existed and presumably had the power to affect the lives of the living, they were accorded the status of minor supernatural powers and given the collective title **dī mānēs*** (*divine Shades*). This term is never used in the singular, even when referring to the Shade of a single person. On tombstones, the usual introductory formula is **dīs mānibus** followed by the name of the dead person in the genitive case (*to the divine Shades of* _____).

*****Mānēs** is the formal word used for the Shades of the dead but, unlike **anima**, has no other meaning.

Hope Not for Immortality

Quintus Horātius Flaccus (*65–8 B.C.*), *known in English as* **Horace**, *was a contemporary of Vergil. In his lyric poetry, he looked to early Greek poets such as Alcaeus (fl. 600 B.C.) rather than the tradition of contemporary Greek poetry as the generation of Catullus had done. The following poem illustrates the meticulous aptness of expression, the* **cūriōsa fēlīcitās** *that Petronius, a later Roman author, ascribes to Horace.*

Diffugere nives, redeunt iam gramina campis
   arboribusque comae;
mutat terra vices et decrescentia ripas
   flumina praetereunt.
Gratia cum Nymphis geminisque sororibus audet   5
   ducere nuda choros.
immortalia ne speres, monet annus et almum
   quae rapit hora diem.

TEXT   Q. Horati Flacci *Opera*, ed. D. R. Shackleton Bailey
       (Bibliotheca Teubneriana, 2001)
METER First Archilochian [§M 6]
       dĭffŭ|gḗrĕ nĭ|vḗs ‖ rĕdĕ|ū́nt iā́m | grā́mĭnă | cā́mpīs
       ā́rbŏrĭ|būsquĕ cŏ|mā́e

1f.   **Diffūgēre** (= **Diffūgērunt**) 3 pl. perf. ind. act. **diffugiō -ere** *scatter, disperse;* **nix nivis** F. *snow;* **grāmen grāminis** N. *grass;* **campīs** and **arboribus** dat. of motion toward [§G 35]; **coma -ae** F. here *leaf.*

3f.   **mūtat terra vicēs** (pl. of — **vicis** F.; the word does not occur in the nom. sg.) lit., *the earth changes [its] successive changes,* i.e., the earth undergoes its regular changes (**vicēs** a type of cognate acc. [§G 17] after **mūtat**); take **dēcrescentia** (pres. pple. of **dēcrescō -ere**) with **flūmina** *shrinking rivers;* **rīpās ... praetereunt** (**praetereō -īre**) *flow within* (lit., *past*) *[their] banks*—in Italy, the melting snows of winter raise the level of rivers and cause them to overflow their banks, but this is corrected in spring when the water level falls.

5f.   **Grātia cum ... geminīs sorōribus** lit., *the Grace with ... [her] twin sisters,* i.e., the three Graces—they were, in fact, triplets; both the Nymphs (**Nympha -ae** F.), of whom there were many, and the Graces, were minor female divinities; **audet** *ventures;* take **nūda** (*naked*) with **Grātia** (l. 5), *the Grace ... ventures to lead the dances* (**chorus -ī** M.) *naked*—any such displays had been impossible in chilly winter.

7f.   **immortālia nē spērēs** (indirect command after **monet** [§G 91]) lit., *that you should not hope for immortal* (**immortālis**) *things,* i.e., not hope that everything, including yourself, will last forever; the subjects of **monet** are **annus** and **hōra**, but the verb agrees with the nearer one only [§G 58]; the normal prose word order after **et** would be **hōra quae diem almum rapit** (*the hour that snatches away the life-giving* (**almus**) *day*)—the year symbolizes the changes of the seasons, the hour the more immediate change from a sunny day in spring.

frigora mitescunt Zephyris, ver proterit aestas
    interitura, simul   10
pomifer autumnus fruges effuderit; et mox
    bruma recurrit iners.
damna tamen celeres reparant caelestia lunae:
    nos ubi decidimus
quo pius Aeneas, quo dives Tullus et Ancus,   15
    pulvis et umbra sumus.
quis scit an adiciant hodiernae crastina summae
    tempora di superi?

9ff.   The next four lines describe the passage of the four seasons; **frīgora** (pl. for sg.
[§G 53]; **frīgus frīgoris** N.) *the cold* (of early spring); **mītescō -ere** *become mild*;
Zephyrīs instrumental abl. [§G 47] *with the west winds* (**Zephyrus -ī** M.)—the
west winds blow in spring; **vēr** (**vēris** N. *spring*) is the object of **prōterit** (**prōterō
-ere** *trample on*), and its subject is **aestās** (**aestātis** F. *summer*), which is qualified
by **interitūra** (fut. pple. of **intereō -īre** *die*); **simul** (= **simulac**) *as soon as*; **pōmifer**
fruit-bearing (**pōmum** + **fer**); **autumnus -ī** M. *autumn*; **frūgēs** (**frux frūgis** F.)
crops; **effūderit** (3 sg. fut. perf. act. **effundō -ere**) trans. by perfect [§G 66], *has
poured forth*; **brūma -ae** F. *winter*; **recurrō -ere** *come back*; take **iners** ((**inertis**)
sluggish) with **brūma**.

13f.   Horace now contrasts the return of the seasons with human life, which *knows
no second spring*; **celerēs ... lūnae** is the subject of **reparant** (**reparō -āre**), and its
object is **damna** (**damnum -ī** N. *loss*) **... caelestia** (**caelestis** *celestial*); trans. *swift
moons make good [their] celestial losses*, i.e., the moon, like the seasons, quickly re-
pairs the loss of its waning phase and is restored as a new entity, hence the pl.
lūnae; its successive losses are described as **caelestia** to emphasize the contrast
with mortal affairs; **nōs** is put before **ubi** (*when*) for emphasis; **dēcidimus** (perf.
ind. act.) *we have gone down* (**dēcidō -ere**).

15f.   **quō** *to where*; **pius** *good* (an epithet often used of **Aenēās** (**-ae** M.) in Vergil);
supply **dēcidit** after the first **quō** and **dēcidērunt** after the second; Tullus was the
third king of Rome, Ancus the fourth; Tullus was supposed to have been wealthy
(**dīves** (**dīvitis**)); after death, all that remains of us is **pulvis** (**pulveris** M. *dust*) on
earth and **umbra** (**-ae** F. *a Shade*) in the Underworld.

17f.   **quis scit** (*who knows*) is followed by an indirect question introduced by **an**
(*whether*); the subject of **adiciant** (**adiciō -ere** *add*) is **dī superī**, and its direct object is **crastina** (adj. from **crās** *tomorrow*) **... tempora** (pl. for sg. [§G 53]); there is
also an indirect object in the dative, **hodiernae** (adj. from **hodiē** *today*) **... summae** (**summa -ae** F. *total*); trans. *whether the gods are adding tomorrow's time to today's total*, i.e., whether we are going to live any longer; on **dī superī**, see note to
Vergil *Aeneid* 1.4, page 66.

19f.   **cuncta** (*all things*) is the subject of **fugient** (here *escape*); take **avidās** (*greedy*)
with **manūs**; **hērēs hērēdis** M./F. *heir*; take **amīcō** (here an adj.) with **animō**
(dat.), lit., *to [your] dear soul*—the expression is a translation of a Greek phrase
and is to be translated *to your own soul*, but **animus** here is conceived as equivalent

cuncta manus avidas fugient heredis, amico
   quae dederis animo.   20
cum semel occideris et de te splendida Minos
   fecerit arbitria,
non, Torquate, genus, non te facundia, non te
   restituet pietas.
infernis neque enim tenebris Diana pudicum   25
   liberat Hippolytum,
nec Lethaea valet Theseus abrumpere caro
   vincula Pirithoo.

~: HORACE *Odes* 4.7

to **genius**, the attendant spirit whose function was to see that a person had a good
time (cf. **indulgē geniō** *indulge your genius*, i.e., *have a good time*); the relative **quae**
(antecedent **cuncta**) is placed second in its clause [§G 4]; **dederīs** (2 sg. fut. perf.
act. **dō dare**) lit., *you will have given*, but trans. *you have given* [§G 66].

21f.   **cum** *when*; **semel** *once*; **occiderīs** (**occidō -ere** *die*) and **fēcerit** are future perfect, but trans. by perfect [§G 66]; **dē tē** lit., *about you*; **Mīnōs Mīnōis** M. one of
three judges of the Underworld—the pronouncements of such an eminent legal
figure were naturally **splendida** (*august*); **splendida ... arbitria** pl. for sg. [§G 53]
august judgment.

23f.   **nōn** and **tē** are repeated for emphasis; **Torquāte** voc.—the ode is addressed
to Torquatus, a friend of Horace; **genus** (here [*high*] *birth*), **facundia** (**-ae** F. *elo-*
quence), and **pietās** (**pietātis** F. *piety*) are the subjects of **restituet** (**restituō -ere**
bring back), which, however, agrees with the nearest and is singular [§G 58]—once
dead, a person cannot be restored to life by virtue of any desirable attributes or
good qualities.

25f.   **infernīs ... tenebrīs** (**tenebrae -ārum** F.PL. with sg. meaning) abl. of separation [§G 40] *from the infernal darkness*, i.e., from the Underworld; **neque enim**
(*for neither*) joins the final four lines of the ode to the preceding lines, although
placed after **infernīs**; **Dīana** (**-ae** F.), although a goddess, was unable to restore a
favored mortal, **Hippolytus** (**-ī** M.), to life, despite the fact that he had died unjustly as the result of the false accusations of his stepmother, Phaedra, who had
tried to seduce him; take **pudīcum** (*chaste*) with **Hippolytum** (who had resisted
his stepmother's advances); **līberō -are** *set free*.

27f.   Theseus, the great Athenian hero, and his friend Pirithous, while still living,
tried to abduct Persephone, the queen of the Underworld; their attempt was un-
successful, and although Theseus was able to return to the upper world, his friend
was made to stay in the Underworld; **nec ... valet** (lit., *be strong*) **Thēseus abrum-**
pere *nor is Theseus able to break* (**abrumpō -ere**); **Lēthaea ... vincula** *the Lethean*
chains—Lethe was one of the five rivers of the Underworld, but **Lēthaea** is used
here by synecdoche [§G 98] for the Underworld itself; **cārō ... Pīrithoō** dat. of
advantage [§G 31], lit., *for* [*the advantage of his*] *dear Pirithous*, but trans. *from* [*his*]
dear Pirithous.

The Death of a Friend

*Consolatory literature had a long history in antiquity, and all possible themes
had been explored long before Horace. This poem, addressed to Vergil on the
death of their friend Quintilius, stands in the tradition. Its finely balanced
phrasing, its mythology and abstractions (**Pudor, Iustitia, Fidēs, Vēritās**)
give it a formality that seems strange to us today, but that illustrates how an
ancient author worked within a framework developed by his predecessors.*

*Horace tells us elsewhere (**Ars poētica** 438ff.) that Quintilius was a competent and tactful literary critic.*

Quis desiderio sit pudor aut modus
tam cari capitis? praecipe lugubris
cantus, Melpomene, cui liquidam pater
    vocem cum cithara dedit.
ergo Quintilium perpetuus sopor   5
urget; cui Pudor et Iustitiae soror
incorrupta Fides nudaque Veritas
    quando ullum inveniet parem?

TEXT   Q. Horati Flacci *Opera,* ed. D. R. Shackleton Bailey
          (Bibliotheca Teubneriana, 2001)
METER   second Asclepiad [§m 12]
        quīs dē|sīdĕrĭō ‖ sīt pŭdŏr āut | mŏdŭs
        tām cā|rī căpĭtīs ‖ prāecĭpĕ lŭ|gŭbrīs
        cāntūs | Mēlpŏmĕnē ‖ cūī lĭquĭdām | pătĕr
        vōcēm | cūm cĭthărā | dĕdĭt

1   **Quis ... pudor aut modus** *what restraint or limit* (**modus -ī** M.); **dēsīderiō** dat.
to longing (**dēsīderium -(i)ī** N.); **sit** potential subj. [§G 68], trans. *could there be.*
2ff.   **tam cārī capitis** objective gen. [§G 23] after **dēsīderiō,** *for so dear a head* (by
synecdoche [§G 98] for *person*); **praecipe** 2 imp. act. of **praecipiō -ere** *begin, lead*—
Melpomene is to take the lead in singing the dirge and the poet is to follow;
lūgubrīs cantūs *mournful song* (pl. for sg. [§G 53]; **cantus -ūs** M.); **Melpomenē
Melpomenēs** F. one of the Muses; **liquidus** *clear(-toned)*; **pater** i.e., Jupiter, father
of the Muses; **cithara -ae** F. *lyre.*
5   **ergō** *so,* expressing resignation; **Quintilius -iī** M.; **perpetuus sopor** *eternal sleep*
(**sopor sopōris** M.).
6ff.   **urgeō -ēre** here *weigh down on;* the remaining words of the stanza are a question introduced by a postponed [§G 4] **quandō** (l. 8) but connected with the preceding clause by **cui** (antecedent **Quintilium;** dat. with **ullum parem** (l. 8), lit., *to
whom);* **Pudor** (here *Modesty*), **Fidēs,** and **Vēritās** (**vēritātis** F. *Truth*) are the subjects of **inveniet,** which agrees with the nearest [§G 58]; **iustitia -ae** *justice* F.;
incorruptus *untainted;* **nūdus** *naked;* **ullum ... parem** *any equal* (**pār (paris)**).

multis ille bonis flebilis occidit,
nulli flebilior quam tibi, Vergili.   10
tu frustra pius, heu, non ita creditum
    poscis Quintilium deos.
quid? si Threicio blandius Orpheo
auditam moderere arboribus fidem,
num vanae redeat sanguis imagini,   15
    quam virga semel horrida

9   Take **multīs ... bonīs** (dat. of reference [§G 32]) with **flēbilis**, lit., *worthy of tears for many good [people]*; **occidō -ere** *die*—rather than *he died ...*, English would say *his death was....*

10   Take **nullī** and **tibi** (dat. of reference [§G 32]) with **flēbilior** (compar. of **flēbilis**); **quam** *than*; **Vergilī** voc. of **Vergilius -(i)ī** M. *Vergil.*

11f. Take **frustrā** with **poscis** (2 sg. pres. ind. act. **poscō -ere**), which is followed by two accusatives [§G 9], *ask the gods for Quintilius*; translate **pius** by an adverbial phrase [§G 55], *in your loyalty* (i.e., toward Quintilius); **heu** *alas!*; take **nōn ita crēditum** (*not thus* (i.e., on such terms) *entrusted*) with **Quintilium**—it seems that when Quintilius was close to death, Vergil, as his loyal friend, entrusted his well-being to the gods in the expectation that Quintilius would be returned to him; the gods, however, did not take Quintilius on such terms.

13   **quid?** *what [then]?*, i.e., what then can be done?—the answer is that even the highest powers of persuasion, such as the music of Orpheus, could not bring Quintilius back; **Thrēiciō ... Orpheō** abl. of comparison [§G 42] *than Thracian Orpheus* (see Vergil *Georgics* 4.464ff., page 60); **blandius** (compar. adv. of **blandē**) *more persuasively.*

14   **audītam ... arboribus fidem** *a lyre* (**fidēs fidis** F.) *heard by trees* (dat. of agent [§G 29]); **moderēre** (= **moderēris**) 2 sg. pres. subj. **moderor -ārī** here *play*—Orpheus, as Shakespeare tells us, *with his lute made trees, and the mountain tops that freeze, bow themselves when he did sing* (*King Henry VIII*, act 3, scene 1).

15   **num** introduces a question expecting a negative answer, trans. *surely ... not*; **vānae ... imāginī** dat. of motion toward [§G 35] *to the empty likeness* (**imāgō imāginis** F.), i.e., to the Shade of a dead person, which lacked blood, the essence of life (see "Roman Beliefs About an Afterlife," page 78); **sī ... moderēre ... num ... redeat sanguis** category 1 conditional sentence referring to the future [§G 94], where both verbs are present subjunctive, *if you were to play ... surely blood would not return.*

16   The antecedent of **quam** is **imāginī**; **virgā ... horridā** instrumental abl. [§G 47] *with [his] terrible wand* (**virga -ae** F.)—Horace is referring to a Greek belief that the god Mercury (**Mercurius -(i)ī** M.) herded the Shades of the dead to the Underworld with a stick.

non lenis precibus fata recludere
nigro compulerit Mercurius gregi?
durum: sed levius fit patientia
   quidquid corrigere est nefas.   20

~: HORACE *Odes* 1.24

17 **nōn lēnis** (with **Mercurius**) *not lenient*; **precibus** abl. of cause [§G 48] *through
    prayers*; **fāta reclūdere** lit., *to open* (**reclūdō -ere**) *death* (pl. for sg. [§G 53]), trans.
    in opening [the gates of] death—the line is grimly euphemistic, since Mercury
    never opened the gates of death to anyone.

18 **nigrō … gregī** dat. of motion toward [§G 35] *to the black crowd* (**grex gregis**
    M.), i.e., to the Shades already in the Underworld, who take their color from the
    surrounding darkness; **compulerit** 3 sg. perf. subj. act. **compellō -ere** *drive* (as one
    would cattle)—the subjunctive follows on from **redeat**, lit., *would have driven*, but
    trans. *has driven*.

19 **dūrum [est]** *[it is] hard*, i.e., to accept Quintilius' death; **levius** n.sg. compar. of
    levis; **fit** *becomes*; **patientiā** instrumental abl. [§G 47] *through endurance* (**patientia
    -ae** F.).

20 **quidquid** *whatever*; **corrigō -ere** *correct*; **nefās** here *an offense against divine
    law*, trans. *wrong*.

HORATIANA ·II·

In the modern world, politicians and writers are often forced to realize that an ill-advised statement they have made cannot be revoked.
In the absence of mass media, politicians of antiquity were probably
less likely to suffer in this way, but it could certainly happen to writers, and Horace gives them this warning:

Nescit vox missa reverti.   *Ars poëtica* 390
A word [once] released knows not how to return.

For more Horatiana, see pages 28, 89, 97, 100, and 176.

A Quiet Drink

In keeping with his preference for a simple life, Horace tells his slave that he requires no frills or elaborate preparations when he is enjoying a drink alfresco.

Persicos odi, puer, apparatus,
displicent nexae philyra coronae,
mitte sectari, rosa quo locorum
    sera moretur.
simplici myrto nihil adlabores   5
sedulus curo: neque te ministrum
dedecet myrtus neque me sub arta
    vite bibentem.

~: HORACE *Odes* 1.38

TEXT   Q. Horati Flacci *Opera*, ed. D. R. Shackleton Bailey
        (Bibliotheca Teubneriana, 2001)
METER Sapphic stanza [§M5]
        Pērsĭ|cōs ō|dī ‖ pŭĕr | āppă|rātūs
        dīsplĭ|cēnt nē|xāē ‖ phĭlȳ|rā cŏ|rōnāē
        mīttĕ | sēctā|rī ‖ rŏsă | quō lŏ|cōrŭm
        sēră mŏ|rētŭr

1f.   **Persicōs ... apparātūs** trans. by sg., *Persian luxury* (**apparātus -ūs** M.)—the Persians had long been notorious for elaborate feasts; **puer** voc. *boy*—male slaves, regardless of age, were referred to as **puerī**; **displicent** [**mihi**] *displease* (**displiceō -ēre**) [*me*]; **nexae ... corōnae** *wreaths* (**corōna -ae** F.) *bound* (**nectō -ere**); **philyrā** instrumental abl. [§G47] *with bast* (**philyra -ae** F.)—Horace is thinking of wreaths made from flowers held together by thin strips of bark from a lime tree.

3f.   **mitte** 2 sg. imp. *refrain from*; trans. **sectārī** by a participle, *hunting for* (**sector -ārī**)—the word implies considerable effort; the indirect question is introduced by **quō** (postponed [§G4]) **locōrum** (lit., *where of places*, trans. *a place where*); **rosa ... sēra** *a late rose* (**rosa -ae** F.); **moror -ārī** *stay behind, linger*—since roses flower in spring, the expression *late rose* probably indicates that it is midsummer, when a person would be most in need of refreshment.

5ff.   The clause of l. 5, which would normally be introduced by *ut*, is subordinate to **sēdulus cūrō** in l. 6, lit., *[that] you take the trouble to add nothing to plain* (**simplex (simplicis)**) *myrtle* (**myrtus -ī** F.)—the verb **adlabōrō -āre** (*take the trouble to add*) is followed by an accusative and a dative; trans. **sēdulus** by an adverb [§G55], *earnestly*; **neque ... neque ...** (ll. 7f.) *neither ... nor ...*; **ministrum** in apposition [§G52] to **tē**, [*as*] *servant* (**minister ministrī** M.); **dēdecet -ēre** + acc. *be unsuitable for* (normally impers., but can be used with a 3 sg. subject, here **myrtus**); take **mē** with **bibentem**; **sub artā vīte** *under a dense vine* (**vītis vītis** F.)—Horace thinks of himself as drinking under a pergola covered by a grapevine, and both he and the slave serving the wine are to wear garlands of myrtle.

Seize the Day!

Horace addresses many women in his odes, but whether they really existed outside his imagination we have no way of knowing. In the following clever seduction poem, which plays on the well-worn theme of life's shortness, he suggests to Leuconoe, who, like his other lovers, has a Greek name, that she should not postpone enjoying life, presumably under Horace's guidance.

Among the many echoes of this poem in modern literature, perhaps the most famous is that of the sixteenth-century French poet Pierre de Ronsard: "Vivez, si m'en croyez, n'attendez à demain, Cueillez dès aujourd'hui les roses de la vie."

Tu ne quaesieris, scire nefas, quem mihi, quem tibi
finem di dederint, Leuconoe, nec Babylonios
temptaris numeros. ut melius, quidquid erit, pati,
seu pluris hiemes seu tribuit Iuppiter ultimam,
quae nunc oppositis debilitat pumicibus mare   5

TEXT   Q. Horati Flacci *Opera*, ed. D. R. Shackleton Bailey
        (Bibliotheca Teubneriana, 2001)
METER   fifth Asclepiad [§M14]
        tū nē | quaēsĭĕrīs ‖ scīrĕ nĕfās ‖ quĕm mĭhĭ quĕm | tĭbĭ
        fīnēm | dī dĕdĕrīnt ‖ Leūcŏnŏĕ ‖ nēc Băbў̆lŏ|nĭŏs

1ff.   **nē quaesierīs** (2 sg. perf. subj. act. **quaerō -ere** *ask*) neg. command with the
       perf. subj. [§G72], followed by an indirect question, **quem … dederint; scīre ne-**
       fās [est] a parenthetical expression, *it is wrong to know,* i.e., *it is not for us to know;*
       quem interr. adj. modifying **fīnem,** *what end;* **Leuconoē** (voc.) is the name of the
       woman addressed; **nec … numerōs** a second neg. command; **temptārīs** (= temp-
       tāverīs) 2 sg. perf. subj. act. **temptō -āre** *try out, play around with;* **Babylōniōs …**
       numerōs i.e., calculations made according to Babylonian astrology to determine
       one's horoscope and so predict the date of one's death; **ut** exclamatory *how* (the
       exclamation ends with **Tyrrhēnum** in l. 6); with **melius** (nom. sg. neuter of **me-**
       lior *better*) supply **est; quidquid** *whatever;* **patī** here *to endure.*
4ff.   **seu … seu …** *whether … or …;* take **plūrīs** (acc. pl. of **plūs**) with **hiemēs**
       (**hiems hiemis** F. *winter*); take **tribuit** (**tribuō -ere** *assign*) **Iuppiter** with what fol-
       lows each **seu; ultimam** (i.e., **hiemem**) **quae …** *[as our] last [winter, the one] which*
       …; **oppositīs … pūmicibus** (**pūmex pūmicis** M. lit., *pumice*) instrumental abl.
       [§G47] *with rocks set opposite [to the sea]*—the rocks are called **pūmicēs** because of
       their corroded appearance; the subject of **dēbilitat** (**dēbilitō -āre** *weaken*) is **quae,**
       and its object is **mare Tyrrhēnum,** the sea on the west coast of Italy.
6ff.   **sapiās** (**sapiō -ere** *be wise*) **… liquēs** (**liquō -āre** *strain*) **… resecēs** (**resecō**
       -āre *cut short*) subj. used to express an order [§G69]; **vīna** (pl. for sg. [§G53])
       liquēs—wine was not prestrained in antiquity as it is today; **spatiō brevī** abl. of
       time within which [§G37]—Leuconoe is being told to cut short her long-term

Tyrrhenum! sapias, vina liques et spatio brevi
spem longam reseces. dum loquimur, fugerit invida
aetas. carpe diem, quam minimum credula postero.

~: HORACE *Odes* I.11

hopes within a brief time span; **dum** here *while*; **fūgerit** 3 sg. fut. perf. act. *will have
fled*; **invida aetās** (**aetātis** F.) *envious time*; **carpe diem** *pluck* (**carpō -ere**) *the day*
(the metaphor is from plucking a flower or fruit), i.e., *seize the day*; **quam minimum** *as little as possible*; **crēdula** (*trusting in*; feminine because it agrees with the
understood subject *you*, i.e., **Leuconoē**) is followed by the dative **posterō** [**diēī**]
(*the next* [*day*]).

HORATIANA ·III·

Making the most of passing time is a recurring theme in Horace (cf.
fugācēs ... lābuntur annī (*the fleeting years slip by*) (*Odes* 2.14.1–2,
page 98) and **carpe diem** (*seize the day*) (l. 8 above)).

Horace urges his friend and patron Maecenas to leave Rome and
visit him on the farm that Maecenas has bought for him:

Eripe te morae. *Odes* 3.29.5

Escape (lit., *Tear yourself away*) *from delay.*

In the midst of a terrible storm, he urges his friends to make the most
of the moment:

Rapiamus, amici,
    occasionem de die, dumque virent genua
et decet, obducta solvatur fronte senectus.
    tu vina Torquato move consule pressa meo. *Epodes* 13.3ff.

*Let us seize the opportunity before the day passes (lit., from
the day), [my] friends, and while our limbs are strong and
[the time] is right, let old age be banished from [our] darkened
brow. Bring [some] wine pressed when Torquatus was my consul.*

Elsewhere, he cautions against putting off what needs to be done:

Dimidium facti, qui coepit, habet: sapere aude,
incipe. *Epistulae* 1.2.40f.
*Once begun, half done. (lit., He who has begun
has half the deed.) Dare to be wise, begin!*

For more Horatiana, see pages 28, 86, 97, 100, and 176.

An Old Love Revived

Horace presents a dialogue with a former mistress, **Lȳdia,** *in which, to all appearances, true love prevails.*

Donec gratus eram tibi
nec quisquam potior bracchia candidae
   cervici iuvenis dabat,
Persarum vigui rege beatior.
   "donec non alia magis   5
arsisti neque erat Lydia post Chloen,
   multi Lydia nominis
Romana vigui clarior Ilia."
   me nunc Thressa Chloe regit,
dulcis docta modos et citharae sciens,   10
   pro qua non metuam mori,
si parcent animae fata superstiti.

TEXT   Q. Horati Flacci *Opera,* ed. D. R. Shackleton Bailey
      (Bibliotheca Teubneriana, 2001)
METER fourth Asclepiad [§M 13]
      dōnēc | grātŭs ĕrām | tĭbĭ
      nēc quīs|quăm pŏtĭōr || brācchĭă cān|dĭdāē

In the first 16 lines, each of Horace's statements is matched in syntax and content by a parallel statement of Lydia's.

2ff. **quisquam ... iuvenis** *any youth;* **potior** lit., *more desired,* trans. *more favored* (i.e., by you); **bracchium** -(i)ī N. *arm;* **candidae cervīcī** dat. (after **dabat**) *around* (lit., *to) [your] white neck* (**cervix cervīcis** F.)—a white complexion and skin were always the ideal of Roman women; **dabat** *used to put;* **Persa** -ae M. *a Persian;* **vigeō** -ēre *flourish;* **rēge** abl. of comparison [§G 42]; **beātior** (compar. of **beātus**) *happier,* but trans. by an adverbial phrase [§G 55], *in greater happiness*—the proverbial wealth of Persian kings was supposed to have made them supremely happy.

5f. **aliā** abl. of cause [§G 48] *because of another [woman];* **ardeō** -ēre *burn* (intr.), here used metaphorically of love; **Chloēn** acc. of **Chloē Chloēs** F., a Greek name.

7 **multī ... nōminis** gen. of description [§G 20] *of much renown.*

8 **Rōmānā ... Īliā** abl. of comparison [§G 42] *than Roman Ilia* (**Īlia** -ae F.)—Ilia was a major figure in Roman legend (see Ennius *Annālēs* I fr. xxix, page 3); **clārior** (compar. of **clārus**) *more famous,* but trans. by an adverbial phrase [§G 55], *in greater fame*—Lydia hints that Horace made her famous with his poetry.

9 **mē ... regit** *rules me,* i.e., has me as her lover; **Thressa** f. adj. *Thracian.*

10 **dulcīs ... modōs** retained acc. [§G 9] after **docta,** lit., *having been taught sweet melodies* (**modus** -ī M.), trans. *skilled in sweet melodies;* **citharae** objective gen. [§G 23] after **sciens,** lit., *knowing of the lyre* (**cithara** -ae F.), trans. *versed in the lyre.*

11 The antecedent of **quā** is **Chloē; metuam** fut. ind. act.

"me torret face mutua
Thurini Calais filius Ornyti,
    pro quo bis patiar mori,   15
si parcent puero fata superstiti."
    quid si prisca redit Venus
diductosque iugo cogit aeneo,
    si flava excutitur Chloe
reiectaeque patet ianua Lydiae?   20
    "quamquam sidere pulchrior
ille est, tu levior cortice et improbo
    iracundior Hadria,
tecum vivere amem, tecum obeam lubens."

~: Horace   *Odes* 3.9

12   **parcō -ere** + dat. *spare*; **animae ... superstitī** dat., lit., *[my] surviving* (**super-stes** (**superstitis**)) *life*, an exaggerated way of referring to Chloe—the adjective is used idiomatically here to express the result of the action of the verb, trans. *spare [my] darling and let her live*.

13ff.   **torreō -ēre** *set on fire*; **face mūtuā** instrumental abl. [§G 47] *with mutual torch* (**fax facis** F.)—the metaphorical language suggests that each is applying a torch to the other; **Thūrīnī ... Ornytī** lit., *of Thurine Ornytus*, i.e., *of Ornytus from Thurii*, a city in southern Italy—for some reason, Chloe is proud of the ancestry of her present lover (**Calais Calais** M.); Lydia continues to trump Horace by saying that she is prepared to die *twice* (**bis**) for her lover.

17   **quid sī** *what if*, i.e., what would be your reaction if; **prisca ... Venus** *[our] former love*—the name of **Venus** (**Veneris** F.), the goddess of love, is used for the emotion she embodies (metonymy [§G 97]).

18   **dīductōs** *[us] separated* (**dīdūcō -ere**); **iugō cōgit aēneō** *forces with [its] bronze yoke* (instrumental abl. [§G 47]; **iugum -ī** N.)—a yoke (see note to Juvenal 10.135, page 209) symbolizes the union of two people; love's yoke is made of bronze, not wood, because bronze is harder to break.

19f.   **flāvus** *fair-haired*—Roman men usually preferred blonde women; **excutiō -īre** *shake off*; **rēiectae ... Lȳdiae** dat. *to cast-off* (**rēiciō -ere**) *Lydia*; **pateō -ēre** *lie open*; **iānua -ae** F. *door*.

21   **sīdere** abl. of comparison [§G 42] (**sīdus sīderis** N. *star*); **pulchrior** compar. of **pulcher.**

22f.   **ille** i.e., Calais, Lydia's current lover; **levior** compar. of **levis**, here *more fickle*; **cortice** abl. of comparison [§G 42] *than a cork* (**cortex corticis** M.), i.e., more unpredictable than a cork bobbing in water; **improbō ... Hadriā** abl. of comparison [§G 42] *than the tempestuous Adriatic* (**Hadria -ae** M.)—because of its shallowness, storms in the Mediterranean begin quickly and unexpectedly; **īrācundior** compar. of **īrācundus** *hot-tempered*.

24   **tēcum** = **cum tē**; **amem, obeam** (**obeō obīre**) potential subj. [§G 68] *I would love, I would die*; trans. **lubens** (= **libens**) by an adverb [§G 55], *willingly*.

Caught by a Bore!

In addition to his lyric poetry, Horace wrote the **Sermōnēs** *(sometimes called* Satirae), **Epistulae,** *and* **Ars poētica.** *The language of these poems (all written in hexameters) is informal, and their subjects vary from personal experiences and homely presentations of Horace's views on life to philosophy and literature.*

Ibam forte via Sacra, sicut meus est mos,
nescio quid meditans nugarum, totus in illis:
accurrit quidam notus mihi nomine tantum
arreptaque manu "quid agis, dulcissime rerum?"
"suaviter, ut nunc est" inquam, "et cupio omnia quae vis."   5
cum adsectaretur, "numquid vis?" occupo. at ille
"noris nos" inquit; "docti sumus." hic ego "pluris

TEXT   Q. Horati Flacci *Opera,* ed. D. R. Shackleton Bailey
             (Bibliotheca Teubneriana, 2001)
METER   hexameter [§M1]
             ībām | fōrtĕ vǐ|ā ‖ Sāc|rā sǐ|cūt mĕǔs | ēst mōs
             nēscǐǒ | quīd mĕdǐ|tāns ‖ nū|gārūm | tōtǔs ǐn | īllīs

1   **viā Sacrā** abl. of place where [§G38] *on the Sacred Way,* a street leading from the
    Esquiline Hill, where Horace lived, to the Forum.
2   **nescio quid** (lit., *I know not what*) is the equivalent of a pronoun meaning
    something or other and is followed by a partitive genitive [§G24], **nūgārum** (**nūgae**
    -ārum F.PL. *trifle*)—trans. *some trifle or other;* **meditor -ārī** *think about;* **tōtus in**
    illīs *entire[ly absorbed] in it* (lit., *them,* i.e., the **nūgae**).
3   **accurrō -ere** *run up*—Horace uses the historic present [§G60] here and later in
    the selection; **quīdam** *someone;* **nōtus** (**noscō -ere**) *known;* **nōmine** (instrumental
    abl. [§G47]) **tantum** *only by name.*
4   **arreptā manū** abl. absolute [§G49], trans. *having seized* (**arripiō -ere**) *[my]*
    hand; in keeping with the colloquial language of the **Sermōnēs** and **Epistulae,**
    Horace omits any equivalent of *he said;* **quid agis?** (lit., *how are you doing?*) a stan-
    dard greeting, trans. *how are you?;* **dulcissime rērum** (lit., *sweetest of things*) a form
    of address appropriate for a close friend, trans. *my dear fellow.*
5   **suāviter [mihi est]** lit., *[it is] sweetly [for me],* trans. *very well;* **ut nunc est** *as it is*
    now, i.e., *as things are;* **cupiō omnia quae vīs** (lit., *I want everything [to happen to*
    you] that you desire) a conventional expression meaning *I hope everything's well with*
    you.
6   **adsector -ārī** *follow closely;* **numquid** (**num** + the indef. pron. **quid**) **vīs** *there*
    isn't something you want?—a formula of leave-taking; **occupō** (-**āre**) *I put [him] off*
    [with].

hoc" inquam "mihi eris." misere discedere quaerens
ire modo ocius, interdum consistere, in aurem
dicere nescio quid puero, cum sudor ad imos   10
manaret talos. "o te, Bolane, cerebri
felicem!" aiebam tacitus, cum quidlibet ille
garriret, vicos, urbem laudaret. ut illi
nil respondebam, "misere cupis" inquit "abire:
iamdudum video; sed nil agis; usque tenebo.   15
prosequar hinc quo nunc iter est tibi." "nil opus est te
circumagi. quendam volo visere non tibi notum;
trans Tiberim longe cubat is, prope Caesaris hortos."

7f.   The bore takes Horace's polite dismissal (**numquid vīs**) literally and gives an
answer: [**ut**] **nōrīs** (= **nōverīs**; 2 sg. perf. subj. act. **noscō -ere**) **nōs** lit., *[that] you
should be acquainted with me*—the perfect of **noscō -ere** (*get to know*) can be used
with a present sense of *know, be acquainted with*; **nōs** pl. for sg. [§G53]—this idiom
is continued in the next clause; **doctī sumus** *I'm a scholar* (**doctus** lit., *learned*); **hīc**
here, at this point; **plūris ... eris** lit., *you will be of greater value* (gen. of value
[§G21]); **hōc** abl. of cause [§G48] *because of that*; **mihi** dat. of reference [§G32];
miserē here *desperately*; **discedō -ere** *get away*.

9ff.   **īre ... puerō** Horace becomes so agitated that he uses historic infinitives
[§G77]: **īre, consistere** (**consistō** *stop*), and **dīcere**—trans. these by indicatives *I
at one time* (**modo**) *went more quickly* (**ōcius**), *occasionally* (**interdum**) *stopped, said
something or other* (**nescio quid**; cf. l. 2) *in [my] slave's ear* (lit., *to [my] slave into
[his] ear*); **sūdor sūdōris** M. *sweat*; **īmōs ... tālōs** *lowest [part of my] ankles* (**tālus
-ī** M.), i.e., *the bottom of my ankles*; **mānō -āre** *pour, run*; **tē ... fēlīcem** acc. of exclamation [§G14]; **Bōlāne** voc. of **Bōlānus** (**-ī** M.), an otherwise unknown person
who, with his bad temper (**cerebrum -ī** N.), would have already dismissed the
bore; **cerebrī** gen. of respect [§G22]; trans. **tacitus** by an adverb [§G55], *silently*,
i.e., *to myself*; **quidlibet** *anything at all*.

13   **garriō -īre** *rattle on about*; **vīcus -ī** M. here *street* (the bore is presumably praising the results of Augustus' building program); **ut** + ind. *when*.

14   **respondeō -ēre** *reply*; **abeō abīre** *get away*.

15   *I've noticed [this] for a long time*—the present, not the perfect, is used with **iamdūdum** in this sense; **nīl agis** lit., *you're doing (accomplishing) nothing*, i.e., *it's no
use*; **usque tenēbō** lit., *I will hold [you] all the way*, i.e., *I'll stick with you the whole
way*.

16f.   **prōsequor -ī** *escort*; **quō** *to where*; **tibi** dat. of possessor [§G30]; **nīl** here used
as an emphatic negative; **opus est** (*there is need*) is followed by an accusative **tē**
and infinitive **circumagī** (**circumagō -ere** *drag around*); **quendam** acc. sg. of
quīdam *someone*; **vīsō -ere** *visit*; **nōtum** *known* (cf. l. 3).

18   **Tiberis Tiberis** M. *the Tiber River*; **longē** *far away*; **cubō -āre** *be [sick] in bed*;
the **Caesaris hortī** were across the Tiber to the west of the city.

"nil habeo quod agam et non sum piger; usque sequar te."
demitto auriculas, ut iniquae mentis asellus,   20
cum gravius dorso subiit onus.

～: HORACE *Sermōnēs* 1.9.1–21

19   **nīl habeō quod agam** *I have nothing to do* (**agam** potential subj. [§G 68]); **piger**
slow; **usque sequar tē** *I will accompany you the whole way* (cf. l. 15).
20   **dēmitto -ere** *let fall*; **auricula -ae** F. *ear*; **inīquae mentis** gen. of description
[§G 20] *of sullen disposition*; **asellus -ī** M. *donkey*.
21   **cum** + ind. *when*; **gravius ... onus** *a heavier* (compar. of **gravis**) *load* (**onus**
oneris N.); **dorsō** instrumental abl. [§G 47], lit., *with [its] back* (**dorsum -ī** N.);
subiit (3 sg. perf. ind. act. **subeō -īre**) lit., *has come under*, trans. *is burdened with*.

Graffiti in Pompeii

Certain elements in Roman society were avid writers of graffiti.
When Pompeii, a Roman town south of Naples, was covered by volcanic dust from the eruption of Mt. Vesuvius in A.D. 79, many thousands of their scribblings were preserved. These have been gathered
in Volume IV of a massive collection of Roman inscriptions, the *Cor-*
pus Inscriptionum Latinarum (*C.I.L.*), and provide valuable linguistic
and sociological information about the lower strata of the Pompeian
population.

In the verse examples that follow, the original spelling has been
standardized. Each poem forms an elegiac couplet, although the pentameter of the second is faulty. In the first, the writer comments on
the literary merit of the graffiti already on the wall he has chosen to
embellish. In the second, a dissatisfied patron of a **taberna** upbraids
the proprietor for the poor quality of his wine.

Admiror, paries, te non cecidisse ruinis,
    qui tot scriptorum taedia sustineas.   *C.I.L.* IV.3512
O wall, I marvel that you have not fallen in ruins,
since you hold up the trash of so many writers.

Talia te fallant utinam mendacia, copo:
    tu vendis aquam et bibis ipse merum.   *C.I.L.* IV.3948
May such deceits (i.e., as you practice) be your downfall, innkeeper.
You sell water and you yourself drink unmixed wine.

The implication is that, although the innkeeper drank straight wine
himself, he sold his customers wine so diluted that it was indistin-
guishable from water.

The Lessons of Homer

One of Horace's **Epistulae** *is a letter addressed to a young friend, Lollius Maximus, who was studying rhetoric in Rome. Horace tells how he is once again reading Homer, who in his opinion is a surer guide for correct conduct than any of the moral philosophers.*

Troiani belli scriptorem, Maxime Lolli,
dum tu declamas Romae, Praeneste relegi;
qui, quid sit pulchrum, quid turpe, quid utile, quid non,
planius ac melius Chrysippo et Crantore dicit.
cur ita crediderim, nisi quid te distinet, audi.   5
fabula, qua Paridis propter narratur amorem
Graecia barbariae lento conlisa duello,

TEXT   Q. Horati Flacci *Opera*, ed. D. R. Shackleton Bailey
         (Bibliotheca Teubneriana, 2001)
METER   hexameter [§M 1]
         Trōiă|nī bēl|lī ‖ scrīp|tōrēm | Māxĭmĕ | Lōllī
         dūm tū | dēclă|mās ‖ Rō|māē Prāe|nēstĕ rĕ|lēgī

1f. The *writer* (**scriptor scriptōris** M.) *of the Trojan War* is Homer, whose two
     epics, the *Iliad* and the *Odyssey*, were an important part of the educational program
     in both Greece and Rome (cf. Lucretius *Dē rērum nātūrā* 3.1037f., page 24)—Hor-
     ace first mentions the moral lessons to be derived from the *Iliad*; **Maxime Lollī**
     voc.—the normal word order (**nōmen, cognōmen**) is inverted, and the friend's
     first name (**praenōmen**) is omitted; **dēclāmō -āre** *make speeches* (by way of prac-
     tice); **Rōmae** loc. *in Rome*; **Praeneste** loc. *in Praeneste* (**Praeneste Praenestis** N.), a
     popular holiday resort southeast of Rome; **relegō -ere** *read again.*
3f. The antecedent of **quī** is **scriptōrem** in l. 1, i.e., Homer, but trans. *he*; the four
     clauses introduced by **quid** (supply **sit** with the last three) are indirect questions
     [§G 91] governed by **dīcit** and pose problems of moral philosophy; **pulchrum**
     (here *good*) has as its opposite **turpe** (*bad*); **ūtile** *useful*; **plānius** (compar. adv. of
     plānē) *more clearly*; **melius** (compar. adv. of **bene**) *better*; **Chrȳsippō et Crantore**
     abl. of comparison [§G 42] *than Chrysippus and Crantor*, earlier Greek philosophers.
5   **cūr ita crēdiderim** indirect question [§G 91] governed by the imp. **audī**; **quid**
     indef. pron. *something*; **distineō -ēre** *distract.*
6f. **fabula** is the subject of **continet** in l. 8; **quā** (antecedent **fābula**) instrumental
     abl. [§G 47], but trans. *in which*; **Paris Paridis** M. the Trojan prince whose elope-
     ment with Helen began the Trojan War; the subject of **narrātur** is **Graecia ...
     conlīsa**, lit., *Greece brought into collision* (**conlīdō -ere** + acc. and dat. *bring [some-
     thing] into collision with [something]*); **barbariae** dat. after **conlīsa**, trans. *with the
     foreign world* (**barbaria -ae** F., referring to Phrygia, of which Troy was the main
     city); **lentō ... duellō** (= **bellō**) instrumental abl. [§G 47] *by a prolonged war*—the
     Trojan War lasted ten years; trans. l. 7 *the collision of Greece with the foreign world
     in a prolonged war*—**Graecia conlīsa** is an example of a noun and participle used
     where English has an abstract noun and a genitive [§G 75].

stultorum regum et populorum continet aestus.
Antenor censet belli praecidere causam:
quid Paris? ut salvus regnet vivatque beatus,   10
cogi posse negat. Nestor componere litis
inter Peliden festinat et inter Atriden:
hunc amor, ira quidem communiter urit utrumque.
quidquid delirant reges plectuntur Achivi.
seditione, dolis, scelere atque libidine et ira   15
Iliacos intra muros peccatur et extra.
rursus quid virtus et quid sapientia possit

8   **stultus** *foolish*; take the genitives with **aestūs** (*passions*; **aestus -ūs** M.), which is
    the object of **continet** (**contineō -ēre** *encompass*).
9   **Antēnor Antēnoris** M. a Trojan prince who suggested that the Trojans hand
    Helen over to the Greeks and so end the siege; **censet** *recommends* (**censeō -ēre**)—
    Horace uses the present tense here and later, since he is retelling Homer's narra-
    tive; **praecīdō -ere** *remove*.
10ff. **quid Paris?** *what [does] Paris [say]?*; **ut** introduces two noun clauses gov-
    erned by **cōgī** (pres. pass. inf. of **cōgō -ere** *force*); **salvus** *safe*, but trans. by an ad-
    verbial phrase [§G55], *in safety*; **regnō -āre** *rule*; trans. **beātus** by an adverb [§G55],
    happily; **posse negat** … *declares that he cannot* …—Paris means that he cannot
    rule Troy in safety without giving up Helen, but without her he cannot be happy;
    Nestor Nestoris M. the elderly warrior whose contribution to the Greek expedi-
    tion consisted wholly of giving advice—the incident referred to here is the quarrel
    between the Greek leader, Agamemnon, and the foremost Greek fighter, Achilles,
    over a captive woman, Briseis; **compōnō -ere** *settle*; **lītīs** acc. pl. of **līs lītis** F. *quar-
    rel*; **inter** is repeated for emphasis; **Pēlīdēn** and **Atrīdēn** Greek acc. sg. of **Pēlīdēs**
    (**-ae** M.) *son of Peleus*, i.e., Achilles, and **Atrīdēs** (**-ae** M.) *son of Atreus*, i.e., Aga-
    memnon—patronymics are common in Homer (cf. English surnames such as
    Adamson and Masterson); **festīnat** (**festīnō -āre** *hasten*) governs **compōnere** in
    l. 11.
13   **hunc** here *the former*, i.e., Achilles, who had fallen in love with Briseis; supply
    ūrit (**ūrō ūrere** *burn, inflame*) with **amor**; **quidem** (lit., *indeed*) contrasts **amor**
    and **īra**, trans. *but*; **commūniter** *alike*.
14   **quidquid dēlīrant rēgēs** *whatever the kings rave* (**dēlīrō -āre**); **plectō -ere** *pun-
    ish*; **Achīvī** (**-ōrum** M.PL.) = **Graecī**—Horace means that the common Greek
    soldiers suffered because of the follies of their leaders (here called **rēgēs**).
15   The nouns are all ablatives of cause [§G48]; **sēditiō sēditiōnis** F. *discord*; **dolus
    -ī** M. *act of treachery*; **libīdō libīdinis** F. *lust*.
16   **Īliacus** *of Troy, Trojan*; both **intrā** and **extrā** govern **mūrōs**; **peccātur** (im-
    pers.) lit., *it is blundered* (**peccō -āre**), trans. *mistakes are made*.
17   **rursus** *on the other hand*—whereas the *Iliad* gives examples of human folly and
    vice, the *Odyssey*, to which Horace now turns, gives a model of virtue and wisdom
    in the character of Ulysses; the two indirect questions are governed by the main
    clause in l. 18, trans. *[as to] what virtue and wisdom* (**sapientia -ae** F.) *can [do]*.

utile proposuit nobis exemplar Ulixen,
qui domitor Troiae multorum providus urbes
et mores hominum inspexit latumque per aequor,   20
dum sibi, dum sociis reditum parat, aspera multa
pertulit, adversis rerum immersabilis undis.

~: HORACE *Epistulae* 1.2.1–22

18   **ūtile … exemplar** acc. in apposition [§G 52] to **Ulixēn** (acc. of **Ulixēs Ulixis** M. *Ulysses*), trans. *Ulysses [as] a useful model* (**exemplar exemplāris** N.); **prōposuit** *he* (i.e., Homer) *has set forth* (**prōpōnō -ere**); **nōbīs** dat. *for us*.

19f.   The antecedent of **quī** is **Ulixēn**; **domitor** (**domitōris** M. *conqueror*) in apposition [§G 52] to **quī**—Ulysses played the major role in the capture of Troy, particularly with his suggestion of the Wooden Horse; take **multōrum … hominum** with **urbēs et mōrēs**, which are accusative after **inspexit** (**inspiciō -ere** *observe*)—Horace uses the perfect tense when telling of the *Odyssey* (cf. note to l. 9); **prōvidus** also in apposition to **quī**, trans. *[and a] prudent [man]*; **lātum per aequor** (*over the broad sea* (**aequor aequoris** N.)) is part of the next clause.

21f.   **dum** (*while*) is repeated for emphasis—it is idiomatically followed by the present [§G 61]; **sibi … sociīs** dat. of advantage [§G 31] *for himself [and his] companions*; **reditus -ūs** M. *return*; **parat** trans. *[tried to] secure*—Ulysses finally managed to return to his home from Troy, but his companions perished along the way; **aspera multa** lit., *many harsh [things]*, trans. *many hardships*; **pertulit** *he endured* (**perferō -ferre**); **immersābilis** (*unsinkable*) is qualified by **adversīs rērum … undīs** (instrumental abl. [§G 47], but trans. *amid the hostile waves of circumstances* (lit., *things*)).

HORATIANA ·IV·

The rat race of modern Western societies existed in Augustan Rome, and moralists were quick to point out the futility of believing that an extravagant lifestyle or excessive material possessions could buy happiness. For Horace, the worries and troubles of the rich could not be alleviated by leisure activities, such as horseback riding, that were available to them alone.

Post equitem sedet atra cura.   *Odes* 3.1.40
Dismal (lit., *black*) *care sits behind the rider.*

His meaning has often been misinterpreted by Latin learners as *The black lady sits cautiously behind the horseman.*

For more Horatiana, see pages 28, 86, 89, 100, and 176.

Live How We Can, Yet Die We Must

Whether the Postumus addressed in this ode was a friend of Horace or simply a convenient name we do not know, but the warning given on the inevitability of death is in keeping with attitudes expressed elsewhere by the poet.

Eheu fugaces, Postume, Postume,
labuntur anni nec pietas moram
   rugis et instanti senectae
     adferet indomitaeque morti:
non si trecenis quotquot eunt dies,   5
amice, places inlacrimabilem
   Plutona tauris, qui ter amplum
     Geryonen Tityonque tristi

TEXT   Q. Horati Flacci *Opera*, ed. D. R. Shackleton Bailey
       (Bibliotheca Teubneriana, 2001)
METER   Alcaic stanza [§M 4]
      ē|hēū fŭ|gācēs ‖ Pōstŭmĕ | Pōstŭ|mĕ
      lā|būntŭr | ānnī ‖ nēc pĭĕ|tās mŏ|răm
        rū|gīs ĕt | īnstān|tī sĕ|nēctāē
        ādfĕrĕt | īndŏmī|tāēquĕ | mōrtī

1ff.   **ēheu** (= **heu**) *alas!*; take **fugācēs** (**fugax** (**fugācis**) *fleeting*) with **annī**; **Postume** voc. of **Postumus -ī** M.; **lābor lābī** *slip by*; **pietās pietātis** F. *piety, reverence toward the gods*; the verb of the second clause, **adferet** (**adferō -ferre** *bring*), is followed by an accusative, **moram** (**mora -ae** F. *delay*), and three datives, **rūgīs** (**rūga -ae** F. *wrinkle*), **senectae** (**senecta -ae** F. *old age*), and **mortī**, lit., *will bring a delay to wrinkles …*; **instans** (pres. pple. of **instō -āre**) *impending*; **indomitus** *invincible*.

5ff.   **nōn sī … plācēs** (potential subj. [§G 68]; **plācō -āre**) *not [even] if you were to placate*—what follows, viz the sacrifice of three hundred bulls a day to Pluto, would be an extreme example of **pietās**; take **trecēnīs quotquot eunt diēs** with **taurīs** (instrumental abl. [§G 47]), lit., *with three hundred bulls each* (**trecēnī** distributive numeral *300 each*; **taurus -ī** M. *bull*) *[for] however many days go* (poetic expression for **quōtīdiē** *daily*), trans. *with three hundred bulls for each day that passes*; **inlacrimābilis** *pitiless*; **Plūtōna** (Greek acc. of **Plūtō Plūtōnis** M., ruler of the Underworld) is the antecedent of **quī**; **ter amplum Gēryonēn** (Greek acc.) *thrice huge Geryones*, a three-bodied monster of mythology (the commoner form of his name is **Gēryōn**); **Tityon** Greek acc. of **Tityos -ī** M., a mythological giant—both he and Geryones were condemned to be punished in Tartarus for their crimes on earth; **tristī conpescit undā** *confines* (**conpescō -ere**) *with the gloomy water* (instrumental abl. [§G 47]; **unda -ae** F. *wave*, but often used in poetry as a synonym for **aqua**)—i.e., the Styx, across which Charon ferried the dead (see "Roman Beliefs About an Afterlife," page 78); agreeing with **undā** is **ēnāvigandā** (l. 11), a gerundive used as an attributive adjective [§G 79], lit., *water needing to be sailed across* (**ēnāvigō**

conpescit unda, scilicet omnibus,
quicumque terrae munere vescimur,   10
   enaviganda, sive reges
      sive inopes erimus coloni.
frustra cruento Marte carebimus
fractisque rauci fluctibus Hadriae,
   frustra per autumnos nocentem   15
      corporibus metuemus Austrum:
visendus ater flumine languido
Cocytos errans et Danai genus
   infame damnatusque longi
      Sisyphus Aeolides laboris: 20

-āre); with **ēnāvigandā** take **omnibus** (dat. of agent [§G29]), which is the antecedent of **quīcumque** (*whoever*); the meaning of the relative clause of l. 10 is *whoever we [are who] feed* (**vescor vescī** + abl., hence **mūnere**) *on the gift of earth*, i.e.,
all mortals—taking this clause and its antecedent, we can translate *with the gloomy
water that must certainly* (**scīlicet**) *be crossed by all of us who feed on earth's gift;* **sīve
... colōnī** lit., *whether we will be kings or poor farmers* (**colōnus -ī** M.).

13   **cruentō Marte** abl. after **carēbimus**, *we will avoid bloody Mars* (**Mars Martis**
M. god of war).

14   **fractīs ... fluctibus** another abl. after **carēbimus**, lit., *broken waves* (**fluctus -ūs**
M.)—the reference is to waves driven against the shore, trans. *crashing waves;* **raucī
Hadriae** *of the raucous Adriatic* (**Hadria -ae** M.).

15f.   **per autumnōs** trans. *in the autumn* (**autumnus -ī** M.); **nocentem corporibus
... Austrum** *the south wind* (**Auster Austrī** M.) *harming* (**noceō -ēre** + dat., hence
corporibus) *[our] bodies*—the south wind (modern *sirocco*), which blows in autumn, was supposed to cause malaria.

17ff.   **vīsendus** (**vīsō -ere**) gerundive used as a predicative adj. [§G80], lit., *needing
to be seen*—supply **est nōbīs** (the subjects are the nominatives in the following
three lines, but **vīsendus** is sg., agreeing with the nearest [§G58]); **āter ... Cōcȳtos**
(Greek nom. sg.) *black Cocytus* (one of the rivers of the Underworld)—because
they had nowhere to flow, the Underworld rivers (see "Roman Beliefs About an
Afterlife," page 78) were always murky and slow moving, hence **flūmine languidō
... errans** *wandering with a sluggish current* (abl. of manner [§G45]; **flūmen
flūminis** N.); **Danaī genus infāme** *the ill-famed family of Danaus* (**Danaus -ī** M.),
i.e., the daughters of Danaus (the **Danaides**), who were condemned to Tartarus,
where they were made to fetch water in sieves; **damnātus longī ... labōris** *condemned to long toil*—the genitive expresses the punishment; **Sīsyphus** (**-ī** M.), son
of Aeolus (hence **Aeolidēs** (**-ae** M.) Greek nom. sg.), was condemned for all eter-
nity to push a large stone up a hill, but when he reached the top, it rolled back and
he was obliged to begin again—the Cocytus, the Danaids, and Sisyphus are se-
lected to symbolize the Underworld.

linquenda tellus et domus et placens
uxor, neque harum quas colis arborum
   te praeter invisas cupressos
      ulla brevem dominum sequetur:
absumet heres Caecuba dignior   25
servata centum clavibus et mero
   tinget pavimentum superbo,
      pontificum potiore cenis.

~: HORACE *Odes* 2.14

21ff.   **linquenda** (**linquō -ere**) gerundive used as a predicative adj. [§G 80], lit.,
needing to be left—supply **est nōbīs** (the subjects are the following nominatives,
but **linquenda** is sg., agreeing with the nearest [§G 58]); **tellūs** (**tellūris** F. *earth*)
here means the upper world; **placens** (with **uxor**) *pleasing*; take **hārum ... arborum ... ulla** together, *any of these trees*; **quās** (antecedent **arborum**) **colis** *that you
cultivate*; **praeter** + acc. *except*; **invīsās cupressōs** *hateful cypresses* (**cupressus -ī**
F.); **tē ... brevem dominum** *you, ... [their] short[-lived] master*—we are to imagine
Postumus among trees he has planted; only the cypress will follow him in death,
since its foliage was placed around funeral pyres.

25ff.   **absūmō -ere** here *drink (up)*; **hērēs** (**hērēdis** M./F.) **... dignior** (*a worthier
heir*) is said sarcastically—Horace supposes that Postumus' heir will waste what
Postumus has carefully stored up; **Caecuba ... servāta centum clāvibus** [*your*]
Caecuban wines (**Caecubum -ī** N., a much-valued wine) *guarded* (**servō -āre**) *by a
hundred keys* (instrumental abl. [§G 47]; **clāvis clāvis** F.); **merō ... superbō** *with
proud wine* (instrumental abl. [§G 47]; **merum -ī** N. lit., *undiluted wine*); **tingō -ere**
wet, stain; **pavīmentum -ī** N. *floor*; take **potiōre** with **merō**, *wine better ...*; **pontifex pontificis** M. *high priest*; **cēnīs** (**cēna -ae** F. *dinner*) abl. of comparison [§G 42]—
lit., *than the dinners of the high priests*, a condensed comparison: the full expression
would be *wine better than that of the dinners ...* (the **pontificēs** were notorious for
their lavish feasts).

HORATIANA ·V·

Some literary questions were never resolved in ancient times. One
was the identity of the first writer of elegiac verse.

   **Quis tamen exiguos elegos emiserit auctor
   grammatici certant et adhuc sub iudice lis est.**   *Ars poētica* 77f.
   *Neverthless, scholars argue about which writer [first] set forth
   unassuming elegiacs, and the case is still before the judge.*

For more Horatiana, see pages 28, 86, 89, 97, and 176.

The Favor of the Muse

*Horace's early attempts at establishing himself as a lyric poet did not meet
with universal approval, but in the latter part of his life, he came to be recognized as the leading exponent of the genre in Rome, as he testifies in the following ode.*

Quem tu, Melpomene, semel
nascentem placido lumine videris,
   illum non labor Isthmius
clarabit pugilem, non equus impiger
    curru ducet Achaico   5
victorem, neque res bellica Deliis
   ornatum foliis ducem,
quod regum tumidas contuderit minas,

TEXT   Q. Horati Flacci *Opera*, ed. D. R. Shackleton Bailey
        (Bibliotheca Teubneriana, 2001)
METER   fourth Asclepiad [§M 13]
        quēm tū | Mēlpŏmĕnē | sĕmĕl
        nāscēn|tēm plăcĭdō ‖ lūmĭnĕ vī|dĕrĭs

1f.   With **Quem** (antecedent **illum** in l. 3) take **nascentem** (*being born*); **Melpomenē** Greek voc. of **Melpomenē Melpomenēs** F. one of the nine Muses; **placidō
lūmine** instrumental abl. [§G 47] *with a kindly eye*; **vīderis** 2 sg. fut. perf. act., but
trans. *you have looked upon* [§G 66].

3f.   **illum** object of **clārābit** (**clārō -āre** *make famous*), **dūcet** (l. 5), **ostendet** (l. 9),
and **fingent** (l. 12); **pugilem** (l. 4), **victōrem** (l. 6), and **ducem** (l. 7) are in apposition [§G 52] to **illum**; **labor Isthmius** *toil in the Isthmian games* (a Greek festival
similar to the Olympic games); **pugilem** [*as*] *a boxer* (**pugil pugilis** M.); **nōn** (l. 4)
trans. *neither*; **impiger** *swift*.

5   **currū ... Achāicō** instrumental abl. [§G 47] *with a Greek* (**Achāicus = Graecus**)
chariot (**currus -ūs** M.)—Horace does not specify where the contest might take
place.

6f.   **rēs bellica** lit., *the military thing*, i.e., *the business of war*; **Dēlius** adj. of Delos, a
Greek island sacred to Apollo—his special tree was the laurel, and a victorious
Roman general was adorned (**ornō -āre**) with a chaplet of its leaves (**folium -(i)ī**
N.) when parading in triumph through Rome.

8   **quod** *because*; **tumidās ... minās** *haughty* (**tumidus** lit., *swollen*) *threats* (**minae
-ārum** F.PL.); **contuderit** 3 sg. fut. perf. act. **contundō -ere**, but trans. *has crushed*
[§G 66].

ostendet Capitolio:
sed quae Tibur aquae fertile praefluunt   10
et spissae nemorum comae
fingent Aeolio carmine nobilem.
Romae, principis urbium,
dignatur suboles inter amabilis
    vatum ponere me choros,   15
et iam dente minus mordeor invido.
    o testudinis aureae
dulcem quae strepitum, Pieri, temperas,
    o mutis quoque piscibus
donatura cycni, si libeat, sonum,   20

9   **Capitōliō** (dat. with **ostendet**) *to the Capitol* (**Capitōlium -(i)ī** N.)—a triumphal procession culminated with the victorious general offering a sacrifice at the
temple of **Iuppiter optimus maximus** on the Capitoline Hill (see the map of
Rome on page xxiv).

10   Horace's fame is due not to athletic or military success but to poetry describing country scenes in the tradition of the Greek lyric poets Sappho and Alcaeus;
quae … aquae the normal prose order would be **aquae quae** *the waters that*;
Tībur Tīburis N. a country retreat near Rome, famous for its picturesque scenery; the waters are those of the Anio, a tributary of the Tiber; **fertilis** *fertile*;
praefluō -ere *flow past*.

11   **spissae … comae** *dense leaves* (**coma -ae** F.); **nemus nemoris** N. *forest*—ll. 10
and 11 give features of a rural setting suitable for Horace's poetry.

12   **fingent … nōbilem** *will make* (**fingō -ere**) *[him] famous*; **Aeoliō carmine** abl.
of respect [§G46] *in Aeolian song,* i.e., in poetry like that of Sappho and Alcaeus,
who wrote in the Aeolic dialect of Greek.

13ff. **Rōmae … subolēs** (**subolis** F.) *the offspring of Rome,* i.e., the Roman youth;
principis (gen. of **princeps** M. *chief, foremost*) in apposition [§G52] to **Rōmae**;
dignor -ārī *think fit*; **inter amābilīs vātum … chorōs** *among the pleasing choirs*
(**chorus -ī** M.) *of poets* (**vātēs vātis** M.).

16   **dente … invidō** instrumental abl. [§G47] *by envious tooth* (**dens dentis** M.),
i.e., by envious people; **minus** adv. *less*; **mordeō -ēre** *bite*.

17f. Horace again addresses Melpomene (hence **ō** in ll. 17 and 19) but calls her
Pīeri (Greek voc. sg. of **Pīeris Pīeridos** F.), an adjective of **Pīeria**, an area in northern Greece associated with the Muses; **Pīeri** is the antecedent of **quae** (here postponed [§G4]); **testūdō testūdinis** F. *tortoise,* here (by synecdoche [§G98]) *lyre*
(cf. Vergil *Georgics* 4.464, page 60); **aureus** *golden*—the lyre is so called because
of the music it produces; **dulcem … strepitum** *sweet sound* (**strepitus -ūs** M.);
temperō -āre *modulate*.

19f. **mūtīs … piscibus** dat. *to dumb fish* (**piscis piscis** M.); **dōnātūra** (fut. pple. of
dōnō -āre) agrees with **Pīeri**, lit., *going to give*; **cycnī … sonum** *the sound* (**sonus**
-ī M.) *of a swan* (**cycnus -ī** M.)—swans were (mistakenly) thought to produce
beautiful sounds; **si libeat** (potential subj. [§G68]) lit., *if it were pleasing [to you]*.

totum muneris hoc tui est,
quod monstror digito praetereuntium
    Romanae fidicen lyrae;
quod spiro et placeo, si placeo, tuum est.

~: HORACE *Odes* 4.3

21   **tōtum ... hoc** (*all this*) is defined by the **quod** clause of ll. 22f.; **mūneris ... tuī** possessive gen. used predicatively [§G18], lit., *of* (i.e., *belongs to*) *your gift*, but trans. simply *your gift*.

22   **quod** [*namely, the fact*] *that*; **monstror** 1 sg. pres. ind. pass. *I am pointed out*; **digitō** instrumental abl. [§G47] *by the finger* (**digitus -ī** M.); **praetereuntium** (gen. pl. pres. pple. of **praetereō -īre** *pass by*) *of passers-by*.

23   **fidicen** (**fidicinis** M.) [*as*] *the player of the Roman* (**Rōmānus**) *lyre* (**lyra -ae** F.), i.e., as the foremost Roman lyric poet.

24   **quod** [*the fact*] *that*; **spīrō -āre** *breathe*; **placeō -ēre** *give pleasure*; **tuum est** *is yours*, i.e., *is due to you*.

A Classics Revival

The scholar/printer Aldus Manutius (latinized from Aldo Manuzio) (1450–1515) printed a great number of Greek and Latin classical texts at his press in Venice, beginning in 1494. Having assembled a group of scholars, he produced editions in a compact format—we would call them "pocketbooks" today—using italic type in small sizes.

Aldus' motto, **Festina lente** (*Hasten slowly*), was a favorite saying of Augustus Caesar in its Greek form, Σπεῦδε βραδέως. The motto was represented visually by his printer's device of a dolphin coiled around an anchor, a symbol used on coins of the emperor Titus struck in A.D. 80. The humanist scholar Erasmus, who collaborated with Aldus, explained the symbolism as follows: **Ad consultandi moram pertineat ancora, ad conficiendi celeritatem delphinus** (*The anchor signifies slowness of deliberation, the dolphin speed of production*).

Prior to Aldus' work, Nicolas Jenson (1420–1480) had been publishing Latin and Greek classics in Venice. Jenson was a pioneer in the development of the roman typeface as we know it today; recognized as a model of beauty and legibility, it has been an inspiration for later type designers. The typeface used for the text of this book is Adobe Jenson Pro, designed by Robert Slimbach; the roman is based on Jenson's roman, the italic on Ludovico degli Arrighi's italic.

An Intoxicated Lover

Sextus *Propertius (fl. 25 B.C.) is one of the three elegiac poets of the Augustan age whose work survives, the others being his contemporary, Tibullus, and Ovid, who was slightly younger. These poets wrote in elegiac couplets, which very often had a love theme. Propertius and Tibullus wrote elegiac verse exclusively, but Ovid used other meters.*

Many of Propertius' elegies are concerned with his love for a woman he calls **Cynthia**. *(Apuleius gives her real name as* **Hostia**. *Propertius was observing the convention of using a metrically equivalent pseudonym for his mistress; see the introduction to Catullus' "Love and Rejection," page 27.) Propertius and Cynthia's torrid relationship was punctuated by the unfaithfulness of each. In the poem whose beginning is given here, Propertius describes how, in an advanced state of drunkenness, he visited the sleeping Cynthia after a period of estrangement.*

Qualis Thesea iacuit cedente carina
   languida desertis Cnosia litoribus;
qualis et accubuit primo Cepheia somno
   libera iam duris cotibus Andromede;

TEXT   Propertius *Elegies*, ed. G. P. Goold (Loeb Classical Library, 1990)
METER elegiac couplet [§M2]
        quālīs | Thēsē|ā ‖ iăcŭ|ĭt cē|dēntĕ că|rīnā
        lānguĭdă | dēsēr|tīs ‖ Cnōsĭă | lītŏrĭ|bŭs

1f.   Propertius makes three learned comparisons to describe the sleeping Cynthia. Each is introduced by the relative adjective of quality **quālis** (*of what sort*), and these are taken up by **tālis** (*of such a sort*) in l. 7—in an idiomatic translation, we can say *just as … even so …*); the subject of the first clause is **Cnōsia** (-ae F. *the Cnossian [woman]*, i.e., Ariadne of Cnossos in Crete, who was abandoned by Theseus on the Aegean island of Naxos (cf. Catullus *Carmina* 64.52ff., page 46)); **Thēsēā … cēdente carīnā** abl. absolute [§G49], lit., *the Thesean keel going away* (**Thēsēā** adj. of **Thēseus**; **carīna** -ae F. *keel*, here *ship* by synecdoche [§G98])— trans. *when the ship of Theseus was going away*; take **languida** (*exhausted*) with **Cnōsia**—Ariadne collapses on the beach as she sees Theseus has forsaken her; **dēsertīs … lītoribus** abl. of place where [§G38] *on the abandoned* (**dēserō -ere**) *shore* (pl. for sg. [§G53]).
3f.   The second comparison is to **Andromedē** (**Andromedēs** F. *Andromeda*), who had been chained to a cliff to be eaten by a sea monster but was freed by Perseus; **et** is postponed [§G3]; the subject of **accubuit** (**accumbō -ere** *lie down*) is **Cēphēia … Andromedē** *Cepheian Andromeda*, i.e., *Andromeda, daughter of Cepheus*

nec minus assiduis Edonis fessa choreis   5
  qualis in herboso concidit Apidano:
talis visa mihi mollem spirare quietem
  Cynthia consertis nixa caput manibus,
ebria cum multo traherem vestigia Baccho
  et quaterent sera nocte facem pueri.   10
hanc ego, nondum etiam sensus deperditus omnis,
  molliter impresso conor adire toro;

(**Cēphēia** adj. of **Cēpheus**); **prīmō ... somnō** abl. of time when [§G 37] *in first sleep*; take **lībera iam** together, *now free*; **dūrīs cōtibus** abl. of place from which [§G 39] *from the hard rocks* (**cōs cōtis** F.).

5f.   **nec minus ... quālis** trans. *nor less like*—the third comparison is no less applicable than the first two; **Ēdōnis** (**Ēdōnidos** F. *an Edonian woman* (the Edoni were a tribe in Thessaly celebrated for their frenzied Bacchic rites)) is **assiduīs ... fessa choreīs** *exhausted from continual dances* (**chorēa -ae** F.; abl. of cause [§G 48]); the relative **quālis** is postponed [§G 4]; **in herbōsō ... Āpidanō** *by* (lit., *on*) *the grassy Apidanus* (a river in Thessaly, whose banks are being referred to as grassy); **concidit** (**concidō -ere**) *collapses*—Propertius uses the present tense because Bacchic dances were still conducted in Thessaly.

7f.   The subject, **Cynthia**, is qualified by the phrase **consertīs nixa caput manibus** (*resting* (**nixa** (perf. pple. of **nītor nītī**) is used in a present sense [§G 74]) *[her] head on joined* (**conserō -ere**) *hands* (abl. of place where [§G 38]))—unlike the English verb *rest*, which can be transitive or intransitive, **nītor** is only intransitive, and consequently **caput** is an accusative of respect [§G 15]; the main verb, **vīsa** **[est]** (*seemed*), is followed by **mihī** (*to me*) and **mollem spīrāre quiētem** (*to breathe gentle sleep*).

9f.   **ēbria ... multō ... vestīgia Bacchō** *steps* (**vestīgium -(i)ī** N.) *[made] drunk with much wine* (abl. of cause [§G 48]; **Bacchus -ī** M.)—Bacchus, the god of wine, is used by metonymy [§G 97] for wine itself; **cum** (*when*) is postponed [§G 4]; the subject in l. 10 is **puerī** (here *slaves*); **quaterent ... facem** *were shaking* (**quatiō -ere**) *[their] torches* (**fax facis** F.; sg. for pl. [§G 53])—since there were no streetlights in ancient Rome, it was normal for a person going out at night to be accompanied by slaves carrying pine torches; when the night was advanced (here **sērā nocte** (abl. of time when [§G 37] *in the late night*)) and torches had burned down, the slaves rekindled them by shaking.

11f.   **hanc** (i.e., Cynthia) is the object of **adīre** (**adeō adīre** *approach*); **nōndum etiam** *not even yet*; **dēperditus** (*lost*; **dēperdō -ere**) is qualified by an accusative of respect [§G 15], **sensūs ... omnīs** (lit., *with respect to all [my] senses*), trans. *deprived of all my senses*; **molliter impressō ... torō** abl. absolute [§G 49] *the couch* (**torus -ī** M.) *having been gently pressed* (**imprimō -ere**), i.e., *having gently pressed* (or *gently pressing*) *the couch*—Propertius is so drunk he must support himself by leaning against the couch where Cynthia is sleeping; **cōnor** historic pres. [§G 60].

et quamvis duplici correptum ardore iuberent
   hac Amor hac Liber, durus uterque deus,
subiecto leviter positam temptare lacerto   15
   osculaque admota sumere tarda manu,
non tamen ausus eram dominae turbare quietem,
   expertae metuens iurgia saevitiae;
sed sic intentis haerebam fixus ocellis,
   Argus ut ignotis cornibus Inachidos.   20

~: PROPERTIUS *Elegies* 1.3.1–20

13f.   In the **quamvīs** clause, the subject of **iubērent** is **hāc Amor hāc Līber** (*on this side Love, on that side Liber* (another name for Bacchus, the god of wine)), with a phrase in apposition [§G 52], **dūrus uterque deus** (*each a pitiless god*); the object of **iubērent** is [**mē**] **duplicī correptum ardōre** [*me,*] *seized* (**corripiō -ere**) *by a double* (**duplex (duplicis**)) *passion* (**ardor ardōris** M.)—the double passion is that inspired by the two gods.

15f.   The two infinitive phrases express what Propertius was being ordered to do; the first is *to touch* (**temptō -āre**) [*her,*] *having been lightly* (**leviter**) *placed* (**positam**) *on* [*my*] *put-underneath* (**subiectō** perf. pple. of **subiciō -ere**) *arm* (**lacertō** abl. of place where [§G 38]; **lacertus -ī** M.), i.e., [*after*] *putting my arm underneath her to place her lightly on it and touch her*; the second infinitive phrase is *to take slow* (**tardus**) *kisses* (**osculum -ī** N.), [*my*] *hand having been moved up* (**admōtā ... manū** abl. absolute [§G 49]; **admōtā** perf. pple. of **admoveō -ēre**), i.e., *moving my hand up to take slow kisses*—Propertius presumably wants to use his free hand to hold Cynthia's mouth as he kisses it.

17   **ausus eram** (1 sg. pluperf. ind. **audeō -ēre**) *I had dared*; **dominae ... quiētem** *the sleep of* [*my*] *mistress* (**domina -ae** F.); **turbō -āre** *disturb*.

18   In the participial phrase, which goes with the subject of l. 17 (*I*, i.e., Propertius), the object of **metuens** is **expertae ... iurgia saevitiae** (*the abuse* (**iurgium -(i)ī** N.; pl. for sg. [§G 53]) *of* [*her*] *having-been-experienced* (**expertae**) *violence* (**saevitia -ae** F.), i.e., *the abuse* [*that was the result*] *of her violent nature* [*and*] *that I had experienced*)—**expertus** (perf. pple. of **experior -īrī**) here has a passive sense, *having been experienced*; it normally means *having experienced*.

19   Propertius' solution to his dilemma is simply to stare at Cynthia; he compares his action to that of **Argus** (for the legend, see the note to ll. 11ff. of Statius, "Insomnia," page 184)—this comparison is expressed by **sīc ... ut** (*in such a way as ...*; for purposes of translation, **sīc** can be ignored); **intentīs ... ocellīs** abl. of manner [§G 45] *with straining* (lit., *stretched*; **intendō -ere**) *eyes* (**ocellus -ī** M.); **haerēbam** (**haereō -ēre**) lit., *I was clinging* [*to her*], but trans. *I stared* [*at her*]; **fixus** perf. pple. of **fīgō -ere** *fasten*, i.e., *fixed to the spot*.

20   **Argus -ī** M. the thousand-eyed guardian of Io; **haerēbam** (l. 19) governs the dative **ignōtīs cornibus** (*at the strange horns* (**cornū -ūs** N.)); **Īnachidos** Greek gen. of **Īnachis** *daughter of Inachus*, i.e., **Īō**.

Love's Miseries

The theme of love's miseries is more frequently and more thoroughly explored in Latin and Greek poetry than in English. Propertius describes here how his love for Cynthia first affected him.

Cynthia prima suis miserum me cepit ocellis,
  contactum nullis ante cupidinibus.
tum mihi constantis deiecit lumina fastus
  et caput impositis pressit Amor pedibus,
donec me docuit castas odisse puellas   5
  improbus, et nullo vivere consilio.
ei mihi, iam toto furor hic non deficit anno,
  cum tamen adversos cogor habere deos.

. . . .

TEXT   Propertius *Elegies*, ed. G. P. Goold (Loeb Classical Library, 1990)
METER   elegiac couplet [§M 2]
          Cȳnthĭă | prīmă sŭ|īs ‖ mĭsĕ|rūm mē | cēpĭt ŏ|cēllīs
          cōntāc|tūm nūl|līs ‖ āntĕ cŭ|pīdĭnĭ|bŭs

1   **suīs … ocellīs** instrumental abl. [§G 47] *with her eyes* (**ocellus -ī** M. a diminutive of **oculus**, but used here in the same sense).

2   **contactum** (*smitten*; **contingō -ere**) is qualified by the adverb **ante** (*previously*); **nullīs … cupīdinibus** instrumental abl. [§G 47] *by no desires* (**cupīdō cupīdinis** F.).

3f. The subject of both verbs is **Amor**, the god of love; **mihi** dat. of reference [§G 32] with **dēiēcit** (**dēiciō -ere**), lit., *cast down for me*, i.e., *cast down my [eyes]*; take **constantis … fastūs** (gen. of description [§G 20]) with **lūmina** (**lūmen lūminis** N.), lit., *eyes of resolute pride* (**fastus -ūs** M.)—the poet had previously scorned love; **impositīs … pedibus** instrumental abl. [§G 47], lit., *with feet* (**pēs pedis** M.) *having been put on* (**impōnō -ere**) *[it]*; **premō -ere** here *trample on*.

5f. The subject is still **Amor**; **castās … puellās** (lit., *chaste girls*) probably does not mean women who preserved their chastity, with whom Propertius seems to have had little, if any, contact, but rather those who, like Cynthia at the beginning of their acquaintance, resisted his sexual advances; trans. **improbus** (lit., *shameless*, qualifying the understood **Amor**) *by the villain*; **nullō … consiliō** instrumental abl. [§G 47] *with no plan*, i.e., *recklessly*.

7   **ei** (one syllable) **mihi** exclamation, lit., *alas for me!*; **tōtō … annō** abl. of time within which [§G 37] *over an entire year*; **furor furōris** M. *madness*; **nōn dēficit** (**dēficiō -ere**) lit., *does not subside*, but trans. *has not abated*.

8   **cum tamen** trans. *while, however*; **adversus** *hostile*; **cōgor** 1 sg. pres. ind. pass. **cōgō -ere**; **habēre** here *to endure*—Propertius does not specify how the gods have afflicted him.

in me tardus Amor non ullas cogitat artes,   17
   nec meminit notas, ut prius, ire vias.
at vos, deductae quibus est pellacia lunae
   et labor in magicis sacra piare focis,   20
en agedum dominae mentem convertite nostrae,
   et facite illa meo palleat ore magis!
tunc ego crediderim Manes et sidera vobis
   posse Cytinaeis ducere carminibus.

. . . .

vos remanete, quibus facili deus annuit aure,   31
   sitis et in tuto semper amore pares.

---

17   **in mē** *in my case;* **Amor** is **tardus** (*slow*) because he does not allow Propertius
      success in his affair with Cynthia; **cōgitō -āre** *devise;* **artēs** here *stratagems,* i.e., to
      win Cynthia's affections.
18   **nōtās … īre viās** *to tread well-known paths*—Propertius' affair is not proceed-
      ing as such matters usually do; **ut prius** *as [he did] previously.*
19   The poet addresses witches, who were commonly approached in matters of
      love; **vōs** (voc.) is the antecedent of the postponed [§G 4] **quibus** (dat. of pos-
      sessor [§G 30]); **dēductae … pellācia lūnae** lit., *the seduction* (**pellācia -ae** F.) *of the
      moon having been drawn down* (**dēdūcō -ere**)—trans. *who seduce the moon and pull
      her down [from the sky]* (a favorite trick of witches).
20   Another adjectival clause follows **quibus; labor [est]** [*whose*] *work* [*it is*]; **in
      magicīs … focīs** *in magical hearths* (**focus -ī** M.); **sacra piāre** *to make propitiatory
      sacrifices* (**piō piāre** *propitiate*).
21   **ēn** exclamation, here as an exhortation to action, which is reinforced by an-
      other exclamation, **agedum** (= **age** + **dum**), trans. the two words *come now!;* **do-
      minae mentem … nostrae** *the heart* (lit., *mind*) *of my* (pl. for sg. [§G 53]) *mistress*
      (**domina -ae** F.); **convertō -ere** *change.*
22   The noun clause [§G 92] after **facite** is not introduced by **ut; illa** i.e., Cynthia;
      meō … ōre abl. of comparison [§G 42] *than my face;* **palleō -ēre** *be pale.*
23f. **crēdiderim** (*I would attribute;* perf. subj. to express a future possibility
      [§G 68]) governs **vōbīs** (dat. *to you*); take the remaining words as follows: **posse**
      (inf. used as a noun) *the power,* **dūcere** *to summon* (lit., *lead*), **Mānēs et sīdera** *the
      dead* (**Mānēs Mānium** M.PL.) *and the stars* (**sīdus sīderis** N.); **Cytīnaeīs … car-
      minibus** instrumental abl. [§G 47] *with Cytinaean spells*—**Cytīnaeus** adj. of the
      town Cytina in Thessaly, a region of Greece notorious for witches.
31   **remanēte** (2 pl. imp. act. **remaneō -ēre**) *stay behind*—in the preceding omitted
      lines, Propertius contemplates traveling abroad; **facilī … aure** instrumental abl.
      [§G 47] *with receptive* (lit., *easy*) *ear;* **deus** i.e., Cupid; **annuō -ere** + dat. (here **qui-
      bus**) *nod to*—Cupid has willingly acceded to their wishes.
32   The clause is joined to what precedes by a postponed **et** [§G 4]; **sītis** subj. to
      express a wish [§G 67]; **parēs** *equally matched* (**pār (paris)**).

nam me nostra Venus noctes exercet amaras,
    et nullo vacuus tempore defit Amor.
hoc, moneo, vitate malum: sua quemque moretur   35
    cura, neque assueto mutet amore torum.
quod si quis monitis tardas adverterit aures,
    heu referet quanto verba dolore mea!

~: PROPERTIUS *Elegies* 1.1.1–8, 17–24, 31–38

33   **nostra Venus** (**Veneris** F.) i.e., *the goddess of us lovers*; **noctēs ... amārās** acc. of time how long [§G 11] *throughout bitter nights*; **exerceō -ēre** here *torment*.

34   **nullō ... tempore** abl. of time when [§G 37]; **vacuus** lit., *empty*, trans. *ungratified*; **dēfīō -fierī** *be absent*.

35f.   **hoc ... malum** *this scourge* (**malum -ī** N.); **sua ... cūra** *his own care*, i.e., the object of his affection (on the use of **sua** here, see §G 56); **quemque** acc. sg. of **quisque** *each*, trans. *every [lover]*; **morētur** jussive subj. [§G 69] *let ... occupy* (**moror -ārī** *keep the attention of, occupy*); **assuētō ... amōre** abl. absolute [§G 49], trans. *when love has become familiar* (**assuescō -ere**); **mūtet** jussive subj. [§G 69]; **torus -ī** M. *bed*—the expression means to transfer one's affections to someone else.

37   **quod sī** *but if*; **quis** indef. pron. *anyone*; **monitīs** dat. with **adverterit** (3 sg. fut. perf. act. **advertō -ere**), lit., *will have turned slow ears* (**tardās ... aurēs**) *to [my] warnings* (**monitum -ī** N.), but trans. *turns* ([§G 66]) *deaf ears to my warnings*.

38   **heu** exclamation *alas!*; **referō -ferre** *recall*; **quantō ... dolōre** abl. of attendant circumstances [§G 45] *with what great grief*; **quantō** is postponed [§G 4].

VERGILIANA ·II·

After suffering shipwreck near Carthage, Aeneas is taken by his mother, Venus, to the city itself. In a temple there, he sees depictions of scenes from the Trojan War, in which he himself has taken part. Amazed that the story of Troy could have reached such distant shores, he concludes:

Sunt lacrimae rerum et mentem mortalia tangunt.

                                      Aeneid 1.462

The interpretation of this line hinges on the enigmatic phrase **lacrimae rērum**, which probably means *tears for [human] things*, that is, for the human condition and the misfortunes to which it is subjected. An appropriate translation would be *There are tears for [life's] hazards, and mortal [troubles] touch the heart*.

For more Vergiliana, see pages 56, 182, 185, and 199.

Therefore Is Love Said to Be a Child ...

The representation of the god of love (**Amor, Cupīdō**) *as a winged boy had a long history in Greek art. Propertius muses on how appropriate the representation is.*

Quicumque ille fuit, puerum qui pinxit Amorem,
    nonne putas miras hunc habuisse manus?
is primum vidit sine sensu vivere amantes,
    et levibus curis magna perire bona.
idem non frustra ventosas addidit alas,   5
    fecit et humano corde volare deum:
scilicet alterna quoniam iactamur in unda,
    nostraque non ullis permanet aura locis.
et merito hamatis manus est armata sagittis
    et pharetra ex umero Cnosia utroque iacet: 10

TEXT   Propertius *Elegies*, ed. G. P. Goold (Loeb Classical Library, 1990)
METER elegiac couplet [§M2]
        quīcūm|qu(e) īllĕ fŭ|ĭt ‖ pŭĕ|rūm quī | pīnxĭt Ă|mōrĕm
        nōnnĕ pŭ|tās mī|rās ‖ hūnc hăbŭ|īssĕ mă|nūs

1   **Quīcumque** *whoever;* **puerum** is in apposition [§G52] to **Amōrem** *[as a] boy;* the antecedent of **quī** (postponed [§G4]) is **ille**; **pingō -ere** *paint.*

2   **nōnne** introduces a question expecting an affirmative answer; **mīrās ... manūs** *skillful hands.*

3f.   **prīmum** adv. *for the first time, first;* **vīdit** is followed by two acc.+inf. constructions [§G10], **vīvere amantēs** (pres. pple. used as a noun, trans. *lovers*) and **magna perīre bona** *great advantages* (**bonum -ī** N.) *are lost;* **sensus -ūs** M. here *judgment;* **levibus cūrīs** abl. of cause [§G48] *through [their] trivial cares.*

5   **īdem** *the same [person],* i.e., the artist of ll. 1–4; **nōn frustrā** *not without good reason;* **ventōsās ... ālās** *quivering wings* (**āla -ae** F.)—**ventōsus** signifies the fickle nature of Love; **addō -ere** *add.*

6   **et** is postponed [§G4]; **fēcit ... volāre deum** *made the god fly* (**volō -āre**), i.e., depicted the god as flying; **hūmānō corde** abl. of place where [§G38].

7   **scīlicet ... quoniam** (lit., *indeed, since*) introduces the reasons for the symbolism of ll. 5–6—trans. *since in fact;* **alternā ... in undā** lit., *on alternating wave,* trans. *on the wave's ebb and flow;* **iactāmur** *we are tossed* (**iactō -āre**)—here and in the next line, Propertius compares lovers to ships at the mercy of waves and the wind.

8   **nostra ... aura** lit., *our breeze* (**aura -ae** F.), trans. *the breeze that drives us;* **nōn ullīs** (= **nullīs**) **... locīs** abl. of place where [§G38], trans. *not ... in one place;* **permaneō -ēre** *remain.*

9   **meritō** *rightly*—the artist's imagery is again considered appropriate; **hāmātīs ... sagittīs** instrumental abl. [§G47] *with barbed arrows* (**sagitta -ae** F.); **manus** *[his]*

ante ferit quoniam tuti quam cernimus hostem,
   nec quisquam ex illo vulnere sanus abit.
in me tela manent, manet et puerilis imago:
   sed certe pennas perdidit ille suas;
evolat heu nostro quoniam de pectore nusquam,   15
   assiduusque meo sanguine bella gerit.
quid tibi iucundumst siccis habitare medullis?
   si pudor est, alio traice tela, puer!
intactos isto satius temptare veneno:
   non ego, sed tenuis vapulat umbra mea.   20

---

hand, i.e., that of Love; **armāta** (f.sg. because **manus** is feminine; **armō -āre**) *armed.*

10   **pharetra … Cnōsia** *Cretan quiver* (**pharetra -ae** F.; **Cnōsius** a learned synonym for Cretan)—Cretan archers were regarded as the best; **umerus -ī** M. *shoulder;* **iaceō -ēre** here *hang down.*

11   Again Propertius explains the symbolism; normal prose order of the first words would be **quoniam ferit antequam …** *since he strikes* (**feriō -īre**) *before …;* **tūtī** *we, [feeling] safe*—a good archer had an arrow in his victim before the latter saw him.

12   **quisquam** *anyone;* **sānus** *unharmed;* **abeō abīre** *get away, escape.*

13   **tēla** *[his] weapons;* **et** is postponed [§G4]; **puerīlis imāgō** lit., *boyish form* (**imāgō imāginis** F.), i.e., Cupid.

14   **certē** *certainly;* **penna -ae** F. *wing.*

15   **ēvolō -āre** *fly away;* **heu** interjection *alas!;* **nostrō … pectore** trans. *my* (pl. for sg. [§G53]) *heart;* **quoniam** is postponed [§G4]; **nusquam** lit., *nowhere,* trans. *to no other place.*

16   Trans. **assiduus** by an adverb [§G55], *constantly;* **meō sanguine** abl. of place where [§G38].

17   Propertius now addresses Cupid; **iucundumst** = **iucundum est** (**iucundus** *pleasant*); **siccīs … medullīs** abl. of place where [§G38], lit., *in dry marrows* (**medulla -ae** F.; the use of the plural **medullae** is normal)—bone marrow was considered the seat of the emotions, but when in an unhealthy state and hence *dry* (**siccus**), it no longer responded to them, trans. *in [my] sick heart.*

18   **sī pudor est** lit., *if there is any shame [in you],* trans. *if you have any shame;* **aliō** adv. *elsewhere;* **trāice** 2 sg. imp. act. **trāiciō -ere** *shoot.*

19   **intactōs** *[those] unscathed,* i.e., people as yet unaffected by love; **istō … venēnō** instrumental abl. [§G47] *with that poison* (**venēnum -ī** N.) *of yours* (**iste** (*that … of yours*) draws attention to something belonging to the person addressed)—Cupid dipped his arrows in poison; **satius** (n.sg. compar. of **satis**) **[est]** *[it is] better [for you];* **temptō -āre** *attack.*

20   Propertius has suffered so much that *not I, but my frail* (**tenuis**) *Shade is being flogged* (**vāpulō -āre** (*be flogged*) is active in form but passive in meaning)—the metaphor changes from Cupid the archer to Cupid the slave owner.

quam si perdideris, quis erit qui talia cantet
  (haec mea Musa levis gloria magna tuast),
qui caput et digitos et lumina nigra puellae
  et canat ut soleant molliter ire pedes?

~: PROPERTIUS *Elegies* 2.12

21f.   The antecedent of **quam** is **umbra**, but trans. *it*; **perdideris** 2 sg. fut. perf. act.,
  but trans. *you destroy* [§G66]; the subjunctive in the **quī** clauses here and in l. 24 is
  potential [§G68]: *who would sing of* (**cantō -āre**), etc.; **tālia** *such things*, i.e., matters
  pertaining to love; **haec mea Mūsa levis** (*this slight Muse* (**Mūsa -ae** F.) *of mine*)
  refers to Propertius' love poetry, which is **levis** (*slight*) compared with other forms
  of verse such as epic; **tuast = tua est.**
23f.   The objects of **canat** are **caput et digitōs** (*fingers*; **digitus -ī** M.) **et lūmina**
  nigra (*dark eyes*; **lūmen lūminis** N.) **... et ... ut ...** (*and how ...*); **puellae** *of [my]*
  sweetheart, i.e., Cynthia (cf. Propertius *Elegies* 1.1, page 107; 1.3, page 104; and 4.8,
  page 113); **molliter** adv. *gracefully*; **pedēs** (*[her] feet*) is the subject of **soleant**—
  Cynthia seems to have had what today would be called a sexy way of walking.

Hadrian's Horse

Hadrian was an avid hunter. The following verse epitaph, for a favorite horse he had used for hunting, was probably composed by Hadrian
himself. The horse's name was Borysthenes, and it was of a breed
famous among the Alani, a Scythian people.

Borysthenes Alanus,   ausus fuit nocere,
  Caesareus veredus   ut solet evenire,
per aequor et paludes   vel extimam saliva
  et tumulos Etruscos   sparsit ab ore caudam;
volare qui solebat   sed integer iuventa,
  Pannonicos et agros,   inviolatus artus,
nec ullus insequentem   die sua peremptus
  dente aper albicanti   hoc situs est in agro.

The Fragmentary Latin Poets (ed. E. Courtney), page 384

Buried in this field is Alanian Borysthenes, the steed of Caesar,
which was accustomed to race over water and swamps and Etruscan
hills and Pannonian fields, (nor did any boar with white tusk dare
to harm it in pursuit, as often happens, or spray the tip of its tail
with foam), but [which], in the prime of its youth (lit., unimpaired
in youth) and with its limbs whole, died on its [appointed] day.

For another example of Hadrian's poetry, see page 33.

The End of a Wild Party

In a futile attempt to forget Cynthia, Propertius hires two prostitutes and has a party while Cynthia is away from Rome.

Cum fieret nostro totiens iniuria lecto,
   mutato volui castra movere toro.
Phyllis Aventinae quaedam est vicina Dianae,
   sobria grata parum: cum bibit, omne decet.   30
altera Tarpeios est inter Teia lucos,
   candida, sed potae non satis unus erit.
his ego constitui noctem lenire vocatis,
   et Venere ignota furta novare mea.

TEXT   Propertius *Elegies*, ed. G. P. Goold (Loeb Classical Library, 1990)
METER elegiac couplet [§M2]
    cūm fĭĕ|rēt nōs|trō ‖ tŏtĭ|ēns īn|iūrĭă | lēctō
    mūtā|tō vŏlŭ|ī ‖ cāstră mŏ|vērĕ tŏ|rō

27 **Cum** *since*; **fieret ... iniuria** *wrong* (**iniuria -ae** F.) *was being done*—Cynthia was being unfaithful; **nostrō ... lectō** dat. of disadvantage [§G31] *to my* (pl. for sg. [§G53]) *bed* (**lectus -ī** M.); **totiens** *so often*.

28 **mūtātō ... torō** abl. absolute [§G49], lit., *bed having been changed*—bed is used by metonymy [§G97] for *partner*; **castra movēre** *to move camp* (a military metaphor).

29 **Phyllis ... quaedam est** *there is a certain Phyllis* (**Phyllis Phyllidos** F. a Greek name); **Aventīnae ... vīcīna Diānae** *a neighbor* (**vīcīna -ae** F.) *of Aventine Diana*—there was a temple of Diana on the Aventine Hill.

30 **sōbria** *[when] sober*; **grāta parum** lit., *too little charming*, i.e., *possessing few charms*; **omne decet** *she adorns everything* (**decet** is not used impersonally here).

31 **altera ... est ... Tēia** *there is another, Teia*—Propertius assumes that the reader will know he is talking about prostitutes; take **Tarpēiōs ... inter ... lūcōs** together, *[from] among the Tarpeian groves* (**lūcus -ī** M.), an area between the two peaks of the Capitol.

32 **candida** *fair* with the implication of both a fair complexion and beauty; **pōtae** (alternate perf. pple. of **pōtō -āre**, *for her [when] drunk*) is dative after **satis** (*enough*); **ūnus** *one [man]*.

33 Take **hīs ... vocātīs** (instrumental abl. [§G47]) with **noctem lēnīre**, *to pass the night pleasantly* (**lēniō -īre** lit., *soften*) *by inviting these* (lit., *by these having been invited*); **constituō -ere** *decide*.

34 **Venere ignōtā** instrumental abl. [§G47] *with a novel* (lit., *unfamiliar*) *sexual experience*—**Venus Veneris** F., the goddess of sexual love, is used for the act itself by metonymy [§G97]; **furta novāre mea** *to resume* (**novō -āre**) *my stolen pleasures* (**furtum -ī** N. lit., *[sexual] thefts*)—Propertius had been unfaithful to Cynthia before, but he seems to think his infidelities of less importance than hers.

unus erat tribus in secreta lectulus herba.   35
  quaeris discubitus? inter utramque fui.

. . . .

cantabant surdo, nudabant pectora caeco: 47
  Lanuvii ad portas, ei mihi, totus eram;
cum subito rauci sonuerunt cardine postes,
  nec levia ad primos murmura facta Lares.   50
nec mora, cum totas resupinat Cynthia valvas,
  non operosa comis, sed furibunda decens.

35   tribus *for three* (**trēs trēs tria**); **in sēcrētā … herbā** *in a secluded garden* (**herba
-ae** F. here *an area covered with grass*—this would have been in the **peristȳlium**
(**-iī** N. *inner courtyard*) of Propertius' house; **lectulus -ī** M. *couch*—a couch
for dining is meant, which could accommodate three people reclining on their
elbows.

36   **discubitūs** *seating [arrangement]* (pl. for sg. [§G53]; **discubitus -ūs** M.); **inter
utramque** lit., *between each of the two*, trans. *between the two*.

47   The party is underway, but Propertius is unable to assume the proper spirit;
cantābant surdō *they were singing* (**cantō -āre**) *to a deaf [man]* (i.e., *me*); **nūdābant
pectora caecō** *they were baring* (**nūdō -āre**) *[their] breasts to a blind [man]*.

48   **Lānuvium -(i)ī** N. a town in the hills south of Rome where Cynthia had gone;
ei (one syllable) an exclamation of distress, often followed by a noun or pronoun
in the dat. (here **mihi**), trans. *woe is me!*; trans. **tōtus** by an adverb [§G55], *I was
entirely at the gates of Lanuvium*, i.e., *my whole mind was…*.

49   **cum** (*when*) is here followed by the indicative (also in l. 51); **subitō** *suddenly*;
raucī … postēs *screechy doors* (**postis postis** M. *doorpost*, here used by metonymy
[§G97] for the door itself—the entrance to a Roman house had double doors;
sonō -āre *make a noise*; **cardine** sg. for pl. [§G53] (**cardō cardinis** M. *(hinge)
pin*)—a Roman door was hinged by two pins (**cardinēs**), one projecting up into
the frame in which the door swung, the other projecting down into the threshold
beneath; unless the pins were constantly lubricated, doors had a tendency to
squeak; trans. *made a noise with their pins*.

50   **nec levia … murmura facta [sunt]** *and no low murmurs* (**murmur murmuris**
N.) *were made*, i.e., *there was a commotion*; **ad prīmōs … Larēs** lit., *at the first
Lares*, trans. *in the front room with the Lares*—the shrine of the Lares (see "Religion at Rome," page 57) was in the first room (**ātrium -iī** N.) after the entrance
(**ostium -(i)ī** N.).

51   **nec mora [erat], cum …** lit., *nor [was] there delay* (**mora -ae** F.) *when …*, trans.
and, without delay, …; although **tōtās** is an adjective qualifying **valvās**, trans. it by
an adverb [§G55], *fully*; **resupīnō -āre** *pull back*; **valvae -ārum** F.PL. *double doors*—
Cynthia has come through the house and pulls open the doors of the **peristȳlium**,
where the party is being held (see the note to l. 35).

52   Cynthia is described as **nōn operōsa comīs** (*not careful with respect to [her] hair*
(abl. of respect [§G46]; **coma -ae** F.)) and **furibunda decens** (*[though] furious, elegant*)—trans. *[her] hair unkempt, but elegant despite her fury*.

pocula mi digitos inter cecidere remissos,
   palluerunt ipso labra soluta mero.
fulminat illa oculis et, quantum femina, saevit,   55
   spectaclum capta nec minus urbe fuit.
Phyllidos iratos in vultum conicit ungues:
   territa "vicini," Teia clamat "aquam!"
crimina sopitos turbant elata Quirites,
   omnis et insana semita voce sonat.   60
illas direptisque comis tunicisque solutis
   excipit obscurae prima taberna viae.

53   **pōcula** pl. for sg. [§G 53] (**pōculum -ī** N. *cup*)—to drink wine, the Romans used what we would call cups, not glasses); **mī** (shorter form of **mihi**) dat. of disadvantage [§G 31]; take **digitōs inter ... remissōs** together, *[from] between [my] slackened* (**remittō -ere**) *fingers* (**digitus -ī** M.); **cecidēre** = **cecidērunt** (**cadō -ere** *fall*).

54   **pallescō -ere** *grow pale*; **ipsō labra solūta merō** *[my] lips* (**labrum -ī** N.) *relaxed* (**solvō -ere**) *from the wine itself* (instrumental abl. [§G 47]; **merum -ī** N.)—**ipsō** is added to give emphasis to the phrase and should be translated by *indeed*; trans. *[though] indeed relaxed from the wine*—Propertius' lips had felt the relaxing effect of the wine, but even so they reacted to the sight of Cynthia.

55f.   **fulminō -āre** *flash with lightning*—the historic present [§G 60] is used here and with most of the verbs that follow; **oculīs** abl. of respect [§G 46]; trans. *[her] eyes flashed with lightning*; **quantum fēmina [potest]** *as much as a woman [can]*; **saeviō -īre** *rage*; **nec** is postponed [§G 3]; **spectāclum -ī** N. *sight, spectacle*; **captā ... urbe** abl. of comparison [§G 42] with **minus**, trans. *nor was the sight anything short of* (lit., *less than*) *[that of] a captured city*.

57f.   Take **Phyllidos** (Greek gen. of **Phyllis**) with **vultum**; **īrātus** *angry*; Cynthia is the understood subject of **conicit** (**coniciō -ere** *thrust*); **unguis unguis** M. *[finger]nail*; *The terrified Teia shouted, "Neighbors!* (**vīcīnus -ī** M.) *[Bring] water!"*— because of shoddy buildings, fire was a greater danger in Rome than in modern Western cities, and consequently to shout **Aquam!**, the equivalent of *Fire!* today, was a certain way of attracting attention.

59f.   Take **crīmina** (**crīmen crīminis** N. here *reproach, abuse*) and **ēlāta** (perf. pple. of **efferō -ferre** *utter*) together as the subject of **turbant** (**turbō -āre** *disturb*); **sōpītōs ... Quirītēs** *the sleeping* (**sōpiō -īre** *put to sleep*) *citizens*—**Quirītēs** (**Quirītium** M.PL.), the formal term for Roman citizens, is used here ironically; **et** is postponed [§G 3]; **omnis ... sēmita** (**-ae** F. *alley*) is the subject of **sonat**, here *rang, resounded*; **insānā ... vōce** abl. of cause [§G 48] *with frenzied voices* (sg. for pl. [§G 53]).

61f.   **illās** (the two prostitutes) is the object of **excipit** (**excipiō -ere** *receive*); **dīreptīs comīs** abl. absolute [§G 49] *with torn* (**dīripiō -ere**) *hair* (see l. 52); **... -que ... -que** *both ... and ...*; **tunicīs solūtīs** abl. of manner [§G 45] *with loose* (**solvō -ere**) *tunics* (**tunica -ae** F.)—the women did not have time to adjust their clothing; **obscūrae ... viae** *on* (lit., *of*) *a dark street*—Roman streets were not illuminated (cf. note to Propertius *Elegies* 1.3.10, page 105), but light would have come from an open **taberna** (**-ae** F. *inn*) and so attracted the fugitives.

Cynthia gaudet in exuviis victrixque recurrit
  et mea perversa sauciat ora manu,
imponitque notam collo morsuque cruentat,   65
  praecipueque oculos, qui meruere, ferit.

~: PROPERTIUS *Elegies* 4.8.27–36, 47–66

63   **exuviae -ārum** F.PL. *spoils*—presumably Cynthia came back carrying something she had torn from the fleeing women; **victrix (victrīcis)** feminine of **victor** *victorious*; **recurrō -ere** *hurry back*.

64   **mea ... ōra** here *my face* (pl. for sg. [§G 53]); **perversā manū** instrumental abl. [§G 47], lit., *with backturned hand*, trans. *with the back of [her] hand*; **saucio -āre** *wound*, trans. *bruise*.

65   **impōnit (impōnō -ere** *put*) is followed by an accusative, **notam (nota -ae** F. *mark*), and dative, **collō (collum -ī** N. *neck*); **morsū ... cruentat** *draws blood* (**cruentō -āre**) *with [her] biting* (**morsus -ūs** M.).

66   **praecipuē** *especially*; **meruēre** (= **meruērunt**) *deserved [it]*—Propertius' eyes deserved the beating because they had attracted him to other women; **feriō -īre** *strike*.

A Divine Injunction Observed

The *Anthologia Latina* is a collection of Latin poems that survive from late antiquity, many of which are of doubtful authorship and of little merit. The following elegiac couplet is an exception.

   Phoebus me in somnis vetuit potare Lyaeum
     pareo praeceptis: tunc bibo cum vigilo.
          Anthologia Latina 1.1.174 (ed. D.R. Shackleton Bailey)

In sleep, Phoebus forbade me to drink wine (**Lyaeus** = **Bacchus** = *wine*); *I obey his orders: I drink [only] while awake.*

The Golden Age

The idea that there was a time when humanity lived happily in a state of primitive simplicity goes back to the early Greek poet Hesiod and was taken up by Roman poets. The Golden Age, the **aurea aetās**, *was the period when Jupiter's father and predecessor, Saturn, was king of the gods and presided over a world where the ready availability of simple food made work unneces-sary; animals were not exploited; no inventions, even of the simplest kind, such as the plow, existed; justice reigned supreme; and all humanity lived in perfect happiness.*

Albius **Tibullus** *(c. 50–19 B.C.), an elegist contemporary with Propertius, had none of the latter's liking for learned and elaborate verse. His poems are both simple and elegant, whether they treat of his loves, his patron, or the plea-sures of country life.*

Quam bene Saturno vivebant rege, priusquam   35
    tellus in longas est patefacta vias!
nondum caeruleas pinus contempserat undas,
    effusum ventis praebueratque sinum,

TEXT   *Tibulli aliorumque carminum libri tres,* ed. J. P. Postgate
        (Oxford Classical Texts, 1924)
METER elegiac couplet [§M 2]
      quām bĕnĕ | Sātūr|nō ‖ vī|vēbānt | rēgĕ prĭ|ūsquăm
      tēllūs | īn lōn|gās ‖ ēst pătĕ|fāctă vĭ|ās

35   The exclamatory **quam** qualifies **bene**, *how well;* **Sāturnō ... rēge** abl. absolute [§G 49], lit., *Saturn [being] king,* trans. *when Saturn was king;* **vīvēbant** *they* (i.e., people) *used to live;* **priusquam** conj. *before.*

36   **tellūs tellūris** F. poetic word for *earth;* **est patefacta** (**patefaciō -ere**) *was opened up, cleared;* **in longās ... viās** *into long roads*—in the Golden Age, people did not move about and so had no need of roads.

37   Take **nōndum** (*not yet*) with this clause and the next (l. 38); **caeruleus** *blue;* **pīnus -ūs** F. [*ship of*] *pine*—ancient ships were made of pinewood (synecdoche [§G 98]); **contempserat** (**contemnō -ere**) *had scorned*—with the subsequent ad-vent of ships, people were no longer afraid of the sea.

38   **-que** is postponed to after the third word for metrical reasons but must be taken in sense at the beginning of this line [§G 3]; **effūsum** (**effundō -ere** *spread*) **... sinum** (**sinus -ūs** M. *fold,* here used of a swelling sail) is the object of **prae-buerat** (**praebeō -ēre** *expose*); **ventīs** dat. *to the winds.*

nec vagus ignotis repetens compendia terris
   presserat externa navita merce ratem.   40
illo non validus subiit iuga tempore taurus,
   non domito frenos ore momordit equus,
non domus ulla fores habuit, non fixus in agris,
   qui regeret certis finibus arva, lapis.
ipsae mella dabant quercus, ultroque ferebant   45
   obvia securis ubera lactis oves.

39f.   **vagus … nāvita** (a poetic variant of **nauta**) *roving sailor*; **ignōtīs … terrīs** abl. of place from which [§G 39] *from unknown lands*; **repetō -ere** *take back*; **compendium -(i)ī** N. *profit*; **presserat** *had weighed down*, lit., *pressed*; **externā … merce** instrumental abl. [§G 47] *with foreign merchandise* (**merx mercis** F.); **ratis ratis** F. poetic word for *ship*.

41   **illō … tempore** abl. of time when [§G 37] *at that time*; take **nōn** with **subiit** (3 sg. perf. ind. act. **subeō -īre** *go under*); **taurus -ī** M. *bull*; **iuga** pl. for sg. [§G 53] (**iugum -ī** N. *yoke*, a heavy wooden frame attached to an animal's neck to harness it for pulling a plow or vehicle).

42   Take **nōn** with **momordit** (3 sg. perf. ind. act. **mordeō -ēre** *bite*, here *take in its teeth*); **domitō** (**domō -āre** *subdue*) **… ōre** (**ōs ōris** N. here *mouth*) instrumental abl. [§G 47]; **frēnōs** trans. *bit* (**frēnī -ōrum** M.PL. normally *bridle*).

43f.   **nōn … ulla** = **nulla**; **foris foris** F. *door*—houses had no doors because everyone was honest; the subject of **fixus [est]** (**fīgō -ere** *drive in, plant*) is **lapis** (**lapidis** M. *stone*); **quī** (antecedent **lapis**) introduces an adjectival clause of purpose [§G 88], as is shown by the subjunctive **regeret** (**regō -ere** here *determine*); **certīs fīnibus** instrumental abl. [§G 47] *with fixed boundaries*; **arva** (**arvum -ī** N. *field*) is the object of **regeret**—in later times, the boundaries of fields were marked by stones planted in the ground; the complete honesty of the Golden Age made these unnecessary; since **ager** and **arvum** have the same meaning (*field*), trans. **in agrīs** *on land*.

45f.   Take **ipsae** with **quercūs** (nom. pl. of **quercus -ūs** F. *oak*—all names of trees are feminine in Latin); trans. **mella** by the singular (**mel mellis** N. *honey*); **ultrō** *of [their] own accord*; the subject of **ferēbant** is **ovēs** (**ovis ovis** F. *sheep*), and its object is **ūbera lactis** *udders* (**ūber ūberis** N.) *of milk* (**lac lactis** N.); **obvia** (**obvius** + dat. *in the way of*), an adjective that has no single-word equivalent in English, agrees with **ūbera** and governs the dative **sēcūrīs** (**sēcūrus** *carefree*)—the meaning is *of [their] own accord, sheep used to bring udders of milk in the way of carefree [people]*, i.e., *to meet people, who were free from care*; sheep's milk was, and still is, commonly used in Mediterranean countries.

47f.   **aciēs -ēī** F. *battle line*; **īra -ae** F. *anger, rage*—because everyone was righteous and no one lost his temper, there was universal peace; the subject of **dūxerat** (**dūcō -ere** here *form*) is **saevus … faber** (**fabrī** M. *blacksmith*), and its object is **ensem** (**ensis ensis** M. poetic word for *sword*); **immītī … arte** abl. of manner [§G 45] *with merciless* (**immītis**) *skill*.

non acies, non ira fuit, non bella, nec ensem
  immiti saevus duxerat arte faber.
nunc Iove sub domino caedes et vulnera semper,
  nunc mare, nunc leti multa reperta via.   50

~: Tıbullus *Elegies* 1.3.35–50

49f. **Iove sub dominō** lit., *under Jupiter* (**Iuppiter Iovis** M.) *[as] ruler*; supply **est**
or **sunt** as appropriate with **caedēs** (**-ēī** F. *slaughter*), **vulnera** (**vulnus vulneris** N.
wound), and **mare**; **nunc mare [est]** *now [there is] the sea*, i.e., now the dangers of
sea travel have become part of our lives; take **lētī** (**lētum -ī** N. poetic word for
death) with **multa ... via** *many a way of death*; **reperta [est]** *has been found* (**reperiō
-īre**).

Dr. Fell

An important figure in 17th-century Oxford, England, was Dr. John
Fell (1625–1686), who, among other things, did much to advance
Oxford University Press, including designing the "Fell types" for its
use. Because of a minor incident, he acquired the reputation of being
a disagreeable person.

On one occasion, he summoned an offending undergraduate in
order to expel him. When the latter presented himself, Fell offered
to set aside the punishment if the student could give an immediate
translation of the following epigram of Martial (set here in a digital
version of Fell's pica roman type).

Non amo te, Sabidi, nec possum dicere quare:
  hoc tantum possum dicere, non amo te.   *Epigrammata* 1.32
I do not love you, Sabidius, and I cannot say why.
I can only say this: I do not love you.

The quick-witted student, whose name was Thomas Brown, replied
immediately—and in verse:

I do not love thee, Dr. Fell.
The reason why I cannot tell,
But only this I know full well,
I do not love thee, Dr. Fell.

Fell kept his word and allowed Brown to stay at the university.
Although both men have now sunk into relative obscurity, Brown's
translation has become one of the better known jingles in English.

A Face That's Best
by Its Own Beauty Blest...

Tibullus' simple tastes, as shown in his praise of the Golden Age, extended to his ideas about female beauty. The affluence of Augustan Rome meant that many luxury items were available to women for their personal adornment, and this, combined with increased leisure and political and social stability, led to elaborations in their toilet and dress to an extent unknown in earlier times. Tibullus was not alone among contemporary poets in his criticism.

Quid tibi nunc molles prodest coluisse capillos
    saepeque mutatas disposuisse comas,   10
quid fuco splendente genas ornare, quid ungues
    artificis docta subsecuisse manu?
frustra iam vestes, frustra mutantur amictus,
    ansaque compressos colligat arta pedes.
illa placet, quamvis inculto venerit ore   15
    nec nitidum tarda compserit arte caput.

TEXT   *Tibulli aliorumque carminum libri tres*, ed. J. P. Postgate
        (Oxford Classical Texts, 1924)
METER   elegiac couplet [§M2]
        quīd tĭbĭ | nūnc mōl‖lēs ‖ prō|dēst cŏlŭ|īssĕ că|pīllōs
        saēpĕquĕ | mūtā|tās ‖ dīspŏsŭ|īssĕ cŏ|mās

9f.   **Quid** lit., *what*, trans. *how*; **mollēs ... capillōs** *soft hair* (**capillus -ī** M. *(a single)* *hair*; **prōdest** (**prōsum prōdesse**) impers., lit., *it benefits*; the perfect active infinitives **coluisse** and **disposuisse** (l. 10) are used in a present sense [§G76], *to adorn* (**colō -ere**) and *to arrange* (**dispōnō -ere**); **coma -ae** F. *hair*—to avoid repetition, trans. **comās** as *locks*.

11f.   Supply **prōdest** after each **quid**; **fūcō splendente** instrumental abl. [§G47] *with shining* (**splendeō -ēre**) *pigment* (**fūcus -ī** M. lit., *dye*); **gena -ae** F. *cheek*; **ornō -āre** *beautify*; **unguis unguis** M. *fingernail*; take **artificis** (**artifex artificis** M. *artist*, here one who trims nails) with **doctā ... manū** *skilled hand* (instrumental abl. [§G47]); take **subsecuisse** (**subsecō -āre**) in a present sense [§G76], lit., *to trim*, but trans. *to have [nails] trimmed*—the verb is used in a causative sense (cf. English *I'm building a house* in the sense *I'm having a house built*).

13f.   **amictus -ūs** M. here an outer garment, trans. *shawl*; **ansa ... arta** *tight loop* (**ansa -ae** F.), a thin piece of leather that attached a type of sandal to one's foot; **compressōs ... pedēs** *constricted* (**comprimō -ere**) *feet*; **colligō -āre** *bind*—Tibullus is thinking of some elaborate, and no doubt uncomfortable, form of footwear.

15f.   **illa** *(that woman)* seems to be a reference to another person of Tibullus' acquaintance; **quamvīs** *(even though)* is followed by two subjunctives, **vēnerit** *(has come)* and **compserit** *(has arranged*; **cōmō -ere**); **incultō ... ōre** abl. of manner

num te carminibus, num te pallentibus herbis
    devovit tacito tempore noctis anus?
cantus vicinis fruges traducit ab agris,
    cantus et iratae detinet anguis iter,   20
cantus et e curru Lunam deducere temptat
    et faceret, si non aera repulsa sonent.
quid queror heu misero carmen nocuisse, quid herbas?
    forma nihil magicis utitur auxiliis:
sed corpus tetigisse nocet, sed longa dedisse   25
    oscula, sed femori conseruisse femur.

~: TIBULLUS *Elegies* 1.8.9–26

[§G 45] *with unadorned face*; **nitidus** here *elegant*; **tardā ... arte** abl. of manner
[§G 45] *with long-drawn-out skill*—Roman women favored very elaborate hair-
styles that would have taken much time to create.

17f.   To account for his mistress' use of beauty aids, Tibullus wonders if a witch
has cast a spell on her; **num** (repeated for emphasis) introduces a question expecting a negative answer and gives an urgency to Tibullus' speculation, trans.
surely ... not; **carminibus ... pallentibus herbīs** instrumental abl. [§G 47], trans.
with spells [and] pale (**palleō** -**ēre**) *herbs* (**herba** -**ae** F.)—**carmen**, normally *song*,
was used for witches' spells; **dēvoveō** -**ēre** *bewitch*; **tacitō tempore** abl. of time
when [§G 37] *at the quiet time*; **anus** -**ūs** F. *old woman*.

19   **cantus** -**ūs** M. *the act of casting spells, incantation*; **vīcīnīs ... ab agrīs** *from neighboring fields*; **frūgēs frūgum** F.PL. *crops*; **trādūcō** -**ere** *bring over*.

20   **et** is postponed [§G 4]; **irātae ... anguis** *of an angry snake* (**anguis anguis**
M./F.); **dētineō** -**ēre** *hold back, stop*; **iter** here *advance*—a spell can stop a snake in
its tracks.

21   **et** is postponed [§G 4]; **currus** -**ūs** M. *chariot*; **Lūna** the goddess of the moon is
meant; **dēdūcō** -**ere** *pull down*; **temptō** -**āre** *attempt*—on this activity of witches,
cf. Propertius *Elegies* 1.1.19, page 108.

22   **faceret ... sonent** two subjunctives in an unreal conditional sentence [§G 94];
aera repulsa lit., *bronzes* (**aes aeris** N.) *having been struck* (**repellō** -**ere**); **sonō** -**āre**
make a noise; trans. *it would do so if gongs were not struck to make a noise*—it was
believed that noise could nullify a spell.

23   Tibullus gives up his speculation and concludes that his trouble has other
causes; **quid** here *why* (repeated for emphasis); **heu** interjection *alas!*; with **miserō**
(dat. after **nocuisse**) supply **mihi**.

24   **forma** -**ae** F. here *beauty*; **nihil** is used as an emphatic negative, *not at all*; **ūtitur**
(**ūtor ūtī** + abl. *use*) governs **magicīs ... auxiliīs** *magic aids*.

25f.   **sed** is repeated for emphasis; in the three infinitive phrases (which are the
subject of **nocet**), the perfect infinitive is used in a present sense (cf. l. 9); **tetigisse**
perf. act. inf. of **tangō** -**ere** *touch*; **osculum** -**ī** N. *kiss*; **femur femoris** N. *thigh*; **conserō** -**ere** *join, press together*.

You Are My Heart's Desire

Nothing is known about Lygdamus, apart from what can be gleaned from the few poems of his that have survived under the name of his contemporary Tibullus. In the following elegy, Lygdamus laments that his prayers have been unable to secure a reunion with his lover, Neaera.

Quid prodest caelum votis implesse, Neaera,
  blandaque cum multa tura dedisse prece,
non, ut marmorei prodirem e limine tecti,
  insignis clara conspicuusque domo,
aut ut multa mei renovarent iugera tauri   5
  et magnas messes terra benigna daret,
sed tecum ut longae sociarem gaudia vitae
  inque tuo caderet nostra senecta sinu,

TEXT   *Tibulli aliorumque carminum libri tres*, ed. J. P. Postgate
        (Oxford Classical Texts, 1924)
METER   elegiac couplet [§M 2]
        quīd prō|dēst cae|lūm ‖ vō|tīs īm|plēssĕ Nĕ|āeră
        blāndăquĕ | cūm mūl|tā ‖ tūră dĕ|dīssĕ prĕ|cĕ

1   The long question that begins **Quid prōdest [mihi]** (*what does it benefit* (**prō-sum prōdesse** + dat.) *[me]*) continues through l. 10; **vōtīs** instrumental abl. [§G 47] *with vows*—Lygdamus would have committed himself to do something for the gods, such as make a sacrifice, if his wishes (ll. 7f.) were fulfilled; **implesse** (= **implēvisse**) *to have filled* (**impleō -ēre**); **Neaera** here voc. (**Neaera -ae** F.).

2   **blanda … tūra** trans. by sg., *beguiling frankincense* (**tūs tūris** N.)—frankincense was used in formal approaches to the gods; **cum multā … prece** *with many a prayer.*

3f. In three purpose clauses expressed by **ut** + subj. [§G 83], Lygdamus first states what he does not want (ll. 3–6) and then what he does; **marmoreī … ē līmine tectī** *from the threshold* (**līmen līminis** N.) *of a marble building* (**tectum -ī** N.); **prōdeō -īre** *come forth*; **insignis** (*famous*) and **conspicuus** (*notable*) agree with the subject of **prōdīrem**, i.e., *I*; take **clārā … domō** (abl. of cause [§G 48]; *because of an impressive house*) with both adjectives.

5f. The second thing that Lygdamus does not want is a large, productive farm; **renovō -āre** *recondition, restore*—the reference is to annual plowing; **iūgerum -ī** N. a measure of land, trans. *acre*; **taurus -ī** M. *bull*; **messis messis** F. *harvest*; **benignus** *bounteous.*

7f. The **ut** introducing Lygdamus' real wishes is postponed [§G 4]; **tēcum** = **cum tē**; **sociō -āre** *unite*, trans. *share*; **gaudium -(i)ī** N. *joy*; **in tuō … sinū** *in your bosom* (**sinus -ūs** M.); **cadō -ere** *die*, trans. *come to an end*; **nostra senecta** *my* (pl. for sg. [§G 53]) *old age* (**senecta -ae** F.).

tum cum permenso defunctus tempore lucis
   nudus Lethaea cogerer ire rate?   10
nam grave quid prodest pondus mihi divitis auri,
   arvaque si findant pinguia mille boves?
quidve in Erythraeo legitur quae litore concha   17
   tinctaque Sidonio murice lana iuvat,
et quae praeterea populus miratur? in illis
   invidia est: falso plurima vulgus amat.   20
non opibus mentes hominum curaeque levantur:
   nam Fortuna sua tempora lege regit.
sit mihi paupertas tecum iucunda, Neaera,
   at sine te regum munera nulla volo.

~: LYGDAMUS [Tibullus] *Elegies* 3.3.1–24 (with omission)

9f. **tum cum** lit., *then when*, trans. simply *when*; take **permensō** (here with a
passive sense, *traversed, travelled over*; **permētior -īrī**) **tempore** with **dēfunctus**
(**dēfungor -ī** + abl. *be finished with*); **lūcis** gen. with **tempore**; **nūdus** *naked*;
Lēthaeā … rate instrumental abl. [§G 47] *with the Lethean boat* (**ratis ratis** F.)—
an inconsistency with general belief, since Charon's boat, which is referred to here,
normally ferried the dead across the river Styx, not the Lethe; **cōgerer** 1 sg. imperf.
subj. pass. **cōgō -ere** *force*.

11f. **quid** (postponed [§G 4]) *what*; the subjects of **prōdest** are **grave … pondus**
(*heavy weight* (**pondus ponderis** N.)) and the **sī** clause in l. 12; **arva … pinguia**
[my] fertile fields (**arvum -ī** N.); **sī** is postponed [§G 4]; **findō -ere** *cleave*, here in
plowing; take **mille** (indecl. adj. *thousand*) with **bovēs**.

17f. **quid** *what*; the prose order would be **concha quae in Erythraeō lītore legitur**
(*the pearl* (**concha -ae** F. normally *shell*) *that is gathered on the Red [Sea] coast*)—
Erythraeus adj. *of the Red Sea* (**mare Erythrum**, which included the Persian Gulf
and the Arabian Sea, as well as what we now call the Red Sea); **concha, lāna** (l. 18;
lāna -ae F. *wool*), and the understood antecedent of **quae** (l. 19) are the subjects of
iuvat (sg. agreeing with its nearest subject [§G 58]); take **tincta** (*dyed*; **tingō -ere**)
with **lāna**; **Sīdoniō mūrice** instrumental abl. [§G 47] *with Sidonian purple* (**mūrex**
mūricis M. a shellfish from which a purple dye was extracted)—cf. Ovid *Fastī*
2.107, page 142, where **mūrex** is called *Tyrian* (Tyre and Sidon were cities 20 miles
apart in the Roman province of Syria).

19f. **quae** trans. *the things that*—with these, which involve **invidia**, Lygdamus is
thinking of other ostentatious displays of wealth; **falsō** *mistakenly*; **plūrima** superl.
used to express a very high degree [§G 54] *very many*.

21 **opibus** instrumental abl. [§G 47] *by wealth*; **levō -āre** *relieve*.

22 **suā … lēge** instrumental abl. [§G 47] *with her own law*; **tempora** here *[their]
circumstances*—Fortune decrees who will be rich and who will be poor.

23 **sit** potential subj. [§G 68] *would be*; **mihi** dat. of reference [§G 32] *for me*; **paupertās paupertātis** F. *poverty*; **iūcundus** *pleasant*.

Mythology

For the Greeks, myths were originally stories that had been passed down by word of mouth because they were regarded as having a particular significance, often of a religious or ritual nature. Many involved divinities and illustrated popular conceptions of their character. Others told of human adventures, and of bizarre situations in which men and women became entangled. Sometimes myths reflected real events, such as the capture of Troy, but with such changes that make it impossible to sort truth from fiction. This vast store, which had accumulated over centuries, was an essential part of Greek culture. From the first, poets mined it for plots and subject matter. The traditional mythology of Greece continued to inspire Greek poets up to the end of the ancient world and beyond.

What happened at Rome was quite different. One myth that seems to have been genuinely Roman was the tale of how the twins Romulus and Remus were suckled by a she-wolf and of how Romulus grew up to become the founder of the city named after him. There were few other myths that are unmistakably Roman, but when Rome came under the influence of Greek culture and Roman divinities were equated with those of Greece (see "Religion at Rome," page 57), the stories connected with the Greek gods were also attributed to their Roman counterparts.

If there were tales about how Zeus, the king of the Greek pantheon, had a penchant for seducing mortal women, then the same tales must be true of his Roman equivalent, Jupiter. This is illustrated in Plautus' comedy *Amphitruō* (produced c. 190 B.C.), which is an adaptation of a Greek play; the original names of the victim, **Alkmene**, and her husband, **Amphitryon**, are simply Latinized to **Alcūmena** and **Amphitruō**, but **Zeus** and his accomplice, **Hermes**, become the Roman **Iuppiter** and **Mercurius**.

Roman authors saw themselves as standing in the Greek tradition and continuing it; the only exception was satire, a purely Roman invention. As genres of Greek poetry were taken over into Latin, with them came the whole body of Greek mythology, whether connected with divinities or not. By the end of the Augustan Age, poems both long and short had been written on tales like that of the Argonauts, and this continued into the imperial era (see Valerius Flaccus, "A Pep Talk," page 180).

Perhaps more significantly, Greek mythology came to be used as a tool to illustrate a poet's meaning. When Propertius describes his sleeping mistress, he begins by comparing her with two mythological heroines, Ariadne and Andromeda (*Elegies* 1.3.1–4, page 104). Statius, in describing his chronic insomnia, cannot refrain from referring to the goddess of the dawn, Aurora, as the wife of Tithonus (**Tithōnia**) and thereby displaying his acquaintance with the myth of their union (*Silvae* 5.4.9, page 184); later in the same poem, he compares himself to the principal insomniac of mythology, the many-eyed Argus (5.4.11ff.).

Many forms of Latin poetry were permeated with Greek mythology, and this continued until Rome collapsed. *The Vigil of Venus* (page 213) employs the Greek concept of the goddess and the Greek myths about her, and the last poet represented in these selections, Claudian (page 218), wrote a lengthy account of the abduction of Proserpina by the king of the Underworld, Pluto (*Dē raptū Prōserpinae*). Roman poets not only adopted the genres and forms of Greek literature—they assimilated Greek mythology as well, and they never abandoned it.

THE ABOVE-MENTIONED STORY of Jason and the Argonauts is an example of a myth that never faded from popularity.

Aeson, the father of Jason, was deprived of the throne of Thessaly by his brother Pelias. On reaching manhood, Jason claimed his inheritance from his uncle, but Pelias attempted to trick Jason by sending him to recover a family possession, the Golden Fleece, from Aeetes, king of Colchis, on the east coast of the Black Sea. This necessitated a sea voyage—something never before attempted—and Jason was obliged to construct the first boat, the Argo. This he manned with the elite of available heroes, who became the Argonauts (Greek for "Argo sailors"), and set out.

Numerous obstacles presented themselves, one of the most threatening being the Clashing Rocks, opposing cliffs that operated like a modern automobile compactor but on a horizontal plane; anything caught in the narrow channel running between them was destroyed. With divine assistance, Jason reached his destination only to discover that he must perform several superhuman tasks before Aeetes would hand over the fleece. Fortunately, the king's daughter, Medea, who possessed magical powers, fell in love with Jason and lent her assistance in return for a promise of marriage.

The fleece won, the newlyweds started back toward Greece, hotly pursued by Aeetes. Medea had foreseen this possibility and, as a precaution, had kidnapped her young brother, whom she now killed; at intervals, she threw his body parts overboard. In retrieving these, the king was delayed, and so the Argo escaped.

On their return to Greece, further adventures and crimes enveloped Jason and Medea, culminating in her murder of their children and her escape from retribution in a flying chariot. Interested readers can consult works on mythology for the many details and variations not included here. ༄༅

Sophistication

Publius Ovidius Nāsō (43 B.C.–A.D. 17), *known in English as* **Ovid**, *was the third of the Augustan elegiac poets whose works survive. When he started to write, Rome was enjoying the stability and prosperity brought by Augustus, and his earlier poetry reflects the satisfaction he felt with the life and society of his day. In his later years, he had the misfortune to incur the displeasure of the emperor and was sentenced to exile in* A.D. 8. *The full reasons for this are not known, but it is certain that one of his principal works, the* **Ars amātōria** (The Art of Love), *from which the following selection is taken, had transgressed the official policies on public morality.*

Simplicitas rudis ante fuit: nunc aurea Roma est,
    et domiti magnas possidet orbis opes.
aspice, quae nunc sunt, Capitolia, quaeque fuerunt: 115
    alterius dices illa fuisse Iovis.
Curia, consilio quae nunc dignissima tanto,
    de stipula Tatio regna tenente fuit.

TEXT   P. Ovidii Nasonis *Amores, Medicamina faciei femineae,*
        Ars amatoria, Remedia amoris, ed. E. J. Kenny
        (Oxford Classical Texts, 1961)
METER   elegiac couplet [§M2]
        sīmplĭcĭ|tās ‖ rŭdĭs | āntĕ fŭ|ĭt ‖ nūnc | āūrĕă | Rōm(a) ēst
        ēt dŏmĭ|tī māg|nās ‖ pōssĭdĕt | ōrbĭs ŏ|pēs

113f.   **Simplicitās simplicitātis** F. *plainness, simplicity;* **rudis** *primitive, unrefined;* **ante** adv. *previously;* take **aurea** (*golden*) as a predicative adjective [§G57]; **domitī** (**domō -āre**) ... **orbis** *of the conquered world* (**orbis orbis** M.); **opēs** here *wealth.*
115f.   **aspice** 2 sg. pres. imp. act. **aspiciō -ere** *observe;* the Capitoline Hill (**Capitōlium -(i)ī** N.) with the temple of **Iuppiter optimus maximus** was the most sacred place in Rome—the plural is used here with reference to its two ridges (cf. note to Ovid *Tristia* I.3.29, page 134, and the map of Rome on page xxiv), trans. *the Capitol with its twin peaks;* **alterius ... Iovis** *of another Jupiter* (**Iuppiter Iovis** M., the principal Roman divinity)—a god was regarded as owning his own temple as well as dwelling in it); **dīcēs** introduces an acc.+inf. construction [§G10]; **illa** i.e., the **Capitōlia** of early Rome, trans. *the latter.*
117   **Cūria -ae** F. *the Senate-house,* situated on the northern edge of the **Forum Rōmānum; consiliō ... tantō** abl. with **dignissima** (superl. of **dignus,** which takes the ablative [§G50]) *most worthy of so great a council;* in the adjectival clause (supply **est**), **quae** is postponed [§G4].
118   **dē stipulā** (**stipula -ae** F.) *from straw,* i.e., *made of straw*—Ovid is probably only thinking of the roof; **Tatiō ... tenente** abl. absolute [§G49]—Tatius was co-regent of Rome with Romulus; **regna** pl. for sg. [§G53].
119f.   The antecedent (**Palātia**) of the adjectival clause (**quae ... fulgent**) has been placed inside the clause itself; it refers to the temple of Apollo that Augustus had

quae nunc sub Phoebo ducibusque Palatia fulgent,
  quid nisi araturis pascua bubus erant?   120
prisca iuvent alios: ego me nunc denique natum
  gratulor; haec aetas moribus apta meis,
non quia nunc terrae lentum subducitur aurum,
  lectaque diverso litore concha venit:
nec quia decrescunt effosso marmore montes,   125
  nec quia caeruleae mole fugantur aquae:
sed quia cultus adest, nec nostros mansit in annos
  rusticitas, priscis illa superstes avis.

~: Ovid *Ars amātōria* 3.113–128

built and to Augustus' own residence (**sub Phoebō ducibusque**, lit., *under Phoe-bus* (= *Apollo*) *and [our] leaders*); **Palātia** pl. for sg. [§G 53]—the Palatine (**Palātium -(i)ī** N.) was a hill south of the **Forum Rōmānum**; **fulgeō -ēre** *shine*—Augustus used white marble for his buildings; trans. *the Palatine, which now shines with [the temple of] Phoebus and [the house of our] leaders*; **quid ... erant** *what was it* (**erant** is plural because of **Palātia**); **nisi** here *except*; **arātūrīs** (fut. pple. of **arō arāre** *plow*) ... **būbus** (irreg. dat. pl. of **bōs bovis** M./F.) dat. of advantage [§G 31], lit., *for oxen [who were] going to plow*, i.e., *for oxen before plowing*; **pascuum -ī** N. *pasture*.

121f.   **prisca** (nom. pl.) **iuvent** (jussive subj. [§G 69]) **aliōs** *let ancient [things] please others*; **mē ... nātum [esse]** *that I was born*, acc.+inf. [§G 10] after **grātulor** (**-ārī** *rejoice*); **dēnique** (adv. *at last*) adds emphasis to **nunc** and need not be translated; **mōribus ... meīs** dat. with **apta** [§G 28] *suited to my character*.

123f.   Lines 123–128, a succession of adverbial clauses of reason [§G 86] introduced by **quia** (*because*), give Ovid's reasons for preferring his own age. Augustan poets often commented on the demand among the wealthy for elaborate dwellings and for luxury items such as gold and pearls, which reflected the prosperity Rome was enjoying; **terrae** dat. after **subdūcitur** (**subdūcō -ere** + acc./dat. *remove [something] from [something]*); **lentus** (*malleable*) refers to the ease with which gold can be worked; **lecta ... concha** (**-ae** F.) *a choice pearl*—pearls were brought to Rome from the East; **dīversō lītore** abl. of place from which [§G 39] *from a distant shore*.

125   **dēcrescō -ere** *grow smaller*; **effossō** (perf. pple. of **effodiō -ere** *dig up, quarry*) **marmore** (**marmor marmoris** N. *marble*) abl. of cause [§G 48], trans. *because of the marble [that has been] quarried.*

126   **caeruleus** *blue*; **mōlēs mōlis** F. *pile* (for the foundations of a building); **fugō -āre** *put to flight*—wealthy Romans were fond of building over water, whether in the sea or in a lake, and this necessitated driving piles to support the building; Ovid exaggerates the slight displacement of water involved.

127f.   **cultus** (**-ūs** M. *refinement*) **adest** (**adsum** *be present*) trans. *there is now refine-ment*; **rusticitās rusticitātis** F. *coarseness*; **priscīs** (*ancient*) **avīs** (**avus -ī** M. here *ancestor, forebear*) dat. after **superstes** (**superstitis** adj. *surviving*) [§G 28]; **illa** lit., *that one*; trans. *nor has that coarseness that survived our ancient forebears persisted* (lit., *stayed*) *up to our times*—the **rusticitās** that existed under Tatius continued after him but had disappeared by Ovid's time.

The Immortality of Verse

Ovid's claim to immortality reflects a common theme in poetry, but in his case it has proved true.

Quid mihi, Livor edax, ignavos obicis annos,
  ingeniique vocas carmen inertis opus;
non me more patrum, dum strenua sustinet aetas,
  praemia militiae pulverulenta sequi,
nec me verbosas leges ediscere nec me   5
  ingrato vocem prostituisse foro?
mortale est, quod quaeris, opus. mihi fama perennis
  quaeritur, in toto semper ut orbe canar.

TEXT   Ovid *Heroides, Amores*, trans. G. Showerman, revised G. P. Gould
        (Loeb Classical Library, 1977)
METER   elegiac couplet [§M2]
        quīd mĭhĭ | Līvŏr ĕ|dāx ‖ īg|nāvōs | ōbĭcĭs | ānnōs
        īngĕnĭ|īquĕ vŏ|cās ‖ cārmĕn ĭ|nērtĭs ŏ|pŭs

1   **Quid** *why*; **mihi ... ignāvōs ... annōs** dat. and acc. after **obicis** (**obiciō -ere** lit.,
    throw [something] (acc.) *at [someone]* (dat.)) *reproach me with idle* (**ignāvus**) *years*;
    Līvor edax voc. *biting* (**edax** (**edācis**)) *Envy* (**līvor līvōris** M.).
2   **vocās** (*do you call*) is followed by an accusative, **carmen** (here *poetry*), and a
    predicative accusative, **opus**, which is qualified by a genitive of description [§G20],
    ingeniī ... inertis (*the work of a lazy mind*).
3ff. Three acc.+inf. constructions [§G10] follow: **nōn mē ... sequī** *that I do not
    pursue*; **nec mē ... ēdiscere** *and that I do not memorize* (**ēdiscō -ere**); and **nec mē
    ... prostituisse** *and that I have not put to unworthy use* (**prostituō -ere**)—Latin
    does not need a specific word to introduce indirect speech when the context
    makes clear who is speaking (here **Līvor**), but in English we must insert *saying,
    claiming,* or something similar; **mōre patrum** *according to the custom* (abl. of man-
    ner [§G45]) *of [our] fathers*—it was normal for young men to enter the army or to
    take up law; **strēnua ... aetās** *vigorous age*, i.e., youth; **sustinet [mē]** *supports*
    (**sustineō -ēre**) *[me]*; **praemia mīlitiae pulverulenta** *the dusty rewards of military
    service* (**mīlitia -ae** F.)—Ovid is thinking of marches over unimproved roads; **ver-
    bōsās lēgēs** *wordy laws*; **ingrātō ... forō** abl. of place where [§G38]—the forum,
    which was the center of legal life, is called **ingrātus** (*thankless*) because it gave no
    adequate reward for a person's ability.
7f.   **mortālis** *mortal*—because the memory of a person's military or legal career
    does not survive him; **mihi** dat. of agent [§G29] *by me*; **perennis** *everlasting*; the
    purpose clause is introduced by a postponed **ut** [§G4]; **orbis orbis** M. *world*; **canar**
    (1 sg. pres. subj. pass. **canō -ere**) *I may be sung*—Ovid will be sung in the sense
    that his poetry will be read.
9f.   Ovid lists some of the great poets of the Greek and Roman past, beginning
    with Homer (**Maeonidēs -ae** M. lit., *the Lydian*), who was universally acknowl-

vivet Maeonides, Tenedos dum stabit et Ide,
    dum rapidas Simois in mare volvet aquas.   10

Ennius arte carens animosique Accius oris   19
    casurum nullo tempore nomen habent.

carmina sublimis tunc sunt peritura Lucreti,   23
    exitio terras cum dabit una dies;

Tityrus et segetes Aeneiaque arma legentur,   25
    Roma triumphati dum caput orbis erit;

donec erunt ignes arcusque Cupidinis arma,
    discentur numeri, culte Tibulle, tui.

ergo, cum silices, cum dens patientis aratri   31
    depereant aevo, carmina morte carent.

edged pre-eminent (cf. Lucretius *Dē rērum nātūrā* 3.1037, page 24); **Tenedos** (-ī F.) and **Īdē** (-ēs F.) are nom. sg. Greek names and are the subject of **stabit** (the sg. verb agreeing with the nearer subject [§G 58])—the former, an island off the coast of Asia Minor, and the latter, a mountain near Troy (in English, *Ida*), are both involved in the Trojan story, part of which is the subject of Homer's *Iliad*; **rapidus** *swift*; **Simoīs** (**Simoentis** M.) a river near Troy mentioned by Homer.

19f.   On Ennius, see page 3; **arte** abl. after **carens** *lacking in art*—Ennius' poetry was regarded as rough by the more refined Augustan poets; Accius (170–c. 80 B.C.) wrote tragedies; **animōsī ... ōris** gen. of description [§G 20] *of spirited mouth*; take **cāsūrum** (fut. pple. of **cadō -ere** *fall*) with **nōmen**, i.e., *a name that will die*; **nullō tempore** abl. of time when [§G 37] *at no time*—it is ironic that, except for meager fragments, the works of neither have survived.

23f.   **sublīmis ... Lucrētī** *of majestic Lucretius* (see page 22); **sunt peritūra** (fut. pple. of **pereō -īre**) = **perībunt** *will perish*; **cum** is postponed [§G 4]; **exitiō** dat. after **dabit** *will give to destruction* (**exitium** -(i)ī N.), i.e., will see the destruction of; **terrās** here *the earth*—Ovid is stating a theory of Lucretius'.

25   Instead of naming Vergil (see page 51), Ovid alludes to his three works by metonymy [§G 97]: **Tītyrus** -ī M. a character in the *Eclogues*; **segetēs** *crops* (**seges segetis** F.)—the subject of the *Georgics* is farming; **Aenēia arma** (*the arms of Aeneas* (**Aenēius** adj. of **Aenēās**)) refers to the *Aeneid*; **legō -ere** here *read*.

26   **Rōma** -ae F. *Rome*; take **triumphātī** with **orbis**, *of the conquered* (**triumphō -āre**) *world*; **dum** (*while, as long as*) is postponed [§G 4].

27   **ignēs arcusque** (*fires and a bow*; **arcus** -ūs M.) (cf. *Pervigilium Veneris*, l. 33, page 215) is the subject of **erunt**, and **Cupīdinis arma** (*the weapons of Cupid*; **Cupīdō Cupīdinis** M.) is the predicate.

28   **discentur** 3 pl. fut. ind. pass. **discō -ere** *learn*; **numerī** *verses* (**numerus** -ī M.); **cultus** *elegant* (on Tibullus, see page 117).

31   **ergō** *therefore, so*; **cum** + subj., here *although*; **silex silicis** M. *flint*, a proverbially hard stone; **dens patientis arātrī** *the tooth* (**dens dentis** M.) *of the long-lasting* (**patiens** (**patientis**)) *plow* (**arātrum** -ī N.).

32   **dēpereō -īre** *perish*; **aevō** instrumental abl. [§G 47] *through age* (**aevum** -ī N.); **morte** abl. after **carent**.

cedant carminibus reges regumque triumphi,
  cedat et auriferi ripa benigna Tagi!
vilia miretur vulgus; mihi flavus Apollo   35
  pocula Castalia plena ministret aqua,
sustineamque coma metuentem frigora myrtum,
  atque a sollicito multus amante legar!

33   **cēdant** (jussive subj. [§G 69]) governs the dative **carminibus**, *let … yield to poetry* (lit., *songs*); **triumphus -ī** M. *triumph*.

34   **et** is postponed [§G 3]; **aurifer** adj. *gold-bearing*; **Tagus -ī** M. *a river in Spain famous for its alluvial gold*; **rīpa benigna** *generous bank* (**rīpa -ae** F.).

35   **vīlia** *worthless [things]* (**vīlis** adj.); **mīrētur** jussive subj. [§G 69]; **vulgus -ī** N. *the common herd*, used here in a derogatory sense; **flāvus** *fair-haired*; **Apollō Apollinis** M. *god of poetry*.

36   Scansion indicates **pōcula Castaliā plēna**, but because the final syllable of a pentameter can be long or short, we must use syntax to determine whether we have **aqua** or **aquā**—since **Apollō** can only be nominative and is therefore the subject of **ministret** (if vocative, **Apollō** could not be qualified by the nominative **flāvus**), **aqua** cannot be nominative (vocative *O water* hardly seems appropriate to the sense), and we are left with **aquā**, with which we can take **Castaliā**; trans. *cups* (**pōculum -ī** N.) *full of* (**plēnus** + abl.) *Castalian water* (**Castalius** adj. of **Castalia -ae** F. *a fountain on Mt. Parnassus at Delphi*, whose waters were supposed to give poetic inspiration—cf. ll. 1f. of Persius' prologue, page 166); **ministret** optative subj. [§G 67] with **Apollō** as subject, *may Apollo serve* (**ministrō -āre**).

37   **sustineam** optative subj. [§G 67] *may I support* (**sustineō -ēre**); **comā** instrumental abl. [§G 47] *with [my] hair* (**coma -ae** F.); **metuentem frīgora myrtum** lit., *myrtle* (**myrtus -ī** F.) *fearing the cold* (**frīgora** pl. for sg. [§G 53]; **frīgus frīgoris** N.)—Ovid wrote on erotic themes and so was a suitable recipient of a myrtle chaplet (myrtle was sacred to Venus—cf. *Pervigilium Veneris*, l. 6, page 214); *myrtle fears the cold* because it does not grow in colder climates.

38   **ā sollicitō … amante** *by an anxious lover* (**amans amantis** M./F.); **multus** *much*, trans. by an adverb [§G 55], *often*; **legar** optative subj. [§G 67] *may I be read*—the reference is to Ovid's manual for lovers, the *Ars amātōria*.

39   **pascitur** 3 sg. pres. ind. pass. **pascō -ere** *feed* (tr.)—the passive is used intransitively in the sense *feed oneself* [§G 59]; **in vīvīs** *on the living*; **fāta** pl. for sg. [§G 53] here *death*; **quiescō -ere** *grows quiet*.

40   **suus … quemque tuētur honōs** (= **honor**) lit., *his renown protects* (**tueor tuērī**) *each [person]*, trans. *each is protected by his renown* [§G 56]; **ex meritō** *according to [his] worth*.

41   **ergō** *therefore, so*; **suprēmus … ignis** *the last fire*—the Romans practiced cremation (see "Roman Beliefs About an Afterlife," page 78); **adēderit** 3 sg. fut. perf. act. **adedō -ere**, lit., *will have consumed*, but trans. *has consumed* [§G 66].

42   **vīvam** fut. *I will live on*; **pars … multa** *a large part*; **meī** gen. of **ego**; **superstes** (**superstitis**) *surviving*.

pascitur in vivis Livor; post fata quiescit,
   cum suus ex merito quemque tuetur honos.   40
ergo etiam cum me supremus adederit ignis,
   vivam, parsque mei multa superstes erit.

~: OVID *Amōrēs* 1.15 (with omissions)

Pick Three Lines ... Any Three Lines

The elder Seneca (born c. 50 B.C.) has been overshadowed by his more famous son of the same name (see page 168), but his surviving writings, which are concerned with instruction in rhetoric, contain a great deal of information about the Rome of his day. In his *Contrōversiae* (*Opposing Arguments*), he tells a curious story about Ovid.

> *The poet was once asked by his friends to remove three lines [from his poems]. In turn, he requested that he himself should exclude three that were not to be touched. The stipulation seemed fair. In private, the friends wrote down the lines they wanted removed, he those he wanted left in.*
>
> *Each of the two tablets had the same lines. One of the witnesses, Albinovanus Pedo, used to say that the first [line] was*

semibovemque virum semivirumque bovem

and the second

et gelidum Borean egelidumque Notum   *Contrōversiae* 2.2.12

The first line, from Ovid's *Ars amātōria* (2.24), is a description of the Minotaur, who was *both half-bull man and half-man bull*; the second line, *and the chilling north wind and the de-chilling south wind*, is from Ovid's *Amōrēs* (2.11.10). The third either was not known to Seneca or was accidentally omitted from manuscripts of the *Contrōversiae*.

The two lines appear to have offended Ovid's friends because of their play on words. By way of excusing the poet, Seneca adds that Ovid, although a person of the highest talent, had the judgment—but not the will—to check the lack of restraint sometimes evident in his work.

Ovid's Last Night in Rome

When sent into exile by Augustus, Ovid was ordered to live in Tomis, an out-post of the Roman Empire on the west coast of the Black Sea (now Constanța in Romania). Though condemned there to live a hard and dangerous life, he continued to write poetry. The following lines describe the last night before he left the Rome he loved—to which he was never to return.

Cum subit illius tristissima noctis imago,
    quae mihi supremum tempus in urbe fuit,
cum repeto noctem, qua tot mihi cara reliqui,
    labitur ex oculis nunc quoque gutta meis.
iam prope lux aderat, qua me discedere Caesar   5
    finibus extremae iusserat Ausoniae.
nec spatium nec mens fuerat satis apta parando:
    torpuerant longa pectora nostra mora.

TEXT   P. Ovidii Nasonis *Tristia*, ed. J. B. Hall (Bibliotheca Teubneriana, 1995)
METER   elegiac couplet [§M 2]
        cūm sŭbĭt | īllī|ūs ‖ trīs|tīssĭmă | nōctĭs ĭ|māgō
        quaē mĭhĭ | sūprē|mūm ‖ tēmpŭs ĭn | ūrbĕ fŭ|ĭt

1   **subit** (3 sg. pres ind. act. **subeō -īre**) here *comes [to my mind]*; take **illīus** with **noctis**, and **tristissima** (superl. of **tristis** *sad*, here used to express a very high degree [§G 54]) with **imāgō** (**imāginis** F. *picture*).

2f.   **mihi** dat. of disadvantage [§G 31] *for me*; **suprēmus** *last*; **in urbe** *in the city*—Rome was often referred to simply as **urbs**; **repetō -ere** *recall, remember*; **quā** abl. of time when [§G 37] *on which*; take **tot** (indecl. adj.) with **mihi cāra** (*so many [things] dear to me*).

4   The subject of **lābitur** (**lābor lābī** *fall*) is **gutta** (**-ae** F. *drop*, i.e., *a tear*); take **ex oculis ... meīs** together; **nunc quoque** *now too*—Ovid cried at the time and cries again when writing the poem.

5f.   **prope ... aderat** (**adsum** *be present*) trans. *had almost come*; **lux** (**lūcis** F.) lit., *light*, but trans. *day*; **quā** as in l. 3; **mē** is the object of **iusserat**; **discēdō -ere** *depart*; **Caesar Caesaris** M. here the emperor Augustus; **finibus** abl. of place from which [§G 39] *from the boundaries*; **extrēmus** *farthest*; **Ausonia -ae** F. a poetic word for Italy—Ovid was not allowed to stay even in its most remote areas.

7   **spatium -iī** N. here *period, time*; **mens mentis** F. *[frame of] mind*; **fuerat** is singular to agree with the nearer of the two subjects [§G 58], **spatium** and **mens**; **satis** adv. *sufficiently, quite*; **apta** (**aptus** *favorable*) agrees with the nearer subject (**mens**) but must be taken in sense with both; **parandō** dat. of gerund to express purpose [§G 33] *for preparing*.

8   **torpuerant** (**torpeō -ēre**) *had become numb*; **longā ... morā** abl. of cause [§G 48] *through long delay*; **pectora nostra** (pl. for sg. [§G 53] *my breast*) is the subject of **torpuerant**—**pectus** was considered, among other things, the seat of intellectual faculties and so here is the equivalent of **mens** (*mind*); however, since **mens** has just occurred (l. 7), this line is best translated *my brain had become numb*.

non mihi servorum, comitis non cura legendi,
    non aptae profugo vestis opisve fuit.   10
non aliter stupui, quam qui Iovis ignibus ictus
    vivit et est vitae nescius ipse suae.
ut tamen hanc animo nubem dolor ipse removit,
    et tandem sensus convaluere mei,
adloquor extremum maestos abiturus amicos,   15
    qui modo de multis unus et alter erant.
uxor amans flentem flens acrius ipsa tenebat,
    imbre per indignas usque cadente genas.
nata procul Libycis aberat diversa sub oris,
    nec poterat fati certior esse mei.   20

9f.   The basic construction is **nōn mihi** (dat. of reference [§G 32]) ... **cūra ... fuit** lit., *there was not concern for me*; with **cūra** take **legendī**, a gerundive [§G 81] that agrees with **comitis** (**comes comitis** M./F. *companion*), but it must also be taken in sense with the genitives **servōrum, aptae ... vestis**, and **opis**, lit., *concern of slaves*, etc. *going to be chosen*, i.e., *concern of choosing slaves, a companion, clothing suitable for an exile* (**profugō** dat. after **aptae**) *or necessities* (**ops opis** F.); **nōn** is repeated in ll. 9 and 10 for emphasis; trans. *I was not concerned with choosing slaves, a companion*, etc.

11f.   **nōn aliter ... quam** lit., *not otherwise than*, i.e., *in the same way as*; **stupuī** (**stupeō -ēre**) *I was stunned*; **quī** *[a person] who*; **Iovis ignibus** (instrumental abl. [§G 47]) **ictus** *struck* (**īciō īcere**) *by the lightning* (lit., *fires*) *of Jupiter* (**Iuppiter Iovis** M.); **vīvit** *lives, is alive*; **nescius** + gen. *unaware of*—the lightning victim is so stunned that he does not realize he is still alive.

13   **ut** + ind. *when*; **hanc ... nūbem** *this cloud* (**nūbēs nūbis** F.); **animō** abl. of separation [§G 40] *from [my] mind*; **dolor dolōris** M. *grief*; **removeō -ēre** *remove*.

14   **tandem** adv. *finally*; **sensūs ... meī** (*my emotions* (**sensus -ūs** M.)) is the subject of **convaluēre** (= **convaluērunt**; **convalescō -ere** *recover*).

15   **adloquor** historic pres. [§G 60], trans. *I addressed*; **extrēmum** adverbial acc. [§G 16] *for the last time*; **maestōs ... amīcōs** *[my] sad friends*; **abitūrus** (fut. pple. of **abeō abīre**) *[when] about to depart*.

16   The antecedent of **quī** is **amīcōs**; **modo** adv. *now*; **dē multīs** *of many*; **ūnus et alter** trans. *one or two*.

17f.   **uxor amans** *[my] loving wife*; with **flentem** (**fleō flēre** *weep*) supply **mē**; take **flens acrius** (compar. adv. of **acriter** *bitterly*) with **uxor**; **imbre ... cadente** abl. absolute [§G 49], trans. *with a rain [of tears]* (**imber imbris** M.) *falling*; **per** (prep. + acc.) *over*; **indignās ... genās** *[her] innocent cheeks* (**gena -ae** F.); **usque** *constantly*.

19   **nāta** (**-ae** F.) *[my] daughter*—Ovid's only child (from a previous marriage) was living with her husband in Africa; the three words **procul** (*far away*) ... **aberat** (**absum** *be distant*) **dīversa** (agreeing with **nāta**, *separated [from me]*) emphasize the fact that the daughter was far away from her father at the time—trans. *was abroad, far away from me*; **Libycīs ... sub ōrīs** *on African shores*.

20   **poterat** 3 sg. imperf. ind. **possum**; **fātī ... meī** *of my fate*; **certior** (compar. of **certus** *certain*) here *informed*.

quocumque aspiceres, luctus gemitusque sonabant,
  formaque non taciti funeris intus erat.
femina virque meo, pueri quoque funere maerent,
  inque domo lacrimas angulus omnis habet.
si licet exemplis in parvo grandibus uti,   25
  haec facies Troiae, cum caperetur, erat.
iamque quiescebant voces hominumque canumque
  Lunaque nocturnos alta regebat equos.
hanc ego suspiciens et ab hac Capitolia cernens,
  quae nostro frustra iuncta fuere Lari,   30

21 **quōcumque aspicerēs** (**aspiciō -ere**) *wherever you/one looked* (generalizing
    relative clause with the subj. [§G88]); sense tells us that **luctūs** (**luctus -ūs** M.
    lament) and **gemitūs** (**gemitus -ūs** M. *groan*) are both nominative plural; **sonābant**
    (**sonō -āre**) lit., *were sounding out*, but trans. *were heard*.

22 **forma … intus erat** lit., *inside [the house] there was the appearance*; **nōn tacitī**
    lit., *not quiet*, but trans. *noisy*—Roman funerals were notorious for their noise;
    fūnus fūneris N. *funeral*.

23 **fēmina virque** trans. *men and women* (the singular is used to represent a class
    [§G53]); **puerī** *children*; **meō … fūnere** abl. of place where [§G38] *at my funeral*;
    quoque *also*—the three preceding nouns are the subjects of **maerent** (historic
    pres. [§G60]; **maereō -ēre** *mourn*).

24 **inque** = **in** + **que**; take **angulus** (**-ī** M.) **omnis** together, *every corner*; **habet**
    historic pres. [§G60].

25 **licet** impers. *it is allowed*; take **exemplīs … grandibus** as the ablative object of
    ūtī (pres. inf. of **ūtor**), *to use prominent examples* (**exemplum -ī** N.); **in parvō** *in an
    insignificant [case]*.

26 **haec faciēs** (**-ēī** F.) **… erat** *this was the appearance*—**faciēs** is the predicate and
    haec, although the subject of **erat**, agrees with it; **caperētur** here *was taken [in
    war]*—the capture of Troy (**Trōia -ae** F.) was naturally a mournful affair for
    the Trojans, and it is typical of Ovid's style that he introduces a mythological
    parallel.

27 **iamque** *and already*; **quiescō -ere** *grow quiet*; **vōcēs** here *sounds* (**vox vōcis** F.);
    … -que … -que *both … and …*; **canum** gen. pl. of **canis canis** M./F. *dog*.

28 Traditional belief regarded the moon as a goddess (hence **Lūna**) who rode in a
    horse-drawn chariot across the sky; **nocturnus** *nocturnal*; **alta** (with **Lūna**) *lofty*;
    regēbat here *drove*.

29 **hanc** and **hāc** both refer to **Lūna**; **suspiciō -ere** *glance up at*; **cernō -ere** *look
    at*—Ovid shifts his eyes from the moon to the twin peaks of the Capitoline Hill
    (hence pl. **Capitōlia** (**Capitōlium -(i)ī** N.)) and its various temples, the most im-
    portant of which was that of **Iuppiter optimus maximus**, the holiest place in
    Rome.

30 The antecedent of **quae** is **Capitōlia**; **nostrō … Larī** (**Lar Laris** M.) dat. after
    iuncta fuēre (= **fuērunt**); **iuncta fuēre** is another form of the perfect indicative
    passive of **iungō -ere** *join* (the normal form is **iuncta sunt**)—the **Lar** was the

"numina vicinis habitantia sedibus," inquam,
  "iamque oculis numquam templa videnda meis,
dique relinquendi, quos urbs habet alta Quirini,
  este salutati tempus in omne mihi."

~: OVID *Tristia* 1.3.1–34

household god that protected the home, and often, as here, the name was used by metonymy [§G 97] to indicate the house itself; **frustrā** *in vain, to no purpose*—Ovid's house was near the Capitol, but this did not save him from being condemned to exile; trans. *which to no purpose were close* (lit., *were joined*) *to my home.*

31   **nūmina ... sēdibus** is a vocative phrase, *divinities living in* (**habitantia** pres. pple. of **habitō -āre**) *neighboring dwellings* (**vīcīnīs ... sēdibus** abl. of place where [§G 38])—a god was believed to live in his temple, and Ovid is addressing those with temples on the Capitoline Hill; **inquam** historic pres. [§G 60] *I said.*

32   Ovid now addresses the temples themselves; **oculīs ... meīs** dat. of agent [§G 29] after the gerundive [§G 81] **videnda**; trans. *and temples now never [again] to be seen by my eyes.*

33   The second category of divinities addressed is **dī ... quōs urbs habet alta Quirīnī** (*gods whom the lofty city of Quirinus* (= **Rōmulus**) *holds* (i.e., gods who had temples elsewhere in Rome)), and these are qualified by the gerundive [§G 81] **relinquendī** (*going to be left,* i.e., *whom I must leave*).

34   Take **este** (2 pl. imp. of **sum**) with **salūtātī** (**salūtō -āre** *greet*); **mihi** dat. of agent [§G 29], lit., *be greeted by me for all time* (**tempus in omne**), i.e., *I greet you now, and this greeting must suffice for all future time*—the Roman gods had no temples in Ovid's place of exile and so would never come there.

Fair-Weather Friends

In exile at Tomis, Ovid wrote two collections of poems, the *Tristia* (*Sad [Poems]*) and the *Epistulae ex Pontō* (*Letters from the Pontus* (the Black Sea)). In these, he often complains of his present life and of how he has been deserted by many of his friends (cf. l. 16, page 133). At *Tristia* 1.9.5, he sums up his plight with these words:

Donec eris sospes, multos numerabis amicos:
  tempora si fuerint nubila, solus eris.
While you are free of troubles, you count many friends.
  If the times are cloudy, you are alone.

Deucalion and Pyrrha

Before his exile, Ovid wrote a long poem in hexameters, the **Metamorphōsēs** (Transformations), *which consists of a large number of stories from mythology and legend involving a change of form or shape (as, for example, humans changed into birds or trees). In the story from which the following selection is taken, Jupiter, exasperated by humanity's wickedness, has ordered a universal flood. Only Deucalion and his wife, Pyrrha, because of their piety, are allowed to survive. When the flood subsides, they go to the temple of Themis, the goddess of justice, and ask how they might restore the human race.*

Ut templi tetigere gradus, procumbit uterque 375
pronus humi gelidoque pavens dedit oscula saxo
atque ita "si precibus" dixerunt "numina iustis
victa remollescunt, si flectitur ira deorum,
dic, Themi, qua generis damnum reparabile nostri
arte sit, et mersis fer opem, mitissima, rebus!" 380
mota dea est sortemque dedit: "discedite templo
et velate caput cinctasque resolvite vestes

TEXT   P. Ovidii Nasonis *Metamorphoses*, ed. W. S. Anderson
       (Bibliotheca Teubneriana, 1996)
METER hexameter [§M1]
       ūt tēm|plī ‖ tĕtĭ|gērĕ gră|dūs ‖ prō|cūmbĭt ŭ|tērquĕ
       prōnŭs hŭ|mī ‖ gĕlĭ|dōquĕ pă|vēns ‖ dĕdĭt | ōscŭlă | sāxō

375   **Ut** + ind. *when;* **tetigēre** (= tetigērunt; **tangō -ere**) *reached;* **gradūs** (**gradus -ūs** M.) *steps;* **prōcumbit** historic pres. [§G60] (**prōcumbō -ere** *fall down*)—the historic present occurs several times later in the selection; **uterque** *each.*
376f. **prōnus** *lying face down, prone;* **humī** loc. sg. of **humus -ī** F., *on the ground;* **gelidō ... saxō** dat. after **dedit**, *to the cold stone;* **paveō -ēre** *be afraid;* **osculum -ī** N. *kiss;* **precibus ... iustīs** instrumental abl. [§G47], lit., *by just prayers,* trans. *by the prayers of the righteous;* **nūmina** here *divinities.*
378   **victa** trans. *won over;* **remollescō -ere** *relent;* **flectō -ere** *turn aside, avert.*
379f. **dīc** 2 sg. imp. of **dīcō -ere**; **Themi** voc. of **Themis Themidis** F. goddess of justice; take **quā** with **arte** (instrumental abl. [§G47]), *by what way, how;* **generis ... nostrī** *of our race;* **damnum -ī** N. *loss;* **reparābile ... sit** subj. in an indirect question [§G91], lit., *can be restored,* i.e., *can be made good;* **mersīs ... rēbus** dat. *to the submerged* (**mergō -ere** *world*) *world;* **fer** 2 sg. imp. of **ferō ferre** *bring;* **opem** *help;* **mītissima** f.sg. voc. of the superl. of **mītis** *gentle.*
381   **mōta ... est** *was moved,* i.e., by their prayers; **sors sortis** F. *oracle, oracular statement;* **discēdite** (2 pl. imp. of **discēdō -ere**) *go out;* **templō** abl. of place from which [§G39] *from [my] temple.*
382   **vēlāte** (**vēlō -āre** *cover*) and **resolvite** (**resolvō -ere** *loosen*) are 2 pl. imperative—both actions indicate a reverent and submissive attitude; **caput** sg. for pl.

ossaque post tergum magnae iactate parentis!"
obstipuere diu: rumpitque silentia voce
Pyrrha prior iussisque deae parere recusat,   385
detque sibi veniam pavido rogat ore pavetque
laedere iactatis maternas ossibus umbras.
interea repetunt caecis obscura latebris
verba datae sortis secum inter seque volutant.
inde Promethides placidis Epimethida dictis   390
mulcet et "aut fallax" ait "est sollertia nobis,
aut (pia sunt nullumque nefas oracula suadent!)

[§G53]; cinctās ... vestēs lit., *girt up* (cingō -ere) *clothes*—because they had been walking, both were wearing a belt (zōna) to hitch up their tunics.

383   os ossis N. *bone*; post tergum sg. for pl. [§G53], lit., *behind [your] back*, i.e., *over your backs*; magnae ... parentis (parens parentis M./F.)—oracles in antiquity were never clear, and the expression *bones of the great [female] parent* was meant to puzzle; iactāte 2 pl. imp. of iactō -āre *throw*.

384   obstipuēre (= obstipuērunt; obstipescō -ere) *they were stunned*; rumpit historic pres. [§G60], trans. *broke*; silentia *silence* (pl. for sg. [§G53]; silentium -(i)ī N.); vōce instrumental abl. [§G47] *with [her] voice*.

385   Pyrrha -ae F.; prior adj. translated by an adverb [§G55], *first*; iussīs (iussum -ī N. *order*) dat. pl. after pārēre (here *obey*); recūsō -āre *refuse*.

386   det ... veniam (venia -ae F. *pardon*) indirect petition (hence the subj. [§G91]) after rogat (the clause would normally be introduced by ut)—the understood subject of det is Themis, but sibī refers to Pyrrha; pavidō ... ōre abl. of manner [§G45] *with frightened mouth*; paveō -ēre (see l. 376).

387   māternās ... umbrās *maternal Shades*, i.e., *[her] mother's Shade* (pl. for sg. [§G53])—Pyrrha wrongly thinks that the bones of her own mother were meant by the oracle; iactātis ... ossibus instrumental abl. [§G47], lit., *by bones having been thrown*; trans. *was afraid to offend [her] mother's Shade by throwing [her] bones*.

388f.   intereā here *nevertheless*; repetō -ere *go back over, reflect on*; obscūra agrees with verba but is qualified by caecīs ... latebrīs (abl. of cause [§G48]), a highly metaphorical expression, *because of [their] dark uncertainty* (lit., *by reason of [their] blind hiding places* (latebra -ae F.)); sortis see l. 381; sēcum and inter sē go with different verbs but mean the same thing: *between themselves, together*; volūtō -āre *think/talk over*.

390ff.   inde here *then*; Promēthīdēs (-ae M.) Greek patronymic, *son of Prometheus* (i.e., Deucalion); placidīs ... dictīs instrumental abl. [§G47] *with calm words*; Epimēthida Greek acc. sg. of Epimēthis (Epimēthidos F.) feminine patronymic, *daughter of Epimetheus* (i.e., Pyrrha)—Roman poets often used such terms for variety; mulceō -ēre *soothe*; aut ... aut ... *either ... or ...*; fallax *deceptive*; ait historic pres. [§G60]; sollertia -ae F. *cleverness*; nōbīs pl. for sg. [§G53], dat. of possessor [§G30]; lit., *either there is deceptive cleverness for us*, i.e., *either my cleverness deceives me*; ōrācula (ōrāculum -ī N.) is the subject of sunt and suādent (suādeō -ēre *counsel*); take pia (*righteous*) predicatively [§G57] after sunt; nefās (indecl.) *crime*.

magna parens terra est: lapides in corpore terrae
ossa reor dici; iacere hos post terga iubemur."
coniugis augurio quamquam Titania mota est,   395
spes tamen in dubio est: adeo caelestibus ambo
diffidunt monitis; sed quid temptare nocebit?
discedunt velantque caput tunicasque recingunt
et iussos lapides sua post vestigia mittunt.
saxa (quis hoc credat, nisi sit pro teste vetustas?)   400
ponere duritiem coepere suumque rigorem
mollirique mora mollitaque ducere formam.

~: OVID *Metamorphōsēs* 1.375–402

393f.   **lapidēs** (**lapis lapidis** M. *stone*) is the subject of **dīcī** in an acc.+inf. construc-
        tion [§G10] after **reor**, *I think that stones are called* (**dīcī**) *bones in the earth's body*;
        take **iacere** after **iubēmur**, *we are being ordered to throw*; the antecedent of **hōs** is
        lapidēs.

395   **coniunx coniugis** M./F. *spouse*; **auguriō** (**augurium -(i)ī** N. here *interpreta-
        tion*) instrumental abl. [§G47] after **mōta est**; **quamquam** (*although*) is postponed
        [§G4]; **Tītānia -ae** F. *daughter of a Titan*, i.e., Pyrrha, whose father, Epimetheus
        (see l. 390), belonged to a class of gods called Titans.

396f.   **spēs … in dubiō est** (historic pres.), lit., *[their] hope is in doubt* (**dubium
        -(i)ī** N.), i.e., *their hopes were faint*; **adeō** *to such an extent*; **caelestibus** (**caelestis
        divine**) … **monitīs** (**monitum -ī** N. *instruction*) dat. after **diffīdunt** (**diffīdō -ere**
        + dat. *be uncertain about*); **ambō** *both*; **quid temptāre nocēbit?** *what would* (lit.,
        will) *it hurt to try* (**temptō -āre**)?

398   The use of the historic present continues; **discēdō -ere** see l. 381—they now
        obey the goddess's instructions to go out, cover their heads, and loosen their
        tunics (**tunica -ae** F.); instead of the earlier **resolvite** (l. 382), we have **recin-
        gunt** (**recingō -ere**), which refers to the same action but is more specific, trans.
        unfasten.

399   **iussōs lapidēs** lit., *ordered stones*, i.e., *stones, as they had been ordered*; **sua post
        vestīgia** a variation of the earlier **post tergum**, lit., *behind their footsteps* (**vestīgium
        -(i)ī** N.), i.e., *behind them*; **mittunt** here *throw*.

400   **saxa** is used instead of **lapidēs** for variety; **crēdat … sit** two present subjunc-
        tives in an unreal conditional sentence referring to the future [§G94], lit., *who
        would believe this unless antiquity* (**vetustās vetustātis** F.) *were for* (**prō** here *fulfill-
        ing the function of*) *a witness*, trans. *… unless it were vouched for by antiquity*.

401f.   The subject of **coepēre** (= **coepērunt**) is **saxa** (l. 400), and three infinitives
        follow: (1) **pōnere** (here *set aside*), which governs **dūritiem** (**dūritiēs -ēī** F. *hard-
        ness*) and **suum rigōrem** (**rigor rigōris** M. *rigidity*); (2) **mollīrī** (pres. pass. inf. of
        molliō -īre *make soft*) *to soften*; **morā** (**mora -ae** F. *delay*) abl. of manner [§G45]
        with delay, i.e., *slowly*; and (3) **dūcere** (here *take on*); take **mollīta** with **saxa**; **forma
        -ae** F. *shape*—we infer from the context that a new shape is meant, each of which
        becomes a human being.

A Storm at Sea

Ovid describes a storm he experienced on his way to Tomis, where he would spend the final ten years of his life in exile.

Me miserum, quanti montes volvuntur aquarum!
   iam iam tacturos sidera summa putes.   20
quantae diducto subsidunt aequore valles!
   iam iam tacturas Tartara nigra putes.
quocumque aspicio, nihil est, nisi pontus et aer,
   fluctibus hic tumidus, nubibus ille minax.
inter utrumque fremunt immani murmure venti;   25
   nescit, cui domino pareat, unda maris;

TEXT   P. Ovidii Nasonis *Tristia*, ed. J. B. Hall (Bibliotheca Teubneriana, 1995)
METER elegiac couplet [§M2]
     mē mĭsĕ|rūm quān|tī ‖ mōn|tēs vōl|vūntŭr ă|quārūm
     iām iām | tāctū|rōs ‖ sīdĕră | sūmmă pŭ|tēs

This poem was no doubt written after the storm, but for vividness Ovid uses the present tense, which can be retained in English.

19 **Mē miserum** acc. of exclamation [§G14] *Unhappy me!*, trans. *Woe is me!*; **quantī** (and **quantae** in l. 21) introduces an exclamation, *what great …!*; **volvuntur** pass. used in an intr. sense, *roll*, trans. *surge up.*

20 **iam iam** lit., *already, already*, i.e., *on the point of*; with **tactūrōs** (fut. pple. of **tangō -ere**) supply **esse**, which is part of the acc.+inf. [§G10] after **putēs** (potential subj. [§G68]), lit., *you would think [them (i.e., **montēs … aquārum**)] already, already to be going to touch the highest stars* (**sīdus sīderis** N.), i.e., *you would think that they were on the point of touching….*

21f. The third and fourth lines are parallel to the first two; **dīductō … aequore** abl. absolute [§G49], lit., *the sea* (**aequor aequoris** N.) *having been parted* (**dīdūcō -ere**); **subsīdō -ere** *sink down*; **vallis vallis** F. *valley*; **Tartara -ōrum** N.PL. the lowest part of the Underworld (in English, *Tartarus*); **niger** *black.*

23 **quōcumque** *wherever*; **aspiciō -ere** *look*; **pontus -ī** M. *sea*; **āēr** (two syllables) **āeris** M. here *sky.*

24 **fluctibus** abl. of respect [§G46] with **tumidus**, *swelling with waves* (**fluctus -ūs** M.); **hic … ille …** *the former … the latter …*; **nūbibus** instrumental abl. [§G47] with **minax** ((**minācis**) adj.), *threatening with clouds* (**nūbēs nūbis** F.).

25 **fremō -ere** *roar*; **immānī murmure** abl. of manner [§G45] *with a terrible rumble* (**murmur murmuris** N.).

26 **nescit** governs the indirect question [§G91] **cui dominō pāreat** (*which master it should obey* (**pāreō -ēre** + dat.))—as explained in the following lines, the competing masters are the different winds.

nam modo purpureo vires capit Eurus ab ortu,
  nunc Zephyrus sero vespere missus adest,
nunc gelidus sicca Boreas bacchatur ab Arcto,
  nunc Notus adversa proelia fronte gerit.   30
rector in incerto est nec quid fugiatve petatve
  invenit: ambiguis ars stupet ipsa malis.
scilicet occidimus, nec spes nisi vana salutis,
  dumque loquor, vultus obruit unda meos.
opprimet hanc animam fluctus, frustraque precanti   35
  ore necaturas accipiemus aquas.

~: OVID *Tristia* 1.2.19–36

27 **modo** adv. *now;* **purpureō … ab ortū** *from the purple east* (**ortus -ūs** M.); **Eurus**
  -ī M. *the east wind;* **vīrēs capit** *gathers* (lit., *takes*) *strength.*
28 *Zephyrus* (**Zephyrus -ī** M. *the west wind*) *is here* (lit., *is present;* **adsum**), *sent*
  from the late evening (abl. of separation [§G40]; **vesper** (no gen.) M.).
29 Take **gelidus** (*cold*) with **Boreās** (**-ae** M. *the north wind;* the name is Greek,
  hence the odd nom. sg.); **siccā … ab Arctō** *from the dry [constellation of the] Bear*
  (**Arctus -ī** F.)—the constellation of the Bear is above the North Pole and so symbolized north; poets called it *dry* because it never sets, whereas other constellations, which do set, were believed to dip themselves into the waters of **Ōceanus**
  (see note to Seneca *Trōades* 383, page 169); **bacchor -ārī** *rage.*
30 **Notus -ī** M. *the south wind;* **adversā … fronte** abl. of manner [§G45] *with an*
  opposing front (**frons frontis** F.)—the phrase indicates a head-on attack.
31f. **rector rectōris** M. *helmsman;* **in incertō** *in doubt,* i.e., uncertain what to do;
  nec … invenit *and is at a loss to know;* **quid fugiatve petatve** (**… -ve … -ve** *either*
  … or …) indirect questions [§G91] governed by **invenit;** **petō -ere** here *head for;*
  ambiguīs … malīs abl. of cause [§G48] *because of conflicting perils;* **ars artis** F. here
  skill; **stupeō -ēre** *be powerless*—the helmsman, despite his skill, cannot take action
  to counter one difficulty of navigation because to do so would aggravate another.
33 **scīlicet occidimus** *of course, we are doomed* (**occidō -ere** lit., *die*)—the plural
  here and in l. 36 indicates all those on board; with **spēs … salūtis** supply **est;**
  vānus *vain.*
34 **dumque** = **dum** + **que;** **vultūs … meōs** pl. for sg. [§G53] *my face;* **obruit** (**ob-**
  ruō -ere) lit., *covers,* trans. *floods over.*
35f. **opprimō -ere** (tr.) *overwhelm* (in the sense of submerge); **hanc animam** lit.,
  this life, i.e., Ovid himself; **frustrāque precantī ōre** instrumental abl. [§G47] *and*
  with vainly praying (**precor -ārī**) *mouth* (sg. for pl. [§G53])—in such circumstances,
  it was advisable to pray to the gods of the sea; **necātūrās … aquās** lit., *waters going*
  to kill (**necō -āre**) *[us],* trans. *the waters that will kill [us];* **accipiō -ere** *admit,* i.e.,
  drink in.

Arion and the Dolphin

Ovid's works contain many stories derived from legend and folklore. One such work, his incomplete **Fastī**, *is a poetic discourse on the religious festivals of the Roman calendar and their mythological roots. The following story concerns Arion, an early Greek poet, who, after a successful tour of the Greek cities of southern Italy and Sicily, survives a criminal assault while returning to his native Corinth.*

Nomen Arionium Siculas impleverat urbes,
    captaque erat lyricis Ausonis ora sonis;
inde domum repetens puppem conscendit Arion,   95
    atque ita quaesitas arte ferebat opes.
forsitan, infelix, ventos undasque timebas,
    at tibi nave tua tutius aequor erat;
namque gubernator destricto constitit ense
    ceteraque armata conscia turba manu.   100

TEXT   Ovid *Fasti*, trans. J. G. Frazer, revised G. P. Gould
        (Loeb Classical Library, 1989)
METER   elegiac couplet [§M 2]
        nōměn Ă|rīŏnĭ|ūm ‖ Sĭcŭ|lās īm|plēvěrăt | ūrbēs
        cāptăqu(e) ě|răt lўrĭ|cīs ‖ Aūsŏnĭs | ōră sŏ|nīs

93f.   **Arīonius** adj. of **Arīōn** (see l. 95); **Siculus** adj. of **Sicilia -ae** F. *Sicily;* **impleō -ēre** *fill;* **capta erat** (3 sg. pluperf. ind. pass. **capiō -ere**) *had been captivated;* **lyricīs ... sonīs** instrumental abl. [§G 47], lit., *by the lyrical sounds* (**sonus -ī** M.), trans. *by the sounds of [his] lyre* (**lyricus** adj. of **lyra -ae** F. *lyre*); take **Ausonis** (f. adj. of **Ausonia -ae** F. *Italy*) with **ōra.**

95f.   **inde** *from there;* **repetō -ere** (tr.) *return to;* **puppis puppis** F. *stern* (of a boat), used by synecdoche [§G 98] for *ship;* **conscendō -ere** *board;* **Arīōn Arīonis** M.— the name is Greek, as is the legend; **ita quaesītās arte ... opēs** *wealth won* (**quaerō -ere**) *in this way by [his] skill* (**arte** instrumental abl. [§G 47]).

97   **forsitan** *perhaps;* **infēlix** voc. *O unfortunate [man]*—Ovid is fond of addresses of this sort that break into the story (cf. ll. 101–102 and 106).

98   **tibi** dat. of reference [§G 32] *for you;* **nāve tuā** abl. of comparison [§G 42] *than your ship;* **tūtius** n.sg. compar. of **tūtus** *safe;* **aequor aequoris** N. here *sea.*

99f.   **namque** = **nam; gubernātor gubernātōris** M. *helmsman;* **destrictō ... ense** abl. absolute [§G 49], lit., *sword* (**ensis ensis** M.) *having been drawn* (**destringō -ere**), trans. *with drawn sword;* **-que** (after **cētera**) trans. *together with;* **constitit** (**constō -āre** *take a stand*) agrees with the nearer of its two subjects [§G 58], **gubernātor** and **turba; cētera ... conscia turba** *the rest of the guilty band;* **armātā ... manū** abl. absolute [§G 49], but trans. *with armed* (**armō -āre**) *hands* (sg. for pl. [§G 53])—the meter tells us that the final ā of **armātā** is long and therefore the participle is ablative and is to be taken with **manū** (and not with the nominative **turba**).

quid tibi cum gladio? dubiam rege, navita, puppem:

    non haec sunt digitis arma tenenda tuis.

ille, metu pavidus, "mortem non deprecor" inquit,

    "sed liceat sumpta pauca referre lyra."

dant veniam ridentque moram. capit ille coronam,   105

    quae possit crines, Phoebe, decere tuos;

induerat Tyrio bis tinctam murice pallam:

    reddidit icta suos pollice chorda sonos.

protinus in medias ornatus desilit undas: 111

    spargitur impulsa caerula puppis aqua.

---

101   To render the scene more vivid, Ovid calls on the helmsman (cf. ll. 97 and 106); supply **est** with the question **quid ... gladiō?** *what [business is there] for you* (dat. of reference [§G 32]) *with a sword?*; **dubius** *uncertain*—the ship (**puppem**, as in l. 95) needs to be controlled, hence **rege** (2 sg. imp. act. of **regō -ere** *steer*); **nāvita -ae** M. (= **nauta**) *sailor*.

102   Take **digitīs ... tuīs** (instrumental abl. [§G 47]) with **tenenda** (gerundive used as a predicative adj. [§G 80], lit., *needing to be held*; trans. *your fingers should not be holding this weapon* (pl. for sg. [§G 53]).

103   **ille** i.e., Arion; **metū pavidus** *trembling with fear* (**metū** instrumental abl. [§G 47]); **dēprecor -ārī** *beg to avoid*.

104   **liceat** subj. to express a wish [§G 67] *may it be allowed [to me]*; **sumptā ... lyrā** abl. absolute [§G 49], lit., *lyre having been taken up*; **pauca** n.pl. acc. *a few [tunes]*; **referō -ferre** *repeat*.

105   **dant** historic pres. [§G 60], as are other verbs later in the narrative; **venia -ae** F. *permission*; **rīdent moram** *they laughed at the delay* (**mora -ae** F.); **capit** here *put on*; **corōna -ae** F. *chaplet*.

106   **possit** potential subj. [§G 68] *could*; **crīnēs ... tuōs** trans. *your own hair* (**crīnis crīnis** M.); **Phoebe** voc. of **Phoebus -ī** M. another name for Apollo; **decēre** (pres. inf. of **decet** normally impers. *it adorns*) can be used with a third-person subject.

107   **induerat** pluperf. used for perf. [§G 64] (**induō -ere**) *he put on*; **Tyriō ... pallam** *a cloak* (**palla -ae** F.) *twice* (**bis**) *dipped* (**tingō -ere**) *in Tyrian* (adj. of **Tyrus -ī** F. *Tyre*) *dye* (**mūrex mūricis** M. shellfish found off the coast of Tyre from which a purple dye was extracted).

108   **reddō -ere** *give back*; **icta** perf. pple. of **īciō īcere** *strike*; **suōs ... sonōs** trans. *sounds [all] their own*; **pollice** instrumental abl. [§G 47] *with [his] thumb* (**pollex pollicis** M.); **chorda** (**-ae** F. *string*) sg. for pl. [§G 53].

111   **prōtinus** adv. *immediately*; **in mediās ... undās** *into the middle of the waves*; **ornō -āre** *adorn*; **dēsiliō -īre** *jump down*—beginning with **dēsilit**, the historic present is used exclusively to the end of the selection.

112   **spargō -ere** *splash*; **impulsā ... aquā** instrumental abl. [§G 47] *by the water [when] hit* (**impellō -ere**); **caerula puppis** *the blue ship* (cf. l. 95).

113f.   **inde** *then*; take **fidē** (abl. of comparison [§G 42]) with **maius** (n. compar. of **maior**), lit., *greater than belief*, i.e., *incredible as it sounds*; **tergō ... recurvō** in-

inde (fide maius) tergo delphina recurvo
　se memorant oneri subposuisse novo;
ille, sedens citharamque tenens, pretiumque vehendi　　115
　cantat et aequoreas carmine mulcet aquas.
di pia facta vident: astris delphina recepit
　Iuppiter et stellas iussit habere novem.

~: OVID *Fastī* 2.93–108, 111–118

strumental abl. [§G 47] *with [its] curved back* (**tergum -ī** N.); **delphīna** Greek acc.
sg. of **delphīn delphīnis** M. *dolphin;* **memorant** (*they* (i.e., people) *say* (**memorō
-āre**)) is followed by an acc.+inf. construction [§G 10], **delphīna … sē subposuisse**—**delphīna** is the subject of the infinitive and **sē** is its object; **onerī … novō**
dat. after **subposuisse** (**subpōnō -ere** + acc./dat. *place [something] under [some-
thing]*), lit., *a dolphin to have placed itself under an unfamiliar burden* (**onus oneris**
N.)—the dolphin was unaccustomed to carrying humans.

115f.　**cithara -ae** F. *lyre;* … **-que** (after **pretium**) **et** … lit., *both … and …,* but
trans. simply *and;* **pretium vehendī** is in apposition [§G 52] to the first clause (**cantat**), *[as] payment for being carried* (lit., *of the carrying*—**vehendī** gerund [§G 78]);
cantō -āre *sing;* **aequoreās … aquās** *waters of the sea* (**aequoreus** adj. of **aequor**
(cf. l. 98); **carmine** instrumental abl. [§G 47] *with [his] song;* **mulceō -ēre** *calm.*

117f.　**vident** here take note of; **astrīs** abl. of place where [§G 38], trans. *among the
constellations* (**astrum -ī** N.); **delphīna** Greek acc. (cf. l. 113); **recipiō -ere** here *admit;* **Iuppiter Iovis** M. *Jupiter;* **stella -ae** F. *star;* **iubeō -ēre** here *direct;* **novem**
nine.

Rhapsody in Verse

Although his *Astronomica* contains many striking passages, Marcus
Manilius (see page 157) has found few readers because of his complex
subject and the difficulty of his language. Among those who have
appreciated his succinct and epigrammatic style was the German
polymath Johann Wolfgang von Goethe. Once, during a visit to the
Harz Mountains in Germany, Goethe was deeply moved by the gran-
deur of the scenery and quoted Manilius in a visitors' book:

Quis caelum posset nisi caeli munere nosse
et reperire deum, nisi qui pars ipse deorum est?　　2.115f.
*Who could know heaven except by heaven's gift and discover the
divine (lit., god) except [a person] who is himself part of the gods?*

Ovid's Early Life

This selection is from the account of his life that Ovid wrote in exile.

Sulmo mihi patria est, gelidis uberrimus undis,   3
   milia qui noviens distat ab urbe decem.
editus hic ego sum, nec non, ut tempora noris,   5
   cum cecidit fato consul uterque pari.
nec stirps prima fui: genito sum fratre creatus,   9
   qui tribus ante quater mensibus ortus erat.   10
Lucifer amborum natalibus adfuit idem:
   una celebrata est per duo liba dies.

TEXT   P. Ovidii Nasonis *Tristia*, ed. J. B. Hall (Bibliotheca Teubneriana, 1995)
METER   elegiac couplet [§M2]
     Sūlmŏ mĭ|hī pătrĭ|(a) ēst ‖ gĕlĭ|dīs ū|bērrĭmŭs | ūndīs
     mīlĭă | quī nŏvĭ|ēns ‖ dīstăt ăb | ūrbĕ dĕ|cĕm

3ff. **Sulmo Sulmōnis** M. a town east of Rome in central Italy (modern Sulmona); **patria -ae** F. here *native place*; take **gelidīs … undīs** (abl. of respect [§G46]) with **ūberrimus** (superl. of **ūber** (**ūberis**) to express a very high degree [§G54]), *very rich in cool waters* (**unda -ae** F. *wave*, but often used in poetry as a synonym for **aqua**); **quī** (antecedent **Sulmo**) is postponed [§G4]; **mīlia** *miles* (**mille passuum** lit., *a thousand paces*, the Roman measure for longer distances); **noviens … decem** lit., *nine times ten*—poets often had difficulty in fitting numbers into verse (cf. l. 10); **distō -āre** *be distant*; **urbe** i.e., Rome; **ēditus … sum** 1 sg. perf. ind. pass. **ēdō ēdere** (tr.) *give birth to*; **hīc** adv. *here*; **nec nōn** *and indeed*—in Latin, two negatives cancel each other out; **ut** introduces an adverbial clause of purpose [§G83]; **tempora** pl. for sg. [§G53]; **nōrīs** (= **nōverīs**, 2 sg. perf. subj. act. **noscō -ere** *get to know*) *you may know*—the perfect of **noscō** can have the present sense of *know*.

6   The line establishes the year of Ovid's birth (43 B.C.) by reference to an event in the civil war between Octavius (the future emperor Augustus) and the forces of Brutus and Cassius; **cecidit** 3 sg. perf. ind. act. **cadō -ere** *fall, be killed*; **fātō … parī** abl. of cause [§G48] *by the same* (**pār** (**paris**) lit., *equal*) *fate*; **consul consulis** M. *consul*, the highest Roman political office; the consuls, killed in the battle of Mutina, were C. Vibius Pansa and A. Hirtius, the latter having written the eighth book of Caesar's *dē bellō Gallicō*.

9f. **stirps stirpis** F. *offspring*; **prīmus** *first*; three verbs are used with the meaning *to be born*: **gignō -ere, creor -ārī**, and **orior orīrī** (lit., *rise*); **genitō** (perf. pple. of **gignō**) **frātre** abl. absolute [§G49], trans. *after the birth of my brother*; the antecedent of **quī** is **frātre**; take **tribus … quater mensibus** (abl. of measure of difference [§G43]) with **ante**, lit., *previously by [the measure of] four times three months* (**mensis mensis** M.).

11f. The brothers had the same birthday; **Lūcifer … īdem** *the same Morning Star* (**Lūcifer Lūciferī** M.); **ambō -ōrum** pron. *both*; **nātālibus** abl. of time when [§G37] *at the birthdays* (**nātālis nātālis** M.); **adsum** *be present*; **ūna … dies** *one day*—**dies**, usually M., is here F.; **celebrō -āre** *celebrate*; **lībum -ī** N. *(a kind of) cake*.

protinus excolimur teneri, curaque parentis 15
  imus ad insignes urbis ab arte viros.
frater ad eloquium viridi tendebat ab aevo,
  fortia verbosi natus ad arma fori:
at mihi iam puero caelestia sacra placebant,
  inque suum furtim Musa trahebat opus. 20
saepe pater dixit "studium quid inutile temptas?
  Maeonides nullas ipse reliquit opes."
motus eram dictis, totoque Helicone relicto
  scribere temptabam verba soluta modis:
sponte sua carmen numeros veniebat ad aptos, 25
  et quod temptabam scribere versus erat.

~: OVID *Tristia* 4.10.3–26 (with omissions)

15f. **prōtinus** *from the start*; **excolimur** historic pres. [§G60], 1 pl. pres. ind. pass. **excolō -ere** *educate*; **tenerī** (adj. **tener tenera tenerum** *tender, at a young age*) agrees with the understood subject, *we*; **cūrā** instrumental abl. [§G47] *through the care*; **parens parentis** M./F. here *father*; **īmus** historic pres. [§G60], 1 pl. pres. ind. act. **eō īre** *go*; **insignēs ... ab arte** *noted for* (lit., *from*) [*their*] *ability*.

17 **ēloquium -(i)ī** N. *oratory*; **viridī ... ab aevō** *from a young age* (**aevum -ī** N.); **tendēbat** *was inclined* (**tendō -ere**).

18 **verbōsī ... forī** *of the wordy Forum*—the Forum was the center of the Roman legal world, and the *strong weapons* (**fortia ... arma**) were the skills needed to cope there; a legal career was one of the options open to a young man (cf. Ovid *Amōrēs* 1.15.3ff., page 128).

19f. **mihi ... puerō** dat. after **placēbant** (*used to delight*); **iam** here *still*; **caelestia sacra** *divine rites* (**sacrum -ī** N.)—we learn from the next line that the rites were those of the Muse (**Mūsa -ae** F.) who inspired poetry; take **inque** (= **in** + **-que**) **suum ... opus** together; **furtim** adv. *secretly*; with **trahēbat** supply **mē**.

21 **quid** (*why*) is postponed [§G4]; **studium ... inūtile** *a useless pursuit* (**studium -(i)ī** N.); **temptō -āre** *attempt, try out*.

22 **Maeonidēs -ae** M. another name for Homer, the greatest of poets (cf. Ovid *Amōrēs* 1.15.9f., page 129, and Lucretius *Dē rērum nātūrā* 3.1037, page 24); **nullās ... opēs** *no wealth*.

23 **mōtus eram** 1 sg. pluperf. ind. pass.—the pluperfect expresses a state in the past, lit., *I was in a state of having been moved*, trans. *I was influenced*; **dictīs** instrumental abl. [§G47] *by* [*his*] *words*; **tōtō Helicōne relictō** abl. absolute [§G49]—Mt. Helicon (**Helicōn Helicōnis** M.) in Boeotia was the home of the Muses (cf. l. 4 of Persius' prologue, page 166) and here symbolizes poetry.

24 **verba solūta modīs** *words freed* (**solvō -ere**) *from meters* (**modus -ī** M.; abl. of separation [§G40], pl. for sg. [§G53]), i.e., prose.

25 **sponte suā** *of its own accord*; **carmen carminis** N. here *poetry*; **numerōs ... ad aptōs** *in suitable rhythms* (**numerus -ī** M.)—**ad** here means *in conformity with*.

26 **versus -ūs** M. (*line of*) *verse*.

Pyramus and Thisbe

Many of the tales in Ovid's **Metamorphōsēs** *explain the origin of a characteristic of an animal or plant. The story of Pyramus and Thisbe tells how the fruit of the mulberry tree was changed from white to dark purple. Shakespeare, who would have read Ovid as a schoolboy, took up the story in* A Midsummer Night's Dream, *where it is turned into farce by Bottom and his fellow tradesmen.*

Pyramus et Thisbe, iuvenum pulcherrimus alter, 55
altera, quas Oriens habuit, praelata puellis,
contiguas tenuere domos, ubi dicitur altam
coctilibus muris cinxisse Semiramis urbem.
notitiam primosque gradus vicinia fecit,
tempore crevit amor; taedae quoque iure coissent, 60

TEXT   P. Ovidii Nasonis *Metamorphoses,* ed. W. S. Anderson
(Bibliotheca Teubneriana, 1996)
METER   hexameter [§M 1]
Pȳrămŭs | ēt Thīs|bē ‖ iŭvĕ|nūm pūl|chērrĭmŭs | āltĕr
āltĕră | quās Ŏrĭ|ēns ‖ hăbŭ|ĭt prāe|lātă pŭ|ēllīs

55f.   **Pȳramus -ī** M. the sweetheart of Thisbe, whose name is Greek (**Thisbē Thisbēs** F.); **pulcherrimus** superl. of **pulcher** *most handsome;* **alter, altera** *the one* (Pyramus), *the other* (Thisbe); the antecedent of **quās** is **puellīs; Oriens Orientis** M. *the East;* **praelāta** perf. pple. of **praeferō -ferre** *give preference to someone* (acc.) *over someone else* (dat., here **puellīs**)—the expression *esteemed above the girls whom the East held* simply means that Thisbe was the most beautiful girl in the East.

57f.   **contiguās … domōs** *adjoining houses*—the houses were part of the same building and shared a common wall (l. 66); **tenuēre** (= **tenuērunt**) here *lived in;* the subject of **dīcitur** is **Semiramis** (**Semiramidis** F.), a legendary queen of Babylon (**altam … urbem** [*her*] *lofty city*), which she was supposed to have enclosed (**cingō -ere**) with Babylon's famous brick walls; **coctilibus mūrīs** instrumental abl. [§G 47], lit., *with baked walls,* i.e., with brick walls.

59   **nōtitiam prīmōsque gradūs** lit., *acquaintance* (**nōtitia -ae** F.) *and first steps* (**gradus -ūs** M.) (hendiadys [§G 96]), trans. *the first steps in [their] acquaintance;* **vīcīnia -ae** F. *proximity.*

60   **tempore** abl. of time when [§G 37]; **crēvit** 3 sg. perf. ind. act. **crescō -ere; taedae … iūre** abl. of manner [§G 45], trans. *by right of marriage* (**taeda -ae** F. *pine torch*—used by metonymy [§G 97] for *marriage* (after a Roman marriage ceremony, the bride was escorted in a torch procession to the bridegroom's house (cf. Vergil *Eclogues* 8.29, page 52); here and later, Ovid gives the story a Roman flavor); **coissent** (3 pl. pluperf. subj. act. **coeō coīre**) lit., *they would have come together,* i.e., *they would have been joined*—the subjunctive is potential [§G 68].

sed vetuere patres; quod non potuere vetare,
ex aequo captis ardebant mentibus ambo.
conscius omnis abest; nutu signisque loquuntur,
quoque magis tegitur, tectus magis aestuat ignis.
fissus erat tenui rima, quam duxerat olim, 65
cum fieret, paries domui communis utrique;
id vitium nulli per saecula longa notatum
(quid non sentit amor?) primi vidistis, amantes,
et vocis fecistis iter, tutaeque per illud
murmure blanditiae minimo transire solebant. 70
saepe, ubi constiterant hinc Thisbe, Pyramus illinc,
inque vices fuerat captatus anhelitus oris,
"invide" dicebant "paries, quid amantibus obstas?

61   vetuēre = vetuērunt; the quod clause is in apposition [§G52] to the main
clause, ex ... ambō (l. 62); potuēre = potuērunt.
62   ex aequō *equally*; captīs ... mentibus abl. of manner [§G45] *with hearts* (lit.,
minds) *overcome*; ardeō -ēre *burn*; ambō pl. pron. *both*.
63f.   The four verbs are in the historic present [§G60] and should be translated by
the English simple past tense; conscius ... abest lit., *any* (omnis) *[person] privy*
(conscius *sharing knowledge*) *[to their love] was absent* (absum), i.e., *no one was
privy [to their love]*; nūtū signīsque instrumental abl. [§G47] *with a nod* (nūtus
-ūs M.) *and with signs* (signum -ī N.)—they were presumably limited to sign language until they discovered the crack in the wall (l. 65); quōque (= quō + que)
lit., *and by how much* (abl. of measure of difference [§G43]); the subject of tegitur
(and aestuat) is ignis; tectus perf. pple. of tegō -ere; aestuō -āre *blaze*; trans. *and
the more it was hidden, the more the hidden fire [of love] blazed.*
65f.   The subject of fissus erat (3 sg. pluperf. ind. pass. findō -ere *split*), duxerat,
and fieret is pariēs (parietis M. *wall*) (l. 66); tenuī rīmā instrumental abl. [§G47]
with a narrow crack (rīma -ae F.); duxerat *had formed*; fieret *was being built*; commūnis + dat. *common to, shared by.*
67ff.   id vitium (*that fault*) is the object of vīdistis (l. 68) and is qualified by
notātum (*noticed*; notō -āre); nullī dat. of agent [§G29] *by no one*; sentiō -īre here
perceive; prīmī agrees with the understood subject of vīdistis, *you first*; amantēs
voc.—Ovid addresses the lovers, using a rhetorical trick common in Latin poetry;
vōcis ... iter lit., *a path of voice*, i.e., *a path for [your] voices*; tūtae agrees with blanditiae (blanditia -ae F. *blandishment*), but trans. by an adverb [§G55], *safely*; per
illud i.e., *through the* iter *just mentioned*; murmure ... minimō abl. of manner
[§G45] *in the lowest whisper* (murmur murmuris N.); transeō -īre *cross.*
71f.   consistō -ere *stand* (intr.); hinc ... illinc ... *on this side ... on that side ...*;
in vicēs *in turn*—vicis (gen. sg.) is a defective noun; captō -āre *catch*; anhēlitus
-ūs M. *breath*; trans. ōris (gen. sg. of ōs *mouth*) by a plural [§G53], *of [their] mouths.*
73   invide ... pariēs voc. *O ill-natured wall*; quid *why*; obstō -āre + dat. *stand in the
way of*; amantibus pple. used as a noun.

quantum erat, ut sineres toto nos corpore iungi,
aut, hoc si nimium est, vel ad oscula danda pateres?   75
nec sumus ingrati: tibi nos debere fatemur,
quod datus est verbis ad amicas transitus aures."
Talia diversa nequiquam sede locuti
sub noctem dixere "vale" partique dedere
oscula quisque suae non pervenientia contra.   80
postera nocturnos Aurora removerat ignes,
solque pruinosas radiis siccaverat herbas:
ad solitum coiere locum. tum murmure parvo
multa prius questi statuunt, ut nocte silenti

74   **quantum erat …?** lit., *how big [a thing] was it …?*—the implication is that the
     matter was insignificant, trans. *was it so much …?*; **ut** introduces two noun clauses
     [§G92]; **tōtō … corpore** abl. of manner [§G45] *with [our] whole bodies* (sg. for pl.
     [§G53]); **iungī** pres. pass. inf. of **iungō -ere** *join*.

75   **hoc** i.e., *to embrace*; **sī** is postponed [§G4]; **nimium** n. acc. sg. of **nimius** *too
     much*; **vel** here *merely, just*; **ad oscula danda** lit., *for kisses* (**osculum -ī** N.) *going to
     be given* (gerundive to express a pres. pass. pple. [§G81]), i.e., *for giving kisses*; **pateō**
     -ēre *be open*—the lovers want a hole large enough to allow them to kiss.

76   **nec** *but … not*; **ingrātus** *ungrateful*; **tibi nōs dēbēre** acc.+inf. [§G10] after **fatē-**
     mur, *we admit that we owe to you*.

77   The clause introduced by **quod** (*[the fact] that*) states what the lovers owe to
     the wall; **verbīs** dat. after **datus est**; take **ad amīcās aurēs** (*to loving ears*) after
     transitus (-ūs M. *passage*).

78   **dīversā … sēde** abl. of place where [§G38], lit., *in separate places* (sg. for pl.
     [§G53]), trans. *from [their] separate positions*; take **nēquīquam** (*to no purpose*) with
     locūtī—the lovers were unable to persuade the wall to be more accommodating.

79f. **sub noctem** lit., *just before night*, trans. *at nightfall*; **dixēre** = **dixērunt**; **valē**
     farewell (**valeō -ēre** *be well*); **partī … suae** lit., *to his/her side*, trans. *to his own side
     [of the wall]*; **dedēre** = **dedērunt**; with **oscula** take **nōn pervenientia contrā**, *kisses
     not passing* (**perveniō -īre**) *across*; **quisque** *each*, although singular, is the subject of
     the two plural verbs (agreement according to sense).

81   **postera … Aurōra** *the following dawn* (**Aurōra -ae** F. goddess of the dawn); **noc-**
     turnōs … ignēs lit., *the nightly fires*, i.e., the stars; **removeō -ēre** *remove, banish*.

82   **pruīnōsās … herbās** *the dewy grasses* (**herba -ae** F.); **radiīs** instrumental abl.
     [§G47] *with [its] rays* (**radius -(i)ī** M.); **siccō -āre** *dry*.

83   **ad solitum … locum** *to the usual place*; **coiēre** = **coiērunt**—**coeō** here has its
     literal meaning *meet* (in l. 60 it is used metaphorically); **murmure parvō** cf. l. 70.

84   **prius** adv. *previously*, trans. *first*; **questī** lit., *having complained* (**queror querī**);
     statuunt (**statuō -ere**) *they decided* (historic pres. [§G60]; further examples will
     not be noted); **ut** (*that*) introduces a series of noun clauses [§G92] stating what
     the lovers decided; **nocte silentī** abl. of time when [§G37] *in the quiet night*.

85   Take **fallere** (**fallō -ere** *elude*) and **excēdere** (**excēdō -ere** *go out*) after **temp-**
     tent (**temptō -āre** *attempt*); **foribus** abl. of place from which [§G39], lit., *from*

fallere custodes foribusque excedere temptent,   85
cumque domo exierint, urbis quoque tecta relinquant,
neve sit errandum lato spatiantibus arvo,
conveniant ad busta Nini lateantque sub umbra
arboris: arbor ibi niveis uberrima pomis,
ardua morus, erat, gelido contermina fonti.   90
pacta placent; et lux, tarde discedere visa,
praecipitatur aquis, et aquis nox exit ab isdem:
callida per tenebras versato cardine Thisbe

[*their*] *doors* (**foris foris** F.)—the doors meant are the front entrances of their separate houses.

86   Trans. **domō** (abl. of place from which [§G 39]) *from* [*their*] *homes* (sg. for pl. [§G 53]); **exierint** 3 pl. perf. subj. **exeō exīre** *depart*; **tectum -ī** N. *building*.

87   **nēve** (= **nē** + **-ve**) **sit errandum** negative purpose clause [§G 83] with an impersonal gerundive to express necessity [§G 80], lit., *so that there must not be an aimless wandering*; **lātō ... arvō** abl. of place where [§G 38], lit., *in the broad countryside* (**arvum -ī** N.); [**eīs**] **spatiantibus** dat. of agent [§G 29], lit., *by* [*them*] *roaming* (**spatior -ārī**); trans. the line *and so that they would not be obliged to wander aimlessly as they roamed over the broad countryside*—since the lovers would not be leaving their homes at the same time, they foresee that they might wander about without coming across each other if they did not fix a place to meet.

88   **conveniant** (**conveniō -īre** *meet*) and **lateant** are the verbs of the last two clauses introduced by **ut** in l. 84; **busta** *tomb* (pl. for sg. [§G 53]; **bustum -ī** N.); **Ninus -ī** M. the legendary founder of Nineveh, an ancient city of Mesopotamia.

89   The lovers' decisions end with **arboris**; **niveīs ... pōmīs** abl. of respect [§G 46], but trans. *with snowy fruits* (**pōmum -ī** N.); **ūberrima** superl. of **ūber** (**ūberis**) to express a very high degree [§G 54] *laden*.

90   **ardua mōrus** is in apposition [§G 52] to **arbor** (l. 89), *a tall mulberry tree* (**mōrus -ī** F.); **gelidō ... fontī** dat. after **contermina**, *close to a cool spring* (**fons fontis** M.).

91   **pacta placent** lit., *the arrangements* (**pactum -ī** N.) *are agreed on*; **lux** *the light* [*of the sun*], but trans. *the sun*; **tardē discēdere vīsa** lit., *having seemed* (the passive of **videō** can have the sense of *seem*) *to depart* (**discēdō -ere**) *slowly*.

92   **praecipitātur** *plunged itself* (pass. used in a reflexive sense [§G 59]; **praecipitō -āre**); **aquīs** (before **et**) abl. of place where [§G 38]; take **aquīs** (after **et**) with **ab īsdem**, *from the same waters*—the Mediterranean is almost 500 miles west of Babylon and the lovers could not see the sun disappear into its waters or those of any other sea, but Ovid is thinking as a Roman on the west coast of Italy; **exeō exīre** *come out*.

93   Take **callida** (*careful*) with Thisbe; **tenebrae -ārum** F.PL. *darkness*; **versātō cardine** abl. absolute [§G 49], lit., *hinge* (**cardō cardinis** M.) *having been turned* (**versō -āre**), trans. *the door having been opened*—in opening the front door, Thisbe had to take extreme care to avoid making noise (cf. Propertius *Elegies* 4.8.49, page 114).

egreditur fallitque suos adopertaque vultum
pervenit ad tumulum dictaque sub arbore sedit: 95
audacem faciebat amor. venit ecce recenti
caede leaena boum spumantes oblita rictus
depositura sitim vicini fontis in unda;
quam procul ad lunae radios Babylonia Thisbe
vidit et obscurum timido pede fugit in antrum,   100
dumque fugit, tergo velamina lapsa reliquit.
ut lea saeva sitim multa conpescuit unda,
dum redit in silvas, inventos forte sine ipsa
ore cruentato tenues laniavit amictus.

94f.   **ēgredior -ī** *go out;* **suōs** *her [family];* **adoperta vultum** *lit., covered* (**adoperiō -īre**) *with respect to [her] face* (acc. of respect [§G15]), *trans. with [her] face covered;* **perveniō -īre** *here arrive;* **tumulus -ī** M. *grave;* **dictā ... arbore** *the appointed tree.*

96f.   *Love made [her] bold* (**audax** (**audācis**)); **ecce** *behold!*—the exclamation marks an unexpected development; take **recentī caede ... boum** (lit., *with [its] recent slaughter* (instrumental abl. [§G47]; **caedēs caedis** F.) *of cattle* (**bōs bovis** M./F.)) with **oblita** (*smeared;* **oblinō -ere**); **leaena -ae** F. *lioness;* **spūmantēs ... rictūs** acc. of respect [§G15] after **oblita**, lit., *foaming* (**spūmō -āre**) *open jaws* (pl. for sg. [§G53]; **rictus -ūs** M.); *trans.* **venit ... rictūs** *behold! a lioness came, [its] open jaws smeared [and] dripping from [its] recent slaughter of cattle.*

98   The phrase **dēpositūra sitim** (lit., *going to put down* (**dēpositūra** fut. pple. of **dēpōnō -ere**) *[its] thirst* (**sitis sitis** F.)) tells the purpose of the lioness' arrival, trans. *in order to quench [its] thirst;* **vīcīnī fontis in undā** *in the water of the nearby spring,* i.e., the spring mentioned in l. 90.

99f.   Trans. **quam** (lit., *whom,* antecedent **leaena**) by *it;* **ad lūnae radiōs** *in the moon's rays;* **Babylōnius** *Babylonian;* **obscūrum ... in antrum** *into a dark cave* (**antrum -ī** N.); **timidō pede** abl. of manner [§G45] *with frightened foot.*

101   **dum** is idiomatically followed by the present tense (**fūgit** [§G61]), although the other verbs in the sentence are perfect (**vīdit, fūgit** (l. 100), and **relīquit**)— trans. *while she was fleeing;* **tergō vēlāmina lapsa** *a garment* (pl. for sg. [§G53]; **vēlāmen vēlāminis** N.) *fallen* (**lābor lābī**) *from [her] back* (abl. of place from which [§G39]; **tergum -ī** N.).

102   **ut** + ind. *when*—the verb of the clause governed by **ut** (**conpescuit**) should be translated by the English pluperfect; **lea** = **leaena**; **multā ... undā** instrumental abl. [§G47]) *with much water;* **conpescō -ere** *relieve.*

103f.   **dum** + pres. (as in l. 101), trans. *while it was returning;* **inventōs ... tenuēs ... amictūs** lit., *the discovered light garment* (pl. for sg. [§G53]; **amictus -ūs** M.), but trans. by a separate clause, *it found the light garment and ...;* **forte** *by chance;* **sine ipsā** lit., *without [her] herself,* trans. *without the girl;* **ōre cruentātō** instrumental abl. [§G47] *with [its] blood-stained* (**cruentō -āre**) *mouth;* **laniō -āre** *tear apart.*

serius egressus vestigia vidit in alto   105
pulvere certa ferae totoque expalluit ore
Pyramus; ut vero vestem quoque sanguine tinctam
repperit, "una duos" inquit "nox perdet amantes,
e quibus illa fuit longa dignissima vita;
nostra nocens anima est. ego te, miseranda, peremi,   110
in loca plena metus qui iussi nocte venires
nec prior huc veni. nostrum divellite corpus
et scelerata fero consumite viscera morsu,
o quicumque sub hac habitatis rupe leones!
sed timidi est optare necem." velamina Thisbes   115

105ff.   For dramatic effect, the subject of the first two clauses (**Pȳramus**) is held back until l. 107; **sērius** *later* (compar. of **sērō**); **ēgressus** *having come out* (**ēgredior -ī**), i.e., from Babylon; **vestīgia ... certa ferae** *the unmistakable footprints* (**vestīgium -(i)ī** N.) *of the wild beast* (**fera -ae** F.); **altus** here *deep*; **pulvis pulveris** M. *dust*; **tōtō ... ōre** abl. of place where [§G 38] (**ōs** here *face*); **expallēscō -ere** *turn pale*.

107f.   **ut** + ind. *when*; **vērō** *however*; **vestem ... sanguine tinctam** *the garment stained* (**tingō -ere**) *with blood* (instrumental abl. [§G 47]); **reperiō -īre** *find*; take **ūna** with **nox** and **duōs** with **amantēs** (pple. used as a noun, *lovers*); **perdet** here *will destroy*.

109   The antecedent of **quibus** is **amantēs**; **longā dignissima vītā** *most worthy* (superl. of **dignus** (+ abl.)) *of a long life.*

110   **nostra ... est** *my* (pl. for sg. [§G 53]) *soul is guilty,* but English would more naturally use *I am the guilty one*; **miseranda** voc. f.sg. of the gerundive used as an attributive adj. [§G 79], lit., *O [woman] worthy to be pitied* (**miserō -āre**), trans. *O unhappy girl*; **perimō -ere** *destroy*.

111f.   Two adjectival clauses modify **ego** (l. 110): **in loca ... quī ... venīres** and **nec prior hūc vēnī**; **plēna** is followed by a genitive, **metūs**, *full of fear*; **quī** (postponed [§G 4]) is the subject of **iussī** and **vēnī**; **iussī** is followed by an indirect command (**nocte venīrēs**) without an introductory **ut** [§G 91]; **nocte** abl. of time when [§G 37]; **nec** *and ... not*; **prior** trans by an adverb [§G 55], *first*; **nostrum** pl. for sg. [§G 53]; **dīvellite** 2 pl. imp. of **dīvellō -ere** *tear apart*—Pyramus is appealing to all the lions in the area (cf. l. 114).

113   **scelerāta ... viscera** trans. *[my] guilty flesh* (**viscera viscerum** N.PL. lit., *internal organs of the body*); **ferō ... morsū** instrumental abl. [§G 47] *with cruel bite* (**morsus -ūs** M.); **consūmō -ere** *devour*.

114   Lit., *O whatever* (**quīcumque**) *lions you [are who] live under this cliff* (**rūpēs rūpis** F.), trans. *O all you lions who live under this cliff*.

115   **timidī** gen. of characteristic [§G 19] *[the mark] of a cowardly [person]*; **optāre necem** (*[simply] to pray for death* (**nex necis** F.)) is the subject of **est**—Pyramus wants to move from words to deeds; **vēlāmina** (cf. l. 101) is the object of **tollit** and **fert** in l. 116; **Thisbēs** Greek gen. of **Thisbē**.

tollit et ad pactae secum fert arboris umbram,
utque dedit notae lacrimas, dedit oscula vesti,
"accipe nunc" inquit "nostri quoque sanguinis haustus!"
quoque erat accinctus, demisit in ilia ferrum.
nec mora, ferventi moriens e vulnere traxit   120
et iacuit resupinus humo; cruor emicat alte,
non aliter quam cum vitiato fistula plumbo
scinditur et tenui stridente foramine longas
eiaculatur aquas atque ictibus aera rumpit.
arborei fetus adspergine caedis in atram   125
vertuntur faciem, madefactaque sanguine radix

116   **pactae ... arboris** *of the designated* (**paciscō -ere** *arrange*) *tree;* **sēcum = cum sē.**

117   **ut** + ind. *when*—the verbs of the clauses governed by **ut** (**dedit ... dedit**) should be translated by the English pluperfect; take **nōtae ... vestī** (dat., lit., *to the recognized garment*) with both verbs.

118   **nostrī** pl. for sg. [§G53]; **quŏque** *also*—distinguish from **quōque** in l. 119; **haustūs** *a draft* (pl. for sg. [§G53]; **haustus -ūs** M.).

119   **quōque = quō + que**—the antecedent of **quō** (*with which,* instrumental abl. [§G47]) is **ferrum** (here *sword*); **erat accinctus** 3 sg. pluperf. ind. pass. **accingō -ere** *gird;* **dēmittō -ere** *plunge;* **īlia īlium** N.PL. here *stomach.*

120   **nec mora [erat]** lit., *nor was there delay* (**mora -ae** F.), trans. *and immediately;* **ferventī ... ē vulnere** *from the hot wound*—the wound is hot because of the fresh blood coming from it; the understood object of **traxit** (**trahō -ere** here *withdraw*) is **ferrum** in l. 119.

121   **resupīnus** *lying face upwards,* trans. *on his back;* **humō** abl. of place where [§G38] *on the ground* (**humus -ī** F.); **cruor cruōris** M. *blood;* **ēmicō -āre** *shoot up* (intr.); **altē** adv. *high.*

122   The stream of blood spurting into the air is compared to a burst water pipe— by ancient standards, Roman plumbing was excellent, and lead pipes were used to convey water from aqueducts to points of end use; **non aliter quam cum** lit., *not otherwise than when,* trans. *just as when;* **vitiātō ... plumbō** abl. absolute [§G49], lit., *lead* (**plumbum -ī** N.) *having been damaged* (**vitiō -āre**); **fistula -ae** F. *[water] pipe.*

123f.   **scindō -ere** *split* (tr.); **tenuī strīdente forāmine** abl. of place from which [§G39] *from the small hissing* (**strīdō -ere**) *opening* (**forāmen forāminis** N.); **longās ... aquās** trans. *long [jets of] water;* the subject of both verbs in l. 124 is still **fistula;** **ēiaculor -ārī** *shoot out;* **ictibus** instrumental abl. [§G47] *with [its] spurts* (**ictus -ūs** M. lit., *blow*); **āera** (3 syllables) Greek acc. of **āēr āeris** M. *air;* **rumpit** lit., *breaks,* but trans. *cleaves.*

125f.   **arboreī fētūs** lit., *arboreal* (**arboreus** adj. of **arbor**) *fruits* (**fētus -ūs** M.), trans. *the fruit of the tree;* **adspergine** instrumental abl. [§G47] *with the spray* (**adspergō adsperginis** F.); **caedis** here *blood;* **in ātram ... faciem** *to a dark color*

purpureo tingit pendentia mora colore.
ecce metu nondum posito, ne fallat amantem,
illa redit iuvenemque oculis animoque requirit,
quantaque vitarit narrare pericula gestit;   130
utque locum et visa cognoscit in arbore formam,
sic facit incertam pomi color: haeret, an haec sit.
dum dubitat, tremebunda videt pulsare cruentum
membra solum, retroque pedem tulit oraque buxo
pallidiora gerens exhorruit aequoris instar,   135
quod tremit, exigua cum summum stringitur aura.
sed postquam remorata suos cognovit amores,

(lit., *appearance*); **vertō -ere** here *change*; **madefacta ... rādix** *the root* (**rādix rādīcis** F.) *soaked* (**madefaciō -ere**) *with blood*.

127   **purpureō ... colōre** instrumental abl. [§G 47] *with a purple tint* (**color colōris** M.); **tingō -ere** *stain*; **pendentia mōra** *the hanging* (**pendeō -ēre**) *mulberries* (**mōrum -ī** N.).

128f.   **metū nōndum positō** abl. absolute [§G 49] *[her] fear not yet laid aside*; **nē** introduces a negative purpose clause [§G 83]; **fallō -ere** here *miss*, i.e., not meet up with; **oculīs, animō** (here *heart*) instrumental abl. [§G 47]; **requīrō -ere** *look for*.

130   **quanta ... vītārit** (= **vītāverit**) **... perīcula** indirect question [§G 91] after **narrāre**—the normal prose order would be **quanta perīcula vītārit narrāre**; **gestiō -īre** *desire, long*.

131f.   **ut** (+ ind.) **... sīc ...** (lit., *just as ... so ...*) links parallel clauses without closely specifying the relationship between them—English would translate **ut** by *although* and use no equivalent for **sīc**; **vīsā ... in arbore** lit., *in the tree having been seen*, trans. *of the tree she had [previously] seen*; **cognoscit ... formam** *recognized the shape*; **facit incertam** *made [her] unsure*; **haereō -ēre** (*be uncertain*) is followed by an indirect question [§G 91], **an haec sit** (lit., *whether this was [the tree]*)—**haec** is fem. sg. because it refers to **arbore** (l. 131), trans. *whether this was [the right tree]*.

133ff.   **tremebunda ... membra** (*the trembling limbs*; **membrum -ī** N.) is the subject of **pulsāre** (**pulsō -āre**) *strike*, and its object is **cruentum ... solum** *bloodstained earth* (**solum -ī** N.); **retrō** *backwards*—Thisbe takes a step back in horror at what she sees; **ōra ... gerens** *wearing a face* (pl. for sg. [§G 53]), but trans. *with a face*; **buxō** abl. of comparison [§G 42] after **pallidiōra** (compar. of **pallidus** and agreeing with **ōra**) *paler than boxwood* (**buxus -ī** F.)—boxwood is a pale yellow; **exhorrescō -ēre** *shudder*; **aequor aequoris** N. here *sea*; **instar** indecl. noun (*equivalent, counterpart*) used as a preposition (+ gen.) *in the same way as, like*.

136   The antecedent of **quod** is **aequoris** (l. 135); **tremō -ere** *tremble*; **exiguā ... aurā** instrumental abl. [§G 47] *by a slight breeze* (**aura -ae** F.); **summum [aequor]** lit., *the highest [part of the sea]*, but trans. *its surface*; **stringō -ere** *graze*.

137   **remorāta** (*having delayed*; **remoror -ārī**) agrees with the understood subject of **cognōvit**, *she*, i.e., Thisbe; **suōs amōrēs** pl. for sg. [§G 53] *her love*, i.e., *her beloved*.

percutit indignos claro plangore lacertos
et laniata comas amplexaque corpus amatum
vulnera supplevit lacrimis fletumque cruori   140
miscuit et gelidis in vultibus oscula figens
"Pyrame" clamavit "quis te mihi casus ademit?
Pyrame, responde! tua te carissima Thisbe
nominat; exaudi vultusque attolle iacentes!"
ad nomen Thisbes oculos iam morte gravatos   145
Pyramus erexit visaque recondidit illa.
quae postquam vestemque suam cognovit et ense
vidit ebur vacuum, "tua te manus" inquit "amorque
perdidit, infelix! est et mihi fortis in unum
hoc manus, est et amor: dabit hic in vulnera vires.   150

138 **percutiō -ere** *strike;* **indignōs … lacertōs** *[her] guiltless arms* (**lacertus -ī** M.
lit., *upper arm*); **clārō plangōre** instrumental abl. [§G 47] *with loud beating* (**plangor plangōris** M.)—hitting oneself and tearing one's hair (l. 139) were regular
manifestations of grief in antiquity.

139 Take **comās** (acc. of respect [§G 15]) with **laniāta,** lit., *torn with respect to hair*
(**coma -ae** F.), trans. *with hair torn;* **amplexa** *embracing* (perf. pple. of a deponent
verb used in a present sense [§G 74]; **amplector -ī**).

140f. **suppleō -ēre** *fill;* **lacrimīs** instrumental abl. [§G 47]; **cruōrī** as in l. 121;
miscuit is followed by an accusative (**flētum**) and a dative (**cruōrī**); **gelidīs in
vultibus** *on [his] cold face* (pl. for sg. [§G 53]); **fīgō -ere** *plant.*

142 **clāmō -āre** *shout;* **quis … cāsus** *what misfortune* (**cāsus -ūs** M.); **mihi** dat. of
disadvantage [§G 31], trans. *from me;* **adimō -ere** *take away.*

143 **respondē** (2 sg. imp. of **respondeō -ēre**) *answer [me];* **cārissimus** superl. of
cārus.

144 **nōminō -āre** *call;* **exaudī** 2 sg. imp. of **exaudiō -īre** *listen (to);* **vultūs … iacen-
tēs** pl. for sg. [§G 53] *[your] drooping head;* **attollō -ere** *raise.*

145f. **ad nōmen Thisbēs** (cf. l. 115) *at [the sound of] Thisbe's name;* **oculōs …
gravātōs** (**gravō -āre** *weigh down*) is the object of **ērexit** (**ērigō -ere** *lift*) and **recondidit** (**recondō -ere** here *close again*); **morte** instrumental abl. [§G 47]; **vīsā …
illā** abl. absolute [§G 49], lit., *her having been seen,* trans. *on seeing her.*

147f. Trans. **quae** (antecedent **illā** (l. 146)) *she;* **ense … ebur vacuum** *the ivory*
(**ebur eboris** N.) *[sheath] empty of* (**vacuus** + abl.) *[its] sword* (**ensis ensis** M.).

149f. **perdidit** is singular to agree with the nearer subject [§G 58], **amor** in l. 148;
infēlix voc. *unhappy [one]!;* **est et mihi** lit., *there is for me* (dat. of possessor [§G 30])
too (**et**), trans. *I too have …* —the subject of **est** is **fortis … manus;** **in ūnum hoc**
for this one thing, i.e., *to kill myself;* with **est et amor** supply **mihi;** **hic** i.e., *amor;*
in vulnera trans. *for the blow* (lit., *wounds*).

persequar extinctum letique miserrima dicar
causa comesque tui; quique a me morte revelli
heu sola poteras, poteris nec morte revelli.
hoc tamen amborum verbis estote rogati,
o multum miseri meus illiusque parentes,   155
ut quos certus amor, quos hora novissima iunxit,
conponi tumulo non invideatis eodem.
at tu quae ramis, arbor, miserabile corpus
nunc tegis unius, mox es tectura duorum,
signa tene caedis pullosque et luctibus aptos   160
semper habe fetus, gemini monimenta cruoris."

151ff.   **persequor -ī** *follow*; [**tē**] **extinctum** lit., *[you] having been extinguished* (**ex-tinguō -ere**), trans. *[you] in death*; **dīcar** (1 sg. fut. pass. *I will be called*) is followed by a predicate [§G6], **lētī miserrima … causa comesque tuī** (*the most unfortunate* (superl. of **miser**) *cause and companion* (**comes comitis** M.) *of your death* (**lētum -ī** N.)); the antecedent of **quī** (**quīque** = **quī** + **-que**) is the understood subject of **poteris**, *you*; **morte … sōlā** instrumental abl. [§G47] *by death alone*; **revellō -ere** *tear away* (tr.); **heu** *alas!*; **nec** postponed [§G3]—the verbal play of ll. 152f. is typical of Ovid.

154   Thisbe addresses Pyramus' father and her own; **hoc … estōte rogātī** *be* (2 pl. imp.) *asked this* (retained acc. [§G9]); **ambōrum verbīs** instrumental abl. [§G47] *by the words of both [of us]*.

155   **multum** adv. *very*; **meus illīusque parentēs** a condensed expression for **meus parens illīusque parens**—as the gender of **meus** shows, **parens** (**parentis** M./F.) here means *father*.

156f.   **ut** introduces the indirect petition [§G91] foreshadowed by **hoc** (l. 154); the antecedent of each **quōs** is the understood subject of **conpōnī**, *we*; **hōra novissima** *last* (superl. of **novus**) *hour*; **tumulō … eōdem** abl. of place where [§G38] *in the same grave*; **invideātis** (**invideō -ēre** *refuse*) is followed by an accusative (**nōs** understood) and infinitive (**conpōnī** pres. pass. inf. of **conpōnō -ere** *put together*).

158f.   Thisbe now addresses the mulberry tree; **rāmīs** instrumental abl. [§G47] *with [your] branches* (**rāmus -ī** M.); **arbor** voc.; with **miserābile corpus** (*pitiable corpse*) take **ūnīus** (*of one*, i.e., of Pyramus); **es tectūra** *you are going to cover* (fut. pple. of **tegō -ere**); with **duōrum** supply **corpora** [*the corpses*] *of two*.

160f.   **signa … caedis** *signs of [our] death*—**caedēs** has a different meaning here than it has in l. 97 (*slaughter*) and in ll. 125 and 163 (*blood*); **tenē, habē** 2 sg. imp. *keep, have*; take **pullōs** (**pullus** *dark*) and **aptōs** (**aptus** + dat. *appropriate to*) with **fētūs**; **luctibus** (**luctus -ūs** M. *grief*) dat. after **aptōs**; **geminī monimenta cruōris** is in apposition [§G52] to **fētūs**, [*as*] *a memorial* (pl. for sg. [§G53]; **monimentum -ī** N.) *of [our] double death*—**cruor** has a different meaning here than it has in ll. 121 and 140 (*blood*).

dixit et aptato pectus mucrone sub imum
incubuit ferro, quod adhuc a caede tepebat.
vota tamen tetigere deos, tetigere parentes:
nam color in pomo est, ubi permaturuit, ater,   165
quodque rogis superest, una requiescit in urna.

~: OVID *Metamorphōsēs* 4.55–166

162f.   **aptātō ... mucrōne** abl. absolute [§G 49], lit., *sword tip* (**mucrō mucrōnis**
     M.) *having been positioned* (**aptō -āre**); **pectus ... sub īmum** *under the lowest [part*
     of her] chest; **incubuit ferrō** *she fell on* (**incumbō -ere** + dat.) *the sword*; **adhūc ā**
     caede tepēbat *was still warm* (**tepeō -ēre**) *with blood*.
164   **tetigēre** (= **tetigērunt**; 3 pl. perf. ind. act. **tangō -ere**) here *move* (emotion-
     ally).
165   **permātūrescō -ere** *become fully ripe*; **āter** here *dark*.
166   **quodque** = **quod** + **-que**—the antecedent of **quod** is the understood subject
     of **requiescit**; **rogīs** (**rogus -ī** M. *pyre*) dat. after **superest** (**supersum** + dat. *be left*
     from); **ūnā ... in urnā** *in one urn* (**urna -ae** F.); **requiescō -ere** *rest*—Ovid attrib-
     utes Roman funeral practices (cremation and the use of an urn to store the ashes
     of the dead) to the Babylonians.

LITTERA SCRIPTA MANET ·III·

Among the many stories from mythology and legend that Ovid tells
in his *Metamorphōsēs* is that of Medea. When Jason and his Argonauts arrive in her father's kingdom to claim the Golden Fleece, Medea falls desperately in love with Jason. Torn between love and duty,
she describes her feelings with words that reflect an old dispute over
human motivation. In the fifth century B.C., Socrates had declared
that bad actions are caused by ignorance and that we do not commit
an evil deed if we are fully aware of what is involved. Ovid's Medea is
of the opposite opinion:

video meliora proboque,
deteriora sequor.   *Metamorphōsēs* 7.20f.
I see [what is] better and I approve, [but] I follow [what is] worse.

For a summary of Jason's quest of the Golden Fleece, see page 125. For
a selection from Valerius Flaccus' *Argonautica*, see page 180.

The Folly of Human Desires

Ancient sources provide no information about **Marcus Mānīlius***, the author of a lengthy work on astrology, the* **Astronomica***, but references in the poem show that he wrote in the early part of the first century* A.D.

Although the outward forms of traditional Roman religion were still kept up in imperial times, the Greek philosophical systems, Stoicism and Epicureanism, had replaced traditional beliefs for many of the educated class. One of the principal tenets of Stoicism was the idea of an immutable Fate that determines human life. For some Stoics, such as Manilius, this led to an acceptance of astrology. In the following selection, he tells that, because the course of our lives has already been fixed at the moment of birth, any anxiety we might have about the future is pointless.

Quid tam sollicitis vitam consumimus annis
torquemurque metu caecaque cupidine rerum
aeternisque senes curis, dum quaerimus, aevum
perdimus et nullo votorum fine beati
victuros agimus semper nec vivimus umquam,   5

TEXT   Manilius *Astronomica*, ed. G. P. Gould (Loeb Classical Library, 1977)
METER   hexameter [§M1]
      quīd tām | sōllĭcĭ|tīs ‖ vī|tām cōn|sūmĭmŭs | ānnīs
      tōrquē|mūrquĕ mĕ|tū ‖ cāe|cāquĕ cŭ|pīdĭnĕ | rērŭm

The first eleven lines contain a series of rhetorical questions complaining of the folly of pursuing material goals.

1   **Quid** *why;* **tam sollicitīs ... annīs** abl. of manner [§G45] *in such anxious years;* **vītam** in English we would use the plural *lives;* **cōnsūmō -ere** *spend.*

2   **torquēmur (torqueō -ēre)** *do we torture ourselves* (reflexive use of the passive [§G59]); **metū** and **cupīdine (cupīdō cupīdinis** F. *desire)* instrumental ablatives [§G47]; the latter is *blind* (**caecus**) because it is irrational; **rērum** (lit., *of things)* objective gen. [§G23] with **caecā cupīdine,** trans. *with blind desire for possessions.*

3f.   **aeternīs senēs cūrīs** *[made] old men by ceaseless worries;* **aevum** (**-ī** N. here *life),* the object of **perdimus,** is also the understood object of **quaerimus,** *while we are seeking [it], we lose life*—a paradoxical statement typical of Silver Age poets; Manilius means that by our seeking what we think are the means to live a full life, we are never able to live such a life; **nullō votōrum fīne beātī** *satisfied* (lit., *happy)* *with no end of [our] desires,* i.e., never satisfied when we achieve our immediate desires but always forming fresh ones—the basic meaning of **vōtum** is a vow to give something to a divinity in return for a favor; here and in l. 9, it is used in the broader sense of *desire, wish,* but in l. 21 it has the sense of *prayer.*

5   **victūrōs** (fut. pple. of **vīvō -ere**) used as a noun, *those [who are] going to live;* **agō** here *play the part of;* **nec vīvimus umquam** lit., *nor do we ever [really] live* (i.e., enjoy life to the full).

pauperiorque bonis quisque est, quia plura requirit
nec quod habet numerat, tantum quod non habet optat,
cumque sibi parvos usus natura reposcat
materiam struimus magnae per vota ruinae
luxuriamque lucris emimus luxuque rapinas,   10
et summum census pretium est effundere censum?
solvite, mortales, animos curasque levate
totque supervacuis vitam deplete querellis.
fata regunt orbem, certa stant omnia lege
longaque per certos signantur tempora casus.   15
nascentes morimur, finisque ab origine pendet.

6   **pauperiōr** compar. of **pauper** *poor*; **bonīs** abl. of cause [§G 48] *through [his]
     possessions*; **quisque** *each [person]*; **plūra** (compar. of **multus**) *more things*; **requīrō**
     -ere *want*.
7   **numerō -āre** *count (up)*; **tantum** adv. *only*; **optō -āre** *desire*; to make a strong
     contrast between the two clauses, Manilius omits *sed (but)*—this should be sup-
     plied in English.
8   **cum** here *although*; **ūsūs** (acc. pl. of **ūsus -ūs** M.) *needs*; **reposcō -ere** *demand,
     claim*.
9   **māteriam ... struimus** (**struō -ere** lit., *build*) *do we put together the material*;
     magnae ... ruīnae dat. of result [§G 33] *for a great downfall*; the sense is *through
     [our] desires* (**per vōta**) *we amass wealth, only to see it fall apart*.
10   **lucrīs** (**lucrum -ī** N. *gain*) and **luxū** (**luxus -ūs** M. *luxury*) instrumental abla-
     tives [§G 47]; **emimus** (**emō emere** *buy*) governs **luxuriam** (**luxuria -ae** F. *luxury*)
     and **rapīnās** (**rapīna -ae** F. *act of plundering*); the last words are paradoxical, lit.,
     and [buy] plunderings with [our] luxury, i.e., *through our luxurious living, we bring it
     about that others plunder us*.
11   **censūs** gen. of **census -ūs** M. *wealth*; **effundō -ere** here *squander*.
12   **solvite** (**solvō -ere** *free*) and **levāte** (**levō -āre** *lighten*) are both 2 pl. imp. act.;
     mortālis mortālis M. *human (being), mortal*.
13   Take **tot** (indecl., *so many*) with **supervacuīs** (*pointless*) **querellīs** (**querella -ae**
     F. *complaint*); trans. **vītam** by *lives*, as in l. 1; **dēplēte** (2 pl. imp. act. of **dēpleō -ēre**
     empty, rid [something] of) is followed by an accusative (**vītam**) and an ablative of
     separation [§G 40] (**tot ... querellīs**).
14   **fāta** should be translated by the singular *Fate*; **orbis orbis** M. *world*; **certā ...**
     lēge instrumental abl. [§G 47] *by unchangeable law*; **stant** *stand [fixed]*.
15   **longa ... tempora** *the long ages* (since all time is meant, we should use the defi-
     nite article in English); **signantur** (**signō -āre**) lit., *are stamped* (the metaphor is
     from stamping coins); **per certōs ... cāsūs** is the equivalent of an instrumental
     ablative, lit., *with immutable happenings* (**cāsus -ūs** M.)—Manilius is saying that
     everything that happens throughout time is predetermined.
16   **nascentēs** (**nascor nascī** *be born*) **morimur** another paradox, *we die as we are
     being born*, i.e., at the moment of birth, the time of our death is fixed; **fīnis** *[our]*

hinc et opes et regna fluunt et, saepius orta,
paupertas, artesque datae moresque creatis
et vitia et laudes, damna et compendia rerum.
nemo carere dato poterit nec habere negatum   20
Fortunamve suis invitam prendere votis
aut fugere instantem: sors est sua cuique ferenda.

~: MANILIUS *Astronomica* 4.1–22

---

end; **ab orīgine pendet** lit., *hangs* (**pendeō -ēre**) *from* (i.e., *results from*) *[our] begin-ning* (**orīgō orīginis** F.)—the second clause makes virtually the same point as the first.

17ff. **hinc** *hence, from this [source]* (i.e., *from Fate*); **opēs** (**ops opis** F.) here *wealth*; **regna** (**regnum -ī** N.) *kingdoms*; **fluunt** (**fluō -ere**) *flow*, i.e., *are derived, come*; **saepius** (compar. of **saepe**) *more often*; take **orta** (**orior orīrī** *arise, occur*) with **paupertās** (**paupertātis** F.), lit., *poverty, occurring more often* (the perf. pples. of deponent verbs are often used in a present sense [§G74]), trans. *poverty, which oc-curs more often*; **artēs ... mōrēsque** *skills and characters*; **datae [sunt] ... creātīs** (**creō -āre** *give birth to*) *are given to [people when] born*; **vitia** (**vitium -(i)ī** N.) *faults*; **laudēs** (**laus laudis** F.) here *virtues*; **damna et compendia rērum** *losses* (**damnum -ī** N.) *and gains* (**compendium -(i)ī** N.) *of property*.

20 **careō -ēre** (*lack, be exempt from*) takes the ablative, here **datō** (*[what is] as-signed*); **poterit** fut. of **possum**; **negātum** *[what is] denied*; both the assigning and denying are done by Fate—trans. *no one will [ever] be able to be exempt from [what is] assigned [to him] or to have [what is] denied [to him]*.

21f. The two infinitive phrases introduced by **-ve** and **aut** (both *or*) are governed by **nēmō ... poterit** of l. 20; **invītam** (with **Fortūnam**) *[if she is] unwilling*—for Manilius, Fortune and Fate are one and the same; **suīs ... vōtīs** instrumental abl. [§G47] *with his prayers*; **prendō -ere** *take hold of*; take **instantem** (**instō -āre** here *approach*) with **Fortūnam**; **sors sortis** F. *destiny*; **cuīque** (**quisque** *each*) dat. of agent [§G29] with the gerundive used predicatively [§G80], **ferenda**, lit., *his own destiny must be borne by each*, i.e., *everyone must endure his own destiny*; on this use of **suus**, see §G56.

Of Arms and the Kings

The German military theorist Carl von Clausewitz said that war was diplomacy by other means, but the same sentiment was more cogently expressed by arms manufacturers of the 18th century who inscribed their cannon with the words **Ultima ratio regum**—*The final argument of kings.*

Editing a Latin Text

The advent of printing had an unprecedented, immense effect on editing Latin (and other) texts. Its invention in the middle of the fifteenth century enabled scholars to achieve a standard of accuracy that had previously been impossible. Printers were able to produce identical copies of a book in whatever quantity was required. As a result, readers could be certain that the printed text of a Latin author was, barring the odd typographical error, exactly as the editor had intended. Subsequent editors could be sure that they had before them the text as their predecessor had meant it to be.

In earlier times, readers had been obliged to cope with mistakes that were the inevitable result of the way in which books were produced (see "The Roman Book," page 18). Such errors were often confined to one manuscript, while the original text was preserved in others; sometimes a mistake was even corrected in the faulty manuscript. An example occurs in Propertius *Elegies* 2.12 (see page 110), where one manuscript has the first line as follows.

Quicumque ille fuit, primus qui pinxit Amorem
Whoever it was who first painted Love (i.e., Cupid)

This reading is intelligible as it stands but, if genuine, would mean that Propertius, at the beginning of his poem about Love, does not mention that the god was universally shown as a child despite the allusion to this in line 13 (**puerilis imago**); with **primus**, there is also a clumsy repetition with **primum** in line 3. A reader of this manuscript corrected **primus** to **puerum**, which is also in the other manuscripts. With this revised reading, Propertius is saying that the artist who painted Love as a boy was the first to see that lovers live without judgment (**is primum vidit sine sensu vivere amantes**, l. 3). This makes much more sense than saying that the artist who first painted Love was the first to recognize this flaw in lovers; it is also a neater fit with the rest of the poem.

It often happens, however, that all surviving manuscripts agree in giving a faulty text. This occurs when at some stage in the transmission of a text over the centuries following its composition, only one copy remained in existence and contained an error that was reproduced in the copies made from it. Very occasionally, the true reading survived in a quotation. The following two examples, from Ovid and Juvenal, show how wrong all manuscripts of an author can be.

In a poem composed during his voyage into exile, Ovid explains why he continues to write. The manuscripts have the following two lines.

Seu stupor huic studio sive est insania nomen,
   omnis ab hac cura mens relevata mea est.   *Tristia* 1.11.11f.
Whether folly or madness is the [correct] name for this pursuit
(i.e., writing poetry),
all my mind is lightened by this concern (i.e., for poetry).

The text here appears sound. However, the elegiac couplet is quoted in an inscription where the pentameter is given as follows.

omnis ab hac cura cura levata mea est.
*all my anxiety (***cūra***) is relieved by this concern (***ab hāc cūrā***).*

This new reading illustrates one of Ovid's favorite tricks, the repetition of a word with two different senses; it is obviously correct. The manuscript corruption was caused by the accidental omission of the second **cura**; a later scribe, seeing that **levata … est** lacked a subject to agree with **mea** and that two syllables ($-\smile$) were missing from the line, supplied **mens** and then altered **levata** to **relevata** to fill out the meter.

   In his eighth satire, Juvenal complains of how a consul, who came from an old and distinguished family, demeaned his office by driving a carriage himself instead of leaving such a lowly task to a slave. The manuscripts of the poet give the pertinent lines as follows.

Praeter maiorum cineres atque ossa volucri
carpento rapitur pinguis Lateranus, et ipse,
ipse rotam adstringit multo sufflamine consul.   *Satires* 8.146ff.
Lateranus, the fatso, dashes past the ashes and bones
of [his] ancestors in a swift carriage and he himself,
[yes] himself, a consul, checks the wheel with a long bar.

The third line describes how Lateranus slows down his vehicle by pressing a long bar against one of the wheels. Such a bar might well have been long, but we would have expected it to be described as **longus** rather than **multus**. Fortunately, the original reading has been preserved in an anthology that quotes this passage.

ipse rotam adstringit sufflamine mulio consul.
[yes] himself, a mule-driver consul, checks the wheel with a bar.

This reading not only eliminates the difficulty with **multo** but also provides the phrase **mulio consul**, which is very much in Juvenal's style. It is easy to see how the corruption came about. The word **mulio** was mistakenly copied as **multo**, and a later scribe, seeing that this would given a highly unusual spondee in the fifth foot, normalized the meter by transposing **sufflamine** and **multo**.

In the vast majority of cases, however, where manuscripts present a suspect or obviously wrong reading, there is no other evidence for what the author wrote, and here scholars are obliged to make informed guesses, or conjectures.

When preparing to edit a Latin text, an editor must consult, compare, and assess all surviving manuscripts. If some are merely copies of others, they can be rejected because they simply present the words of the manuscripts from which they were copied as well as their own mistakes. Next, the variations of the remaining manuscripts must be noted. From these variants the editor must decide which, if any, is the original reading, that is, what the author wrote. In what is called a critical edition, important variants are given at the bottom of each page, because the editor, although he has rejected them, thinks that they may possibly be correct or that they illustrate some significant feature of the manuscripts in which they occur. The name given to these footnotes is *critical apparatus*. The following example is taken from Otto Zwierlein's edition of Seneca's tragedy *Trōades* (see pages 169–170).

> **quidquid bis veniens et fugiens lavat,**
> **aetas Pegaseo corripiet gradu.**   385
> **quo bis sena volant sidera turbine,**
> **quo cursu properat volvere saecula**

384 bis … et E: vel … vel A lavat A: labat E   386 quo bis sena A: bis quos s. E volant A: voc- E   387 volvere secula E: s. v. A

> [*whatever [Oceanus], coming and fleeing twice [in a day] washes,*
> *time will sweep away with Pegasean pace. With the same revolution*
> *as the twelve constellations fly, with the same motion as [the lord*
> *of the stars] hastens to bring around periods of time*]

For the sake of brevity, manuscripts are indicated by capital letters, and here E is the designation of a particular manuscript, A that of a combination of several. The reader is left to deduce why the text of a manuscript has been adopted, but the reason is usually obvious.

LINE 384: The manuscript E has the reading **bis … et**, which the editor considers correct and has adopted in the text, while the manuscripts indicated by A have **vel … vel**. The latter makes sense (*whatever [Oceanus], either coming or fleeing, washes*), but the former gives a more precise description of tidal action (*whatever [Oceanus], coming and fleeing twice [in a day], washes*) and so is to be preferred. The last word of the line in A is **lavat** (*washes*), in E **labat** (*totters*); **lavat** makes perfect sense, but **labat** does not; in addition, because **labō -āre** is an intransitive verb, **quidquid** cannot be fitted into the clause as an object or in any other way.

LINE 386: There is a variation in word order between A and E (here and throughout the notes, Latin words are abbreviated) and for A's **quo** E has **quos**, which, as the masculine accusative plural of the relative pronoun, has no antecedent and cannot be fitted into the overall construction. In addition, the word order of A is to be preferred, since an adverb generally comes immediately before the word it qualifies. The variant in E, **vocant** (for **volant**), seems to have been a deliberate alteration to accommodate the corruption of **quo** to **quos** and would give the meaning *whom the twelve constellations call*, which makes no sense.

LINE 387: A interchanges the final two words as they appear in E (**secula** is the normal medieval spelling of **saecula** and is of no importance). The transposition makes no difference in sense, and since **vōlvĕrĕ** has exactly the same metrical value as **saēcŭlă**, no decision can be made on internal grounds. The editor has been forced to choose **volvere saecula** simply because E appears elsewhere to be a superior witness to A.

TWO IMPORTANT SERIES of critical editions are the German *Bibliotheca Teubneriana* and the English *Oxford Classical Texts*; both give the text of an author together with critical apparatus and an account of the manuscripts, but with no explanatory notes. The American *Loeb Classical Library* and its French counterpart, the *Budé* series, have a translation facing the text, as well as explanatory notes and an account of the author; they also have a critical apparatus, but that of the *Loeb* series is confined to the most significant variants.

The Horse and the Wild Boar

Gaius Iūlius *Phaedrus* *(c. 15 B.C.–c. A.D. 50), a freedman of Augustus, wrote fables derived from Aesop and other Greek sources. He presents somewhat banal material in an elegant and concise style.*

Equus sedare solitus quo fuerat sitim,
dum sese aper volutat turbavit vadum.
hinc orta lis est. sonipes iratus fero
auxilium petiit hominis, quem dorso levans
rediit ad hostem laetus. hunc telis eques   5
postquam interfecit, sic locutus traditur:
"Laetor tulisse auxilium me precibus tuis,
nam praedam cepi et didici quam sis utilis."
atque ita coegit frenos invitum pati.

TEXT   Phaedri *Fabulae Aesopiae*, ed. J. P. Postgate (Oxford Classical Texts, 1919)
METER   iambic senarius [§M 8]

  ĕquŭs | sēdā|rĕ ‖ sŏlĭ|tūs quō | fŭĕrāt | sĭtĭm
  dūm sē|s(e) ăpēr | vŏlŭ|tāt ‖ tūr|bāvīt | vădŭm

1 The conjunction introducing the clause, **quō** (*where*), is postponed [§G 4]; **sēdō -āre** *quench*; **solitus ... fuerat** (= **solitus erat**) *had been accustomed*; **sitis sitis** F. *thirst.*

2 The present **volūtat** after **dum** is idiomatic [§G 61]—trans. by a past tense; **sēsē = sē**; **aper aprī** M. *wild boar*; **volūtō -āre** *roll*, trans. (with **sēsē**) *wallow*; **turbō -āre** here *muddy*; **vadum -ī** N. *ford*.

3 **hinc** adv. *from this*, i.e., *because of this*; **līs lītis** F. *quarrel*; **sonipēs sonipedis** M. lit., *hoof-beater*, poetic word for *horse*; **īrātus** *angry*; **ferō** (**ferus -ī** M. *wild animal*) abl. of cause [§G 48].

4f. Take **auxilium ... hominis** together; **petiit = petīvit**; **dorsō** (instrumental abl. [§G 47]; **dorsum -ī** N. *back*); **levans** (**levō -āre** *lift*) agrees with the understood subject of **rediit**, i.e., the horse; **hostem** i.e., the boar; trans. **laetus** by an adverb [§G 55], *happily*; **hunc** i.e., the boar, trans. *the latter*; **tēlīs** pl. for sg. [§G 53], instrumental abl. [§G 47] *with [his] spear*; **eques equitis** M. *horseman*.

6 **postquam** is postponed [§G 4]; **sīc locūtus [esse] trāditur** *he (the horseman) is reported* (**trādō -ere**) *to have spoken thus.*

7 **laetor** (-**ārī** *be glad*) is followed by an acc.+inf. construction [§G 10], **tulisse auxilium mē**, trans. *I am glad that I brought help*; **precibus tuīs** dat., lit., *to your prayers* (**precēs precum** F.PL.), trans. *to you when you asked.*

8 The booty (**praeda**) is the dead boar; **didicī** (1 sg. perf. ind. act. **discō -ere** *learn*) is followed by an indirect question [§G 91]; **quam** *how*.

9 **atque ita** *and so*; **frēnī -ōrum** M.PL. *bridle*; **invītum** (*unwilling*) **[eum]** refers to the horse.

10f. Trans. **maestus** by an adverb [§G 55], *sadly*; **ille** *it [said]*; the conjunction **dum** is postponed [§G 4]; **Parvae vindictam reī** *retribution* (**vindicta -ae** F.) *for* (lit., *of*)

tum maestus ille: "Parvae vindictam rei   10
dum quaero demens, servitutem repperi."
   Haec iracundos admonebit fabula
impune potius laedi quam dedi alteri.

~: PHAEDRUS *Fābulae* 4.4

> *a small matter*; on the present **quaerō,** cf. l. 2; **dēmens** (**dēmentis**) *crazy*, trans. by
> an adverb [§G55], *foolishly*; **servitūs servitūtis** F. *slavery*; **repperī** 1 sg. perf. ind. act.
> **reperiō -īre** *find*.
>
> 12   A moral is typical in the Aesopean type of fable; **Haec ... fābula** *this fable*;
> **īrācundōs** *angry* [*people*].
> 13   The acc.+inf. [§G10] **potius** [**esse**] (*[that] it is better*) governs **impūne ... laedī**
> (*to be harmed without redress*) and **quam dēdī alterī** (*than to surrender oneself to*
> *another*)—**dēdī** (pres. pass. inf. of **dēdō -ere** *surrender*) is used here in a reflexive
> sense [§G59].

A Hexameter for Benjamin Franklin

When Benjamin Franklin was in Paris in the 1780s as ambassador of
his newly independent country, a medal was struck in his honor. On
the obverse side, his portrait was encircled with this Latin hexameter,
attributed to the French statesman Anne-Robert-Jacques Turgot:

Eripuit coelo fulmen sceptrumque tyrannis.
He snatched the lightning bolt from heaven and the scepter
from tyrants.
(**Coelum** is an alternative spelling of **caelum.**)

The references are to Franklin's invention of the lightning rod and the
role he played in the American War of Independence.

   The line was not wholly original, however. It was cleverly modeled
on a line from Manilius. In a passage praising **ratiō** (*human reason*),
the poet says this:

Cur imbres ruerent, ventos quae causa moveret
pervidit, solvitque animis miracula rerum
eripuitque Iovi fulmen viresque tonandi.   *Astronomica* 1.102ff.
It (i.e., human reason) discerned why rains pour down and what
cause sets the winds in motion, and it explained for humanity
(lit., [human] minds) the wonders of the world, and from Jupiter
it snatched the lightning bolt and the power to thunder.

An Atypical Poet

Aulus *Persius* Flaccus (A.D. 34–62) *wrote six satires in the manner of Horace but in a much sharper vein. The following short poem is generally regarded as a prologue to them.*

Nec fonte labra prolui caballino
nec in bicipiti somniasse Parnaso
memini, ut repente sic poeta prodirem.
Heliconidasque pallidamque Pirenen
illis remitto quorum imagines lambunt   5
hederae sequaces; ipse semipaganus
ad sacra vatum carmen adfero nostrum.

TEXT   A. Persi Flacci et D Iuni Iuvenalis *Saturae*, ed. W. V. Clausen
          (Oxford Classical Texts, 1992)
METER   limping iambic [§M 10]
          nēc fŏn|tĕ lāb|ră ‖ prō|lŭī | căbāl|līnō
          nēc īn | bĭcĭpĭ|tī ‖ sōm|nĭās|sĕ Pār|nāsō

1ff.   Persius mocks conventional expressions taken from the traditions of Greek poetry: A poet was supposed to gain inspiration by drinking from the Muses' spring or by sleeping on Mt. Parnassus. **Nec ... nec ...** *neither ... nor ...*; **fonte ... caballīnō** abl. of place where [§G 38] *in the nag's spring*—a derogatory translation of the Greek name **Hippocrēnē** (lit., *horse's fountain*), a spring on Mt. Helicon in Boeotia created by the hoof of the flying horse Pegasus; it was frequented by the Muses and was supposed to inspire poets; **caballīnus** adj. of **caballus -ī** M., a disparaging term for a horse, comparable to English *nag*; **labrum -ī** N. *lip*; **prōluō -ere** *wash thoroughly, douse*; **in bicipitī ... Parnāsō** *on twin-peaked* (**biceps (bicipitis)**) *Parnassus* (**Parnāsus -ī** M.)—Parnassus, the mountain behind Apollo's oracle at Delphi, was associated with poetic inspiration because of the god's own patronage of poets; take **somniasse** (= **somniāvisse**; **somniō -āre** *dream*) with **meminī**; **ut** introduces an adverbial clause of result [§G 84], trans. *so that I should suddenly* (**repente**) *come forth* (**prōdeō -īre**) *in this way [as] a poet.*

4   **Helicōnidas** Greek acc. pl. of **Helicōnides** *the daughters of Mt. Helicon*, i.e., the Muses, who were supposed to live there; **Pīrēnēn** Greek acc. of **Pīrēnē**, a fountain in Corinth also associated with poetic inspiration and supposed to have been created by Pegasus—it is called **pallida** (*pale*) because poets were supposed to be somewhat anemic and colorless.

5   **illīs** (dat.) is the antecedent of **quōrum**; **remittō** (**-ere** *leave*) governs the two accusatives of l. 4; **imāginēs** (**imāgō imāginis** F. *image*) is accusative after **lambunt** (**lambō -ere** *wreathe*)—the **imāginēs** would have been portraits or busts in libraries.

6f.   Trans. **hederae** (subject of **lambunt**; **hedera -ae** F. *ivy*) by sg.—ivy was associated with poets; **sequax** (**sequācis**) *pliant*; **ipse** agrees with the understood subject of **adferō**, viz *I*; **sēmipāgānus -ī** M. *half-peasant*—a **pāgānus** (*peasant*) be-

quis expedivit psittaco suum "chaere"
picamque docuit nostra verba conari?
magister artis ingenique largitor   10
venter, negatas artifex sequi voces.
quod si dolosi spes refulserit nummi,
corvos poetas et poetridas picas
cantare credas Pegaseium nectar.

~: PERSIUS prologue

longed to a **pāgus** (*country community*) that held a festival, the **pāgānālia** (**pāgānā-lium** N.PL.), with contributions from each member; by way of humorous self-deprecation, Persius describes his contribution to a supposed festival (**sacra**) of poets as that of one who is only half-qualified; **vātēs vātis** M. a poetic word for poet, trans. *bard*; **adferō -ferre** *bring*—Persius is bringing his poem (**carmen**) as a peasant would bring his contribution; **nostrum** pl. for sg. [§G 53], trans. *my*.

8   **expediō -īre** *make easy*; **psittacō** dat. of **psittacus -ī** M. *parrot*; **suum "chaere"** (*its "hello"*) is accusative after **expedīvit**—parrots and other birds were kept and taught to speak; **chaere** is the sg. pres. imp. of the Greek verb χαίρω—there was a fashion to teach birds to say this.

9   **pīca -ae** F. *magpie* (a common European bird); **nostra verba** *our words*, i.e., human speech.

10f.   The two lines give the answer to the questions of ll. 8 and 9; **magister artis** *teacher of skill*; **ingenī** alternative gen. of **ingenium -(i)ī** N. *talent*; **largītor largītōris** M. *bestower*; **venter** (**ventris** M. *stomach*) is in apposition [§G 52] to **magister** and **largītor**, and **artifex** (**artificis** M. *expert*) is in apposition to **venter**—Persius uses **venter** to represent greed as the motivation to write poetry (cf. l. 12); **negātās … vōcēs** *forbidden words*—*forbidden* because it is not in the nature of birds to talk; take **sequī** (pres. inf.) with **artifex**, trans. *expert in imitating* (lit., *following*).

12ff.   **quod sī** *moreover if*; **dolōsus** *deceitful*; **refulgeō -ēre** *shine, gleam*, here *appear*; **nummus -ī** M. *money*, here called *deceitful* because it motivates poets to make their audiences think that they are really inspired; in each of the phrases **corvōs poētās** (*raven* (**corvus -ī** M.) *poets*) and **poētridas pīcās** (*magpie poetesses* (Greek **poētris poētridos** F.)), two nouns are juxtaposed as in English—Persius is implying that poets of both sexes resemble mimicking birds in their willingness to perform for material gain; **cantāre** (**cantō -āre** *sing*) is part of the acc.+inf. construction [§G 10] after **crēdās** (the accusative is the nouns in l. 13); the subjunctive is used in the **sī** clause (**refulserit**) and the main clause (**crēdās**) [§G 94], trans. *if the hope … has appeared, you would believe …*; **Pēgasēium nectar** *Pegasean nectar*, acc. after **cantāre**—**nectar** (**nectaris** N.) was normally the drink of the gods, but here **Pēgasēium** (adj. of **Pēgasus**) shows that the waters of the **Hippocrēnē** (see note to l. 1), the drink of the Muses, are meant; *to sing Pegasean nectar* means to write poetry as though inspired by the very drink of the Muses.

Is There Life After Death?

We possess a large body of philosophical writings by **Lūcius Annaeus Seneca** *(c. 2 B.C.–A.D. 65). In addition, ten plays have come down under his name, of which eight—all tragedies—are probably genuine. They were likely intended to be read aloud at* **recitātiōnēs** *(cf. Juvenal Satires 1.1–18, page 202) rather than to be performed on stage. Though modeled on Greek tragedy, the plays exemplify the rhetorical style in vogue at Rome in the first century A.D.*

Seneca's plays were extremely popular in Renaissance Europe and influenced the development of tragedy in most Western countries. After falling from favor in the nineteenth century, they have lately been revived, and amid the upheavals of current times, their exaggerated violence has found sympathetic ears.

The following choral passage is spoken by Trojan women whom the Greeks have captured after the sack of Troy.

Verum est an timidos fabula decipit
umbras corporibus vivere conditis,
cum coniunx oculis imposuit manum
supremusque dies solibus obstitit
et tristis cineres urna coercuit?   375

TEXT   L. Annaei Senecae *Tragoediae*, ed. Otto Zwierlein
(Oxford Classical Texts, 1986)
METER   first Asclepiad [§M 11]
vēr(um) ēst | ān tǐmǐdōs ‖ fābǔlǎ dē|cǐpǐt
ūmbrās | cōrpǒrǐbūs ‖ vīvěrě cōn|dǐtīs

371   **Vērum est an ...** *is it true or ...*; **timidōs** adj. used as a masculine noun, *the fearful*; **fābula -ae** F. here *tale*; **dēcipiō -ere** *deceive*.
372   An acc.+inf. [§G 10] follows the double question of l. 371, **umbrās ... vīvere** *that the Shades* (**umbra -ae** F.) *[of the dead] live [on]*; trans. the abl. absolute [§G 49] **corporibus ... conditīs** (**condō -ere** *bury*) by a clause, *after their bodies have been buried*—there is a slight inconsistency between this and l. 375, which refers to the normal Roman practice of cremation; however, urns with the ashes of the dead were often buried beneath a tombstone.
373   **cum** (*when*) introduces three clauses, all with verbs in the indicative; **imposuit** (**impōnō -ere** *place on*) governs an accusative, **manum**, and a dative, **oculīs**— the dead person's eyelids are being closed.
374   **suprēmus** (*last, final*) agrees with **diēs**, which is masculine here; **sōlibus** dat. after **obstitit** (**obstō -āre**), *has stood in the way of [further] suns*—the plural reflects the fanciful notion that a new sun rises every day.
375   **tristīs cinerēs** (*sad ashes* (**cinis cineris** M.)) is the object of **coercuit** (**coerceō -ēre** *confine*), whose subject is **urna** (**-ae** F. *urn*).

non prodest animam tradere funeri,
sed restat miseris vivere longius?
an toti morimur nullaque pars manet
nostri, cum profugo spiritus halitu
immixtus nebulis cessit in aera   380
et nudum tetigit subdita fax latus?
Quidquid sol oriens, quidquid et occidens
novit, caeruleis Oceanus fretis
quidquid bis veniens et fugiens lavat,
aetas Pegaseo corripiet gradu.   385

376   **nōn prōdest** impers. *is it of no use* (**prōsum prōdesse**); **animam** here *soul*;
trādō -ere *hand over*; **fūnus fūneris** N. here *death*.

377   **restat** impers. *it remains* (**restō -āre**); **miserīs** (dat.) adj. used as a noun, *for
the wretched*; **longius** compar. adv. of **longus**, *longer, further*.

378ff.   **an** (*or*) introduces the alternative to the preceding two lines; trans. **tōtī** by
an adverb [§G 55], *wholly*; take **nostrī** (gen. of **nōs**) with **nulla pars** *no part of us*;
cum + ind. *when*; **profugō ... hālitū** abl. of attendant circumstances [§G 45], trans.
with fleeting breath (**hālitus -ūs** M.); **spīritus** (**-ūs** M. *spirit, soul*) is here the equivalent of **anima**; **immixtus** (**immisceō -ēre**) governs the dative **nebulīs**, *mingled
with the clouds* (**nebula -ae** F.); **cessit** (**cēdō -ere**) *has gone*; **āĕrã** (three syllables)
Greek acc. of **āēr āĕris** M. *air*.

381   **nūdum ... latus** (*naked side*) is the object of **tetigit**, and **subdita** (perf. pple.
of **subdō -ere** *place under*) **fax** (**facis** F. *torch*) is its subject, lit., *the torch, having
been placed under, has touched the naked side* (**latus** here *the side of the upper part of
the human body*, but to avoid ambiguity trans. *corpse*), trans. *the torch has been
placed under and touched the naked corpse.*

382   **Quidquid** (*whatever*) is repeated for emphasis; **sōl oriens ... et occidens**
(**occidō -ere**) *the rising and setting sun.*

383   **nōvit** (**noscō -ere** *get to know*) is a perfect used with a present meaning, trans.
knows; in the next clause, the introductory **quidquid** is postponed [§G 4]; **caeru-
leīs ... fretīs** instrumental abl. [§G 47] *with [its] blue waters* (**fretum -ī** N.); for
Homer and early Greek writers, who thought the earth was flat, **Ōceanus** (**-ī** M.)
was a mighty river that flowed in a circle around Europe, Africa, and Asia, the
only known lands—this view of world geography became traditional in poetry.

384   The phrase **bis veniens et fugiens** (*coming and fleeing twice* (i.e., in a day))
agrees with **Ōceanus** and refers to the action of the tides; **lavat** (*washes*; **lavō -āre**)
has **Ōceanus** as its subject and the preceding **quidquid** as its object.

385   The noun clauses *whatever the sun knows* and *whatever Oceanus washes* are the
object of **aetās ... corripiet** (*time will sweep away* (**corripiō -ere**)); **Pēgaseō ...
gradū** abl. of manner [§G 45] *with Pegasean pace* (**gradus -ūs** M.), i.e., *with the speed
of Pegasus* (a flying horse in Greek mythology).

quo bis sena volant sidera turbine,
quo cursu properat volvere saecula
astrorum dominus, quo properat modo
obliquis Hecate currere flexibus:
hoc omnes petimus fata nec amplius,   390
iuratos superis qui tetigit lacus,
usquam est; ut calidis fumus ab ignibus
vanescit, spatium per breve sordidus,
ut nubes, gravidas quas modo vidimus,

386   In ll. 386–390, Seneca compares the speed with which human life passes to
the passage of various celestial bodies; this is contained in three adjectival clauses
introduced by phrases expressing the speed of the zodiac, the sun, and the moon:
quō ... turbine (*with what revolution* (**turbō turbinis** M.)), **quō cursū** (*with what
motion* (**cursus -ūs** M.)), and **quō ... modō** (*in what way* (**modus -ī** M.)); **bis sēna**
twice six—Roman poets regularly use a periphrasis for larger numbers (here the
distributive **sēnī** *six each* is used instead of the cardinal **sex**); **volō -āre** *fly, move
quickly*; **sīdus sīderis** N. normally *star*, but here *constellation*—the twelve signs of
the zodiac are meant.

387f.   **properō -āre** *hasten*; **volvere saecula** *bring around* (lit., *turn*) *periods of time*
(**saeculum -ī** N.); **astrōrum dominus** *the lord of the stars* (**astrum -ī** N.), i.e., the
sun—Seneca is thinking in terms of Ptolemaic astronomy, according to which the
sun revolves around the earth.

389   Hecatē (**Hecatēs** F.) was another name for the moon, whose course in Ptolemaic astronomy was conceived as swerving to the south, hence **oblīquīs ... flexibus** (abl. of manner [§G 45] *in slanting curves* (**flexus -ūs** M.)).

390ff.   **hōc [modō]** *in this way*, i.e., with similar speed (**hōc** is the antecedent of the
three adjectival clauses); **petimus fāta** lit., *we head for death*—in this sense, **petō**
does not imply a willing search for a goal; **fāta** pl. for sg. [§G 53], here *death, doom*;
nec amplius ... usquam est *nor is [he] any longer* (**amplius**) *anywhere* (**usquam**),
i.e., *nor does he exist any longer in any place*—the understood subject of **est** is the
antecedent of the adjectival clause of l. 391; **iūrātōs superīs ... lacūs** *the lakes*
(**lacus -ūs** M.) *sworn* (**iūrō -āre**) *by the gods* ([**dī**] **superī**—see note to Vergil *Aeneid* 1.4, page 66)—the river Styx is meant, but it is called *lakes* because, like the
other Underworld rivers, it was stagnant, having nowhere to discharge its waters;
the Styx was used by the gods in their oaths, and such an oath could not be broken; **quī** is postponed in its clause [§G 4]; **tetigit** (**tangō -ere**) *has reached*—instead of simply saying *[a person] who has died*, Seneca, rather illogically, uses an
expression that implies the continued existence of his **umbra** in the Underworld.

392   **ut** + ind. here (and in l. 394) introduces a comparison, trans. *as*; **calidīs ... ab
ignibus** *from hot fires*; **fūmus -ī** M. *smoke*.

393   **vānescō -ere** *vanish*; **spatium -iī** N. here *span of time*; **sordidus** lit., *dirty,
grimy*, trans. *of a grimy color*.

arctoi Boreae dissipat impetus: 395
sic hic, quo regimur, spiritus effluet.
post mortem nihil est ipsaque mors nihil,
velocis spatii meta novissima;
spem ponant avidi, solliciti metum:
tempus nos avidum devorat et chaos. 400
mors individua est, noxia corpori
nec parcens animae: Taenara et aspero
regnum sub domino, limen et obsidens
custos non facili Cerberus ostio

394 **nūbēs** (**nūbēs nūbis** F. *cloud*) is here accusative plural and is the object of **dissipat** (l. 395); **gravidās** *swollen* (i.e., with rain); the relative **quās** (antecedent **nūbēs**) is postponed [§G4]; **modo** here an adv., *recently*; **vīdimus** *we have seen*.

395 **arctōī Boreae … impetus** *the blast* (**impetus -ūs** M.) *of northern Boreas* (**Boreās -ae** M. the north wind); **dissipō -āre** *scatter*.

396 **sīc** (*in this way*) introduces the other half of the comparison; **hic … spīritus** *this soul*; **quō regimur** *by which we are governed*; **effluō -ere** *dissolve* (intr.).

397 **ipsa mors** supply **est**.

398 Seneca uses a metaphor from horse racing (**mēta** is in apposition [§G52] to **mors**); **vēlox** (**vēlōcis**) *swift*; **spatium -iī** N. here *racetrack*, but used by metonymy [§G97] for the race itself; **mēta -ae** F. the turning point at either end of a racetrack, *trans. goal*; **novissimus** superl. of **novus**, *last*.

399 **pōnant** (**pōnō -ere**) here *lay aside* (the subjunctive is jussive [§G69]); **avidī** adj. used as a masculine noun, *the greedy*; supply **pōnant** with **sollicitī** (adj. used as a masculine noun, *the worried*).

400 The subject of **dēvorat** (**dēvorō -āre** *swallow up*) is **tempus … et chaos**, but the verb agrees with the nearer noun (**tempus**) [§G58]; **chaos** (**-ī** N.) a Greek noun partly assimilated into the second declension, trans. *primordial matter*.

401 **indīviduus** *indivisible* (death of the body necessarily entails death of the soul—the two cannot be divided); **noxius** + dat. *harmful to*.

402ff. **parcens** pres. pple. of **parcō -ere** (+ dat.) *spare*; in the next sentence supply **sunt** (**Taenara … regnum … custōs … Cerberus** constitute the subject, and **rūmōrēs … verba … fābula** the predicate); **Taenara** (**-ōrum** N.PL.; also **Taenarus -ī** M./F.) *Taenarus*, a promontory in Laconia with a cave leading down to the Underworld (see Vergil *Georgics* 4.467, page 60); **asperō … sub dominō** *under a harsh master* (i.e., **Plūtō**, the king of the Underworld); **līmen** (**līminis** N. *threshold*) is the object of **obsidens** (**obsideō -ēre** *block*); **et** is placed second in its clause [§G3]; **nōn facilī … ostiō** (**ostium -(i)ī** N.) abl. of description [§G44] *with no easy entrance*; **Cerberus** (**-ī** M.) the three-headed dog that guarded the entrance of the Underworld—trans. *the guardian Cerberus blocking the threshold with [its] difficult entrance*.

rumores vacui verbaque inania   405
et par sollicito fabula somnio.
quaeris quo iaceas post obitum loco?
    quo non nata iacent.

~: SENECA *Trōades* 371–408

405f.   **rūmōrēs** (**rūmor rūmōris** M.) **vacuī** *idle* (lit., *empty*) *gossip*; **inānis** *empty*;
take **pār** ((**paris**) + dat. *similar to*) with **fābula**; **sollicitō** (*troubled*) ... **somniō** dat.
after **pār**.

407f.   The indirect question [§G 91] after **quaeris** is introduced by **quō ... locō**
(abl. of place where [§G 38]); **obitus -ūs** M. *death*—the whole sentence is a direct
question, *do you ask ...?*; the half line giving the answer (*where* (lit., *in what [place]*)
[things] not born lie, i.e., nowhere) adds to the dramatic effect.

The Discovery of America Foretold

In a choral ode of his tragedy *Mēdēa*, Seneca describes how navigation, which began with the voyage of the Argonauts, had become
commonplace by his own time and had extended the known world.
He goes on to predict that a new land would someday be discovered
beyond Oceanus, the mighty river presumed to encircle Europe, Asia,
and Africa.

> Venient annis saecula seris,
> quibus Oceanus vincula rerum
> laxet et ingens pateat tellus
> Tethysque novos detegat orbes
> nec sit terris ultima Thule.   *Mēdēa* 375ff.
>
> *Times will come in later years when* (lit., *in which) Oceanus*
> *will loosen the bonds of the world and a huge land will lie*
> *revealed and Tethys will uncover new regions and Thule will*
> *not be the farthest [land] on earth.*

(**Tēthys** was the wife of Oceanus and queen of the seas.
Thūlē was a fabled land in the far north.)

After Columbus' voyages, it was natural that these lines were interpreted as foretelling his discovery of America. In fact, the navigator's
son Ferdinand wrote this in his copy of Seneca:

> Haec prophetia expleta est per patrem meum, Cristoforum
> Colon admirantem, anno 1492.
>
> *This prophecy was fulfilled by my father, Admiral Christopher*
> *Columbus, in the year 1492.*

Pompey and Caesar

The idea of an epic on a historical topic was not new to Latin, but **Marcus Annaeus Lūcānus** (A.D. *39–65*), *known in English as* **Lucan**, *chose a dangerous topic with his* Bellum cīvīle, *a poem on the civil war between Pompey and Julius Caesar that began the final disintegration of republican government in Rome. The following selection, which compares the two opposing leaders, shows Lucan's rhetorical technique, and in particular his mastery of the* **sententia**, *the brief striking phrase or sentence that was the hallmark of Silver Age writers, whether of prose or verse.*

Quis iustius induit arma
scire nefas: magno se iudice quisque tuetur;
victrix causa deis placuit sed victa Catoni.
nec coiere pares. alter vergentibus annis
in senium longoque togae tranquillior usu   130

TEXT   Lucan *The Civil War*, trans. J. D. Duff (Loeb Classical Library, 1928)
METER   hexameter [§M1]
      scīrĕ nĕ|fās māg|nō ‖ sē | iūdĭcĕ | quīsquĕ tŭ|ētŭr
      vīctrīx | cāusă dĕ|īs ‖ plăcŭ|it sēd | vīctă Că|tōnī

126   **iustius** *more rightly* (compar. adv. of **iustē**); **induit arma** *put on* (3 sg. perf. ind. act. **induō -ere**) *arms.*

127   **scīre nefās [est]** *it is wrong to know*—Caesar's victory ultimately led to the establishment of the Julio-Claudian line of emperors, one of whom, Nero, was ruling when the poem was written; Lucan's open criticism of Caesar and his admiration of Pompey were certainly among the reasons why Nero ordered him to commit suicide; **magnō ... iūdice** instrumental abl. [§G47] *with a mighty judge*; **sē ... tuētur** *defends* (**tueor tuērī**) *himself.*

128   **victrix victrīcis** fem. of **victor**, here used as an adj. with **causa**, *victorious*; **deīs** dat. with **placuit** *pleased the gods*; with **victa Catōnī** (dative of **Catō Catōnis** M.) supply **causa placuit**—the meaning is that Caesar had the favor of the gods and so won; Pompey lost but he attracted the support of one of the most respected figures of the day, the younger Cato, who is idealized by Lucan (see the next selection, page 177).

129f.   **coiēre** (= **coiērunt**) *came together [in war]* (**coeō coīre**); **parēs** *[as] equals* (**pār paris** M./F.); **alter** *the one*, i.e., Pompey; **vergentibus annīs in senium** abl. absolute [§G49], lit., *[his] years declining* (**vergō -ere**) *into old age* (**senium -iī** N.)—Pompey at 58 was six years older than Caesar; **longō ... ūsū** instrumental abl. [§G47] *through long use*; **togae** *of the toga* (**toga -ae** F.)—the toga symbolized civil life (Pompey had not been engaged in military activities for some time); **tranquillior** *more peaceful* (compar. of **tranquillus**), i.e., than he otherwise would have been.

dedidicit iam pace ducem, famaeque petitor
multa dare in vulgus, totus popularibus auris
impelli plausuque sui gaudere theatri,
nec reparare novas vires, multumque priori
credere fortunae. stat magni nominis umbra,   135
qualis frugifero quercus sublimis in agro
exuvias veteres populi sacrataque gestans
dona ducum nec iam validis radicibus haerens
pondere fixa suo est, nudosque per aera ramos
effundens trunco, non frondibus, efficit umbram,   140
et quamvis primo nutet casura sub Euro,

131   dēdidicit *he unlearned* (**dēdiscō -ere**), i.e., *he forgot*: **pāce** instrumental abl. [§G 47] *through peace*; **ducem** *[the role of] leader*—extremely condensed expressions of this sort are a feature of Silver Age rhetoric; **petītor petītōris** M. *seeker*.

132   Although we have already had a finite verb (**dēdidicit**), a series of historic infinitives [§G 77] follows: **dare, impellī, gaudēre, reparāre,** and **crēdere; in vulgus** *to the common people*; trans. **tōtus** by an adverb [§G 55], *wholly*; **populāribus aurīs** lit., *by the public* (**populāris**) *breezes* (**aura -ae** F.), trans. *by the breath of popular favor.*

133   **impellī** (pres. pass. inf. of **impellō -ere**) historic inf. [§G 77] *he was swayed*; **plausū** (**plausus -ūs** M. *applause*) abl. with **gaudēre; suī theātrī** *of his own theater* (**theātrum -ī** N.)—Pompey had built the first stone theater in Rome (see the map of Rome on page xxiv).

134f.   **nec reparāre novās vīrēs** lit., *nor did he rebuild* (**reparō -āre**) *new power*, trans. *and he did not acquire fresh power*; **multum** adv. *much*; **priōrī ... fortūnae** dat. with **crēdere** (here *trust*); **stat** (historic pres. [§G 60]) **... umbra** *he stood, the shadow of a mighty name.*

136ff.   **quālis** (*of what sort*) introduces a simile, trans. *just as*; **frūgifer** *fertile*; **quercus -ūs** F. *oak tree*; **sublīmis** *lofty*; **exuviae -ārum** F.PL. *trophies*; **sacrāta ... dōna** *consecrated* (**sacrō -āre**) *gifts*; **gestō -āre** *bear, carry*; *the ancient trophies of a people and the consecrated gifts of leaders are fastened on the old oak tree*—this custom was reserved for oak trees, considered sacred to Jupiter; **nec iam** *but no longer* (**nec** negates **haerens** only); **validīs rādīcibus** instrumental abl. [§G 47] *with strong roots* (**rādix rādīcis** F.); **haereō -ēre** *be firmly attached, cling.*

139f.   **pondere ... suō** instrumental abl. [§G 47] *by its own weight* (**pondus ponderis** N.); **fixa ... est** lit., *has been fixed* (**fīgō -ere**), trans. *is held*; **nūdōs ... rāmōs** *naked branches* (**rāmus -ī** M.)—the old tree has no leaves; **āera** Greek acc. of **āēr āeris** M. *air*; **effundens** (**effundō -ere** here *stretch out, spread*) governs **rāmōs; truncō, nōn frondibus** instrumental ablatives [§G 47] *with [its] trunk* (**truncus -ī** M.), *not with [its] leaves* (**frons frondis** F. *foliage*); **efficiō -ere** *make, create.*

141   **quamvīs** is followed by the subjunctives **nūtet** (**nūtō -āre** *nod, sway*) and **tollant** (**tollō -ere** *raise*); **prīmō ... sub Eurō** *under* (i.e., *due to*) *the first east wind* (**Eurus -ī** M.); **cāsūra** (**cadō -ere**) lit., *going to fall*, trans. by a finite verb, *and is going to fall.*

tot circum silvae firmo se robore tollant
sola tamen colitur. sed non in Caesare tantum
nomen erat nec fama ducis, sed nescia virtus
stare loco, solusque pudor non vincere bello.   145
acer et indomitus, quo spes quoque ira vocasset,
ferre manum et numquam temerando parcere ferro,
successus urguere suos, instare favori
numinis, impellens quidquid sibi summa petenti
obstaret gaudensque viam fecisse ruina,   150
qualiter expressum ventis per nubila fulmen

142ff. There is no conjunction between the first clause introduced by **quamvīs**
and the second, but English requires that we supply *and*; take **tot** (*so many*) with
silvae (here *trees*); **circum** here an adv. *round about*; **firmō … rōbore** instrumental
abl. [§G 47] *with solid growth* (lit., *strength*; **rōbur rōboris** N.); **sē … tollant** lit.,
raise themselves, trans. *rise*; *it alone* (i.e., the old oak tree) *is revered* (**colō -ere**);
tantum adv. *only*; with **nec** supply **tantum erat**; **fāma dūcis** trans. *reputation as a
[military] leader* (**dūcis** possessive gen. [§G 18]); **nescia** *not knowing* agrees with
virtūs and governs **stāre locō**, lit., *vigor not knowing [how] to stand in [one] place*,
trans. *vigor that did not know …*; **sōlus pudor** [**erat**] *his only shame* (**pudor pudōris**
M.) *was*, i.e., *the only thing that caused him shame*; **nōn vincere bellō** (instrumental abl. [§G 47]) *not to conquer by war*—Caesar always won, but he felt shame if he
achieved his ends by peaceful means.

146f. **ācer et indomitus** (*energetic and headstrong*) qualifies the understood subject (Caesar) of the following historic infinitives [§G 77]; **quō spēs quōque** (= quō
+ -que) **īra vocāsset** (= **vocāvisset**) *wherever* (lit., *to wherever*) *hope and wherever
anger had summoned [him]*—the subjunctive **vocāsset** gives the clause a general
sense [§G 88], which is conveyed in English by *wherever*; **ferre manum** = prose
conferre manum, a common expression for joining battle, trans. *fight*; **temerandō**
(gerundive of **temerō -āre** *violate*) **… ferrō** dat. after **parcere** (**parcō -ere** + dat.
spare, refrain from), lit. *refrained from his sword going to be violated*, i.e., *refrained
from violating [his] sword*—Caesar never refrained from using war for unjust purposes (on the use of the gerundive, see §G 81).

148 **successūs … suōs** *his successes* (**successus -ūs** M.); **urg(u)eō -ēre** *press*, i.e.,
make the most of; **īnstō -āre** + dat. *pursue*; **favor favōris** M. *favor, support*.

149ff. Lucan uses the vague term **nūmen** (*divinity*), presumably to imply that Caesar enjoyed the favor of several divine powers; **impellō -ere** here *overcome*; **quidquid … obstāret** *whatever stood in [his] way* (**obstō -āre** + dat.)—**quidquid** and
the use of the subjunctive give the clause a general sense [§G 88]; **sibi summa
petentī** (dat. after **obstāret**) *for him seeking supreme power* (lit., *highest things*);
gaudēns (*rejoicing*) is followed by the infinitive construction **viam fēcisse ruīnā**
(*to make a path by devastation* (**ruīna -ae** F.))—the perfect infinitive is used in a
present sense [§G 76]; **quāliter** (rel. adv.) introduces a simile (see **quālis** in l. 136),
just as; **expressum ventīs per nūbila fulmen** *lightning* (**fulmen fulminis** N.) *driven
forth* (**exprimō -ere**) *by winds through clouds* (**nūbilum -ī** N.)—an allusion to the
theory that lightning was produced by clouds colliding.

aetheris impulsi sonitu mundique fragore
emicuit rupitque diem populosque paventes
terruit obliqua praestringens lumina flamma:
in sua templa furit, nullaque exire vetante   155
materia magnamque cadens magnamque revertens
dat stragem late sparsosque recolligit ignes.

~: LUCAN *Bellum cīvīle* 1.126–157

152   Take **impulsī** (perf. pple. of **impellō -ere**) with **aetheris** (**aethēr aetheris** M.)
      of the smitten sky; **sonitū … fragōre** ablatives of attendant circumstances [§G45]
      with the sound (**sonitus -ūs** M.) *… with the crash* (**fragor fragōris** M.); **mundus -ī**
      M. (here with virtually the same meaning as **aethēr**) *heavens.*
153   The subject of **ēmicuit** (**ēmicō -āre** *flash*) and the following finite verbs is **ful-
      men** in l. 151—trans. **ēmicuit** and **rūpit** (**rumpō -ere** *break*) by the present (the
      perfect is sometimes used for the present in similes); **diēs -ēī** M. here *the light of
      day;* **paveō -ēre** *be frightened.*
154   **terruit** trans. by the present (see the note to l. 153); **oblīquā … flammā** in-
      strumental abl. [§G47] *with [its] zigzag flame;* **praestringō -ere** *dazzle;* **lūmen
      lūminis** N. here *eye.*
155ff.   **sua templa** *its own area [of the sky]* (pl. for sg. [§G53])—**templum** here has
      the sense used by augurs, who divided the sky into various parts (**templa**) and
      made predictions according to where lightning appeared; **furō -ere** *rush;* **nullā
      exīre vetante māteriā** abl. absolute [§G49] *no [solid] matter preventing [it] from
      leaving*—only clouds stood in the way of the lightning when it left its quarter of
      the sky to strike the earth; both when falling and returning (**revertor -ī**), the light-
      ning causes (**dat**) great devastation (**strāgēs strāgis** F.)—**magnam** is repeated for
      emphasis; **lātē** (adv. of **lātus**) *over a wide area;* **sparsōs … ignēs** *[its] scattered*
      (**spargō -ere**) *fires;* **recolligō -ere** *gather up again.*

HORATIANA ·VI·

Tua res agitur paries cum proximus ardet.   *Epistulae* 1.18.84
It's your business when a neighbor's (lit., *the nearest*) *wall is on fire.*

Most people in Rome and other Italian cities lived in adjoining buildings with a common wall (see OVID *Metamorphōsēs* 4.57, page 146,
and 4.66, page 147). Consequently, when a neighbor's house caught
on fire, as frequently happened, it was a matter for serious concern.
(See also PUBLILIUS SYRUS *Sententiae* 670, page 50.)

For more Horatiana, see pages 28, 86, 89, 97, and 100.

Cato at the
Oracle of Jupiter Ammon

After the death of Pompey in 48 B.C., Cato continued fighting in north Africa for the cause of the Senate. In the Bellum cīvīle, Lucan brings Cato to the shrine of Jupiter Ammon, the seat of a famous oracle. Cato's subordinate, La-biēnus, suggests that he consult the god about the nature of virtue, a vital question for Cato, who, as a convinced Stoic, held that virtue was the touch-stone against which all human conduct must be judged. Cato's reply eloquently sets forth Stoic doctrine on the matter and his own opinion of oracles.

Quid quaeri, Labiene, iubes? an liber in armis   566
occubuisse velim potius quam regna videre?
an, sit vita brevis, nil, longane, differat, aetas?
an noceat vis nulla bono fortunaque perdat

TEXT   Lucan *The Civil War*, trans. J. D. Duff (Loeb Classical Library, 1928)
METER   hexameter [§M1]
         quīd quae͞e|rī ‖ Lăbĭ|ēnĕ iŭ|bēs ‖ ān | lībĕr ĭn | ārmīs
         ōccŭbŭ|īssĕ vĕ|līm ‖ pŏtĭ|ūs quām | rēgnă vĭ|dērĕ

566   **Quid** (*what*) is the subject of the passive infinitive **quaerī** (**quaerō -ere** *ask* (a question))—take both words with **iubes**, lit., *what do you order to be asked [by me]?*, i.e., *what do you bid me ask?*; a series of indirect questions follow, with the first three introduced by **an** (here *whether*).
567   **occubuisse** perf. act. inf. of **occumbō -ere** *fall, meet one's death*, but trans. as a pres. act. inf. (a common idiom in Latin verse [§G76]); **velim** (pres. subj. of **volō velle** *wish*), trans. *prefer* because of **potius quam** *rather than*; **regna** pl. for sg. [§G53] (**regnum -ī** N. here *autocratic rule, tyranny*)—Cato is sarcastically referring to the possibility of Caesar becoming sole ruler of the Roman state (which, in fact, happened); trans. the first indirect question as *whether I prefer to fall in arms [as a] free [man] rather than witness* (lit., *see*) *a tyranny?*
568   Normal word order is disrupted in this line, in which an indirect question, **an ... nīl ... differat**, is followed by a double indirect question, **sit vīta brevis ... longane ... aetās**; in prose, we would have **an nīl differat** (**differō -ferre** *make a difference*) [utrum] **vīta brevis sit longane aetās** [sit], lit., *whether it makes no* (**nīl** = **nihil**, here used as an emphatic negative) *difference whether* (**utrum**, which normally introduces the first part of a double question, is omitted) *a life is short or* (**-ne** introduces the second element of the double question) *a life* (**aetās** here has the same meaning as **vīta**) *[is] long?*
569   **noceō** + dat. *harm*; **vīs** here *violence*; **bonō** (dat. after **noceat**) adj. used as a masculine noun, *a virtuous man*; **perdō -ere** *waste*.

opposita virtute minas, laudandaque velle   570
sit satis et numquam successu crescat honestum?
scimus, et hoc nobis non altius inseret Hammon.
haeremus cuncti superis, temploque tacente
nil facimus non sponte dei; nec vocibus ullis
numen eget, dixitque semel nascentibus auctor   575
quidquid scire licet. sterilesne elegit harenas
ut caneret paucis, mersitque hoc pulvere verum,

570   Take **opposită** (**oppōnō -ere** *place in opposition*) with **virtūte** as an ablative
absolute [§G 49], lit., *virtue having been placed in opposition* (viz to Fortune)—according to Stoic doctrine, the virtuous man is self-sufficient and is unaffected by
external violence or chance happenings; **minās** (**minae -ārum** F.PL. *threats*) is the
object of **perdat**; **laudanda** (n.pl. of the gerundive [§G 79] of **laudō -āre**) *[things]*
worthy of praise is the object of **velle** (pres. inf. of **volō** here *desire*).

571   **successū** instrumental abl. [§G 47] *through success* (**successus -ūs** M.); **crescō**
-ere *increase*; **honestum** (adj. used as a neuter noun, *[that which is] honorable*) is a
synonym of **virtūs**—a virtuous person does not become more virtuous through
worldly success.

572   **scīmus** pl. for sg. [§G 53] *I know [the answer to these questions]*; **hoc** i.e., the
answer; **nōbīs** pl. for sg. [§G 53], dat. with **inseret** *in me*; **altius** (comp. adv. of **altē**)
more deeply; **inseret** (3 sg. fut. ind. act. **inserō -ere** (+ acc. and dat.)) *will fix*;
Hammōn Hammōnis M. Latin form of the Egyptian god Ammon, who was
equated with the Roman Jupiter.

573ff.   **haereō -ēre** (+ dat.) *be closely attached to*; **cunctī** *all*; **superīs** (**superī -ōrum**
M.PL. *gods*; see note to Vergil *Aeneid* 1.4, page 66) dat. with **haerēmus**; **templō ...**
tacente (**taceō -ēre** *be silent*) abl. absolute [§G 49], which in this context has a
concessive sense—trans. *[even if] an oracle* (lit., *temple*) *is silent*; **nīl** *nothing*; **sponte**
(a noun that occurs only in the gen. and abl. sg.) **deī** *by the will of the god* (i.e., Jupiter)—Cato says *we do nothing [that is] not in accordance with the will of the god*,
because for a Stoic all human actions are predetermined; take **vōcibus ullīs** (abl.)
with **eget** (**egeō -ēre** *need*); **nūmen** here a synonym of **deus**, trans. *nor does the*
divinity have need of any voices (of oracles and the like); take **semel** (*once and for*
all) with **dixit**; with **nascentibus** (dat. pl. of the pres. pple. of **nascor nascī** *be*
born) supply **nōbīs**, since Cato is speaking here of all humanity, including himself—trans. *[our] creator* (**auctor auctōris** M.) *has once and for all told [us as we are]*
being born.

576   **quidquid** (indef. rel. pron.) *whatever*; **scīre licet** *it is allowed [for us] to know*;
sterilis *barren*; **-ne** introduces a rhetorical question; **ēlēgit** (3 sg. perf. ind. act.
ēligō -ere) *did he choose*; **harēna -ae** F. *sand*—Ammon's temple was on an oasis in
the Libyan desert.

577   **ut** introduces an adverbial clause of purpose [§G 83]; **canō -ere** *sing*—oracles
were given in chanted verse; **paucīs** dat. pl. *to a few*, i.e., only those able to get to
Ammon's temple; **mersit** (3 sg. perf. ind. act. **mergō -ere**) *did he bury*; **hōc pulvere**
abl. of place where [§G 38] (**pulvis pulveris** M. *dust*—a disparaging remark about
the site of the oracle); **vērum -ī** N. *truth*.

estque dei sedes nisi terra et pontus et aer
et caelum et virtus? superos quid quaerimus ultra?
Iuppiter est quodcumque vides, quodcumque moveris.   580
sortilegis egeant dubii semperque futuris
casibus ancipites: me non oracula certum,
sed mors certa facit. pavido fortique cadendum est:
hoc satis est dixisse Iovem.

~: Lucan *Bellum cīvīle* 9.566–584

578f.   **estque deī sēdēs nisi ...?** *is there [any] abode of the god except ...?;* **pontus -ī**
M. *sea;* **āēr** (two syllables) *air*—the Stoics regarded the supreme god, Jupiter, as
immanent in the whole universe (this is stated even more forcefully in the next
line); **superōs quid quaerimus ultrā?** *why do we look for gods further?,* i.e., what is
the point of further investigation?

580   **quodcumque** (indef. pron.) *whatever,* trans. *everything;* **movēris** 2 sg. pres.
ind. pass. **moveō -ēre** *move*—the passive is used here in a reflexive sense [§G59],
you move yourself, you move (intr.), and the preceding **quodcumque** is an accusative of respect [§G15], lit., *in respect to whatever you move yourself,* i.e., *everything
that causes you to act,* a somewhat obscure way of saying again that all human actions are divinely predetermined (cf. l. 574).

581ff.   **sortilegus -ī** M. *soothsayer;* **egeant** jussive subj. [§G69] (**egeō egēre** *need*);
dubiī adj. used as a masculine noun, *the irresolute;* take **semper** with **ancipitēs**
(**anceps (ancipitis)**) *[those] always uncertain,* which is qualified by an ablative of
respect [§G46], **futūrīs** (fut. pple. of **sum**) **cāsibus** (**cāsus -ūs** M.), trans. *let the irresolute and those [who are] always uncertain about future events have a use for* (lit.,
need) *soothsayers;* in the next sentence, the prose order would be **nōn ōrācula sed
mors certa mē certum facit,** i.e., *I am made certain [of the future] not by oracles but
by the certainty of death* (lit., *certain death*)—for Cato, as a Stoic, the only significant future event for any human is death; **facit** agrees with the nearer of its two
subjects [§G58], **ōrācula** (**ōrāculum -i** N. *oracle*) and **mors**; **pavidō** and **fortī** (adjectives used as masculine nouns) are both datives of agent [§G29] with the impersonal gerundive [§G80] **cadendum** (**cadō -ere** here *die*), lit., *there must be a
dying by a timid man and by a brave man,* i.e., *the timid and brave must [both] die.*

584   **Iovem** (acc. of **Iuppiter Iovis** M. *Jupiter*) is the subject of **dixisse** (perf. act.
inf. of **dīcō -ere**) and **hoc** is the object, lit., *that Jupiter has said this is sufficient*
(**satis est**), i.e., *this is all that Jupiter needs to have said [about the future].*

A Pep Talk

Valerius Flaccus was one of the many poets of the Silver Age who retold stories from Greek mythology. The only evidence for when he lived is a reference he makes to the eruption of Vesuvius in A.D. 79. His epic poem, the Argonautica, tells how Jason sailed from Greece with a band of warriors to regain the Golden Fleece, which was in the possession of Aeetes, king of Colchis, on the east coast of the Black Sea.

Valerius owed much to the Greek poet Apollonius Rhodius (fl. 250 B.C.), whose epic of the same name had been translated into Latin by Terentius Varro Atacīnus (b. 82 B.C.). (The Greek poem has survived, but the Latin translation has not.) However, the rhetorical flavor that permeates Valerius' work marks him as a writer of the same mold as those criticized by Juvenal for their pompous regurgitation of Greek myths (see Juvenal Satires 1.1–18, page 202).

The following selection describes how Jason gives his men much-needed encouragement when, on arriving at Colchis by night after an exhausting voyage, they must face unknown dangers in the next stage of their quest.

Tunc defixa solo coetuque intenta silenti
versus ad ora virum "quod pridem ingentibus ausis
optavistis" ait "veterumque quod horruit aetas,
adsumus en tantumque fretis enavimus orbem.   315

TEXT   Valerius Flaccus *Argonautica*, ed. W.-W. Ehlers
       (Bibliotheca Teubneriana, 1980)

METER hexameter [§M1]

       tūnc dē|fīxă sŏ|lō ‖ cōē|tūqu(e) īn|tēntă sĭ|lēntī
       vērsŭs ăd | ōră vĭ|rūm ‖ quōd | prīd(em) īn|gēntĭbŭs | āusīs

312ff.   The understood subject of **ait** (l. 314) is Jason, who is described as **versus ad ōra virum** (= **virōrum** [§G95]), lit., *having turned* (**versus** passive used in a reflexive sense [§G59]) *to the faces of [his] men*; **dēfixa** (**dēfīgō -ere** *fix*) agrees with **ōra** and is followed by **solō** (*on the ground* (abl. of place where [§G38])); trans. **-que** by *or*—*some men were looking at the ground and others were looking around the group*; **intenta** (**intendō -ere** *direct [something]* (acc.) *to [something]* (dat.)) also agrees with **ōra** and is followed by **coetū ... silentī** (*toward the silent group* (**coetus -ūs** M.—**coetū** is an alternative form of the dat. sg. of the fourth declension)—*the silent group is the men themselves*); the two **quod** clauses (ll. 313 and 314) are in apposition [§G52] to the two main clauses in l. 315; **prīdem** *previously*; **ingentibus ausīs optāvistis** i.e., *you wished [would happen] through [your] mighty exploits* (instrumental abl. [§G47]; **ausum -ī** N.); **veterum ... aetās** *the age of past [men]*; **quod** postponed rel. pron. [§G4]; **horreō -ēre** *shudder at* (tr.)—*previous generations had, out of fear, not undertaken any sea travel, and the voyage of the Argo, the vessel of the Argonauts, represented the first attempt at navigation.*

nec pelagi nos mille viae nec fama fefellit
soligenam Aeeten media regnare sub Arcto.
ergo ubi lux altum sparget mare, tecta petenda
urbis et ignoti mens experienda tyranni.
adnuet ipse, reor, neque inexorabile certe   320
quod petimus. sin vero preces et dicta superbus
respuerit, iam nunc animos firmate repulsae
quaque via patriis referamus vellera terris,
stet potius: rebus semper pudor absit in artis."

315   **adsumus** *we are here* (**adsum**), i.e., at Colchis; **ēn** interjection *behold!*; **tantum
... orbem** lit., *the world* (**orbis orbis** M.) *as large [as it is]*; **fretīs** *on the seas* (abl. of
place where [§G38]; **fretum -ī** N.); **ēnō ēnāre** *sail over* (tr.).

316f.   **pelagī ... mille viae** (*the thousand paths of the sea* (**pelagus -ī** N.)) and **fāma**
(here *report*) are the subjects of **fefellit**, which agrees with the nearer subject
[§G58]; the acc.+inf. [§G10] explains **fāma** in l. 316; **sōligena -ae** M. *offspring of the
sun*; **Aeētēn** Greek acc. of **Aeētēs -ae** M., king of Colchis, whose father was the
sun god; **mediā ... sub Arctō** lit., *under the middle of [the constellation of] the Bear*
(**Arctus -ī** F.), trans. *in the farthest north* (the constellation of the Bear is above the
North Pole; cf. Ovid *Tristia* 1.2.29, page 140)—Valerius' geography is badly at
fault, since the east coast of the Black Sea is at much the same latitude as Italy.

318f.   **ergō** *accordingly*; **ubi** *when*; **spargō -ere** here *spread over* (tr.); **tecta petenda
[sunt]** lit., *the buildings* (**tectum -ī** N.) *must be sought* (gerundive used as a predicative adjective [§G80]); **ignōtī mens ... tyrannī** *the attitude* (lit., *mind*) *of the
unknown monarch* (**tyrannus -ī** M.—the word does not always have a negative
connotation); **experienda [est]** lit., *must be put to the test* (gerundive used as a
predicative adjective [§G80]; **experior -īrī**).

320ff.   **adnuet** *he will grant* (**adnuō -ere**) *[our request]*—the Argonauts had come
for the fleece of a golden (and flying) ram that had transported a persecuted
Greek, Phrixus, to Colchis; after sacrificing the ram, Phrixus had presented its
fleece (the Golden Fleece) to Aeetes, but later, when Phrixus was dead, Jason was
ordered to retrieve it; the subject of the **neque** clause is **quod petimus** (*[that]
which we seek*, trans. *what we seek*), and **est** must be supplied; **inexōrābilis** *not to be
obtained by entreaty*; **certē** *certainly*; **sīn vērō** *but if*; **dicta** *[our] words*; **superbus**
agrees with the understood subject, Aeetes—trans. *he, in his pride*; **respuerit** 3 sg.
fut. perf. act. **respuō -ere**, but trans. with the English present tense [§G66], *rejects*;
iam nunc lit., *already now*, but trans. *here and now*; **firmō -āre** *strengthen*; **repulsae**
poetic use of dat. for **ad repulsam**, *to* (i.e., *in the face of*) *a rebuff* (**repulsa -ae** F.).

323   An indirect question [§G91] is introduced by **quā ... viā** (instrumental abl.
[§G47] *by what way*, i.e., *by what means*); **patriīs ... terrīs** dat. of motion toward
[§G35] *to [our] native land* (pl. for sg. [§G53]); **referō -ferre** *bring back*; **vellera**
fleece (pl. for sg. [§G53]; **vellus velleris** N.).

324   **stet potius** lit., *let it rather stand [fixed for us]* (jussive subj. [§G69] used impersonally), trans. *rather let us resolve*; **rēbus ... in artīs** *in difficult* (lit., *tight*) *circumstances*; **pudor** here *scruple*; **absit** (jussive subj. [§G69]; **absum** *be absent*)—
Jason is urging his men to resort to any means to achieve their goal.

dixerat et Scythicam qui se comitentur ad urbem   325
sorte petit numeroque novem ducuntur ab omni.
inde viam, qua Circaei plaga proxima campi,
corripiunt regemque petunt iam luce reducta.

~: VALERIUS FLACCUS *Argonautica* 5.312–328

325   **dixerat** trans. by the English simple past [§G64]; **Scythicam ... ad urbem** *to the Scythian city*—the people to the north and east of Greece were indiscriminately called Scythians; the postponed rel. pron. [§G4] **quī** introduces an adjectival clause of purpose [§G88], with its verb, **comitentur** (**comitor -ārī** *accompany*), in the subjunctive; **sē** (*him*) refers to the subject of the main verb, **petit** (l. 326), i.e., Jason.

326   The verbs of the last three lines are all historic presents [§G60]; the understood object of **sorte petit** is the antecedent of **quī** (l. 325), *he sought by lot [men] who would accompany him*; **numerō ... ab omnī** *from the whole company*; **novem** *nine*.

327f.   **viam** here *road*; with **quā** (instrumental abl. [§G47] *by which*) supply **est**; **Circaeī plaga ... campī** *the land* (**plaga -ae** F.) *of the Circaean plain*, an extreme example of a learned allusion—Circe, the witch of Homer's *Odyssey* who lived on a Mediterranean island, was the niece of Aeetes, and Valerius imagined this relationship sufficient justification to call the king's territory *Circaean*; **proxima** (*closest*) is used predicatively [§G57] after the understood **est**; **corripiō -ere** *hurry over*; **iam lūce reductā** abl. absolute [§G49], lit., *light already having been brought back* (**redūcō -ere**)—dawn had arrived.

VERGILIANA ·III·

When Aeneas finally reaches Italy, his first concern is to consult the Sibylla, a priestess of Apollo, and inquire how he can use a nearby entrance to the Underworld to visit his dead father, Anchises (cf. VERGIL *Aeneid* 6.791ff., page 74). The Sibylla prefaces her not very encouraging reply with this sentence:

Facilis descensus Averno.   *Aeneid* 6.126
The descent to Avernus (i.e., the Underworld) *[is] easy.*

She goes on to say that the real problem is how to return from the abode of the dead. Her initial remark is often misinterpreted, from a Christian perspective, as *The road to Hell is easy.*

For more Vergiliana, see pages 56, 109, 185, and 199.

Insomnia

From **Publius Papinius Stātius** (*c.* A.D. *50–c. 96*) *we possess the* Silvae, *a collection of occasional poems, and two mythological epics, the* Thebaid *and the unfinished* Achilleid.

The subjects of the Silvae *range from the trivial, such as the death of a parrot, to the celebration of a friend's marriage. The following selection shows how a bad bout of insomnia can be set against a mythological background.*

Crimine quo merui iuvenis, placidissime divum,
quove errore miser, donis ut solus egerem,
Somne, tuis? tacet omne pecus volucresque feraeque
et simulant fessos curvata cacumina somnos,
nec trucibus fluviis idem sonus; occidit horror   5
aequoris, et terris maria adclinata quiescunt.
septima iam rediens Phoebe mihi respicit aegras

TEXT   Statius *Silvae*, ed. D. R. Shackleton Bailey (Loeb Classical Library, 2003)
METER   hexameter [§M I]
crīmĭně | quō mĕrŭ|ī ‖ iŭvĕ|nīs plăcĭ|dīssĭmě | dīvŭm
quōv(e) ĕr|rōrě mĭ|sēr ‖ dō|nīs ūt | sōlŭs ĕg|ĕrĕm

1ff.   **Crīmine quō ... quōve** (= **quō** + **-ve**) **errōre** abl. of cause [§G 48] *through what misdeed ... or what mistake* (**error errōris** M.); **merui** *did I deserve*; **iuvenis ... miser** is in apposition [§G 52] to the understood subject of **meruī**; take **placidissime** (superl. of **placidus**) **dīvum** (gen. pl. of **dīvus -ī** M. [§G 95]) and **Somne** (voc.) in l. 3 together, *O Sleep, kindest of the gods*; **ut** (here postponed [§G 4]) introduces a noun clause [§G 92]; **dōnīs ... tuīs** abl. after **egērem** (**egeō egēre** + abl. *lack*); three nouns, **pecus**, **volucrēs** (**volucris volucris** F. *bird*), and **ferae** (**fera -ae** F. *wild beast*), are the subjects of **tacet**, but it agrees with the nearest [§G 58].

4   **simulō -āre** *imitate*; **fessōs ... somnōs** *weary sleep* (pl. for sg. [§G 53]); **curvāta** (**curvō -āre** *bend*) **cacūmina** (**cacūmen cacūminis** N. *top*—trees are probably meant) is the subject of the verb.

5f.   Supply **est** with the first clause; **trucibus** (**trux** (**trucis**) *raging*) **fluviīs** (**fluvius -(i)ī** M. *river*) dat. of possessor [§G 30]; **īdem sonus** (**-ī** M.) *the same sound*—trans. *raging rivers do not have the same sound*; **occidō -ere** here *drop*; **horror aequoris** *the turbulence* (**horror horrōris** M.) *of the sea* (**aequor aequoris** N.); **terrīs** dat. with **adclīnāta** (**adclīnō -āre**), *resting on* (lit., *laid on*) *the lands*; **quiescō -ere** *become quiet*.

7   Lit. (including the first two words of l. 8), *the seventh* (**septimus**) *Phoebe* (i.e., the moon; **Phoebē Phoebēs** F., a Greek noun), *now returning* (**rediens**), *sees that, for me* (**mihi** dat. of disadvantage [§G 31]), *weary eyes* (**gena -ae** F.) *stand out* (**stāre**), i.e., *Phoebe, now returning for the seventh time, sees my staring weary eyes* (**gena** here does not have its usual meaning of *cheek*); **respiciō -ere** (here simply *see*) is followed by an acc.+inf. construction [§G 10]—Statius has apparently been sleepless for a week.

stare genas; totidem Oetaeae Paphiaeque revisunt
lampades et totiens nostros Tithonia questus
praeterit et gelido spargit miserata flagello.   10
unde ego sufficiam? non si mihi lumina mille,
quae sacer alterna tantum statione tenebat
Argus et haud umquam vigilabat corpore toto.
at nunc heu! si aliquis longa sub nocte puellae
brachia nexa tenens ultro te, Somne, repellit,   15

8ff.   Take **totidem** (indecl. adj. *as many*, i.e., seven) with **lampades** (**lampas lampadis** F. *torch*); **Oetaeus** *Oetaean*, adj. of **Oeta**, a mountain in Thessaly traditionally associated with the Evening Star; **Paphius** *Paphian*, adj. of **Paphos**, a city on
Cyprus associated with Venus—*the Oetaean and Paphian torches are the evening
and morning stars* (it was known that both are the planet Venus, but in poetry
they were often regarded as separate stars); with **revīsunt** (**revīsō** -ere *visit again*)
supply **mē**; **totiens** adv. *as many times, as often*; **nostrōs** (pl. for sg. [§G53]) ...
questūs (*my complaints* (**questus** -ūs M.)) is the object of **praeterit** (**praetereō**
-īre *pass by*); **Tīthōnia** -ae F. the wife of **Tīthōnus**, i.e., **Aurōra**, the goddess of the
dawn; **gelidō ... flagellō** instrumental abl. [§G47] *with [her] cold whip* (**flagellum**
-ī N.); with **spargit** (**spargō** -ere *sprinkle*) supply **mē**; **miserāta** (**miseror** -ārī) *pitying [me]* (the perfect participle of a deponent verb may be used in a present sense
[§G74])—the cold whip is the morning dew; such heavy-handed use of mythology is typical of much of Silver Age poetry.

11ff.   **unde ego sufficiam?** *how am I to manage?* (deliberative subj. [§G70]; **sufficiō**
-ere); **nōn** i.e., *[I could] not [manage]*; with **sī mihi** (dat. of possessor [§G30])
lūmina (**lūmen lūminis** N. here *eye*) **mille** (indecl. adj. *thousand*) supply **essent**,
lit., *if [there were] to me the thousand eyes*, i.e., *if I had the thousand eyes* (*the* because
of what follows); **sacer ... Argus** *sacred Argos*, a man endowed with prodigious
eyesight who was appointed by Juno (hence the epithet **sacer**) to watch over the
maiden **Īō**, a love interest of Jupiter; Argos performed his duty by keeping 500
eyes awake and 500 asleep, as Statius explains in **quae ... alternā tantum statiōne
tenēbat** *that Argos kept only in alternating guard duty*; **alternā ... statiōne** (**statiō
statiōnis** F.) abl. of manner [§G45]—the number of Argos' eyes differs in other
authors; **haud umquam** (= **numquam**) trans. *never*; **vigilō** -āre *be awake*; **corpore
tōtō** abl. of respect [§G46] *with [his] whole body*—the implication is that if even
Argos was only half awake, Statius cannot be expected to be wholly so.

14f.   Statius' ingenious solution to his insomnia is that the god Sleep should come
to him from some lover who wants to stay awake with his girlfriend; **heu** interjection *alas!*; **longā sub nocte** *during the long night*; **brachium** -(i)ī N. *arm*; **nexus**
perf. pple. of **nectō** -ere *twine together, join*; **tenens** governs **brachia**—trans. *holding his girl's arms, [which are] joined [to his]*; **repellit** (**repellō** -ere *drive away*) governs **tē**; **ultrō** adv. *of his own accord*.

16f.   **inde venī** (2 sg. imp.) *come from there!*, i.e., from the lover to me—the lover
wants, of course, to ward off sleep; **compellō** (l. 17) is followed by an acc.+inf.
construction [§G10], **tē ... infundere ...**; **infundō** -ere (+ acc. and dat.) *pour*

inde veni; nec te totas infundere pennas
luminibus compello meis (hoc turba precetur
laetior); extremo me tange cacumine virgae
(sufficit), aut leviter suspenso poplite transi.

~: STATIUS *Silvae* 5.4

[something] over [something]—tē is the subject and **pennās** (**penna -ae** F. *wing*) the
object of **infundere**; **lūminibus … meīs** dat.; **compellō -ere** lit., *force*—trans. *nor
do I insist that you spread the whole of [your] wings over my eyes.*

17f.　**turba … laetior** *a more fortunate crowd*, i.e., people more fortunate than Statius; **precētur** jussive subj. [§G 69] (**precor -ārī** (tr.) *pray for*); **extrēmō … cacū-
mine virgae** instrumental abl. [§G 47] *with the very* (**extrēmus** lit., *farthest*) *tip*
(**cacūmen cacūminis** N.) *of [your] wand* (**virga -ae** F.).

19　**sufficit** [*that*] *is enough* (**sufficiō -ere**); take **leviter** with **transī** (2 sg. imp. of
transeō -īre) *lightly pass over* [*me*]; **suspensō poplite** abl. of manner [§G 45] *with
[your] hovering* (**suspendō -ere** lit., *hang over*) *knee* (**poples poplitis** M.)—Sleep is
conceived as flying over Statius.

VERGILIANA ·IV·

When Aeneas is making his way down to the Underworld, he finds a
vast horde of the recent dead waiting on the banks of the Styx to be
ferried across by Charon. In their eagerness to cross, they beg the god
to take them:

> Stabant orantes primi transmittere cursum
> tendebantque manus ripae ulterioris amore.　　*Aeneid* 6.313f.
> *They stood begging to make the crossing (lit., to cross
> the passage) first, and they stretched out [their] hands
> in yearning for the opposite shore.*

The divine ferryman, however, is pitiless in his choice, and those
whose bodies remain unburied in the world above must wait a hundred years before crossing.

For more Vergiliana, see pages 56, 109, 182, and 199.

Scipio and Syphax

The Pūnica of Sīlius Italicus (c. A.D. 26–c. 102), the longest surviving poem in Latin (more than 12,000 lines), is a verse account of the Second Carthaginian War (218–201 B.C.). It describes how Hannibal, after many years of successful campaigning in Italy, was forced to return to defend Carthage and was finally defeated by Scipio Africanus (see note to Lucretius Dē rērum nātūrā 3.1034, page 23).

Silius faced problems similar to those of a modern poet writing a conventional epic on the Napoleonic wars. His methods for coping with these, which include introducing gods in the same way as Vergil did in the Aeneid, were not as successful as those of his predecessor Lucan. The highest praise usually accorded him is that he sometimes rises above the mediocre.

The following selection, from the account of Scipio's mission to gain the support of Syphax, king of the Massyli in northern Africa, shows how Silius gives a poetic gloss to a historical event.

Iamque novum terris pariebat limine primo
egrediens Aurora diem, stabulisque subibant   230
ad iuga solis equi, necdum ipse ascenderat axem,
sed prorupturis rutilabant aequora flammis:

TEXT   Silius Italicus *Punica*, ed. J. D. Duff (Loeb Classical Library, 1934)
METER   hexameter [§M1]

    iāmquĕ nŏ|vūm tēr|rīs ‖ părĭ|ēbāt | līmĭnĕ | prīmō
    ēgrĕdĭ|ēns Aū|rōră dĭ|ēm ‖ stăbŭ|līsquĕ sŭb|ībānt

229ff.   **novum ... diem** is the object of **pariebat**; **terrīs** dat. pl. *for the world*; take **līmine prīmō** (abl. of place from which [§G39]) with **ēgrediens** (**ēgredior -ī**), *going out from the edge of her threshold* (lit., *from the first [part of her] threshold*; **līmen līminis** N.); **Aurōra -ae** F. the goddess of the dawn; **stabulīs** abl. of place where [§G38] *in [their] stables* (**stabulum -ī** N.); *the sun's horses* (**sōlis equī**) *were going up* (**subeō -īre**) *to [their] yokes* (**iugum -ī** N.)—in mythology, the sun was a god who drove his horses and chariot across the heavens every day; a yoke was a pole fastened over the necks of two horses and attached to a vehicle; **necdum** *and not yet*; **ipse** i.e., the sun; **ascendō -ere** *mount*; the basic meaning of **axis** (**axis** M.) is *axle*, hence, by metonymy [§G97], *a chariot*.

232   **prōruptūrīs** (fut. pple. of **prōrumpō -ere**) **flammīs** abl. of cause [§G48], lit., *with flames about to burst forth*, i.e., *with flames that would soon burst forth*; **aequora** (pl. for sg. [§G53]; **aequor aequoris** N. *sea*) is the subject of **rutilābant** (**rutilō -āre** *glow red*).

233f.   The subject of the two verbs in the historic present [§G60], **exigit** (**exigō -ere** *remove*) and **contendit** (**contendō -ere** *go quickly*), is **Scīpio**; **ē strātīs** *from [his] bed* (pl. for sg. [§G53]; **strātum -ī** N.)—note how Silius here uses **ē** + ablative

exigit e stratis corpus vultuque sereno
Scipio contendit Massyli ad limina regis.
illi mos patrius fetus nutrire leonum   235
et catulis rabiem atque iras expellere alendo.
tum quoque fulva manu mulcebat colla iubasque
et fera tractabat ludentum interritus ora.
Dardanium postquam ductorem accepit adesse,
induitur chlamydem, regnique insigne vetusti   240
gestat laeva decus. cinguntur tempora vitta
albente, ac lateri de more adstringitur ensis.
hinc in tecta vocat, secretisque aedibus hospes

to express place from which, whereas four lines earlier he uses the plain ablative (such variation is common in Latin poetry); the body (**corpus**) is that of Scipio; **vultū serēnō** abl. of manner [§G45] *with a calm face;* **Massȳlī ... rēgis** *of the Massylian king;* **līmina** pl. for sg. [§G53].

235   Take **illī** (i.e., Syphax; dat. of possessor [§G30]) with **mōs patrius** and supply **erat**, lit., *there was to him ...,* i.e., *he observed the native custom;* **fētūs nutrīre leōnum** *of rearing* (lit., *to rear;* **nutriō -īre**) *the offspring* (**fētus -ūs** M.; English uses the collective singular for the Latin plural) *of lions* (**leō leōnis** M.).

236   **catulīs** abl. of separation [§G40] (**catulus -ī** M., here *cub*); **rabiēs -ēī** F. *ferocity;* **īrās** pl. for sg. [§G53], trans. *rage;* **expellō -ere** *drive away;* **alendō** instrumental abl. [§G47] of the gerund [§G78] of **alō alere** *feed.*

237   **fulva ... colla** *tawny necks* (**collum -ī** N.); **manū** instrumental abl. [§G47]; **mulceō -ēre** *caress;* **iuba -ae** F. *mane.*

238   **fera ... lūdentum ... ōra** *the wild mouths of the playing [animals];* **tractō -āre** *stroke;* **interritus** *unafraid.*

239   **Dardanium ... ductōrem ... adesse** acc.+inf. [§G10] *that the Dardanian leader* (**ductor ductōris** M.) *was present* (**adsum**)—*Dardanian* (= Trojan = Roman) is a learned epithet used here by Silius to confer a poetic flavor; **postquam** postponed conj. [§G4]; **accēpit** here *he heard.*

240ff.   **induitur** *he put on* (historic pres. [§G60]—further examples will not be pointed out; **induō -ere**)—the passive can be used for an action performed on oneself [§G59 and §G15]; **chlamys chlamydis** F. *cloak;* **regnī ... vetustī** *of the ancient kingdom;* **insigne ... decus** *distinguished symbol* (**decus decoris** N.)—this would have been a scepter or something of the sort); **gestat laeva [manus]** *his left [hand] carried* (**gestō -āre**); **cingō -ere** *encircle;* **tempora** (**tempus temporis** N.) here *temples* (of the head); **vittā albente** instrumental abl. [§G47] *with a white* (**albens (albentis)**) *headband* (**vitta -ae** F.); take **laterī** (dat.) with **adstringitur** (**adstringō -ere**), *was fastened to [his] side;* **dē mōre** *according to custom;* **ensis ensis** M. *sword.*

243   **hinc** here *then, next;* **tecta** pl. for sg. [§G53] *building* (**tectum -ī** N.); with **vocat** supply **eum** (*him*), i.e., Scipio; **sēcrētīs ... aedibus** abl. of place where [§G38] *in secluded rooms* (**aedēs aedis** F.); **hospes hospitis** M. here *guest.*

sceptrifero cum rege pari sub honore residunt.
tum prior his infit terrae pacator Hiberae: 245
"Prima mihi, domitis Pyrenes gentibus, ire
ad tua regna fuit properantem et maxima cura,
o sceptri venerande Syphax, nec me aequore saevus
tardavit medio pontus. non ardua regnis
quaesumus aut inhonora tuis: coniunge Latinis   250
unanimum pectus sociusque accede secundis.
non tibi Massylae gentes extentaque tellus
Syrtibus et latis proavita potentia campis

244   **sceptrifer** *scepter-bearing;* **parī sub honōre** *in equal honor;* **resīdō -ere** *sit down*—the pl. **resīdunt** agrees according to sense (the two sat down), not according to strict grammar (the subject is singular, viz **hospes**).

245   **prior** *first;* **hīs** instrumental abl. [§G 47] *with these [words];* **infit** *begins to speak* (no other form of this verb occurs); **terrae ... Hibērae** *of the Spanish land;* **pācātor pācātōris** M. *subduer.*

246f.   **Prīma ... et maxima cūra** (*the first and greatest concern*) is the subject of the clause and is followed by **mihi ... īre ... fuit** *was for me to go;* **domitīs Pyrēnēs gentibus** abl. absolute [§G 49], trans. *after conquering* (**domō -āre**) *the peoples of the Pyrenees* (**Pyrēnē Pyrēnēs** F. a Greek word); **regna** pl. for sg. [§G 53]; **properantem** (*hurrying;* **properō -āre**) is accusative as though Silius had written **mē** as the subject of **īre** (another agreement according to sense rather than strict grammar).

248f.   **sceptrī** (gen. of respect [§G 22]; **sceptrum -ī** N. *scepter*) goes with **venerande** (m.sg. voc. of the gerundive of **veneror -ārī**) **Syphax** (**Syphācis** M.), lit., *Syphax, to be venerated with respect to [your] scepter,* i.e., *Syphax of venerable scepter;* **aequore ... mediō** instrumental abl. [§G 47], lit., *with [its] middle sea,* trans. *with its intervening water;* **tardō -āre** *delay;* **pontus -ī** M. *sea.*

249ff.   **ardua regnīs ... aut inhonōra tuīs** [*things*] *difficult or dishonorable for your kingdom* (pl. for sg. [§G 53]); **quaesumus** = **quaesimus** (pl. for sg. [§G 53]; **quaesō -ere** *seek*); **coniungō -ere** *join;* **Latīnīs** dat. *to the Latins* (= Romans); trans. **ūnanimum** (*sharing a single aim*) by an adverb [§G 55], *unreservedly;* **pectus pectoris** N. here *heart;* **socius** is in apposition [§G 52] to the understood subject of the verb, trans. [*as*] *an ally;* **accēde secundīs** lit., *come over* (**accēdō -ere**) *to [their] successful [things],* i.e., *share in [their] success.*

252ff.   **tibi ... amplius attulerint decoris** lit., *would bring* (**afferō -ferre**; the perfect subjunctive is potential [§G 68]) *you* (**tibi** dat. of advantage [§G 31]) *more* (**amplius**) *of honor* (partitive gen. [§G 24]; **decus decoris** N.)—trans. the last two words *more honor;* **extentaque tellūs Syrtibus** *land* (**tellūs tellūris** F.) *extending* (lit., *stretched;* **extendō -ere**) *to the Syrtes* (dat. of motion toward [§G 35]; **Syrtis Syrtis** F. as plural, dangerous shallows in the southern Mediterranean Sea east of Carthage); **latīs ... campīs** abl. of place where [§G 38] *over* (lit., *in*) *wide fields;* **proavīta potentia** *ancestral power* (**potentia -ae** F.); **quam** *than;* **Rōmula virtūs certā iuncta fidē** *Roman courage joined [to you] by sure faith*—the Romans prided

amplius attulerint decoris, quam Romula virtus
certa iuncta fide et populi Laurentis honores.   255
cetera quid referam? non ullus scilicet ulli
aequus caelicolum, qui Dardana laeserit arma."

~: SILIUS ITALICUS *Pūnica* 16.229–257

themselves on being trustworthy; **populī Laurentis honōrēs** *the esteem* (pl. for sg.
[§G53]) *of the Laurentine people* (**Laurēns** (**Laurentis**) yet another synonym for
Roman).

256f. **cētera quid referam?** *why should I mention* (potential subjunctive [§G68];
referō -ferre) *the other [considerations]?*; with the next clause supply **est** (*is*); **nōn
ullus ... caelicolum** (= **nullus caelicolārum** [§G95]) *none of the gods* (**caelicola
-ae** M./F. lit., *sky-dweller*); **scīlicet** *of course*—Scipio now casually tosses in the
most important argument of all; **ullī aequus ... quī** *favorable to anyone who*; **Dardana** cf. l. 239; **laeserit** subj. in a generalizing adjectival clause [§G88], trans. *has
harmed*.

Changing with the Times

Tempora mutantur, nos et mutamur in illis.
Times change, and we change with them.
(lit., *Times are changed, and we are changed in them.*)

This common quotation is a hexameter:

tēmpŏră | mūtān|tūr || nōs | ēt mū|tāmŭr ĭn | īllīs

It also appears in a form where the **et** of the second clause is not
postponed:

Tempora mutantur et nos mutamur in illis.

The first version is certainly the original, since the second does not
scan properly (the syllable **-tur** would be short before **et**).

A widely held notion is that this line is from Ovid, as a search of
the Internet shows. However, it is neither from Ovid nor from any
other classical writer. Its author is, in fact, unknown. According to the
Oxford Dictionary of Quotations, it first appears in William Harrison's
Description of Britain (1577) and is modeled on a saying of a grandson
of Charlemagne, the Frankish emperor Lothair I (795–855):

Omnia mutantur, nos et mutamur in illis.
All things change, and we change with them.

Lost Latin Poetry

After the collapse of Rome in the fifth century A.D., the survival of many Latin authors was largely a matter of chance (see page xv). Many quotations from lost poetic works were preserved in prose writers. Cicero, for example, was fond of quoting from Ennius and other early poets in his letters and philosophical treatises. Still, the main source of information on what has been lost is grammarians and writers on antiquities, who quote from earlier literature to illustrate the meaning of a word, a point of grammar, or some facet of Roman history or society. These quotations, which may consist of a single word or run to several lines, have been collected by scholars and classified under the original authors' names.

The possibility exists that a medieval manuscript of an otherwise lost work may still come to light, although the chances are slim, since monasteries and old libraries where it might be preserved have long since been thoroughly searched. Over the past 200 years, however, many ancient papyri have been discovered in Egypt, where dry conditions have protected them from disintegration. The majority of these have been of Greek authors and have yielded many works previously thought lost. The most interesting of the Latin finds has been nine lines from a poem of Cornelius Gallus (d. 26 B.C.), a contemporary and friend of Vergil who introduced the love elegy to Rome. Although celebrated as a poet during his lifetime and after his death, he was previously known only by a single line quoted by a later writer.

The other source of ancient papyri is Herculaneum, one of the towns destroyed by the eruption of Vesuvius in A.D. 79. Nearby Pompeii was covered with hot volcanic dust, which destroyed most material of a combustible nature, but the ash that engulfed Herculaneum solidified into rock, and some objects made of organic matter, such as wood and the papyrus plant, were preserved. Since the first excavations in the eighteenth century, over 1700 rolls have been found. Because of their charred and brittle state, these could only be opened by breaking or slicing off successive pieces from the outer end of a roll. This unsatisfactory method, which was attempted on several hundred rolls, has for the most part produced prose works in Greek by a minor philosopher and rhetorician, Philodemus. Among the few Latin finds is a 52-line fragment from a poem on the final phase of the civil war between Octavian and Marcus Antonius after the former's victory at the naval battle at Actium in 31 B.C. About 900 rolls remain unopened, and it is possible that scanning technology (for example, computed tomography (CT) and magnetic resonance imaging (MRI)) will allow these to be read without damage. Perhaps some treasures of Latin literature are still waiting to be revealed. ~:~

A Pleasant Retirement

*Marcus Valerius Martiālis (c. A.D. 40–c. 102), known in English as **Martial**, was born in Bilbilis, a small provincial city in northeastern Spain. After coming to Rome as a young man, he was dependent on the patronage of the wealthy and eventually established himself as a writer of short poems (**epigrammata**), mainly of a satirical nature. His success is shown in the poems he addresses to the emperor Domitian, but he eventually returned to Spain in A.D. 98.*

*The following poem, written to a friend still in Rome called **Iuvenālis** (who may be the poet Juvenal), expresses the pleasure he felt in no longer being constricted by the social conventions of the Roman capital (cf. Martial 4.8.1, page 200).*

Dum tu forsitan inquietus erras
clamosa, Iuvenalis, in Subura,
aut collem dominae teris Dianae;
dum per limina te potentiorum
sudatrix toga ventilat vagumque   5
maior Caelius et minor fatigant:

TEXT   *Martial,* ed. D. R. Shackleton Bailey (Loeb Classical Library, 1993)
METER   hendecasyllable [§M3]
        dūm tū | fōrsĭtăn | īnquĭ|ētŭs | ērrās
        clāmō|sā Iŭvĕ|nālĭs | īn Sŭ|būrā

In ll. 1–6, Martial supposes that his friend is performing the **salūtātiō**, the formal morning call of a **cliens** on his patrons (**patrōnī**), on whom his livelihood might depend. This visit had to be made in a **toga**, which was made of wool and not suited for strenuous walking, as Martial points out in l. 5.

    The first six lines consist of four subordinate clauses introduced by **dum**, which is repeated in l. 4.

1   **forsitan** *perhaps;* trans. **inquiētus** (*restless*) by an adverb [§G55].
2f. **clāmōsā … in Subūrā** *in noisy Subura,* a lively and densely populated part of Rome, northeast of the Forum; the hill (**collis collis** M.) of mistress Diana was the Aventine in southwest Rome, where there was an old temple of Diana (**domina** here indicates ownership); in Martial's time, the area was largely inhabited by the wealthy; **terō -ere** here *tread.*
4ff. **per līmina … potentiōrum** *across the thresholds* (**līmen līminis** N.) *of the more powerful* (**potentior** compar. of **potens** (**potentis**)); the object of **ventilat** (**ventilō -āre** *fan*) is **tē**, and its subject is **toga**; **sūdātrix** (with **toga**) *sweaty*—as Martial's friend enters the houses of the wealthy, his sweaty toga is flapping against his body; **vagum** (adj. *wandering*) agrees with **tē**, the understood object of **fatigant** (**fatigō -āre** *make weary*); the greater and lesser Caelius are the two peaks of the **mons Caelius** in southeast Rome, an area favored by the wealthy.

me multos repetita post Decembres
accepit mea rusticumque fecit
auro Bilbilis et superba ferro.
hic pigri colimus labore dulci   10
Boterdum Plateamque—Celtiberis
haec sunt nomina crassiora terris.
ingenti fruor improboque somno,
quem nec tertia saepe rumpit hora,
et totum mihi nunc repono, quidquid   15
ter denos vigilaveram per annos.
ignota est toga, sed datur petenti
rupta proxima vestis a cathedra.

7ff.   The subject of the two clauses is **mea ... Bilbilis**, and with it go both **multōs repetīta post Decembrēs** (*returned to* (**repetō -ere** *seek again*) *after many Decembers*) and **aurō ... et superba ferrō** (*proud with [its] gold and iron* (**aurō** and **ferrō** abl. of cause [§G 48])—Bilbilis was famous for its mines); the object of both clauses is **mē**; in the second, the verb **fēcit** has a predicate **rusticum**, trans. *has made me a rustic* (in contrast to the sophisticated life Martial had lived in Rome).

10ff.   **hīc** *here*; trans. **pigrī** (**piger** *idle*) by an adverb [§G 55]; **colimus** pl. for sg. [§G 53] (**colō -ere** here *visit*); **labōre dulcī** abl. of manner [§G 45] *with pleasant toil*; **Bōterdum** and **Platea** were villages near Bilbilis; **Celtibērīs ... terrīs** abl. of place where [§G 38] *in the Celtiberian lands* (an area in northeastern Spain); **crassiōra** (compar. of **crassus**, here expressing a high degree [§G 54]) *rather uncouth*.

13   *I enjoy a huge and indecent [amount of] sleep* (**fruor** takes the ablative); **improbus** (*morally unsound*) is used humorously here—in his retirement, Martial enjoys rising late.

14   The antecedent of **quem** is **somnō**; **nec** here *not even*; **tertia ... hōra** *the third hour*, i.e., between 8 and 11 A.M., depending on the time of year—in the Roman day, the hours of sunlight were divided into twelve **hōrae** and hence varied in length according to the season; **rumpō -ere** here *disturb*.

15f.   **tōtum ... quidquid** lit., *all whatever*, i.e., *all [the time] that*; **repōnō -ere** *pay back*; **ter dēnōs ... per annōs** *over thrice ten years*—Roman poets regularly use a periphrasis for larger numbers (here the distributive **dēnī** (*ten each*) is used instead of the cardinal **decem**); trans. the pluperfect **vigilāveram** (**vigilō -āre**) by the English past tense [§G 64], *I stayed awake*—in Rome, the noise at night made it difficult to sleep, and in addition Martial had been obliged to rise early to perform the **salūtātiō**.

17f.   **ignōtus** *unknown*; **petentī** pres. pple., dat. after **datur** *to [the person] asking*, trans. *to you when you ask* (i.e., for an article of clothing); **ruptā ... ā cathedrā** *from a broken* (**rumpō -ere**) *chair* (**cathedra -ae** F.); **proxima vestis** *the nearest [article of] clothing*—the absence of the toga and the use of a broken chair as a clothes stand indicate the lack of formality at Bilbilis and its easy lifestyle.

surgentem focus excipit superba
vicini strue cultus iliceti,   20
multa vilica quem coronat olla.
venator sequitur, sed ille quem tu
secreta cupias habere silva;
dispensat pueris rogatque longos
levis ponere vilicus capillos.   25
sic me vivere, sic iuvat perire.

~: Martial *Epigrammata* 12.18

19f.   **surgentem** (**surgō -ere** here *rise from bed*) lit., *[a person] rising*, but Martial is
obviously referring to himself, trans. *[you] when you rise*; **focus -ī** m. *fireplace*;
excipiō -ere here *greet*; **superbā ... strue cultus** *fed* (**colō -ere**) *by a noble pile*
(**struēs struis** f.) (instrumental abl. [§G 47]); **vīcīnī ... īlicētī** *from* (lit., *of*) *a nearby*
(**vīcīnus**) *holm-oak grove* (**īlicētum -ī** n.).

21   The antecedent of the postponed **quem** [§G 4] is **focus**; **multā ... ollā** instrumental abl. [§G 47] *with many [a] pot* (**olla -ae** f.); **vīlica -ae** f. the female associate
of the overseer (**vīlicus**), who, whether a slave or a freeman, was in charge of running a farm or estate; **corōnō -āre** *crown*—the verb is used here because the pots
surround the fire.

22f.   **vēnātor vēnātōris** m. *a hunter*, who has presumably caught some small game
for the meal; **ille quem tū** *one whom you*; **sēcrētā ... silvā** abl. of place where
[§G 38] *in a secluded woods*; **cupiās** (potential subj. [§G 68]) **habēre** *you would like
to have*—the hunter's good looks stir Martial's emotions (homosexuality is frequently hinted at or explicitly mentioned in his poems).

24f.   The subject of both verbs is **lēvis ... vīlicus** *the smooth-skinned overseer* (**lēvis**
smooth—distinguish from **lĕvis** *light*), smooth-skinned because he has not yet
reached puberty; **dispensat** (**dispensō -āre**) *gives a handout* (i.e., of the daily food
rations); **puerīs** dat. *to the slaves*; **rogat longōs ... pōnere ... capillōs** *asks [to be
allowed] to set aside* (lit., *put down*, i.e., *cut*) *[his] long hair* (**capillus -ī** m.)—owners
allowed the hair of young male slaves to grow long; here the **vīlicus** wants to cut
his hair and so be accepted as an adult male; Martial's young overseer is another
indication of his homosexual tendencies.

26   **sīc** *in this way*; **mē ... iuvat** impers. *it pleases me*, i.e., *I want*.

Some Odd Characters

Martial often makes fun of particular people and their failings or defects. These he names as though they were contemporaries, but we cannot know whether they existed outside his own imagination.

A Gellius aedificat semper: modo limina ponit,
    nunc foribus claves aptat emitque seras,
    nunc has, nunc illas reficit mutatque fenestras;
    dum tantum aedificet, quidlibet ille facit
    oranti nummos ut dicere possit amico   5
    unum illud verbum Gellius "Aedifico."   (9.46)

B Solvere dodrantem nuper tibi, Quinte, volebat
    lippus Hylas; luscus vult dare dimidium.
    accipe quam primum; brevis est occasio lucri:
    si fuerit caecus, nil tibi solvet Hylas.   (8.9)

TEXT   *Martial,* ed. D. R. Shackleton Bailey (Loeb Classical Library, 1993)
METER elegiac couplet [§M2]
      Gēllĭŭs | āēdĭfĭ|cāt ‖ sēm|pēr mŏdŏ | līmĭnă | pōnĭt
      nūnc fŏrĭ|būs clā|vēs ‖ āptăt ĕ|mītquĕ sĕ|rās

A 1   **aedificō -āre** *build;* **modo** *now;* **līmen līminis** N. *threshold;* **pōnit** *he lays.*
2   **foribus** (**foris foris** F. *door*) dat. after **aptat** (**aptō -āre** *fit [something]* (acc.) *to [something]* (dat.)); **clāvis clāvis** F. *key;* **sera -ae** F. *bar,* which was placed across a door to fasten it.
3   **reficiō -ere** *remodel;* **fenestra -ae** F. *window.*
4   **dum** + subj. *provided that;* **tantum** adv. *only;* **quidlibet** *anything.*
5f.   The final lines are a purpose clause [§G83] introduced by a postponed **ut** [§G4]; **ōrantī nummōs ... amīcō** *to a friend asking for money* (**nummus -ī** M.); **ūnum illud verbum ... "Aedificō"** *that single word "I'm building"*—Gellius tactfully implies that he has no money to lend.

B 1f.   **Hylās** (**-ae** M., a Greek name), who has trouble with his eyes, *was recently* (**nūper**) *willing,* when he was merely *bleary-eyed* (**lippus**), *to pay* (**solvō -ere**) *three quarters* (**dōdrans dōdrantis** M.) of his debt to Quintus; now that he has lost an eye and become *one-eyed* (**luscus**), his offer is reduced to *half* (**dīmidium -iī** N.).
3   **accipe** 2 sg. imp. act. of **accipiō -ere**; **quam prīmum** *as soon as possible;* **occāsiō occāsiōnis** F. *opportunity;* **lucrum -ī** N. *gain*—to get anything from Hylas will be to Quintus' advantage.
4   **fuerit** 3 sg. fut. perf. **sum**, lit., *will have been* (i.e., *become*), trans. by the present [§G66], *becomes;* **caecus** *blind.*

C Si memini, fuerant tibi quattuor, Aelia, dentes:
     expulit una duos tussis et una duos.
    iam secura potes totis tussire diebus:
     nil istic quod agat tertia tussis habet.   (1.19)

D Dicere de Libycis reduci tibi gentibus, Afer,
     continuis volui quinque diebus "have":
    "non vacat" aut "dormit" dictum est bis terque reverso.
     iam satis est: non vis, Afer, havere: vale.   (9.6)

E Mentiris iuvenem tinctis, Laetine, capillis,
     tam subito corvus, qui modo cycnus eras.
    non omnes fallis; scit te Proserpina canum:
     personam capiti detrahet illa tuo.   (3.43)

~: Martial *Epigrammata*

C 1f. **tibi** dat. of possessor [§G 30]; **dens dentis** M. *tooth*; **expellō -ere** *knock out*; **tussis tussis** F. *cough*—each of Aelia's two coughs knocked out two of her four remaining teeth.

3 **sēcūrus** *carefree*, trans. *without care*; **tōtīs ... diēbus** abl. to express time how long *for entire days*—this is a Silver Age use [§G 11]; **tussiō -īre** *cough*.

4 **istīc** adv. *there*, i.e., in Aelia's mouth; **agat** potential subj. [§G 68]; **tertius** *third*.

D 1f. **Dīcere**, which is governed by **voluī**, has as its object "**have**" ("*hello*," 2 sg. imp. of **haveō** (often spelled **aveō**) **-ēre** *greet*); **Libycus** adj. of *Libya*, a name given to north Africa; **reducī tibi** dat. after **dīcere** *to you, having returned*—the adjective **redux** (**reducis**) functions as a perfect active participle; **Āfer** voc. of the cognomen **Āfer Āfrī** M.; **continuīs ... quinque diēbus** abl. of time during which [§G 37] *over five days in a row* (lit., *continuous*).

3 **vacō -āre** *be unoccupied, be free*; **bis terque** *two and three times*; supply **mihi** with **reversō** (perf. pple. of **revertor -ī**) after **dictum est**, lit., *[to me] having returned*.

4 **vīs** 2 sg. pres. ind. **volō velle** *wish*; **havēre** *to be greeted with* **have**.

E 1f. **mentior -īrī** here *pretend to be*; **tinctīs ... capillīs** instrumental abl. [§G 47] *with [your] dyed* (**tingō -ere**) *hair* (**capillus -ī** M.); **Laetīne** voc. of the cognomen **Laetīnus -ī** M.; **tam subitō corvus** (*so suddenly a raven* (**corvus -ī** M.)) is in apposition [§G 52] to the understood subject *you*—Laetinus' hair has suddenly become as black as a raven's feathers; **modo** *recently, just now*; **cycnus -ī** M. *swan*.

3f. **Prōserpina -ae** F. *Proserpine*—as queen of the Underworld, she is not deceived, and after death Laetinus' hair will revert to white (**cānus**); **persōna -ae** F. *mask*; **capitī ... tuō** dat. of disadvantage [§G 31] *from your head*; **dētrahō -ere** *pull off*.

Wisecracks

Martial wrote many short poems whose final words give a humorous or un-expected twist to what has preceded.

A   Numquam se cenasse domi Philo iurat, et hoc est:
    non cenat, quotiens nemo vocavit eum.   (5.47)

B   Callidus imposuit nuper mihi copo Ravennae:
    cum peterem mixtum, vendidit ille merum.   (3.57)

C   Tu Setina quidem semper vel Massica ponis,
    Papyle, sed rumor tam bona vina negat.
    diceris hac factus caelebs quater esse lagona.
    nec puto nec credo, Papyle, nec sitio.   (4.69)

D   Quod tam grande sophos clamat tibi turba togata,
    non tu, Pomponi, cena diserta tua est.   (6.48)

TEXT   *Martial*, ed. D. R. Shackleton Bailey (Loeb Classical Library, 1993)
METER   elegiac couplet [§M2]
    nūmquām | sē ‖ cē|nāssĕ dŏ|mī ‖ Phĭlŏ | iūrăt ĕt | hōc ēst
    nōn cē|nāt quŏtĭ|ēns ‖ nēmŏ vŏ|cāvĭt ĕ|ŭm

A   Philo boasts that he is always being invited out to dinner; **sē cēnasse** (= **cēnā-visse**, *himself to have dined* (**cēnō -āre**)) is acc.+inf. [§G10] after **iūrat**; **domī** (loc. of **domus**) *at home*; **hoc est** *this is [so]*; **quotiens** *whenever*; **vocō -āre** here *invite*.

B   **Callidus** *cunning*; **impōnō -ere** + dat. *trick*; **nūper** *recently*; **cōpo cōpōnis** M. *innkeeper*; **Ravennae** loc.—in Ravenna, a city in northern Italy, water was in such short supply that it was said to be more expensive than wine; **mixtum [vī-num]** *mixed [wine]*, i.e., wine and water; **merum [vīnum]** *neat [wine]*, i.e., undiluted wine.

C   Papylus always serves (**pōnō -ere**) good-quality wines at his dinner parties; **Sētīna [vīna]**, **Massica [vīna]** superior varieties of wine; **quidem** emphasizes the preceding word, but in English we would convey this by the tone with which **Sētīna** is pronounced; **Pāpyle** voc.; **rūmor rūmōris** M. *gossip*; **negat** here *forbids [us]*, i.e., suggests that it would not be a good idea to drink Papylus' wines; **dīceris** 2 sg. pres. ind. pass. *you are said*; **hāc ... lagōnā** *with this wine bottle* (**lagōna -ae** F.), i.e., with this wine of yours; **caelebs caelibis** M. *bachelor*; **quater** *four times*—Papylus is rumored to have rid himself of four wives with poisoned wine (poisoning was more common in ancient Rome than it is today); **nec puto nec crēdō** *I neither think nor believe [this]*; in Silver Age poetry, the ō of the 1 sg. pres. ind. act. of verbs is sometimes shortened, hence Martial has **puto**, not **putō**, here; trans. the third **nec** *but ... not*; **sitiō -īre** *be thirsty*.

D   **Quod** here introduces a noun clause and means *with respect to the fact that*, but trans. *when*; the reference is to a **recitātiō** (cf. the introductions to "Is There Life After Death?", page 168, and "The Necessity of Writing Satire," page 202), where an author read his work to invited guests, but in this case Pomponius also gave

E Quid mihi reddat ager quaeris, Line, Nomentanus?
  hoc mihi reddit ager: te, Line, non video. (2.38)

F Nescio tam multis quid scribas, Fauste, puellis:
  hoc scio, quod scribit nulla puella tibi. (11.64)

G Quid recitaturus circumdas vellera collo?
  conveniunt nostris auribus ista magis. (4.41)

H Nil recitas et vis, Mamerce, poeta videri.
  quidquid vis esto, dummodo nil recites. (2.88)

I Septima iam, Phileros, tibi conditur uxor in agro.
  plus nulli, Phileros, quam tibi, reddit ager. (10.43)

J Cum tua non edas, carpis mea carmina, Laeli.
  carpere vel noli nostra vel ede tua. (1.91)

~: MARTIAL *Epigrammata*

them dinner; take **grande** (**grandis** *loud*) with **sophōs** (an exclamation of admiration), *a loud bravo!*; **clāmō -āre** *shout*; **turba togāta** *toga'd crowd*—on a formal occasion such as this, the guests wore togas; **nōn tū ...** lit., *not you, [but] your dinner*
(**cēna -ae** F.) *is eloquent* (**disertus**); **Pompōnī** voc.—both poetry and prose of the
Silver Age were permeated with the current style of rhetoric, and to be considered
eloquent was the supreme accolade for a writer.

E **quaeris** governs the indirect question [§G91] **Quid mihi reddat** (**reddō -ere**
  return [in rent]) **ager ... Nōmentānus** (adj. of **Nōmentum -ī** N., a town near
  Rome); **Line** voc.; **hoc** (*this*, i.e., the return) is spelled out in the second half of the
  line: Martial was able to stay on his field, which would have been a small farm,
  and so not be troubled by Linus.

F **quid** introduces an indirect question [§G91] after **Nescio** but is postponed
  [§G4]; **multīs ... puellīs** dat. after **scrībās**; **Fauste** voc.; **hoc scio quod ...** *I know
  this, [namely] that....*

G **Quid** *why*; **recitātūrus** (**recitō -āre** *recite*) *[when] about to recite* (at a **recitātiō**);
  circumdō -are + acc./dat. *put [something] around [something]*; **vellera** pl. for sg.
  [§G53] *wool* (**vellus velleris** N.); **collum -ī** N. *neck*—to protect the reciter's voice;
  conveniō -īre + dat. *be suited to*; **nostrīs auribus** dat. *our ears*, i.e., the ears of the
  audience, who would prefer not to listen; take **magis** (*more*) with **conveniunt**.

H **vīs** 2 sg. pres. ind. **volō velle**; **Māmerce** voc.; **vidērī** *to appear*; **quidquid** *whatever*; **estō** 2 sg. imp. of **sum**; **dummodo** + subj. *provided that*.

I **Septima ... uxor** *seventh wife*; **Philerōs** voc.; **tibi** is to be taken as both a dative
  of possessor [§G30] (*your seventh wife*) and a dative of agent [§G29] (*by you*);
  condō -ere *bury*; **in agrō** *in [your] field*; **plūs nullī ... quam tibi** *to no one more
  than to you*; **reddit** cf. epigram E above; **ager** trans. *a field*—Martial is suggesting
  that Phileros is killing his wives.

J **Cum** + subj. here *although*; **tua [carmina]** *your [poems]*; **ēdō ēdere** *publish*;
  carpō -ere *criticize*; **Laelī** voc.; **vel ... vel ...** *either ... or ...*; **nōlī** (2 sg. imp. of **nōlō
  nolle**) + inf. *don't ...* [§G72]; **nostra** pl. for sg. [§G53].

The Happy Life

In a poem addressed to a friend with the same name as his own, Martial details the ingredients of a happy life. The list agrees with what one might draw up today, except that it contains nothing that we might interpret as job satisfaction. The puritan work ethic was more than a thousand years in the future, and a Roman saw no virtue in having to earn a living. Certain careers (advocate, politician, soldier, farmer) were held in esteem, but to work with one's hands was considered degrading, and merchants and traders were despised. The ideal was to lead a life of ōtium *(leisure), such as Martial describes here.*

Vitam quae faciant beatiorem,
iucundissime Martialis, haec sunt:
res non parta labore, sed relicta;
non ingratus ager, focus perennis;
lis numquam, toga rara, mens quieta;   5
vires ingenuae, salubre corpus;
prudens simplicitas, pares amici;

TEXT   *Martial,* ed. D. R. Shackleton Bailey (Loeb Classical Library, 1993)
METER   hendecasyllable [§M 3]
      vītām | quaē făcĭ|ānt bĕ|ātĭ|ōrĕm
      iūcūn|dīssĭmĕ | Mārtĭ|ālĭs | haēc sūnt

1   The antecedent of **quae** (postponed [§G 4]) is **haec** in l. 2; **faciant** potential subj. [§G 68]; **beātior** compar. of **beātus** *happy.*
2   **iūcundissimus** superl. of **iūcundus** *charming.*
3   **rēs** here *wealth;* **parta** (perf. pple. of **pariō** -ere) here *obtained;* **labōre** instrumental abl. [§G 47]; **relicta** (perf. pple. of **relinquō** -ere) here *inherited.*
4   **nōn ingrātus** (*not unrewarding*) is used of an **ager** (*farm*) that returns a profit— Martial would have seen himself as enjoying rural life while underlings and slaves performed the manual labor; **focus** -ī M. *fireplace;* **perennis** *year-round, constant,* i.e., always burning—the kitchen fire would be in constant use to provide cooked food.
5   **līs lītis** F. *lawsuit;* **toga rāra** trans. *a toga* (**toga** -ae F.) *rarely used*—the toga was the formal Roman dress, and the need to wear it was much less in the country than in Rome (cf. Martial, "A Pleasant Retirement," page 191); **quiētus** *quiet, at rest.*
6   **vīrēs ingenuae** lit., *freeborn strength,* i.e., the strength of a freeborn man, not that of a slave, who, through hard manual labor, might have been much stronger than the average citizen; **salūber** *healthy.*
7   **prūdens** (**prūdentis**) *prudent, sensible;* **simplicitās simplicitātis** F. *openness;* **pār** (**paris**) *matching, equal,* i.e., of equal status.

convictus facilis, sine arte mensa;
nox non ebria, sed soluta curis;
non tristis torus, et tamen pudicus;   10
somnus, qui faciat breves tenebras:
quod sis, esse velis nihilque malis;
summum nec metuas diem nec optes.

~: Martial *Epigrammata* 10.47

8   **convictus** -ūs M. *companionship*; **mensa** -ae F. *table*, used here by metonymy
     [§G97] for food.
9   **ēbrius** *drunken*; **solūta** perf. pple. of **solvō** -**ere** *(set) free*; **cūrīs** abl. of separation
     [§G40].
10   **tristis** here *austere, straitlaced*; **torus** -ī M. lit., *bed*, used here by metonymy
     [§G97] for marriage; **pudīcus** *chaste*.
11   **faciat** potential subj. [§G68]; **tenebrae** -ārum F.PL. *darkness*, trans. *the night*.
12f.   The two final requisites are expressed by clauses; **velīs ... mālīs** (2 sg. pres.
     subj. **volō velle** and **mālō malle**) potential subj. [§G68], *[that] you would wish to be*
     (**esse**) *whatever you are* (**quod sīs**) *and would prefer nothing [else]*—**quod sīs** is a
     generalizing relative clause (hence the subj. [§G88]); **summum ... diem** *the final*
     day, i.e., the day of one's death; **metuās, optēs** potential subj. [§G68].

Vergiliana ·V·

Like his contemporaries, Vergil was always quick to praise the simple
way of life believed to have been practiced by Romans and their
neighbors in earlier centuries. To this he attributed not only Rome's
present greatness, but also the prosperity formerly enjoyed by the
Etruscans:

> **Sic fortis Etruria crevit**
> **scilicet et rerum facta est pulcherrima Roma.**   *Georgics* 2.533f.
> *In this way* (i.e., by following a simple way of life),
> *of course, Etruria grew strong and Rome has become*
> *the fairest [city] of the world.*

The first line has often been used, especially in Australia, as a motto
by such unlikely institutions as banks and insurance companies.

For more Vergiliana, see pages 56, 109, 182, and 185.

A Roman's Day

Martial hints to Euphemus, Domitian's dining-room steward, that the emperor might enjoy the poet's works over dinner. By way of tactfully introducing this suggestion, he describes, hour by hour, the daily activities of a person such as himself.

Mechanical clocks were unknown to the Romans, and their system of time-keeping, based on the sundial, differed from ours; the sunlight hours of each day were divided into twelve equal **hōrae,** *and consequently a* **hōra** *varied in length through the year. The* **hōra prīma** *of a day in midsummer would have been long and early, but in midwinter short and late (cf. Martial Epigrammata 12.18.14, page 192).*

Prima salutantes atque altera conterit hora,
    exercet raucos tertia causidicos,
in quintam varios extendit Roma labores,
    sexta quies lassis, septima finis erit,
sufficit in nonam nitidis octava palaestris,   5
    imperat extructos frangere nona toros:

TEXT   *Martial,* ed. D. R. Shackleton Bailey (Loeb Classical Library, 1993)
METER   elegiac couplet [§M2]
        prīmă să|lūtān|tēs ‖ āt|qu(e) āltĕră | cōntĕrĭt | hōră
        ēxēr|cĕt rāu|cōs ‖ tērtĭă | cāusĭdĭ|cōs

1 **prīmus** *first;* **salūtantēs** (pres. pple. of **salūtō -āre** *greet*) trans. *the callers*—these were the **clientēs** (**cliens clientis** M. *client*), who in return for loyalty toward their **patrōnus** (**-ī** M.) received material support from him in the form of food or money; one of their duties was the **salūtātiō** (**salūtātiōnis** F.), an early-morning call on the patron's house in a toga, the Roman formal dress (cf. Martial *Epigrammata* 12.18.1–6, page 191); **altera** *the other* (of two), trans. *second;* **conterit** (**conterō -ere** *make weary*) agrees with the nearer of its two subjects [§G58].

2f. **exerceō -ēre** *occupy, keep busy;* **raucōs ... causidicōs** *hoarse advocates* (**causidicus -ī** M.)—the law courts (and presumably other public activities) began with the third (**tertius**) hour and extended up to (the end of) the fifth (**quintus**) hour; **extendō -ere** *extend* (tr.).

4 The sixth (**sextus**) and seventh (**septimus**) hours were for the siesta; with **sexta** supply **hōra est;** **lassīs** dat. *for the weary;* **septima fīnis erit** *the seventh will be [its] end,* i.e., the end of the siesta that concludes with the end of the seventh hour.

5 **sufficit ... nitidīs ... palaestrīs** *is for* (**sufficiō -ere** + dat. *be available for*) *shining wrestling schools* (**palaestra -ae** F.)—the **palaestra** (called *shining* because wrestlers rubbed their bodies with oil) was part of the **thermae** (**-ārum** F.PL. *hot baths*), large recreational centers with various sports facilities, of which Martial mentions one; **in nōnam ... octāva** *the eight [hour] up to the ninth.*

hora libellorum decuma est, Eupheme, meorum,
temperat ambrosias cum tua cura dapes
et bonus aetherio laxatur nectare Caesar
ingentique tenet pocula parca manu.　　　　10
tunc admitte iocos: gressu timet ire licenti
ad matutinum nostra Thalia Iovem.

～: MARTIAL *Epigrammata* 4.8

6　The ninth hour was to prepare for dinner and begin the meal; **imperat [nōs]** (*orders [us]*) is followed by an infinitive, **frangere** (*to crush*); **extructōs ... torōs** lit., *heaped up* (**ex(s)truō -ere**) *couches* (**torus -ī** M.)—at dinner, the Romans lay on couches; these did not have attached upholstery but were covered with cushions, which were *crushed*, i.e., compressed, by the weight of the diner.

7　**libellōrum ... est ... meōrum** broader use of a possessive genitive [§G18], *belongs to my little books* (**libellus -ī** M.), i.e., is a suitable time to read, etc.; **decumus** *tenth*; **Euphēme** voc.

8　Three clauses are introduced by the postponed **cum** [§G4]; the subject of **temperat** (**temperō -āre** *direct*) is **tua cūra**; **ambrosiās ... dapēs** *ambrosial feasts* (**daps dapis** F.)—ambrosia and nectar (l. 9) were the food and drink of the gods, and Martial, who was shameless in his flattery of the emperor, supposes Domitian to be a god on earth.

9　**aetheriō ... nectare** instrumental abl. [§G47] *with heavenly nectar* (**nectar nectaris** N.); **laxātur** pass. used reflexively [§G59] *relaxes himself*; **Caesar** (**Caesaris** M.) had become the term for the emperor, in this case Domitian.

10　**ingentī ... manū** instrumental abl. [§G47] *with mighty hand*—the expression is meant to suggest that Domitian's physique is of divine proportions; **pōcula parca** *moderate cups* (**pōculum -ī** N.)—as befits a responsible emperor, Domitian does not overindulge in his drinking.

11f.　**admitte** 2 sg. imp. act. of **admittō -ere** *let in*; **iocus -ī** M. *jest*—Martial is referring to his poems; the subject of the final clause is **nostra Thalīa** (*my* (pl. for sg. [§G53]) *Thalia*), who, as the muse of comedy and light verse, was the source of Martial's inspiration; **gressū ... licentī** abl. of manner [§G45] *with unrestrained step* (**gressus -ūs** M.); **mātūtīnum ... Iovem** *Jupiter* (**Iuppiter Iovis** M.) *in the morning* (**mātūtīnus** adj.)—Domitian, the earthly Jupiter, spent his mornings in serious work and was not to be distracted by a frivolous poet.

The Necessity of Writing Satire

Very little is known about **Decimus Iūnius Iuvenālis** (*in English,* Juvenal), *who was born about* A.D. *60 and lived on into the next century. He did not have the success in attracting patrons that his elder contemporary Martial had enjoyed, and a hard and poverty-stricken life seems to have prompted him to attack those aspects of Roman society of which he disapproved. With him, satire became more strongly focused as a vehicle for pungent and bitter criticism, a characteristic that it has retained.*

In his first poem, which is intended as an introduction to his satires, Juvenal gives his reasons for choosing the genre. He is infuriated by contemporary society and insists on making his protest heard. His first complaint is about poets who wrote on mythological subjects and then recited their efforts to bored (and perhaps captive) audiences. These **recitātiōnēs** *were a regular feature of Roman literary circles of the time.*

Semper ego auditor tantum? numquamne reponam
vexatus totiens rauci Theseide Cordi?
inpune ergo mihi recitaverit ille togatas,
hic elegos? inpune diem consumpserit ingens
Telephus aut summi plena iam margine libri   5

TEXT   A. Persi Flacci et D. Iuvenalis *Saturae*, ed. W. V. Clausen
        (Oxford Classical Texts, 1992)
METER   hexameter [§M1]
        sēmpĕr ĕg|(o) āūdī|tōr ‖ tān|tūm nūm|quāmnĕ rĕ|pōnăm
        vēxā|tūs tŏtĭ|ēns ‖ rāu|cī Thē|sēĭdĕ | Cōrdī

1f.   **audītor audītōris** M. *listener;* **tantum** *only;* supply **erō** in the first sentence: *Will I always be only a listener?;* **-ne** introduces the second question; **repōnam** 1 sg. fut. ind. act. **repōnō -ere** here *retaliate;* **vexō -āre** *harass;* **totiens** *so often;* **raucus** *hoarse;* **Thēsēide** instrumental abl. [§G47] (**Thēsēis Thēsēidis** F.) *Theseid,* i.e., an epic about Theseus; we know nothing about Cordus, who is hoarse from reading his long poem.

3   **inpūne** adv. *without punishment, with impunity;* **ergo** *so, then* with strong sarcasm; **recitāverit ille** *will that person have recited* (**recitō -āre**—the fut. perf. expresses a result in the future); **togātās [fābulās]** comedies of Roman life, so called because they were performed in Roman dress (**toga**).

4ff.   **elegī -ōrum** M.PL. *elegies,* which were poems in elegiac verse, usually with a love theme; the first subject of **consumpserit** (3 sg. fut. perf. act. **consūmō -ere** *take up*) is **ingens Tēlephus** (*a huge [poem about]* Telephus (a mythological hero)—

scriptus et in tergo necdum finitus Orestes?
nota magis nulli domus est sua quam mihi lucus
Martis et Aeoliis vicinum rupibus antrum
Vulcani; quid agant venti, quas torqueat umbras
Aeacus, unde alius furtivae devehat aurum   10
pelliculae, quantas iaculetur Monychus ornos,

the poem is so long that a day is required to read it); the second subject, **Orestēs** (another mythological hero), is qualified by two participial phrases, **scriptus et in tergō necdum fīnītus** (*written also* (et) *on the back* (**tergum -ī** N.) *and not yet* (**necdum**) *finished*), and these are preceded by an abl. absolute [§G 49], **summī plēnā iam margine librī** (*the margin* (**margō marginis** here F.) *at the end of the book [being] already full*)—the **liber** (*book*) is an ordinary papyrus roll; when the author of the Orestes came to the end of the roll, he filled in the margins and then turned the roll over and tried unsuccessfully to complete the poem on the back; a papyrus roll was normally written on only one side (see "The Roman Book," page 18).

7ff.   **nōta … est** 3 sg. perf. ind. pass. **noscō -ere**; **nullī … mihi** dat. of agent [§G 29]; **magis … quam** *more than*; take **lūcus** (**-ī** M. *grove*) and **Martis** (gen. of **Mars**, god of war) together, lit., *his own house is more known by no one than the grove of Mars [is known] by me*, i.e., *no one knows his own house better than I know the grove of Mars*; take the dative **Aeoliīs** (**Aeolius** adj. of **Aeolus**, god of the winds) … **rūpibus** (**rūpēs rūpis** F. *cliff*) with the nominative **vīcīnum … antrum** (**-ī** N.) **Vulcānī** (**Vulcānus -ī** M., god of fire), *the cave of Vulcan near the cliffs of Aeolus*— the grove of Mars at Colchis held the Golden Fleece, sought by the Argonauts (cf. Valerius Flaccus, "A Pep Talk," page 180); the cliffs of Aeolus are the Lipari Islands (in Italian, *Isole Eolie*) north of Sicily—Vulcan's forge was under these cliffs or the nearby Mt. Etna; Juvenal's sarcasm indicates that such places were forever being mentioned in the mythological epics that were popular with his fellow poets.

9ff.   Four indirect questions with the subjunctive [§G 91] (**quid …**, **quās …**, **unde …**, and **quantās …**), which refer to the subject matter of mythological epics, precede the main clause in ll. 12–13 (**Frontōnis … columnae**) with its verb **clāmant**; **quid agant ventī** *what the winds are doing*—in mythology, the winds are personified as minor deities; **torqueat** 3 sg. pres. subj. act. **torqueō -ēre** *torture*; **umbrās** *Shades [of the dead]*; **Aeacus** (**-ī** M.) was one of the three judges of the Underworld who, according to some beliefs, passed sentence on the dead—Juvenal is deliberately demeaning his office by describing Aeacus as torturing the Shades; the third indirect question is a scornful reference to the recovery of the Golden Fleece by Jason, whom Juvenal offhandedly calls **alius** *another [fellow]*; **unde** *from where* (i.e., Colchis); **furtīvae … aurum pelliculae** *the gold of the stolen [sheep]skin* (**pellicula -ae** F.); **dēvehat** 3 sg. pres. subj. act. **dēvehō -ere** *carry off*; **quantās iaculētur Mōnychus ornōs** a condensed expression for *how large* (**quantās**) *[are] the ash trees* (**ornus -ī** F.) *[that] Monychus hurls [as missiles]* (**iaculor -ārī**)—Monychus was a centaur.

Frontonis platani convolsaque marmora clamant
semper et adsiduo ruptae lectore columnae.
expectes eadem a summo minimoque poeta.
et nos ergo manum ferulae subduximus, et nos　　　　15
consilium dedimus Sullae, privatus ut altum
dormiret. stulta est clementia, cum tot ubique
vatibus occurras, periturae parcere chartae.

~: JUVENAL *Satires* 1.1–18

12f.　We are to imagine **Frontō** (**Frontōnis** M.) as some wealthy person who al-
lows his garden to be used for **recitātiōnēs** by poets; the preceding indirect questions are governed by **clāmant** (**clāmō -āre** *shout*)—for rhetorical effect, Juvenal
supposes that objects in the garden are reciting poetry themselves or echoing
the reciters; **platanus -ī** F. *plane tree*; **convolsa** perf. pple. of **convellō -ere** *shatter*;
marmor marmoris N. *marble* (here the slabs of marble on the floor and walls);
take **adsiduō … lectōre** (instrumental abl. [§G 47] *by the constant reciter* (**lector
lectōris** M.)) with **ruptae** (perf. pple. of **rumpō -ere**)—the reciter breaks the columns (**columna -ae** F.) unintentionally and so is an instrument, not an agent.

14　**expectēs** potential subj. [§G 68] *you can expect* (**expectō -āre**); **eadem** (acc.
n.pl. of **īdem**) *the same [things]*; **ā summō minimōque poētā** *from the best and
worst* (lit., *least*) *poet*.

15ff.　Juvenal says that he himself has been to school as well and has had the same
training in rhetoric as the poets he condemns, thereby implying that he has an
equal right to compose poetry—the underlying assumption that a training in
rhetoric is essential for a poet is borne out by Silver Age Latin verse, which is
permeated with all the devices of rhetorical theory; **et nōs ergo** pl. for sg. [§G 53]
well, I too; **manum ferulae subduximus** *have withdrawn* (**subdūcō -ere** (*withdraw*) takes acc. and dat. objects) *[my] hand from the rod* (**ferula -ae** F.), i.e., in an
attempt to avoid being hit—Roman schoolteachers were fond of corporal punishment; **consilium -(i)ī** N. *advice*; **Sullae** (dat. of **Sulla -ae** M.) *to Sulla*, a Roman
general who in the early years of the first century B.C. established himself as sole
ruler of Rome by utterly brutal methods—a standard exercise in the school cur-
riculum of Juvenal's time was the **suāsōria**, a speech giving advice to a historical
figure at a critical point in his career, and a favorite topic for a **suāsōria** was to
urge Sulla, when on the point of attacking Rome, to retire to a normal civilian life:
prīvātus ut altum dormīret *that he should sleep soundly [as] a private citizen* (**prīvātus -ī** M.)—the postponed **ut** [§G 4] introduces an indirect command [§G 91];
altum n.sg. adj. used as an adverb [§G 55].

17f.　**stultus** *foolish*; **clēmentia -ae** F. *clemency*; **tot** (indecl.) **… vātibus** (**vātēs vātis**
M. *poet*) dat. with **occurrās** (generalizing subj. [§G 88]; **occurrō -ere** *run into,
meet*); **ubīque** *everywhere*; **peritūrae** (fut. pple. of **pereō -īre** *perish*) **… chartae**
(**charta -ae** F. *paper* (made from the papyrus reed—see "The Roman Book," page
18)) dat. with **parcere**, *to spare the paper [that is] going to perish*, trans. *to spare the
doomed paper*—doomed because if Juvenal did not use it for poetry, someone else
would.

An Adventurous Woman

Women at Rome enjoyed greater freedom than women in almost all other ancient societies, but by modern Western standards, they were certainly not on an equal footing with men. The structure and attitudes of Roman society meant that women were expected to content themselves with duties related to family and home, that is, producing and raising children, as well as attending to household chores (consisting mainly in supervising slaves). It is not surprising that some women cast off social restraints, usually to the horror of their contemporaries.

Juvenal, who appears to have been an inveterate misogynist, gives a vivid and unsympathetic account of Eppia, a married woman of the previous generation who had run off with a gladiator.

Nupta senatori comitata est Eppia ludum
ad Pharon et Nilum famosaque moenia Lagi
prodigia et mores urbis damnante Canopo.
inmemor illa domus et coniugis atque sororis   85
nil patriae indulsit, plorantisque improba natos

TEXT   A. Persi Flacci et D. Iuvenalis *Saturae*, ed. W. V. Clausen
       (Oxford Classical Texts, 1992)

METER   hexameter [§M 1]
       nūptă sĕ|nātō|rī ‖ cŏmĭ|tāt(a) ēst | Ēppĭă | lūdŭm
       ād Phărŏn | ēt Nī|lūm ‖ fă|mōsăquĕ | mōēnĭă | Lāgī

82   **nūbō -ere** + dat. *marry* (of a woman); **senātor senātōris** M. *member of the Roman Senate, senator;* **comitor -ārī** *accompany;* **lūdus -ī** M. here *gladiatorial troupe.*

83   **Pharon** Greek acc. of **Pharos** (-ī F.), an island off the coast of Egypt near Alexandria; **Nīlus -ī** M. *the Nile River;* **fāmōsus** here *infamous;* **moenia Lāgī** i.e., Alexandria (**Lāgus** (-ī M.) was the father of the first Greek ruler of Egypt, Ptolemy I, whose capital was Alexandria)—for Juvenal, contemporary Egypt was a sink of depravity.

84   **prōdigia et mōrēs** (*the monstrosities* (**prōdigium -iī** N.) *and morals*) is the object of the participle in the ablative absolute [§G 49] **damnante Canōpō** (lit., *Canopus* (**Canōpus -ī** M.) *condemning* (**damnō -āre**)); take **urbis** (*of the city,* i.e., of Rome; cf. Ovid *Tristia* 1.3.2, page 132, and elsewhere) with the accusatives—Juvenal pretends that even Canopus, an Egyptian city with an evil reputation, felt itself superior to Rome.

85   **inmemor** (+ gen. *forgetful of*) is followed by **domūs** (here *home*), **coniugis**, and **sorōris**.

86   **nīl** (= **nihil**) here an emphatic negative, *not at all;* **patriae** dat. after **indulsit** (**indulgeō -ēre** + dat. *have regard for*); **plōrantīs … nātōs** *weeping* (**plōrō -āre**) *children,* acc. after **relīquit** (l. 87); trans. **improba** by an adverb [§G 55], *shamefully.*

utque magis stupeas ludos Paridemque reliquit.
sed quamquam in magnis opibus plumaque paterna
et segmentatis dormisset parvula cunis,
contempsit pelagus; famam contempserat olim,   90
cuius apud molles minima est iactura cathedras.
Tyrrhenos igitur fluctus lateque sonantem
pertulit Ionium constanti pectore, quamvis
mutandum totiens esset mare. iusta pericli
si ratio est et honesta, timent pavidoque gelantur   95
pectore nec tremulis possunt insistere plantis:
fortem animum praestant rebus quas turpiter audent.

87   **ut magis stupeās** adv. clause of result [§G84], lit., *so that you would be more
     amazed* (**stupeō -ēre**); **lūdōs** here *public games*, which included gladiatorial dis-
     plays and theatrical performances; **Paris Paridis** M. a popular actor in panto-
     mimes—Juvenal's heavy-handed sarcasm suggests that Eppia and women of her
     class were devoted to popular entertainment.
88f. **quamquam ... dormisset** (= **dormīvisset**) *although she had slept*—**quam-
     quam** can take the subjunctive in Silver Latin; **in** governs the three abl. phrases
     that follow; **plūmā paternā** *[her] father's down* (**plūma -ae** F.); **segmentātīs ...
     cūnīs** *decorated cradle* (**cūnae -ārum** F.PL.)—the decoration was made of pieces of
     colored cloth (**segmentum -ī** N.); **parvula** *[as a] tiny [child]* (**parvulus** diminutive
     of **parvus**).
90f. **contemnō -ere** *scorn*; **pelagus -ī** N. *sea*—the rigors and dangers of ancient sea
     travel would likely have terrified a woman brought up in luxury; **fāmam** (*[her]
     reputation*) is the antecedent of **cuius** (*whose*), which qualifies **iactūra** (**-ae** F. *loss*);
     apud mollēs ... cathedrās *among soft easy chairs* (**cathedra -ae** F.), i.e., among
     women of status and wealth—an example of metonymy [§G97], because such
     women were associated with soft easy chairs; **minimus** superl. of **parvus** used to
     express a very high degree [§G54], trans. *trivial*.
92f. **Tyrrhēnōs ... fluctūs** *the Tyrrhenian waves* (**fluctus -ūs** M.); **igitur** *therefore,
     so*; **lātē sonantem ... Īonium** *the loudly resounding* (**sonō -āre**) *Ionian sea* (**Īonium
     [mare]**)—the Tyrrhenian and Ionian seas were on the route from Rome to
     Egypt; **perferō -ferre** *endure*; **constantī pectore** abl. of manner [§G45] *with reso-
     lute heart*.
94   Take **mūtandum** (gerundive [§G80]) with **esset**, *had to be passed from one to
     another*; **totiens** adv. *so many times*—to reach Egypt from Rome, several seas were
     crossed; trans. *although she had to travel from sea to sea*; **iustus** *legitimate*; **periclī** =
     perīculī.
95f. **ratiō ratiōnis** F. *reason*; **timent** *they* (i.e., women) *are afraid*; **pavidō ... pec-
     tore** abl. of respect [§G46] *in [their] timid hearts* (sg. for pl. [§G53]); **gelō -āre**
     freeze (tr.); **tremulīs ... plantīs** abl. of cause [§G48] *on [their] trembling feet* (**planta
     -ae** F. lit., *sole of the foot*); **insistō -ere** *stand*.

si iubeat coniunx, durum est conscendere navem,
tunc sentina gravis, tunc summus vertitur aer:
quae moechum sequitur, stomacho valet. illa maritum   100
convomit, haec inter nautas et prandet et errat
per puppem et duros gaudet tractare rudentis.
qua tamen exarsit forma, qua capta iuventa
Eppia? quid vidit propter quod ludia dici
sustinuit? nam Sergiolus iam radere guttur   105
coeperat et secto requiem sperare lacerto;
praeterea multa in facie deformia, sulcus

97   **praestō -āre** *apply [something]* (acc., here **fortem animum**) *to [something]* (dat.,
     here **rēbus** *actions*); **turpiter audent** lit., *they disgracefully dare*, trans. *they, in their*
     disgrace, dare to do.
98   The potential subjunctive [§G 68] **iubeat** indicates repeated action; **dūrum est**
     impers. *it is hard*; **conscendō -ere** *board.*
99   With **sentīna** (-ae F. *bilge water*) supply **est**; **gravis** here *offensive*; **summus ...**
     āēr lit., *the highest air* (**āēr āeris** M.), trans. *the sky*; **vertitur** trans. *spins round—*
     they get dizzy.
100 **quae** *[a woman] who*; **moechus -ī** M. *adulterer*; **stomachō** abl. of respect
     [§G 46] *in [her] stomach* (**stomachus -ī** M.); **illa** trans. *the former*, i.e., the wife who
     is with her husband.
101 **convomō -ere** (tr.) *vomit over*; **haec** trans. *the latter*; **nauta -ae** M. *sailor*; **et ...**
     et ... *both ... and ...*; **prandeō -ēre** *take breakfast.*
102 **puppis puppis** F. *poop* (of a ship), trans. *deck*; **dūrōs ... rudentīs** *rough ropes*
     (**rudens rudentis** M.); **tractō -āre** *handle.*
103 Juvenal asks a question implying that one might have thought that Eppia had
     run off with a handsome young gigolo; **quā ... formā** abl. of cause [§G 48], trans.
     with what good looks; **exardescō -ēre** *be inflamed*; **quā ... iuventā** instrumental abl.
     [§G 47] *by what youthfulness* (**iuventa -ae** F.); with **capta** supply **est.**
104 **propter quod** *on account of which*; **lūdia -ae** F. *female slave in a school of*
     gladiators, trans. *gladiator's woman*; **dīcī** (pres. pass. inf. of **dīcō -ere**) *to be called.*
105 **sustineō -ēre** *put up with, endure*; **nam** (*for*) suggests that because her lover
     had no physical attractions, Eppia must have had some other compelling reason
     for running away with him—this is given in l. 110; **Sergiolus -ī** M. diminutive of
     Sergius, the name of Eppia's lover, trans. *[her] darling Sergius*; **rādō -ere** *shave*;
     guttur gutturis N. *neck*—since it appears to have been fashionable for young men
     to wear beards, Juvenal implies that her lover was of mature years.
106 **sectō ... lacertō** abl. of cause [§G 48] *because of [his] wounded* (lit., *cut*; **secō**
     -āre) *arm* (**lacertus -ī** M.); **requiem spērāre** *to hope for rest* (**requiem** usual acc. of
     requiēs requiētis F.), i.e., to retire from being a gladiator.
107 Take **multa** with **dēformia** (*unsightly [marks]*; **dēformis** adj.) and supply
     erant; **faciēs -ēī** F. *face*; **sulcus -ī** M. *furrow.*

attritus galea mediisque in naribus ingens
gibbus et acre malum semper stillantis ocelli.
sed gladiator erat. facit hoc illos Hyacinthos.   110

~: JUVENAL *Satires* 6.82–110

108   **atterō -ere** *rub*; **galeā** instrumental abl. [§G 47] *by [his] helmet* (**galea -ae** F.);
nārēs nārium F.PL. *nose.*
109   **gibbus -ī** M. *lump*; **ācre malum** trans. *severe* (**ācer**) *complaint* (**malum -ī** N.);
stillantis ocellī gen. of definition [§G 25] *of a constantly* (**semper**) *weeping* (**stillō**
-āre *drip*) *eye* (**ocellus -ī** M. diminutive of **oculus** but used here in the same
sense).
110   **gladiātor gladiātōris** M. *gladiator*; **illōs** i.e., gladiators in general; **Hyacyn-**
thus -ī M. a handsome youth of Greek mythology.

Quis custodiet ...?

In his sixth satire, *On Women*, Juvenal considers how husbands keep
watch over their potentially adulterous wives.

                           Novi
consilia et veteres quaecumque monetis amici,
"pone seram, cohibe." sed quis custodiet ipsos
custodes, qui nunc lascivae furta puellae
hac mercede silent?   *Satires* 6.O29ff.
I'm acquainted with [your] advice and all [your] warnings,
[my] old friends: "Put a bolt [on the door], confine [her]."
But who will guard the guards, who now receive this payment
for keeping quiet about the love affairs of the loose woman
(lit., who now for this payment are quiet ...)?
(The guards receive sexual favors in return for their silence.)

The question **Quis custodiet ipsos custodes?** is often used in politics
as an expression of concern regarding the reliability and accountability
of those in positions of public trust.

The Emptiness of Military Glory

Juvenal's tenth satire is a biting attack on the vanity of human wishes and desires. One of his particular targets is the ambitions of military leaders.

Bellorum exuviae, truncis adfixa tropaeis
lorica et fracta de casside buccula pendens
et curtum temone iugum victaeque triremis   135
aplustre et summo tristis captivus in arcu
humanis maiora bonis creduntur. ad hoc se
Romanus Graiusque et barbarus induperator
erexit, causas discriminis atque laboris
inde habuit: tanto maior famae sitis est quam   140
virtutis. quis enim virtutem amplectitur ipsam,

TEXT   A. Persi Flacci et D. Iuvenalis *Saturae*, ed. W. V. Clausen
      (Oxford Classical Texts, 1992)
METER hexameter [§M I]
     bēllōr(um) | ēxŭvĭ|āē ‖ trūn|cīs ād|fixă trŏ|pāēīs
     lōrīc(a) | ēt frāc|tā ‖ dē | cāssĭdĕ | būccŭlă | pēndēns

133 **exuviae -ārum** F.PL. *spoils;* **truncīs ... tropaeīs** dat. *to lopped-off trophies* (**tropaeum -ī** N.)—the original trophy, or symbol of victory, was a tree stump adorned with weapons of the defeated enemy; **adfīgō -ere** + acc. and dat. *fasten [something] to [something].*

134 **lōrīca -ae** F. *breastplate;* **fractā dē casside** *from a broken helmet* (**cassis cassidis** F.); **buccula -ae** F. *cheek-piece;* **pendeō -ēre** *hang* (intr.).

135f. **curtus** + abl. *stripped of;* **tēmō tēmōnis** M. *pole,* a shaft joining the yoke to a chariot; **iugum -ī** N. *yoke,* a wooden beam fastened over the necks of two horses harnessed together; **victae trirēmis aplustre** *the sternpost* (**aplustre aplustris** N.) *of a captured trireme* (**trirēmis trirēmis** F.)—parts of captured ships were displayed as symbols of victory; **summō ... in arcū** *on the top of a [triumphal] arch* (**arcus -ūs** M.); **tristis captīvus** *sad captive* (**captīvus -ī** M.)—he would have been depicted in relief on the arch.

137ff. Take **hūmānīs ... bonīs** (abl. of comparison [§G 42]) with **maiōra,** *greater than human glories* (**bonum -ī** N.), trans. *glories greater than human,* i.e., glories worthy of the gods; **ad hoc** *to this,* i.e., to attain this; **sē ... ērexit** lit., *has raised himself* (**ērigō -ere**), trans. *have aspired*—both **ērexit** (sg. to agree with the nearest subject [§G 58]) and **habuit** in l. 140 should be translated by the plural; **Grāius** *Greek;* **barbarus** *foreign,* i.e., not Roman or Greek; **induperātor** (**induperātōris** M.; = **imperātor** [§G 95]) *general;* **causās ... labōris** *incentives for [enduring]* (lit., *of*) *danger* (**discrīmen discrīminis** N.) *and toil;* **inde** *from this;* **tantō** abl. of measure of difference [§G 43], lit., *by so much;* **sitis sitis** F. *thirst;* **quam** *than;* **virtūtem ... ipsam** *virtue itself,* i.e., virtue for its own sake; **amplector -ī** *embrace.*

praemia si tollas? patriam tamen obruit olim
gloria paucorum et laudis titulique cupido
haesuri saxis cinerum custodibus, ad quae
discutienda valent sterilis mala robora fici,   145
quandoquidem data sunt ipsis quoque fata sepulcris.
expende Hannibalem: quot libras in duce summo
invenies? hic est quem non capit Africa Mauro
percussa oceano Niloque admota tepenti,

142   **tollās** (**tollō -ere**) potential subj. [§G 68] *you/one were to remove*; **obruit** perf.
has overwhelmed (**obruō -ere**); **ōlim** *in the past.*

143ff.   **glōria -ae** F. *(desire for) glory, ambition*; **laus laudis** F. *praise*; **titulus -ī** M. *inscription, here* **epitaph**; **cupīdō cupīdinis** F. *desire*; **haesūrī** (agreeing with **titulī**)
fut. pple. of **haereō -ēre** *cling (to)*; **saxīs** (dat. after **haesūrī**) **cinerum custōdibus**
to [tomb]stones, the guardians (**custōs custōdis** M.) *of [their] ashes* (**cinis cineris**
M.)—a Roman tomb contained the cremated ashes of the dead person, not the
corpse (the expression *an epitaph that will cling to tombstones* alludes to the imper-
manent nature of such records and anticipates the next two lines); **ad quae** (antecedent **saxīs**) **discutienda** lit., *for which going to be shattered* (gerundive [§G 81]),
trans. *and to shatter these*; **valent ... mala rōbora** *the weak strength* (pl. for sg.
[§G 53]; **rōbur rōboris** N.) *is sufficient* (lit., *strong enough*); **sterilis ... fīcī** *of a sterile
fig tree* (**ficus -ī** F.).

146   **quandoquidem** *since*; **data ... sepulcrīs** *destruction* (**fāta** pl. for sg. [§G 53])
has also been assigned to the graves (**sepulcrum -ī** N.) *themselves*, i.e., as it had been
for the occupants.

147   **expendō -ere** *weigh* (trans.); **Hannibal Hannibalis** M. a Carthaginian general who invaded Italy in the Second Carthaginian War (218–201 B.C.); **quot
lībrās** *how many pounds* (weight; **lībra -ae** F.)—Hannibal's ashes are meant; **in
duce summō** *in the greatest of generals*—the Romans themselves acknowledged
Hannibal's military genius.

148f.   **nōn capit** *does not hold*, i.e., *cannot contain* because of his ambition—the
historic present [§G 60], used here and continued in the following lines, can be retained in translation; **Āfrica** (**-ae** F.) refers to what we think of today as the northern part of the continent; **Maurō percussa ōceanō** *lashed* (**percutiō -ere**) *by the
Moorish* (= Atlantic) *ocean* (instrumental abl. [§G 47]; **ōceanus -ī** M.); **admōta**
(lit., *stretched*, but trans. *extending*; **admoveō -ēre**) is followed by the dative **Nīlō**
(**Nīlus -ī** M.) **tepentī** (**tepeō -ēre**) *(to the warm Nile).*

150   Supply **et admōta** with **rursus** *[and extending] southward* (lit., *backward*—
from the perspective of a Roman, going south in Africa could be described as
going backward); instead of the dative (as in l. 149), we have **ad** + acc.; **Aethiops
Aethiopis** M. *an Ethiopian*; **aliōs elephantōs** *different elephants* (**elephantus -ī**
M.)—the more familiar type were those of northwest Africa.

rursus ad Aethiopum populos aliosque elephantos.　150
additur imperiis Hispania, Pyrenaeum
transilit. opposuit natura Alpemque nivemque:
diducit scopulos et montem rumpit aceto.
iam tenet Italiam, tamen ultra pergere tendit.
"acti" inquit "nihil est, nisi Poeno milite portas　155
frangimus et media vexillum pono Subura."
o qualis facies et quali digna tabella,
cum Gaetula ducem portaret belua luscum!
exitus ergo quis est? o gloria! vincitur idem

151　**addō -ere** *attach, add*; **imperiīs** dat. *to [his] empire* (pl. for sg. [§G 53]; **impe-rium -(i)ī** N.); **Hispānia -ae** F. strictly speaking, the whole Iberian peninsula, but usually translated *Spain*; **Pȳrēnaeus [mons]** *the Pyrenees.*

152　**transiliō -īre** *jump over*—the verb indicates the ease with which Hannibal made the crossing, which was the first step in his invasion of Italy; **oppōnō -ere** *place in the way*; **Alpis Alpis** F. *the Alps*; **nix nivis** F. *snow.*

153　**dīdūcō -ere** *split*; **scopulus -ī** M. *rock*; **rumpit** here *breaks through*; take **acētō** (instrumental abl. [§G 47] *with vinegar*; **acētum -ī** N.) with both verbs—legend had it that in making a way for his troops and elephants, Hannibal removed rocks by first heating them with fire and then softening them with vinegar (whether this was possible on any large scale is doubtful).

154　**tenet** *he occupies*—Hannibal's successes in his first three years in Italy brought a large part of the peninsula under his control, although Rome still resisted; **ultrā** *farther*; **pergō -ere** *proceed*; **tendō -ere** *strive.*

155　Take **actī** (partitive gen. [§G 24]) with **nihil**, lit., *nothing of achievement* (**ac-tum -ī** N.)—trans. the clause *nothing has been achieved*; **Poenō mīlite** instrumental abl. [§G 47] *with Carthaginian soldier*; **portās**—Hannibal means the gates of Rome.

156　Trans. both **frangimus** and **pōno** by the first-person singular; **mediā ... Subūrā** abl. of place where [§G 38] *in the middle of the Subura* (a central district of Rome northeast of the Forum; cf. Martial *Epigrammata* 12.18.2, page 191); **vexil-lum -ī** N. *[military] standard*—to plant (**pōnere**) it in a particular spot symbolized victory.

157　**quālis** here introduces an exclamation; **faciēs -ēī** F. *sight*; **quālī digna tabellā** *worthy of* (**dignus** + abl.) *what a picture* (**tabella -ae** F.).

158　**Gaetūla ... bēlua** *a Gaetulian* (= African) *monster* (**bēlua -ae** F.), i.e., an ele-phant; **ducem ... luscum** *the one-eyed general*—Hannibal had lost an eye to dis-ease early in his Italian campaign; **portō -āre** *transport, carry.*

159　**exitus ... est?** *so* (**ergō**), *what is [his] fate* (**exitus -ūs** M. lit., *end*)?; **vincitur**—Hannibal was defeated at the battle of Zama in 202 B.C.; **īdem** lit., *the same [man].*

nempe et in exilium praeceps fugit atque ibi magnus   160
mirandusque cliens sedet ad praetoria regis,
donec Bithyno libeat vigilare tyranno.

◠: JUVENAL *Satires* 10.133–162

160f.   **nempe** (*of course*) is used here ironically; **exilium -(i)ī** N. *exile*—Hannibal
lived for some time in exile in Bithynia, a small kingdom in northwest Asia Minor
(cf. l. 162); **praeceps (praecipitis)** *headlong*; the phrase **magnus mīrandusque cliens** is in apposition [§G 52] to the understood subject, trans. *[as] an important and
remarkable* (**mīrandus** gerundive used as an attributive adj. [§G 79]) *client* (**cliens
clientis** M., cf. Martial *Epigrammata* 12.18.1–6, page 191); **ad** + acc. here *at*;
praetōria *palace* (pl. for sg. [§G 53]; **praetōrium -(i)ī** N.); **rēgis** (*of the king*) refers
to the same person mentioned in l. 162.

162   *until the Bithynian tyrant should deign to rise*, lit., *until it might be pleasing to*
(**libet** + dat.) *the Bithynian tyrant* (**tyrannus -ī** M.) *to be awake* (**vigilō -āre**).

The Satirist on Satire

If not born to write satire, Juvenal at least felt that circumstances
obliged him to do so.

Difficile est saturam non scribere.   *Satires* 1.30
*It is difficult **not** to write satire.*

Si natura negat, facit indignatio versum.   *Satires* 1.79
*Even if nature tells me not to (lit., says no), indignation
prompts me to write verse (lit., makes the verse).*

Scoffing at the Scofflaws

The two Gracchi brothers, Tiberius and Gaius, were would-be
reformers of the second century B.C. Having caused a great deal of
trouble for the conservative clique that controlled Rome, they came to
be regarded as dangerous revolutionaries. What Juvenal wrote of
them more than two centuries later has passed into proverb for people who complain about how others behave even though they themselves have acted in exactly the same way.

Quis tulerit Gracchos de seditione querentes?   *Satires* 2.24
Who would tolerate the Gracchi complaining about rebellion?

The Vigil of Venus

No author's name is given in the manuscripts of the Pervigilium Veneris (The Vigil of Venus), *but it is thought to be the work of* **Tiberiānus,** *an obscure poet of about* A.D. 300. *The poem is in the form of a song to be sung on the night before the first day of spring, but the highly personal note of the final lines shows that it was not intended to be part of a real festival. The poem's setting is in Hybla, a town in eastern Sicily near Mt. Etna, whose rich volcanic soil would have promoted the lush spring growth and accompanying abundance of animal life that the poet celebrates.*

The enthusiastic appreciation of nature that we see in the Pervigilium Veneris *is something new in Latin literature, but which reappears in the poetry of the Middle Ages. For parallels in English, we must turn to poets of the early nineteenth-century romantic movement, such as Byron and Keats.*

The following is a selection from the poem's 93 lines.

Cras amet qui numquam amavit, quique amavit cras amet!
ver novum, ver iam canorum, vere natus orbis est;
vere concordant amores, vere nubunt alites,
et nemus comam resolvit de maritis imbribus.
cras amorum copulatrix inter umbras arborum   5

TEXT   *Catullus, Tibullus, Pervigilium Veneris,* (various editors) rev. G. P. Gould (Loeb Classical Library, 1988)
METER   trochaic septenarius [§M7]
      crās ă|mēt quī | numqu(am) ă|māvīt ‖ quīqu(e) ă|māvīt | crās ă|mĕt
      vēr nŏ|vūm vēr | iām că|nōrūm ‖ vērĕ | nātŭs | ōrbĭs | ēst

The first line is the refrain, which occurs at irregular intervals throughout the poem.

1   **amet** jussive subj. [§G69] *let him love;* **quīque** = **quī** + **-que.**
2   **vēr vēris** N. (season of) *spring;* supply **est** with **novum** and **canōrum** *spring is new* (i.e., is just beginning), *spring is full of song* (i.e., of birds; **canōrus** adj. of **canor canōris** M. *song of a bird*); **vēre** abl. of time when [§G37]; **nātus orbis est** *the world* (**orbis orbis** M.) *has been born*—the lush growth of spring after winter's bleakness is seen as a new birth.
3   **concordō -āre** *bring hearts together, create harmony;* **amōrēs** i.e., individual instances of love, but trans. *love;* **nūbō -ere** here *mate* (intr.); **āles ālitis** M./F. *bird.*
4   **nemus nemoris** N. *forest;* **coma -ae** F. *foliage;* **resolvō -ere** *release;* **dē** + abl. *because of* (late use); **marītus** adj. *connubial;* **imber imbris** M. *rain*—the metaphor is of the (male) rains fertilizing the (female) forest and so producing leaves.
5   **cōpulātrix cōpulātrīcis** F. *female coupler,* trans. *she who unites* (i.e., Venus).

implicat casas virentes de flagello myrteo;
cras Dione iura dicit fulta sublimi throno.

. . . .

Cras amet qui numquam amavit, quique amavit cras amet!   27
ipsa nymphas diva luco iussit ire myrteo.
it Puer comes puellis; nec tamen credi potest
esse Amorem feriatum, si sagittas vexerit: 30
"ite, nymphae, posuit arma, feriatus est Amor!
iussus est inermis ire, nudus ire iussus est,

6   **implicō -āre** *weave*—for vividness the present is used of a future event (cf. **dīcit**
     in l. 7); **casa -ae** F. *arbor*; **vireō -ēre** *be green*; **dē** + abl. here *from*; **flagellum -ī** N.
     here *shoot* (of a plant); **myrteus** adj. *myrtle*—to provide suitable trysting places for
     lovers, Venus will create shady recesses with shoots of the plant sacred to her, the
     myrtle.

7   **Diōnē** (**Diōnēs** F. a Greek noun) was the mother of Venus in some myths, but
     occasionally, as here, the name is used for Venus herself, who is described as **fulta**
     sublīmī thronō *seated* (**fulciō -īre** lit., *support*) *on [her] lofty* (**sublīmis**) *throne* (in-
     strumental abl. [§G 47]; **thronus -ī** M.); **iūs iūris** N. here *judgment*; **dīcō -ere** here
     deliver.

28   **ipsa ... dīva** *the goddess* (**dīva -ae** F.) *herself*, i.e., Venus; **nympha -ae** F. *nymph*—
     nymphs were minor female divinities who inhabited trees, fountains, and other
     natural phenomena (cf. ll. 53f.) and so were associated with spring and its re-
     growth; **lūcō ... myrteō** dat. of motion toward [§G 35] *to the myrtle grove* (**lūcus -ī**
     M.).

29   **Puer** *the Boy*, i.e., Cupid, Venus' son; **comes** (**comitis** M./F. *companion*) is in
     apposition [§G 52] to **Puer**; **puellīs** dat. *for the girls*, i.e., the nymphs, who were al-
     ways being subjected to sexual overtures by male divinities and so are depicted as
     being wary of Cupid; **crēdī potest** (impers. *it can be believed*) is followed by an
     acc.+inf. [§G 10].

30   **Amor** *Love*, i.e., Cupid; **fēriātus** *keeping a holiday*, trans. *observing the holiday*;
     sagitta -ae F. *arrow*; **vexerit** 3 sg. perf. subj. act. **vehō -ere** *carry*—the subjunctive
     is required in a subordinate clause within an acc.+inf. [§G 87].

31   Venus tries to reassure the nymphs; **īte** 2 pl. imp. of **eō īre** *go*; **posuit arma**
     he has laid down (**posuit** here = **dēposuit**) *[his] weapons.*

32   **inermis** *unarmed*; **nūdus** *naked*, but the word also means *without weapons*—
     Cupid was always naked as far as clothes were concerned.

33   **neu ... neu ... neu ...** (lit., *lest ... nor ... nor ...*) expresses purpose; **quid**
     (indef. pron.) **... laederet** (*do any harm* (**laedō -ere**)) is followed by three instru-
     mental ablatives [§G 47] that refer to the two ways in which Cupid incited love, viz
     with a bow (**arcus -ūs** M.) and arrow or with a lighted torch (**igne** lit., *with fire*)
     that he hurled into a victim's heart.

neu quid arcu neu sagitta neu quid igne laederet.
sed tamen, nymphae, cavete, quod Cupido pulcher est:
totus est in armis idem quando nudus est Amor." 35

· · · · · · · · · · · · · · · · · · · ·

Cras amet qui numquam amavit, quique amavit cras amet! 48
iussit Hyblaeis tribunal stare diva floribus:
praeses ipsa iura dicet, adsidebunt Gratiae. 50
Hybla, totos funde flores, quidquid annus adtulit;
Hybla, florum sume vestem, quantus Aetnae campus est.
ruris hic erunt puellae vel puellae montium,
quaeque silvas, quaeque lucos, quaeque fontes incolunt:
iussit omnes adsidere Pueri mater alitis, 55
iussit, et nudo, puellas nil Amori credere.

· · · · · · · · · · · · · · · · · · · ·

34   **cavēte** 2 pl. imp. of **caveō -ēre** *to take care*; **quod** *because*; **Cupīdō Cupīdinis** M.
     Cupid.
35   Translate **tōtus** by an adverb [§G 55], *fully*; **īdem ... Amor** (*[that] same Love*,
     i.e., Cupid) is the subject of the main clause and the **quandō** clause—there is a
     play on the two senses of **nūdus** (cf. l. 32): even when he is unarmed, he is danger-
     ous because in his nakedness his beauty can of itself generate love.
49   The subject of **iussit** is **dīva** (*the goddess*, i.e.,Venus); **Hyblaeīs ... flōribus** abl.
     of place where [§G 38] *amid the flowers of Hybla*; **tribūnal tribūnālis** N. *court* (of
     law); **stāre** here *be set up*.
50   **praeses** (**praesidis** M./F.) is in apposition [§G 52] to **ipsa** (*she herself [as] adju-*
     dicator); **adsideō -ēre** lit., *sit by [her]*, i.e., *assist [her]*; **Grātiae -ārum** F.PL. *the*
     Graces—see note to Horace *Odes* 4.7.5, page 81.
51   **Hybla** (voc. of **Hybla -ae** F.) itself is now addressed—the region around the
     town is meant; **tōtōs funde flōrēs** *pour forth* (**fundō -ere**) *all [your] flowers*; **quid-**
     quid indef. rel. pron. *whatever*; **adtulit** 3 sg. perf. ind. act. **adferō -ferre** *bring.*
52   **flōrum ... vestem** *garment of flowers*; **sumō -ere** here *put on*; **quantus** (rel. adj.
     of quantity *of what size, how big*) agrees with **campus** (**-ī** M. *plain*) in gender and
     number but has as its antecedent **vestem**, lit., *of what size is Etna's* (**Aetna -ae** F.)
     plain, trans. *as big as is Etna's plain*—Hybla's garment is to be the whole plain to
     the west of the volcano of Mt. Etna.
53f. Various types of nymphs are to be present; each **quaeque** = **quae** + **-que** *and*
     [those] who; **incolō -ere** *inhabit, dwell in.*
55   **omnēs** i.e., all the nymphs; **Puerī ... ālitis** *of the winged Boy*, i.e., Cupid, who
     was always represented as having wings (**āles** here an adj.).
56   **et** *even*; **nūdō ... Amōrī** dat. after **crēdere** (here *put trust in*); **nīl** here used as
     an emphatic negative.

Cras amet qui numquam amavit, quique amavit cras amet!   80
ecce iam subter genestas explicant tauri latus,
quisque tutus, quo tenetur, coniugali foedere!
subter umbras cum maritis, ecce, balantum greges!
et canoras non tacere diva iussit alites:
iam loquaces ore rauco stagna cygni perstrepunt;   85
adsonat Terei puella subter umbram populi,
ut putes motus amoris ore dici musico,
et neges queri sororem de marito barbaro.
illa cantat, nos tacemus. quando ver venit meum?
quando fiam uti chelidon, ut tacere desinam?   90

81 **ecce** interjection *behold!*; **subter** + acc. *under*; **genesta -ae** F. (the shrub called) *broom*; **explicō -āre** *stretch*; **taurī** nom. pl. of **taurus -ī** M. *bull*; **latus lateris** N. *flank*—trans. by the plural, *[their] flanks.*

82 **quisque** *each* (i.e., of the bulls) is in apposition [§G 52] to **taurī**; **tūtus** *secure*; the antecedent of **quō** (instrumental abl. [§G 47]) is **foedere**; **coniugālī foedere** abl. of respect [§G 46] *in the conjugal bond.*

83 **cum marītīs** *with [their] mates*; **bālans bālantis** M./F. (lit., *bleater*) poetic word for *sheep*, but here only ewes are meant; **grex gregis** M. *flock.*

84 **canōrās … ālitēs** *tuneful birds* (cf. ll. 2f.).

85 **loquācēs … cygnī** *noisy* (**loquax (loquācis)**) *swans* (**cygnus -ī** M.); **ōre raucō** instrumental abl. [§G 47] *with harsh-sounding voices* (lit., *mouth*; on the use of the sg. **ōre**, cf. **latus** in l. 81); **stagna** (**stagnum -ī** N. *pool*) is accusative plural after **perstrepunt** (**perstrepō -ere** *fill with a din*).

86 **adsonō -āre** *sing in accompaniment*; **Tēreī puella** lit., *Tereus' girl*, viz **Philomēla**—**Tēreus** (-ī M.), king of Thrace, married Philomela, an Athenian princess, and had a son, **Itys**, by her; later he raped Philomela's sister, **Procnē**, and cut out her tongue to ensure her silence; Philomela, however, discovered what had happened; in revenge she killed Itys and used his body for a meal she prepared for Tereus; when Tereus learned what he had eaten, he immediately started to chase the two sisters, but the gods resolved the matter by turning the three into birds: Philomela became a nightingale and forever lamented the loss of Itys and the mutilation of Procne; Procne became a swallow and regained the power of speech, though only as chirping (cf. l. 90); Tereus became a hoopoe, which was supposed to chase the other two birds (in earlier versions of the story, the roles of Philomela and Procne are reversed); **pōpulus -ī** F. *poplar (tree).*

87 **ut putēs … negēs** adv. clauses of result [§G 84] *so that you would think … and you would not say*, both followed by acc.+inf. constructions [§G 10]; **mōtūs** here *feelings* (**mōtus -ūs** M.); **ōre … mūsicō** instrumental abl. [§G 47] *with [her] melodious voice*; **dīcī** pres. pass. inf. of **dīcō -ere** here *declare.*

88 **querī sorōrem** acc.+inf. after **negēs**, trans. *that a sister* (i.e., Philomela) *was complaining*; **dē** here *about*; **barbarus** adj. *barbarous, cruel*—Tereus' conduct was typical of Thracians, who, according to Greek tradition, were considered uncivilized barbarians.

perdidi Musam tacendo, nec me Phoebus respicit.

sic Amyclas, cum tacerent, perdidit silentium.

Cras amet qui numquam amavit, quique amavit cras amet!

∾: ∾

89   **illa** i.e., Philomela; **cantō -āre** *sing*; **nōs** pl. for sg. [§G53]—in a personal note, the poet laments his own silence, presumably because he is unable to declare his love through lack of confidence; **quandō …?** here the interrogative *when …?*

90   **fīam** I sg. fut. **fīō fierī** *become*; **utī** conj. *like, as*; **chelīdōn chelīdonis** F. *swallow*—the poet wishes to regain his voice as Procne had done (cf. note to l. 86).

91   **perdidī** I sg. perf. ind. act. **perdō -ere** here *lose*; **Mūsa -ae** F. *Muse,* i.e., the source of poetic inspiration; **tacendō** instrumental abl. [§G47] of the gerund [§G78] *by being silent*; **Phoebus** (-ī M., = **Apollō**) was the god of poets; **respiciō -ere** *take notice of.*

92   The reference is to a story that became proverbial: the town of **Amyclae** (-ārum F.PL.) had been disturbed by false alarms about invaders so often that a law was passed forbidding such rumors; when a genuine enemy approached, no one dared report the fact and so the town was captured; the subject of **perdidit** (here *destroy*) is **silentium** (-(i)ī N. *silence*), and its object is **Amyclās**; the understood subject of **tacērent** is **Amyclae**.

"Bread and Circuses"

By the beginning of the second century A.D., the Roman populace had long since forgotten the power it wielded under the Republic. Juvenal saw the **plebs** of his day as having only two concerns:

> qui dabat olim
> **imperium, fasces, legiones, omnia, nunc se**
> **continet atque duas tantum res anxius optat,**
> **panem et circenses.**   *Satires* 10.78ff.
> [*The people*] *who once used to grant* [*military*] *command,*
> *public offices, legions, everything, now limits itself and longs*
> *eagerly for just two things, bread and public games.*

The common interpretation *bread and circuses* is a mistranslation. The **circensēs** (circensium M.PL.; = **lūdī**) were public games held in a **circus** (-ī M.), a circular or oval arena surrounded by seating for spectators.

"Bread and circuses," in today's political parlance, continues to be a derogatory catchword for policies intended to mitigate discontent among the people.

The Happy Peasant

Claudian (**Claudius Claudiānus**, *c.* A.D. *370–c. 404*) *lived when Rome and the western portion of the old empire were in decline. Although living centuries after the great figures of the Silver Age, he continued in their traditions and style and produced poetry that, in its technique, can bear comparison with that of earlier writers.*

Felix, qui patriis aevum transegit in arvis,
  ipsa domus puerum quem videt, ipsa senem;
qui baculo nitens in qua reptavit harena
  unius numerat saecula longa casae.
illum non vario traxit fortuna tumultu,   5
  nec bibit ignotas mobilis hospes aquas.
non freta mercator tremuit, non classica miles,
  non rauci lites pertulit ille fori.

TEXT   Claudiani *Carmina*, ed. J. B. Hall (Bibliotheca Teubneriana, 1985)
METER   elegiac couplet [§M 2]
        fēlīx | quī pătrĭ|īs ‖ āē|vūm trān|sēgĭt ĭn | ārvīs
        īpsă dŏ|mūs pŭĕ|rūm ‖ quēm vĭdĕt | īpsă sĕ|nēm

1f. **Fēlīx** [**est**] *he is happy*; **patriīs ... in arvīs** *in ancestral fields* (**arvum -ī** N.); **aevum -ī** N. *age, life*; **transigō -ere** *spend*; **quem**, which introduces the second adjectival clause, is postponed [§G 4]; **ipsa domus** *the very house*, i.e., the one in his ancestral fields; **puerum** [*as*] *a boy*; **ipsa senem** i.e., *the very* [*house sees as*] *an old man*—trans. *whom the very* [*same*] *house sees as a boy and sees as an old man.*

3   **baculum -ī** N. *staff*; **nītor nītī** + abl. *lean on*; **in quā ... harēnā** abridged expression for **in harēnā in quā**; trans. *leaning on* [*his*] *staff on the sand* (**harēna -ae** F.) *on which he crawled* (**reptō -āre**)—in his old age, the peasant totters over the same sand on which he crawled as a young child.

4   **numerō -āre** *count*, i.e., look back over; the *long generations* (**saeculum -ī** N.) are his own and those of his forebears, who lived in the one cottage (**casa -ae** F.).

5   **variō ... tumultū** instrumental abl. [§G 47] *with unstable turmoil* (**tumultus -ūs** M.); **traxit** (**trahō -ere**) *has dragged off*—the reference is to foreign invasion.

6   *nor has he drunk unfamiliar* (**ignōtās**) *waters* [*as*] *a restless* (**mōbilis**) *stranger*—**hospes** is in apposition [§G 52] to the understood subject *he*.

7   **fretum -ī** N. *sea*; **mercātor mercātōris** M. *merchant*, trans. [*as*] *a merchant*—**mercātor** and **mīles** are in apposition [§G 52] to the understood subject *he*; **tremō -ere** *tremble at*; **classicum -ī** N. *trumpet call*; **mīles** [*as*] *a soldier*—supply **tremuit**.

8   **raucī lītēs ... forī** *the disputes* (**līs lītis** F.) *of the noisy forum*—in every Roman city there was a **forum**, around which legal activity was centered; **pertulit** 3 sg. perf. ind. act. **perferō -ferre** *endure, put up with*—the poem's hero had not been a lawyer.

9   **indocilis rērum** *ignorant of the world* (lit., *things*); **vīcīnus** *neighboring*—the city is Verona in northern Italy (cf. l. 17); **nescius** + gen. *unacquainted with.*

indocilis rerum, vicinae nescius urbis,
    aspectu fruitur liberiore poli.   10
frugibus alternis, non consule computat annum:
    autumnum pomis, ver sibi flore notat.
idem condit ager soles idemque reducit,
    metiturque suo rusticus orbe diem,
ingentem meminit parvo qui germine quercum   15
    aequaevumque videt consenuisse nemus,
proxima cui nigris Verona remotior Indis
    Benacumque putat litora Rubra lacum.
sed tamen indomitae vires firmisque lacertis
    aetas robustum tertia cernit avum.   20

10   **aspectū ... līberiōre** abl. after **fruitur**, *he enjoys a freer* (compar. of **līber**) *view* (**aspectus -ūs** M.); **polus -ī** M. *sky.*

11f.   **frūgibus alternīs, nōn consule** instrumental abl. [§G 47] *by alternating crops* (**frux frūgis** F.), *not by the consul* (**consul consulis** M.)—a year was normally designated by the names of the consuls who held office, but our peasant distinguishes one year from another by the crops he planted; **computō -āre** *calculate;* **autumnus -ī** M. *autumn;* **pōmum -ī** N. *fruit;* **vēr vēris** N. *spring;* **sibi ... notat** *marks* (**notō -āre**) *for himself*—the implication is that he makes no use of a normal calendar.

13f.   Because he never leaves his field, it is said to set (**condō -ere** lit., *bury*) and bring back (**redūcō -ere**) the sun; the plural **sōlēs** is used for emphasis (cf. Catullus *Carmina* 5.4, page 27); **mētior -īrī** *measure;* **suō ... orbe** instrumental abl. [§G 47] *with his own luminary* (**orbis orbis** M. lit., *orb,* i.e., of the sun)—the world of our peasant (**rusticus -ī** M.) is so confined that he seems to have his own sun.

15   The antecedent of the postponed **quī** [§G 4] (and of **cui** in l. 17) is **rusticus** in l. 14—trans. both adjectival clauses by separate sentences; **ingentem ... quercum** *the huge oak* (**quercus -ūs** F.); **parvō ... germine** abl. of origin [§G 41] *from a small seedling* (**germen germinis** N.).

16   **aequaevum ... nemus** lit., *the forest* (**nemus nemoris** N.) *of the same age*—the forest had been planted at the same time he was born; **consenuisse** (**consenescō -ere**) *to have grown old,* i.e., *with him* (as implied by con-).

17f.   **proxima ... Vērōna** *neighboring* (lit., *very close*) *Verona* (**Vērōna -ae** F.); **cui** dat. of reference [§G 32] *for whom;* with **remōtior** (compar. of **remōtus**, *more distant*) supply **est;** **nigrīs ... Indīs** abl. of comparison [§G 42] *than the dark Indians* (**Indus -ī** M.); **Bēnācum ... lacum** *Lake* (**lacus -ūs** M.) *Benacus* (a lake near Verona); with **lītora Rubra** *the Red shores,* i.e., *the Red Sea* (cf. Lygdamus 3.3.17, page 123) supply **esse.**

19f.   **sed tamen** lit., *but however,* trans. *however*—the peasant might be ignorant of geography, but he enjoys healthy old age and has grandchildren; with **indomitae vīrēs** supply **sunt,** *[his] strength [is] unbroken;* **firmīs ... avum** *the third age* (**aetās aetātis** F.) *sees [him as] a grandfather* (**avus -ī** M.), *vigorous* (**robustus**) *with strong arms* (**lacertus -ī** M.; **firmīs ... lacertīs** abl. of respect [§G 46])—the third age is that of an old man.

erret et extremos alter scrutetur Hiberos:
   plus habet hic vitae, plus habet ille viae.

~: CLAUDIAN *Shorter poems*, 20

21   **erret … scrūtētur** jussive subj. [§G69] *let another* (**alter**) *wander and explore* (**scrūtor -ārī**); **extrēmos … Hibērōs** *farthest Spaniards* (**Hibērus -ī** M.)—for the Romans, Spain was at the western extremity of the known world.

22   **hic … ille …** *the former* (i.e., the peasant) … *the latter* (the traveler of l. 21) …; **plūs … vītae, plūs … viae** partitive gen. [§G24] *more life, more traveling* (lit., *journey*).

Stoicism Embraced

Stoicism was developed in Greece from the end of the fourth century B.C. While the philosophical doctrine encompassed intellectual fields such as logic and physics, it was the ethical teaching of Stoicism that had the most appeal in Rome, where its influence continued to grow under the Empire.

Central to the Stoic position was fate, which was identified with Jupiter. Everything in our lives is predestined, and a good Stoic accepted this with good grace. This attitude is aptly described in a translation made by the younger Seneca from a leading Greek Stoic, Cleanthes. The god addressed is Jupiter himself.

Duc, o parens celsique dominator poli,
quocumque placuit: nulla parendi mora est;
adsum inpiger. fac nolle, comitabor gemens
malusque patiar facere quod licuit bono.
ducunt volentem fata, nolentem trahunt.   *ad Lūcīlium* 107.11

Lead, O father and lord of the lofty sky, wherever you have decided (lit., it has been pleasing [to you]). I do not hesitate to obey (lit., there is no delay in obeying). I am here [and am] eager. Suppose that [I am] unwilling—I will complain and follow (lit., will follow complaining), and as a wicked man, I will put up with doing what I could have done as a virtuous one (lit., what was allowed to [me to do as] a virtuous [one]). The fates lead the willing [but] drag the unwilling.

GRAMMAR

Formal Latin poetry, such as that of Vergil, employed a language that had developed over the two centuries preceding the Augustan Age (see the time line on page xix). Despite changes in style, it remained the language used by subsequent poets, and we call it *Latin poetic diction*. It diverged somewhat from that of Cicero's speeches, which scholars have taken as the standard of classical Latin and have used as a convenient yardstick to describe the language of other writers, both of prose and verse.

Latin literature was written in the shadow of Greek originals. The influence of the latter extended even to language, and Roman poets introduced constructions that were foreign to their native tongue. An example is the accusative of respect (§G15 below), which is not found in Cicero but was used by Augustan poets and even by prose writers of the Silver Age, who affected a style tinged with poetic idiom.

Latin poetic diction also differed from formal Ciceronian prose in its use of archaisms. In addition to individual words that had passed out of normal use, Latin poets employed word forms and modes of expression no longer current: obsolete forms such as the genitive plural **deum** (= **deōrum**) (§G95 below), as well as points of syntax that reflect an earlier stage of the language. This is especially noticeable in certain case uses. In prose, for example, the use of the accusative to express motion toward is restricted to towns, small islands, and a few other words. In verse, however, it is used indiscriminately, and here, as elsewhere, poetic use reflects an earlier age when the accusative was regularly used in this way (§G13 below).

Some words and forms were neither archaisms nor part of the language of Cicero's speeches. Within a limited range, poets could coin new words, such as **squāmeus** (*scaly,* from **squāma -ae** *scale* + **-eus**; VERGIL *Georgics* 2.154, 3.426). They could also use forms not accepted in educated speech, for example, the third-person plural, perfect indicative active ending **-ēre**, which was a useful metrical alternative to the standard **-ērunt**.

Not all Latin poetry was formal. Poetry of an informal type is represented in this book by the plays of Plautus and Terence, Catullus' personal poems, Publilius Syrus' aphorisms, and Horace's *Sermōnēs.* These authors wrote in a language close to the everyday speech of the educated, as exemplified in Cicero's letters.

THE GRAMMAR SUMMARY that follows will help you toward a full under-standing of the poetry selections in this book. It deals mainly with syntax, that is, the ways in which words are combined to form sentences. We as-sume that you are familiar with the following points of grammar.

- The different categories of words in Latin, that is, the parts of speech: noun, pronoun, adjective, adverb, preposition, verb, conjunction, and interjection
- The declension of nouns, pronouns, and adjectives
- The comparison of adjectives and adverbs
- The conjugation of verbs
- The form of a simple Latin sentence (subject/predicate, agreement of adjectives, agreement of subject and verb, and so on)
- The different types of clauses (main and subordinate clauses (adverbial, adjectival, and noun))

It is important that you understand the following terms.

- **Sentence** A syntactic unit that expresses a complete thought or action. It normally contains at least one main clause and may be either a state-ment, question, or command.
- **Clause** A group of words forming a sense unit and containing one fi-nite verb, for example, *the Gauls* **feared** *Caesar* and *I* **disapprove** *of orgies at Baiae* (the finite verb is in bold type). Clauses are divided into **main clauses**, which can stand on their own, and **subordinate clauses**, which cannot. Subordinate clauses are further divided into **adverbial clauses**, which function as adverbs in the sentence, **adjectival clauses**, which function as adjectives, and **noun clauses**, which function as nouns.
- **Phrase** An intelligible group of words, none of which is a finite verb, for example, *on the sea* and *Hannibal's blind eye*. A phrase can be used by it-self only in certain circumstances, such as in responding to a question.

The grammar points are referenced by number in the notes to the selec-tions, as follows.

assiduīs ... luctibus instrumental abl. [§G 47] *with constant sorrows*

All examples, except those marked with an asterisk (*), are taken from the poetry selections. The Latin word or words that illustrate a particular use are italicized.

WORD ORDER

Because poets were restricted by considerations of meter and rhythm, word order in Latin verse was much freer than in prose. The most striking differences are the following.

G1   *Adjectives* and the nouns with which they agree are sometimes separated to an extent that would be unusual in prose.

Tālibus **Aenēās ardentem et torva tuentem lēnībat** *dictīs* **animum.**
> VERGIL *Aeneid* 6.467f.
With such words Aeneas tried to soothe [her] burning anger and grim looks.

G2   *Adverbs* in prose are usually placed immediately before the word they qualify; this norm is often broken in verse.

Illō *nōn* **validus** *subiit* **iuga tempore taurus.**   TIBULLUS *Elegies* 1.3.41
At that time, a strong bull did not go under the yoke.

Conveniunt nostrīs auribus ista *magis.*   MARTIAL *Epigrammata* 4.41.2
That is more suited to our ears.

... contactum nullīs *ante* **cupīdinibus.**   PROPERTIUS *Elegies* 1.1.2
... previously smitten by no desires.

G3   *Coordinating conjunctions*, such as **et** (*and*) and **nec** (*nor*), are sometimes placed after the first word or words of the phrase or clause that they join to what precedes.

... cēdat *et* **auriferī rīpa benigna Tagī!**   OVID *Amōrēs* 1.15.34
... and let the generous bank of gold-bearing Tagus yield!
(in prose, **et cēdat ...**)

Fulminat illa oculīs et, quantum fēmina, saevit,
    spectaclum captā *nec* minus urbe fuit.   Propertius *Elegies* 4.8.55f.
[Her] eyes flashed with lightning and she raged as much
    as a woman [can], nor was the sight anything short of
    [that of] a captured city.
    (in prose, **nec spectaclum captā ...**)

In verse, **-que** *and* is sometimes placed after the second, third, or even fourth word of the clause that it joins to what precedes.

Nōndum caeruleās pīnus contempserat undās,
    effūsum ventīs praebuerat*que* sinum.   Tibullus *Elegies* 1.3.37f.
[A ship of] pine had not yet scorned the blue waves and exposed
    [its] billowing sail to the winds.
    (in prose, **effūsumque ventīs praebuerat ...**)

(G4) *Subordinating conjunctions, relative pronouns,* and *interrogative pronouns* can be placed after the first word or words of the clause they introduce.

Coniugis auguriō *quamquam* Tītānia mōta est ...
                              Ovid *Metamorphōsēs* 1.395
Although the Titan's daughter was moved by the interpretation
    of [her] spouse ...
    (in prose, **quamquam coniugis auguriō ...**)
... in tōtō semper *ut* orbe canar.   Ovid *Amōrēs* 1.15.8
... so that I may be sung forever in the whole world.
    (in prose, **ut in tōtō semper ...**)
Eurydicā prognāta, pater *quam* noster amāvit ...
                         Ennius *Annālēs* 1 fr. xxix.3
Daughter of Eurydica, whom our father loved ...
    (in prose, **quam pater ...**)
Nescio tam multīs *quid* scrībās, Fauste, puellīs.
                       Martial *Epigrammata* 11.64.1
I don't know, Faustus, what you write to so many girls.
    (in prose, **quid tam multīs ...**)

(G5) An antecedent can be placed after the adjectival clause referring to it. (This also occurs in prose.)

Quem tū, Melpomenē, semel nascentem placidō lūmine vīderis,
    illum nōn labor Isthmius clārābit.   Horace *Odes* 4.3.1ff.
[The one] whom you, Melpomene, have once looked upon with a kindly eye
    at his birth, toil in the Isthmian Games will not make [him] famous.
    (**illum** is the antecedent of **quem**)

NOUNS AND PRONOUNS

Uses of Cases

A striking feaure of the Romance languages, which have descended from Latin, is how prepositional use has expanded to assume the meanings covered by cases in classical Latin; for example, **mīles hostem gladiō interficit** (*the soldier kills an enemy with a sword*) is in French **le soldat tue un ennemi** *avec* **une épée**.

In its earliest form (of which we have no direct evidence), Latin seems to have employed cases mainly, if not completely, without prepositions. As the language developed, prepositions were sometimes added for greater clarity. In classical Latin, the process was in midcourse, and yet poets retained certain constructions where the accusative and ablative cases were used by themselves but where ordinary speech added a preposition.

It is important to remember that a Roman did not speak or write with a list of case uses in the back of his head. These have been devised to help in learning Latin and in analyzing texts; distinctions are not always clearcut, and a particular example can often be interpreted in different ways.

Nominative

G6 The *nominative* is used for the *subject* of a finite verb.

Ipse Epicūrus obīt.   Lucretius *Dē rērum nātūrā* 3.1042
Epicurus himself died.

It is also used for the *predicate* of a finite copulative verb, that is, a verb such as *to be*, *seem*, *appear*, or *be called* that is followed by a description or definition of the subject.

Sum *pius* Aenēās.   *Vergil *Aeneid* 1.378
I am good Aeneas.

Quod nisi concēdās, habeāre *insuāvis*.   *Horace *Sermōnēs* 1.3.85
If you were not to concede this, you would be considered harsh.

Vocative

G7 The *vocative* is used to address another person.

Exī ē culīnā sīs forās, *mastīgia*.   Plautus *Mostellāria* 1
Come out into the open from the kitchen, if you please, [you] rascal.

Nīl recitās et vīs, *Māmerce*, poēta vidērī.
          Martial *Epigrammata* 2.88.1
You recite nothing, and [yet] wish to appear a poet, Mamercus.

Accusative

G8 The *accusative* is used for the *direct object* of transitive verbs and *after certain prepositions.*

Quid tam sollicitīs *vītam* consūmimus annīs?

MANILIUS *Astronomica* 4.1

Why do we spend our lives in such anxious years?

... priusquam tellūs in *longās* est patefacta *viās*.

TIBULLUS *Elegies* 1.3.35f.

... before the earth was cleared into long roads.

G9 Because of their meaning, some verbs can take *two accusatives*.

❨ *Factitive* verbs, that is, verbs of *making, calling, thinking*, etc. (The English construction is usually the same.)

Ingeniī ... vocās *carmen* inertis *opus*. OVID *Amōrēs* 1.15.2
You call poetry the work of a lazy mind.

❨ Verbs of *asking, teaching*, and a few others

Tū frustrā ... poscis *Quintilium* deōs. HORACE *Odes* 1.24.11f.
You in vain ask the gods for Quintilius.

Is *hunc hominem cursūram* docet. *PLAUTUS *Trinummus* 1016
He teaches this man [the art of] running.

When a verb of the second type is put into the passive, one of the accusatives can be kept (**retained accusative**).

Chloē ... *dulcīs* docta *modōs*. HORACE *Odes* 3.9.9f.
Chloe, skilled (lit., having been taught) sweet melodies.

G10 The *accusative-and-infinitive* construction is used after verbs of *saying, thinking, believing, showing, perceiving*, etc., where English normally uses a noun clause introduced by *that*. The subject of the infinitive is put into the accusative, and the tense of the infinitive (present, future, or perfect) is that of the finite verb in the original statement.

Necdum etiam *sēsē* quae vīsit *vīsere* crēdit.

CATULLUS *Carmina* 64.55

Not even yet does she believe that she is seeing what she sees.

Lapidēs in corpore terrae ossa reor *dīcī*.

OVID *Metamorphōsēs* 1.393f.

*I think that stones are called (**dīcī**) bones in the earth's body.*

G11 The accusative is used to express *time how long.*

Diēs noctēsque bibite.   Plautus *Mostellāria* 22
Drink for days and nights.

In Silver Latin, the ablative can be used for this purpose.

Sēcūra potes *tōtīs* tussīre *diēbus*.   Martial *Epigrammata* 1.19.3
You can cough without care for entire days.

G12 The accusative is used to express *spatial extent.*

Sulmo mihī patria est, ... *mīlia* quī noviens distat ab urbe *decem*.
                                        Ovid *Tristia* 4.10.3f.
My native place is Sulmo, which is nine times ten (i.e., ninety) miles
  from the city (i.e., Rome).

G13 *Motion toward* is expressed by the accusative more freely in verse
than in prose, where it is confined to certain nouns.

Arma virumque canō, Trōiae quī prīmus ab ōrīs
  Ītaliam fātō profugus Lāvīniaque vēnit lītora.   Vergil *Aeneid* 1.1ff.
I sing of arms and of the man who, an exile by fate,
  first came from the shores of Troy to Italy and the coasts
  of Lavinium.

G14 The accusation of *exclamation* indicates amazement, admiration,
or distress. It is sometimes preceded by **ō** or some other word of
exclamation.

Ō tē, Bōlāne, cerebrī *fēlīcem*!   Horace *Sermōnēs* 1.9.11f.
O Bolanus, [how] fortunate [you are] in [your] bad temper!

Mē *miserum*, quantī montēs volvuntur aquārum!   Ovid *Tristia* 1.2.19
Unhappy me! What great mountains of water are surging up!

G15 *Accusative of respect* is the term used for a noun that qualifies an
adjective or verb and defines the sphere in which the adjective or
verb is to be applied. For a literal translation, *with respect to* is prefixed to
the noun so used, but some change is needed for an idiomatic English
translation.

Nōndum etiam *sensūs* dēperditus *omnīs*.   Propertius *Elegies* 1.3.11
Not even yet deprived of all my senses.
  (lit., *Not even yet lost with respect to all [my] senses.*)

… nōn teretī strophiō lactentēs vincta papillās.

Catullus *Carmina* 64.65

… nor [were] her milk-white breasts bound with a smooth band.
(lit., *[she was] not bound with respect to [her] milk-white breasts …*)

Caeruleōs … implexae crīnibus anguīs Eumenidēs.

Vergil *Georgics* 4.482f.

The Furies, with blue snakes intertwined in [their] hair.
(lit., *The Furies, intertwined with respect to blue snakes in [their] hair.*)

When the accusative is used in this way with the passive of verbs meaning *put on* (**induō**), *take off* (**exuō**), and the like, the verb is to be translated as active.

Induitur chlamydem. Silius Italicus *Pūnica* 16.240
He put on a cloak.

Compare the genitive of respect (§G 22) and ablative of respect (§G 46).

G 16 The *adverbial accusative* involves the use of a neuter singular pronoun or a neuter adjective (singular or plural) as an adverb. **Nihil** (*nothing*) is so used as an emphatic negative and may be literally translated *not at all* or *in no way*.

Forma nihil magicīs ūtitur auxiliīs. Tibullus *Elegies* 1.8.24
Beauty has no use for the aids of magic (lit., *does not use magic aids at all*).

… tē spectat et audit dulce rīdentem. Catullus *Carmina* 51.3ff.
… [who] looks at you and hears you laughing sweetly.

… torva tuentem. Vergil *Aeneid* 6.467
… looking grimly (lit., *… looking grim [things]*).

G 17 A *cognate accusative* is an accusative noun that is etymologically related to the verb by which it is governed.

Nōmen parentēs nōminārunt Claudiam. *Verse Epitaphs* B.3
[Her] parents gave her the name of Claudia
(lit., *named [her] the name Claudia*).

Included here are accusatives used in exactly the same way but with nouns not etymologically related to the verb.

Mūtat terra vicēs. Horace *Odes* 4.7.3
The earth undergoes [its] regular changes (lit., *changes [its] successive changes*). (**vicēs** = **mūtātiōnēs**)

Genitive

A noun in the genitive qualifies another word, which can be a noun, adjective, verb, or adverb. Most uses of the genitive are to be translated by *of;*

sometimes, the English genitive is a possible alternative (**gladius** *mīlitis* (*the sword of the soldier* or *the soldier's sword*)). However, certain uses require a different translation.

G18 A *possessive genitive* can be used to indicate simple possession.

> **Dēformis harundō Cōcȳtī.**   VERGIL *Georgics* 4.478f.
> *The ugly reed of the Cocytus* (or *Cocytus' ugly reed*).

It can also be used of a person (for example, an author or sculptor) who has created something.

> **Accipe *fācundī* Culicem ... *Marōnis*.**   *MARTIAL *Epigrammata* 14.185.1
> *Receive the* Culex *of the eloquent Maro.*

Sometimes the relationship between a noun and a qualifying genitive is one of association rather than actual possession.

> **Hōra *libellōrum* decuma est ... *meōrum*.**   MARTIAL *Epigrammata* 4.8.7
> *The tenth hour belongs to my little books* (i.e., *is the time for my little books*).
>
> **Fāma *ducis*.**   LUCAN *Bellum cīvīle* 1.144
> *A reputation as a leader.*

G19 The *genitive of characteristic* is used with a third-person singular form of **sum** to mean *it is the part/duty/mark/habit/characteristic of someone [to do something]*. Context shows which of these nouns should be used in the translation.

> **Pauperis est numerāre pecus.**   *OVID *Metamorphōsēs* 13.824
> *It is [characteristic] of a poor man to count [his] livestock.*
>
> **Nunc ea mē exquīrere *inīquī patris* est.**   TERENCE *Andria* 186f.
> *For me to inquire into these things now would be* (lit., *is*) *[the action] of a harsh father.*

G20 The *genitive of quality/description* is an attribute of the noun it qualifies, just as in English phrases such as *a person **of great talent***. In Latin, this genitive must always be accompanied by an adjective.

> **Inīquae mentis asellus.**   HORACE *Sermōnēs* 1.9.20
> *A donkey of sullen disposition.*
>
> **Animōsī ... Accius ōris.**   OVID *Amōrēs* 1.15.19
> *Accius of spirited mouth.*

The genitive of quality/description coincides with a use of the ablative (see §G44). The distinction usually observed in prose (the genitive for an inherent characteristic, the ablative for an external one) is ignored in verse.

(G21) The *genitive of value* is used when a person or thing is assessed or valued.

Rūmōrēs ... senum sevēriōrum omnēs *ūnius* aestimēmus *assis*.

CATULLUS *Carmina* 5.2f.

Let us value all the gossip of too narrow-minded old men
at a single as.
(**as** assis N. a coin of small value)

Plūris hōc ... mihi eris.   HORACE *Sermōnēs* 1.9.7f.

I'll value you all the more because of that (lit., *because of that*
you will be of greater value to me).

(G22) A wide range of adjectives or their equivalents can be followed by a *genitive of respect*, that is, a noun in the genitive that defines the sphere in which an adjective is to be applied in a particular context. This genitive can be roughly translated *with respect to.*

Ō *sceptrī* venerande Syphax.   SILIUS ITALICUS *Pūnica* 16.248

O Syphax of venerable scepter.
(lit., *O Syphax to be venerated with respect to [your] scepter.*)

Ō tē, Bōlāne, *cerebrī* fēlīcem!   HORACE *Sermōnēs* 1.9.11f.

O Bolanus, [how] fortunate [you are] in [your] bad temper!

This use is common in poetry from the time of Vergil and Horace, but does not occur in prose until the Silver Age. Compare the accusative of respect (§G15) and ablative of respect (§G46).

(G23) A noun used as an *objective genitive* stands in the same relation to the noun or adjective that it qualifies as an object does to a finite verb. **Ēmathiōn, *aequī* cultor timidusque *deōrum*** (*Emathion, lover of what is right and [a man] fearful of the gods* (*OVID *Metamorphōsēs* 5.100)) could also be translated *Emathion, who loved what is right and feared the gods*, because **aequī** and **deōrum** are objective genitives after **cultor** and **timidus**, respectively. The objective genitive is often translated by *for* or some other preposition.

Torquēmur ... caecā ... cupīdine *rērum*.

MANILIUS *Astronomica* 4.2

We torture ourselves with (or *are tortured by*) *a blind*
desire for possessions.

... dēsīderiō ... tam *cārī capitis*.   HORACE *Odes* 1.24.1f.

... to longing for so dear a head (i.e., *a person*).

The *subjective genitive*, where a noun in the genitive stands in the same relation to the noun that it qualifies as a subject does to a verb, occurs less frequently.

G24 The *partitive genitive* occurs in phrases where a noun in the genitive expresses a whole and the noun or noun substitute that it qualifies expresses a part. The noun substitute may be a pronoun, adjective, or adverb.

> **Fortissima *Tyndaridārum*.**   *Horace Sermōnēs 1.1.100
> The bravest of the daughters of Tyndareus.

When the word qualified is a pronoun or adjective, a particular emphasis or nuance is sometimes implied.

> **… cum tantum sciat esse *bāsiōrum*.**   Catullus Carmina 5.13
> … when he knows there are so many kisses (lit., *so much of kisses*—
> Catullus wants to emphasize the tremendous number of kisses
> involved).

Sometimes a partitive expression is little more than the equivalent of a noun with an adjective in agreement.

> **Plūs habet hic *vītae*, plūs habet ille *viae*.**
>   Claudian Shorter poems 20.22
> This one has more life, that one more traveling (lit., *journey*).

G25 The *genitive of definition* specifies more precisely what is meant by the noun it governs, and stands in the same relation to it as a noun in apposition (§g52). It is sometimes translated by *of,* sometimes simply by using apposition.

> **Virtūtēs *continentiae, gravitātis, iustitiae*.**   *Cicero prō Mūrēnā 23
> The virtues [of] self-restraint, seriousness, justice.

> **Ācre malum semper *stillantis ocellī*.**   Juvenal Satires 6.109
> The severe complaint of a constantly weeping eye.

G26 A few *adjectives* and **intransitive verbs** take the *genitive*; this use is indicated in the Glossary.

> **Vīcīnae *nescius* urbis.**   Claudian Shorter poems 20.9
> Unacquainted with the neighboring city.

Dative

The dative indicates the person involved in an action or state (for instance, the recipient or person advantaged or disadvantaged) or, in the case of things, a purpose or final result. A noun in the dative can be governed by a verb, an adjective or, very occasionally, a noun or adverb. The dative is usually translated by *to* or *for*.

G27 *Transitive verbs* of *saying, giving, promising, showing,* etc. can be followed by a direct object (accusative) and an indirect object (dative). The English idiom is similar, although the preposition *to* can often be omitted (*he gave a book to me = he gave me a book*).

> **Dā mī (= mihi) bāsia mille.**   CATULLUS *Carmina* 5.7
> *Give me a thousand kisses.*

Other verbs, mainly compounds, that are also followed by a direct object in the accusative and an indirect object in the dative require some change for an idiomatic translation.

> **Rūs *mihi* tū obiectās?**   PLAUTUS *Mostellāria* 16
> *Do you throw the country in my face?*
>   (**obiectō -āre** lit., *throw [something]* (acc.) *at [someone]* (dat.))

G28 The dative is used with certain *adjectives*, for example, **aptus** (*suitable*), **fidēlis** (*faithful*), and **similis** (*similar*).

> **... aptae *profugō* vestis.**   OVID *Tristia* 1.3.10
> *... of clothing suitable for an exile.*

G29 The dative without a preposition is used for the *agent* with gerundives expressing necessity (see §G80).

> ***Tibi* sunt ... gerendae aerumnae.**   ENNIUS *Annālēs* 1 fr. xxix.11f.
> *You must endure troubles.* (lit., *Troubles must be endured by you.*)

The dative of agent is sometimes used in other situations.

> **... amāta *nōbīs* quantum amābitur nulla.**   CATULLUS *Carmina* 8.5
> *... loved by me as much as no [woman] will be loved.*

> **... audītam ... *arboribus* fidem.**   HORACE *Odes* 1.24.14
> *... the lyre heard by trees.*

G30 The dative is used with **sum** and sometimes with other verbs to indicate the *owner* or *possessor*.

> **Nec *trucibus fluviīs* īdem sonus.**   STATIUS *Silvae* 5.4.5
> *And raging rivers do not have the same sound.* (lit., *Nor is there the same sound for raging rivers.* (**est** is understood)

> **Fuerant *tibi* quattuor ... dentēs.**   MARTIAL *Epigrammata* 1.19.1
> *You had four teeth.*

G31 The *dative of advantage/disadvantage* is used for a person who is affected by the action expressed by a verb, whether advantageously or the opposite. This can sometimes be translated by *for*, but often the translation must be adapted to the context.

Fulsēre quondam candidī *tibī* sōlēs.   Catullus *Carmina* 8.3
Bright suns once shone for you. (dative of advantage)

Fūneris ... *tibi* causa fuī?   Vergil *Aeneid* 6.458
Was I the cause of your death? (lit., *Was I the cause of death*
  for you?) (dative of disadvantage)

Tam bellum *mihi* passerem abstulistis.   Catullus *Carmina* 3.15
You have taken so beautiful a sparrow from me (lit., *to my disadvantage*).

> **G 32** The ***dative of reference*** is used for a person who is interested or in-
> volved in the action or state expressed by a verb.

Nōn *mihi* servōrum, comitis nōn cūra legendī ... fuit.
                                             Ovid *Tristia* 1.3.9f.
I was not concerned with choosing slaves [or] a companion.
  (lit., *There was not concern for me in choosing ...*)

***Multīs* ille *bonīs* flēbilis occidit.**   Horace *Odes* 1.24.9
His death was (lit., *He died*) *worthy of tears for many good people.*

Sometimes this dative has the meaning *in the eyes of* or *in the judgment of.*

Cui vidēberis bella?   Catullus *Carmina* 8.16
To whom will you seem beautiful?

It is sometimes difficult to distinguish between a dative of possessor (§G 30),
a dative of advantage/disadvantage (§G 31), and a dative of reference (§G 32).

> **G 33** The ***dative of purpose*** or ***final result*** expresses the purpose for which
> something exists or is done, or the result of an action. This can be
concrete or abstract.

Nec mens fuerat satis apta *parandō*.   Ovid *Tristia* 1.3.7
Nor had [my frame of] mind been sufficiently favorable for preparing.
  (**parandō** is a gerund)

Māteriam struimus *magnae* per vōta *ruīnae*.
                                             Manilius *Astronomica* 4.9
We put together material for a great downfall through [our] desires.
  (*a great downfall* is the result of our activity)

> **G 34** The ***predicative dative*** predicates, or asserts, something about the
> subject (hence the term; see §G 6). It is generally accompanied by
another dative (of reference or advantage/disadvantage). Instead of *this was*
an honor for him, Latin prefers **hoc eī honōrī fuit**, lit., *this was for an honor*
for him, where **honōrī** is a predicative dative and **eī** is a dative of advantage.

Tibi est *odiō* mea fistula.   Vergil *Eclogues* 8.33
You dislike my pipe. (lit., *My pipe is for hatred for you.*)
  (**odiō** is a predicative dative, **tibi** is a dative of reference)

Exitiō est avidum mare nautīs.   *Horace Odes 1.28.18
The greedy sea is death to sailors (lit., is for death for sailors).
   (**exitiō** is a predicative dative, **nautīs** is a dative of disadvantage)

$\boxed{\text{G35}}$ The *dative expressing motion toward* is often used by poets where classical prose writers would use **ad** or **in** plus the accusative.

   ... **dum conderet urbem inferretque deōs *Latiō*.**   *Vergil Aeneid 1.5f.
   ...until he would establish a city and bring [his] gods to Latium.

$\boxed{\text{G36}}$ A few *intransitive verbs* take the dative; this use is indicated in the Glossary.

   ... **an *noceat* vīs nulla bonō?**   *Lucan Bellum cīvīle 9.569
   ... whether no violence harms a virtuous man? (**noceō -ēre** + dat. *harm*)

Two impersonal verbs, **libet/lubet** (*it is pleasing*) and **licet** (*it is allowed*), are followed by the dative.

   Nunc, dum tibi *lubet licetque*, pōtā, perde rem.
                                                    *Plautus Mostellāria 20
   Now, while you want to and can, drink, waste property.

Ablative

The ablative was used without a preposition more often in Latin poetry than in Ciceronian prose. (For the reasons, see pages 221 and 225.)
   The ablative case in classical Latin is an amalgam of the following cases.

⊂ The original ablative case, which expressed removal and separation only
⊂ The instrumental case, which was used for both agent (without a preposition) and instrument
⊂ The locative case in most of its original uses, which expressed *place where* and *time when* (For what is left of the locative case, see §G51.)

Both the instrumental and the locative cases originally had distinctive endings of their own.
   The expanded ablative had more uses than any other case. In prose, many were differentiated with a preposition.

$\boxed{\text{G37}}$ *Time when, time within which,* and *time during which* are expressed by the ablative.

   Dīvōs ... *extrēmā* moriens tamen adloquor *hōrā*. *Vergil Eclogues 8.19f.
   Nevertheless, as I die, I address the gods in [my] final hour. (time when)

   Spatiō brevī spem longam resecēs.   *Horace Odes 1.11.6f.
   Within a brief time span cut short far-reaching hope. (time within which)

Dīcere ... tibi ... *continuīs* **voluī** *quinque diēbus* **"havē."**

MARTIAL Epigrammata 9.6.1f.

Over five days in a row, I wanted to say "hello" to you.
(time during which)

G38 *Place where* is occasionally expressed by the plain ablative.

Iacuit ... languida *dēsertīs* **Cnōsia** *lītoribus.*   PROPERTIUS *Elegies* 1.3.1f.
The Cnossian [woman] lay exhausted on the abandoned shore.

G39 *Place from which* is often expressed by the plain ablative in verse, where Cicero would have used the ablative with a preposition. Because this generally occurs with verbs of motion or in expressions implying motion, it can be easily distinguished from the ablative to express place where (§G38), which accompanies a verb of rest.

Lecta ... *dīversō lītore* **concha venit.**   OVID *Ars amātōria* 3.124
A choice pearl comes from a distant shore.

Discēdite *templō.*   OVID *Metamorphōsēs* 1.381
Go out from [my] temple.

... lībera iam *dūrīs cōtibus* **Andromedē.**   PROPERTIUS *Elegies* 1.3.4
... Andromeda, now free from the hard rocks.
(**lībera** implies that Andromeda was physically removed from the rocks)

G40 The *ablative of separation* is very close to the ablative of place from which (§G39). It is generally translated by *from* and is found with verbs and adjectives indicating removal or separation.

Tē ... *aspectū* **nē subtrahe** *nostrō.*   VERGIL *Aeneid* 6.465
Do not withdraw yourself from my sight.

Exterrita *somnō.*   ENNIUS *Annālēs* 1 fr. xxix.2
Frightened out of sleep.

G41 The *ablative of origin* indicates the ancestry or source of a person or thing.

Eurydicā prognāta.   ENNIUS *Annālēs* 1 fr. xxix.3
Daughter of Eurydica. (lit., *Born of/from Eurydica.*)

G42 The *ablative of comparison* is used after a comparative adjective.

Mortālis vīsus pulchrior esse *deō.*   CATULUS B.4
The mortal seemed fairer than a god.

G43 The *ablative of measure of difference* is used with a comparative to indicate the degree by which something is greater, smaller, etc.

> *Tantō maior fāmae sitis est quam virtūtis.* JUVENAL *Satires* 10.140f.
> *So much greater is the thirst for fame than for virtue.*
> (lit., *By so much is the thirst for fame greater …*)

G44 The *ablative of quality/description* differs little from the same use of the genitive (§G20). Like the genitive, it must always be accompanied by an adjective.

> [Erat] *sermōne lepidō,* tum autem *incessū commodō.* *Verse Epitaphs* B.7
> *Her conversation was charming, yet her bearing was proper.*
> (lit., *[She was] with charming conversation, but then with proper bearing.*)

G45 The *ablative of manner* and the *ablative of attendant circumstances* are classified together because they have the same construction. These are used in adverbial phrases of the type *the ship set sail* **with a broken mast** (manner) and *the ship set sail* **amid great rejoicing** (attendant circumstances). The preposition **cum** is optional if the noun in the ablative is qualified by an adjective or another noun in the genitive.

> *Dulcī … adfātus amōre est.* VERGIL *Aeneid* 6.455
> *He spoke with tender love.* (manner)
>
> *Pāce mihī liceat, caelestēs, dīcere vestrā …* CATULUS B.3
> *May I be allowed, O heavenly beings, to say without offense*
> (lit., *by your leave*) … (attendant circumstances)
>
> *Fulmen aetheris impulsī sonitū mundīque fragōre ēmicuit.*
> LUCAN *Bellum cīvīle* 1.151ff.
> *Lightning flashes with the sound of the smitten sky and the crash*
> *of the heavens.* (attendant circumstances)
>
> *Cum tremulīs anus attulit artubus lūmen.* ENNIUS *Annālēs* I fr. xxix.1
> *With trembling limbs, the old woman brought a torch.* (manner)

With an unqualified noun, **cum** is used.

> *Rem hanc cum cūrā gerās.* *PLAUTUS *Persa* 198
> *You should handle this matter with care.* (manner)

However, exceptions occur.

> *Saxa … pōnere dūritiem coepēre … mollīrīque morā.*
> OVID *Metamorphōsēs* 1.400ff.
> *The stones began to set aside their hardness and to soften slowly.* (manner)

G46 The *ablative of respect* is the normal form of this construction in classical Latin. (The accusative in this use (§G15) comes from Greek, and the genitive (§G22) is a poetic development.) The ablative of respect can accompany nouns, adjectives, and verbs and defines the sphere in which these words are to be applied. It can be roughly translated by *with respect to*, but this can be replaced by a single preposition, most commonly *in* or *with*.

Haud umquam vigilābat *corpore tōtō*.   STATIUS *Silvae* 5.4.13
He was never awake with [his] whole body.

... quī melior *multīs* quam tū fuit.   LUCRETIUS *Dē rērum nātūrā* 3.1026
... who was better than you in many [ways].

G 47 The *instrumental ablative* is used for the tool with which something is done and is usually translated by *by* or *with*; it is occasionally used of something living.

At *cantū* commōtae Erebī dē sēdibus īmīs umbrae ...
                                   VERGIL *Georgics* 4.471f.
But the Shades, stirred by [his] song from the deepest abodes of Erebus ...

... nisi *Poenō mīlite* portās frangimus.   JUVENAL *Satires* 10.155f.
... unless I break the gates with the Carthaginian soldier.
   (the Carthaginian soldier is regarded as the instrument
   with which the gates are to be broken)

G 48 The *ablative of cause* gives the reason for something and is close in meaning to the instrumental ablative.

Fātō profugus.   VERGIL *Aeneid* 1.2
An exile by fate.

Omnis et *insānā* sēmita *vōce* sonat.   PROPERTIUS *Elegies* 4.8.60
And the whole alley rang with frenzied voices.

G 49 The term *ablative absolute* (*absolute* here means *independent*) is used for the construction that, in its simplest form, involves a noun or pronoun and a participle, both of which are in the ablative case and are grammatically independent of the rest of the sentence. There is, however, a connection in sense between the ablative absolute and the rest of the sentence; otherwise, there would be no point in putting the two together (compare the English nominative absolute in *Gaul having been pacified, Caesar returned to Rome*). This construction is not as common in verse as it is in prose.

Vērum est ... umbrās *corporibus* vīvere *conditīs*?   SENECA *Trōades* 371f.
Is it true that the Shades live after [their] bodies have been buried
   (lit., *bodies having been buried*)?

The participle may govern an accusative.

Cūria ... dē stipulā *Tatiō regna tenente* fuit.   OVID *Ars amātōria* 3.117f.
The Senate-house was [made] of straw when Tatius held the kingdom
   (lit., *Tatius holding the kingdom*).

Since the verb **sum** does not have a present participle, in an ablative absolute that would otherwise require this, two nouns or a noun and an adjective are used.

> **Quam bene *Sāturnō* vīvēbant *rēge*.**   Tibullus *Elegies* 1.3.35
> *How well [people] used to live when Saturn was king*
>   *(lit., Saturn [being] king).*

G 50 **Dignus** (*worthy (of)*) and a few ***intransitive verbs*** take the ablative; this use is indicated in the Glossary.

> **Illa fuit longā *dignissima* vītā.**   Ovid *Metamorphōsēs* 4.109
> *She was most worthy of a long life.*

> **Simulācra ... lūce *carentum*.**   Vergil *Georgics* 4.472
> *The ghosts of those lacking the light [of day].*
>   (**careō -ēre** + abl. *lack*)

Locative

G 51 The locative denotes ***place where*** and is used in verse with the same words as in prose (towns, small islands, and a few common nouns, the most frequent of which are **domus -ūs** F. *house*, **rūs rūris** N. *country*, and **humus -ī** F. *ground*); **animī** *in the mind* also occurs.

> **Callidus imposuit nūper mihi cōpo *Ravennae*.**
>   Martial *Epigrammata* 3.57.1
> *A cunning innkeeper recently tricked me at Ravenna.*

> **Numquam sē cēnasse *domī* Philo iūrat.**   Martial *Epigrammata* 5.47.1
> *Philo swears that he has never dined at home.*

Apposition

G 52 A noun or noun phrase is in apposition to another noun or a pronoun when it follows by way of explanation and is in the same case.

> **Tū *urbānus vērō scurra, dēliciae poplī*, rūs mihi tū obiectās?**
>   Plautus *Mostellāria* 15f.
> *Do you, a real city smart aleck, a darling of the people,*
>   *throw the country in my face?*

> **Quamvīs ... iubērent hāc Amor hāc Līber, *dūrus uterque deus* ...**
>   Propertius *Elegies* 1.3.13f.
> *Although on this side Love, on that side Liber, each a pitiless god,*
>   *were ordering [me] ...*

A noun or phrase can be in apposition to an entire clause.

> **Ille ... *pretium* ... *vehendī* cantat.**   Ovid *Fastī* 2.115f.
> *He sang [as] payment for being carried.*

A noun clause introduced by **quod** can even be in apposition to a main clause (see VALERIUS FLACCUS *Argonautica* 5.313ff., page 180).

Plural for Singular/Singular for Plural

G53 A common feature of Latin verse is the use of the plural form of a noun instead of the singular, with no difference in meaning.

Iacuit ... languida *dēsertīs* Cnōsia *lītoribus*.   PROPERTIUS *Elegies* 1.3.1f.
The Cnossian [woman] lay exhausted on the abandoned shore.

Rumpit ... *silentia* vōce Pyrrha prior.   OVID *Metamorphōsēs* 1.384f.
Pyrrha first broke the silence with [her] voice.

Sometimes, the opposite occurs.

Postīs ... ā *cardine* vellit.   VERGIL *Aeneid* 2.480
He wrenched the rails from [their] hinge pins.

Omnis et *insānā* sēmita *vōce* sonat.   PROPERTIUS *Elegies* 4.8.60
And the whole alley rang with frenzied voices.

Similar to this is the use of the first-person plural pronoun or possessive adjective (or a first-person plural verb) for the corresponding singular form.

Et *nōs* ... manum ferulae *subdūximus*.   JUVENAL *Satires* 1.15
I too have withdrawn [my] hand from the rod.

Tē ... aspectū nē subtrahe *nostrō*.   VERGIL *Aeneid* 6.465
Do not withdraw yourself from my sight.

ADJECTIVES AND ADVERBS

G54 The *comparative* and *superlative* of adjectives can be used without any idea of comparison but to express a high or very high degree; for example, instead of meaning *more beautiful* and *most beautiful*, **pulchrior** and **pulcherrimus** can mean *rather beautiful* and *very beautiful*, respectively. (Sometimes the translation *very* can also be used for the comparative.)

Sulmo mihī patria est, gelidīs *ūberrimus* undīs.   OVID *Tristia* 4.10.3
My native place is Sulmo, very rich in cold waters.

The same applies to adverbs.

Hic vir, hic est, tibi quem prōmittī *saepius* audīs.   VERGIL *Aeneid* 6.791
This, this is the man whom you very often hear promised to you.

G55 A Latin adjective should sometimes be translated by an adverb or adverbial phrase in English.

Concordēs ... parī vīximus ingeniō.   *Verse Epitaphs* c.6
We lived harmoniously with matching temperaments.

... **ut** *salvus* **regnet vīvatque** *beātus.*   Horace *Epistulae* 1.2.10
... *to rule in safety and to live happily.*

G56 Latin has *possessive adjectives* corresponding to the English *my*
(**meus**), *your* (sg. **tuus**, pl. **vester**), and *our* (**noster**), but the third-
person possessive adjective **suus** (*his, her, its, their*) is reflexive and refers to
the subject of its clause.

In ... *suum* **furtim Mūsa trahēbat opus.**   Ovid *Tristia* 4.10.20
The Muse used to draw [me] secretly to her work.

Some exceptions occur and are of the following type.

Sua **quemque morētur cūra.**   Propertius *Elegies* 1.1.35f.
Let everyone be occupied with his own care.
  (lit., *Let his own care occupy each person.*)

In other cases, where English uses a third-person possessive adjective, a
Latin author uses the genitive of a demonstrative pronoun (**eius, huius,
illius,** etc.).

Sīc semper avunculus *eius* **... dixerat.**   Catullus *Carmina* 84.5f.
In this way, his maternal uncle ... had always spoken.

Compared with English, Latin is very sparing in its use of possessive adjectives, and more often than not it must be deduced from context if a particular possessive adjective must be supplied in the translation.

Solvite, mortālēs, animōs cūrāsque levāte.
        Manilius *Astronomica* 4.12
Mortals, free [your] minds and lighten [your] cares.

G57 *Attributive* and *predicative* are terms for the two ways in which adjectives can be used.

An adjective used attributively forms a phrase with the noun it qualifies;
in English, the adjective always comes immediately before the noun: *modern
Italy, a fat Gaul, the boring poet.*

The predicate is what is said about the subject of a clause (§G6) or the
subject of an infinitive in an accusative-and-infinitive construction (§G10).
In **erunt ignēs arcusque Cupīdinis arma** (*fires and a bow are* (lit., *will be*)
the weapons of Cupid (Ovid *Amōrēs* 1.15.27)), the subject is **ignēs arcusque**
and the remaining words form the predicate. When an adjective is used
predicatively, it indicates what is predicated of, or asserted about, the subject: *the gods are immortal, Catullus was passionate.* This use frequently involves the verb *to be.*

Pia **sunt nullumque nefās ōrācula suādent!**   Ovid *Metamorphōsēs* 1.392
Oracles are righteous and counsel no crime!

Gerundives can be used both attributively (§ G 79) and predicatively (§ G 80); there is a distinction in meaning between the two.

VERBS

Agreement

G58 In Latin, as in English, a verb agrees with its subject in person and number, with one exception. When two singular nouns (or one singular and one plural noun) are the subject of a clause in English, its verb is plural: *Joanne and her partner go to the supermarket together.* Latin can have the same construction, but very often a singular verb is used when the nearer of the two subjects is singular.

> **Nec spatium nec mens *fuerat* satis apta parandō.** OVID *Tristia* 1.3.7
> *Neither the time nor [my frame of] mind had been sufficiently*
>   *favorable for preparing.* (**fuerant** would be possible
>   grammatically and metrically)

> ***Tacet* omne pecus volucrēsque feraeque.** STATIUS *Silvae* 5.4.3
> *All cattle and birds and wild beasts are silent.*
>   (**tacent** would be possible grammatically, but not metrically)

Voice

G59 An important difference between the uses of the passive voice in English and in Latin is that the Latin passive can be used in a ***reflexive sense***; for example, **lavor** (first-person singular, present indicative passive of **lavō -āre** *wash*) can mean either *I am washed* or *I wash myself.* Context shows which meaning is intended.

> ***Pascitur* in vīvīs Līvor.** OVID *Amōrēs* 1.15.39
> *Envy feeds* (lit., *feeds itself*) *on the living.*

> **Bonus aetheriō *laxātur* nectare Caesar.** MARTIAL *Epigrammata* 4.8.9
> *Good Caesar relaxes himself with heavenly nectar.*

Tense

G60 The ***present indicative*** normally expresses an action or state occurring at the present time. According to context, it is translated by the English simple present (*we live in Baiae*), continuous present (*we are living in Baiae*), or emphatic present (*we do live in Baiae*).

The present indicative is also used to describe a past event in order to give a vivid effect (***historic present***, sometimes called the ***vivid present***); this is normally translated by the English past tense.

> **Tālia tum *memorat* ... exterrita somnō.** ENNIUS *Annālēs* 1 fr. xxix.2
> *Then she, frightened out of sleep, spoke thus.*

A historic present and a past tense can occur within the same sentence.

> **Adloquor extrēmum maestōs abitūrus amīcōs,**
>   **quī modo dē multīs ūnus et alter *erant*.**   Ovid *Tristia* 1.3.15f.
> *[When] about to leave, I addressed for the last time [my] sad friends,*
>   *who now were one or two of many.*

Occasionally, the historic present may be retained for stylistic reasons in English (for an example, see Juvenal *Satires* 10.148ff., pages 210–211).

G61 The present indicative is used after **dum** (*while*) when the action of the verb in the **dum** clause covers a longer period than that of the verb in the main clause.

> **Parvae vindictam reī**
>   ***dum* quaerō dēmens, servitūtem repperī.**   Phaedrus *Fābulae* 4.4.10f.
> *While I was foolishly seeking retribution for a small matter,*
>   *I found slavery.*

G62 The *imperfect indicative* expresses continuous or habitual action in the past.

> **Quōcumque aspicerēs, luctūs gemitūsque *sonābant*.**
>   Ovid *Tristia* 1.3.21
> *Wherever you looked, laments and groans were heard*
>   *(lit., were being heard).* (continuous action)

> **... cum *ventitābās* quō puella *dūcēbat*.**   Catullus *Carmina* 8.4
> *... when you used to go where [your] girl used to lead [you].*
>   (habitual action; a more idiomatic translation would be
>   *... when you always went to where your girl used to lead you*)

The imperfect indicative also expresses an action that was begun in the past but not completed.

> **Tālibus Aenēās ardentem et torva tuentem**
>   ***lēnībat* dictīs animum.**   Vergil *Aeneid* 6.467f.
> *With such words Aeneas tried to soothe (lit., was soothing)*
>   *[her] burning anger and grim looks.*
>   (conative imperfect)

Similarly, it can express the beginning of an action in the past.

> **Umbrae *ībant* tenuēs.**   Vergil *Georgics* 4.472
> *The insubstantial Shades began to move.*
>   (inceptive imperfect)

The exact meaning of a verb in the imperfect depends on context; however, the conative and inceptive uses are less common. The simple past tense in English can very often be used to translate a Latin imperfect.

Nec sēsē ā gremiō illius *movēbat*.   CATULLUS *Carmina* 3.8
And it did not stir (lit., move itself) from her lap.
     (the more literal translation *it used not to move itself* ...
     is also possible)

G63   The *perfect indicative* describes both a simple past action (*I shut the
     city gates yesterday*) and a present state resulting from a past action
or actions (*I have now shut the city gates*); context shows which meaning is
intended.

Subita incautum dēmentia *cēpit* amantem.   VERGIL *Georgics* 4.488
A sudden madness seized the unwary lover.
     (a single past action)

Hoc *intellextīn* (= intellexistī + -ne)?   TERENCE *Andria* 201
Have you understood this? (i.e., Are you now in a state
*   of understanding this?)*
     (the perfect expressing a present state)

G64   The *pluperfect indicative* describes an action or state two stages
     back in the past.

Nōn tamen *ausus eram* dominae turbāre quiētem.
                                                    PROPERTIUS *Elegies* 1.3.17
I had nevertheless not dared to disturb the sleep of [my] mistress.

In poetry, the pluperfect is sometimes used to describe a simple event in the
past and is translated by the simple past tense in English.

***Induerat* Tyriō bis tinctam mūrice pallam.**   OVID *Fastī* 2.107
He put on a cloak twice dipped in Tyrian dye.

G65   The *future indicative* describes something that is expected to hap-
     pen in the future. English has a continuous future (*I will be going*) as
well as a simple future (*I will go*); this distinction does not exist in Latin.

Tē rūrī, sī vīvam, *ulciscar*.   PLAUTUS *Mostellāria* 4
If I'm alive (lit., will live), I will take vengeance on you
*   in the country.*

G66   The *future perfect indicative* places one event before another in the
     future. In a subordinate clause, it is usually translated by the English
perfect.

Cum mīlia multa *fēcerīmus*, conturbābimus.
                                                    CATULLUS *Carmina* 5.10f.
When we have made up many thousands, we will declare
*   ourselves bankrupt. (lit., When we will have made up ...)*

Sometimes the English present yields a more appropriate translation.

> **Quod sī quis monitīs tardās *adverterit* aurēs,**
> **heu referet quantō verba dolōre mea!** PROPERTIUS *Elegies* 1.1.37f.
> *But if anyone turns deaf ears to [my] warnings,*
> *alas! with what great grief will he recall my words!*

The Subjunctive

The subjunctive in a main clause expresses what is willed, wished, or considered possible. It is used in four ways in Latin poetry. (A fifth, the concessive subjunctive, is rare in verse.)

[G 67] The *optative subjunctive* (negated by **nē**) expresses a wish. It may be reinforced by **utinam**. In the present tense, an optative subjunctive expresses a wish for the future.

> **Tē Iuppiter dīque omnēs *perdant*!** PLAUTUS *Mostellāria* 38
> *May Jupiter and all the gods destroy you!*

An imperfect subjunctive expresses a wish for the present.

> **Tēcum lūdere, sīcut ipsa, *possem*.** CATULLUS *Carmina* 2.9
> *I wish I could play with you as she herself [does]. (lit., Would that I could …)*

A pluperfect subjunctive expresses a wish for the past.

> **Utinam nē … Cnōsia Cecropiae *tetigissent* lītora puppēs.**
>   *CATULLUS *Carmina* 64.171f.
> *Would that the Cecropian ships had not touched the Cnossian shores.*

[G 68] The *potential subjunctive* (negated by **nōn**) expresses an action or state that has or had the potentiality of happening. In English, this is normally expressed by the auxiliary *would* (or sometimes *should, could/can*). The tense is determined by the following rules.

❡ The present or perfect subjunctive is used with a present or future reference.

> **Quis dēsīderiō *sit* pudor aut modus tam cārī capitis?**
>   HORACE *Odes* 1.24.1f.
> *What restraint or limit could there be to longing for*
> *so dear a head (i.e., a person)?*
> **Nōn tibi Massȳlae gentēs … amplius *attulerint* decoris.**
>   SILIUS ITALICUS *Pūnica* 16.252ff.
> *The Massylian peoples would not bring you more honor.*

The second-person singular is used with a general reference and may be translated by either *you* or *one*.

Expectēs **eadem ā summō minimōque poētā.**   JUVENAL *Satires* 1.14
You/One can expect the same from the best and worst poet.

❈ The imperfect subjunctive is used with a past reference.

At tū dictīs, Albāne, *manērēs!*   *VERGIL *Aeneid* 8.643
But you, man of Alba, should have stayed true to [your] words!

When the potential subjunctive occurs in a conditional sentence, different rules apply (see §G94).

G69   The *jussive subjunctive* (negated by **nē**) expresses an order. In the first-person plural, it expresses self-encouragement or self-exhortation and is translated *let us....*

Vīvāmus, mea Lesbia, atque *amēmus.*   CATULLUS *Carmina* 5.1
Let us live, my Lesbia, and let us love.

In the second and third persons, its meaning coincides with the imperative.

Miser Catulle, *dēsinās* **ineptīre.**   CATULLUS *Carmina* 8.1
Unhappy Catullus, stop being foolish.

Prisca *iuvent* **aliōs.**   OVID *Ars amātōria* 3.121
Let ancient [things] please others.

G70   The *deliberative subjunctive* (negated by **nōn**) is used in questions to indicate the uncertainty of the speaker about the future and what should be done.

Quid nōn *spērēmus* **amantēs?**   VERGIL *Eclogues* 8.26
What are [we] lovers not to expect?

Unde ego *sufficiam?*   STATIUS *Silvae* 5.4.11
How am I to manage?

Commands

G71   The *imperative* is used to express a positive command.

Incipe **Maenaliōs mēcum, mea tībia, versūs.**   VERGIL *Eclogues* 8.21
Begin, my flute, Maenalian verses with me.

G72   Negative commands can be expressed in one of three ways.

❈ **Nē** with the imperative. In classical Latin, this construction occurs only in poetry.

Tē ... **aspectū** *nē subtrahe* **nostrō.**   VERGIL *Aeneid* 6.465
Do not withdraw yourself from my sight.

❨ **Nē** with the perfect subjunctive, which is used in a jussive sense and is translated by the English present.

Tū *nē quaesierīs* **… quem mihi, quem tibi fīnem dī dederint.**
Horace Odes 1.11.1f.

Do not ask what end the gods have assigned (lit., given)
to me [and] what to you.

Occasionally, the present subjunctive is used with **nē**.

Nē *quaerātis* **honōre quī minus sit mandātus.**   Verse Epitaphs A.7
Do not ask why he was not entrusted with public office.

❨ The imperative of **nōlō** (**nōlī, nōlīte**) with the infinitive.

Carpere vel **nōlī** **nostra vel ēde tua.**   Martial *Epigrammata* 1.91.2
Either don't criticize my [poems] or publish yours.

Participles

Latin has fewer participles than English does, but the way they are used in Latin is similar. The following differences should be noted, however.

$\boxed{\text{G 73}}$ Participles in Latin are not qualified by words corresponding to English *when, while,* etc. (*while staying in Greece, we made a visit to Delphi*). In English translations, these words must often be supplied from the overall sense.

Nec sēsē dedit in conspectum corde *cupītus.*
Ennius Annālēs 1 fr. xxix.14

Nor did he, [though] desired by [my] heart, appear
to [my] sight.

$\boxed{\text{G 74}}$ The *perfect participle of deponent verbs* is often used in a present sense.

Totiens … Tīthōnia … gelidō spargit *miserāta* **flagellō.**
Statius Silvae 5.4.9f.

As often does the wife of Tithonus, pitying [me], sprinkle [me]
with [her] cold whip.

$\boxed{\text{G 75}}$ In certain types of phrases where English uses an abstract noun followed by a concrete noun in the genitive, Latin prefers the concrete noun with a participle that expresses the sense of the English abstract noun; thus, instead of **mūtātiō terrae** (*change of land*), Latin uses **terra mūtāta** (*Livy *Ab urbe conditā* 37.54.18) with the same meaning.

Fābula, quā ... narrātur ... *Graecia* barbariae lentō *conlīsa* duellō ...
HORACE *Epistulae* 1.2.6f.
The story in which is told the collision of Greece with the foreign world
  in a prolonged war ...

Infinitives

A Latin infinitive can usually be translated by an infinitive in English, but
the following points should be noted.

For *accusative-and-infinitive* constructions, see §G10.

G76 The *perfect infinitive* is often used in poetry in a present sense.

... an līber in armīs *occubuisse* velim potius quam regna vidēre?
LUCAN *Bellum cīvīle* 9.566f.
... whether I would prefer to fall in arms [as a] free [man]
  rather than witness a tyranny?

Sed corpus *tetigisse* nocet. TIBULLUS *Elegies* 1.8.25
But to touch the body does harm.

G77 The *historic present* can be used to create a vivid narrative (§G60),
but when an even stronger effect is desired, the *historic infinitive*,
replacing the imperfect indicative, is used. Nouns, pronouns, and adjectives
remain in the same case that they would take if the verb were finite. The
construction is usually confined to main clauses.

Multa *dare* in vulgus, tōtus populāribus aurīs
  impellī plausūque suī *gaudēre* theātrī. LUCAN *Bellum cīvīle* 1.132f.
[He] gave much to the common people; he was wholly swayed
  by the breath of popular favor and delighted in the applause
  of his own theater.

Gerunds and Gerundives

G78 The *gerund* is a verbal noun and is active in meaning. Its English
equivalent is the verbal noun in *-ing*. (The English verbal noun in
-ing is identical to the present active participle, but context shows which is
involved. The word *fighting* is a verbal noun in *the Romans loved fighting*, but
a participle in *the Romans, fighting against the Gauls, were almost always victorious*.) The gerund cannot be used in the nominative or vocative.

Pretiumque *vehendī* cantat. OVID *Fastī* 2.115f.
And he sang [as] payment for being carried (lit., *of carrying*).
  (objective genitive [§G23])

Nec mens fuerat satis apta *parandō*.   OVID *Tristia* 1.3.7
Nor had [my frame of] mind been sufficiently favorable for preparing.
(dative of purpose [§G 33])

... catulīs rabiem atque īrās expellere *alendō*.
                                          SILIUS ITALICUS *Pūnica* 16.236
... to drive away ferocity and rage from the cubs by feeding [them].
(instrumental ablative [§G 47])

The *gerundive* is a verbal adjective that has no single-word equivalent in
English. It can be used in three ways.

(G 79) As an ***attributive adjective*** (see §G 57), passive in sense and ex-
        pressing what could or should happen, for example, **rēs metuendae**
(*things worthy to be feared, i.e., terrible things*).

Magnus *mīrandusque* cliens.   JUVENAL *Satires* 10.160f.
An important and remarkable (lit., worthy to be marvelled at) client.

Sometimes, the idea of necessity is uppermost.

Undā ēnāvigandā.   HORACE *Odes* 2.14.9ff.
With the water that must be crossed (lit., water needing to be sailed across).

(G 80) As a ***predicative adjective*** with the same meaning, except that it
        always expresses the idea of necessity, that is, what must happen,
not what could happen. This use involves a form of **sum**, which is often
understood.

Nōbīs, cum semel occidit brevis lux,
  nox *est* perpetua ūna *dormienda*.   CATULLUS *Carmina* 5.5f.
When [our] short light has once set, we must sleep one continuous night
  (*lit., one continuous night must be slept by us*).

In this sense, the gerundive can also be used impersonally; with intransitive
verbs, the impersonal use is the only possibility.

Pavidō fortīque *cadendum* est.   LUCAN *Bellum cīvīle* 9.583
The timid and brave must [both] die. (lit., There must be a dying
  by a timid man and a brave man.)

(G 81) As an adjective with the sense of a ***present*** or ***future passive parti-***
        ciple. In this sense, the gerundive cannot be used in the nominative
and is always combined with a noun or pronoun. While this noun or pronoun is the grammatical subject of the gerundive, the logical subject is
the verbal concept of the gerundive. The literal meaning of **haec arma ad**
bellum gerendum ūtilia sunt is *these weapons are useful for war going to be*

waged, but the real meaning can only be brought out in English by translating it as *these weapons are useful for waging war*, where *waging* is a verbal noun of *wage*. Context shows when an author is employing this use of the gerundive, which is similar to that of participles described in §G 75.

> ... numquam *temerandō* parcere ferrō.   Lucan *Bellum cīvīle* 1.147
> ... *[he] never refrained from violating his sword*
> *(lit., from [his] sword going to be violated).*
> *(violating is a verbal noun)*

A further change is often needed for an idiomatic translation.

> Mihi ... comitis nōn cūra *legendī* ... fuit.   Ovid *Tristia* 1.3.9f.
> *I was not concerned with choosing a companion.*
> *(lit., There was not concern for me of a companion*
> *going to be chosen.)*
> ... saxīs ... ad quae *discutienda* valent sterilis mala rōbora fīcī.
>   Juvenal *Satires* 10.144f.
> ... *to [tomb]stones, [and] to shatter these (lit., to stones,*
> *for which going to be shattered ..., i.e., to stones, for*
> *shattering which ...) the weak strength of a sterile fig*
> *tree is sufficient.*

Supines

G 82 The supine in -um (the accusative singular) is used to express purpose after verbs of motion.

> Ībimus *quaesītum.*   Catulus a.5
> *We (i.e., I) will go to look for [it].*

The supine in -ū is used in phrases such as **mīrābile dictū** (*wonderful to relate* (*Vergil *Aeneid* 1.439)).

SUBORDINATE CLAUSES

Only those types of subordinate clauses that occur in the selections are given here.

G 83 An *adverbial clause of purpose* is expressed by **ut** (negative **nē**) and the subjunctive.

> Sterilēsne ēlēgit harēnās *ut caneret paucīs?*
>   Lucan *Bellum cīvīle* 9.576f.
> *Did he choose barren sands to give oracles (lit., so that he might sing)*
> *to a few?*

G84 An *adverbial clause of result* is expressed by **ut** (negative **ut nōn**) and the subjunctive.

Adsonat Tēreī puella ... *ut putēs mōtūs amōris ōre dīcī mūsicō.*

Pervigilium Veneris 86f.

The young wife (lit., girl) of Tereus sings in accompaniment ... so that you would think feelings of love were being declared with [her] melodious voice.

G85 An *adverbial clause of time* that expresses something anticipated (not something that has already taken place) has its verb in the subjunctive.

... multa quoque et bellō passus, *dum conderet urbem.*

VERGIL *Aeneid* 1.5

... having suffered many things also in war as well, until he would establish a city.

G86 An *adverbial clause of reason* has its verb in the indicative, unless the reason is an alleged one.

Haec aetās mōribus apta meīs ... *quia cultus adest.*

OVID *Ars amātōria* 3.122ff.

This age is suited to my character ... because now there is refinement.

Noctū ambulābat in pūblicō Themistoclēs, *quod somnum capere nōn posset.* *CICERO *Tusculan Disputations* 4.44

Themistocles used to walk in public at night, on the grounds that he could not get to sleep. (**posset** is subjunctive because the reason given is alleged and not necessarily true)

G87 A *subordinate clause in indirect speech* has its verb in the subjunctive if it was part of the original statement.

Nec tamen crēdī potest esse Amōrem fēriātum, *sī sagittās vexerit.*

Pervigilium Veneris 29f.

However, it would be beyond belief (lit., it cannot be believed) that Love is observing the holiday if he is carrying arrows. (the original statement was Love is observing the holiday if he is carrying arrows)

G88 An *adjectival clause expressing purpose, a general class, consequence, cause,* or *concession* has its verb in the subjunctive.

Nōn fixus in agrīs, *quī regeret certīs fīnibus arva,* lapis.

TIBULLUS *Elegies* 1.3.43f.

A stone [was] not planted on land (lit., fields) to determine (lit., which should determine) fields with fixed boundaries. (purpose)

... impellens quidquid sibi summa petentī obstāret.

LUCAN Bellum cīvīle 1.149f.

... overcoming whatever stood in [his] way as he sought supreme power
(lit., for him seeking highest things). (a general class)

Necdum ... crēdit, ... quae ... dēsertam ... sē cernat.

CATULLUS Carmina 64.55ff.

Not even yet does she believe, since she sees herself
abandoned. (cause)

Of the same type is an *adjectival clause of a generalizing nature.*

... quod sīs, esse velīs.   MARTIAL *Epigrammata* 10.47.12

... [that] you would wish to be whatever you are.

G 89   Verbs of fearing are followed by **nē** and the subjunctive.

Nē ipsī teneāmur formīdō.   CATULUS A.5f.

I am afraid lest I myself may be caught.

G 90   *Verbs of hindering, preventing,* and *forbidding* can be followed
by a noun clause introduced by **quīn, quōminus,** or **nē** and the
subjunctive.

Sī sēnserō hodiē quicquam in hīs tē nuptiīs fallāciae
cōnārī *quō fīant minus ...* (quō ... minus = quōminus)

TERENCE Andria 196f.

If I perceive today that you are trying any deceit in this
marriage to prevent it from happening (lit., so that it
does not happen) ...

G 91   An *indirect question, indirect command,* or *indirect petition* has its
verb in the subjunctive.

Quaeris, quot mihi bāsiātiōnēs
tuae, Lesbia, sint satis superque.   CATULLUS *Carmina* 7.1f.

You ask, Lesbia, how many of your kisses are enough and more for me.
(indirect question)

Immortālia nē spērēs, **monet annus et ... hōra.**   HORACE *Odes* 4.7.7f.

The year and the hour warn you not to hope that this
will last forever (lit., that you should not hope for immortal
things). (indirect command)

Det ... sibī veniam **pavidō rogat ōre.**   OVID *Metamorphōsēs* 1.386

With frightened mouth, she asked that [the goddess] pardon her.
*(indirect petition; **ut**, which would normally introduce the*
petition, is omitted)

G92 Some *noun clauses* not included in §G89, §G90, and §G91 are expressed by **ut/nē** and the subjunctive.

Nec vērī simile loquere nec vērum, frutex,
comesse quemquam ut quisquam absentem possiet.

PLAUTUS *Mostellāria* 13f.

What you say is neither likely nor true, [you] blockhead,
[namely] that a person can eat someone [who is] absent.

G93 *Sequence of tenses* requires that the tense of the subjunctive in a subordinate clause is generally restricted by the tense of the verb in the main clause. In such cases, a primary tense in the main verb (present, future, future perfect, or perfect expressing a present state) is followed by a primary tense of the subjunctive (present or perfect); a secondary tense in the main verb (imperfect, perfect expressing a simple past action, or pluperfect) is followed by a historic tense of the subjunctive (imperfect or pluperfect).

Nescit, **cui dominō** *pāreat*, **unda maris.**   OVID *Tristia* 1.2.26
The waves of the sea do not know which master they should obey.
   (primary sequence: present indicative, present subjunctive)

Illa *placet*, **quamvīs incultō** *vēnerit* **ōre.**   TIBULLUS *Elegies* 1.8.15
That [other] woman is pleasing even though she has come
   with [her] face not made up.
   (primary sequence: present indicative, perfect subjunctive)

Sterilēsne *ēlēgit* **harēnās ut** *caneret* **paucīs?**

LUCAN *Bellum cīvīle* 9.576f.

Did he choose barren sands to give oracles (lit., *so that he might sing*)
   to a few?
   (secondary sequence: perfect indicative, imperfect subjunctive)

Rogabat **denique, cur umquam** *fugisset.*   *HORACE *Sermōnēs* 1.5.67f.
He finally asked why he had ever fled.
   (secondary sequence: imperfect indicative, pluperfect subjunctive)

The construction in CATULLUS *Carmina* 101.1ff., page 44, is complicated by the fact that the purpose clauses introduced by **ut** follow not from the main verb **adveniō**, but from the perfect participle **vectus**, which expresses a simple past action (lit., *having traveled*); consequently, their verbs, **dōnārem** and **alloquerer**, are imperfect subjunctive in a secondary sequence.

G94 A *conditional sentence* consists of an *if* clause and a main clause. There are two types.

❰ **Category 1** Conditional sentences that have the *subjunctive* in both clauses in Latin and that have *would* or *should* in the main clause in English.

Sī urbānus *essēs* ... tamen renīdēre usque quāque tē *nollem.*

CATULLUS CARMINA 39.10ff.

If you were a city man, nevertheless I would not want you to smile
everywhere. (the reference is to the present)

Quis hoc *crēdat,* nisi *sit* prō teste vetustās? OVID *Metamorphōsēs* 1.400
Who would believe this unless it were vouched for by antiquity?
(the reference is to the future)

Sī duo ... tālīs Īdaea *tulisset* terra virōs, ... Īnachiās *vēnisset*
ad urbēs Dardanus. *VERGIL *Aeneid* 11.285ff.

If the Idaean land had produced two such men, Dardanus would
have come to the cities of Greece (lit., *Inachian* (= *Greek*) *cities*).
(the reference is to the past)

The time references of the subjunctive tenses are as indicated. Note that
these are different from those of the potential subjunctive when used alone
(§G 68), and that English does not make a distinction between a sentence
with a present reference and one with a future reference.

In TIBULLUS *Elegies* 1.8.22, page 121, a present subjunctive (**sonent**) in the
sī clause follows an imperfect subjunctive (**faceret**) in the main clause, even
though the reference is to the present. This irregularity is probably due to
considerations of meter.

❲ Category 2   Conditional sentences that have the *indicative* in both
clauses in Latin and that do not have *would* or *should* in the main clause in
English. The main difference between the Latin and English formations is
in sentences of the following type.

Cēnābis bene ... sī tēcum *attuleris* bonam atque magnam cēnam.

CATULLUS *Carmina* 13.1ff.

You will dine well if you bring with you a good and large dinner.

Because the dinner must be brought before it can be eaten, Latin uses the
future perfect **attuleris** (see §G 66).

ARCHAIC AND POETIC FORMS

Early Latin writers used older forms of words that subsequently under-
went one or more changes. These were sometimes retained in poetic diction,
partly to give a poet's language a certain remoteness from that of everyday
speech, and partly because these forms were often metrically convenient. An
example of the latter is the use of **induperātor** (*general*) in JUVENAL *Satires*
10.138, which would have been replaced long before his time by the shorter
form **imperātor**. The former, which scans as **indŭpĕrātŏr**, can be used in a
hexameter, whereas **īmpĕrātŏr**, which has a short syllable between two long
syllables, cannot.

A few other forms used by poets do not occur in Ciceronian Latin, but were not necessarily archaisms. These are termed *poetic*, although some may have been part of popular speech.

G95 The following poetic forms occur in the poetry selections in this book.

Verbs

❡ The present passive infinitive can end in **-ier** instead of **-ī**, for example, **vertier** (= **vertī**, LUCRETIUS *Dē rērum nātūrā* 5.1199).

❡ The ending for the third-person plural, perfect indicative active **-ēre** (instead of **-ērunt**) is common, for example, **fulsēre** (= **fulsērunt**, CATULLUS *Carmina* 8.3) and **stupuēre** (= **stupuērunt**, VERGIL *Georgics* 4.481). The shorter ending also occurs in some prose writers, such as Livy and Tacitus; it appears to have been used in popular speech.

❡ Forms with a perfect stem ending in **-v** are often contracted, for example, **vocāsset** (= **vocāvisset**, LUCAN *Bellum cīvīle* 1.146) and **temptārīs** (= **temptāverīs**, HORACE *Odes* 1.11.3).

Nouns and Pronouns

❡ Archaic forms, such as **duellum** (= **bellum**, HORACE *Epistulae* 1.2.7), are used as metrical variants. Forms such as **istuc** (= **istud**, TERENCE *Andria* 186) and **hōrunc** (= **hōrum**, *Verse Epitaphs* B.5) were current at the time of their writing and are occasionally found in later authors.

❡ The old ending of the genitive plural of the second declension (**-um**) is common, for example, **virum** (= **virōrum**, VERGIL *Georgics* 2.142) and **superum** (= **superōrum**, VERGIL *Aeneid* 1.4).

Other Parts of Speech

❡ By the Augustan Age, an original **uo** had changed to **uu** or **u**. Older forms are found in Plautus and Terence, for example, **quom** (= **cum**, PLAUTUS *Mostellāria* 25) and **suom** (= **suum**, TERENCE *Andria* 188).

FIGURES OF SPEECH

A figure of speech is an expression in which the normal use of words is varied for some rhetorical effect. Some figures, such as simile and metaphor, occur often and require no explanation; of the many others, three are common in Latin poetry.

G96 *Hendiadys* is the use of two words connected by a conjunction (in English, *and*) to express a single complex idea. Often, two substantives are so joined instead of one substantive and an adjective or attributive genitive, for example, *by length of time and siege* (= *by a long siege*). When hendiadys occurs in a Latin author, the two elements are usually combined into a single phrase in translation.

Tēlīs et lūce coruscus aēnā.   VERGIL *Aeneid* 2.470
Shining with the bronze gleam of [his] weapons. (lit., Shining
   with respect to [his] weapons and [their] bronze light.)

(G97) **Metonymy** is the substitution of one word for another to which it stands in some close relation. In the sentence *In his despair, the Latin professor took to the bottle*, it is obvious that the unfortunate pedagogue did not consume a bottle, but rather what can be inside bottles, viz alcohol. Metonymy always depends on associations that are commonly made, for example, alcohol and bottles.

An example of metonymy in Latin can sometimes be kept in translation. In *arma* **virumque canō …** (VERGIL *Aeneid* 1.1), **arma** (*arms, weapons*) is used for *wars*, because the two are normally associated. The figure of speech may be kept in English and the words may be translated *I sing of arms and the man….*

However, in **mūtātō voluī castra movēre torō** (lit., *I wanted to move camp, with [my] bed having been changed* (PROPERTIUS *Elegies* 4.8.28)), **torus** is used for what Propertius associated with a bed, viz a sex partner. A narrow translation could suggest that he wanted to change beds in a literal sense; to avoid this, the translation should be *I wanted to change my partner and move camp.*

(G98) **Synecdoche** is the use of a part for the whole, or the whole for a part. If the cry goes out on a ship "All hands on deck!", those on board are expected to present not just their hands but themselves **in tōtō**. It is sometimes necessary to abandon the figure in translation.

Puppem conscendit Arīōn.   OVID *Fastī* 2.95
Arion boarded a ship (lit., a poop; the name of a part of a ship
   (an enclosed structure at the stern of the ship above the
   main deck) is used for the ship itself).

METRICS

Scansion is the analysis of how Latin poetry is constructed, and to scan a line is to divide it into its metrical units. Because of the differences between English and Latin verse, scansion is by no means easy for a beginner to grasp. However, mastery of its principles through deliberate application and practice is the key to appreciation of the rhythmic beauty of Latin poetry.

English poetry is constructed in lines of stressed syllables arranged in certain patterns; there can be the additional feature of rhyme. As an example, consider the following stanza from Latin scholar A. E. Housman's *The Oracles*, where lines of seven and five stressed syllables alternate, combined with a rhyming pattern of *abab*.

> 'Tis múte, the wórd they wént to heár on hígh Dodóna moúntain
>> When wínds were in the oákenshaws and áll the caúldrons tólled,
> And múte's the mídland nável-stóne besíde the sínging foúntain,
>> And échoes list to sílence now where góds told líes of óld.

Classical Latin poetry was composed in an entirely different way; patterns of stressed syllables were of secondary importance, and rhyme was never used. In spite of this, the structure of Latin verse was much more formal and prescribed than that of English.

The basic unit of Latin verse was a syllable's length. Each syllable of a Latin word was regarded as either long or short according to fixed rules. Poets used different arrangements of long and short syllables, depending on the type of poetry they were composing. A particular arrangement is called a meter, but before these metrical varieties are described, it is necessary to specify what constitutes a syllable in Latin and to consider the rules governing its length.

The Syllable

A syllable contains one and only one vowel or diphthong (two vowels pronounced as one, like **ae** in **saevus**). It may also contain one or more consonants: **ē**, **heu**, and **stat** are all monosyllabic words. In order to scan a line of Latin poetry, that is, to analyze the meter in which it is composed, it is necessary not only to mark the syllables of each word as long or short, but also to indicate where one syllable ends and the next begins, as follows.

❈ In words of more than one syllable, a single consonant belongs to the following vowel, except that a final consonant belongs to the preceding vowel: **a-mī-cus**. The consonant or consonants before the first vowel of a word belong to that vowel: **vī-vō, sta-tim, proe-li-um**.

❈ If two or more consonants occur together within a word, the syllable is divided immediately before the last consonant: **as-pe-ra, dig-nus, pulch-rum**. However, note the following.

A Compound words are divided between their parts: **con-spectus** (not **cons-pectus**).

B The letter **h** is completely disregarded: **e-le-phan-tus**.

C The combination **qu** counts as one consonant and is not divided: **se-qui-tur**.

D The letters **x** and **z** count as double consonants and are resolved into their constituent elements, **c + s** and **d + s**, respectively: **axis = ac-sis**.

E Special rules apply if the second consonant of a two-consonant group is **l** or **r**; see below.

The Length of a Syllable

When words have been divided into their constituent syllables, the syllables are marked as long or short. A macron, or bar (ˉ), above a vowel or diphthong indicates that its syllable is long; a micron, or half-moon (˘), indicates that the syllable is short.

❈ A syllable is long if …

F It contains a long vowel or diphthong: **a-mō, a-ci-ēs** (the final vowels in both words are long), or

G It ends in two consonants: **a-mānt**, or

H It ends in a consonant and is followed by a syllable that begins with a consonant: **āb-sum**. The second syllable may even belong to the next word: **mu-rūs novus**.

❈ A syllable is short if …

I It contains a short vowel and does not end in a consonant: **ă-mant**, or

J It contains a short vowel and is the final syllable of a word ending in a single consonant: **mo-nĕt** (to count as short in verse, such a syllable must be followed by a word beginning with a vowel or **h: monĕt am-icus** (see H above)), or

K It contains a short vowel and is the final syllable of a prefix that is followed by a syllable beginning with a vowel: **ăb-it**. The syllable division is determined by rule A above.

❡ If the second consonant of a two-consonant group is **l** or **r**, the preceding syllable, if it contains a short vowel, can be long or short, as indicated by the syllable division: **āp-rī** or **ă-prī**.

A long syllable does not necessarily contain a long vowel or diphthong. Under either G or H above, the vowel itself may be short (and be pronounced as short), even though its syllable is long.

If the rules above seem complicated at this point, learn the following rule of thumb.

> A syllable is long if it contains a long vowel or diphthong, or if its vowel is followed by two (or more) consonants, of which the second is not **l** or **r** (**h** is not counted, **qu** counts as one consonant, and **x** and **z** count as two). Other syllables are short, except that if a short vowel is followed by two consonants of which the second is **l** or **r**, the syllable may be either long or short, at the poet's option.

It is important to remember the difference between the length of vowels and the length of syllables. Every vowel in a Latin word had a fixed pronunciation, which was either long or short; the difference was the same as that between the *o* sounds in English *note* (long) and *not* (short). This information is given in works of reference by placing a macron over long vowels; short vowels are left unmarked except where ambiguity is possible, and in such cases they are marked with a micron.* Vowel length was an integral part of the Latin language, and if a foreigner pronounced a long vowel as short or vice versa, he ran the risk of not being understood; for example, to confuse **occīdō** (*I kill*) with **occidō** (*I die*) could have had serious consequences.

Syllable length is the fundamental element of Latin poetry. It is based not only on vowel length, but also on the consonants following vowels. To mark long and short syllables, scholars have, unfortunately, used the same signs (macrons and microns) as for vowels. This can be confusing unless it is remembered that, while all short syllables, by definition, contain a short vowel, the same is not true of long syllables. A long vowel can, by itself, make a syllable long, but a short vowel followed by two consonants also has this effect. In the latter case, however, the short vowel remains short in pronunciation; **monent** has a metrical value of **mŏnēnt**, but a Roman would have pronounced both vowels as short.

---

*This system is followed in the *Oxford Latin Dictionary*, as well as in the Glossary and examples in this book. It ignores the problem of so-called hidden quantity, that is, a vowel followed by two consonants. The length of such a vowel cannot always be determined and is, in any case, of no importance to scanning Latin verse.

Elision

Elision (from **ēlīdō -ere** *to eject*) occurs when a vowel/diphthong at the end of a word is followed by a word beginning with a vowel/diphthong; the former is *ejected*, that is, it is not pronounced and does not count metrically. Elided vowels are enclosed in parentheses for purposes of scansion. The following examples are taken from Vergil unless otherwise indicated.

Since punctuation has no significance in scansion, it is not indicated.

siste gradum tequ(e) aspectu ne subtrahe nostro	*Aeneid* 6.465
errabat silv(a) in magna quam Troius heros	*Aeneid* 6.451
at cantu commot(ae) Erebi de sedibus imis	*Georgics* 4.471

Since **h** does not count metrically, elision also occurs when a word beginning with **h** is preceded by a word ending in a vowel/diphthong.

nesciaqu(e) humanis precibus mansuescere corda	*Georgics* 4.470

Further, elision occurs even with words ending in a vowel plus **m**. This reflects the weak pronunciation of final **m** in Latin.

talibus Aeneas ardent(em) et torva tuentem	*Aeneid* 6.467

These last two features are combined in the following line.

magnanim(um) heroum pueri innuptaeque puellae	*Georgics* 4.476

Hiatus (absence of elision) occurs, but is rare. The purpose of elision is to facilitate pronunciation by eliminating the slight pause necessary when pronouncing two adjacent vowels (compare **tequ(e) aspectu** with **teque aspectu**). Elision does not, however, take place inside words or between lines.

Metrical Feet

A metrical foot is a combination of two or more long or short syllables. A regular succession of metrical feet is called a meter.

The most common metrical feet are the following.

Feet of Two Syllables	Trochee	—◡
	Iamb	◡—
	Spondee	——
Feet of Three Syllables	Dactyl	—◡◡
	Anapest	◡◡—
	Tribrach	◡◡◡
Foot of Four Syllables	Choriamb	—◡◡—

In scanning a line, all syllables are first marked as long or short by applying the rules given above. The length of a vowel followed by a single consonant within a word determines the length of its syllable; in cases of doubt, a dictionary and/or grammar should be consulted.

> fŏēdĕră tērquĕ frăgōr stāgnīs āudītŭs Ăvērnīs   *Georgics* 4.493

Assuming that we know the meter in which the poem is written (all works of Vergil are in hexameters), we apply the metrical scheme, given in "Meters" below, for that meter and mark the division between feet with a vertical bar.

> fŏēdĕră | tērquĕ fră|gōr stāg|nīs āu|dītŭs Ă|vērnīs

Care must be taken to mark elided vowels if any occur. These can then be ignored.

> rēddĭtăqu(e) Eūrўdīcē sŭpĕrās vĕnĭēbăt ăd āurās   *Georgics* 4.486
> rēddĭtă|qu(e) Eūrўdĭ|cē sŭpĕ|rās vĕnĭ|ēbăt ăd | āurās

Caesura and Diaeresis

For purposes of overall rhythm in some meters, poets arranged the words of a line so that there was a break between words inside a particular foot. This is called a *caesura* (lit., *cutting*) and is marked with a double vertical bar.

> fŏēdĕră | tērquĕ fră|gōr || stāg|nīs āu|dītŭs Ă|vērnīs

A *diaeresis* (lit., *splitting*) occurs where there is a break between words at the end of a foot. This too is marked with a double vertical bar. For an example of diaeresis, see "Pentameter" below.

In the majority of meters, there is only one mandatory caesura or diaeresis, and it is this that is marked. Because a caesura occurs inside a foot and a diaeresis at the end of a foot, they cannot be confused despite being indicated by the same sign.

Meters

Only the meters that occur in this book are described below.

In every meter, it is assumed that all long syllables require equal time to articulate, and that the same is true for all short syllables, but this is, at best, a very rough approximation of the real time needed in normal pronunciation.

In some meters described below (for example, the hexameter and pentameter, except for the final foot of each), all short syllables are presumed to take exactly half the time required to pronounce a long syllable. Consequently, in certain feet, a dactyl (−∪∪) can be replaced with a spondee (−−).

In other meters (for example, the iambic senarius), long and short syllables are interchangeable, and so an iamb (∪−) can be replaced by a spondee (−−) in certain feet.

One feature common to all meters is that the last syllable of the final foot can be either long or short.

Individual meters are used either by themselves (for example, the hendecasyllable and iambic senarius) or in combination (for example, the Sapphic stanza). Some meters are employed in both ways; for instance, the hexameter is used alone and as the first line in the elegiac couplet and the first Archilochian.

When two meters are combined in a poem, one is distinguished from the other by being indented. An example is the elegiac couplet.

> **Me miserum, quanti montes volvuntur aquarum!** (hexameter)
> **iam iam tacturos sidera summa putes.**　　(pentameter)
> OVID *Tristia* 1.2.19f.

In a three-meter combination, the second and third meters are successively indented; see the Alcaic stanza below.

In some meters (for example, the various Asclepiads), the length of each syllable except the last is prescribed, while in others (for example, the iambic senarius), there is considerable freedom.

As indicated below, certain meters were associated with particular genres of poetry. All examples are taken from the selections in this book.

(M1) Hexameter

The hexameter is used for epic, pastoral, satire, and certain other poetic genres. It is the meter of the selections from Ennius, Lucretius, Catullus (*Carmina* 64), Vergil, Horace (*Sermōnēs* and *Epistulae*), Ovid (*Metamorphōsēs*), Manilius, Lucan, Valerius Flaccus, Statius, Silius Italicus, and Juvenal.

The hexameter has six feet. The first four may be either dactyls or spondees, the fifth is a dactyl, and the sixth is a trochee or spondee.

−∪∪|−∪∪|−∪∪|−∪∪|−∪∪|−∪

To give the hexameter a more rhythmic effect, a caesura occurs either after the first syllable of the third foot or after the first syllables of the second and fourth feet.

$$—\smile\smile|—\smile\smile|—\|\smile\smile|—\smile\smile|—\smile\smile|—\smile$$

spārgĕrĕ | quādrŭpĕ|dūm || nĕc | vōtīs | nēctĕrĕ | vōtă

LUCRETIUS Dē rērum nātūrā 5.1202

$$—\smile\smile|—\|\smile\smile|—\smile\smile|—\|\smile\smile|—\smile\smile|—\smile$$

īndŏmĭ|tōs || īn | cōrdĕ gĕ|rēns || Ărĭ|ādnă fŭ|rōrēs

CATULLUS Carmina 64.54

(M2) Elegiac couplet

In an elegiac couplet, a hexameter is followed by a pentameter. Used for love poetry, epigrams, and occasional poetry, this is the meter of the selections from *Verse Epitaphs* c, Catulus, Catullus (*Carmina* 84, 85, and 101), Propertius, Tibullus, Lygdamus, Ovid (*Amōrēs, Ars amātōria, Fastī,* and *Tristia*), Martial (*Epigrammata* 4.8 and poems under the titles "Some Odd Characters" and "Wisecracks"), and Claudian.

A pentameter consists of two halves of two and a half feet each; between the two there is a break between words, which is called a diaeresis—not a caesura—because it occurs at the end of a metrical unit, not inside it.

$$—\smile\smile|—\smile\smile|—\|—\smile\smile|—\smile\smile|\smile$$

An example of an elegiac couplet follows.

dānt vĕnĭ|ām || rī|dēntquĕ mŏ|rām || căpĭt| īllĕ cŏ|rōnăm (hexameter)
   quāe pōs|sīt crī|nēs || Phōēbĕ dĕ|cērĕ tŭ|ōs   (pentameter)

OVID Fastī 2.105f.

The pentameter is always used to form an elegiac couplet; it is never used alone.

An elegiac couplet normally forms a self-contained sense unit and is usually followed by a mark of punctuation indicating this.

(M3) Hendecasyllable

A hendecasyllable (from Greek **hendeka** *eleven*) is a line of eleven syllables and is used in occasional poetry. It is the meter of the selections from Catullus (*Carmina* 2, 3, 5, 7, and 13) and Martial (*Epigrammata* 10.47 and 12.18). Its metrical pattern follows.

$$\smile—|—\smile\smile|—\smile|—\smile|—\smile$$

dōnā|rūnt Vĕnĕ|rēs Cŭ|pīdĭ|nēsquĕ   CATULLUS *Carmina* 13.12

A caesura sometimes occurs after the fifth syllable, but practice varies.

M 4   **Alcaic stanza**

Named for the early Greek poet Alcaeus, the Alcaic stanza was brought into Latin by Horace, who used it for lyric poems on a variety of topics, usually of a serious nature. It is the meter of Horace *Odes* 2.14.

An Alcaic stanza consists of four lines with three different meters. The first two lines have the following metrical pattern.

—|—∪|——‖—∪∪|—∪≍

Each line normally begins with a single long syllable (an exception is Horace *Odes* 2.14.6, where the initial syllable is short). Diaeresis occurs after the fifth syllable.

The third line, which also begins with a single long syllable, has the following pattern.

—|—∪|——|—∪|—≍

The fourth line has the following pattern.

—∪∪|—∪∪|—∪|—≍

The third and fourth lines have neither caesura nor diaeresis.

cōn|pēscĭt|ūndā ‖ scīlĭcĕt|ōmnĭbŭs
quī|cūmquĕ|tērrāē ‖ mūnĕrĕ|vēscĭmŭr
ē|nāvĭ|gāndā|sīvĕ|rēgēs
sīv(e) ĭnŏ|pēs ĕrĭ|mūs cŏ|lōnī   HORACE *Odes* 2.14.9ff.

M 5   **Sapphic stanza**

The Sapphic stanza, named for the most famous woman poet of antiquity, Sappho, is a lyric meter used for love poetry, as well as for poetry on other topics. It is the meter of Catullus *Carmina* 51 and Horace *Odes* 1.38.

A Sapphic stanza consists of four lines with two different meters. The first three lines have the following metrical pattern.

—∪|——|—∪∪|—∪|—≍

There is usually a caesura after the fifth syllable.

The fourth line, which does not have a caesura or diaeresis, has the following pattern.

—∪∪|—≍

līnguă|sēd tōr|pēt ‖ tĕnŭ|īs sŭb|ārtūs
flāmmă|dēmā|nāt ‖ sŏnĭ|tū sŭ|ōptĕ
tīntĭ|nānt āū|rēs ‖ gĕmĭ|nā tĕ|gūntŭr
lūmĭnă|nōctĕ   CATULLUS *Carmina* 51.9ff.

⎡M 6⎤ First Archilochian

The first Archilochian, employed by Horace in *Odes* 4.7, is a couplet consisting of a hexameter and a shorter verse (technically known as a lesser Archilochian).

—⏗|—⏗|—⏗|—⏗|—⏗|—⏗   (hexameter; the caesura
                                    occurs as indicated above)
—⏑⏑|—⏑⏑|⏒   (lesser Archilochian)

**Grātĭă | cūm Nȳm|phīs ‖ gĕmĭ|nīsquĕ sŏ|rōrĭbŭs | aūdĕt
dūcĕrĕ | nūdă chŏ|rōs**   HORACE *Odes* 4.7.5f.

⎡M 7⎤ Trochaic septenarius

A trochaic septenarius (also called trochaic tetrameter catalectic) is a line of seven trochees (—⏑) with the addition of an extra syllable at the end; trochees in the even-numbered feet can be replaced by spondees. It is the meter of the *Pervigilium Veneris*. Its basic pattern follows.

—⏑|—⏒|—⏑|—⏒‖—⏑|—⏒|—⏑|⏒

There is a diaeresis after the fourth foot, as indicated.

īpsă | nȳmphās | dīvă | lūcō ‖ iūssĭt | īrĕ | mȳrtĕ|ō
                                       Pervigilium Veneris 28

Some variations on this pattern occur in the *Pervigilium Veneris*.

⎡M 8⎤ Iambic senarius

The iambic senarius was the meter commonly used in drama for dialogue (here in Plautus (*Mostellāria*), Terence (*Andria* 196–198), and Publilius Syrus), but it also occurs elsewhere, for example, in Phaedrus' *Fābulae* and in epitaphs (see *Verse Epitaphs* B). Its basic pattern follows.

⏑—|⏑—|⏑—‖—|⏑—|⏑—|⏑⏒

A caesura is usual in the third foot, but is sometimes postponed to the fourth foot. Considerable variation is allowed in the first five feet, where a foot may have ⏑⏑⏑ or —— or —⏑ or —⏑⏑ or ⏑⏑— or ⏑⏑⏑⏑.

nēc vē|rī sĭmĭ|lĕ lŏquĕ|rĕ ‖ nēc | vērum | frŭtēx
                                    PLAUTUS *Mostellāria* 13

pōstqu(am) īn|tērfē|cīt ‖ sīc | lŏcū|tūs trā|dĭtŭr
                                    PHAEDRUS *Fābulae* 4.4.6

M 9 | Iambic octonarius

The iambic octonarius occurs in Terence (*Andria* 185–195 and 199–202). Its basic pattern follows.

⏑—|⏑—|⏑—|⏑—|⏑⏑‖—|⏑—|⏑—|⏑⏓

A caesura is usual in the fifth foot. The same variations occur in the first seven feet as in the iambic senarius.

hōc quīd | sĭt ōm|nēs qu(i) ă|mānt grăvĭ|tēr ‖
sĭbĭ | dăr(i) ū|xōrēm | fĕrūnt   TERENCE *Andria* 191

M 10 | Limping iambic

The limping iambic is used for occasional poetry, as in Catullus (*Carmina* 8 and 39) and Persius (prologue). It is an iambic senarius, but with a trochee or spondee (—⏓) as the sixth foot. Because the final foot interrupts the iambic rhythm, the line is said to limp. Its basic pattern follows.

⏑—|⏑—|⏑‖—|⏑—|⏑—|—⏓

Most variations allowed in the iambic senarius can occur in the first three feet of the limping iambic.

āut Trāns|pădā|nŭs ‖ ūt | mĕōs | quŏqu(e) āt|tīngăm
                                         CATULLUS *Carmina* 39.13

Asclepiad Meters

The four meters that follow consist of a number of choriambic feet (—⏑⏑—) preceded by a spondee (——) and followed by an iamb (⏑—). Since the second syllable of the iamb is the last syllable in the line, the final foot may also be ⏑⏑. Each choriambic foot except the last is followed by a diaeresis.

These meters were used by Horace in his lyric poetry and by Seneca in the choral odes of his tragedies. Three metrical patterns are used, differing in the number of choriambic feet they contain.

A One choriambic (there is no diaeresis)

——|—⏑⏑—|⏑⏓

B Two choriambics (the first is followed by a diaeresis)

——|—⏑⏑—‖—⏑⏑—|⏑⏓

c Three choriambics (the first and second are followed by a diaeresis)

——|—⏑⏑—‖—⏑⏑—‖—⏑⏑—|⏑⏚

M11 **First Asclepiad*** (Seneca *Trōades* 371–408)

The first Asclepiad consists solely of pattern B.

   īmmīx|tūs něbŭlīs ‖ cēssĭt ĭn ā|ěrǎ   SENECA *Trōades* 380

M12 **Second Asclepiad** (Horace *Odes* 1.24)

The second Asclepiad is a stanza of four lines, of which the first three are pattern B and the fourth is pattern A.

   ērgō|Quīntĭlĭūm ‖ pērpětŭŭs|sŏpŏr
   ūrgēt|cūī Pŭdŏr ēt ‖ Iūstĭtĭāē|sŏrŏr
   īncŏr|rūptǎ Fĭdēs ‖ nūdǎquě Vē|rĭtǎs
   quānd(o) ūl|l(um) īnvěnĭēt|pǎrěm   HORACE *Odes* 1.24.5ff.

M13 **Fourth Asclepiad** (Horace *Odes* 3.9 and 4.3)

The fourth Asclepiad is a couplet consisting of patterns A and B.

   cērvī|cī iŭvěnīs|dǎbǎt
   Pērsā|rūm vĭgŭī ‖ rēgě běā|tĭŏr   HORACE *Odes* 3.9.3f.

M14 **Fifth Asclepiad** (Horace *Odes* 1.11)

The fifth Asclepiad consists solely of pattern C.

   āetās|cārpě dĭēm ‖ quām mĭnĭmūm ‖ crēdŭlǎ pōs|těrō
                                   HORACE *Odes* 1.11.8

---

*The numbers given to the Asclepiad meters are those of Nisbet and Hubbard in their commentaries on Horace's *Odes*. The third Asclepiad is not represented in this book.

TRANSLATIONS

❦ Explanations and more literal interpretations are given in parentheses. Words that have no specific equivalent in the Latin original but that must be supplied in English are enclosed in square brackets.

❦ Translations are as literal as possible and are not to be taken as models of English style or as reflecting the style of the original Latin.

The Dream of Ilia

ENNIUS *Annālēs* 1 fr. xxix

And with trembling limbs, the old woman quickly brought a torch. Then she (Ilia), crying [and] frightened out of sleep, spoke thus, "Daughter (*lit.*, born) of Eurydica, whom our father loved, strength and life now abandon my whole body. For a handsome man seemed to carry me off through pleasant willow groves and [river] banks and strange places. [And] thus afterwards, sister of mine (*lit.*, full sister), I seemed to wander alone and slowly search and look for you but not be able to grasp you in [my] heart. No path guided [my] foot. Then [our] father seemed to address me with [his] voice in these words, 'O daughter, you must first (*lit.*, before) endure troubles, later [your] fortune will rise again from a river.' After saying this (*lit.*, these [things]), [our] father suddenly went away, sister, nor did he, [though] desired by [my] heart, appear to [my] sight, although many [times] in tears (*lit.*, crying) I stretched [my] hands to the blue regions of the sky and called with coaxing voice. Just now sleep left me with my heart sick."

A Quarrel Between Slaves

PLAUTUS *Mostellāria* 1–39

GRUMIO. Come out into the open from the kitchen, if you please, [you] rascal, [you] who are displaying [your] verbal wit to me amid your dishes. Come out of the house, [you] ruin of [our] master. By Pollux, if I'm alive (*lit.*, will live), I will take vengeance on you thoroughly in the country. Come out of the kitchen, I'm telling [you], [you] smell-lover. Why are you hiding?

TRANIO. Why are you shouting, damn it, here in front of the house? Do you think you are [still] in the country? Go away from the house! Go away to the country, go away immediately, go away from the door! (*hitting* Grumio) There [you are]! Is this what you wanted?

GRUMIO. Yikes! Why are you hitting me?

TRANIO. Because you are alive.

GRUMIO. I will put up with [it]. Just let the old man come. Just let him come safely whom you are ruining (*lit.*, eating) in his absence (*lit.*, [when] absent).

267

TRANIO. What you say is neither likely nor true, [you] blockhead, [namely] that a person can eat someone [who is] absent.

GRUMIO. Do you, a real city smart aleck, a darling of the people, throw the country in my face? [You] certainly [do this], I think, because you know that in the near future you will be consigned to the mill. By Hercules, within a few seasons, Tranio, you will increase the country population, [namely] the iron mob. Now, while you want to and can, drink, waste property, corrupt [our] excellent young master, drink night and day, act like Greeks, buy mistresses, set [them] free, feed parasites, stock up for sumptuous banquets. Did the old man give you these instructions when he went abroad from here? Will he find [his] property here looked after in this way? Do you think that this is the duty of a good slave, [namely] that he should ruin both the property and the son of his master? For I consider that [person] ruined when he devotes himself to these actions. He who previously was considered to surpass all the Athenian youth in sobriety and self-restraint (*lit.*, than whom no one from all the Athenian youth was previously considered equally sober and more self-restrained), now takes the prize (*lit.*, holds the palm) for the very opposite. This has been done through you and your instruction.

TRANIO. Damn it, why do you care about me or what I do? Tell me, aren't there cattle in the country that you should be tending? We like to drink, fornicate, bring prostitutes home. I'm doing these things on the responsibility of my back, not yours.

GRUMIO. How audaciously he talks!

TRANIO. But may Jupiter and all the gods destroy you! Yuck! You have a stink of garlic [about you].

An Insolent Slave
TERENCE *Andria* 185–202

SIMO. There is a rumor that my son is in love.

DAVOS. Of course, people are interested in that.

SIMO. Are you paying attention to this or not?

DAVOS. I [am] indeed [paying attention] to that.

SIMO. But for me to inquire into these things now would be (*lit.*, is) [the action] of a harsh father; for what he did previously is of no concern at all to me. While circumstances were suited to this [sort of] thing, I allowed him to follow his inclination. Now this day brings a different life[style] [and] calls for different behavior. Consequently, I am asking, or, if it is right, I am begging you that he return now to the [proper] path. What is this? All those who are in love take it badly that a wife is being presented to them.

DAVOS. So they say.

SIMO. In these circumstances (*lit.*, then), if anyone gets a rascally guide for the matter, [the latter] often leads [his] heart, itself [love]sick, in a worse direction.

DAVOS. By Hercules, I do not understand.

SIMO. No? Really?

DAVOS. No, I'm Davos, not Oedipus.

SIMO. So, of course, you want me to state frankly what else I have (*lit.*, what remains [for me]) to say?

DAVOS. Yes, indeed.

SIMO. If I perceive today that you are trying any deceit in this marriage to prevent it from happening (*lit.*, so that it does not happen), or that, in this matter, [you] want to show how clever you are, I will deliver you, Davos, after being flogged, to a mill until you die, on this condition and expectation, that if I take you away from there, I [am to] grind in your place. Well, have you understood this? Or even now do you not [understand] this?

DAVOS. But [I do], thoroughly, for you have now stated the matter itself clearly; you have not used a circumlocution.

Verse Epitaphs

A Lucius Cornelius Scipio, son of Gnaeus, grandson of Gnaeus. This [tomb]-stone holds great wisdom and many virtues with a short life. This [man], whose life, not [his own] probity, ran short for gaining public office (*lit.*, ran short with respect to public office), [and] who was never surpassed in virtue, is buried here. Twenty years of age (*lit.*, born twenty years), he has been entrusted to the places (*i.e.*, the Underworld). Do not ask why he was not entrusted with public office.

B Stranger, what I [have to] say is short; stand by and read [it] through. Here is the not beautiful tomb of a beautiful woman. [Her] parents gave her the name of Claudia. She loved her husband with [all] her heart. She gave birth to two sons; of these one she leaves on earth, the other she puts below the earth. Her conversation was charming, yet her bearing was proper. She kept house, she made wool. I have spoken [what I have to say]. Go on your way (*lit.*, go away).

C You who walk leisurely with carefree mind, traveler, and [who] direct your gaze at my funeral offerings, if you ask who I am, look! [I am now simply] ashes and burned remains; before [my] sad death I was Helvia Prima. I enjoyed Cadmus Scrateius [as my] spouse, and we lived harmoniously with matching temperaments. Now I have been given to Pluto to stay for a long age, having been taken down by destructive fire and the water of the Styx.

The New Eroticism
CATULUS epigrams

A My heart has run away. It has gone off, I think, to Theotimus, as it is accustomed [to do]. So it is, [my heart] avails itself of (*lit.*, has) that refuge. [But] didn't I tell Theotimus not to admit that runaway into his house, but, on the contrary, to throw it out? I will go to look for [it]. But I am afraid lest I myself may be caught. What am I to do? Venus, give [me] advice.

B By chance I had stood addressing the dawn when suddenly Roscius came into view on the left. May I be allowed, O heavenly beings, to say without offense, the mortal seemed fairer than a god.

The Inevitability of Death

LUCRETIUS *Dē rērum nātūrā* 3.1024–1044

This too you could at times say to yourself, "Even good Ancus abandoned the light with his eyes, who was better than you in many ways, [you] shameless [person]. Since then many other kings and lords of the world have died who ruled over great nations. Even that [man] himself (*i.e.,* Xerxes I) who once paved a road over the mighty sea and allowed his legions to go on a way over the deep, and taught [them] to go over the salt pools (*i.e.,* the sea) with their feet, and showed [his] contempt for the sea's mutterings [by] prancing on [it] with horses, when deprived of the light [of day], breathed out [his] soul from [his] dying body.

"Scipio, the thunderbolt of war, the terror of Carthage, gave [his] bones to the earth in the same way as [if] he were the lowliest house slave. Add the creators of philosophies and arts that give pleasure, add the followers of the dwellers on Helicon, of whom Homer alone having won the scepter [of poetry], fell asleep in (*lit.,* with) the same slumber as the others.

"Finally, after ripe old age had warned Democritus that [his] faculty of memory (*lit.,* remembering activities) was becoming feeble, of his own accord he himself presented (*lit.,* presenting) and gave up [his] head to death. Epicurus himself died after he had run through the light of life, [he] who surpassed the human race in intellect and extinguished all just as the rising sun in the heavens [extinguishes] the stars."

True Piety

LUCRETIUS *Dē rērum nātūrā* 5.1194–1203

O unhappy human race, when it attributed such actions to the gods and added bitter anger. How much misery (*lit.,* how many groans) did they themselves produce for themselves, how many wounds [and] how many tears for us and our descendants. Nor is it any piety to be often seen veiled [and] turning to a stone and to approach every altar, nor to lie stretched out on the ground and to spread open [one's] palms before the shrines of the gods, nor to sprinkle altars with an abundance of (*lit.,* much) blood of animals, nor to make vow upon vow (*lit.,* join vows with vows), but rather [it is piety] to be able to observe everything with a tranquil mind. (*A more idiomatic translation of the last sentence would be* Nor is there any piety in being often seen, *etc. or* Nor does piety consist in being often seen, *etc.*)

Love and Rejection

CATULLUS *Carmina* 5, 7, 8, and 85

A Let us live, my Lesbia, and let us love, and let us value all the gossip of too narrow-minded old men at a single *as.* Suns can set and rise again (*lit.,* come back); when [our] short light has once set, we must sleep one continuous night. Give me a thousand kisses, then a hundred, then another thousand, then a second hundred, then, without stopping, another thousand, then a hundred. Then, when we have made up many thousands, we will declare ourselves bankrupt so that we do not know their number or so that some malicious person cannot cast the evil eye [on us] when he knows there are so many kisses.

B   You ask, Lesbia, how many of your kisses are enough and more for me. To give you as many kisses as [there are] Libyan sands [that] lie in silphium-bearing Cyrene between the oracle of parched Jupiter and the sacred tomb of old Battus, or stars [that] see the stolen loves of mortals when night is silent, [that] is enough and more for demented Catullus. This number (*lit.*, which) neither busybodies would be able to count nor an evil tongue [would be able] to bewitch.

C   Unhappy Catullus, stop being foolish and consider that what you see to have vanished has been lost. Bright suns once shone for you when you always went where [your] girl used to lead [you], [she who was] loved by me as much as no [woman] will be loved. Then, when those many playful things happened, which you wanted and the girl was not unwilling, bright suns really shone for you. But now she is unwilling; you also, [although] irresolute, be unwilling, and do not pursue her who is fleeing, nor live in unhappiness, but with resolute mind bear up, be firm!

Farewell, girl, Catullus is now firm, and he will not seek you out and will not ask for your favors [if you are] unwilling. But you will be sorry when no one asks for your favors (*lit.*, you will not be asked). Wretched [woman], damn you! What life is left for you? Who will approach you now? To whom will you seem beautiful? Whom will you love now? Whose will you be said to be? Whom will you kiss? Whose lips will you bite? But you, Catullus, be steadfast and firm.

D   I hate and I love. Perhaps you ask why I do this. I do not know, but I feel [it] happening and I am in torment.

The Effect of Love
CATULLUS *Carmina* 51.1–12

That man seems to me to be equal to a god, that man, if it is right [to say so], [seems to me] to surpass the gods, who, sitting opposite (*i.e.*, facing [you]), looks at you continually and hears you laughing sweetly, [something] that snatches every sense (*lit.*, all senses) from wretched me; for as soon as I have looked at you, Lesbia, no voice remains in [my] mouth (*lit.*, for me in the mouth), but [my] tongue is paralyzed, a subtle flame runs down into [my] limbs, [my] ears ring with their own sound, [my] eyes are covered with double night.

Lesbia's Sparrow
CATULLUS *Carmina* 2 (with omission of l. 7) and 3

A   Sparrow, my girl's darling, with whom [she is accustomed] to play, whom [she is accustomed] to hold in her bosom, to whom, [when] pecking at [it], she is accustomed to give the tip of her finger and provoke sharp bites when my radiant sweetheart is pleased to play some sweet game, I believe, so that her burning (*lit.*, heavy) passion may then subside. I wish I could play with you as she herself [does] and lighten the gloomy cares of [my] mind.

B   Lament, O Loves and Cupids and all those of finer feelings (*lit.*, how much of more refined people there are), my girl's sparrow has died, the sparrow [that was] my girl's darling, whom she loved more than her own eyes. For it was honey-sweet and knew its mistress as well as a girl [knows her own] mother, and it did not stir (*lit.*, move itself) from her lap, but hopping around now here, now there, it always chirped to its mistress alone.

Now it goes along the gloomy way to the place from where they say that no one returns. But a curse on you (*lit.*, may it be badly for you), wicked Shades of Orcus that swallow up everything beautiful; so beautiful a sparrow have you taken from me. O wicked deed! O poor little sparrow! Because of you, my girl's swollen eyes are red from weeping.

Dental Hygiene in the Provinces
CATULLUS *Carmina* 39

Egnatius, because he has white teeth, smiles everywhere. If he has come to a defendant's bench, when the speaker is provoking tears (*lit.*, weeping), that [fellow] smiles; if there is mourning at the funeral pyre of a dutiful son, when a bereaved mother bewails her only boy, that [fellow] smiles. Whatever it is, wherever he is, whatever he is doing, he smiles: he has this disease, neither refined, in my opinion (*lit.*, as I think), nor polite.

So (*lit.*, wherefore) I must warn you, [my] good Egnatius. If you were a city man or a Sabine or a Tiburtine or a stout Umbrian or a fat Etruscan or a dark Lanuvian with good teeth or a Transpadane, to touch on my [own people] as well, or anyone who washes [his] teeth cleanly, nevertheless I would not want you to smile everywhere, for nothing is more foolish than foolish laughter.

As it is, you are a Celtiberian; in the Celtiberian land, everyone is accustomed in the morning to rub [their] teeth and red gums with what they have urinated (*lit.*, what each person has urinated, with this he is accustomed ...), so that the more polished those teeth of yours are, the greater amount of urine they (*i.e.*, the teeth) declare that you have drunk.

A Social Climber
CATULLUS *Carmina* 84

Whenever Arrius wanted to say "advantages" he would say "hadvantages," and "hambushes" [for] "ambushes," and hoped that he had spoken wonderfully when he had pronounced (*lit.*, said) "hambushes" with as much emphasis as he could. In this way, I expect, his mother, his maternal uncle, his maternal grandfather and grandmother had always spoken. When he was sent to Syria, everyone's ears got a rest. They would hear these same [words] [pronounced] smoothly and lightly and were not afraid of such words for the future (*lit.*, afterwards), when suddenly the spine-chilling news was brought that the Ionian waves, after Arrius had passed (*lit.*, gone) there, were no longer Ionian but Hionian.

An Invitation to Dinner
CATULLUS *Carmina* 13

You will dine well, my Fabullus, at my house within a few days if the gods are favorable to you, if you bring with you a good and large dinner, not forgetting (*lit.*, not without) a pretty girl and wine and wit and all manner of laughter. If, I say, you bring these things, my charming [friend], you will dine well, for the purse of your Catullus is full of cobwebs. But in return you will receive pure affection or if there is anything more pleasant or graceful; for I will give [you] an unguent that the Loves and Cupids have given to my girl. When you smell this (*lit.*, which when you will smell), you will ask the gods to make you, Fabullus, all nose.

A Brother's Tears
CATULLUS *Carmina* 101

I come, brother, after traveling through many peoples and over many seas for this sad offering, so that I might present you with the last gift [owed to] the dead and vainly address [your] silent ashes. Since fortune has taken you yourself from me—alas! unhappy brother undeservedly snatched from me—now, however, accept these [things], which, by the ancient custom of [our] ancestors, have been presented for an offering by way of sorrowful gift [and which are] drenched with a brother's tears, and forever, brother, hail and farewell.

Ariadne on Naxos
CATULLUS *Carmina* 64.52–75

For Ariadne, looking out from the resounding shore of Dia (Naxos), watches Theseus going with [his] swift fleet, bearing unbridled passions in [her] heart, and not even yet does she believe that she is seeing what she sees; no wonder, since she, then first awakened from treacherous sleep, sees herself abandoned [and] miserable on the lonely sand. But the forgetful youth strikes the waters with oars in his flight (*lit.*, fleeing), leaving [his] empty promises to the windy storm. Him (*lit.*, whom) the daughter of Minos with sad eyes watches from the seaweed at a distance, like the stone image of a bacchante, alas! she watches and is tossed on great waves of troubles; [she was] not holding [her] finely woven bonnet on her blonde head, nor [was] her chest, previously covered with a light garment, concealed (*lit.*, not concealed with respect to [her] chest, *etc.*), nor [were] her milk-white breasts bound with a smooth band (*lit.*, [she was] not bound with respect to [her] milk-white breasts, *etc.*).

All this (*lit.*, all of which things, *i.e.*, the articles of clothing), fallen at random from [her] whole body, the waves of the sea were lapping at in front of her feet. But then, caring for neither bonnet nor floating clothes, she, ruined, was hanging on you, Theseus, with [her] whole heart, with [her] whole soul, with [her] whole mind. Alas! unhappy [woman], whom Erycina (Venus), sowing thorny troubles in [her] breast, drove mad with constant sorrows at that time when cruel Theseus, having left from the winding shores of Piraeus (the port of Athens), arrived at the Cretan palace of the unjust king (Minos).

Worldly Wisdom
Publilius Syrus assorted *sententiae*

22 To be in love and to be wise is scarcely granted to a god (and so a mortal cannot expect to combine the two).

26 What trouble would you wish for a greedy person except "May he live long"?

41 Misfortune reveals whether you have a friend or [just] a name (*i.e.*, a real friend or one in name only).

92 Life itself is short, but it is made longer by troubles.

186 Even a single (*lit.*, even one) hair has its own shadow (*i.e.*, a shadow of its own).

222 Fortune is of more value to a person than intelligence.

258 The weeping of an heir is laughter beneath the mask.

275 Poverty lacks many things, greed everything.

296 The judge is condemned when a guilty person is acquitted.

298 In a difficult position, boldness is of the greatest value.

307 In love, beauty avails more than authority.

331 It is unreasonable for a person who is shipwrecked for a second time to blame Neptune (*lit.*, [A person] ... unreasonably blames ...).

339 A guilty person fears the law, an innocent person [fears] fortune.

358 When a bad person pretends to be good (*lit.*, himself to be good), he is then worst.

397 It is a misfortune to many when a good man dies. (*lit.*, A good man dies to the misfortune of many.)

478 No one can escape either death or love.

670 It is foolish to take revenge on a neighbor with fire (*i.e.*, by setting his house on fire).

711 It is better to trust virtue than fortune.

Unrequited Love
Vergil *Eclogues* 8.17–42

Rise (*lit.*, be born), Morning Star, and precede and bring on the life-giving day, while I, deceived by the unworthy love of [my] partner, Nysa, complain and, although I achieved nothing with them (*i.e.*, the gods) as witnesses, nevertheless, as I die (*lit.*, dying), I address the gods in [my] final hour. (Begin, my flute, Maenalian verses with me.)

Maenalus always has both rustling forest and whispering pines; it is always hearing the loves of herdsmen and Pan, who first did not allow reeds to be idle. (Begin, my flute, Maenalian verses with me.)

Nysa is being given to Mopsus. What are [we] lovers not to expect? Griffins will now be mated with horses, and in the following age timid deer will come to drink with dogs. (Begin, my flute, Maenalian verses with me.)

Mopsus, cut new torches; a wife is being brought to you. Husband, scatter nuts; for you the Evening Star leaves [Mt.] Oeta. (Begin, my flute, Maenalian verses with me.)

O [you], joined to a worthy husband, while you look down on everyone and while you dislike my pipe and nanny goats and shaggy eyebrow and long beard, and you do not believe that any of the gods tends to human [affairs]. (Begin, my flute, Maenalian verses with me.)

In our enclosure I saw you [when you were] small with your mother (I was your guide) picking dewy apples. The next year after [my] eleventh had already received me; already I was able to reach fragile branches from the ground. As soon as I saw [you], I was lost and foul madness swept me away. (Begin, my flute, Maenalian verses with me.)

Italy
Vergil *Georgics* 2.136–157

But neither the groves of the Medes, the richest land, nor the fair Ganges and Hermus, thick with gold, could contend with the praises of Italy, nor (*lit.*, not) Bactra nor the Indians and all Panchaia, rich with [its] incense-bearing sands. Bulls breathing fire from [their] nostrils have not plowed (*lit.*, turned over) these places for sowing the teeth of a savage dragon, nor has a crop of men bristled with helmets and closely packed spears; but abundant harvests and the Massic juice of Bacchus have filled [them (*i.e.*, these places)]; olive trees and fat herds cover [them].

From here the warhorse advances proudly on the plain, from here, Clitumnus, white herds and a bull, the largest sacrifice, dipped in your sacred river, have often led Roman triumphal processions to the temples of the gods. Here [there is] constant spring and summer in months not its own. [Farm] animals [are] pregnant twice [a year], twice [a year] a tree shows its use (*lit.*, [is] useful) with [its] fruits. But raging tigers and the fierce offspring of lions are not here, nor does aconite deceive the unfortunate reapers, nor does a scaly snake hurry [its] huge coils over the ground nor does it gather itself into a spiral with a mighty upward movement. Add so many splendid cities and the toil of [human] achievements, so many towns raised up by hand on precipitous rocks and rivers flowing at the base of ancient walls.

Orpheus and Eurydice
VERGIL *Georgics* 4.464–503

He himself, comforting his ailing love with a hollow tortoise shell (*i.e.*, a lyre), used to sing of you, sweet wife, of you by himself (*lit.*, with himself) on the lonely shore, of you when day was rising, of you when it was setting. After entering (*lit.*, having entered) even the jaws of Taenarus, Dis' lofty portal, and the grove gloomy with black fear, he approached both the Shades and [their] fearsome king and hearts not knowing [how] to become gentle through human prayers.

But stirred by [his] song from the deepest abodes of Erebus, the insubstantial Shades began to move, and the ghosts of those lacking the light [of day], as numerous as the thousands of birds [that] hide themselves in the leaves when it is evening or [when] winter rain drives [them] from the mountains, mothers and men and the figures of brave heroes [who had] finished with life, boys and unmarried girls, and young men placed on funeral pyres before the faces of their parents, whom the black mud and ugly reed of the Cocytus and the loathsome swamp with its sluggish water confine in a circle and the Styx, with its nine intervening streams (*lit.*, poured nine times in between), encloses. Indeed, the abodes themselves and Death's innermost region and the Furies, with blue snakes intertwined in [their] hair, were stunned, and Cerberus held his three mouths agape and the revolving wheel of Ixion stopped with the wind.

And now, returning, he had escaped all dangers, and Eurydice, given back [to him], was coming to the upper breezes, following behind (for Proserpine had laid down (*lit.*, given) this condition), when a sudden madness seized the unwary lover, pardonable indeed, if the Shades knew [how] to pardon; he stopped and, already under the light itself, forgetful, alas! and with mind overcome, looked back at his Eurydice. Then all [his] effort was wasted and the agreement with (*lit.*, of) the cruel tyrant was broken, and three times a crash was heard in the infernal swamps.

She said, "What terrible madness (*lit.*, what so great madness) has destroyed both unhappy me and you, Orpheus? See, again the cruel fates call me back and sleep closes my swimming eyes. And now, farewell. I am borne [back] surrounded by thick night and, alas! not (*i.e.*, no longer) yours, stretching out my weak hands to you." She spoke and suddenly fled from his eyes in the opposite direction, like smoke mixed with (*lit.*, into) the thin breezes, nor did she see him thereafter as he clutched vainly at the shadows, wishing to say many things (*lit.*, vainly clutching at the shadows and wishing …); nor did the ferryman of Orcus allow [him] to cross again the swamp that stood in [his] way.

Of Arms and the Man
VERGIL *Aeneid* 1.1–11

I sing of arms and of the man who, an exile by fate, first came from the shores of Troy to Italy and the coasts of Lavinium, much tossed both on land and on the deep through the violence of the gods because of the unforgetting anger of fierce

Juno, [and] having suffered many things also in war as well, until he would establish a city and bring [his] gods to Latium. From this source [arose] the Latin race and the Alban fathers and the walls of lofty Rome.

Muse, recount to me the reasons—through offense to what aspect of her divinity or because of what resentment (*lit.*, grieving over what) did the queen of the gods drive a man, distinguished by piety, to suffer so many misfortunes [and] to take on so many labors. [Is there] such great anger in divine hearts?

The Capture of a Royal Palace
VERGIL *Aeneid* 2.469–495

In front of the entrance hall itself and on the edge of the threshold, Pyrrhus swaggered, shining with the bronze gleam of his weapons; just as when a snake, which, in a swollen state (*lit.*, swollen), the cold winter covered below the earth, having eaten harmful plants, now fresh after shedding [its] skin and shining with youth, raises [its] breast and rolls [its] slippery back toward the light, rearing up to the sun, and flashes with a three-forked tongue from [its] mouth.

Together [with Pyrrhus], huge Periphas and the armor-bearer Automedon, [once] driver of Achilles' horses, [and] together [with Pyrrhus], all the force of Scyros moved up to the building and tossed flames onto the roof. Among the first, [Pyrrhus] himself, snatching an ax, broke through the stout door and wrenched the bronze-clad rails from [their] hinge pins; and now he made a hole in the solid oak by cutting through a panel and made a huge window with a wide opening.

The palace (*lit.*, house) inside was visible and the long hall was disclosed. Visible were the chambers of Priam and the old kings, and they (*i.e.*, the Trojans inside) saw armed [men] standing on the threshold's edge. But the palace inside (*lit.*, the inner house) was in confusion with wailing and woeful uproar, and the hollow rooms within howled with the lamentations of women; the clamor struck the golden stars. Then frightened mothers wandered in the huge building and embraced and clung to the doors and planted kisses [on them].

Pyrrhus pressed on with the force of his father; nor were the bars or the guards themselves [sufficiently] strong to withstand [him]. The door gave way with frequent blows from a battering ram, and the rails, dislodged from their pins, collapsed. A way is made by violence, and the Greeks, after gaining entry, forced the entrance and slaughtered those in front, and filled the place (*lit.*, places) with soldiers over a wide area.

The Shade of Dido
VERGIL *Aeneid* 6.450–474

Among whom Phoenician Dido, her wound still fresh, was wandering in the great forest. When the Trojan hero first stood near her and recognized her, [a] dim [figure] in (*lit.*, through) the shadows, just as at the beginning of the month a man sees or thinks he has seen the moon rising through the clouds, he (*i.e.*, Aeneas) shed tears and spoke with tender love:

"Unhappy Dido, so [was] the message true [that] had come to me that you had died and that you had sought [your own] end with a sword? Alas, was I the cause of your death (*lit.*, of death for you)? I swear by the stars, by the gods, and if there is any faith below the deepest earth, unwillingly, [O] queen, I went from your shore. But the commands of the gods, which now force [me] to pass through these Shades, through places squalid with neglect, and [through] bottomless night, drove me with their orders; nor could I believe that I was bringing such great grief as this (*lit.*, this so great grief) for you by [my] leaving. Halt [your] step and do not withdraw yourself from my sight. From whom are you fleeing? The words I am saying to you are the last allowed by fate."

With such words Aeneas tried to soothe (*lit.*, was soothing) her burning anger and grim looks and stirred (*lit.*, was stirring) up [his] tears. She, not facing him (*lit.*, turned away), kept [her] eyes fixed on the ground, nor did her expression change from the beginning of his words more than if hard flint or Marpessian rock were standing [there]. Finally, she snatched herself away and, [still] hostile, fled back to the shady grove, where Sychaeus, [her] former husband, responded to [her] sorrows and reciprocated [her] love.

The Emperor Augustus
Vergil *Aeneid* 6.791–807

This, this is the man whom you very often hear promised to you: Augustus Caesar, offspring of a god, who will again establish golden generations in Latium through fields once ruled over by Saturn, and will extend the empire beyond the Garamantes and Indians; the land [at its boundaries] lies beyond the constellations [of the zodiac], beyond the yearly path of the sun (*lit.*, the paths of the year and the sun), where, on [his] shoulder, sky-bearing Atlas turns the sky, furnished with blazing stars. In anticipation of the coming of this man, both Caspian kingdoms and the Maeotic territory already now tremble because of replies of the gods, and the anxious mouths of the sevenfold Nile are alarmed.

Nor indeed did Hercules visit so much of the earth, although he shot the bronze-footed stag or pacified the groves of Erymanthus and made Lerna tremble with [his] bow. Nor [did] triumphant Liber [visit so much of the earth], who controlled the yoke with reins of vine shoots, driving [his] tigers from the lofty peak of Nysa. And do we still hesitate to enlarge [our] worth by deeds, or does fear prevent [us] from settling on Ausonian land?

The Roman Mission
Vergil *Aeneid* 6.847–853

Others will fashion breathing bronze (*i.e.*, statues) more delicately (indeed I believe [so]) [and] will shape lifelike (*lit.*, living) faces from marble; they will plead cases better and with a rod will trace the movements [of the celestial bodies] in the sky and will predict the rising stars.

[You], Roman, be sure to rule peoples with [your] government (these will be your skills) and to impose civilized practice on pacified lands (*lit.*, on peace), [and] to spare the submissive and subdue the proud.

Hope Not for Immortality
HORACE *Odes* 4.7

The snows have scattered, grasses now return to the fields and leaves to the trees; the earth undergoes its regular changes and shrinking rivers flow within their banks. The Grace, with the Nymphs and her twin sisters, ventures to lead the dances naked. The year and the hour, which snatches away the life-giving day, warn you not to hope that this will last forever (*lit.*, warn that you should not hope for immortal things). The cold becomes mild with the west winds, spring is trampled on by summer (*lit.*, summer tramples on spring), [itself] going to die as soon as fruit-bearing autumn has poured forth [its] crops, and soon sluggish winter returns.

However, swift moons make good [their] celestial losses; when we have gone down to where good Aeneas, to where rich Tullus and Ancus [have gone], we are dust and a Shade. Who knows whether the gods are adding tomorrow's time to today's total? All things that you have given to your own soul will escape the greedy hands of [your] heir. When once you have died and Minos has passed [his] august judgment on you, Torquatus, neither [high] birth nor eloquence nor piety will bring you back, for neither does Diana set the chaste Hippolytus free from the infernal darkness, nor is Theseus able to break the Lethean chains from [his] dear Pirithous.

The Death of a Friend
HORACE *Odes* 1.24

What restraint or limit could there be to longing for so dear a head (*i.e.*, a person)? Lead the mournful song, Melpomene, [you] to whom [your] father has given a clear voice [together] with the lyre. So, an eternal sleep weighs down on Quintilius. When will Modesty and untainted Faith, the sister of Justice, and naked Truth find any equal to him? His death was (*lit.*, he died) worthy of tears for many good people, [but] for no one more worthy of tears than for you, Vergil. In your loyalty (*lit.*, loyal [to your friend]), you in vain ask the gods for Quintilius, alas! not entrusted [by you to them] on such terms (*lit.*, thus).

What [then]? If you were to play the lyre heard by trees more persuasively than Thracian Orpheus, surely blood would not return to the empty likeness that Mercury, not lenient in opening [the gates of] death through prayers, has once driven to the black crowd with [his] terrible wand? [It is] hard. But whatever it is wrong to correct becomes lighter through endurance.

A Quiet Drink
HORACE *Odes* 1.38

I hate Persian luxury, boy. Wreaths bound with bast displease me. Refrain from hunting for a place where a late rose lingers. I am earnestly concerned [that] you do not take the trouble to add anything to plain myrtle. Myrtle is unsuitable neither for you as servant nor for me as I drink (*lit.*, drinking) under a dense vine.

Seize the Day!
HORACE *Odes* 1.11

Do not ask—it is not for us to know (*lit.*, it is wrong to know)—what end the gods have assigned (*lit.*, given) to me [and] what to you, Leuconoe, and do not try out Babylonian numbers. How better [it is] to endure whatever will be, whether Jupiter has assigned [to us] many winters or [he has assigned as our] last [the one] that now breaks the Tyrrhenian Sea on opposing rocks! Be wise, strain the wine, and within a brief time span cut short far-reaching (*lit.*, long) hope. While we are talking, envious time will have fled. Pluck the day, trusting in the next as little as possible. (*This last sentence is often translated as* Seize the day; put little trust in the morrow.)

An Old Love Revived
HORACE *Odes* 3.9

While I was pleasing to you and no more (*lit.*, nor did any more) favored youth put [his] arms around [your] white neck, I flourished in greater happiness (*lit.*, more happy) than the king of the Persians.

"While you did not burn more because of another [woman] (*i.e.*, than because of me), and Lydia (*i.e.*, I myself) was not behind Chloe, I, Lydia of much renown, flourished in greater fame (*lit.*, more famous) than Roman Ilia."

Thracian Chloe now rules me, skilled in sweet melodies and versed in the lyre; for her (*lit.*, whom) I will not fear to die if the fates spare [my] darling and let her live.

"Calais, son of Ornytus from Thurii, sets me on fire with a mutual torch; for him (*lit.*, whom) I will suffer death twice (*lit.*, to die twice) if the fates spare [my] boy and let him live."

What if [our] former love returns and forces us, [now] separated, with [its] bronze yoke, if fair-haired Chloe is shaken off and [my] door lies open to cast-off Lydia?

"Although he is more beautiful than a star [and] you are more fickle (*lit.*, lighter) than a cork and more hot-tempered than the tempestuous Adriatic, I would love to live with you [and] would willingly die with you."

Caught by a Bore!
HORACE *Sermōnēs* 1.9.1–21

I was going by chance on the Sacred Way, as is my habit, thinking about some trifle or other [and] entire[ly absorbed] in it. Somebody known to me only by name ran up and, having seized [my] hand, [said], "How are you, my dear fellow?" "Very well, as things are," I said, "and I hope everything's well with you." When he followed, I put [him] off [with] "There isn't something you want?" But he said, "[Yes, that] you should be acquainted with me. I'm a scholar." At this point I said, "I'll value you all the more because of that."

Desperately wanting to get away, I at one time walked more quickly, occasionally stopped, said something in [my] slave's ear as (*lit.*, when) sweat poured [down] to the bottom of my ankles. "O Bolanus, [how] fortunate [you are] in [your] bad temper!" I was saying to myself, while (*lit.*, when) he rattled on about anything at all [and] praised the streets [and] the city.

When I was not replying to him, he said, "You desperately want to get away. I've noticed [this] for a long time, but it's no use; I'll stick with you the whole way. I'll escort you from here to where you are going (*lit.*, to where your journey is)." "There is no need for you to be dragged around. I want to visit someone not known to you. He's [sick] in bed a long way off across the Tiber, near Caesar's gardens." "I have nothing to do, and I'm not slow; I'll keep following you." I let my ears fall like a donkey of sullen disposition when it is burdened with a heavier load on [its] back.

The Lessons of Homer
HORACE *Epistulae* 1.2.1–22

While you are making speeches in Rome, Lollius Maximus, I, in Praeneste, have read again the writer of the Trojan War. He tells more clearly and better than Chrysippus and Crantor what is good, what [is] bad, what [is] useful, what [is] not [useful]. Unless something distracts you, listen to why I am of this opinion (*lit.*, have believed thus).

The story, in which is told the collision of Greece with the foreign world in a prolonged war on account of Paris' love, encompasses the passions of foolish kings and peoples. Antenor recommends the removal of (*lit.*, to remove) the cause of the war. What [does] Paris [say]? He declares that he cannot be forced to rule in safety and to live happily. Nestor hastens to settle the quarrels between the son of Peleus (*i.e.*, Achilles) and the son of Atreus (*i.e.*, Agamemnon). Love inflames the former, but anger inflames both (of them) alike. Whatever the kings rave, the Greeks are punished. Inside and outside the walls of Troy mistakes are made because of sedition, acts of treachery, crime, and lust and anger.

On the other hand, he (*i.e.*, Homer) has set forth Ulysses [as] a useful model [as to] what virtue and wisdom can [do]. He (*lit.*, who, *i.e.*, Ulysses), the conqueror of Troy [and a] prudent [man], observed the cities and customs of many people, and endured many hardships over the broad sea while he tried to secure a return for himself and [his] companions, [but he was] unsinkable amid the hostile waves of circumstances.

Live How We Can, Yet Die We Must
HORACE *Odes* 2.14

Alas! the fleeting years, Postumus, Postumus, slip by, and piety will not bring a delay to wrinkles and impending old age and invincible death, not [even] if, [my] friend, you were to placate with three hundred bulls for each day that passes the pitiless Pluto, who confines three-bodied (*lit.*, thrice huge) Geryones and Tityos with the gloomy water that must certainly be crossed by all of us who feed on earth's gift, whether we are (*lit.*, will be) kings or poor farmers.

In vain will we avoid bloody Mars and the crashing waves of the raucous Adriatic; in vain will we, in the autumn, fear Auster as it harms (*lit.*, harming) [our] bodies. We must see black Cocytus, wandering with a sluggish current, and the ill-famed family of Danaus, and Sisyphus, son of Aeolus, condemned to long toil. We must leave the earth and [our] home and pleasing wife, nor will any of these trees that you cultivate, except for hateful cypresses, follow you, [their] short[-lived] master. A worthier heir will drink up [your] Caecuban wines, [which were] guarded by a hundred keys, and he will stain the floor with proud wine, better than [that of] the dinners of the high priests.

The Favor of the Muse
HORACE *Odes* 4.3

[The one] whom you, Melpomene, have once looked upon with a kindly eye at his birth (*lit.*, being born), toil in the Isthmian games will not make [him] famous [as] a boxer, nor will a swift horse bring [him in as] winner with a Greek chariot, nor will the business of war display [him] to the Capitol [as] a leader decorated with Delian leaves because he has crushed the haughty threats of kings; but the waters that flow past the fertile Tibur and the dense leaves of forests will make him famous in Aeolian song.

The offspring of Rome, chief of cities, thinks fit to place me among the pleasing choirs of poets, and now I am bitten less by envious tooth. O Pierian [woman] (*i.e.*, Muse), who modulate the sweet sound of the golden lyre, O [you] who would give (*lit.*, going to give) the sound of a swan to dumb fishes if you pleased, all this is your gift, [namely, the fact] that I am pointed out by the finger of passers-by [as] the player of the Roman lyre; [the fact] that I breathe and give pleasure, if I do give pleasure, is due to you (*lit.*, is yours).

An Intoxicated Lover
PROPERTIUS *Elegies* 1.3.1–20

Just as the Cnossian [woman] lay exhausted on the abandoned shore when the ship of Theseus was going away; and just as Andromeda, the daughter of Cepheus, lay down in first sleep, now free from the hard rocks; nor less like [is] an

Edonian woman [who], exhausted from continual dances, collapses by the grassy Apidanus; even so Cynthia, resting [her] head on joined hands, seemed to me to breathe gentle sleep, when I was dragging steps [made] drunk with much wine and the slaves were shaking [their] torches in the late night.

I, not even yet deprived of all my senses, tried to approach her as I gently pressed [her] couch; and although on this side Love, on that side Liber, each a pitiless god, were ordering [me], seized by a double passion, [after] putting my arm underneath her to place her lightly on it and touch her, and moving my hand up to take slow kisses, I had nevertheless not dared to disturb the sleep of [my] mistress, fearing the abuse [that was the result] of her violent nature [and] that I had experienced; but, fixed [to the spot], I stared [at her] with straining eyes as Argus [stared] at the strange horns of the daughter of Inachus.

Love's Miseries
PROPERTIUS *Elegies* 1.1.1–8, 17–24, 31–38

Cynthia first captured me, unhappy wretch (*lit.*, miserable me), previously smitten by no desires, with her eyes. Then Love cast down my eyes in their resolute pride (*lit.*, of resolute pride) and put [his] feet on [my] head and trampled it (*lit.*, pressed [my] head with [his] feet having been put on [it]), until the villain taught me to hate unresponsive (*lit.*, chaste) girls and to live recklessly (*lit.*, with no plan). Alas for me! Now this madness has not abated over an entire year, while I, however, am forced to endure (*lit.*, have) hostile gods.

In my case, slow Love does not devise any stratagems nor does he remember to tread well-known paths as [he did] previously. But you who seduce the moon and pull her down [from the sky] and [whose] work [it is] to make propitiatory sacrifices in magical hearths, come now! change the heart (*lit.*, mind) of my mistress and make her be paler than my face. Then I would attribute to you the power to summon the dead and the stars with Cytinaean spells.

Remain behind, you to whom the god nods with receptive (*lit.*, easy) ear, and may you always be equally matched in a secure love. For our Venus torments me throughout bitter nights, and at no time is ungratified Love absent. Avoid this scourge, I warn [you]; let everyone be occupied with his own care (*lit.*, let his own care occupy each person), nor let him change [his] bed when love has become familiar (*lit.*, love having become familiar). But if anyone turns deaf ears to [my] warnings, alas! with what great grief will he recall my words!

Therefore Is Love Said to Be a Child ...
PROPERTIUS *Elegies* 2.12

Whoever it was who painted Love [as a] boy, don't you think that he had skillful hands? He first saw that lovers live (*i.e.*, behave) without judgment and that great advantages are lost through [their] trivial cares. Not without good reason, the same [person] added quivering wings and made the god fly in the human heart, since in fact we are tossed on the wave's ebb and flow (*lit.*, on alternating wave) and the breeze that drives us (*lit.*, our breeze) does not remain in one place. And rightly is [his] hand armed with barbed arrows and a Cretan quiver hangs down from each shoulder, since he strikes before we, [feeling] safe, see the enemy, nor does anyone escape (*lit.*, go away) unharmed. In me [his] weapons remain, and the boyish form remains, but certainly he has lost his wings, since—alas!—he flies away from my heart to no other place and constantly wages war in my blood.

What pleasure is there for you (*lit.*, what pleasant [thing] is there for you) in dwelling in [my] sick heart (*lit.*, dry marrows)? If you have any shame (*lit.*, if there is shame [to you]), shoot [your] weapons elsewhere, boy! [It is] better [for you] to shoot unscathed people with that poison of yours. [It is] not I, but my frail Shade [that] is being flogged. If you destroy it, who will there be who would sing of such things—this slight Muse of mine is your great glory—[and] who would sing of [my] sweetheart's head and fingers and dark eyes and how [her] feet are accustomed to step (*lit.*, go) in a graceful fashion (*lit.*, gracefully)?

The End of a Wild Party
PROPERTIUS *Elegies* 4.8.27–36, 47–66

Since wrong was being done to my bed so often, I wanted to change my partner (*lit.*, with [my] bed having been changed) and move camp. There is a certain Phyllis, a neighbor of Aventine Diana, possessing few charms (*lit.*, too little charming) when sober, [but] when she drinks, she adorns everything. There is another, Teia, [from] among the Tarpeian groves, fair, but one [man] will not be enough for her [when] drunk. I decided to pass the night pleasantly by inviting these (*lit.*, by these having been invited) and to resume my stolen pleasures with a novel sexual experience. There was one couch for three in a secluded garden. You ask about the seating? I was between the two....

They were singing to a deaf [man], they were baring [their] breasts to a blind [man]; woe is me! my whole mind was (*lit.*, I was entirely) at the gates of Lanuvium, when suddenly the screechy doors made a noise with their pins and loud (*lit.*, no low) murmurs were made in the front room with the Lares (*lit.*, at the first Lares). And without delay, Cynthia pulled back the double doors fully, [her] hair unkempt, but elegant despite her fury. The cup fell [from] between [my] slackened fingers, [my] lips, [though] indeed relaxed from the wine, grew pale. [Her] eyes flashed with lightning (*lit.*, she flashed with lightning with respect to her eyes) and she raged as much as a woman [can], nor was the sight anything short of [that of] a captured city. She thrust [her] angry nails into Phyllis' face; the terrified Teia shouted, "Neighbors! [Bring] water!" The abuse [that was] uttered disturbed the sleeping citizens, and the whole alley rang with frenzied voices. The first inn on a dark street received them (*i.e.*, the two prostitutes), with torn hair and loose tunics.

Cynthia rejoiced in the spoils and hurried back victorious and bruised my face with the back of [her] hand and put a mark on [my] neck and drew blood with [her] biting, and especially struck my eyes, which deserved [it]. (*The historic presents have been translated by the English past tense.*)

The Golden Age
TIBULLUS *Elegies* 1.3.35–50

How well [people] used to live when Saturn was king, before the earth was cleared into long roads. [A ship of] pine had not yet scorned the blue waves and exposed [its] billowing sail to the winds, nor had a roving sailor, taking back profits from unknown lands, weighed down [his] ship with foreign merchandise. At that time, a strong bull did not go under (*i.e.*, submit to) the yoke, a horse did not take a bit in its teeth with subdued mouth, no house had doors, a stone [was] not planted on land (*lit.*, in fields) to determine (*lit.*, which should determine) fields with fixed boundaries. The oak trees themselves used to give honey, and of [their] own accord, sheep used to bring udders of milk to meet people, who were free from care. There was no battle line, no anger, no wars, nor did a cruel blacksmith form a sword with merciless skill. Now under Jupiter's rule, [there are] constantly slaughter and wounds, now [there is] the sea, now many a way of death has been found.

A Face That's Best
by Its Own Beauty Blest...
TIBULLUS *Elegies* 1.8.9–26

How does it now benefit you to adorn [your] soft hair and to arrange [your] altered locks often, how [does it benefit you] to beautify [your] cheeks with shining pigment (*lit.*, dye), how [does it benefit you] to have your fingernails trimmed by the skilled hand of an artist? To no purpose now [your] clothes [are changed], to no purpose [your] shawls are changed, and a tight loop binds [your] constricted feet. That [other] woman is pleasing even though she has come with [her] face not made up (*lit.*, unadorned) and has not arranged [her] elegant head with long-drawn-out skill.

Surely an old woman has not bewitched you with spells [and] pale herbs at the quiet time of night? An incantation brings crops over from neighboring fields, and an incantation stops the advance of an angry snake, and an incantation attempts to pull the Moon down from [her] chariot and would do [so] if gongs were not struck to make a noise (*lit.*, if bronzes having been struck did not make a noise).

Alas! why do I complain that a spell [or] herbs has harmed me in my misery (*lit.*, miserable [me])? Beauty has no use for the aids of magic (*lit.*, does not use magic aids at all). But to touch the body does harm, to give long kisses [does harm], [or] to join thigh to thigh [does harm].

You Are My Heart's Desire
LYGDAMUS [Tibullus] *Elegies* 3.3.1–24 (with omission)

What does it benefit [me], Neaera, to have filled the heavens with vows and to have given beguiling frankincense with many a prayer, not that I should come forth from the threshold of a marble building, famous and notable because of

an impressive house, or that my bulls should restore many acres and the bounteous earth should give large harvests, but that I should share the joys of a long
life with you and my old age should come to an end in your bosom, when, finished with the time of light [that I had] traversed, I am forced to go naked in
the Lethean boat?

For what does a heavy weight of rich gold benefit me, or if a thousand oxen
cleave [my] fertile fields? Or what does a pearl that is gathered on the Red [Sea]
coast help [me] and wool dyed with Sidonian purple, and, in addition, the
things that the populace admires? Envy is [involved] in those things. The common people mistakenly love very many things. The minds and cares of human
beings are not relieved by wealth, for Fortune governs [their] circumstances
with her own law. For me, poverty would be pleasant with you, Neaera, but
without you I have no wish for the (*lit.*, I want no) gifts of kings.

Sophistication
Ovid *Ars amātōria* 3.113–128

Previously there was unrefined simplicity. Now Rome is golden and possesses
the great wealth of the conquered world. Observe what the twin peaks of the
Capitol are now and what they were; you will say that the latter belonged to
(*lit.*, was of) another Jupiter. The Senate-house, which now is most worthy of
so great a council, was [made] of straw when Tatius held the kingdom. What
was the Palatine that now shines with [the temple of] Phoebus and [the house
of] our leaders, except pastures for oxen before plowing?

Let ancient [things] please others; I rejoice that I was born now; this age is
suited to my character, not because malleable gold is now removed from the
earth and a choice pearl comes from a distant shore, nor because mountains
grow smaller because of the marble quarried, nor because blue waters are put to
flight by a pile, but because now there is refinement, and that coarseness that
survived our ancient forebears has not persisted (*lit.*, stayed) up to our times.

The Immortality of Verse
Ovid *Amōrēs* 1.15 (with omissions)

Why, biting Envy, do you reproach me with idle years and call poetry the work
of a lazy mind, [saying] that, while vigorous age supports me, I do not, according to the custom of [our] fathers, pursue the dusty rewards of military service,
and that I do not memorize wordy laws, and that I have not put [my] voice to
unworthy use in the thankless forum?

The work you ask [of me] is mortal. I seek everlasting fame (*lit.*, everlasting
fame is sought by me) so that I may be sung forever in the whole world. Maeonides (*i.e.*, Homer) will live while Tenedos and Ida stand [and] while Simois
rolls [its] swift waters to the sea (*lit.*, will stand, will roll). Ennius, [though]
lacking in art, and Accius of spirited mouth have a name that will at no time die.
The poems of majestic Lucretius will then perish when one day will give the
earth to destruction. Tityrus and crops and the arms of Aeneas will be read

while Rome is (*lit.*, will be) the head of the conquered world. While fires and a bow are (*lit.*, will be) the weapons of Cupid, your verses, elegant Tibullus, will be learned.

So, although flints, although the tooth of the long-lasting plow may perish through age, poetry is exempt from death (*lit.*, poems lack death). Let kings and the triumphs of kings yield to poetry, and let the generous bank of gold-bearing Tagus yield [as well]! Let the common herd marvel at worthless [things]. May fair-haired Apollo serve me cups full of Castalian water. And may I wear on my head (*lit.*, support with my hair) [a chaplet of] myrtle, which fears the cold, and may I be read often by an anxious lover! Envy feeds on the living; it grows quiet after death, when according to [his] worth, each person is protected by his renown. So, even when the last fire has consumed me, I will live on, and a large part of me will survive (*lit.*, will be surviving).

Ovid's Last Night in Rome
OVID *Tristia* 1.3.1–34

When there comes [to my mind] the very sad picture of that night that was my last time in the city, when I recall the night on which I left so many [things] dear to me, now too a [tear]drop falls from my eyes. Already the day (*lit.*, light) had almost come, on which Caesar had ordered me to depart from the farthest boundaries of Ausonia. Neither the time nor [my frame of] mind had been sufficiently favorable for preparing; my brain had become numb through long delay. I was not concerned with choosing slaves, a companion, clothing suitable for an exile, or necessities. I was stunned in the same way as [a person] who, struck by the lightning of Jupiter, lives and yet does not know he is alive (*lit.*, is himself unaware of his life).

When, however, grief itself removed this cloud from [my] mind and my emotions recovered at last, [when] about to leave I addressed for the last time [my] sad friends, who now were one or two of many. As I wept (*lit.*, weeping), [my] loving wife, weeping more bitterly herself, held [me] with a rain [of tears] falling constantly over [her] innocent cheeks. [My] daughter was abroad, far away from me, on African shores, and could not be informed of my fate. Wherever you looked, laments and groans were heard, and inside [the house] there was the appearance of a noisy funeral. Men and women, [and] children too, wept at my funeral, and in the house there was crying in every corner (*lit.*, every corner had tears). If I may (*lit.*, if it is allowed to) use prominent examples in an insignificant [case], this was the appearance of Troy when it was taken.

And already the sounds of men and dogs were growing quiet, and the lofty Moon was driving [her] nocturnal horses. Glancing up at her (*i.e.*, the moon) and from her looking at the Capitol's twin peaks (*lit.*, the Capitols), which to no purpose were close to my home, "[You] divinities living in neighboring dwellings," I said, "and temples now never [again] to be seen by my eyes, and gods whom the lofty city of Quirinus holds [and] whom I must leave, I greet you now and never again (*lit.*, be greeted by me for all time).

Deucalion and Pyrrha

OVID *Metamorphōsēs* 1.375–402

When they reached the steps of the temple, each fell down prone on the ground and, being afraid, gave kisses to the cold stone, and they spoke thus, "If the divinities relent, won over (*lit.*, conquered) by just prayers (*i.e.*, by the prayers of the righteous), if the anger of the gods is turned aside, tell, Themis, how the loss of our race can be made good (*lit.*, restored), and bring help, O gentlest [one], to the submerged world." The goddess was moved and gave [them] an oracle, "Go out from [my] temple and cover [your] heads and loosen [your] clothes, [now] girt up, and throw the bones of the great mother over your backs!"

For a long time they were stunned, and Pyrrha first broke the silence with [her] voice and refused to obey the orders of the goddess, and with frightened mouth asked that [the goddess] pardon her; and she [Pyrrha] was afraid to offend [her] mother's Shade by throwing [her] bones. Nevertheless, they reflected between themselves on the words of the oracle given [to them], obscure because of [their] dark uncertainty (*lit.*, of [their] blind hiding places), and talked over [the oracle] together. Then the son of Prometheus [Deucalion] soothed the daughter of Epimetheus [Pyrrha] with calm words and said, "Either my cleverness deceives me or (oracles are righteous and counsel no crime!) the great mother is the earth; I think that stones are called bones in the earth's body; we are being ordered to throw these (*i.e.*, stones) over [our] backs."

Although the Titan's daughter was moved by the interpretation of [her] spouse, [their] hopes were faint, to such an extent were they both uncertain about the divine instructions; but what would it hurt to try? They went out and covered [their] heads and unfastened [their] tunics and threw stones, as they had been ordered, behind them (*lit.*, behind [their] footsteps). The stones (who would believe this unless it were vouched for by antiquity?) began to set aside their hardness and rigidity and to soften slowly and, [when] softened, to take on a [new] shape.

A Storm at Sea

OVID *Tristia* 1.2.19–36

Woe is me! (*lit.*, Unhappy me!) What great mountains of water are surging up (*lit.*, rolling)! You would think that they were on the point of touching the highest stars. What great valleys sink down when the sea parts! You would think that they were on the point of touching black Tartarus. Wherever I look, there is nothing except sea and sky, the former swelling with waves, the latter threatening with clouds. Between the two, the winds roar with a terrible rumble. The waves of the sea do not know which master they should obey; for now Eurus gathers strength from the purple east, now Zephyrus is here (*lit.*, is present), sent from the late evening, now cold Boreas rages from the dry [constellation of the] Bear, now Notus wages battles in a head-on attack (*lit.*, with an opposing front).

The helmsman is in doubt and is at a loss to know (*lit.*, does not find) either what he should flee from or what he should head for; because of conflicting perils, [his] very skill is powerless. Of course, we are doomed and any hope of being saved is vain (*lit.*, nor [is there] hope of safety except [a] vain [one]), and while I speak, a wave floods over my face. The wave will overwhelm this life [of mine], and with vainly praying mouths we will drink in (*lit.*, admit) the waters that will kill [us].

Arion and the Dolphin
OVID *Fastī* 2.93–108, 111–118

The name of Arion had filled the cities of Sicily, and the Ausonian shore had been captivated by the sounds of [his] lyre. Returning from there to [his] home, Arion boarded a ship and took the wealth won in this way by [his] skill. Perhaps, unfortunate [man], you feared the winds and the waves, but for you the sea was safer than your ship; for the helmsman took a stand with drawn sword, together with (*lit.*, and) the rest of the guilty band with armed hands. What business do you have with a sword? (*lit.*, What [business is there] for you with a sword?) Sailor, steer the uncertain ship. Your fingers should not be holding this weapon.

He (*i.e.*, Arion), trembling with fear, said, "I do not beg to avoid death, but let me take up my lyre and repeat a few [tunes] (*lit.*, may it be allowed [to me], lyre having been taken up, to repeat …)." They gave permission and laughed at the delay. He put on a chaplet, [one] that could adorn your own hair, Phoebus. He put on a cloak twice dipped in Tyrian dye; the strings, struck by [his] thumb, gave back sounds [all] their own. Immediately, he, adorned [as he was], jumped into the middle of the waves. The blue ship was splashed by the water [when] hit (*i.e.*, by Arion). Then, incredible as it sounds (*lit.*, greater than belief), they say that a dolphin placed itself under an unfamiliar burden with [its] curved back. And he, sitting and holding [his] lyre, sang [as] payment for being carried and calmed the waters of the sea with [his] song.

The gods take note of good deeds: Jupiter admitted the dolphin among the constellations and directed [it] to have nine stars.

Ovid's Early Life
OVID *Tristia* 4.10.3–26 (with omissions)

My native place is Sulmo, very rich in cold waters, which is ninety (*lit.*, nine times ten) miles from the city. I was born here, and indeed, so that you may know the time, when both consuls fell by the same fate. And I was not the first offspring; I was born after the birth of [my] brother (*lit.*, [my] brother having been born), who had come into the world twelve (*lit.*, four times three) months before. The same Morning Star was present at the birthdays of both; one day was celebrated with two cakes.

From the start, at a tender age, our education began (*lit.*, we were educated), and through the care of [our] father we went to men in the city noted for their ability. From a young age, [my] brother was inclined to oratory, born for the

strong weapons of the wordy Forum. But [when] still a boy, divine rites used
to delight me, and the Muse used to draw [me] secretly to her work. Often [my]
father said, "Why do you attempt a useless pursuit? Homer himself left no
wealth." I was influenced by [his] words and, abandoning the whole of Helicon,
I attempted to write prose (*lit.*, words freed from meter). Of its own accord,
poetry came in suitable rhythms, and what I was trying to write was verse.

Pyramus and Thisbe
OVID *Metamorphōsēs* 4.55–166

Pyramus and Thisbe—the one the most handsome of young men, the other
esteemed (*lit.*, preferred) above the girls whom the East held—lived in adjoining houses where Semiramis is said to have enclosed [her] lofty city with baked
(*i.e.*, brick) walls. Proximity brought about (*lit.*, made) the first steps in [their]
acquaintance; in time, [their] love grew. They would have also been joined by
right of marriage, but [their] fathers forbade [it]. They both [however] equally
burned with hearts overcome, which (*i.e.*, something that) [their fathers] could
not forbid. No one was privy [to their love]. They spoke with a nod and with
signs, and the more it was hidden, the more the hidden fire [of love] blazed.

The wall common to each house had split with a narrow crack, which it had
long ago formed when it was being built. That fault, noticed by no one over long
ages, you, O lovers, first saw (what does love not perceive?), and you made [it] a
path for [your] voices, and through it blandishments used to cross safely in the
lowest whisper. Often when Thisbe had been standing on this side [and] Pyramus on the other, and the breath of [their] mouths had been caught in turn,
they used to say, "O ill-natured wall, why do you stand in the way of lovers? Was
it so much that you should allow us to be joined with [our] whole bodies, or if
that is too much, that you should open just for giving kisses? But we are not ungrateful. We admit that we owe to you that a passage to loving ears has been
given to [our] words."

Having spoken such [words] to no purpose from [their] separate positions,
they said "Farewell!" at nightfall, and each to his own side [of the wall] gave
kisses that could not pass across (*lit.*, not passing across). The following dawn
had banished the fires of night (*i.e.*, the stars), and the sun had dried the dewy
grasses with [its] rays. They came together at (*lit.*, to) the usual place. Then after
first making many complaints (*lit.*, having first complained many [things]) in a
low whisper, they decided that in the quiet night they would attempt to elude
the guards and go out from [their] doors, and when they departed from [their]
homes, they would also leave the city's buildings behind; and so that they would
not be obliged to wander aimlessly as they roamed over the broad countryside,
they would meet at the tomb of Ninus and hide under the shadow of a tree—
there was a tree there, a tall mulberry, laden with snowy fruits [and] close to a
cool spring. They agreed on the arrangements (*lit.*, the arrangements are agreed
on); and the sun (*lit.*, light), after seeming to depart slowly, plunged itself in the
waters [of the sea], and from the same waters night came out.

Careful Thisbe, after the door had been opened (*lit.*, after the hinge had been turned) in the darkness, went out and eluded her [family] and, with [her] face covered, arrived at the grave and sat under the appointed tree. Love made [her] bold. [But] behold! a lioness, [its] open jaws smeared [and] dripping from [its] recent slaughter of cattle, came in order to quench [its] thirst in the water of the nearby spring. Babylonian Thisbe saw it at a distance in the moon's rays and with frightened foot fled into a dark cave, and while she was fleeing, she left behind a garment that fell (*lit.*, fallen) from [her] back. When the savage lioness [had] relieved [its] thirst with much water, while it was returning to the woods, by chance it found the light garment without the girl and tore it apart with [its] blood-stained mouth.

Pyramus, having come out later, saw the unmistakable footprints of the wild beast in the deep dust and his whole face turned pale (*lit.*, he turned pale over [his] whole face). When, however, he also found the garment stained with blood, he said, "One night will destroy [us] two lovers, of whom she was most worthy of a long life. I am the guilty one (*lit.*, my soul is guilty). I destroyed you, O unhappy girl, [I] who bade you come by night to places full of fear, and I did not come here first. Tear apart my body and devour [my] guilty flesh with cruel bites, O all you lions who live under this cliff! But [simply] to pray for death is [the mark] of a cowardly [person]." He raised Thisbe's garment and carried it with him to the shadow of the designated tree. And when he had given tears [and] given kisses to the garment he had recognized, he said, "Take now a draft of my blood too," and he plunged into [his] stomach the sword with which he had been girded. And immediately, [as he was] dying, he withdrew [it] from the hot wound and lay on the ground on his back. The blood shot up high, just as when a [water] pipe splits after [its] lead has been damaged and from the small hissing opening shoots out long [jets of] water and cleaves the air with [its] spurts. The fruit of the tree was changed to a dark color with the spray of blood, and [its] root, soaked with blood, stained the hanging mulberries with a purple tint.

Behold! Thisbe (*lit.*, she), her fear not yet laid aside, returned so that she would not miss her lover, and looked for the young man with [her] eyes and [her] heart, and longed to tell what great dangers she [had] escaped. And although she recognized the place and the shape of the tree she had [previously] seen (*lit.*, in the tree having been seen), the color of [its] fruit made her unsure. She was uncertain whether this was [the right tree]. While she hesitated, she saw the trembling limbs striking the blood-stained earth, and she took a step backwards and, with (*lit.*, wearing) a face paler than boxwood, she shuddered in the same way as the sea, which trembles when its surface is grazed by a slight breeze. But when, after having delayed, she recognized her beloved, she struck her guiltless arms with loud beating, and, with hair torn, she, embracing the body she loved (*lit.*, the loved body), filled the wounds with tears and mixed [her] weeping with the blood, and planting kisses on [his] cold face, she shouted, "Pyramus, what misfortune has taken you away from me? Pyramus, answer [me]! Your dearest Thisbe calls you. Listen [to me] and raise [your] drooping face!" At [the sound of] Thisbe's name, Pyramus lifted [his] eyes, already weighed down by death, and on seeing her, closed (*lit.*, hid) [them] again.

After she recognized her garment and saw the ivory [sheath] empty of [its] sword, she said, "Your own hand and love have destroyed you, unhappy one! [But] I too have a hand strong [enough] for this one thing, [and] I have love as well (*lit.*, there is for me too a hand ... there is [for me] love too). This will give [me] strength for the blow (*lit.*, wounds). I will follow [you] in death, and I will be called the most unfortunate cause and companion of your death. And you, who—alas!—could have been torn away from me by death alone, will not be able to be torn away by death. But, O very unhappy fathers of us two, be asked this by the words of both [of us], that you do not refuse that we, whom sure love, whom our last hour joined, be put together in one grave. But you, O tree, who now cover the pitiable corpse of one [and] are soon going to cover [the corpses] of two, keep the signs of [our] death and always have dark fruit appropriate to grief [as] a memorial of [our] double death."

She spoke, and after putting the sword tip under the lowest [part of her] chest, she fell on the blade (*lit.*, sword), which was still warm with blood. [Her] prayers, however, moved the gods [and] moved [their] fathers, for the color on the fruit, when it becomes fully ripe, is dark, and what was left from [their] pyres rests in one urn.

The Folly of Human Desires
MANILIUS *Astronomica* 4.1–22

Why do we spend [our] lives in such anxious years and torture ourselves with fear and blind desire for possessions and, [made] old (*lit.*, old men) by ceaseless worries, lose life while we are seeking [it] and, satisfied with no end of [our] desires, always play the part of those [who are] going to live but we never really live, and [why] is each [person] poorer through [his] possessions because he wants more and does not count up what he has, [but] only desires what he does not have, and although nature demands minor needs for herself, [why] do we put together material for a great downfall through [our] desires and buy luxury with [our] gains and plunderings with [our] luxury, and [why] is the greatest reward of wealth to squander wealth?

Mortals, free [your] minds and lighten [your] cares and rid [your] lives of so many pointless complaints. Fate rules the world, everything stands fixed by unchangeable law, and the long ages are stamped with an unchangeable [series of] events. We die as we are being born, and [our] end results from [our] beginning. From this [source] wealth and kingdoms come, and poverty, which occurs more often; and [from this source] skills and characters are given to [people when] born, as well as (*lit.*, and) faults and virtues, losses and gains of property. No one will [ever] be able to be exempt from [what is] assigned [to him] or to have [what is] denied [to him], or with his prayers to take hold of Fortune [if she is] unwilling or to escape [her] when she approaches (*lit.*, approaching); everyone must endure his own destiny.

The Horse and the Wild Boar
PHAEDRUS *Fābulae* 4.4

While a wild boar was wallowing (*lit.*, rolling itself), it muddied a ford where a horse had been accustomed to quench [its] thirst. Because of this a quarrel arose. The horse, angry with the wild animal, sought the help of a man and, lifting him (*lit.*, whom lifting) on his back, returned happily to [its] enemy. After the horseman killed the latter with [his] spear, he is reported to have spoken thus: "I am glad that I brought help to you when you asked, for I took booty and I learned how useful you are." And so he forced the unwilling [horse] to endure a bridle. Then it [said] sadly, "While I was foolishly seeking retribution for a small matter, I found slavery."

This fable will warn angry [people] that it is better to be harmed without redress than to surrender oneself to another.

An Atypical Poet
PERSIUS prologue

Neither have I doused my lips in the nag's spring nor do I remember to have dreamed on twin-peaked Parnassus so that I should suddenly come forth in this way [as] a poet. I leave the daughters of Mt. Helicon and pale Pirene to those whose images pliant ivy wreathes. I myself, a half-peasant, bring my poem to the festival of bards. Who made it easy for a parrot [to say] its "hello" (*lit.*, made its "hello" easy for a parrot) and taught a magpie to try [to speak] human (*lit.*, our) words? [That] teacher of skill and bestower of talent, the stomach, [which is] an expert in imitating forbidden words. Moreover, if the hope of deceitful money has appeared (*lit.*, shone), you would believe that the raven poets and magpie poetesses were singing [pure] Pegasean nectar.

Is There Life After Death?
SENECA *Trōades* 371–408

Is it true or does a tale deceive the fearful that the Shades [of the dead] live [on] after [their] bodies have been buried, when a spouse has placed a hand on the eyes (*i.e.*, of the corpse) and the final day has stood in the way of [further] suns and an urn confines the sad ashes? Is it of no use to hand over a soul to death but there remains further life for the wretched (*lit.*, it remains for the wretched to live further)? Or do we wholly die and no part of us remains, when with fleeting breath the soul, mingled with the clouds, has gone into the air and the torch has been placed under and touched the naked corpse (*lit.*, side)?

Whatever the rising and setting sun knows, whatever Oceanos, coming and fleeing twice [in a day], washes with [its] blue waters, time will sweep away with Pegasean pace. With the same revolution as the twelve constellations fly, with the same motion as the lord of the stars hastens to bring around periods of time, in the same way as Hecate hastens to run in slanting curves, do we make our journey toward death (*lit.*, with what revolution the twice six constellations fly, with what motion the lord of the stars hastens to bring around periods of time, in what way Hecate hastens to run in slanting curves, in this [way] we head for death), nor does [the person] who has reached the lakes used as an oath (*lit.*, sworn) by the gods exist any longer in any place. As smoke vanishes from hot fires, of a grimy color for a short span of time, as clouds, which we have seen recently swollen [with rain], are scattered by the blast of northern Boreas (*lit.*, as the blast of northern Boreas scatters clouds …): in this way this soul by which we are governed will dissolve.

There is nothing after death and death itself is nothing, the last goal of a swift race (*lit.*, racetrack). Let the greedy lay aside [their] hope, [and] the worried [their] fear. Greedy time and primordial matter swallow us up. Death is indivisible, harmful to the body and not sparing the soul. Taenarus and the kingdom ruled by (*lit.*, under) a harsh master and the guardian Cerberus blocking the threshold with [its] difficult entrance [are] idle gossip and empty words and a story similar to a troubled dream.

Do you ask where you lie after death? Where things not born lie.

Pompey and Caesar
Lucan *Bellum cīvīle* 1.126–157

It is wrong to know who more justly put on arms. Each defends himself with a mighty judge. The victorious side pleased the gods, but the conquered [side pleased] Cato. Nor did they come together [as] equals.

The one (*i.e.*, Pompey), on the threshold of (*lit.*, [his] years declining into) old age and [made] more peaceful through long use of the toga, now forgot the [role of] leader through peace, and as a seeker of popularity gave much to the common people; he was wholly swayed by the breath of popular favor and delighted in the applause of his own theater; and he did not acquire (*lit.*, rebuild) fresh power, and he trusted much in [his] earlier fortune. He stood, the shadow of a mighty name; just as a lofty oak tree in a fertile field, bearing the ancient trophies of a people and the consecrated gifts of leaders but no longer clinging [to the earth] with strong roots, is held by its own weight; and spreading [its] naked branches through the air, it creates shade with [its] trunk, not with [its] leaves; and although it sways and is going to fall under the first east wind, [and] so many trees round about rise with solid growth, nevertheless it alone is revered.

But in Caesar there was not only a name and a reputation as a [military] leader, but vigor that did not know how to stand in [one] place, and the only thing that caused him shame (*lit.*, his only shame) was not to conquer by war. Energetic and headstrong, he fought wherever hope and anger had summoned [him] and never refrained from violating his sword (*i.e.*, using his sword unjustly). He made the most of (*lit.*, pressed) his successes and pursued the favor of a divinity, overcoming whatever stood in [his] way as he sought supreme power (*lit.*, for him seeking highest things), and rejoicing to make a path by devastation; just as lightning, driven forth by winds through clouds, flashes with the sound of the smitten sky and the crash of the heavens, and breaks the light of day and terrifies frightened peoples, dazzling eyes with [its] zigzag flame; it rushes to its own area [of the sky] and, with no material preventing [it] from leaving, it causes great devastation over a wide area in falling and great [devastation] returning, and it gathers up [its] scattered fires again.

Cato at the Oracle of Jupiter Ammon
LUCAN *Bellum cīvīle* 9.566–584

What do you bid me ask, Labienus? Whether I would prefer to fall in arms [as a] free [man] rather than witness (*lit.*, see) a tyranny? Whether it makes no difference if a life is short or a life [is] long? Whether no violence harms a virtuous man and fortune wastes [its] threats [when] opposed by virtue, and [whether] to desire what is praiseworthy is sufficient and [whether] what is honorable never increases through success? I know [the answer], and Ammon will not fix this more deeply in me.

　　We are all closely attached to the gods, and [even if] an oracle (*lit.*, temple) is silent, we do nothing [that is] not in accordance with the will of the god, nor does the divinity have need of any voices (*i.e.*, of oracles and the like), and [our] creator has once and for all told [us as we are] being born whatever it is allowed [for us] to know. Did he choose barren sands to give oracles (*lit.*, sing) to a few, and did he bury truth in this dust, and is there [any] abode of the god except earth and sea and air and sky and virtue?

　　Why do we look for gods further? Jupiter is everything (*lit.*, whatever) you see and everything that causes you to act. Let the irresolute and those [who are] always uncertain about future events have a use for (*lit.*, need) soothsayers. I am made certain [of the future] not by oracles but by the certainty of death (*lit.*, certain death). The timid and brave must [both] die. It is sufficient that Jupiter has said this.

A Pep Talk
VALERIUS FLACCUS *Argonautica* 5.312–328

Then, after turning to the faces of [his] men, [which were] fixed on the ground or (*lit.*, and) directed toward the silent group, he said, "Behold! We are here and we have sailed over the world, as huge [as it is], on the seas, [something] which you wished [would happen] through [your] mighty exploits and which the age of past [men] shuddered at. Neither have the thousand paths of the sea misled us, nor has the report that Aeetes, offspring of the sun, rules in the farthest north. Accordingly, when light spreads (*lit.*, will spread) over the deep sea, we must seek the buildings of the city and put the attitude of the unknown monarch to the test. He himself will, I think, grant [our request], and what we seek can certainly be obtained by entreaty (*lit.*, nor is [that] which we seek certainly not to be obtained by entreaty). But if, in his pride, he rejects [our] prayers and words, strengthen [your] minds here and now against (*lit.*, to) a rebuff, and rather let us resolve (*lit.*, let it rather stand [fixed for us]) by what means we can bring the fleece back to [our] native land. Let any scruple (*lit.*, let scruple always) be absent in difficult circumstances."

He spoke and sought by lot [men] who would accompany him to the Scythian city, and nine were taken (*lit.*, led) from the whole company. Then they hurried over the road by which the land of the Circaean plain was closest, and when light had already returned, they sought the king.

Insomnia
Statius *Silvae* 5.4

Through what misdeed or through what mistake, O Sleep, kindest of the gods, did I, unhappy youth, deserve that I alone should lack your gifts? All cattle and birds and wild beasts are silent, and bent [tree]tops imitate weary sleep, and raging rivers do not have the same sound (*lit.*, nor is there the same sound for raging rivers); the turbulence of the sea drops and [its] waters (*lit.*, the seas), resting on the lands, become quiet. Phoebe, now returning for the seventh time, sees my staring weary eyes; as many times do the Oetaean and Paphian torches (*lit.*, as many Oetaean and Paphian torches) visit [me] again, and as often does the wife of Tithonus pass by my complaints and, pitying [me], sprinkle [me] with [her] cold whip.

How am I to manage? [I could] not, [even] if I had the thousand eyes that sacred Argos kept only in alternating guard duty and was never awake with [his] whole body. But now, alas! if someone during the long night, holding [his] girl's arms, [which are] joined [to his], drives you away of his own accord, come from there; nor do I insist that you spread the whole of [your] wings over my eyes (let a more fortunate crowd pray for this); touch me with the very tip of your wand ([that] is enough) or lightly pass over [me] with [your] hovering knee.

Scipio and Syphax
Silius Italicus *Pūnica* 16.229–257

And already the Dawn, going out from the edge of her threshold, was bringing forth a new day for the world, and the sun's horses were going up to the yokes in [their] stables, and he himself had not yet mounted [his] chariot, but the sea was glowing red with flames that would soon burst forth; Scipio got out of bed (*lit.*, removed [his] body from bed) and, with a calm face, went quickly to the threshold of the Massylian king.

The latter observed the native custom of rearing the offspring of lions and driving away ferocity and rage from [lion] cubs by feeding [them]. Then too he was caressing [their] tawny necks and manes with [his] hand and, unafraid, was stroking the wild mouths of the playing [animals]. After he heard that the Dardanian leader was present, he put on a cloak and his left [hand] carried the distinguished symbol of the ancient kingdom. [His] temples were encircled with a white headband, and according to custom a sword was fastened to [his] side.

Then he summoned [Scipio] into the building, and in secluded rooms the guest sat down with the scepter-bearing king in equal honor.

Then the subduer of the Spanish land began to speak first with these [words], "My first and greatest concern, after conquering the peoples of the Pyrenees, was to go in haste (*lit.*, hurrying) to your kingdom, O Syphax of venerable scepter, nor did the wild sea delay me with its intervening water. I do not seek [things] difficult or dishonorable for your kingdom: join your heart unreservedly to the Latins and [as] an ally share in [their] success. The Massylian peoples and land extending to the Syrtes and ancestral power over wide fields would not bring you more honor than Roman courage, joined [to you] by sure faith, and the esteem of the Laurentine people. Why should I mention the other [considerations]? Of course, none of the gods [is] favorable to anyone who has harmed Dardanian arms."

A Pleasant Retirement
MARTIAL *Epigrammata* 12.18

While you perhaps are restlessly wandering in noisy Subura, Juvenal, or you are treading the hill of mistress Diana, while [your] sweaty toga fans you across the thresholds of the more powerful, and the greater and lesser [peaks of the] Caelian Hill weary [you] as you wander (*lit.*, wandering), my Bilbilis, proud with [its] gold and iron, [which I have] returned to after many Decembers, has received me and made me a rustic.

Here with pleasant toil, I idly visit Boterdum and Platea—these are rather uncouth names in the Celtiberian lands. I enjoy a huge and indecent [amount of] sleep, which often not even the third hour disturbs, and I now repay myself [for] all [the time] that I stayed awake over thrice ten years. The toga is unknown, but the nearest [article of] clothing from a broken chair is given [to you] when you ask. A fireplace fed by a noble pile from a nearby holm-oak grove greets [you] when you rise, and it is surrounded by the female overseer (*lit.*, which the female overseer crowns) with many a pot. There follows a hunter, but one whom you would like to have in a secluded woods. The smooth-skinned overseer gives a handout to the slaves and asks [to be allowed] to set aside (*i.e.*, cut) [his] long hair. In this way I want to live, in this way to die.

Some Odd Characters
MARTIAL assorted epigrams

A Gellius is always building; now he is laying thresholds, now he is fitting keys to doors and buying bars, now he is remodelling and changing these windows, now those. Provided only that he is building, that man does anything so that when a friend asks for money (*lit.*, to a friend asking for money), he, Gellius, can say that single word, "I'm building."

B Bleary-eyed Hylas recently was willing to pay you three quarters [of his debt], Quintus; [now that he is] one-eyed, he is willing to give [you] half. Accept as soon as possible. The opportunity for gain is fleeting. If he becomes blind, Hylas will pay you nothing.

C If I remember, you had four teeth, Aelia. A single cough knocked out two, and [another] single [cough knocked out] two. Now you can cough without care for entire days: a third cough has nothing that it could do there (*i.e.*, in your mouth).

D Over five days in a row, Afer, I wanted to say "hello" to you [when you had] returned from the peoples of Libya. Coming back two and three times, I was told (*lit.*, [to me] having returned ... it was said), "He's not free" or "He's sleeping." That's enough [for] now! You don't wish to be greeted, Afer. Good-bye!

E You pretend to be a young man with [your] dyed hair, Laetinus, so suddenly [you], who just now were a swan, [have become] a crow. You do not deceive everyone. Proserpine knows you [to be] white; she will pull the mask from your head.

Wisecracks
MARTIAL assorted epigrams

A Philo swears that he has never dined at home, and this is so; whenever no one has invited him, he does not dine (*i.e.*, he goes without dinner).

B A cunning innkeeper recently tricked me at Ravenna; when I asked for mixed [wine], he gave (*lit.*, sold) me neat (*i.e.*, straight).

C Papylus, you always serve Setine or Massic wine, but gossip forbids [us] such good wines. You are said to have been made a bachelor four times with this wine bottle [of yours]. I don't think [this] nor do I believe [this], Papylus, but I'm not thirsty.

D When a crowd in togas shouts a loud *bravo!* for you, Pomponius, your dinner is eloquent, not you.

E Do you ask, Linus, what my farm (*lit.*, field) at Nomentum returns me [in rent]? It returns me this: I don't see you, Linus.

F I don't know, Faustus, what you write to so many girls, [but] I know this, that no girl writes to you.

G When [you are] about to recite, why do you put wool around your neck? That is more suited to our ears.

H You recite nothing and [yet] wish to appear a poet, Mamercus. Be whatever you like, provided that you don't recite anything.

I Phileros, you are now burying your seventh wife in your field. No one gets a better return from a field than you. (*lit.*, your seventh wife is now being buried by you in [your] field. A field returns more to no one than to you.)

J Although you don't publish your [poems], you criticize my poems, Laelius. Either don't criticize mine or publish yours.

The Happy Life
MARTIAL *Epigrammata* 10.47

The things that would make life happier, most charming Martial, are these: wealth not obtained by labor but inherited; a farm not without rewards (*i.e.*, a profitable farm), a fireplace always burning; never a lawsuit, a toga rarely used, a mind at rest; the strength of a freeborn man, a healthy body; a sensible openness, friends of equal status; easy companionship, a simple (*lit.*, without art) table; a night not drunken but free from cares; a marriage (*lit.*, bed) not strait-laced but nevertheless chaste; sleep that would make the night short; [that] you would wish to be whatever you are and would prefer nothing [else]; [that] you would neither fear nor wish for [your] final day.

A Roman's Day
MARTIAL *Epigrammata* 4.8

The first and second hours weary the callers; the third occupies hoarse advocates; Rome extends [her] different labors up to [the end of] the fifth; the sixth [hour is] rest for the weary; the seventh will be [its] end; the eighth up to the ninth is for shining wrestling schools; the ninth orders us to crush heaped-up couches; the tenth hour belongs to my little books, Euphemus, when your care directs ambrosial feasts and good Caesar relaxes himself with heavenly nectar and holds moderate cups with [his] mighty hand. Then let [my] jests in; my Thalia fears to go with unrestrained step to Jupiter in the morning.

The Necessity of Writing Satire
JUVENAL *Satires* 1.1–18

Will I always be only a listener? Will I never retaliate after being harassed so often by the Theseid of hoarse Cordus? So, then with impunity will that person have recited comedies to me, this person elegies? Will a huge [poem about] Telephus have taken up a day with impunity, or a [poem about] Orestes, which, after the margin at the end of the book was already full, was written also on the back and is not yet finished (*lit.*, Orestes, the margin of the end of the book [being] already full, written also on the back and not yet finished)?

No one knows his own house better than I know the grove of Mars and the cave of Vulcan near the cliffs of Aeolus; what the winds are doing, what Shades Aeacus is torturing, from where another [fellow] carries off the gold of the stolen [sheep]skin, [and] how large [are] the ash trees [that] Monychus hurls [as missiles], [these are matters that] the plane trees of Fronto and shattered marble and columns broken by the constant reciter are always shouting. You can expect the same from the best and worst poet.

Well, I too have withdrawn [my] hand from the rod, and I have given advice to Sulla that he should sleep soundly as a private citizen. It is foolish clemency, when you run into so many poets everywhere, to spare the doomed paper (*lit.*, paper going to perish).

An Adventurous Woman

JUVENAL *Satires* 6.82–110

Eppia, married to a senator, accompanied a gladiatorial troupe to Pharos and the Nile and the infamous walls of Lagus, with [even] Canopus condemning the monstrosities and morals of the city (*i.e.*, Rome). She, forgetful of [her] home and [her] husband and sister, had no regard at all for [her] country, and shamefully abandoned [her] weeping children and, to amaze you more, the public games and Paris (a popular mime in Rome). But although [as a] tiny [child], she had slept amid great wealth and on [her] father's down and in a decorated cradle, she scorned the sea; she had long ago scorned [her] reputation, whose loss is trivial (*lit.*, very small) among [women accustomed to] soft easy chairs.

So with resolute heart she endured the Tyrrhenian waves and the roaring (*lit.*, loudly resounding) Ionian Sea, although she had to travel from sea to sea (*lit.*, a sea had to be passed from one to another [by her]) so many times. If the reason for danger is legitimate and honorable, [women] are afraid and [their] timid hearts are frozen (*lit.*, they are frozen with respect to [their] timid heart) and they cannot stand on [their] trembling feet. They apply a brave heart to actions that they, to their disgrace, dare [to do] (*lit.*, things that they disgracefully dare). If ever a husband bids [them], it is hard to board a ship; that's when (*lit.*, then) the bilge water is offensive, that's when the sky spins round (*i.e.*, they get dizzy). A woman who follows an adulterer has a strong stomach (*lit.*, is strong in [her] stomach). The former vomits over her husband, the latter both takes breakfast among the sailors and wanders over the deck and takes joy in handling the rough ropes.

Yet with what good looks was Eppia inflamed? By what youthfulness was she captivated? What did she see that caused her to put up with (*lit.*, on account of which she endured) being called a gladiator's woman? For [her] darling Sergius had already begun to shave [his] neck and to hope for rest (*i.e.*, retirement) because of [his] wounded arm; moreover, there were many unsightly [marks] on [his] face, a furrow rubbed by [his] helmet, and a huge lump in the middle of [his] nose, and the severe complaint of a constantly weeping eye. But he was a gladiator; this makes them the equals of Hyacinthus (*lit.*, makes them Hyacinthuses).

The Emptiness of Military Glory

JUVENAL *Satires* 10.133–162

The spoils of wars, a breastplate fastened to lopped-off trophies and a cheek-piece hanging from a broken helmet and a yoke stripped of [its] pole and the sternpost of a captured trireme and a sad captive on the top of a [triumphal] arch are believed [to be] glories greater than human (*lit.*, greater than human glories). To this have Roman and Greek and foreign general aspired, [and] from this they had incentives for [enduring] danger and toil; so much greater is the thirst for fame than [that] for virtue. For who embraces virtue itself (*i.e.*, for its own sake) if you were to remove rewards? However, in the past the ambition of a few has overwhelmed [their] country, and the desire for praise and an epitaph that will cling to [tomb]stones, the guardians of [their] ashes, [and] to shatter these (*lit.*, which) the weak strength of a sterile fig tree is sufficient, since destruction has also been assigned to the graves themselves.

Weigh Hannibal; how many pounds will you find in the greatest of generals? This is [the man] who cannot be held by Africa (*lit.*, whom Africa … does not hold), lashed by the Moorish ocean and extending to the warm Nile [and] southward to the peoples of the Ethiopians and different elephants. Spain is added to [his] empire; he jumps over the Pyrenees. In [his] way nature places the Alps and snow; he splits rocks and breaks through a mountain with vinegar. Now he occupies Italy, yet he strives to proceed farther. "Nothing has been achieved," he says, "unless I break the gates [of Rome] with the Carthaginian soldier and place [our] standard in the middle of the Subura."

O what a sight and worthy of what a picture when a Gaetulian monster (*i.e.*, an elephant) was carrying the one-eyed general. So what is [his] fate? O glory! The same [man] is, of course, conquered and flees headlong into exile and there, [as] an important and remarkable client, he sits at the king's palace until the Bithynian tyrant should deign to rise.

The Vigil of Venus

Let him who has never loved love tomorrow, and let him who has loved love tomorrow! Spring [is] new, spring [is] now full of song, the world has been born in spring. In spring love brings hearts together, in spring the birds mate and the forest releases its foliage (*i.e.*, the trees leaf out) because of the connubial rains. Tomorrow she who unites lovers weaves green arbors from myrtle shoots amid the shades of trees. Tomorrow Dione (*i.e.*, Venus) delivers (*lit.*, says) [her] judgments, seated on [her] lofty throne.

Let him who has never loved love tomorrow, and let him who has loved love tomorrow! The goddess herself has ordered the nymphs to go to the myrtle grove. The Boy goes [as] a companion for the girls (*i.e.*, the nymphs). However, it would be beyond belief (*lit.*, it cannot be believed) that Love is observing the holiday if he is carrying arrows. "Go, nymphs, he has laid down [his] weapons. Love is observing the holiday. He has been ordered to go without weapons, he has been ordered to go naked lest he do any harm with bow or arrow or with [his] torch. But nevertheless, take care, nymphs, because Cupid is beautiful. [That] same Love is fully armed when he is naked."

Let him who has never loved love tomorrow, and let him who has loved love tomorrow! The goddess has ordered the court to be set up amid the flowers of Hybla. She herself [as] adjudicator will deliver [her] judgments, the Graces will assist (*lit.*, sit by) [her]. Hybla, pour forth all [your] flowers, everything that (*lit.*, whatever) the year has brought. Hybla, put on [your] garment of flowers, as big as is Etna's plain. The girls of the country will be here, or the girls of the mountains, and [those] who [dwell in] woods and [those] who [dwell in] groves, and [those] who dwell in fountains. The mother of the winged Boy has ordered all [of them] to assist [her]. She has ordered the girls not to trust Love at all, even [when he is] naked.

Let him who has never loved love tomorrow, and let him who has loved love tomorrow! Behold! bulls now stretch their flanks under broom shrubs, each secure in the conjugal bond by which he is held. Under the shades, behold! [there are] flocks of ewes with [their] mates. And the goddess has ordered birds not to be silent. Now noisy swans with harsh-sounding voices fill the pools with a din. The young wife (lit., girl) of Tereus sings in accompaniment under the shade of a poplar, so that you would think feelings of love were being declared with [her] melodious voice, and [so that] you would not say that a sister was complaining about her barbarous husband. She sings, [but] I am silent. When is my spring coming? When will I become like a swallow, so that I cease to be silent? I have lost my Muse by being silent, and Apollo does not take notice of me. In this way silence destroyed Amyclae when it was silent.

Let him who has never loved love tomorrow, and let him who has loved love tomorrow!

The Happy Peasant
CLAUDIAN Shorter poems, 20

Happy is he who has spent his life in ancestral fields, whom the very [same] house sees as a boy [and sees] as an old man, who, leaning on [his] staff on the sand on which he crawled [as a child], counts the long generations of a single humble dwelling (lit., cottage). Fortune has not dragged him off with unstable turmoil, nor has he drunk unfamiliar waters [as] a restless stranger. He has not trembled at seas [as] a merchant, he [has not trembled at] trumpet calls [as] a soldier, nor has he endured the disputes of the noisy forum.

Ignorant of the world [and] unacquainted with the neighboring city, he enjoys a freer view of the sky. He calculates the year by alternating crops, not by [the name of] the consul; he marks for himself autumn by [its] fruits [and] spring by [its] flowers (lit., flower). The same field sets the sun and the same [field] brings [it] back, and he, a peasant, measures the day with his own luminary (i.e., sun). He remembers the huge oak from a small seedling. He sees that the forest of the same age [as he is] has grown old [with him]. For him, neighboring Verona is more distant than the dark Indians, and he thinks that Lake Benacus is the Red Sea. However, [his] strength [is] unbroken, and the third age sees [him as] a grandfather, vigorous with strong arms. Let another wander and explore the farthest Spaniards. The former has more life, the latter more traveling.

GLOSSARY

❦ A list of abbreviations is given on page xxvi.

❦ Entries preceded by ✦ are basic vocabulary words whose meanings are not given in the notes to the selections.

❦ Meanings given here reflect a word's use in the selections, not necessarily the entire range of meanings the word may have.

❦ Words with three endings are adjectives (e.g., **acerbus -a -um, amābilis -is -e**, and **ācer ācris ācre**).

❦ The genitive of third-declension nouns is given in full (e.g., **adspergō adsperginis**), as is that of nouns of other declensions whose stems change (e.g., **ager agrī**).

❦ The genitive of third-declension adjectives is given in parentheses (e.g., **fēlix (fēlīcis)**).

❦ Case government is indicated for prepositions (e.g., **ā (ab)** PREP. (+ ABL.)) and, where applicable, for adjectives (e.g., **cupidus -a -um** (+ GEN.)) and verbs (e.g., **careō -ēre** INTR. (+ ABL.)).

❦ For verbs whose perfect and supine forms are regular, only the first-person singular present indicative and the present infinitive are given (e.g., **accūsō -āre** and **audiō -īre**). For all other verbs, all principal parts are given (e.g., **abrumpō -ere abrūpī abruptum**). A missing principal part is indicated by a dash (e.g., **accidō -ere accidī —**).

❦ Alternative forms are given in parentheses (e.g., for the noun **Dāvos (Dāvus) -i**, the pronoun **quīdam quaedam quiddam (quoddam)**, the verb **abeō abīre abiī (abīvī) abitum**, the conjunction **ac (atque)**, and the preposition **ā (ab)**). Some alternative forms are abridged to the ending only (e.g., **appetō -ere appetīvī (-iī) appetītum**). Parentheses are also used to indicate alternative spellings or forms in words such as **sepulc(h)rum -ī**.

❦ Principal parts in square brackets are rare (e.g., **canō -ere cecinī [cantum]**) or are not attested but given to aid identification (e.g., **[ecfor] ecfārī ecfātus sum**).

A

ā INTERJECTION *ah!, alas!*

✦**ā (ab)** PREP. (+ ABL.) *by; (away) from; after*

abeō abīre abiī (abīvī) abitum INTR. *go away, depart; get away, escape*

abrumpō -ere abrūpī abruptum TR. *break*

abscēdō -ere abscessī abscessum INTR. *go away*

absens (absentis) *absent, not present*

absolvō -ere absoluī absolūtum TR. *release; acquit*

absum abesse āfuī āfutūrus INTR. *be distant; be absent*

absūmō -ere absumpsī absumptum TR. *drink (up); waste*

✦**ac (atque)** CONJ. *and, and also*

✦**accēdō -ere accessī accessum** INTR./TR. *approach, come near, come over*

✦**accidō -ere accidī —** INTR. *fall down; happen*

accingō -ere accinxī accinctum TR. *gird*

✦**accipiō -ere accēpī acceptum** TR. *take; accept, receive; admit; hear; grasp, learn*

Accius -(i)ī M. *a Roman poet (170–c. 85 B.C.)*

accumbō -ere accubuī accubitum INTR. *lie down*

accurrō -ere ac(cu)currī accursum INTR. *run up*

accūsō -āre TR./INTR. *blame*

ācer ācris ācre *sharp, severe; energetic*

acerbus -a -um *bitter*

acētum -ī N. *vinegar*

Achāicus -a -um a poetic term for Greek

Achillēs Achillis M. the greatest of the Greek warriors

Achīvī -ōrum M.PL. another name for Greeks

◆aciēs -ēī F. *keenness, edge; battle line*

aconītum -ī N. *aconite* (a poisonous plant)

acquiescō -ere acquiē(v)ī — INTR. *relax; subside*

ācrius COMPAR. ADV. *more bitterly*

actum -ī N. *deed; achievement*

actūtum ADV. *in the near future*

acus -ūs F. *needle*

◆ad PREP. (+ ACC.) *to, toward; until; for (the purpose of)*

adaequē ADV. *equally*

adc- SEE ALSO acc-

adclīnō -āre TR. *lay on, rest on*

addō -ere addidī additum TR. *add, attach*

adedō -ere adēdī adēsum TR. *exhaust; consume*

adeō adīre ad(i)ī aditum INTR./TR. *approach; take on*

◆adeō ADV. *so, to such an extent; to that point*

adf- SEE ALSO aff-

adfīgō -ere adfīxī adfīxum TR. *fasten*

adfor adfārī adfātus sum TR. *speak to, address*

adhūc ADV. *still*

adiciō -ere adiēcī adiectum TR. *add*

adimō -ere adēmī ademptum TR. *take away, snatch away*

aditus -ūs M. *entrance*

adiungō -ere adiunxī adiunctum TR. *add, attach, connect*

adiuvō -āre adiūvī adiūtum TR. *help; favor*

adl- SEE ALSO all-

adlabōrō -āre — — INTR./TR. *take the trouble to add (to)*

adloquor adloquī adlocūtus sum TR. *address, speak to*

admīrans admīrantis M. *admiral* (NONCLASSICAL)

admīror -ārī TR. *marvel (at)*

admittō -ere admīsī admissum TR. *let in, admit*

◆admoneō -ēre TR. *remind; advise, warn*

admoveō -ēre admōvī admōtum TR. *move (up); stretch, extend*

adnuō -ere adnuī adnūtum INTR./TR. *nod (assent to); grant*

adoperiō -īre adoperuī adopertum TR. *cover (over)*

adp- SEE ALSO app-

adplicō -āre adplicāvī (adplicuī) adplicātum (adplicitum) TR. *lead*

adq- SEE acq-

adr- SEE arr-

ads- SEE ALSO ass-

adsector -ārī TR. *follow closely; escort*

adsideō -ēre adsēdī adsessum INTR./TR. *sit by; assist*

adsiduus -a -um *constant, continuous*

adsonō -āre — — INTR. *sing in accompaniment*

adspergō adsperginis F. *sprinkling, spray*

adstō -āre astitī — INTR. *stand by/at/on*

adstringō -ere adstrinxī adstrictum TR. *fasten; check*

adsum adesse adfuī adfutūrus INTR. *be present, be here*

◆adulescens adulescentis M./F. *young person;* ADJ. *young*

adveniō -īre advēnī adventum INTR. *come (to)*

adventus -ūs M. *coming, arrival*

◆adversus -a -um *facing; opposed, opposing; opposite; hostile*

◆adversus PREP. (+ ACC.) *against; toward, facing, opposite*

advertō -ere advertī adversum TR. *turn (to)*

Aeacus -ī M. one of the three judges of the Underworld

◆aedēs (aedis) aedis F.SG. *room;* F.PL. *house; rooms*

◆aedificium -(i)ī N. *building*

aedificō -āre INTR./TR. *build*

Aeētēs -ae M. a king of Colchis, father of Medea

◆aeger aegra aegrum *sick, ill, ailing, lovesick; weary*

aegrōtus -a -um *sick*

Aenēās -ae M. the son of Venus and Anchises, founder of the Roman race

Aenēius -a -um *of Aeneas*

aēn(e)us -a -um *(made of) bronze*

Aeolidēs -ae M. a son of Aeolus

Aeolius -a -um *Aeolian, of Aeolus* (the god of the winds)

aequaevus -a -um *of the same age*

aequō -āre TR. *requite; make even*

aequor aequoris N. *sea*

aequoreus -a -um *of the sea*

aequum -ī N. *equal footing; what is right*

◆aequus -a -um *level, even, calm; equal; just, right; favorable*

◆āēr āeris M. *air, atmosphere; sky*

aerātus -a -um *bronze-clad*

aeripēs (aeripedis) *bronze-footed*

aerumna -ae F. *trouble*

aes aeris N. *copper, bronze, brass; something made of one of these metals*

aestās aestātis F. *summer*

aestimō -āre TR. *value; consider*

aestuō -āre INTR. *burn fiercely, blaze*

aestuōsus -a -um *parched, sweltering*

aestus -ūs M. *heat; passion*

◆aetās aetātis F. *age, time of life; period of time; life; time*

aeternus -a -um *everlasting; ceaseless*

aethēr aetheris M. *sky*

aetherius -a -um *heavenly, in the heavens*

Aethiops Aethiopis M. *an Ethiopian*

Aetna -ae F. *Mt. Etna*

aevum -ī N. *age, period of time; life*

Āfer Āfrī M. *a person addressed in Martial's epigrams*

afferō afferre attulī allātum TR. *bring; raise*

Āfrica -ae F. *Africa*

agedum EXHORTATION TO ACTION *come!*

◆ager agrī M. *field; land; farm*

agitātor agitātōris M. *driver, charioteer*

agnoscō -ere agnōvī agnitum TR. *recognize*

◆agō agere ēgī actum TR./INTR. *do, perform, accomplish, manage, play the part of; drive; bring on; spend (time); pay attention to*

agrestis -is -e *rustic*

◆āiō — — — DEFECTIVE, TR. *say; affirm*

āla -ae F. *wing*

Alānus -a -um *of the Alani people (of Scythia)*

Albānus -a -um *of Alba Longa, Alban*

albens (albentis) *white*

albicans (albicantis) *white*

albus -a -um *white*

Alcīdēs -ae M. *a descendant of Alceus, especially Hercules*

āles (alitis) *winged*

āles alitis M./F. *bird*

alga -ae F. *seaweed*

◆aliēnus -a -um *foreign; strange; belonging/ relating to another*

◆aliquī aliqua aliquod ADJ. *some*

◆aliquis aliqua aliquid PRON. *someone, something*

◆aliter ADV. *otherwise*

ālium -(i)ī N. *garlic*

◆alius alia aliud PRON./ADJ. *another; other, different*

all- SEE ALSO adl-

alligō -āre TR. *fasten; restrict, confine*

allūdō -ere allūsī allūsum INTR. *play with; lap at*

almus -a -um *life-giving; gracious*

alō alere aluī al(i)tum TR. *feed*

Alpis Alpis F. *the Alps*

altē ADV. *to a great height, high*

◆alter altera alterum PRON./ADJ. *one/ other (of two), another, the next, second*

alternus -a -um *alternating*

altum -ī N. *sea, the deep*

◆altus -a -um *high, lofty; deep*

amābilis -is -e *lovable; pleasing*

amans amantis M./F. *lover*

amārus -a -um *bitter*

amātōrius -a -um *of love or lovers, amatory*

ambiguus -a -um *doubtful, hesitant; conflicting*

ambō -ae -ō PL. PRON./ADJ. *both*

ambrosius -a -um *ambrosial, divine*

ambulō -āre INTR. *walk*

amīca -ae F. *(girl)friend; sweetheart, mistress*

amictus -ūs M. *garment, shawl*

amīcus -a -um *dear, loving, friendly; favorable*

◆amīcus -ī M. *friend*

◆amnis amnis M./F. *river*

◆amō -āre TR./INTR. *love, like; enjoy; fornicate*

amoenus -a -um *pleasant, attractive*

◆amor amōris M. *love, affection; yearning; darling, beloved; (PERSONIFIED) the god of love*

amplector -ī amplexus sum TR. *embrace*

amplius INDECL. NOUN *more, a larger amount/number, longer*

amplus -a -um *huge*

Amyclae -ārum F.PL. *the name of towns in Laconia and Latium*

◆an CONJ. *whether; or (INTRODUCING THE SECOND PART OF A QUESTION)*

anceps (ancipitis) *double; wavering, uncertain*

ancora -ae F. *anchor*

Ancus -ī M. *the fourth king of Rome*

Andromedē Andromedēs GREEK F. *Andromeda, a character in Greek mythology rescued by Perseus from a sea monster*

angō -ere anxī anctum TR. *choke*

anguis anguis M./F. *snake*

angulus -ī M. *corner*

angustus -a -um *narrow, confined, limited*

anhēlitus -ūs M. *breath*

◆anima -ae F. *soul, spirit, breath; life; heart*

animōsus -a -um *spirited, courageous*

animula -ae F. *soul*

◆animus -ī M. *soul; mind, intellect; heart; courage; anger; inclination*

ann- SEE adn-

◆annus -ī M. *year*

ansa -ae F. *loop*

◆ante ADV./PREP. (+ ACC.) *first, previously, before; in front (of), before*

◆anteā ADV. *before, previously*

antehāc ADV. *previously*

Antēnor Antēnoris M. a Trojan prince

anthologia -ae F. *anthology*

◆antīquus -a -um *ancient; previous*

antrum -ī N. *cave*

anus -ūs F. *old woman*

anxius -a -um *worried; painstaking*

aper aprī M. *wild boar*

aperiō -īre aperuī apertum TR. *open; reveal*

◆apertē ADV. *openly, frankly*

Āpidanus -ī M. a river in Thessaly

aplustre aplustris N. *sternpost (of a boat)*

Apollō Apollinis M. the son of Jupiter and Leto, the god of poetry and music

apparātus -ūs M. *trapping; luxury*

appāreō -ēre appāruī appāritum INTR. *be visible*

◆appellō -āre TR. *address; call (to); name*

appetō -ere appetīvī (-iī) appetītum TR. *seek, try to reach*

aptō -āre TR. *fit to/on, put in position*

aptus -a -um *favorable, suitable, appropriate; furnished*

◆apud PREP. (+ ACC.) *at, near, with, among, amid; at the house of; in the works of*

◆aqua -ae F. *water; body of water*

āra -ae F. *altar*

arānea -ae F. *cobweb*

arātrum -ī N. *plow*

arbitrium -(i)ī N. *judgment*

arbitror -ārī TR./INTR. *think*

◆arbor (arbōs) arboris F. *tree*

arboreus -a -um *arboreal, of trees*

Arcadia -ae F. the central district of the Peloponnese

◆arceō -ēre arcuī — TR. *keep away; prevent*

arctōus -a -um *northern*

Arctus -ī F. the constellation of the Bear; the north

arcus -ūs M. *bow (for shooting arrows); arch*

ardeō -ēre arsī — INTR. *burn, blaze, be on fire*

ardor ardōris M. *fire; passion*

arduus -a -um *steep; tall; difficult; rearing up, proud*

◆argentum -ī N. *silver; money*

Argus -ī M. the hundred- or thousand-eyed guardian of Io

argūtiae -ārum F.PL. *verbal wit*

argūtus -a -um *rustling*

Ariadna -ae F. Ariadne (the daughter of king Minos of Crete who helped Theseus and was abandoned by him on Naxos)

ariēs arietis M. *battering ram*

Ariōn Ariōnis M. a poet and singer of Lesbos, said to have been saved from drowning by a dolphin

Ariōnius -a -um of the poet Arion

◆arma -ōrum N.PL. *weapons, arms*

armentum -ī N. *herd*

armiger armigerī M. *armor-bearer*

armō -āre TR. *arm*

arō -āre TR. *plow*

arripiō -ere arripuī arreptum TR. *grasp, seize*

Arrius -ī M. a person named in Catullus' *Carmina*

◆ars artis F. *art, skill, ability; knowledge; character; artificiality; stratagem*

artifex artificis M. *artist; expert*

artus -a -um *tight, close, dense; difficult*

artus artūs M. *limb, arm, leg*

arvum -ī N. *field; countryside*

◆arx arcis F. *citadel, fortress*

as assis M. *as (a copper coin of small value)*

ascendō -ere ascendī ascensum TR./INTR. *climb, mount*

asellus -ī M. *donkey*

aspectus -ūs M. *sight, view*

asper aspera asperum *harsh; difficult*

aspiciō -ere aspexī aspectum TR. *look (at), observe*

assiduus -a -um *continuous, constant*

assuēscō -ere assuēvī assuētum TR./INTR. *accustom; become familiar*

astrum -ī N. *star; constellation*

◆at CONJ. *but, moreover*

āter ātra ātrum *black; dark*

Atlās Atlantis M. a Titan, condemned to support the sky on his shoulders

◆atque (ac) CONJ. *and, and also*

Atrīdēs -ae M. a son of Atreus, especially Agamemnon

ātrium -iī N. the first main room in a Roman house

atterō -ere attrīvī attrītum TR. *rub*

Atticus -a -um *Athenian*

attineō -ēre attinuī attentum TR./INTR. *hold back; concern*

attingō -ere attigī attactum TR. *touch (on); arrive at*

attollō -ere — — TR. *raise, lift up*

auctor auctōris M. *creator, writer; authority*

auctōritās auctōritātis F. *authority; reputation*

audācia -ae F. *boldness*

◆audax (audācis) *bold; foolhardy*

◆audeō -ēre ausus sum TR./INTR. *dare, venture; be bold*

◆audiō -īre TR. *hear, listen to*

audītor audītōris M. *listener*

auferō auferre abstulī ablātum TR. *carry/take away; sweep away*

aufugiō -ere aufūgī — INTR./TR. *run away*

◆augeō -ēre auxī auctum TR. *increase, enlarge*

augurium -(i)ī N. *augury; interpretation*

Augustus -ī M. a title given to Octavius Caesar after he had established himself as sole ruler at Rome

aura -ae F. *breeze; breath*

aureus -a -um *golden*

auricula -ae F. *ear*

aurifer aurifera auriferum *gold-bearing*

◆auris auris F. *ear*

Aurōra -ae F. the goddess of the dawn

◆aurum -ī N. *gold*

Ausonia -ae F. *Italy*

Ausonis (Ausonidis) *Italian*

Ausonius -a -um *Italian, Roman*

Auster Austrī M. *the south wind*

ausum -ī N. *exploit*

◆aut CONJ. *or*

◆aut ... aut ... CONJ. *either ... or ...*

◆autem CONJ. *however, on the other hand; and indeed*

Automedōn Automedontis M. Achilles' charioteer and Pyrrhus' armor-bearer

autumnus -ī M. *autumn*

◆auxilium -(i)ī N. *help, aid, assistance*

avāritia -ae F. *greed*

avārus -a -um *greedy*

avē IMP. OF avēre (*to be greeted*) *hail, hello*

āvellō -ere āvellī (āvolsī, āvulsī) āvolsum (āvulsum) TR. *tear away*

Aventīnus -a -um *of the Aventine Hill*

Avernus -a -um *of the Underworld, infernal*

Avernus -ī M. the lake reputed to be an entrance to the Underworld; the Underworld itself

aversus -a -um *facing away*

avia -ae F. *grandmother*

avidus -a -um *greedy*

avis avis F. *bird*

avunculus -ī M. *maternal uncle*

avus -ī M. *grandfather; ancestor, forebear*

axis axis M. *axle, axis; chariot; heavens, sky*

B

Babylōnius -a -um *Babylonian*

bacchans bacchantis F. *a female devotee of Bacchus, bacchante*

bacchor -ārī TR. *rage, rave, rant*

Bacchus -ī M. *Dionysus, Liber* (the son of Jupiter and Semele); *wine*

Bactra -ōrum N.PL. the capital of Bactria (a province of Parthia in what is now northeast Iran)

baculum -ī N. (*walking*) *staff*

bālans bālantis M./F. *sheep*

barba -ae F. *beard*

barbaria -ae F. *the foreign world*

barbarus -a -um *cruel, savage; barbarian, foreign*

bāsiātiō bāsiātiōnis F. *kiss, kissing*

bāsiō -āre TR. *kiss*

bāsium -(i)ī N. *kiss*

Battus -ī M. the legendary founder of Cyrene

beātus -a -um *happy, satisfied*

bellātor bellātōris M. *warrior;* ADJ. *warlike;* bellātōr equus M. *warhorse*

bellicus -a -um *military, warlike*

◆bellum -ī N. *war*

bellus -a -um *beautiful, handsome*

bēlua -ae F. *monster; elephant*

Bēnācus -ī M. a lake near Verona

◆bene ADV. *well, properly, honorably*

benignus -a -um *generous, bounteous*

◆bibō -ere bibī — TR./INTR. *drink*

biceps (bicipitis) *with two peaks*

Bilbilis Bilbilis F. a small city in northeast Spain, the birthplace of Martial

bipennis bipennis F. *double-edged ax*

bis ADV. *twice*

Bīthȳnus -a -um *Bithynian, of Bithynia* (a district on the northwest coast of Asia Minor)

blanditia -ae F. *blandishment*

blandulus -a -um DIMINUTIVE OF blandus *sweet, charming*

blandus -a -um *coaxing, persuasive; beguiling*

Bōlānus -ī M. a person reputed by Horace to have a bad temper

bonum -ī N. *the good, advantage;* (USUALLY PL.) *possessions, glories*

◆bonus -a -um *good; kind, beneficent; virtuous; advantageous, beneficial*

Boreās -ae M. *the north wind*
Borysthenēs Borysthenis M. the name
of a horse belonging to the emperor
Hadrian
◆**bōs bovis** M./F. *ox, bull, cow;*
(PL.) *cattle*
Bōterdum -ī N. a village near Bilbilis in
Spain
bra(c)chium -(i)ī N. *arm*
◆**brevis -is -e** *short, brief; meager*
brūma -ae F. *winter; winter solstice*
buc(c)ula -ae F. *cheek-piece*
bustum -ī N. *tomb*
buxus -ī F. *boxwood*

C

caballīnus -a -um *of a horse; a nag's*
cachinnus -ī M. *laughter*
cacūmen cacūminis N. *top, tip*
Cadmus -ī M. the legendary founder
of Thebes; the first name of the husband
of Helvia Prima (Verse Epitaph C)
◆**cadō -ere cecidī cāsum** INTR. *fall; sink;*
set (of the sun or wind); die, come to
an end
Caecubus -a -um *Caecuban, of Caecubum*
(a district in southern Latium noted
for its wine)
caecus -a -um *blind*
◆**caedēs caedis** F. *slaughter, massacre; blood;*
death
◆**caedō -ere cecīdī caesum** TR. *cut down;*
beat; kill
caelebs caelibis M. *bachelor*
caelestis -is -e *celestial, of the sky; divine*
caelicola -ae M./F. *god*
caelifer caelifera caeliferum *supporting*
the sky
Caelius (mons) M. one of the seven hills
of Rome
◆**caelum -ī** N. *sky, heaven(s)*
caerul(e)us -a -um *blue*
Caesar Caesaris M. *Caesar; emperor*
Caesareus -a -um *of the emperor, imperial*
Calais Calais M. a lover of Lydia,
Horace's former mistress
calamitās calamitātis F. *misfortune,*
disaster
calamus -ī M. *reed; reed pipe*
◆**calidus -a -um** *warm, hot*
cālīgō -āre —— —— INTR. *be dark/gloomy*
callidē ADV. *cleverly; thoroughly*
callidus -a -um *cunning, clever; careful*
◆**campus -ī** M. *plain, open space, field*
candidus -a -um *white; bright; fair; pretty*
◆**canis canis** M./F. *dog*
◆**canō -ere cecinī [cantum]**
INTR./TR. *sing (of); celebrate*

Canōpus -ī M. an Egyptian city with
an evil reputation
canor canōris M. *song of a bird*
canōrus -a -um *tuneful, melodious*
cantō -āre TR./INTR. *sing*
cantus -ūs M. *song; incantation*
cānus -a -um *white*
capella -ae F. *nanny goat*
capessō -ere capessīvī (-iī) [capessītum]
TR. *grasp*
capillus -ī M. *(a single) hair*
◆**capiō -ere cēpī captum** TR. *take, get;*
capture, overcome; captivate, seize;
contain; gather; reach (a position);
don
Capitōlium -(i)ī N. *the Capitoline Hill*
captīvus -ī M. *captive, prisoner of war*
captō -āre TR. *catch*
captus -ūs M. *ability*
◆**caput capitis** N. *head; summit; leader*
cardō cardinis M. *(hinge) pin, hinge*
◆**careō -ēre** INTR. (+ ABL.) *lack; be free*
from, be exempt from; avoid
carīna -ae F. *keel; ship*
◆**carmen carminis** N. *song; poem; poetry;*
spell
carpentum -ī N. *carriage*
carpō -ere carpsī carptum TR. *pluck,*
seize; criticize; make one's way along
Carthāgō Carthāginis F. *Carthage*
◆**cārus -a -um** *dear, beloved; costly;*
sweet
casa -ae F. *arbor; hut, cottage*
Caspius -a -um *Caspian*
cassis cassidis F. *helmet*
Castalius -a -um *of Castalia* (a fountain
on Mt. Parnassus)
◆**castra -ōrum** N.PL. *military camp*
castus -a -um *chaste*
cāsus -ūs M. *accident; misfortune; danger;*
happening, event
cathedra -ae F. *chair, easy chair*
Catō Catōnis M. a Roman cognomen;
Cato the Younger (95–46 B.C.)
Catullus -ī M. a Roman poet
(c. 84–c. 54 B.C.)
catulus -ī M. *cub*
cauda -ae F. *tail*
◆**causa -ae** F. *reason; cause; incentive,*
interest; side (in a dispute), *case*
causidicus -ī M. *lawyer, advocate*
cautēs cautis F. *rock*
caveō -ēre cāvī cautum INTR./TR. *beware*
(of), guard against
cavō -āre TR. *hollow out, make a hole in*
cavus -a -um *hollow*
Cecropius -a -um *of Cecrops or his*
descendants; Athenian

◆ cēdō -ere cessī cessum INTR. (+ DAT.)/
   TR. *go (away), withdraw; proceed;*
   yield (to), make way
celebrō -āre TR. *celebrate*
celer celeris celere *swift*
celeritās celeritātis F. *speed*
celsus -a -um *lofty*
Celtibēr Celtibēra Celtibērum
   of Celtiberia
Celtibēria -ae F. an area in central
   Spain
cēna -ae F. *dinner*
cēnō -āre INTR./TR. *dine*
◆ censeō -ēre censuī censum TR. *have/give*
   an opinion, think; value; recommend
census -ūs M. *wealth*
◆ centum INDECL. NUMBER *(a) hundred*
Cēphēius -a -um *of Cepheus* (the father
   of Andromeda)
Cerberus -ī M. the three-headed dog
   that guarded the entrance to the
   Underworld
cerebrum -ī N. *brain; anger, bad temper*
◆ cernō -ere crēvī crētum TR. *discern;*
   decide; look at, see
certē ADV. *certainly*
certior -ior -ius *informed*
certō -āre INTR. (+ ABL.) *contend with,*
   argue
◆ certus -a -um *fixed, certain, sure, settled,*
   definite, unmistakable, unchangeable
cerva -ae F. *deer, stag*
cervix cervīcis F. *neck*
◆ cēteri -ae -a PL. NOUN/ADJ. *the others,*
   the rest (of)
ceu ADV. *in the same way as, like*
chaere GREEK INTERJECTION *hello*
chaos -ī N. *primordial matter*
charta -ae F. *paper*
chelīdōn chelīdonis F. *swallow*
chlamys chlamydis F. *cloak*
Chloē Chloēs GREEK F. a mistress of
   Horace
chorda -ae F. *string*
chorēa -ae F. *dance*
chorus -ī M. *dance; choir*
Chrȳsippus -ī M. a Greek Stoic
   philosopher (c. 280–c. 206 B.C.)
cibus -ī M. *food*
Cicerō Cicerōnis M. a Roman orator,
   writer, and statesman (106–43 B.C.)
◆ cieō ciēre cīvī citum TR. *stir up,*
   excite
cingō -ere cinxī cinctum TR. *surround,*
   encircle, enclose; gird
cinis cineris M./F. *ash(es)*
◆ circā ADV. *about;* PREP. (+ ACC.) *about,*
   around, near

Circaeus -a -um *Circaean, of Circe*
   (a daughter of the Sun, a sorceress who
   could turn men into animals)
circensēs circensium M.PL. *games held*
   in an arena
circum ADV. *round about*
circumagō -ere circumēgī circumactum
   TR. *drag around*
circumdō -are circumdedī circumdatum
   TR. *put around; surround*
circumsiliō -īre —— —— INTR./TR. *hop*
   around
circus -ī M. a circular or oval arena where
   games are held
cis PREP. (+ ACC.) *within*
cithara -ae F. *lyre*
citus -a -um *quick, moving quickly*
◆ cīvis cīvis M./F. *citizen*
◆ cīvitās cīvitātis F. *community; state;*
   citizenship
clāmitātiō clāmitātiōnis F. *shouting*
clāmō -āre INTR./TR. *shout; resound with*
clāmor clāmōris M. *clamor*
clāmōsus -a -um *noisy*
clārō -āre clārāvī —— TR./INTR. *make*
   clear; make famous
◆ clārus -a -um *loud; bright; distinguished,*
   famous; impressive
classicum -ī N. *trumpet call*
◆ classis classis F. *fleet; class*
Claudia -ae F. a Roman woman's name
claustrum -ī N. *bolt, bar* (for securing
   a door or gate)
clāvis clāvis F. *key*
clēmentia -ae F. *clemency*
cliens clientis M. *client*
Clītumnus -ī M. a river in a region in
   Umbria famous for its white cattle
Cnōsia -ae F. *a Cnossian woman,*
   viz Ariadne
Cnōsius -a -um *Cretan, of Crete*
coctilis -is -e *baked; made of bricks*
Cōcȳtos (Cōcȳtus) -ī M. one of the
   Underworld rivers
◆ coelum SEE caelum
coeō coīre coiī coitum INTR./TR. *come*
   together, meet; join battle; unite
◆ coepī coepisse coeptum INTR./TR. *have*
   begun
coerceō -ēre coercuī coercitum
   TR. *confine*
coetus -ūs M. *group*
◆ cōgitō -āre TR./INTR. *think, reflect on;*
   devise
◆ cognōscō -ere cognōvī cognitum
   TR. *get to know, learn; recognize;*
   (PERF.) *know*

◆cōgō -ere coēgī coactum TR. *gather
  together; force*
cohibeō -ēre cohibuī cohibitum
  TR. *contain, confine*
colligō -ere collēgī collectum TR. *gather,
  collect*
colligō -āre TR. *tie (up), bind*
collis collis M. *hill*
collum -ī N. *neck*
◆colō -ere coluī cultum TR. *cultivate, till;
  feed; revere, worship; visit; dwell (in);
  adorn*
colōnus -ī M. *farmer*
color colōris M. *color, tint*
coluber colubrī M. *snake*
columba -ae F. *dove*
columbārium -(i)ī N. *dovecote (a nesting
  box for doves); sepulcher with niches for
  the ashes of the dead*
columna -ae F. *column, pillar*
coma -ae F. *leaf, foliage; hair (of the head)*
comedō comēsse comēdī comēs(s)um
  TR. *eat (up); squander*
comes comitis M./F. *companion, follower*
comitor -āri TR. *accompany*
commisceō -ēre commiscuī commixtum
  TR. *mix together*
commodum -ī N. *advantage*
commodus -a -um *suitable, proper*
commoveō -ēre commōvī commōtum
  TR. *shake, stir*
commūnis -is -e *common, shared*
commūniter ADV. *alike*
cōmō -ere compsī comptum TR. *adorn;
  arrange*
compellō -ere compulī compulsum
  TR. *drive (together), force; insist*
compellō -āre TR. *address, speak to*
compendium -(i)ī N. *profit, gain*
compleō -ēre complēvī complētum
  TR. *fill*
complexus -ūs M. *embrace*
compōnō -ere composuī compositum
  TR. *put together; settle*
comprimō -ere compressī compressum
  TR. *crush, constrict*
computō -āre TR. *calculate, reckon*
concēdō -ere concessī concessum
  INTR./TR. *grant, allow; withdraw*
concha -ae F. *shell; pearl*
concidō -ere concidī — INTR. *collapse*
concordō -āre INTR. *bring hearts together,
  create harmony*
concors (concordis) *harmonious*
condō -ere condidī conditum
  TR. *found, establish; bury; hide; close; set*
conficiō -ere confēcī confectum
  TR. *perform, accomplish*

confīdenter ADV. *audaciously*
congerō -ere congessī congestum
  TR. *pile up, raise up, amass*
coniciō -ere coniēcī coniectum
  TR. *throw, thrust*
coniugālis -is -e *conjugal, marital*
coniungō -ere coniunxī coniunctum
  TR. *join, connect*
◆coniu(n)x coniugis M./F. *spouse*
◆conl- SEE ALSO coll-
conlīdō -ere conlīsī conlīsum TR. *crush;
  bring into collision*
◆cōnor -ārī TR./INTR. *try, attempt*
◆conp- SEE ALSO comp-
conpescō -ere conpescuī — TR. *confine,
  imprison; relieve*
conscendō -ere conscendī conscensum
  TR./INTR. *go on board*
conscius -a -um *criminal, guilty; privy*
consenescō -ere consenuī —
  INTR. *grow old*
conserō -ere conseruī consertum
  TR. *join, press together*
◆consilium -(i)ī N. *counsel, advice; plan;
  council; intelligence*
consistō -ere constitī — INTR. *stop,
  stand; settle*
conspectus -ūs M. *sight, view*
conspicuus -a -um *noteworthy; visible*
constans (constantis) *resolute, firm*
constituō -ere constituī constitūtum
  TR. *decide; set up*
constō -āre constitī —
  TR./INTR. *take a stand*
consul consulis M. *consul*
consultō -āre TR./INTR. *deliberate*
consūmō -ere consumpsī consumptum
  TR. *use up, take up; spend; devour*
contegō -ere contexī contectum
  TR. *cover; conceal*
contemnō -ere contempsī contemptum
  TR. *scorn, show contempt for*
contendō -ere contendī contentum
  TR./INTR. *stretch; go quickly*
conterminus -a -um *neighboring, close*
conterō -ere contrīvī contrītum
  TR. *make weary*
contiguus -a -um *neighboring, adjoining*
continens (continentis) *self-restrained*
continentia -ae F. *self-restraint*
contineō -ēre continuī contentum
  TR. *join; encompass; limit*
contingō -ere contigī contactum
  TR./INTR. *touch; reach; smite*
continuus -a -um *continuous, in a row*
◆contrā ADV. *in return; across, on the
  opposite side;* PREP. (+ ACC.) *opposite
  (to); against*

Contrōversiae -ārum F.PL. *Opposing Arguments* (the title of a work by the elder Seneca)

contundō -ere contudī contūsum TR. *crush*

conturbō -āre TR./INTR. *go bankrupt*

convalescō -ere convaluī — INTR. *recover*

convellō -ere convellī convulsum (convolsum) TR. *shatter; tug at*

conveniō -īre convēnī conventum INTR. *meet;* (+ DAT.) *be suited to*

convertō -ere convertī conversum TR. *change; rotate*

convictus -ūs M. *companionship*

convīvium -(i)ī N. *banquet*

convolvō -ere convolvī convolūtum TR. *roll (up)*

convomō -ere convomuī convomitum TR. *vomit over*

✦cōpia -ae F. *abundance;* (PL.) *supplies, provisions; forces, troops*

cōpō cōpōnis M. *innkeeper*

cōpulātrix cōpulātrīcis F. *female coupler*

✦cor cordis N. *heart*

Cordus -ī M. a person named in Juvenal's *Satires*

Cornēlius -a -um the name of a Roman gens

cornū -ūs N. *horn*

✦corōna -ae F. *wreath, garland, chaplet, crown*

corōnō -āre TR. *crown; surround*

✦corpus corporis N. *body; corpse*

corrigō -ere correxī correctum TR. *straighten; correct, put right*

corripiō -ere corripuī correptum TR. *snatch (away), seize, sweep away; hurry over*

corrumpō -ere corrūpī corruptum TR. *destroy, ruin*

cortex corticis M. *cork, bark* (of a tree)

coruscus -a -um *shining*

corvus -ī M. *raven*

cōs cōtis F. *stone, rock*

Crantōr Crantoris M. a Greek philosopher (4th century B.C.)

✦crās ADV. *tomorrow*

crassus -a -um *coarse; uncouth*

crastinus -a -um *tomorrow's*

crēber crēbra crēbrum *frequent, plenty of*

✦crēdō -ere crēdidī crēditum TR./INTR. (+ DAT. OF PERSON, + ACC. OF THING) *entrust, trust; attribute;* (+ DAT.) *believe; think*

crēdulus -a -um *trusting*

✦creō -āre TR. *procreate, give birth to; elect;* (PASS.) *be born*

✦crescō -ere crēvī crētum INTR. *arise; grow, increase*

✦crīmen crīminis N. *accusation, charge; reproach, abuse; misdeed*

crīnis crīnis M. *hair, lock of hair*

✦crūdēlis -is -e *cruel, savage*

cruentō -āre TR. *draw blood, cause to bleed; stain with blood*

cruentus -a -um *bloody*

cruor cruōris M. *blood*

cubō -āre cubuī cubitum INTR. *lie down, be in bed; be sick in bed*

Culex Culicis M. the title of a poem attributed to Vergil

culīna -ae F. *kitchen*

culmen culminis N. *roof*

✦culpa -ae F. *guilt; fault*

cultor cultōris M. *one who cherishes, lover*

cultus -a -um *elegant, polished*

cultus -ūs M. *refinement*

✦cum PREP. (+ ABL.) *with, together with*

✦cum CONJ. *when; since; whenever; although*

cūnae -ārum F.PL. *cradle*

✦cunctus -a -um *all, the whole (of)*

cupīdō cupīdinis F. *desire*

Cupīdō Cupīdinis M. *Cupid*

✦cupidus -a -um (+ GEN.) *desirous (of), eager (for)*

✦cupiō -ere cupīvī (-iī) cupītum TR. *desire, wish for*

cupressus -ī F. *cypress (tree)*

✦cūr ADV. *why?*

✦cūra -ae F. *care, worry, concern, trouble, anxiety; sorrow*

cūrātiō cūrātiōnis F. *concern*

Cūria -ae F. *the Senate-house*

cūriōsus -a -um *curious, meddlesome*

✦cūrō -āre TR. *care (for), tend to, look after, be concerned (about), be interested (in); undertake, see to it (that)*

✦currō -ere cucurrī cursum INTR. *run; travel quickly, race*

currus -ūs M. *chariot*

✦cursus -ūs M. *course; motion; passage, journey; race*

curtus -a -um *mutilated, stripped (of)*

curvō -āre TR. *bend*

curvus -a -um *curved, winding*

custōdiō -īre TR. *protect, guard*

✦custōs custōdis M. *guard, guardian, custodian*

cycnus (cygnus) -ī M. *swan*

Cynthia -ae F. the pseudonym of Propertius' mistress in his *Elegies*

Cȳrēnae -ārum F.PL. a Greek city in the northeast of what is now Libya

Cytīnaeus -a -um *of the city Cytina* (in Thessaly)

D

damma -ae F. (M.) *deer*

damnō -āre TR. *condemn*

damnum -ī N. *loss, waste*

Danaī -ōrum M.PL. *another name for Greeks*

Danaus -ī M. *the son of Belus, brother of Aegyptus*

daps dapis F. *feast, banquet*

Dardan(i)us -a -um *Trojan; Roman*

Dardanus -ī M. *an ancestor of Priam*

Dāvos (Dāvus) -ī M. *a typical slave name in Roman comedy*

✦dē PREP (+ ABL.) *down from, away from; about, concerning; (made) of; because of*

✦dea -ae F. *goddess*

dēbellō -āre INTR./TR. *fight; subdue*

✦dēbeō -ēre TR. *owe; (+ INF.) be obliged to, must*

dēbilitō -āre TR. *weaken*

dēcēdō -ere dēcessī dēcessum INTR. *depart; set*

decem INDECL. NUMBER *ten*

December Decembris M. *December (the twelfth and last month of the year)*

decens (decentis) *appropriate; elegant*

decet -ēre decuit — INTR./TR. *adorn; it is fitting*

dēcidō -ere dēcidī — INTR. *go down*

decimus (decumus) -a -um *tenth*

dēcipiō -ere dēcēpī dēceptum TR. *deceive, cheat*

dēclāmō -āre INTR. *make speeches*

dēcrescō -ere dēcrēvī dēcrētum INTR. *shrink, grow smaller*

dēcurrō -ere dē(cu)currī dēcursum INTR./TR. *run down/through*

decus decoris N. *symbol; honor, esteem*

dēdecet -ēre dēdecuit — TR./INTR. *be unsuitable for*

dēdiscō -ere dēdidicī — TR. *unlearn, forget*

✦dēdō -ere dēdidī dēditum TR. *give up, surrender; devote (oneself to)*

dēdūcō -ere dēduxī dēductum TR. *pull down, take down*

✦dēfendō -ere dēfendī dēfensum TR. *defend, protect; ward off*

dēferō dēferre dētulī dēlātum TR. *carry, bring*

dēficiō -ere dēfēcī dēfectum TR./INTR. *fail; run short, subside, abate*

dēfīgō -ere dēfixī dēfixum TR. *fix*

dēfīō -fierī — INTR. *be absent, be lacking*

dēformis -is -e *ugly, unsightly*

dēfricō -āre dēfricuī dēfric(ā)tum TR. *rub (thoroughly)*

dēfungor -ī dēfunctus sum INTR. (+ ABL.) *be finished with, bring to an end*

dehinc ADV. *after this; consequently*

dēiciō -ere dēiēcī dēiectum TR. *throw down, cast down*

✦dein/deinde ADV. *afterward, next, then*

dēlābor -ī dēlapsus sum INTR. *fall*

✦dēleō -ēre dēlēvī dēlētum TR. *destroy; kill*

dēliciae -ārum F.PL. *sweetheart, favorite, pet, darling*

dēlīrō -āre — — INTR. *be mad, rave*

Dēlius -a -um *of Delos (an island in the Aegean Sea)*

delphīn delphīnis (delphīnus -ī) M. *dolphin*

dēlūbrum -ī N. *temple, shrine*

dēmānō -āre -āvī — INTR. *run down*

dēmens (dementis) *crazy; foolish*

dēmentia -ae F. *madness*

dēmittō -ere dēmīsī dēmissum TR. *let fall, shed; plunge*

Dēmocritus -ī M. *a Greek philosopher (c. 460–c. 370 B.C.)*

dēnī -ae -a PL. ADJ. *ten each*

dēnique ADV. *at last, finally*

dens dentis M. *tooth*

densus -a -um *closely packed*

dentātus -a -um *having good teeth*

dēperdō -ere dēperdidī dēperditum TR. *lose*

dēpereō -īre dēperiī — INTR./TR. *perish, die*

dēpleō -ēre dēplēvī dēplētum TR. *empty, rid of*

dēpōnō -ere dēposuī dēpos(i)tum TR. *put/lay down*

dēprecor -ārī TR./INTR. *beg to avoid*

descensus -ūs M. *descent*

describō -ere descripsī descriptum TR. *trace, represent*

dēserō -ere dēseruī dēsertum TR. *abandon, leave*

dēses (dēsidis) *lazy*

dēsīderium -(i)ī N. *longing, desire; sweetheart*

dēsiliō -īre dēsiluī (-īvī, -iī) — INTR. *jump down*

✦dēsinō -ere dēsīvī (-iī) dēsitum INTR./TR. *cease, stop*

despiciō -ere despexī despectum INTR./TR. *look down on, despise*

destinātus -a -um *steadfast; stubborn*

destringō -ere destrinxī districtum TR. *draw, unsheathe*

dēsum dēesse dēfuī — INTR. *be lacking*

dētegō -ere dētexī dētectum
TR. *uncover*

dēterior -ior -ius *worse*

dētineō -ēre dētinuī dētentum
TR. *hold back, stop*

dētrahō -ere dētraxī dētractum
TR. *pull off, remove*

✦deus -ī M. *god*

dēvehō -ere dēvexī dēvectum
TR. *carry off*

dēveniō -īre dēvēnī dēventum
INTR. *arrive, turn up (at), go off to*

dēvorō -āre TR. *swallow up*

dēvoveō -ēre dēvōvī dēvōtum TR. *vow; bewitch*

✦dexter dext(e)ra dext(e)rum *right, on the right-hand side; favorable*

Dīa -ae F. *Naxos (an island in the Aegean Sea)*

Dĭāna -ae F. *a sister of Apollo, the moon goddess*

✦dīcō -ere dīxī dictum TR./INTR. *say, speak, declare, deliver; mention; pronounce; predict; call*

✦dictum -ī N. *what is said, saying, speech; (PL.) words*

Dīdō Dīdōnis F. *the queen of Carthage, lover of Aeneas*

dīdūcō -ere dīduxī dīductum TR. *divide, split, part, separate*

dīērectē ADV. *immediately*

✦diēs diēī M./F. (USUALLY M.) *day; light of day*

differō differre distulī dīlātum
TR./INTR. *disperse; publish; make a difference*

✦difficilis -is -e *difficult, troublesome*

diffīdō -ere diffīsus sum
INTR. *be uncertain (about)*

diffugiō -ere diffūgī — INTR. *scatter, disperse*

digitus -ī M. *finger*

dignor -ārī TR. *think fit (to)*

✦dignus -a -um (+ ABL.) *worthy (of)*

✦dīligens (dīligentis) (+ DAT.) *devoted (to); attentive; thrifty*

✦dīligō -ere dīlexī dīlectum TR. *love*

dīmidium -iī N. *a half*

Diōnē Diōnēs GREEK F. *the mother of Venus; Venus herself*

Dionȳsus -ī M. *Bacchus (the god of wine)*

dīrigō -ere dīrexī dīrectum TR. *direct, guide*

dīripiō -ere dīripuī dīreptum TR. *tear (to shreds); grab*

dīs (dītis) *rich*

Dīs Dītis M. *another name for Pluto (a brother of Jupiter, king of the Underworld)*

discēdō -ere discessī discessum
INTR. *depart, go out; get away*

discessus -ūs M. *departure*

✦discō -ere didicī — TR. *learn*

discrīmen discrīminis N. *distinction; crisis, danger*

discubitus -ūs M. *seating (arrangement)*

discutiō -ere discussī discussum
TR. *shatter*

disertus -a -um *eloquent*

dispensō -āre TR. *distribute, apportion*

displiceō -ēre displicuī displicitum
INTR. *displease, offend*

dispōnō -ere disposuī dispositum
TR. *arrange; distribute*

dissipō -āre TR. *scatter*

distineō -ēre distinuī distentum
TR. *keep apart; distract*

distō -āre — — INTR. *be distant*

✦diū ADV. *for a long time*

dīva -ae F. *goddess*

dīvellō -ere dīvellī (dīvulsī) dīvulsum (dīvolsum) TR. *tear apart*

dīversus -a -um *separate(d); distant; turned in different directions*

✦dīves (dīvitis) *rich*

✦dīvitiae -ārum F.PL. *riches, wealth*

dīvus -ī M. *god*

✦dō dare dedī datum TR. *give; put, place; make; lay down; assign (to); allow*

✦doceō -ēre docuī doctum TR. *teach*

doctrīna -ae F. *instruction; (system of) philosophy*

doctus -a -um *learned, skilled*

dōdrans dōdrantis M. *three quarters*

✦doleō -ēre INTR. *grieve, be sorry; feel pain*

✦dolor dolōris M. *pain; grief*

dolōsus -a -um *deceitful*

dolus -ī M. *act of treachery*

domina -ae F. *mistress*

dominātor dominātōris M. *lord*

✦dominus -ī M. *master; ruler, lord*

domitor domitōris M. *conqueror*

domō -āre domuī domitum TR. *subdue (by taming), break in; conquer*

✦domus -ūs F. *house, home, abode*

✦dōnec CONJ. *until; while, as long as*

✦dōnō -āre TR. *present, give*

✦dōnum -ī N. *gift; offering*

✦dormiō -īre INTR. *sleep*

dorsum -ī N. *back (of the body)*

✦dubitō -āre INTR./TR. *doubt; hesitate, be hesitant*

dubium -(i)ī N. *doubt*

✦dubius -a -um *uncertain, doubtful; difficult*

♦dūcō -ere duxī ductum TR. *lead, bring; summon; consider; marry (of a man); prolong, continue; draw (out); form, shape; take on*

ductor ductōris M. *leader*

duellum -ī N. *war*

♦dulcis -is -e *sweet, tender, pleasant*

♦dum ADV. *yet, now;* CONJ. *while, as long as; provided that; until*

dummodo CONJ. *provided that*

duo -ae -o *two*

duplex (duplicis) *double, twofold*

dūritiēs -ēī F. *hardness*

♦dūrus -a -um *hard, tough, stout, rough; pitiless*

♦dux ducis M. *leader, guide; general*

E

♦ē (ex) PREP. (+ ABL.) *out of, from; since*

ēbrius -a -um *intoxicated, drunk*

ebur eboris N. *ivory; object made of ivory*

ecce INTERJECTION *behold!, see!*

ecf- SEE ALSO eff-

[ecfor] ecfārī ecfātus sum TR. *say*

edax (edācis) *greedy; biting*

ēdiscō -ere ēdidicī — TR. *memorize*

ēdō -ere ēdidī ēditum TR. *put forth, publish; give birth to*

Ēdōnis Ēdōnidos GREEK F. *an Edonian woman, especially a worshipper of Bacchus*

efferō efferre extulī ēlātum TR. *carry out; utter*

efficiō -ere effēcī effectum TR. *make, create*

effigiēs effigiēī F. *image*

effluō -ere effluxī — INTR. *flow out; dissolve*

effodiō -ere effōdī effossum TR. *dig up, quarry*

effugiō -ere effūgī — TR./INTR. *escape*

effundō -ere effūdī effūsum TR. *spread; pour forth; squander, waste*

ēgelidus -a -um *de-chilling, moderately warm*

♦egeō egēre eguī — INTR. (+ GEN./ABL.) *lack; need*

Egnātius -(i)ī M. *a person addressed in Catullus' Carmina*

♦egō (mē meī mihi mē) PRON. *I/me*

ēgredior -ī ēgressus sum INTR./TR. *come/go out, leave*

ēgregius -a -um *splendid*

ēheu INTERJECTION *alas!*

ei AN EXCLAMATION OF DISTRESS

ēiaculor -ārī TR. *shoot out, discharge*

ēiciō -ere ēiēcī ēiectum TR. *throw out*

ēlegans (ēlegantis) *graceful, refined*

elegī -ōrum M.PL. *elegies*

elephantus -ī M. *elephant*

ēligō -ere ēlēgī ēlectum TR. *choose*

ēloquium -(i)ī N. *oratory*

em INTERJECTION *here/there (you are)!*

ēmicō -āre ēmicuī ēmicātum INTR. *flash; shoot up*

ēmittō -ere ēmīsī ēmissum TR. *send out; set forth*

♦emō emere ēmī emptum TR. *buy, procure*

ēmoveō -ēre ēmōvī ēmōtum TR. *remove, dislodge*

ēn INTERJECTION *behold!, look!*

ēnāvigō -āre INTR./TR. *sail across*

♦enim CONJ. *for; for instance; of course, indeed*

Ennius -(i)ī M. *a Roman poet (239–169 B.C.)*

ēnō -āre INTR./TR. *sail over*

ensis ensis M. *sword*

♦eō īre iī (īvī) itum INTR. *go, proceed; pass; tread*

♦eō ADV. *to there, to that point; for this reason*

Epicūrus -ī M. *a Greek philosopher (341–270 B.C.)*

Epimēthis Epimēthidos GREEK F. *Pyrrha (the daughter of Epimetheus)*

♦epistula -ae F. *letter, epistle*

Eppia -ae F. *a woman named in Juvenal's sixth Satire*

♦eques equitis M. *horseman, rider; knight*

♦equidem ADV. *indeed*

♦equus -ī M. *horse*

Erebus -ī M. *the Underworld*

ergō ADV. *therefore, so, accordingly*

ērigō -ere ērexī ērectum TR. *raise, lift*

erīlis -is -e *of a master*

ēripiō -ere ēripuī ēreptum TR. *snatch, tear away*

♦errō -āre INTR. *wander (aimlessly); err, be wrong*

error errōris M. *mistake; madness*

♦erus -ī M. *master; owner*

Erycīna -ae F. *Venus (in an association with Mt. Eryx in Sicily, which had a temple of Venus at its top)*

Erymanthus -ī M. *a mountain in Arcadia*

Erythraeus -a -um *of the Red Sea*

♦et CONJ. *and;* ADV. *even, too, as well*

♦et ... et ... CONJ. *both ... and ...*

♦etiam ADV. *also; even*

Etrūria -ae F. *a region north of Latium in Italy*

Etruscus -a -um *Etruscan*

Etruscus -ī M. *an Etruscan*

♦etsī CONJ. *even if, although*

Eumenis Eumenidos GREEK F. one of the Furies

Euphēmus -ī M. the emperor Domitian's dining-room steward, addressed in Martial's *Epigrammata*

Eurus -ī M. *the east wind*

Eurydica -ae F. *Eurydica* (the mother of Īlia)

Eurydicē Eurydicēs GREEK F. *Eurydice* (the wife of Orpheus)

ēvādō -ere ēvāsī ēvāsum INTR./TR. *go out; escape*

ēveniō -īre ēvēnī ēventum INTR. *emerge; happen*

ēvolō -āre INTR. *fly out/away*

✦**ex (ē)** PREP. (+ ABL.) *out of, from; since*

exardescō -ere exarsī [exarsum] INTR. *be inflamed*

exaudiō -īre TR. *hear, listen to*

excēdō -ere excessī excessum INTR./TR. *go out/away*

excīdō -ere excīdī excīsum TR. *cut out, cut through*

exciō -īre TR. *rouse, awaken*

excipiō -ere excēpī exceptum TR. *gather, receive; give shelter to; greet*

✦**excitō -āre** TR. *stir up, arouse, provoke*

excolō -ere excoluī excultum TR. *instruct*

excruciō -āre TR. *torture, torment*

excūdō -ere excūdī excūsum TR. *hammer out, fashion*

excutiō -ere excussī excussum TR. *shake off*

✦**exd-** SEE **ēd-**

exemplar exemplāris N. *model, example*

✦**exemplum -ī** N. *model, example*

exeō exīre exīvī (-iī) exitum INTR./TR. *come/go out, leave*

exerceō -ēre TR. *occupy, keep busy; torment*

exhibeō -ēre TR. *display*

exhorrescō -ere exhorruī — INTR./TR. *shudder (at)*

exigō -ere exēgī exactum TR. *remove*

exiguus -a -um *small, slight; unassuming*

exilium -(i)ī N. *exile*

exim (= exinde) ADV. *then*

eximius -a -um *outstanding, magnificent*

eximō -ere exēmī exemptum TR. *take away, remove*

existimō -āre TR. *think*

exitium -(i)ī N. *destruction; death*

exitus -ūs M. *end; fate; outcome*

exorior -īrī exortus sum INTR. *rise, come into view*

expallescō -ere expalluī — INTR. *turn pale*

expectō -āre TR./INTR. *expect*

expediō -īre TR./INTR. *make easy; release*

expellō -ere expulī expulsum TR. *drive away*

expendō -ere expendī expensum TR. *weigh; judge*

experior -īrī expertus sum TR. *experience; put to the test*

expleō -ēre explēvī explētum TR. *fill (up); fulfill*

explicō -āre explicāvī (explicuī) explicātum (explicitum) TR. *straighten; stretch*

expolītus -a -um *polished*

exprimō -ere expressī expressum TR. *squeeze out, drive forth*

exquīrō -ere exquīsīvī exquīsītum TR. *ask about, inquire into*

ex(s)pectō -āre TR./INTR. *expect*

ex(s)ternō -āre TR. *drive mad*

ex(s)tinguō -ere ex(s)tinxī ex(s)tinctum TR. *put out; kill, cause to die; (PASS.) die*

ex(s)truō -ere ex(s)truxī ex(s)tructum TR. *heap up*

ex(s)ultō -āre ex(s)ultāvī — INTR. *exult; swagger*

extendō -ere extendī extentum (extensum) TR. *extend, stretch*

✦**exterior -ior -ius** *outer, exterior; outward*

externō -āre TR. *drive mad*

externus -a -um *external; foreign*

exterreō -ēre TR. *frighten*

extimus -a -um *outermost, the tip of*

extorris -is -e *exiled*

✦**extrā** ADV. *outside;* PREP. (+ ACC.) *beyond, outside (of); without*

extrēmum ADV. *for the last time*

✦**extrēmus -a -um** *at the end/edge, last, final; farthest; uttermost; extreme*

exuviae -ārum F.PL. *trophies, spoils; dead skin (of a snake)*

F

faber fabrī M. *craftsman, blacksmith*

✦**fābula -ae** F. *story, tale; drama, play*

Fabullus -ī M. a person addressed in Catullus' *Carmina*

✦**faciēs faciēī** F. *shape, form, appearance, color; sight; face*

✦**facilis -is -e** *easy; affable; clever*

✦**facinus facinoris** N. *crime, villainy*

✦**faciō -ere fēcī factum** TR. *make, create; cause; do*

✦**factum -ī** N. *deed, action*

fācundia -ae F. *eloquence*

fācundus -a -um *eloquent*

fallācia -ae F. *deceit*

fallax (fallācis) *deceptive, treacherous*

◆fallō -ere fefellī falsum TR. *deceive, trick, mislead, elude, be the downfall of; miss;* (PASS.) *be mistaken*

◆falsus -a -um *untrue, wrong, false, mistaken*

◆fāma -ae F. *rumor, report; reputation; fame*

◆familia -ae F. *family; household*

fāmōsus -a -um *famous; infamous, notorious*

famul (famulus) famulī M. *house slave*

◆fās INDECL. N. *(what is) right/lawful; divine law*

fascinō -āre TR. *bewitch, cast a spell on*

fascis fascis M. (USUALLY PL.) *magistrates, public offices*

fastus -ūs M. *pride*

fātālis -is -e *destructive*

◆fateor -ērī fassus sum TR. *confess, admit*

fatīgō -āre TR. *weary, exhaust*

◆fātum -ī N. *fate, divine will, destiny; death, destruction*

faucēs faucium F.PL. *jaws, mouth*

Faustus -ī M. *a person named in Martial's* Epigrammata

◆faveō -ēre fāvī fautum INTR. (+ DAT.) *favor, help*

favilla -ae F. *ash(es), remains*

favor favōris M. *favor, support*

fax facis F. *torch*

fēlix (fēlīcis) *fortunate; happy*

◆fēmina -ae F. *woman, female*

fēmineus -a -um *female, of a woman, of women*

femur feminis (femoris) N. *thigh*

fenestra -ae F. *window; hole*

fera -ae F. *wild beast*

◆ferē ADV. *almost; about; generally*

fēriātus -a -um *keeping/observing a holiday*

feriō -īre —— TR. *strike*

◆ferō ferre tulī lātum TR. *carry (off), bear, bring; endure, tolerate; lead (of a road); say, tell; propose (a law); be suited (to)*

ferox (ferōcis) *savage, fierce; cruel*

ferrātilis -is -e *having to do with iron*

◆ferrum -ī N. (NO PL.) *iron; sword(s)*

fertilis -is -e *fertile*

ferula -ae F. *rod*

◆ferus -a -um *wild, rough; savage; cruel*

ferus -ī M. *wild animal*

fervens (ferventis) *hot, boiling*

fessus -a -um *exhausted, weary*

festīnō -āre INTR. *hasten*

fētus -ūs M. *offspring; fruit*

fīcus -ī F. *fig tree*

◆fidēs -eī F. *faith, belief, trust; honesty; protection*

fidēs fidis F. *lyre*

fidicen fidicinis M. *lyre player; lyricist*

◆fīdō -ere fīsus sum INTR. (+ DAT./ABL.) *trust (in)*

fīdūcia -ae F. *responsibility*

fīgō -ere fīxī fixum (fictum) TR. *fasten, fix; plant; shoot*

◆fīlia -ae F. *daughter*

◆fīlius -(i)ī M. *son*

findō -ere fidī fissum TR. *cleave, split; plow*

◆fingō -ere finxī fictum TR. *make, devise; invent, fabricate*

◆fīniō -īre TR. *finish; limit, restrain*

◆fīnis fīnis M. *end, limit;* (PL.) *boundary, territory, region*

◆fīō fierī factus sum INTR. *be made, be built; become; happen*

firmō -āre TR. *strengthen*

firmus -a -um *strong, solid*

fistula -ae F. *pipe*

flagellum -ī N. *whip; shoot (of a plant)*

◆flamma -ae F. *flame, fire; passion*

flāvus -a -um *fair-haired, blonde*

flēbilis -is -e *worthy of tears*

◆flectō -ere flexī flexum TR. *bend; turn (aside), avert; guide, control; influence*

◆fleō flēre flēvī flētum INTR./TR. *weep (for); lament, bewail*

◆flētus -ūs M. *weeping, tears*

flexus -ūs M. *curve*

◆flōreō -ēre flōruī —— INTR. *flower, bloom; prosper, thrive, flourish*

◆flōs flōris M. *flower, bloom*

flosculus -ī DIMINUTIVE OF flōs M. *(small) flower*

fluctuō -āre INTR. *float; be tossed*

fluctus -ūs M. *wave*

fluentisonus -a -um *resounding* (with the sound of waves)

fluitō -āre fluitāvī —— INTR. *flow; float*

◆flūmen flūminis N. *river, stream*

◆fluō -ere fluxī fluxum INTR. *flow, pass (by); be derived*

fluvius -(i)ī M. *river, stream*

focus -ī M. *fireplace, hearth*

◆foedus foederis N. *agreement, treaty, compact; bond; league*

folium -(i)ī N. *leaf*

◆fons fontis M. *fountain, spring*

◆[for] fārī fātus sum INTR. *speak, say*

forāmen forāminis N. *opening*

forās ADV. *outside*

foris foris F. *door*

◆forma -ae F. *shape; appearance; beauty*

formīdō -āre TR. *fear, dread*

formīdō formīdinis F. *fear, terror*

forsan ADV. *perhaps*

forsitan ADV. *perhaps*
✦ fortasse ADV. *perhaps*
✦ forte ADV. *by chance, accidentally; perhaps*
✦ fortis -is -e *strong, powerful; brave, courageous*
✦ fortūna -ae F. *fate, fortune; good fortune, luck*
✦ forum -ī N. *public square; marketplace*
fragilis -is -e *fragile, brittle*
fragor fragōris M. *crash, roar*
✦ frangō -ere frēgī fractum TR. *break, shatter; crash; crush*
✦ frāter frātris M. *brother*
frāternus -a -um *brotherly; of a brother*
fremō -ere fremuī fremitum INTR. *roar, rumble, hum*
frēnī -ōrum M.PL. *bridle; bit*
fretum -ī N. *sea, waters*
frīgidus -a -um *cold, chilly*
frīgus frīgoris N. *cold*
✦ frons frondis F. *leaf, foliage*
✦ frons frontis F. *forehead, brow; front, battle line*
Frontō Frontōnis M. a person named in Juvenal's *Satires*
✦ fructus -ūs M. *fruit, crop; profit, advantage*
frūgifer frūgifera frūgiferum *fertile*
✦ frūmentum -ī N. *grain, corn*
✦ fruor fruī fructus (fruitus) sum INTR. (+ ABL.)/TR. *enjoy, have the use of*
✦ frustrā ADV. *in vain, to no purpose, without good reason*
frutex fruticis F. *shrub; blockhead*
frux frūgis F. (ESPECIALLY PL.) *crop, fruit; harvest*
fu INTERJECTION *yuck!*
fūcus -ī M. *dye, pigment*
✦ fuga -ae F. *flight; exile*
fugax (fugācis) *fleeing; fleeting*
✦ fugiō -ere fūgī —— INTR./TR. *flee (from), escape; avoid*
fugitīvus -ī M. *runaway (slave)*
✦ fugō -āre TR. *put to flight, rout; deter*
fulciō -īre fulsī fultum TR. *support; seat*
fulgeō -ēre fulsī —— INTR. *shine*
fulmen fulminis N. *lightning*
fulminō -āre INTR./TR. *flash like lightning*
fulvus -a -um *tawny*
fūmus -ī M. *smoke*
fundō -ere fūdī fūsum TR. *pour out*
fūnus fūneris N. *funeral; death*
furibundus -a -um *furious, frenzied*
✦ furō -ere —— —— INTR. *rage; rush*
furor furōris M. *madness, passion*
furtim ADV. *secretly*
furtīvus -a -um *stolen; secret*

furtum -ī M. *theft; secret love, stolen pleasure*
futūrus -a -um *future*

G

Gaetūlus -a -um *Gaetulian; African*
galea -ae F. *helmet*
Gangēs Gangis M. a river in northern India
Garamantēs Garamantium M.PL. a people of north Africa
garriō -īre garrīvī —— INTR. *rattle on, jabber*
✦ gaudeō -ēre gāvīsus sum INTR./TR. *rejoice (in), take joy (in)*
gaudium -(i)ī N. *joy*
gelidus -a -um *cold, cool, chilling, icy*
Gellius -(i)ī M. a person named in Martial's *Epigrammata*
gelō -āre TR./INTR. *freeze, chill*
geminus -a -um *twin; double*
gemitus gemitūs M. *groan, wailing*
gemō -ere gemuī gemitum INTR./TR. *groan, moan; complain*
gena -ae F. *cheek; eye*
genesta -ae F. *broom (a shrub)*
✦ gens gentis F. *tribe, people, nation; family, clan*
genu genūs N. *knee; limb*
✦ genus generis N. *birth, origin; high birth; family, class; race; offspring; mob, bunch; type*
germānus -a -um *full brother/sister; having the same mother and father*
germen germinis N. *seedling, sprout*
✦ gerō -ere gessī gestum TR. *carry, bring, bear; wear; wage, conduct*
Gēryōn Gēryonis (Gēryonēs -ae) M. a mythical three-bodied monster
gestiō -īre gestīvī (-iī) —— INTR. *desire, long*
gestō -āre TR. *bear, carry*
gibbus -ī M. *lump*
✦ gignō -ere genuī genitum TR. *give birth to; produce*
gingīva -ae F. *gum (surrounding the teeth)*
gladiātor gladiātōris M. *gladiator*
✦ gladius (gladium) -(i)ī M./N. *sword*
✦ glōria -ae F. *glory; fame; ambition*
Gnaeus -ī M. a Roman praenomen
gnāta -ae SEE nāta
✦ gnātus -ī SEE nātus
Gortȳnius -a -um *of Gortyn (a city of Crete); Cretan*
Gracchus -ī M. one of two brothers who were would-be reformers of the second century B.C.

gradus -ūs M. *step, pace*
Graecia -ae F. *Greece*
Grāius -a -um *Greek*
grāmen grāminis N. *grass; plant*
grammaticus -ī M. *scholar*
✦grandis -is -e *great; large; loud*
✦grātia -ae F. *favor, goodwill; charm;*
(PERSONIFIED) *Grace* (one of three
sister goddesses, givers of charm and
beauty)
✦grātiā PREP. (+ GEN.) *for the sake of,*
by reason of
grātulor -ārī INTR. *rejoice*
✦grātus -a -um *pleasant, charming, pleasing;*
grateful
gravidus -a -um *swollen; pregnant;*
abundant
✦gravis -is -e *heavy; important, serious;*
burdensome; offensive
gravitās gravitātis F. *seriousness*
graviter ADV. *grievously, badly*
gravō -āre TR. *make heavy, weigh down*
✦gremium -iī N. *lap*
gressus -ūs M. *step*
grex gregis M. *flock, herd; crowd*
gryps grȳpis M. *griffin*
gubernātor gubernātōris M. *helmsman,*
pilot
gutta -ae F. *drop (of liquid)*
guttur gutturis N. *neck*

H

habēna -ae F. *rein*
✦habeō -ēre TR. *have, hold, possess;*
contain; (PASS.) *be considered;*
(WITH REFL.) *be in (a condition);*
endure
✦habitō -āre TR./INTR. *inhabit; dwell,*
live
hāc ADV. *in this way; on this side*
hāc … hāc … *on this side … on that …*
Hadria -ae M. *the Adriatic Sea*
haereō -ēre haesī haesum INTR. *be firmly*
attached (to), cling (to); be uncertain
hālitus -ūs M. *breath*
hāmātus -a -um *barbed*
Hammōn Hammōnis M. *the Egyptian*
god *Ammon*
Hannibal Hannibalis M. *a Carthaginian*
general who invaded Italy in the Second
Carthaginian War
harēna -ae F. *sand, beach;* (PL.) *grains of*
sand
harundō harundinis F. *reed*
hasta -ae F. *spear*
✦haud ADV. *not (at all), by no means*
haustus -ūs M. *draft*
havē havēre SEE avē

Hecatē Hecatēs GREEK F. *a divinity*
identified with Diana in the latter's
function of moon goddess; the goddess
of the black arts
hedera -ae F. *ivy*
Helicōn Helicōnis M. *Mt. Helicon*
Helicōniades Helicōniadum
GREEK F.PL. *dwellers on Helicon*
(the Muses)
Helicōnis (Helicōnidos) GREEK ADJ.
of Mt. Helicon
Helvia -ae F. *a Roman woman's name*
hem INTERJECTION *really?, ah!*
herba -ae F. *garden; herb; grass*
herbōsus -a -um *grassy*
hercle INTERJECTION *by Hercules!*
hērēs hērēdis M./F. *heir*
Hermus -ī M. *a river in Asia Minor*
noted for its alluvial gold
hērōs hērōos GREEK M. *hero*
Hesperus -ī M. *the Evening Star*
heu INTERJECTION *alas!*
hībernus -a -um *of winter*
Hibērus -a -um *Spanish*
✦hic haec hoc PRON./ADJ. *this (near me)*
✦hīc ADV. *here, at this point*
hiems hiemis F. *winter*
✦hinc ADV. *from here, hence; on this side;*
henceforth; from this; then, next
Hippolytus -ī M. *the son of Theseus*
and Hippolyta
hirsūtus -a -um *hairy, shaggy*
Hispānia -ae F. *Spain*
✦hodiē ADV. *today*
hodiernus -a -um *today's*
Homērus -ī M. *Homer*
✦homō hominis M. *human being, person*
✦honestus -a -um *honorable, respectable*
✦honor (honōs) honōris M. *honor, renown;*
probity; high public office
✦hōra -ae F. *hour; time*
horreō -ēre horruī —
INTR./TR. *tremble (at), shudder (at);*
bristle
horribilis -is -e *terrible, spine-chilling*
horridus -a -um *rough; terrible*
horror horrōris M. *turbulence; terror*
✦hortor -ārī TR. *urge, encourage*
✦hortus -ī M. *garden*
✦hospes hospitis M./F. *host; guest; stranger*
✦hostis hostis M./F. *enemy; opponent*
✦hūc ADV. *to this place*
hūmānus -a -um *human*
humus -ī F. *earth, ground*
Hyacinthus -ī M. *a handsome youth of*
Greek mythology
Hybla -ae F. *a town in eastern Sicily near*
Mt. Etna

Hyblaeus -a -um *of Hybla*
hydrus -ī M. *dragon; snake*
Hylās -ae M. a person named in Martial's
Epigrammata

I

◆**iaceō -ēre** INTR. *lie, be recumbent;
be inactive; hang down, droop*
◆**iaciō -ere iēcī iactum** TR. *throw, cast;
lay, build*
iactō -āre TR. *throw, toss (about)*
iactūra -ae F. *loss*
iaculor -ārī INTR./TR. *hurl*
◆**iam** ADV. *already, now; still*
iam nōn ADV. *no longer*
iamdūdum ADV. *already for a long time*
iānua -ae F. *door*
◆**ibĭ** ADV. *there, at that place; then*
īciō īcere īcī ictum TR. *strike*
ictus -ūs M. *blow; spurt*
Īdaeus -a -um *of Mt. Ida; Trojan*
Īdē Īdēs GREEK F. *Mt. Ida (near Troy)*
◆**īdem eadem idem** PRON./ADJ. *the same*
identidem ADV. *repeatedly, continually*
igitur ADV. *therefore, so*
ignāvus -a -um *idle, lazy*
◆**ignis ignis** M. *fire; torch; heavenly body,
star; passion*
◆**ignōscō -ere ignōvī ignōtum**
TR. (+ DAT. OF PERSON, + ACC. OF
THING) *overlook, forgive, pardon*
ignōtus -a -um *strange, unknown,
unfamiliar*
īlia īlium N.PL. *groin, stomach*
Īlia -ae F. the legendary mother of
Romulus and Remus
Īliacus -a -um *of Troy, Trojan*
Īlias Īliadis F. the *Iliad* of Homer
īlicētum -ī N. *grove of holm-oaks*
◆**ille illa illud** PRON./ADJ. *that (over there)*
◆**illīc** ADV. *there, at that place*
illinc ADV. *on that side; from that place*
◆**illūc** ADV. *(to) there, to that place*
imāgō imāginis F. *picture, image, likeness,
form*
imber imbris M. *rain*
immānis -is -e *savage, terrible, frightful*
immemor (immemoris) *forgetful*
immensus -a -um *huge*
immersābilis -is -e *unsinkable*
immisceō -ēre immiscuī immixtum
TR. *mix, mingle*
immītis -is -e *merciless, cruel*
immittō -ere immīsī immissum
TR. *admit; grant entry to*
immō PARTICLE INTRODUCING A
CORRECTION OF THE PRECEDING
STATEMENT

immortālis -is -e *immortal*
imp- SEE ALSO **inp-**
impatiens (impatientis) *impatient*
impellō -ere impulī impulsum TR. *drive,
compel; sway; hit; overcome, smite*
imperātor imperātōris M. *general*
imperitō -āre INTR. (+ DAT.)/TR. *rule
over*
◆**imperium -(i)ī** N. *authority; rule,
command, government; empire*
◆**imperō -āre** INTR./TR. (+ DAT. OF
PERSON, + ACC. OF THING) *order;
govern*
◆**impetus -ūs** M. *attack; blast*
impiger impigra impigrum *swift,
energetic; eager*
implectō -ere implexī implexum
TR. *intertwine*
impleō -ēre implēvī implētum TR. *fill*
**implicō -āre implicāvī (implicuī)
implicātum (implicitum)** TR. *weave*
implōrō -āre TR. *ask for, beg*
impōnō -ere imposuī impositum
TR. *place on, put on; impose on*
impotens (impotentis) *lacking in
self-control, irresolute*
imprimō -ere impressī impressum
TR. *press*
improbus -a -um *indecent, morally
unsound, rascally, shameful, shameless;
unreasonable; tempestuous*
impūne ADV. *without redress, with
impunity*
īmus -a -um *deepest, lowest*
◆**in** PREP. (+ ACC.) *to, into, against, up to;
(+ ABL.) in, on, among; in anticipation
of*
Īnachis Īnachidos GREEK F. *a daughter
of Inachus, especially Io*
Īnachius -a -um *of Inachus; Greek*
inamābilis -is -e *disagreeable, loathesome*
inānis -is -e *empty*
incautus -a -um *unwary*
incendium -(i)ī N. *fire*
◆**incendō -ere incendī incensum**
TR. *kindle, burn; excite*
incertus -a -um *undefined, doubtful,
uncertain, unsure*
incessus -ūs M. *bearing*
◆**incidō -ere incidī incāsum** INTR. *fall
(into); occur*
incīdō -ere incīdī incīsum TR. *cut*
◆**incipiō -ere incēpī inceptum**
TR./INTR. *begin, embark on*
◆**incitō -āre** TR. *hasten; provoke*
incolō -ere incoluī — TR./INTR. *inhabit,
dwell in*
incorruptus -a -um *untainted*

incultus -a -um *not cultivated, untilled; unadorned; uncouth*

incumbō -ere incubuī — INTR. *lean (over), fall (on)*

◆**inde** ADV. *thence, from there, from this, since then; then*

indignātiō indignātiōnis F. *indignation*

indignē ADV. *undeservedly*

indignus -a -um (+ ABL./GEN.) *undeserving, unworthy; innocent, guiltless; cruel*

indīviduus -a -um *indivisible*

indocilis -is -e *ignorant*

indomitus -a -um *invincible; headstrong; unbridled, unbroken*

indulgeō -ēre indulsī indultum INTR./TR. *have regard for*

induō -ere induī indūtum TR. *put on*

induperātor induperātōris M. *general*

Indus -ī M. *an Indian, inhabitant of India*

ineptiō -īre — — INTR. *be foolish*

ineptus -a -um *foolish, silly*

inermis -is -e *unarmed*

iners (inertis) *sluggish; idle, lazy*

inexōrābilis -is -e *that cannot be obtained by entreaty*

inex(s)tinctus -a -um *that is never extinguished*

infāmis -is -e *ill-famed*

infandus -a -um *unspeakable*

infēlix (infēlīcis) *unhappy, unfortunate*

inferiae -ārum F.PL. *offerings made to the dead*

infernus -a -um *infernal, of the Underworld*

inferō inferre intulī illātum TR. *bring; (WITH REFL.) advance*

infimus -a -um *lowest*

infit (NO OTHER FORMS) INTR. *begin to speak*

◆**infrā** ADV. *below, underneath;* PREP. (+ ACC.) *below; inferior to*

infundō -ere infūdī infūsum TR. *pour over*

◆**ingenium -(i)ī** N. *talent; temperament, character; mind; intellect*

◆**ingens (ingentis)** *huge, enormous; mighty; thick*

ingenuus -a -um *freeborn*

ingrātus -a -um *thankless; unrewarding; ungrateful*

ingredior -ī ingressus sum TR./INTR. *enter*

inhiō -āre INTR./TR. *open one's mouth, gape (at)*

inhonōrus -a -um *dishonorable*

inhumātus -a -um *unburied*

inimīcus -a -um *hostile, unfriendly*

inīquus -a -um *unfair, unequal, harsh; sullen*

◆**initium -(i)ī** N. *beginning*

iniūria -ae F. *wrong, injustice*

iniustus -a -um *unfair, unjust*

inlacrimābilis -is -e *pitiless*

inm- SEE imm-

innocens (innocentis) *innocent, guiltless*

innuptus -a -um *unmarried*

inopia -ae F. *poverty*

inops (inopis) *poor*

inp- SEE imp-

◆**inquam — — —** DEFECTIVE, INTR. *say, tell*

inquiētus -a -um *restless*

inr- SEE irr-

insānia -ae F. *madness*

insānus -a -um *frenzied, mad*

inscriptiō inscriptiōnis F. *(the action of) writing; inscription*

insector -ārī TR. *harass*

insequens (insequentis) *following, in pursuit*

inserō -ere inseruī insertum TR. *insert; fix*

insidiae -ārum F.PL. *ambush*

insignis -is -e *distinguished, noted, famous; remarkable*

insistō -ere institī — TR./INTR. *stand (on)*

inspiciō -ere inspexī inspectum TR. *observe*

instar N. (ONLY NOM. AND ACC. SG.) *equivalent, counterpart;* PREP. (+ GEN.) *in the same way as, like*

instō -āre institī — TR./INTR. *press (on), pursue; approach, threaten*

insuāvis -is -e *harsh, unpleasant*

◆**insula -ae** F. *island*

insultō -āre INTR. *jump on; mock*

intactus -a -um *untouched; unharmed, unscathed*

integer integra integrum *whole, unimpaired, fresh*

intellegō -ere intellexī intellectum TR. *understand*

intendō -ere intendī intentum TR./INTR. *stretch; direct (toward); strain*

◆**inter** PREP. (+ ACC.) *among, between, amid*

interdīcō -ere interdixī interdictum TR./INTR. *forbid*

interdum ADV. *occasionally, at times*

◆**intereā** ADV. *meanwhile; nevertheless; as it is*

intereō -īre interiī interitum INTR. *die*

✦interficiō -ere interfēcī interfectum
TR. *kill, destroy*

interfūsus -a -um *poured in between*

interior -ior -ius *inner*

interritus -a -um *unafraid*

intimus -a -um *innermost*

✦intrā ADV./PREP. (+ ACC.) *inside, within*

intrō mittō -ere intrō mīsī intrō
missum (ALSO OCCURS AS SINGLE
FORMS) TR. *allow in, admit*

✦intus ADV. *inside, within*

inūtilis -is -e *useless*

invalidus -a -um *weak*

✦inveniō -īre invēnī inventum TR. *find,
discover; devise;* (WITH NEG.) *be at a
loss to know*

invertō -ere invertī inversum TR. *turn
upside down; turn over, plow*

✦invideō -ēre invīdī invīsum
INTR. (+ DAT. OF PERSON)/TR.
envy; cast the evil eye (on); refuse

✦invidia -ae F. *envy, jealousy*

invidus -a -um *malevolent, ill-natured;
envious*

inviolātus -a -um *whole, unharmed*

invīsus -a -um *hateful; unpopular*

invītus -a -um *unwilling, reluctant*

Īō (NO GEN.) F. *the daughter of Inachus
who was loved by Jupiter and who was
changed into a cow*

iocor -ārī INTR. *jest, joke*

iocōsus -a -um *playful*

iocus -ī N. *jest; trifle*

Īonius -a -um *Ionian*

✦ipse ipsa ipsum PRON./ADJ. *-self,
the very*

✦īra -ae F. *anger, wrath, rage*

īrācundus -a -um *angry; hot-tempered*

✦īrascor -ī īrātus sum
INTR. (+ DAT.) *be angry (with)*

īrātus -a -um *angry, furious*

irritus -a -um *not valid; empty*

✦is ea id PRON./ADJ. *he, she, it; this, that*

✦iste ista istud PRON./ADJ. *that (near you),
that (of yours)*

Isthmius -a -um *Isthmian, of the Isthmus
(of Corinth) (site of the Isthmian
games)*

istīc ADV. *there, over there*

✦ita ADV. *thus, so, to such an extent*

Ītalia -ae F. *Italy*

✦iter itineris N. *road, path, way; journey;
advance*

✦iterum ADV. *again, for a second time*

itiō itiōnis F. *(the action of) going*

iuba -ae F. *mane*

✦iubeō -ēre iussī iussum TR. *order, direct;
decree; bid*

iūcundus -a -um *pleasant, charming*

iūdex iūdicis M. *judge*

iūgerum -ī N. *a measure of land, acre*

iugum -ī N. *yoke*

Iūlus -ī M. *the son of Aeneas*

✦iungō -ere iunxī iunctum TR. *join,
connect, attach; mate*

Iūnō Iūnōnis F. *Juno, queen of the gods,
the wife and sister of Jupiter*

Iuppiter Iovis M. *Jupiter, king of the gods
and men*

iurgium -(i)ī N. *quarrel; abuse*

✦iūrō -āre INTR. *swear (on oath), vow*

✦iūs iūris N. *law; judgment; right, privilege*

iussum -ī N. *command, order*

iustitia -ae F. *justice*

iustus -a -um *just, right, righteous,
legitimate*

Iuvenālis Iuvenālis M. *a person named
in Martial's* Epigrammata, *perhaps the
poet Juvenal*

✦iuvenis iuvenis M. *young man;*
ADJ. *young, youthful*

iuventa -ae F. *youth, youthfulness*

iuventūs iuventūtis F. *youth*

✦iuvō -āre iūvī iūtum TR. *help;* (IMPERS.)
it is pleasing

iuxtā ADV./PREP. (+ ACC.) *nearby; near,
beside*

Ixīōn Ixīonis M. *a mortal who tried to
seduce Juno and was punished in the
Underworld by being spread-eagled on
a constantly turning wheel*

Ixīonius -a -um *of Ixion*

L

labellum -ī N. *lip*

Labiēnus -ī M. *a subordinate addressed
by Cato in Lucan's* Bellum cīvīle

labō -āre labāvī — INTR. *give way,
totter*

lābor lābī lapsus sum INTR. *fall; slip by;
flow*

✦labor labōris M. *labor, toil, exertion, effort,
work; task*

✦labōrō -āre INTR./TR. *labor, toil; be in
trouble, suffer*

labrum -ī N. *lip*

lac lactis N. *milk*

lacertus -ī M. *arm*

✦lacrima -ae F. *tear*

lacrimō -āre INTR./TR. *weep (for)*

lactens (lactentis) *full of milk;
milk-white*

lacūna -ae F. *pool*

lacus -ūs M. *lake, pond*

✦laedō -ere laesī laesum TR. *hurt, harm;
offend*

..a. a person named in
..*Epigrammata*

-ī M. a person named in
..al's *Epigrammata*

.·-ārī INTR. be glad

..us -a -um happy; fortunate; fat

..evus -a -um left, left-hand; unfavorable

lagōna -ae F. wine bottle

Lāgus -ī M. the father of the first Greek ruler of Egypt, Ptolemy I

lambō -ere lambī — TR. lick; wreathe

lampas lampadis F. torch

lāna -ae F. wool

languescō -ere languī — INTR. become weak/feeble

languidus -a -um weary, exhausted; sluggish

laniō -āre TR. tear apart

Lānuvīnus -ī M. a Lanuvian

Lānuvium -(i)ī N. a town in the hills south of Rome

lapis lapidis M. stone

Lar Laris M. household god; dwelling

larārium -(i)ī N. shrine (in the atrium of a home)

largītor largītōris M. bestower, benefactor

lāsarpīcifer lāsarpīcifera lāsarpīciferum silphium-bearing

lascīvus -a -um playful; loose

lassus -a -um weary, exhausted

lātē ADV. widely, over a wide area; loudly

latebra -ae F. hiding place

◆lateō -ēre latuī — INTR. lie, hide, be hidden (from)

Laterānus -ī M. a person named in Juvenal's *Satires*

Latīnus -a -um of Latium, Latin

Latium -(i)ī N. an area of central Italy; Italy itself

lātus -a -um wide, broad

◆latus lateris N. side, flank

◆laudō -āre TR. praise, approve

Laurens (Laurentis) Laurentian; Roman

laus laudis F. praise; praiseworthiness, virtue

Lāvīnius -a -um of Lavinium (a settlement in central Italy founded by Aeneas)

lavō -āre (-ere) lāvī lāvātum (lōtum, lautum) TR./INTR. wash

laxō -āre TR. loosen; relax

lea -ae F. lioness

leaena -ae F. lioness

lector lectōris M. reader, reciter

lectulus -ī M. couch, bed

lectus -a -um choice, excellent

lectus -ī M. bed

legiō legiōnis F. legion

legō -ere lēgī lectum TR. gather, choose; read

lēniō -īre TR. soothe, calm; soften; pass pleasantly

lēnis -is -e gentle, lenient

lēniter ADV. smoothly

lentus -a -um soft, malleable; slow, prolonged

◆leō leōnis M. lion

lepidus -a -um charming

lepōs lepōris M. charm; wit

Lerna -ae F. a district in Argolis in southeastern Greece

Lesbia -ae F. the pseudonym of Catullus' mistress in his *Carmina*

Lēthaeus -a -um Lethean, of Lethe (a river of the Underworld)

lētum -ī N. death (SOMETIMES PERSONIFIED)

Leuconoē Leuconoēs GREEK F. a woman addressed in Horace's *Odes*

◆levis -is -e light, not heavy; slight, trivial; fickle

lēvis -is -e smooth, smooth-skinned

leviter ADV. softly, lightly

levō -āre TR. lift, lighten; relieve

◆lex lēgis F. law; contract; condition, term

libellus -ī M. small book

libens (libentis) pleased, willing, glad

Līber Līberī M. Bacchus, Dionysus

◆liber lībera līberum free (from)

◆liber librī M. book

◆līberī -ōrum M.PL. children

liberō -āre TR. free, set free

◆lībertās lībertātis F. freedom

◆libet libēre libuit (libitum est) INTR., IMPERS. it pleases, it is agreeable

libīdō libīdinis F. lust

lībra -ae F. pound (weight)

lībum -ī M. a kind of cake

Libycus -a -um African

Libyssa -ae F. ADJ. of North Africa, African

◆licet licēre licuit (licitum est) INTR., IMPERS. it is allowed, one may

licet CONJ. (+ SUBJ.) although

līmen līminis N. threshold; door

līmus -ī M. mud, slime

◆lingua -ae F. tongue; language

linquō -ere līquī — TR. leave; abandon

Linus -ī M. a person named in Martial's *Epigrammata*

lippus -a -um bleary-eyed

liquidus -a -um fluid; clear(-toned)

liquō -āre TR. strain

līs lītis F. *quarrel, dispute; lawsuit, case*

✦littera -ae F. *letter (of the alphabet);* (USUALLY PL.) *epistle; literature*

✦lītus lītoris N. *shore, coast*

līvor līvōris M. *envy*

locō -āre TR. *put, place*

✦locus -ī M. *place*

Lollius -a -um the name of a Roman gens

longē ADV. *far away*

✦longus -a -um *long; far-reaching*

loquax (loquācis) *noisy*

✦loquor loquī locūtus sum INTR./TR. *speak, talk, say; whisper*

lōrīca -ae F. *breastplate*

lōtium -(i)ī N. *urine*

✦lubet SEE libet

lūbricus -a -um *slippery*

✦Lūcifer Lūciferī M. *the Morning Star*

Lūcius -(i)ī M. a Roman praenomen

Lucrētius -(i)ī M. a Roman poet (c. 94–c. 55 B.C.)

lucrum -ī N. *profit, gain*

luctus luctūs M. *lament, sorrow, grief*

lūcus -ī M. *sacred grove; woods, grove*

lūdia -ae F. *female slave in a school of gladiators*

✦lūdō -ere lūsī lūsum INTR. *play at/with; trifle with*

✦lūdus -ī M. *game, sport; school; gladiatorial troupe;* (PL.) *public games*

lūgeō -ēre luxī luctum INTR./TR. *mourn, bewail, lament*

lūgubris -is -e *mournful*

✦lūmen lūminis N. *light; lamp, torch; eye*

✦lūna -ae F. *moon*

luscus -a -um *blind in one eye, one-eyed*

✦lux lūcis F. *light*

luxuria -ae F. *luxury, extravagance*

luxus -ūs M. *luxury*

Lyaeus -ī M. *Dionysus; wine*

Lȳdia -ae F. a former mistress of Horace

lyra -ae F. *lyre*

lyricus -a -um *of the lyre, lyrical*

M

madefaciō -ere madefēcī madefactum TR. *soak*

Maenalius -a -um *of Mt. Maenalus*

Maenalus -ī M. *Mt. Maenalus* (in Arcadia)

Maeonidēs -ae M. *the Lydian, viz Homer*

Maeōtius -a -um *of Lake Maeotis or the surrounding territory*

maereō -ēre —— INTR./TR. *mourn*

maestus -a -um *sad*

mage SEE magis

magicus -a -um *magical*

✦magis ADV. *more, rather*

✦magister magistrī M. *schoolmaster, teacher, guide; director*

magisterium -(i)ī N. *instruction*

magnanimus -a -um *brave*

✦magnus -a -um *great, large, tall; important, mighty*

maior -or -us COMPAR. OF magnus *greater*

maiōrēs maiōrum M.PL. *ancestors*

male ADV. *badly, wickedly*

✦mālō malle māluī —— TR. *prefer*

malum -ī N. *trouble, complaint, scourge; peril*

malum INTERJECTION *damn it!*

mālum -ī N. *apple*

✦malus -a -um *bad, evil, malicious, foul, wicked; harmful; poor, weak*

Māmercus -ī M. a person named in Martial's *Epigrammata*

mandō -āre TR. *enjoin, bid; entrust*

māne ADV. *in the morning*

maneō -ēre mansī mansum INTR./TR. *stay, remain; endure, persist*

mānēs mānium M.PL. *Shades (of the dead), the dead*

mānō -āre mānāvī —— INTR. *pour, run, drip*

mansuescō -ere mansuēvī mansuētum INTR. *become gentle/tame*

✦manus -ūs F. *hand; band of men*

✦mare maris N. *sea*

margō marginis M. (F.) *margin*

✦marītus -a -um *wedded, connubial*

✦marītus -ī M. *husband; mate*

marmor marmoris N. *marble*

marmoreus -a -um *of marble*

Marō Marōnis M. *Vergil's cognomen*

Marpēsius -a -um *of Mt. Marpessa, Marpessian*

Mars Martis M. *the god of war*

Martiālis Martiālis M. *Martial, a friend of Martial addressed in his Epigrammata*

massa -ae F. *bundle*

Massicus -a -um *of Mt. Massicus* (noted for its wine)

Massȳlus -a -um *Massylian; Numidian*

mastīgia -ae M. *rascal*

✦māter mātris F. *mother*

māteria -ae F. *material, (solid) matter*

māternus -a -um *of a mother*

mātūrus -a -um *ripe, mature*

mātūtīnus -a -um *of (early) morning*

Maurus -a -um *Moorish*

✦maximus -a -um *greatest, largest*

Maximus -ī M. a Roman cognomen

meātus -ūs M. *movement*

Mēdī -ōrum M.PL. *Medes (inhabitants of Media, a country in what is now northwestern Iran)*

meditor -ārī TR./INTR. *think about*

✦medius -a -um *middle, the middle of; mediocre, middling*

medulla -ae F. *marrow*

meiō -ere mi(n)xī mi(n)ctum INTR. *urinate*

mel mellis N. *honey*

melior -ior -ius COMPAR. OF bonus *better*

mellītus -a -um *honey-sweet*

Melpomenē Melpomenēs GREEK F. *one of the Muses*

membrāna -ae F. *parchment*

membrum -ī N. *limb*

✦meminī meminisse — TR./INTR. *(+ GEN.) remember, recall; be sure (to)*

✦memor (memoris) *(+ GEN.) mindful (of), remembering, unforgetting*

✦memoria -ae F. *memory; history*

memorō -āre TR. *utter, say; recount*

mendācium -(i)ī N. *lie, deceit*

✦mens mentis F. *mind, intellect; attitude; heart*

mensa -ae F. *table*

mensis mensis M. *month*

mentior -īrī mentītus INTR./TR. *lie; pretend to be, feign*

mercātor mercātōris M. *merchant, trader*

mercēs mercēdis F. *payment*

Mercurius -(i)ī M. *Mercury, a son of Jupiter, the messenger of the gods*

✦mereō -ēre (mereor -ērī) TR. *deserve; earn*

mergō -ere mersī mersum TR. *immerse; submerge; bury*

meritō ADV. *rightly, deservedly*

meritum -ī N. *worth*

merum -ī N. *(undiluted) wine*

✦merus -a -um *undiluted, pure*

merx mercis F. *merchandise*

messis messis F. *harvest*

-met PARTICLE ATTACHED TO PRONOUNS FOR EMPHASIS

mēta -ae F. *turning point at the end of a racetrack; goal*

mētior -īrī mensus (mētītus) sum TR. *measure*

✦metuō -ere metuī metūtum TR. *fear, be afraid of*

✦metus -ūs M. *fear, anxiety; awe*

✦meus -a -um *my*

micō -āre micuī — INTR. *flash, gleam*

✦mīles mīlitis M. *soldier*

mīlitia -ae F. *military service*

mille INDECL ADJ. *thousand;* mīlia mīlium N.PL. *thousands*

minae -ārum F.PL. *threats*

minax (minācis) *threatening*

Minerva -ae F. *a daughter of Jupiter, the patroness of handicrafts*

minimum ADV. *to the least extent*

minimus -a -um SUPERL. OF parvus *least, lowest; trivial; worst*

minister ministrī M. *servant*

ministrō -āre INTR./TR. *serve*

Mīnōis Mīnōidis F. *a daughter of Minos, especially Ariadne*

✦minor -or -us COMPAR. OF parvus *smaller; lesser; younger;* M.PL. NOUN *descendants*

Mīnōs Mīnōis M. *one of the three judges of the Underworld*

minus ADV. *less, to a smaller extent; not*

mīrābilis -is -e *wonderful*

mīrāculum -ī N. *marvel, wonder*

mīrificē ADV. *wonderfully*

✦mīror -ārī INTR./TR. *marvel (at), hold in awe, admire*

✦mīrus -a -um *remarkable, marvelous; skillful*

✦misceō -ēre miscuī mixtum (mistum) TR. *mix, mingle; combine;* (PASS. USED AS INTR.) *be in confusion*

misellus -a -um DIMINUTIVE OF miser *poor, wretched*

✦miser misera miserum *unhappy, sad, miserable, unfortunate, wretched, woeful*

miserābilis -is -e *pitiable*

miserē ADV. *desperately*

miseror -ārī TR. *pity, feel sorry for*

mītescō -ere — — INTR. *become mild; ripen*

mītis -is -e *gentle*

mitra -ae F. *bonnet*

✦mittō -ere mīsī missum TR. *send; dismiss, release; refrain (from); throw*

mōbilis -is -e *restless, on the move*

moderor -ārī INTR./TR. *control; play*

modo ADV. *just, only; now; at one time; recently*

modus -ī M. *manner, method, way; limit; moderation; meter; melody*

moechus -ī M. *adulterer*

✦moenia moenium N.PL. *walls; ramparts*

mōlēs mōlis F. *pile (for the foundation of a building)*

molliō -īre TR. *make soft*

mollis -is -e *soft, gentle, delicate*

molliter ADV. *softly, gently; gracefully*

molō -ere moluī molitum TR./INTR. *grind (in a mill)*

◆moneō -ēre TR./INTR. *remind; advise,
warn*

monimentum -ī N. *memorial*

monitum -ī N. *counsel, instruction,
warning*

◆mons montis M. *mountain*

◆monstrō -āre TR./INTR. *show, reveal,
point out*

Mōnychus -ī M. *a centaur*

Mopsus -ī M. *the future husband of
Nysa, who spurned Damon in Vergil's
Eclogues*

mora -ae F. *delay; slowness*

◆morbus -ī M. *sickness, disease*

mordeō -ēre momordī (memordī)
morsum TR. *bite*

moribundus -a -um *dying*

◆morior morī mortuus sum INTR. *die*

moror -ārī TR./INTR. *delay; stay behind,
linger; occupy*

◆mors mortis F. *death*

morsus -ūs M. *bite*

mortālis -is -e *mortal; human*

mortālis mortālis M. *mortal, human being*

◆mortuus -a -um *dead*

mōrum -ī N. *mulberry*

mōrus -ī F. *mulberry tree*

◆mōs mōris M. *custom, habit; civilized
practice; (PL.) habits, character, conduct,
behavior*

mōtus -ūs M. *motion; emotion, feeling;
activity*

◆moveō -ēre mōvī mōtum TR. *move,
set in motion; bring; influence; provoke;
(WITH REFL.) stir*

◆mox ADV. *soon*

mucrō mucrōnis M. *sword tip*

mulceō -ēre mulsī mulsum (mul(c)tum)
TR. *soothe, calm; stroke*

◆mulier mulieris F. *woman; wife*

mūliō mūliōnis M. *mule-driver*

multiplex (multiplicis) *multiple,
numerous*

multum ADV. *much; very*

◆multus -a -um *much; large; numerous,
many*

◆mundus -ī M. *the world, earth; sky,
heavens; the universe*

◆mūnus mūneris N. *gift; office, duty*

mūrex mūricis M. *shellfish; dye (extracted
from the shellfish)*

murmur murmuris N. *roar, rumble;
murmur, whisper, muttering*

◆mūrus -ī M. *wall*

Mūsa -ae F. *one of the nine Muses,
goddesses presiding over the arts*

mūsicus -a -um *melodious*

mūtātiō mūtātiōnis F. *change*

◆mūtō -āre TR. *change, alter, replace; pass
from one to another*

mūtus -a -um *dumb; silent*

mūtuus -a -um *mutual*

myrteus -a -um *of the myrtle*

myrtus -ī F. *myrtle*

N

◆nam CONJ. *for*

namque EMPHATIC FORM OF nam

nāris nāris F. (ALSO AS PL.) *nose,
nostril(s)*

◆narrō -āre TR./INTR. *narrate, tell*

◆nascor nascī nātus sum INTR. *be born,
come into existence; rise*

Nāsō Nāsōnis M. *Ovid's cognomen*

nāsus -ī M. *nose*

nāta -ae F. *daughter*

nātālis nātālis M. *birthday*

natō -āre INTR. *swim*

◆nātūra -ae F. *nature; quality, character*

◆nātus -ī M. *son; (PL.) children*

naufragium -(i)ī N. *shipwreck*

nauta -ae M. *sailor*

◆nāvis nāvis F. *ship*

nāvita -ae M. *sailor*

◆nē CONJ. *lest, (so) that ... not; NEG. ADV.*

nē ... quidem ADV. *not even*

-ne INTERR. PARTICLE

Neaera -ae F. *the pseudonym of
Lygdamus' mistress in his Elegies*

nebula -ae F. *cloud; fog*

◆nec (neque) CONJ. *nor, and ... not, but
not; not even*

◆nec ... nec ... CONJ. *neither ... nor ...*

necdum ADV. *not yet*

◆necesse est IMPERS. *it is necessary, it is
unavoidable*

◆necessitās necessitātis F. *necessity,
inevitability*

necō -āre TR. *kill*

nectar nectaris N. *nectar (the drink of
the gods)*

nectō -ere nexī nexum TR. *join, string
together, weave, bind*

◆nefās INDECL. N. *wickedness; crime;
wrong*

◆negō -āre TR. *deny; say ... not; refuse;
forbid*

◆nēmō nēminis M./F. *no one*

nempe CONJ. *of course*

nemus nemoris N. *forest, grove*

nepōs nepōtis M. *grandson*

Neptūnus -ī M. *Neptune, a brother of
Jupiter, the god of the sea*

◆nēquāquam ADV. *by no means*

◆neque (nec) CONJ. *nor, and ... not,
but not; not even*

✦neque ... neque ... CONJ. *neither ...
nor ...*

nēquīquam ADV. *vainly, to no purpose*

✦nesciō -īre TR. *not know*

nescioquis (-quī) -quis -quid (-quod)
PRON./ADJ. *I know not who/what;
someone/something or other*

nescius -a -um (+ GEN.) *unaware of,
unacquainted with, unknowing*

Nestor Nestoris M. *a king of Pylos
who took part in the Greek expedition
to Troy*

neu ... neu ... CONJ. *lest ... nor ...*

✦neuter neutra neutrum PRON./ADJ.
neither (of two)

nex necis F. *death*

✦nī SEE nisi

nīdōricupius -(i)ī M. *person who loves
the smell of cooking*

niger nigra nigrum *black, dark*

✦nihil (nīl) INDECL. N. *nothing*

nīl ADV. (EMPHATIC) *not (at all)*

Nīlus -ī M. *the Nile River*

✦nimis ADV. *excessively, too much*

✦nimium ADV. *excessively, too (much)*

nimius -a -um *too much*

Nīnus -ī M. *the legendary founder of
Nineveh*

✦nisi (nī) CONJ. *unless, if not; except*

nitens (nitentis) *radiant*

nitidus -a -um *shiny, shining; elegant*

nītor nītī nixus (nīsus) INTR. *rest,
lean on*

niveus -a -um *snowy*

nix nivis F. *snow*

✦nōbilis -is -e *famous; noble*

✦noceō -ēre INTR. (+ DAT.) *harm, hurt,
injure; be guilty*

nocturnus -a -um *nightly, nocturnal*

nōdus -ī M. *knot*

✦nōlō nolle nōluī — INTR./TR. *not want;
be unwilling (to)*

✦nōmen nōminis N. *name; family name;
renown*

Nōmentānus -a -um *of Nomentum
(a town near Rome)*

nōminō -āre TR. *name; call*

✦nōn ADV. *not; no*

✦nōndum ADV. *not yet*

✦nōnne? INTERR. ADV. *Is it not the case
that ...?*

✦nōnnullī -ae -a PRON./ADJ. *some; several*

nōnus -a -um *ninth*

✦nōs (nōs nostrum (nostrī) nōbīs nōbīs)
we/us

✦noscō -ere nōvī nōtum TR. *get to know,
get acquainted; (PERF.) know*

✦noster nostra nostrum *our*

nota -ae F. *mark*

nōtitia -ae F. *acquaintance*

notō -āre TR. *mark; notice*

nōtus -a -um *known, well-known, familiar,
recognized*

Notus -ī M. *the south wind*

novem INDECL. ADJ. *nine*

noviens (noviēs) ADV. *nine times*

novō -āre TR. *replace; resume*

✦novus -a -um *new, fresh, recent; unusual;
unfamiliar, strange*

✦nox noctis F. *night*

noxius -a -um (+ DAT.) *harmful (to)*

nūbēs nūbis F. *cloud*

nūbilum -ī N. *cloud*

nūbilus -a -um *cloudy*

nūbō -ere nupsī nuptum INTR. (+ DAT.)
mate; get married (to) (of a woman)

nūdō -āre TR. *strip bare, uncover*

nūdulus -a -um DIMINUTIVE OF
nūdus *naked, desolate*

nūdus -a -um *naked*

nūgae -ārum F.PL. *nonsense, trifle*

✦nullus -a -um PRON./ADJ. *no one; none,
not any, no*

✦num INTERR. ADV. *surely ... not;*
CONJ. INTRODUCING INDIR. QUESTIONS
whether

✦nūmen nūminis N. *divinity, divine being
(of either sex); divine power*

numerō -āre TR. *count, enumerate*

✦numerus -ī M. *number; company; rhythm,
meter, verse*

nummus -ī M. *money*

✦numquam ADV. *never*

numquis numquis numquid INTERR./
INDEF. PRON./ADJ. INTRODUCING
INDIR. QUESTIONS *anyone, anything;
someone, something*

✦nunc ADV. *now, at this moment; as it is*

✦nuntiō -āre TR. *announce, report*

✦nuntius -(i)ī M. *messenger; message, news*

nūper ADV. *recently*

nuptiae -ārum F.PL. *marriage, wedding*

nusquam ADV. *nowhere*

nūtō -āre INTR. *nod; sway*

nūtriō -īre TR. *feed*

nūtus -ūs M. *nod*

nux nucis F. *nut*

nympha -ae F. *nymph*

Nȳsa -ae F. *the former lover of Damon
in Vergil's Eclogues; a legendary
mountain in India*

O

ō INTERJECTION (WITH VOC.) *O*

✦ob PREP. (+ ACC.) *because of; in front of*

obc- SEE occ-

obdūcō -ere obduxī obductum
TR. *obstruct, darken*
obdūrō -āre INTR. *be firm*
obeō obīre obiī (obīvī) obitum
TR. *meet with; visit; die*
obēsus -a -um *fat*
obiciō -ere obiēcī obiectum TR. (+ DAT.
AND ACC.) *throw at; put in front*
obiectō -āre TR. (+ DAT. OF PERSON,
+ ACC. OF THING) *throw in [someone's]
face*
obitus -ūs M. *death*
oblinō -ere oblēvī (oblīvī) oblitum
TR. *smear*
oblīquus -a -um *slanted, slanting, zigzag*
oboleō -ēre oboluī — INTR. *smell,
stink*
obrēpō -ere obrepsī obreptum
INTR. *creep up*
obruō -ere obruī obrutum TR. *cover,
smother, flood; overwhelm*
obscūrus -a -um *dim, dark, faint; unclear,
obscure*
obsideō -ēre obsēdī obsessum
INTR./TR. *block*
obsōnō -āre INTR./TR. *stock up (with
food)*
obstinātus -a -um *resolute*
obstipescō -ere obstipuī — INTR. *be
stunned*
obstō -āre obstitī obstātum INTR. *stand
in the way (of)*
obvius -a -um *in the way of, placed so as
to meet, presenting*
occāsiō occāsiōnis F. *opportunity*
occidō -ere occidī occāsum INTR. *fall,
drop; die; be doomed; set*
occumbō -ere occubuī — INTR. *fall,
meet one's death*
occupō -āre TR. *seize; forestall, put off*
occurrō -ere oc(cu)currī occursum
INTR. (+ DAT.) *run into, meet*
Ōceanus -ī M. *the ocean*
ocellus -ī M. *eye*
ōcior -ior -ius *quicker*
octāvus -a -um *eighth*
◆oculus -ī M. *eye*
◆ōdī ōdisse ōsum TR. *hate*
◆odium -(i)ī N. *hatred*
Oedipus -ī M. *a king of Thebes, solver
of the riddle of the Sphinx*
Oeta -ae F. *a mountain in Thessaly*
Oetaeus -a -um *of Oeta*
offendō -ere offendī offensum
TR./INTR. *strike; annoy; come upon,
find*
offerō offerre obtulī oblātum
TR. *deliver; put in the path of*

◆officium -(i)ī N. *(sense of) duty;
employment, office*
olea -ae F. *olive tree*
olfaciō -ere olfēcī olfactum TR. *smell*
◆ōlim ADV. *once, in the past, in times past,
long ago; at some future time, one day*
olla -ae F. *(cooking) pot*
ōmen ōminis N. *omen; expectation*
◆omittō -ere omīsī omissum TR. *let go of,
release; abandon*
◆omnis -is -e *every, all*
onus oneris N. *burden, load*
◆opera -ae F. *work, effort; services*
operōsus -a -um *diligent, careful*
◆oportet -ēre oportuit —
INTR., IMPERS. *it is right, one should*
◆oppidum -ī N. *town*
oppōnō -ere opposuī oppositum
TR. *place in opposition, place in the way*
opportūnus -a -um *available*
oppositus -a -um *set opposite, opposing*
opprimō -ere oppressī oppressum
TR. *squeeze, suffocate; overwhelm*
◆ops opis F. *power, (power to) aid;
(USUALLY PL.) resources, wealth*
optimus -a -um SUPERL. OF bonus *best,
(of the) highest (degree)*
◆optō -āre TR. *choose; desire, wish (for),
long for*
optumus -a -um SEE optimus
◆opus operis N. *work, undertaking; need;
literary work, work of art*
◆ōra -ae F. *edge; shore, coast*
ōrāc(u)lum -ī N. *oracle*
ōrātor ōrātōris M. *speaker*
orbis orbis M. *orb; world; region;
revolution; coil*
orbus -a -um *bereaved*
Orcus -ī M. *the Underworld*
◆ordō ordinis M. *line, row; line of soldiers;
rank, class*
Orestēs Orestis M. *the son of
Agamemnon and Clytaemnestra, who
killed his mother to avenge his father's
death and was thereafter haunted by
the Furies*
Oriens Orientis M. *the East*
orīgō orīginis F. *beginning*
◆orior orīrī ortus sum INTR. *rise, arise;
be born; occur*
ornō -āre TR. *adorn, beautify*
ornus -ī F. *ash tree*
Ornytus -ī M. *the father of Calais, who
was the lover of Lydia, Horace's former
mistress*
◆ōrō -āre TR./INTR. *beg, ask, plead;
pray*
Orpheus -ī M. *the husband of Eurydice*

ortus -ūs M. *rising, daybreak; the East*

✦**ōs ōris** N. *mouth; face; beak; voice; opening*

✦**os ossis** N. *bone*

osculum -ī N. *kiss*

✦**ostendō -ere ostendī ostentum (ostensum)** TR. *show, display*

ostium -(i)ī N. *entrance; mouth*

✦**ōtium -(i)ī** N. *leisure*

ovis ovis F. *sheep*

P

pācātor pācātōris M. *subduer*

pācātus -a -um *calm, tranquil*

paciscō -ere — pactum TR. *arrange*

pācō -āre TR. *pacify, subdue*

pactum -ī N. *arrangement*

✦**paene** ADV. *almost, practically*

palaestra -ae F. *wrestling school*

Palātium -(i)ī N. *the Palatine Hill; its residences and temples*

palla -ae F. *cloak*

palleō -ēre [palluī] — INTR. *be pale*

pallescō -ere palluī INTR. *grow pale*

pallidulus -a -um DIMINUTIVE OF **pallidus** *pale*

pallidus -a -um *pale, colorless*

palma -ae F. *palm, hand; first place, prize*

palūs palūdis F. *swamp*

pampineus -a -um *of vine shoots*

Pān Pānos GREEK M. *an Arcadian pastoral god, half-man and half-goat*

Panchāia -ae F. *a legendary island off the coast of Arabia*

pandō -ere — passum (pansum) TR. *spread (open)*

pānis pānis M. *bread*

Pannonicus -a -um *of Pannonia (a Roman province southwest of the Danube River)*

Paphius -a -um *of Paphos (a city in Cyprus)*

papilla -ae F. *nipple; breast*

Pāpylus -ī M. *a person named in Martial's* Epigrammata

pār (paris) (+ DAT.) *equal, similar (to), matching; of equal status*

pār paris M./F. *equal*

parasītus -ī M. *parasite*

parcō -ere pepercī (parcuī, parsī) — INTR. (+ DAT.)/TR. *spare, be economical with, refrain from*

parcus -a -um *sober; moderate*

parens parentis M./F. *parent; father*

Parentālia Parentālium N.PL. *the Roman festival of the family dead*

✦**pāreō -ēre** INTR. (+ DAT.) *appear; obey*

pariēs parietis M. *wall*

✦**pariō -ere peperī partum** TR. *bring forth, give birth to; produce, create; acquire, obtain*

Paris Paridis M. *a Trojan prince; a popular Roman actor in pantomimes*

Parnāsus -ī M. *a mountain in Phocis (in central Greece)*

✦**parō -āre** TR. *prepare, make ready; obtain; (try to) secure*

✦**pars partis** F. *part, section, share; side; region; direction*

parum ADV. *too little*

parvulus -a -um DIMINUTIVE OF **parvus** *tiny*

✦**parvus -a -um** *small, short, low; young; weak, insignificant*

pascō -ere pāvī pastum TR./INTR. *eat; feed*

pascuum -ī N. *pasture*

passer passeris M. *sparrow*

passim ADV. *at random; in every direction*

pastor pastōris M. *herdsman*

patefaciō -ere patefēcī patefactum TR. *open (up), clear*

pateō -ēre patuī — INTR. *be open, lie revealed*

✦**pater patris** M. *father;* M.PL. *forefathers*

paternus -a -um *of a father; ancestral*

patescō -ere patuī — INTR. *be exposed, be disclosed*

patiens (patientis) *long-lasting*

patientia -ae F. *patience, endurance*

patina -ae F. *dish*

✦**patior patī passus sum** TR. *allow, suffer; endure, put up with*

✦**patria -ae** F. *country, native land, native place*

patrius -a -um *paternal, native; ancestral*

✦**paucī -ae -a** *(a) few*

paul(l)us -a -um *small, little*

✦**pauper (pauperis)** *poor*

paupertās paupertātis F. *poverty*

paveō -ēre — — INTR./TR. *be afraid*

pavidus -a -um *frightened, trembling, timid*

pavīmentum -ī N. *floor*

✦**pax pācis** F. *peace; (IN ABL.) with all due respect, by one's leave*

peccō -āre INTR. *blunder, make a mistake*

✦**pectus pectoris** N. *breast, chest; heart*

✦**pecūnia -ae** F. *money, wealth*

✦**pecus pecoris** N. *cattle, herd, flock*

✦**pecus pecudis** F. *an individual domestic animal*

Pēgasēius -a -um *of Pegasus*

Pēgaseus -a -um *of Pegasus*

Pēgasus -ī M. *a mythological flying horse*

pelagus -ī N. *sea*

Pēlīdēs -ae M. *the son of Peleus, viz Achilles*

pellācia -ae F. *seduction*

pellicula -ae F. *(sheep)skin*

◆**pellō -ere pepulī pulsum** TR. *strike; drive away; defeat*

Penātēs Penātium M.PL. *household gods*

pendeō -ēre pependī — INTR. *hang; result (from)*

penetrāle penetrālis N. *chamber; inner(most) part*

penitus ADV. *from within*

penna -ae F. *wing; feather*

◆**per** PREP. (+ ACC.) *through; across, over, along; during; by means of, by; because of*

percutiō -ere percussī percussum TR. *strike, blast, lash*

◆**perdō -ere perdidī perditum** TR. *destroy, ruin; lose; waste*

peregrē ADV. *to foreign parts, abroad*

perennis -is -e *year-round; constant; everlasting*

◆**pereō -īre periī (-īvī) peritum** INTR. *disappear, vanish, be lost; perish, die; be ruined*

perferō perferre pertulī perlātum TR. *bear up; endure, put up with*

perfugium -(i)ī N. *refuge*

perfundō -ere perfūdī perfūsum TR. *flow through; dip*

pergō -ere perrēxī perrectum INTR. *proceed*

pergraecor -ārī INTR. *behave like a Greek, make merry*

◆**perīc(u)lum -ī** N. *danger*

perimō -ere perēmī peremptum TR. *put an end to, destroy*

Periphās Periphantis M. *a Greek warrior*

peristȳlium -iī N. *inner courtyard*

perlegō -ere perlēgī perlectum TR. *scan, read through*

permaneō -ēre permansī permansum INTR. *remain*

permātūrescō -ere permātūruī — INTR. *become fully ripe*

permētior -īrī permensus sum TR. *traverse, travel over*

permitiēs permitiēī F. *ruin*

pernumerō -āre TR. *count in full*

perpetuus -a -um *continuous; eternal;* **in perpetuum** ADV. *forever*

perrumpō -ere perrūpī perruptum TR./INTR. *break through*

Persa -ae M. *a Persian*

persequor -ī persecūtus sum TR. *follow (all the way)*

Persicus -a -um *Persian*

persōna -ae F. *mask*

perstrepō -ere — — INTR./TR. *fill with a din*

pertineō -ēre pertinuī — INTR. *refer to*

perveniō -īre pervēnī perventum INTR. *pass/get through; arrive*

perversus -a -um *reversed, backturned; depraved*

pervideō -ēre pervīdī pervīsum TR. *see fully; discern*

pervigilium -(i)ī N. *vigil*

pēs pedis M. *foot*

pessimus -a -um SUPERL. OF **malus** *worst*

petītor petītōris M. *seeker*

◆**petō -ere petīvī (-iī) petītum** TR. *seek, look for; head for; ask for, request*

pharetra -ae F. *quiver*

Pharos -ī F. *an island off the coast of Egypt near Alexandria*

Philerōs Philerōtis M. *a person named in Martial's Epigrammata*

Philo Philōnis M. *a person named in Martial's Epigrammata*

philyra -ae F. *bast (the bark of a lime tree)*

Phoebē Phoebēs GREEK F. *the goddess of the moon*

Phoebus -ī M. *another name for Apollo*

Phoenissa -ae F. *a Phoenician woman*

Phyllis Phyllidos GREEK F. *a prostitute named in Propertius' Elegies*

pīca -ae F. *magpie*

Pīeris Pīeridos GREEK F. *a Pierian woman, a Muse*

pietās pietātis F. *piety*

piger pigra pigrum *slow, sluggish; idle*

pingō -ere pinxī pictum TR. *paint*

pinguis -is -e *fat, stout; rich, fertile*

pīnus -ūs F. *pine tree; ship*

piō -āre TR. *propitiate*

pīpiō -āre — — INTR. *chirp*

Pīraeus -ī M. *the port of Athens*

Pīrēnē Pīrēnēs GREEK F. *a fountain in Corinth, associated with Pegasus and the Muses*

Pīrithous -ī M. *the son of Ixion, a friend of Theseus*

piscis piscis M. *fish*

pistrīnum -ī N. *mill*

◆**pius -a -um** *pious, good, upright, righteous, dutiful, loyal*

◆**placeō -ēre placuī (placitus sum) placitum** INTR. (+ DAT.) *please, be pleasing to, delight; placate; (OFTEN IMPERS.) be agreed upon*

placidus -a -um *kind, kindly*

plaga -ae F. *(expanse of) land*
plānē ADV. *clearly*
plangor plangōris M. *beating;*
lamentation
planta -ae F. *sole (of a foot)*
platanus -ī F. *plane tree*
Platea -ae F. a village near Bilbilis
in Spain
plausus -ūs M. *clapping, applause*
✦plebs plēbis F. *the common people*
plectō -ere — — TR. *punish*
✦plēnus -a -um (+ GEN./ABL.) *full (of),*
abounding (in)
✦pleō -ēre — — TR. *fill (up)*
plērumque ADV. *often*
plōrō -āre INTR./TR. *weep; lament*
plūma -ae F. *feather, down*
plumbum -ī N. *lead*
plūrēs plūrēs plūra PL. ADJ. *more;*
many, several
plūrimus -a -um *most, a very great*
number of
✦plūs plūris N. *more*
✦plūs ADV. *more*
Plūtō Plūtōnis GREEK M. a brother
of Jupiter, the god of the Underworld
pōculum -ī N. *cup; drink*
✦poena -ae F. *punishment*
Poenus -a -um *of Carthage, Carthaginian*
✦poēta -ae M. *poet*
poētris poētridos GREEK F. *poetess*
pol INTERJECTION *by Pollux!*
pollex pollicis M. *thumb*
pollūcibiliter ADV. *sumptuously*
polus -ī M. *sky*
pōmifer pōmifera pōmiferum
fruit-bearing
Pompōnius -(i)ī M. a person named
in Martial's *Epigrammata*
pōmum -ī N. *fruit*
pondus ponderis N. *weight*
pōne ADV. *behind*
✦pōnō -ere posuī positum TR. *place, put,*
lay; lay/set aside, lay down, shed; pitch
(camp); serve
pontifex pontificis M. *high priest*
pontus -ī M. *sea*
Pontus -ī M. *the Black Sea*
poples poplitis M. *knee*
populāris -is -e *popular*
✦pop(u)lus -ī M. *people, the populace*
pōpulus -ī F. *poplar tree*
✦porta -ae F. *gate*
portiō portiōnis F. *part, share*
portitor portitōris M. *ferryman*
portō -āre TR. *transport, carry*
✦poscō -ere poposcī — TR. *demand,*
call for; request, ask

✦possideō -ēre possēdī possessum
TR. *hold, possess; occupy; control*
✦possum posse potuī — INTR. *be able*
(to), can
✦post ADV. *later; behind; afterwards;*
PREP. (+ ACC.) *behind, after*
✦posteā ADV. *afterwards, later*
posterus -a -um *later; next, following*
postillā ADV. *afterwards*
postis postis M. *doorpost, rail (of a door)*
✦postquam CONJ. *after*
postrēmus -a -um *last, final*
postulō -āre TR. *ask for; demand,*
require
Postumus -ī M. a person addressed
in Horace's *Odes*
potens (potentis) *powerful*
potentia -ae F. *power*
✦potior -īrī (-ī) potītus sum TR./INTR.
(+ GEN./ABL.) *acquire, gain possession of,*
win; control
potior -ior -ius *better, preferable, more*
desired, more favored
potius ADV. *rather*
pōtō -āre pōtāvī pōtātum (pōtum)
TR./INTR. *drink*
pōtor pōtōris M. *drinker*
✦prae PREP. (+ ABL.) *in front of, before*
✦praebeō -ēre TR. *put forward, present;*
provide
praeceps (praecipitis) *headlong*
praeceptum -ī N. *instruction, order*
praecīdō -ere praecīdī praecīsum
TR. *cut short; remove*
✦praecipiō -ere praecēpī praeceptum
TR. *take before(hand), anticipate, begin,*
lead; advise, command
praecipitō -āre TR./INTR. *hurl down;*
plunge
praecipuē ADV. *especially*
✦praeda -ae F. *booty, plunder*
praedicō -āre TR./INTR. *declare*
praeferō praeferre praetulī praelātum
TR. *carry past; give preference to*
praefluō -ere — — INTR./TR. *flow past*
✦praemium -(i)ī N. *reward*
Praeneste Praenestis N. a town about
20 miles southeast of Rome
praeruptus -a -um *precipitous*
✦praesens (praesentis) *present, at hand;*
immediate
praeses praesidis M./F. *judge,*
adjudicator
praestans (praestantis) *superior,*
outstanding
praestō -āre praestitī (praestāvī)
praestātum (praestitum)
INTR./TR. *excel; apply to*

praestringō -ere praestrinxī praestrictum
TR. *dazzle*

✦praeter PREP. (+ ACC.) *except; beyond;*
past

✦praetereā ADV. *in addition, as well as;*
thereafter

praetereō -īre praeteriī (-īvī) praeteritum
INTR./TR. *pass by; flow past*

praetōrium -(i)ī N. *palace*

praeveniō -īre praevēnī praeventum
INTR./TR. *precede*

prandeō -ēre prandī pransum
INTR./TR. *eat breakfast/lunch*

✦precēs precum F.PL. *prayers*

precor -ārī TR. *pray (for)*

pre(he)ndō -ere pre(he)ndī pre(he)nsum
TR. *grasp, take hold of*

✦premō -ere pressī pressum TR. *press;*
propel; crush, trample on; weigh down

prensō -āre TR. *clutch at, grasp*

✦pretium -(i)ī N. *reward, payment; value,*
worth

Priamus -ī M. *Priam (the king of Troy*
when it fell to the Greeks)

prīdem ADV. *previously*

prīmum ADV. *first;* quam prīmum
as soon as possible

prīmus -a -um *first; the first part of;*
foremost

✦princeps principis M. *chief*

✦principium -(i)ī N. *beginning, origin*

✦prior prior prius *earlier, former; superior,*
better; first (of two)

priscus -a -um *ancient, old-fashioned;*
former

pristinus -a -um *former*

prius ADV. *previously, first*

priusquam CONJ. *before*

prīvātus -ī M. *private citizen*

✦prō PREP. (+ ABL.) *before; on behalf of;*
fulfilling the function of, as; in place of

proavītus -a -um *ancestral*

probē ADV. *thoroughly*

✦probō -āre TR. *approve (of)*

procella -ae F. *storm*

✦procul ADV. *at a distance, far away*

prōcumbō -ere prōcubuī prōcubitum
INTR. *bow down, fall down, collapse,*
prostrate oneself

prōdeō -īre prōdiī prōditum
INTR. *come forth*

prōdigium -iī N. *monstrosity*

✦prōdō -ere prōdidī prōditum TR. *give*
rise to, produce; give up; betray; hand
down, transmit

✦proelium -(i)ī N. *battle*

prōferō prōferre prōtulī prōlātum
TR. *bring forth; extend*

prōficiō -ere prōfēcī prōfectum
INTR. *achieve, progress*

✦prōficiscor -ī profectus sum
INTR. *start out; originate (from)*

profugus -a -um *fleeing, fleeting*

profugus -ī M. *exile*

profundus -a -um *bottommost;*
boundless

prōgnātus -a -um *born (of);*
NOUN *child; son, daughter*

✦prohibeō -ēre TR. *prevent; hinder,*
restrain

proinde ADV. *in the same way (as)*

prōluō -ere prōluī prōlūtum TR. *wash*
thoroughly, douse

Promēthīdēs -ae M. *Deucalion, the son*
of Prometheus

prōmissum -ī N. *promise*

prōmittō -ere prōmīsī prōmissum
TR. *send forth, let loose; let grow long;*
promise

prōnus -a -um *lying face down, prone*

✦prope ADV. *near(by), close; nearly;*
PREP. (+ ACC.) *near (to)*

properō -āre INTR./TR. *hurry, hasten*

prophētia -ae F. *prophecy*
(NONCLASSICAL)

prōpōnō -ere prōposuī prōpositum
TR. *exhibit, set forth*

✦propter PREP. (+ ACC.) *on account of*

✦proptereā ADV. *therefore*

prōrumpō -ere prōrūpī prōruptum
INTR./TR. *burst forth*

proscaenium -(i)ī N. *stage*

prōsequor -ī prōsecūtus sum TR. *escort,*
accompany

Prōserpina -ae F. *the wife of Pluto,*
queen of the Underworld

prospectō -āre TR./INTR. *watch, gaze*
out at

prospiciō -ere prospexī prospectum
TR./INTR. *watch*

prostituō -ere prostituī prostitūtum
TR. *put to an unworthy use, prostitute*

prostrātus -a -um *flat, prostrate*

prōsum prōdesse prōfuī — INTR. *be of*
use, benefit

prōterō -ere prōtrīvī prōtrītum
TR. *trample on*

prōtinus ADV. *immediately, without*
hesitation, from the start

prōverbium -iī N. *proverb*

prōvidus -a -um *prophetic; prudent*

✦proximus -a -um *nearest, neighboring;*
next (to); last (in time)

prūdens (prūdentis) *prudent, sensible*

pruīnōsus -a -um *frosty, dewy*

psittacus -ī M. *parrot*

-pte PARTICLE ATTACHED TO A
PERSONAL PRON. OR POSS. ADJ.
FOR EMPHASIS

pūbēs pūbis F. *force* (*of men*)

pūblicum -ī N. *public, the open*

pudīcus -a -um *chaste*

◆pudor pudōris M. (*feeling of*) *shame,
scruple; modesty; honor; restraint*

◆puella -ae F. *girl; sweetheart, girlfriend;
nymph*

◆puer puerī M. *boy; male slave;*
(PL.) *children*

puerīlis -is -e *childish*

pugil pugilis M. *boxer*

◆pugna -ae F. *fight, battle*

◆pugnō -āre INTR. *fight*

◆pulcher pulchra pulchrum *beautiful,
handsome, fair; good*

pullus -a -um *dark*

pulsō -āre TR. *strike, beat*

pulverulentus -a -um *dusty*

pulvis pulveris M. *dust*

pūmex pūmicis M. *pumice, rock*

◆pūniō -īre TR. *punish; avenge*

puppis puppis F. *stern; deck; ship*

pūriter ADV. *cleanly*

purpureus -a -um *purple, crimson*

◆putō -āre TR. *think, consider, suppose*

Pȳramus -ī M. *the sweetheart of Thisbe*

Pȳrēnaeus -a -um *of the Pyrenees*

Pȳrēnē Pȳrēnēs GREEK F. *the Pyrenees*

Pyrrha -ae F. *the wife of Deucalion*

Pyrrhus -ī M. *a son of Achilles*

Q

quadrupēs quadrupedis M./F./N.
(*four-footed*) *animal;* ADJ. *four-footed*

◆quaerō -ere quaesīvī (-iī) quaesītum
TR. *seek, look for; ask, make inquiries;
acquire, win*

quaesō [quaesere] — — TR./INTR. *ask,
seek*

◆quālis -is -e *what* (*kind of*); *of which sort;
just as*

quāliter *just as*

◆quam ADV. *in what way; how; as, than*

quam prīmum ADV. *as soon as possible*

◆quamquam CONJ. *although, however much*

◆quamvīs CONJ. *although, even though,
however much*

◆quandō ADV. *ever;* CONJ. *when?*

quandōquidem CONJ. *since*

quantum ADV. *as much* (*as*)

◆quantus -a -um *how much, how great;
as much as*

◆quāque SEE usque

◆quārē ADV. *how?; why?; whereby,
wherefore*

◆quasi ADV./CONJ. *as if, as though*

quater ADV. *four times*

quatiō -ere — quassum TR. *shake*

quattuor *four*

◆-que CONJ. *and*

... -que ... -que CONJ. *both ... and ...*

◆queō quīre quīvī (-iī) — INTR. *be able*

quercus -ūs F. *oak tree*

querella -ae F. *complaint*

◆queror querī questus sum
INTR./TR. *complain* (*of*)

questus -ūs M. *complaint*

◆quī (quis) quae (qua) quod (quid) REL./
INTERR./INDEF. PRON./ADJ. *who, which;
which?, what kind of?; what, that*

◆quia CONJ. *because*

quīcumque quaecumque quodcumque
INDEF. PRON./ADJ. *whoever, whatever,
whichever*

◆quid ADV. *why?, how?; well*

quīdam quaedam quiddam (quoddam)
PRON./ADJ. *a certain person/thing;
someone*

◆quidem ADV. *indeed, even; but*

◆quiēs quiētis F. *rest, quiet; sleep*

quiescō -ere quiēvī quiētum
INTR. *subside; grow/become quiet*

quiētus -a -um *quiet, at rest*

quīlibet quaelibet quidlibet
PRON. *anyone/anything at all*

quīlubet quaelubet quidlubet
SEE quīlibet

◆quīn ADV./CONJ. *indeed, in fact; but that,
that ... not*

quinque *five*

Quintilius -iī M. *a person whose death
is mourned in Horace's Odes*

quintus -a -um *fifth*

Quintus -ī M. *a person addressed in
Martial's Epigrammata*

Quirīnus -ī M. *another name for
Romulus*

Quirītēs Quirītium M.PL. *Roman citizens*

quis quis quid SEE quī

quisquam quisquam quicquam
(quidquam) PRON. *any*(*one*),
any(*thing*)

quisque quaeque quidque (quodque)
PRON./ADJ. *each* (*person*), *every* (*person*)

quisquis quisquis quidquid
GENERALIZING REL. PRON./ADJ.
whoever, whatever

◆quō ADV. (*to*) *where?; how far?; to which
*(*place*); *where*

quōcumque ADV. *wherever*

quod CONJ. *because; with regard to the fact
that*

quod sī CONJ. *but if*

quōminus (quō ... minus) CONJ.
   so that ... not

✦quondam ADV. *once, formerly*

✦quoniam CONJ. *because, since*

✦quoque ADV. *also, too*

✦quot INDECL. PL. ADJ. *how many?;*
   as many as

quotiens ADV. *whenever*

quotquot INDECL. PL. ADJ. *however many*

R

rabidus -a -um *raging*

rabiēs -ēī F. *ferocity*

radius -(i)ī M. *(pointed) rod; ray*

rādix rādīcis F. *root*

rādō -ere rāsī rāsum TR. *scrape, scratch;*
   shave

rāmus -ī M. *branch*

rapidus -a -um *swift*

rapīna -ae F. *plundering; plunder*

✦rapiō -ere rapuī raptum TR. *seize, snatch*
   away, carry off; hurry, dash

raptō -āre TR. *carry off (in order to ravish)*

raptus -ūs M. *abduction*

✦rārus -a -um *uncommon, rare*

ratiō ratiōnis F. *reason, argument*

ratis ratis F. *ship, boat*

raucus -a -um *hoarse; raucous, noisy,*
   harsh(-sounding), screeching

Ravenna -ae F. *a city in northern Italy*

recēdō -ere recessī recessum
   INTR. *withdraw, go away*

recens (recentis) *recent, fresh*

recingō -ere recinxī recinctum
   TR. *unfasten, ungird*

recipiō -ere recēpī receptum TR. *receive,*
   admit

recitātiō recitātiōnis F. *reading aloud,*
   recitation

recitō -āre TR. *recite*

reclūdō -ere reclūsī reclūsum TR. *open*

recolligō -ere recollēgī recollectum
   TR. *gather up again*

recondō -ere recondidī reconditum
   TR. *put back; close again*

rector rectōris M. *helmsman*

recurrō -ere recurrī recursum
   INTR. *come back; hurry back*

recurvus -a -um *bent, curved*

recūsō -āre INTR./TR. *refuse*

✦reddō -ere reddidī redditum
   TR. *give back; hand over, deliver; render;*
   cause to be, produce

✦redeō -īre rediī reditum INTR. *go back,*
   return

reditus -ūs M. *return*

redūcō -ere reduxī reductum
   TR. *bring back*

redux (reducis) *returning, having returned*

referō referre rettulī relātum
   TR. *mention, repeat; bring back; recall*

reficiō -ere refēcī refectum TR. *restore,*
   remodel

refugiō -ere refūgī — INTR./TR. *flee back*

refulgeō -ēre refulsī — INTR. *shine,*
   gleam; appear

✦rēgīna -ae F. *queen*

✦regiō regiōnis F. *area, district, region*

✦regnō -āre INTR. *reign, rule; control*

✦regnum -ī N. *kingdom; royal power;*
   tyranny

✦regō -ere rexī rectum TR. *guide, manage,*
   steer; rule, govern; drive; determine

rēiciō -ere rēiēcī rēiectum TR. *throw*
   back; cast off

relegō -ere relēgī relectum TR. *pick up*
   again; read again

relevō -āre TR. *relieve, lighten*

✦relinquō -ere relīquī relictum
   TR. *leave (behind), abandon; leave*
   as an inheritance; disregard

remaneō -ēre remansī — INTR. *stay*
   behind

remittō -ere remīsī remissum
   TR. *send back; concede, leave; slacken*

remollescō -ere — — INTR. *become soft;*
   relent

remoror -ārī INTR./TR. *delay*

remōtus -a -um *distant*

removeō -ēre remōvī remōtum
   TR. *remove, banish*

rēmus -ī M. *oar*

renīdeō -ēre — — INTR. *smile back (at)*

renovō -āre TR. *recondition, restore; recall*

✦reor rērī ratus sum INTR. *think*

reparābilis -is -e *able to be restored*

reparō -āre TR. *recover, make good;*
   rebuild, renew

repellō -ere reppulī repulsum TR. *drive*
   away; strike

repente ADV. *suddenly*

reperiō -īre repperī repertum TR. *find,*
   discover

repertor repertōris M. *inventor, creator*

repetō -ere repetīvī (-iī) repetītum
   TR. *return to; take back; reflect on,*
   go back over

repōnō -ere reposuī repos(i)tum
   TR. *replace; pay back; retaliate*

reposcō -ere — — TR. *demand, claim*

reptō -āre INTR. *crawl*

repulsa -ae F. *rebuff*

requiēs requiētis (ACC. USUALLY requiem)
   F. *rest*

requiescō -ere requiēvī requiētum
   INTR. *take repose, rest, get a rest*

requīrō -ere requīsīvī (-iī) requīsītum
   TR. *seek (out), look for; ask; want*
♦**rēs reī** F. *thing; matter, business; property;*
   *wealth; (*PL.*) the world; the universe;*
   circumstances; actions
resecō -āre [resecuī] resectum
   TR. *cut short*
resīdō -ere resēdī (resīdī) —
   INTR. *sit down*
resistō -ere restitī — INTR. *stop, resist;*
   rise again, be restored
resolvō -ere resolvī resolūtum
   TR. *loosen, untie*
♦**respiciō -ere respexī respectum**
   TR./INTR. *look back (at), take notice (of),*
   see
respondeō -ēre respondī responsum
   INTR. *reply, answer; respond (to)*
responsum -ī N. *reply, answer (given by*
   an oracle)
respuō -ere respuī — TR. *reject*
restinguō -ere restinxī restinctum
   TR. *extinguish*
♦**restituō -ere restituī restitūtum**
   TR. *restore, revive, bring back*
restō -āre restitī — INTR. *remain*
resupīnō -āre TR. *pull back*
resupīnus -a -um *lying face upwards*
retineō -ēre retinuī retentum
   TR. *hold (fast), keep*
retrō ADV. *back, backwards*
reus -ī M. *defendant*
revellō -ere revellī (revulsī) revulsum
   (revolsum) TR. *tear away*
revertor -ī reversus sum INTR. *return*
revīsō -ere — — TR./INTR. *visit again*
♦**rex rēgis** M. *king, ruler*
rictus -ūs M. *open mouth/jaws*
♦**rīdeō -ēre rīsī rīsum** INTR./TR. *laugh*
   (at); smile (at)
rigidus -a -um *stiff*
rigor rigōris M. *rigidity*
rīma -ae F. *crack*
rīpa -ae F. *river bank*
rīsus -ūs M. *laughter*
rōbur rōboris N. *oak (tree), timber;*
   strength
rōbustus -a -um *vigorous, robust*
♦**rogō -āre** TR. *ask, request; ask for sexual*
   favors
rogus -ī M. *funeral pyre*
Rōma -ae F. *Rome*
Rōmānus -a -um *Roman*
Rōmulus -a -um *Roman*
rosa -ae F. *rose*
roscidus -a -um *dewy*
Roscius -(i)ī M. *a person named in a*
   poem of Catulus

rota -ae F. *wheel*
rubeō -ēre — — INTR. *be red*
ruber rubra rubrum *red;*
   mare Rubrum *the Red Sea;*
   lītus Rubrum *the Red Sea coast*
rudens rudentis M. *rope*
rudis -is -e *primitive, unrefined*
rūga -ae F. *wrinkle*
♦**ruīna -ae** F. *fall, downfall, collapse,*
   destruction, devastation; PL. *ruins*
rūmor rūmōris M. *noise; gossip, rumor*
♦**rumpō -ere rūpī ruptum** TR. *break, burst,*
   break through, cleave, force; overcome;
   disturb
♦**ruō ruere ruī —** INTR./TR. *rush, hurry*
   on; fall, collapse; pour down; cause to rush
rūpēs rūpis F. *cliff*
♦**rursum (rursus)** ADV. *again; back(wards);*
   on the other hand
♦**rūs rūris** N. *country; land; country estate*
russus -a -um *red*
rusticitās rusticitātis F. *coarseness*
rusticus -a -um *rustic, peasant*
rusticus -ī M. *peasant*
rutilō -āre INTR./TR. *glow red*

S

Sabidius -(i)ī M. *a person addressed*
   in Martial's Epigrammata
Sabīnus -ī M. *a Sabine*
sacculus -ī M. *little purse*
♦**sacer sacra sacrum** *sacred*
sacerdōs sacerdōtis M./F. *priest,*
   priestess
sacrō -āre TR. *consecrate, hallow*
♦**sacrum -ī** N. *ceremony, rite; festival*
♦**saec(u)lum -ī** N. *lifetime, generation; age,*
   period of time, year
♦**saepe** ADV. *often*
saepēs saepis F. *fence*
saeviō -īre saeviī saevītum INTR. *rage*
saevitia -ae F. *cruelty; violence*
♦**saevus -a -um** *fierce, savage, cruel, wild*
sagitta -ae F. *arrow*
sāl salis M. *salt; sea; wit*
salictum -ī N. *willow grove*
salīva -ae F. *saliva; foam*
salsus -a -um *salty*
salūber salūbris salūbre *healthy*
♦**salūs salūtis** F. *safety, welfare*
♦**salūtō -āre** TR. *greet, address, call on,*
   salute
♦**salvē salvēte** IMP. *hail! hello!*
♦**salvus -a -um** *safe, secure; alive*
sānē ADV. *certainly*
♦**sanguis sanguinis** M. *blood*
♦**sānus -a -um** *healthy; sane, rational;*
   unharmed

sapiens (sapientis) *wise*

sapientia -ae F. *wisdom*

sapiō -ere sapīvī (-iī) — INTR. *be wise*

✦sat (satis) INDECL. N./ADJ. (+ GEN.) *sufficient, enough (of)*; ADV. *sufficiently, adequately, enough*

satura -ae F. *satire*

Sāturnus -ī M. *Saturn*, the father of Jupiter

sauciō -āre TR. *wound*

saxeus -a -um *stony*

✦saxum -ī N. *stone, rock; reef; tombstone*

scelerātus -a -um *guilty*

scelestus -a -um *wretched*

✦scelus sceleris N. *crime; calamity*

sceptrifer sceptrifera sceptriferum *bearing a scepter*

sceptrum -ī N. *scepter*

scīlicet ADV. *certainly, of course, in fact*

scindō -ere s(ci)cidī scissum TR. *split*

✦sciō scīre sciī (-īvī) scītum TR. *know*

Scīpiadās -ae M. one of the Scipios, usually *Publius Cornelius Scipio Africanus*

Scīpiō Scīpiōnis M. a cognomen of the gens Cornēlia; the Roman general who, by defeating Hannibal in 202 B.C., brought the Second Carthaginian War to an end

scirpus -ī M. *bulrush*

scopulus -ī M. *rock*

scortum -ī N. *prostitute*

Scrateius -ī M. the second name of the husband of Helvia Prima (Verse Epitaph C)

✦scrībō -ere scrīpsī scrīptum TR. *write; compose*

scriptor scriptōris M. *writer*

scrūtor -ārī TR. *examine; explore*

scurra -ae M. *smart aleck, man about town*

Scȳrius -a -um *of Scyros* (a small island in the northern Aegean Sea)

Scythicus -a -um *Scythian*

✦sē (sēsē) suī sibi sē (sēsē) 3RD-PERS. REFL. PRON.

secō -āre secuī sectum TR. *cut*

sēcrētus -a -um *secluded, hidden*

sector -ārī TR. *pursue; hunt for*

secundus -a -um *(a) second; favorable, successful*

sēcūrus -a -um *carefree*

✦sed CONJ. *but, however*

✦sedeō -ēre sēdī sessum INTR. *sit; be idle; be settled*

✦sēdēs sēdis F. *seat; dwelling place, home, abode; position*

sēditiō sēditiōnis F. *discord, rebellion*

sēdō -āre TR. *relieve, calm down; quench*

sēdulus -a -um *painstaking, earnest*

seges segetis F. *crop*

segmentātus -a -um *decorated*

✦semel ADV. *once, just (once), a single time; once and for all*

sēmen sēminis N. *seed; offspring*

sēmibōs (sēmibovis) *half-bull*

sēmipāgānus -ī M. *half-peasant*

Semīramis Semīramidis F. a legendary queen of Babylon

sēmita -ae F. *path, alley*

sēmivir (sēmivirī) *half-man*

✦semper ADV. *always, constantly*

senātor senātōris M. *member of the Roman senate, senator*

senecta -ae F. *old age*

senectūs senectūtis F. *old age*

✦senex senis M. *old man*; ADJ. *old*

sēnī -ae -a PL. ADJ. *six each*

senium -iī N. *old age*

sensus sensūs M. *emotion; sense, judgment*

sententia -ae F. *a terse and pointed expression; opinion*

sentīna -ae F. *bilge (water)*

✦sentiō -īre sensī sensum TR./INTR. *feel, perceive; get an inkling of*

sentus -a -um *rough, squalid*

septemgeminus -a -um *sevenfold*

septimus -a -um *seventh*

sepulc(h)rum -ī N. *tomb*

sequax (sequācis) *pliant*

✦sequor sequī secūtus sum TR. *follow, accompany; chase, pursue*

sera -ae F. *bar (for a door)*

serēnus -a -um *calm*

Sergiolus -ī DIMINUTIVE OF Sergius M. a gladiator named in Juvenal's *Satires*

sermō sermōnis M. *speech, words; conversation*

✦serō -ere sēvī satum TR. *plant, sow*

sērō ADV. *late*

✦serta -ōrum N.PL. *garlands*

sērus -a -um *late, later; slow*

✦serviō -īre INTR. (+ DAT.) *be a slave (of), be subject (to)*

servitūs servitūtis F. *slavery, bondage*

servō -āre TR. *watch, guard; keep*

✦servus -ī M. *slave*

Sētīnus -a -um *of Setia* (noted for its wine)

✦seu (sīve) CONJ. *or if*

seu ... seu ... *whether ... or ...*

sevērus -a -um *strict, narrow-minded*

sextus -a -um *sixth*

✦sī CONJ. *if*

◆ sīc ADV. *so, thus; in such a way; to such a degree*

siccō -āre TR. *dry (up)*

siccus -a -um *dry*

Sicilia -ae F. *Sicily*

Siculus -a -um *Sicilian*

◆ sīcut CONJ. *as, just as*

Sīdonius -a -um *of Sidon (a city on the Phoenician coast famous for its purple dye)*

sīdus sīderis N. *heavenly body, star; constellation*

signō -āre TR. *imprint, stamp*

signum -ī N. *sign*

silens (silentis) *silent, quiet*

silentium -(i)ī N. *silence*

sileō -ēre siluī — INTR. *be quiet*

silex silicis M./F. *flint, hard rock*

◆ silva -ae F. *forest, woods, grove*

◆ similis -is -e *similar, like*

Simoīs Simoentis M. *a river near Troy*

simplex (simplicis) *plain*

simplicitās simplicitātis F. *simplicity, plainness, openness*

◆ simul ADV. *at the same time, together;* CONJ. *as soon as*

simulācrum -ī N. *image; ghost*

simulō -āre TR. *imitate*

sīn CONJ. *but if*

◆ sine PREP. (+ ABL.) *without*

◆ sinister sinistra sinistrum *left, on the left-hand side; unfavorable*

◆ sinō -ere sīvī (siī) situm TR. *allow; let be*

sinus -ūs M. *fold (of cloth); bosom*

◆ sistō -ere stetī (stitī) statum TR. *stop, halt; erect; station*

Sīsyphus -ī M. *a king of Corinth proverbial for his trickery*

sitiō -īre — — INTR. *be thirsty*

sitis sitis F. *thirst*

situs -a -um *buried*

situs -ūs M. *neglect, deterioration*

◆ sīve (seu) CONJ. *or if*

sīve … sīve … *whether … or …*

sōbrius -a -um *sober*

sociō -āre TR. *unite; share*

◆ socius -(i)ī M. *companion, ally*

◆ sōl sōlis M. *sun*

◆ soleō -ēre solitus sum INTR. *be accustomed (to)*

sōligena -ae M. *offspring of the Sun*

solitus -a -um *usual, accustomed*

sollertia -ae F. *cleverness*

sollicitus -a -um *anxious, restless, worried, troubled*

sōlor -ārī TR. *comfort*

solum -ī N. *floor; ground, soil*

◆ sōlus -a -um *alone; lonely*

solvō -ere solvī solūtum TR. *loosen; (set) free; banish; pay; explain*

somniō -āre INTR. *dream*

◆ somnium -(i)ī N. *dream*

◆ somnus -ī M. *sleep*

sonipēs sonipedis M. *horse;* ADJ. *making noise with the feet*

sonitus -ūs M. *sound, noise*

◆ sonō -āre sonuī sonitum INTR./TR. *make a noise; utter (a sound); ring, resound*

sonus -ī M. *sound, noise*

sophōs INTERJECTION *bravo!*

sōpiō -īre TR. *put to sleep*

sopor sopōris M. *sleep*

sordidus -a -um *dirty, grimy*

◆ soror sorōris F. *sister*

◆ sors sortis F. *destiny, fate; oracle; lot*

sortilegus -ī M. *soothsayer*

sospes (sospitis) *free of troubles, safe and sound*

spargō -ere sparsī sparsum TR. *sprinkle, scatter, splash, spray, spread over*

spatior -ārī INTR. *walk leisurely, stroll; roam*

◆ spatium -iī N. *area, space; distance; (period of) time*

spectāc(u)lum -ī N. *sight, spectacle*

◆ spectō -āre TR. *watch, look (at)*

◆ spērō -āre TR. *hope (for/to/that)*

◆ spēs speī F. *hope*

spīnōsus -a -um *thorny*

spīra -ae F. *spiral, coil*

spīritus -ūs M. *spirit, soul*

spīrō -āre INTR./TR. *breathe*

spissus -a -um *dense*

splendeō -ēre — — INTR. *shine*

splendidus -a -um *bright; august*

sponte WITH POSS. ADJ. OR GEN. NOUN *of (one's) own accord, in accordance with*

spūmō -āre INTR. *foam*

squāmeus -a -um *scaly*

stabiliō -īre stabilīvī stabilītum TR. *make steady*

stabulum -ī N. *stable*

stagnum -ī N. *pool, swamp*

◆ statim ADV. *immediately*

statiō statiōnis F. *guard duty*

statuō -ere statuī statūtum TR. *decide*

stella -ae F. *star*

sterilis -is -e *barren, sterile*

◆ sternō -ere strāvī strātum TR. *spread, scatter; pave; overthrow*

stillō -āre INTR. *drip; weep*

stipula -ae F. *straw*

stirps stirpis F. *offspring*

+ **stō stāre stetī statum** INTR. *stand, be standing, be set up; stand out*
stomachus -ī M. *stomach*
strāgēs strāgis F. *destruction, devastation*
strātum -ī N. *bed*
strēnuus -a -um *vigorous, active*
strepitus -ūs M. *sound*
strīdō -ere strīdī — INTR. *hiss*
stringō -ere strinxī strictum TR. *confine; graze, scratch*
strophium -iī N. *band supporting a woman's breasts*
struēs struis F. *pile*
struō -ere struxī structum TR. *put together, assemble; compose*
studeō -ēre studuī — INTR. *devote oneself to; study; concentrate on*
studium -(i)ī N. *pursuit, activity*
stultitia -ae F. *folly, stupidity*
stultus -a -um *foolish*
stupeō -ēre stupuī — INTR. *be amazed, be stunned; be powerless*
stupor stupōris M. *folly*
Stygius -a -um *of the river Styx*
Styx Stygis F. *the river Styx (one of the Underworld rivers)*
suādeō -ēre suāsī suāsum TR./INTR. *counsel, recommend*
+ **suāvis -is -e** *sweet, pleasant*
suāviter ADV. *sweetly*
+ **sub** PREP. (+ ACC.) *up to, under, down into;* (+ ABL.) *under, beneath, in front of; by; during*
subdō -ere subdidī subditum TR. *place under*
subdūcō -ere subduxī subductum TR. *remove (from), withdraw (from)*
subeō -īre subiī (-īvī) subitum INTR./TR. *go under; come; go up*
subf- SEE **suff-**
subiciō -ere subiēcī subiectum TR. *place underneath*
subiectus -a -um *submissive, subject (to)*
subitō ADV. *suddenly*
subitus -a -um *sudden*
sublīmis -is -e *lofty, elevated; majestic*
subolēs subolis F. *offspring*
subp- SEE ALSO **supp-**
subpōnō -ere subposuī subpositum TR. *place under*
subsecō -āre subsecuī subsectum TR. *cut off, trim*
subsellium -(i)ī N. *bench*
subsīdō -ere subsēdī (subsīdī) — INTR./TR. *sink*
subter PREP. (+ ACC.) *under, at the base of*

subtīlis -is -e *fine, finely woven*
subtrahō -ere subtraxī subtractum TR. *drag away, withdraw*
Subūra -ae F. *an area of Rome northeast of the Forum*
succēdō -ere sucessī successum INTR. *advance, move up (to)*
successus -ūs M. *success*
sūdātrix (sūdātrīcis) *sweaty*
sūdor sūdōris M. *sweat*
sufferō sufferre sustulī sublātum TR. *raise; withstand*
sufficiō -ere suffēcī suffectum TR./INTR. (+ DAT.) *manage; be available for; be enough*
sufflāmen sufflāminis N. *brake (a bar used for braking a wheeled vehicle)*
+ **suī** SEE **sē**
sulcus -ī M. *furrow*
Sulla -ae M. *a Roman dictator (c. 138–78 B.C.)*
Sulmo Sulmōnis M. *a town 90 miles east of Rome in central Italy, the birthplace of Ovid*
+ **sum esse fuī** — INTR. *be; exist*
summa -ae F. *total*
+ **summus -a -um** *highest; greatest, at the top; final*
+ **sūmō -ere sumpsī sumptum** TR. *take, take up; put on; consume, eat*
sumptus -ūs M. *expenditure*
+ **super** ADV. *over, above, more than;* PREP. (+ ACC./ABL.) *over, above; beyond; besides*
+ **superbus -a -um** *proud; splendid; noble*
supercilium -(i)ī N. *eyebrow*
+ **superior -ior -ius** *higher, upper; earlier*
+ **superō -āre** TR. *overcome; surpass; be left, survive*
superstes (superstitis) *surviving*
supersum superesse superfuī — INTR. *remain, be left (from)*
+ **superus -a -um** *upper, on earth;* M.PL. *gods dwelling in the upper world (as distinct from the* **inferī,** *the gods of the Underworld)*
supervacuus -a -um *superfluous; pointless*
suppetō -ere suppetīvī (-iī) — INTR. (+ DAT.) *back up*
suppleō -ēre supplēvī supplētum TR. *fill*
+ **suprā** ADV. *above, on top;* PREP. (+ ACC.) *on top of, over*
suprēmus -a -um *last, final*
surdus -a -um *deaf*
+ **surgō -ere surrexī surrectum** INTR. *rise, get up (from bed)*
suspendō -ere suspendī suspensum TR. *hang; raise*

suspiciō -ere suspexī suspectum
  TR. *glance up (at)*
sustineō -ēre sustinuī — TR. *support,*
  hold up; put up with, endure
✦**suus -a -um** 3RD-PERS. REFL. POSS.
  ADJ. *his, her, its, their (own)*
Sychaeus -ī M. *the husband of Dido*
Syphax Syphācis M. *a Numidian prince*
  at the time of the Second Carthaginian
  War
Syria -ae F. *Syria*
Syrtis Syrtis F. (ESPECIALLY PL.)
  shallows in the Mediterranean Sea
  southeast of Carthage

T

tabella -ae F. *tablet; picture*
taberna -ae F. *inn, shop*
✦**taceō -ēre** INTR./TR. *be silent (about)*
tacitus -a -um *silent, quiet*
taeda -ae F. *pinewood; pine torch*
taedium -(i)ī N. *boredom; trash*
Taenara -orum N.PL. *a promontory in*
  Laconia with a cave leading down to the
  Underworld
Taenarius -a -um *of Taenara*
Tagus -ī M. *a river in Spain noted for its*
  alluvial gold
✦**tālis -is -e** *such, of such a kind, even so*
tālus -ī M. *ankle*
✦**tam** ADV. *so, to such a degree, such*
✦**tamen** ADV. *however, nevertheless, yet*
✦**tamquam** CONJ. *just as, in the same*
  way as
✦**tandem** ADV. *finally, after some time*
✦**tangō -ere tetigī tactum** TR. *touch; reach*
tantum ADV. *only*
✦**tantus -a -um** *so great, so much, as much*
tardē ADV. *slowly*
tardō -āre TR./INTR. *delay*
tardus -a -um *slow, sluggish, moving slowly,*
  long-drawn-out
Tarpēius -a -um *Tarpeian (used of the*
  Capitoline Hill)
Tartara -ōrum N. PL. *Tartarus*
  (the lowest part of the Underworld)
Tatius -(i)ī M. *co-regent of Rome with*
  Romulus
taurus -ī M. *bull*
tectum -ī N. *roof; building, palace*
✦**tegō -ere texī tectum** TR. *cover, hide;*
  shield
Tēia -ae F. *a prostitute named in*
  Propertius' Elegies
Tēlephus -ī M. *the son of Heracles and*
  Auge, king of Mysia, wounded and
  healed by Achilles
✦**tellūs tellūris** F. *land, ground; the earth*

✦**tēlum -ī** N. *spear, missile; weapon*
temerō -āre TR. *violate*
tēmō tēmōnis M. *pole*
temperō -āre INTR./TR. *exercise*
  moderation; direct; modulate
tempestās tempestātis F. *season;*
  (period of) time
✦**templum -ī** N. *temple; region, area,*
  open space; oracle
temptō -āre TR. *try, try out, attempt, test;*
  touch; attack
✦**tempus temporis** N. *time; period of time,*
  age; temple (of the head); circumstances
  (at a particular time)
tendō -ere tetendī tentum (tensum)
  TR./INTR. *stretch; be inclined; strive*
tenebrae -ārum F.PL. *darkness, shades*
tenebricōsus -a -um *gloomy*
Tenedos -ī F. *an island off the coast of*
  Asia Minor
✦**teneō -ēre tenuī tentum** TR. *hold (to),*
  cling (to); stick with; catch; occupy; keep,
  maintain; restrain, prevent; live in
✦**tener tenera tenerum** *tender, delicate;*
  young
tenuis -is -e *slender, small, thin, light,*
  narrow; insubstantial; subtle; frail
tepeō -ēre — INTR. *be warm*
ter ADV. *thrice, three times*
teres (teretis) *smooth*
✦**Tēreus Tēreī** M. *a king of Thrace, the*
  husband of Philomela
✦**tergum -ī** N. *back, rear; hide, skin*
terō -ere trīvī trītum TR. *tread*
✦**terra -ae** F. *land, earth, ground, soil;*
  world
✦**terreō -ēre** TR. *frighten, terrify*
tertius -a -um *third*
testis testis M./F. *witness*
testūdō testūdinis F. *tortoise; tortoise*
  shell, lyre
Tēthys Tēthyos GREEK F. *the wife of*
  Oceanus, queen of the seas
Thalīa -ae F. *the muse of comedy and*
  light verse
theātrum -ī N. *theater*
Themis Themidos GREEK F. *the goddess*
  of justice
Themistoclēs Themistoclis M. *an*
  Athenian statesman (c. 524–c. 460 B.C.)
Theotīmus -ī M. *a person named in a*
  poem of Catulus
thermae -ārum F.PL. *hot baths*
Thēsēis Thēsēidis GREEK F. *an epic*
  about Theseus
Thēseus Thēseī GREEK M. *a hero of Attic*
  legend
Thēsēus -a -um *of Theseus*

Thisbē Thisbēs GREEK F. the sweetheart
of Pyramus
Thrēicius -a -um *Thracian*
Thressa (Thressae) F. ADJ. *Thracian*
thronus -ī M. *throne*
Thūlē Thūlēs GREEK F. a fabled land in
the far north
Thūrīnus -a -um *of Thurii (a city in
southern Italy)*
Tiberis Tiberis M. *the Tiber River*
tībia -ae F. *flute*
Tibullus -ī M. a Roman elegiac poet
(c. 50–19 B.C.)
Tībur Tīburis N. a country retreat near
Rome
Tīburs Tīburtis M. *a Tiburtine, an
inhabitant of Tibur*
tigris tigris F. *tiger*
◆ timeō -ēre timuī — INTR./TR. *fear,
be afraid (of)*
timidus -a -um *timid, fearful, frightened;
cowardly*
◆ timor timōris M. *fear*
tingō -ere tinxī tinctum TR. *wet, dip;
stain; dye*
tintinō -āre — — INTR. *ring*
Tītānia -ae F. *daughter of a Titan*
Tīthōnia -ae F. *Aurora, the wife of
Tithonus*
titulus -ī M. *inscription; epitaph*
Tityos -ī GREEK M. a giant punished
in the Underworld
Tītyrus -ī M. a herdsman named in
Vergil's *Eclogues*
toga -ae F. *toga*
togātus -a -um *wearing a toga;* fābula
togāta *Latin comedy*
◆ tollō -ere sustulī sublātum TR. *raise;
remove, take; destroy*
tonō -āre tonuī — INTR. *thunder*
torpeō -ēre torpuī — INTR. *be numb,
become numb; be paralyzed*
Torquātus -ī M. a person addressed in
Horace's *Odes;* a Roman consul
torqueō -ēre torsī tortum TR. *turn, wind
up; torture*
torreō -ēre torruī tostum TR. *scorch,
burn, set fire to*
torus -ī M. *couch, bed*
torvus -a -um *grim, stern, fierce*
◆ tot INDECL. ADJ. *so many, as many*
totidem INDECL. ADJ. *as many*
totiens ADV. *as often, so often, so many
times*
◆ tōtus -a -um *entire, the whole (of), all*
trabs trabis F. *panel (of a door)*
tractō -āre TR. *stroke, handle*
tractus -ūs M. *pulling*

trādō -ere trādidī trāditum
TR. *hand over/down, surrender, consign;
report, relate*
trādūcō -ere trāduxī trāductum
TR. *bring across/over*
◆ trahō -ere traxī tractum
TR. *draw; drag (off)*
trāiciō -ere trāiēcī trāiectum
TR. *throw across; shoot, pierce*
tranquillus -a -um *calm, peaceful*
◆ trans PREP. (+ ACC.) *across, over*
transeō -īre transīvī (-iī) transitum
INTR./TR. *come/go across, cross;
pass over*
transigō -ere transēgī transactum
TR./INTR. *pass/spend (time)*
transiliō -īre transiluī —
INTR./TR. *jump over*
transitus -ūs M. *passage*
transmittō -ere transmīsī transmissum
TR./INTR. *send over; cross*
Transpadānus -ī M. *a Transpadane,
person living north of the Po River*
trecēnī -ae -a PL. ADJ. *three hundred
each*
tremebundus -a -um *trembling*
tremefaciō -ere tremefēcī tremefactum
TR. *make tremble*
tremō -ere tremuī —
INTR./TR. *tremble (at)*
tremulus -a -um *trembling, shaking*
trepidus -a -um *anxious*
trēs trēs tria PL. ADJ. *three*
tribūnal tribūnālis N. *court (of law)*
tribuō -ere tribuī tribūtum TR. *attribute,
assign*
trirēmis trirēmis F. *trireme (a boat with
three banks of oars)*
◆ tristis -is -e *sad, gloomy, sorrowful, sullen;
austere, strait-laced*
trisulcus -a -um *three-forked,
three-pronged*
triumphō -āre INTR./TR. *conquer,
triumph*
triumphus -ī M. *triumph; triumphal
procession*
Trōia -ae F. *Troy*
Trōiānus -a -um *Trojan*
Trōius -a -um *Trojan*
tropaeum -ī N. *trophy*
trucīdō -āre TR. *slaughter*
truncus -a -um *lopped off*
truncus -ī M. *trunk*
trux (trucis) *raging, savage*
◆ tū (tē tuī tibi tē) PRON. *you* (SG.)
tueor -ērī tuitus (tūtus) sum TR. *look at,
watch, view; defend, protect*
Tullus -ī M. the third king of Rome

◆ tum (tunc) ADV. *then, at that time; next*

tumidus -a -um *swollen, swelling; haughty*

tumultus -ūs M. *turmoil, uproar*

tumulus -ī M. *grave; hill*

◆ tunc (tum) ADV. *then, at that time; next*

tunc ... tunc ... *at one time ... at another time ...*

tunica -ae F. *tunic*

◆ turba -ae F. *crowd, mob, band*

turbidus -a -um *muddy; thick*

turbō -āre TR./INTR. *stir up, rouse; disturb; muddy; be alarmed*

turbō turbinis M. *revolution*

turgidulus -a -um DIMINUTIVE OF turgidus *swollen*

tūrifer tūrifera tūriferum *incense-bearing*

◆ turpis -is -e *ugly; disgraceful; bad*

turpiter ADV. *disgracefully*

tūs tūris N. *frankincense*

tussiō -īre — — INTR. *cough*

tussis tussis F. *cough*

◆ tūtus -a -um *safe, secure*

◆ tuus -a -um *your* (SG.)

Tyndaridēs -ae M. *a descendant of Tyndareus, especially Castor or Pollux*

tyrannus -ī M. *ruler, monarch; tyrant*

Tyrius -a -um *of Tyre*

Tyrr(h)ēnus -a -um *Tyrrhenian; Tuscan*

Tyrus -ī F. *Tyre (a city on the Phoenician coast, famous for its purple dye)*

U

ūber ūberis N. *breast, udder*

ūber (ūberis) *rich, abundant*

◆ ubĭ CONJ. *when; where*

ubĭcumque ADV. *wherever*

◆ ubīque ADV. *everywhere*

ulciscor -ī ultus sum TR. *take vengeance on*

Ulixēs Ulixis M. *Ulysses*

◆ ullus -a -um PRON./ADJ. *any (one/thing)*

ulterior -ior -ius *more distant*

◆ ultimus -a -um *last, final; most distant, farthest*

ultrā ADV. *further, farther, beyond*

ultrō ADV. *of one's own accord*

ululō -āre INTR./TR. *howl*

Umber Umbrī M. *an Umbrian, inhabitant of Umbria (a region of Italy east of Etruria)*

◆ umbra -ae F. *shade; shadow; soul of a dead person, ghost*

umbrifer -a -um *shady*

umerus -ī M. *shoulder*

ūmor ūmōris M. *liquid, juice*

◆ umquam ADV. *ever, at any time*

ūnā ADV. *together*

ūnanimus -a -um *sharing a single aim*

◆ unda -ae F. *wave, ripple; water*

◆ unde ADV. *from where, whence*

undecimus -a -um *eleventh*

unguentum -ī N. *ointment, unguent*

unguis unguis M. *(finger)nail*

ūnicus -ī M. *only son*

◆ ūnus -a -um PRON./ADJ. *one, a single; alone*

urbānus -a -um *urban, of the city; polite*

◆ urbs urbis F. *city*

urg(u)eō -ēre ursī — TR. *press, push, squeeze; weigh down on*

urna -ae F. *urn*

ūrō -ere ussī ustum TR. *burn; inflame*

usquam ADV. *anywhere, in any place*

◆ usque ADV. *as far (as), all the way; continuously, constantly, without stopping, always;* usque quāque *everywhere*

ūsus -ūs M. *use; need*

◆ ut (utī) ADV. *how;* CONJ. *as; (so) that; when*

ut ... ut ... CONJ. *just as ... so ...*

◆ uter utra utrum *which (of two)?; one (of two)*

◆ uterque utraque utrumque *each (of two), either, both*

◆ utī (ut) ADV. *how;* CONJ. *as; (so) that; when*

◆ ūtilis -is -e *useful, beneficial*

◆ utinam ADV. THAT REINFORCES THE OPTATIVE SUBJ. *Would that ...!*

ūtor ūtī ūsus sum INTR. (+ ABL.) *use; have use for*

utpote ADV. *no wonder*

utrum ... an ... *whether ... or ...*

◆ uxor uxōris F. *wife*

V

vacō -āre INTR. *be empty; be free*

vacuus -a -um *empty; idle; ungratified*

vadum -ī N. *ford, shallow water; water*

vae INTERJECTION *woe!*

vagulus -a -um DIMINUTIVE OF vagus *wandering*

vagus -a -um *roving, wandering*

◆ valē valēte IMP. *good-bye, farewell*

◆ valeō -ēre INTR. *be well, be strong; have strength/power/resources; avail, be of value*

◆ validus -a -um *strong, powerful*

vallis vallis F. *valley*

valvae -ārum F.PL. *double doors*

vānescō -ere — — INTR. *vanish*

vānus -a -um *hollow, empty; vain, futile*

vāpulō -āre INTR. *be beaten, be flogged*

◆ varius -a -um *diverse, various, different; changeable, unstable* vātēs vātis M. *prophet; poet*

-ve CONJ. *or*

✦vehō -ere vexī vectum TR. *carry;* (PASS.) *ride, travel*

✦vel CONJ. *or;* ADV. *even*

vel ... vel ... CONJ. *either ... or ...*

vēlāmen vēlāminis N. *garment*

vellō -ere vellī (vulsī, volsī) vulsum (volsum) TR. *pull out, wrench*

vellus velleris N. *wool; fleece*

vēlō -āre TR. *veil, cover*

vēlox (vēlōcis) *swift; transient*

✦velut (velutī) ADV. *as, like, in the same way as*

vēnātor vēnātōris M. *hunter*

✦vendō -ere vendidī venditum TR. *sell*

venēnum -ī N. *poison*

veneror -ārī TR. *venerate, worship*

venia -ae F. *favor; pardon; permission*

✦veniō -īre vēnī ventum INTR. *come, approach*

venter ventris M. *stomach*

ventilō -āre TR. *fan*

ventitō -āre INTR. *go frequently*

ventōsus -a -um *windy; quivering*

✦ventus -ī M. *wind*

Venus Veneris F. *the goddess of procreation and sexual love; love*

venustus -a -um *charming; refined*

vēr vēris N. *spring* (season)

verber verberis N. *lash*

verberō -āre TR. *hit*

verbōsus -a -um *wordy, long-winded*

✦verbum -ī N. *word*

vērē ADV. *really*

verēdus -ī M. *a fast breed of horse; steed*

✦vereor -ērī veritus sum TR./INTR. *respect; fear*

Vergilius -(i)ī M. *Vergil*

vergō -ere — — INTR./TR. *decline*

vēritās vēritātis F. *truth*

vērō ADV. *really, honestly, truly, indeed; however*

Vērōna -ae F. *a town of Gallia Transpadana (northeast Italy)*

versō -āre TR. *spin, turn, swing*

versus -ūs M. (*line of*) *verse*

vertex verticis M. *whirlpool;* (*crown of the*) *head; peak*

✦vertō -ere vertī versum TR. *turn; change; spin around*

vērum -ī N. *truth*

vērum CONJ. *but*

✦vērus -a -um *true, real, genuine*

vēsānus -a -um *demented*

vescor vescī — INTR./TR. *enjoy; feed on*

vesper (NO GEN.) M. *evening*

Vesta -ae F. *the goddess of the hearth*

Vestālis -is -e *Vestal*

✦vester vestra vestrum *your* (PL.)

vestibulum -ī N. *forecourt; entrance hall*

vestīgium -(i)ī N. *footstep, step; footprint*

vestīgō -āre TR. *search for*

✦vestis vestis F. *clothes,* (*article of*) *clothing, garment*

✦vetō -āre vetuī vetitum TR. *forbid; prevent, reject*

✦vetus (veteris) *old; ancient; former*

vetustās vetustātis F. *old age; antiquity*

vetustus -a -um *ancient*

vexillum -ī N. (*military*) *standard*

vexō -āre TR. *harass, constantly attack*

✦via -ae F. *road, street; journey, traveling; way, path; means*

viātor viātōris F. *traveler*

vicem PREP. (+ GEN.) *on account of, for*

vīcīnia -ae F. *proximity*

vīcīnus -a -um *neighboring, nearby, near to;* NOUN *neighbor*

vicis GEN. SG., F. (NOM. SG. DOES NOT OCCUR) *successive change;* in vicēs *in turn*

victima -ae F. *victim, sacrifice*

✦victor victōris M. *victor, conqueror, winner;* ADJ. *triumphant, victorious*

✦victōria -ae F. *victory*

victrix victrīcis F. *victor*

victus -ūs M. *food*

vīcus -ī M. *village; street*

✦videō -ēre vīdī vīsum TR. *see, look at/ upon; take note of; witness;* (PASS.) *seem*

vigeō -ēre viguī — INTR. *flourish*

vigilō -āre INTR. *stay awake, be awake*

vīlica -ae F. *wife of an overseer*

vīlicus -ī M. *overseer*

vīlis -is -e *cheap; worthless*

✦villa -ae F. *country house, estate*

vinciō -īre vinxī vinctum TR. *fasten, bind*

✦vincō -ere vīcī victum TR. *conquer, defeat, overcome; capture; win over; surpass*

✦vinc(u)lum -ī N. *chain; bond, fetter*

vindicta -ae F. *retribution*

✦vīnum -ī N. *wine*

✦vir virī M. *man; male; husband; hero*

vireō -ēre viruī — INTR. *be green, be strong*

✦vīrēs vīrium SEE vīs

virga -ae F. *rod, wand*

✦virgō virginis F. *girl, maiden*

viridis -is -e *green; young*

✦virtūs virtūtis F. *virtue; courage, valor; merit, worth; vigor*

✦vīs DEFECTIVE SG., ACC. vim, ABL. vī; PL. NOM./ACC. vīrēs, GEN. vīrium, DAT./ABL. vīribus, F. (SG.) *power, force, violence;* (PL.) *strength*

viscera viscerum N.PL. *internal organs of the body*

vīsō -ere vīsī — TR./INTR. *visit, go and see; see*

◆**vīta -ae** F. *life*

vitiō -āre TR. *damage, harm*

vītis vītis F. *vine*

◆**vitium -(i)ī** N. *fault, defect, moral failing; vice*

◆**vītō -āre** TR. *avoid, shun; escape*

vitta -ae F. *headband*

vitula -ae F. *calf*

◆**vīvō -ere vixī victum** INTR. *live, be alive; enjoy life*

◆**vīvus -a -um** *alive, living; lifelike*

◆**vix** ADV. *scarcely, just now; with difficulty*

◆**vocō -āre** TR. *call, summon, invite; name*

volō -āre INTR. *fly*

◆**volō velle voluī —** TR./INTR. *wish, want, be willing (to)*

volucer volucris volucre *flying, swift*

volucris volucris F. *bird*

◆**voluntās voluntātis** F. *choice, wish*

◆**voluptās voluptātis** F. *pleasure, delight*

volūtō -āre TR. (WITH REFL.) *roll (about), wallow; think over, talk over*

◆**volvō -ere volvī volūtum**
    TR. *bring around; suffer, go through;* (PASS. USED AS INTR.) *roll, surge; turn*

◆**vōs (vōs vestrum (vestrī) vōbīs vōbīs)** *you* (PL.)

◆**vōtum -ī** N. *vow, promise; wish, desire, prayer*

◆**vox vōcis** F. *voice; word; sound, noise (of animals)*

Vulcānus -ī M. *Vulcan, the god of fire*

◆**vulgus -ī** N. *the common people*

◆**vulnus vulneris** N. *wound, injury*

◆**vultus -ūs** M. *face; expression; gaze, glance*

Z

Zephyrus -ī M. *the west wind*

zōna -ae F. *belt*